Oxford
Learner's Dictionary
of English Idioms

Oxford Learner's Dictionary of English Idioms

Edited by Helen Warren

Oxford University Press 1994

Oxford University Press, Walton Street, Oxford OX2 6DP

Oxford   New York
Athens   Auckland   Bangkok   Bombay   Calcutta
Cape Town   Dar es Salaam   Delhi   Florence   Hong Kong
Istanbul   Karachi   Kuala Lumpur   Madras   Madrid
Melbourne   Mexico City   Nairobi   Paris   Singapore
Taipei   Tokyo   Toronto

and associated companies in Berlin Ibadan

OXFORD and OXFORD ENGLISH are trade marks of Oxford
University Press

ISBN 0 19 4312771

Typeset in Great Britain by Tradespools Limited, Frome, Somerset
Printed and bound in Great Britain

Preface

The word 'idiom' is used to describe the 'special phrases' that are an essential part of a language. Idioms may be 'special' in different ways: for example, the expression *to kick the bucket* seems to follow the normal rules of grammar, although we cannot say 'kick a bucket' or 'kick the buckets', but it is impossible to guess that it means 'to die'. Phrases like *all right*, *on second thoughts*, and *same here*, which are used in everyday English, and especially in spoken English, are 'special' because they are fixed units of language that clearly do not follow the normal rules of grammar.

In this new dictionary we have used the Oxford Corpus, a collection of contemporary written and spoken English stored on computer, to make a selection of the most frequently used of these 'units of language', which are such an important part of written and spoken English.

My thanks are due to Gary Dexter, John Hughes and Fergus McGauran for their work in writing the dictionary and to Angela Crawley, Gary Johns, Christine Rickards and Margaret Deuter for their editorial work, as well as to the team of people involved in the production of the dictionary.

Oxford 1994   Helen Warren

A guide to using the dictionary

Finding an idiom

Idioms are listed under a **keyword**, usually the first noun or verb in the idiom.

Idioms are listed alphabetically in each keyword group, ignoring only **sb**, **sth**, **a**, **the**, possessive adjectives like **his**, **your**, etc and words in brackets

followed by cross-references, also listed alphabetically, showing which keyword to go to to find the idiom you are looking for.

Some short sections combine two keywords, as **hill** and **hills** here.

When one idiom is listed as a variant of another, a cross-reference shows you where to find it.

What the dictionary tells you about the idioms

Different meanings of an idiom

New words formed from an idiom

Words that can be added are shown in brackets.

Sometimes words that are added change the meaning and the change of meaning is shown in the definition.

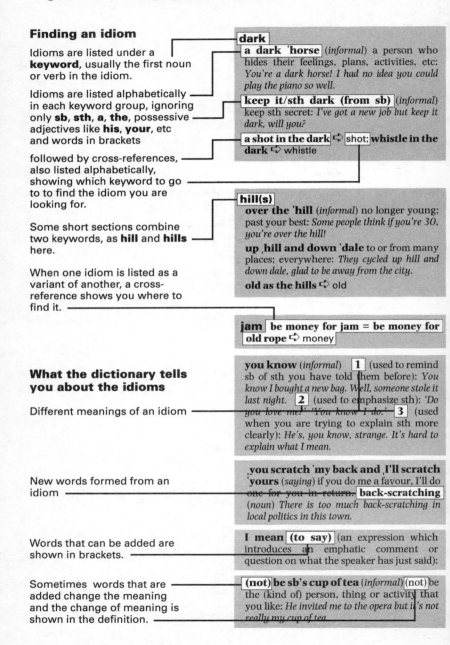

dark

a dark 'horse (*informal*) a person who hides their feelings, plans, activities, etc: *You're a dark horse! I had no idea you could play the piano so well.*

keep it/sth dark (from sb) (*informal*) keep sth secret: *I've got a new job but keep it dark, will you?*

a shot in the dark ⇨ shot; **whistle in the dark** ⇨ whistle

hill(s)

over the 'hill (*informal*) no longer young; past your best: *Some people think if you're 30, you're over the hill!*

up ,hill and down 'dale to or from many places; everywhere: *They cycled up hill and down dale, glad to be away from the city.*

old as the hills ⇨ old

jam be money for jam = be money for **old rope** ⇨ money

you know (*informal*) **1** (used to remind sb of sth you have told them before): *You know I bought a new bag. Well, someone stole it last night.* **2** (used to emphasize sth): *'Do you love me?' 'You know I do.'* **3** (used when you are trying to explain sth more clearly): *He's, you know, strange. It's hard to explain what I mean.*

,you scratch 'my back and ,I'll scratch 'yours (*saying*) if you do me a favour, I'll do one for you in return. **back-scratching** (*noun*) *There is too much back-scratching in local politics in this town.*

I mean (to say) (an expression which introduces an emphatic comment or question on what the speaker has just said):

(not) be sb's cup of tea (*informal*) (not) be the (kind of) person, thing or activity that you like: *He invited me to the opera but it's not really my cup of tea.*

When there are several words that you can use, they are shown separated by slashes. ──────

new/fresh/young blood new members of a group or organization who have fresh ideas, skills, etc and so make the group more efficient: *What this committee really needs is some new blood.*

When a wider range of words can be used, typical words are shown, followed by **etc**. ──────

a matter of 'days, 'miles, 'pounds, etc

variant forms ──────

your 'luck is in *or* **you're in 'luck** you

related idioms ──────

on the 'market be available for sale: *This computer isn't on the market yet. You should be able to buy one early next year.* also **come on (to) the market** be offered for sale: *This house only came on the market yesterday.* also **put/bring sth on (to) the market** offer sth for sale: *We're putting a new range of cosmetics on the market next month.*

Using idioms

Labels help you to know when idioms are used only in particular situations. Labels used in the dictionary are *formal, informal, humorous, ironic, approving, disapproving,* and *offensive.* ──────

rub sb's 'nose in it *or* **rub it in** (*informal*)

If an idiom is used only or usually in British or American English, this is also shown. ──────

get to first base (with sb/sth) *or* **reach/make first base (with sb/sth)** (*especially US, informal*)

Idioms that are well-known proverbs or catchphrases have the label *saying.* ──────

there's a first time for everything (*saying, humorous*) the fact that something

If the stress pattern is unusual, a mark shows where the main stress falls when you say the idiom and, if there is another stressed word, that is marked too. ──────

the ˌsilent maˈjority the great majority of

Notes about the use of an idiom are given in brackets. ──────

by 'all means (*quite formal*) (used for giving permission to sb, or for saying yes to a request) yes, of course; certainly: *'Can I smoke?' 'By all means.'* ○ *'Do you think I could borrow this dictionary?' 'Yes, by all means.'*

Examples show typical uses of the idiom in suitable contexts to help you use the idiom correctly. ──────

Notes show where idioms come from. ──────

(as) mad as a 'hatter (*informal*) mad. (mercury used to be used in making hats and fumes from mercury can cause brain damage. In *Alice in Wonderland* by Lewis Carrol one of the characters is called the Mad Hatter.)

abbreviations used in the dictionary:
sb somebody
sth something

USING IDIOMS

On the pages that follow you will find some examples of the ways idioms are used in daily life:

Idioms all around

Idioms form an important part of our everyday lives. As well as using them in our own speech and writing, we see them all around us: in shop and restaurant names, advertisements, book titles and many other places. They are used to attract our attention, very often in a humorous way, and to make us remember them easily.

Pick of the Bunch

for the freshest flowers, fruit and veg in town!

HOT STUFF
MEXICAN RESTAURANT

Book your table for this weekend

Visit
'Sitting Pretty'
for the best selection of armchairs and sofas.

PLAIN SAILING

An introduction to yachting

ODEON
CINEMA
Dressed to Kill

KIDS' STUFF

clothes your children will love to wear

The Upper Crust

Bread baked fresh twice a day

The Icing on the Cake

Cakes for special occasions made to order

'GOING FOR A SONG'

discount CDs and cassettes, the cheapest in town!

A3

Idioms in conversation

When you are having a conversation, a discussion, or an argument, or when you write an article, an essay, or a report, you want to express your own ideas. But there are many fixed expressions and idioms that you can use to link these ideas, for example, to show the listener or reader that you are making a new point, or disagreeing, or closing the argument. Using these phrases gives you time to think about what you are going to say next, and helps your listeners or readers to know what they can expect and so understand your argument better.

starting a conversation

Look also at:
by the way
guess what

> **I say**, have you heard? Richard Smith's leaving. You could apply for his job at the London office.

saying something that will surprise the other person

Look also at:
believe it or not
as it happens
as a matter of fact

> **Oddly enough**, you're the third person who's said that today. Actually, I did know about it, but I wasn't planning to apply.

giving your opinion

Look also at:
to my mind
in my view
in sb's book
for my money
for my (own) part

> Why ever not? **If you ask me**, it's a great opportunity. You'd be living in London and travelling around a lot, not doing the same thing every day, like here.

giving the first reason for something

Look also at:
for a start

giving another, perhaps more important reason

Look also at:
what's more
into the bargain

> Yes, but I don't want to live in London. **For one thing**, it would mean leaving all my friends, and for another, I'd be further away from my parents, and they're not getting any younger. And **on top of that**, I'd have to find somewhere to live in London.

A4

Idioms in conversation

*showing that you see
somebody's point of view*

Look also at:
**have (got) a point
(there)**

*Introducing a different,
often contrasting point*

There is that. It is very difficult to find
nice flats in London and it would be
more expensive.

On the other hand, you could afford
to pay more because you'd have a
better salary.

emphasizing something

Look also at:
**without (a) doubt
for certain
the thing is
get sth straight**

Believe me, I have thought about it,
but I really don't think I want to take on
more responsibility.

*showing that you have
considered all the various
aspects of the question*

Look also at:
**in the end
all in all
all things considered
when all is said and
done**

Well, **at the end of the day** it's your
decision. You have to do what you
think is best.

*putting an end to an
argument*

**(and/so) that's that
full stop
your last word**

Yes, and I've made my decision. I'm
happy here, so can we **leave it at
that?**

A5

Idioms in reports

① *Referring to something*

Look also at:
as regards sb/sth
on that/this score

② *emphasizing the most important point*

Look also at:
first and foremost

③ *generalizing*

Look also at:
on the whole
in general
as a (general) rule
in the main
for the most part

④ *giving examples*

Look also at:
for instance
a case in point

⑤ *summing up*

Look also at:
in brief

⑥ *showing that you have considered various aspects of a question*

Look also at:
all things considered

⑦ *Referring to an unspecified time in the future*

Look also at:
in the fullness of time
sooner or later

At the staff meeting held on Tuesday 3 May a number of future plans were discussed. **With respect to** ① the provision of new leisure facilities for staff, the most popular idea was the building of a swimming pool. This would, **above all** ②, give employees the opportunity to increase their physical fitness as well as to relax. The firm's medical adviser, Dr Smith, confirmed that **by and large** ③, the staff were not fit, and, in her opinion, the number of working days lost through stress-related illnesses and problems **such as** ④ back pain could be reduced considerably if staff were encouraged to take regular exercise. **In short** ⑤, the benefits to the company would outweigh the cost. Representing the management, Mr James agreed that, **on balance** ⑥, the scheme seemed to have considerable advantages over the other suggestions and said that the management would now discuss the idea and announce a decision **in due course** ⑦.

Idioms you can use when ...

... you don't know the answer to something

I haven't the faintest idea
I haven't a clue
search me
your guess is as good as mine
goodness knows

... you are surprised

well I never!
good heavens!
get away!
good grief!
no kidding
you don't say

... somebody hasn't understood you

talk at cross-purposes
get your wires crossed
get hold of the wrong end of
  the stick

... you are annoyed with somebody and want to tell them to go away

get lost!
beat it!
go to hell
go and jump in the lake
drop dead

... you want to tell somebody to keep calm

keep your hair on
don't get your knickers in a twist
don't make a mountain out of a
  molehill
it's not the end of the world

... you want to tell somebody to stop doing something annoying

pack it in
give it a rest!
get off my back

... you want somebody to hurry up

get your skates on
jump to it
get a move on
make it snappy

... you tell somebody to be careful

watch it
mind your step
steady on!
mind how you go

From the cradle ....to the grave

The **ups and downs**, the **thrills and spills** – we use idioms to describe the good times, the bad times and all the major events in our lives from birth to death: **from the cradle to the grave**.

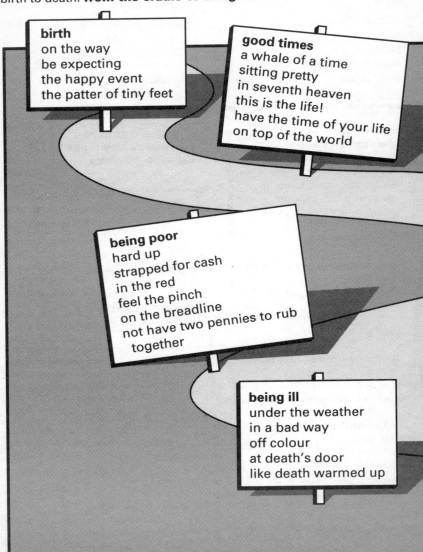

birth
on the way
be expecting
the happy event
the patter of tiny feet

good times
a whale of a time
sitting pretty
in seventh heaven
this is the life!
have the time of your life
on top of the world

being poor
hard up
strapped for cash
in the red
feel the pinch
on the breadline
not have two pennies to rub
    together

being ill
under the weather
in a bad way
off colour
at death's door
like death warmed up

A8

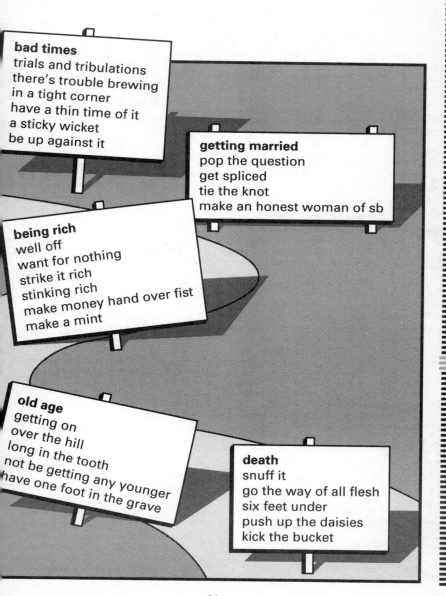

bad times
trials and tribulations
there's trouble brewing
in a tight corner
have a thin time of it
a sticky wicket
be up against it

getting married
pop the question
get spliced
tie the knot
make an honest woman of sb

being rich
well off
want for nothing
strike it rich
stinking rich
make money hand over fist
make a mint

old age
getting on
over the hill
long in the tooth
not be getting any younger
have one foot in the grave

death
snuff it
go the way of all flesh
six feet under
push up the daisies
kick the bucket

A

A
from A to B from one place to another: *I don't care what kind of car it is as long as it gets me from A to B.*

from A to Z very thoroughly and in detail: *We need an expert who knows the subject from A to Z.*

ABC (as) **easy as ABC/anything/pie/ falling off a log** ⇨ easy

about
be about to do sth be going to do sth immediately: *I was about to phone him when he walked into the room.*

how/what about...? (used before a suggestion): *How about us going to Turkey for our holidays?* ○ *What about having lunch with me on Friday?*

above
above all (else) especially: *Don't spend too much money, don't forget to write, but above all, have a good time!* ○ *He misses his family above all else.*

a‚bove and be'yond sth (*formal*) more than (your duty, etc): *They showed commitment to the job above and beyond what was expected of them.*

be/get a'bove yourself behave as if you are better or more important than you really are: *She's getting a bit above herself. She's only been working for me for two weeks and already she's telling me what to do!*

over and above ⇨ over

absence **leave of absence** ⇨ leave

accidentally
accidentally on 'purpose (*informal, ironic*) intending to do sth, but wanting to appear to have done it by accident: *'We'd just finished our meal when John realized he'd accidentally left his cheque-book at home.' 'Accidentally on purpose, you mean!'*

accidents
‚accidents ‚will 'happen (*saying*) (said when a small accident has happened, for example when sth has been spilt or broken, to show that you do not consider it to be serious, or to excuse yourself for causing it): *'I'm so sorry, I've just broken a plate.' 'Oh, never mind, accidents will happen.'*

a chapter of accidents ⇨ chapter

accord
of your own ac'cord without being asked or forced: *I didn't need to tell her to apologize; she did it of her own accord.*

account
of no ac'count (*formal*) not considered important: *His past achievements were of no account when it came to competing with the younger men.*

on account of sth/sb *or* **on sb's account** because of sth/sb: *Flights were delayed on account of the bad weather.* ○ *I can't go, but don't stay in on my account.*

on 'no account *or* **not on 'any account** (*quite formal*) not for any reason: *On no account (should you) try to fix the heater yourself. All repairs should be done by a trained engineer.*

put/turn sth to good account (*formal*) use (money, an ability, etc) profitably: *He put his experience as a teacher to good account as a writer of children's books.*

take sth into account *or* **take account of sth** consider sth when making a calculation or decision: *It's clear he didn't take his family's wishes into account when deciding to change jobs.* ○ *We mustn't forget to take account of price increases when we do the budget for next year.*

call sb to account ⇨ call; **settle your/an account** = **settle a score** ⇨ settle; **square your/an account** ⇨ square

accounting
there's no accounting for 'tastes (*saying*) (used to express surprise at another person's likes and dislikes which are different from your own): *'She's just painted her whole room purple.' 'Well, there's no accounting for tastes!'*

1

accounts

by/from 'all accounts (used when the speaker does not have direct experience of the thing mentioned but is reporting the ideas, etc of others): *I've never seen any of her films but she's a brilliant director, by all accounts.* ○ *It was, from all accounts, a very interesting discussion.*

square accounts = square your/an account ⇨ square

ace(s)

have/hold (all) the aces be in a controlling position because you have certain advantages over another person: *The Labour candidate holds all the aces – he's local and well liked.* (from card-playing)

have an ace/trick up your sleeve = have sth up your sleeve ⇨ sleeve

Achilles

an/sb's Achilles 'heel a hidden weakness or fault in sb which may be used to harm them: *The opposition realized they had found the Prime Minister's Achilles heel.* (from Greek mythology: Achilles could not be wounded, except in his heel)

acid

the acid test (of sth) a situation which finally proves whether sth is good or bad, true or false, etc: *They've always been good friends, but the acid test will come when they have to share a flat.*

acorns great/tall oaks from little acorns grow ⇨ oaks

acquaintance have a nodding acquaintance with sb/sth ⇨ nodding; **scrape an acquaintance with sb** ⇨ scrape

acquired

an acquired 'taste a thing which you find unpleasant or do not appreciate at first but which you gradually learn to like: *Whisky is an acquired taste.*

act

an ,act of 'God (*law*) an event caused by natural forces which people cannot control or prevent, for example a hurricane, earthquake, etc: *The insurance policy covers your house against all types of damage, excluding those caused by acts of God.*

be/get in on the 'act (*informal*) be/become involved in a particular activity only after it has become successful: *Sales of 'green' products have increased dramatically and now a lot of manufacturers are trying to get in on the act.*

act/be your age ⇨ age; **act/play the fool** ⇨ fool; **act/play the goat** ⇨ goat; **do a disappearing act** ⇨ disappearing; **get sth/it/your act together** ⇨ together; **read the riot act** ⇨ read

action(s)

'action stations (*becoming dated*) (used as an order to get ready for action): *Action stations! There's a bus full of tourists arriving in five minutes.*

,actions speak ,louder than 'words (*saying*) what you do is more important than what you say.

in action working, operating, etc; doing a particular activity: *John's a great organizer – you should see him in action.*

out of 'action not working or operating as normal because of illness, injury, damage, etc: *Jane's broken leg will put her out of action for a while.* ○ *He can't give you a lift today – his car's out of action.*

where the 'action is where the most exciting or important events are happening: *I'd hate to live out in the country – I like to be where the action is.*

a course of action ⇨ course; **spring to life/action** ⇨ spring; **swing into action** ⇨ swing

Adam not know sb from Adam ⇨ know

add

add ,fuel to the 'fire/'flames do or say sth which makes a difficult situation worse, or makes sb even more angry, etc: *She was already furious and his apologies and excuses only added fuel to the flames.*

add ,insult to 'injury hurt the feelings of, or harm, sb who has already been harmed in some other way: *She forgot to send me an invitation to her party and then added insult to injury by asking to borrow my earrings!*

advance be ahead of/before/in advance of your time ⇨ time

advantage

take advantage (of sb, sb's kindness, etc) 1 use sb, etc unfairly to get what you want: *He takes advantage of his aunt's good nature.* ○ *I know we said she could stay for a few days but two months is really taking advantage!* **2** (*dated*) seduce sb: *Helen's mother believed that every strange man they met was trying to take advantage of her daughter.*

take (full) advantage of sth make good use of sth: *She takes full advantage of the facilities at the sports centre and practises there every day.* ○ *Take advantage of our special offer and get two books for the price of one!*

to sb's advantage so that sb benefits: *The rise in the value of the pound will work to the advantage of those planning a holiday abroad this summer.*

to (better, etc) ad'vantage in a way that produces a good or profitable result: *You would be spending your time to better advantage if you did what I suggested.* ○ *That's a lovely picture but it's not seen to (it's best) advantage on that wall. Why don't you hang it nearer the light?*

press your advantage ⇨ press; **turn sth to your advantage** ⇨ turn

advocate
a/the devil's advocate ⇨ devil

affairs
a state of affairs ⇨ state

afraid

I'm afraid (that)... (used as a polite way of introducing information which may be unwelcome or unpleasant): *I'm afraid (that) I can't come to your party.* ○ *'Have you got change for ten pounds?' 'I'm afraid not.'* ○ *'I've got some bad news, I'm afraid – John's had an accident.'* ○ *'Is this the best you can do?' 'I'm afraid so.'*

after

after 'all 1 contrary to what you first intend to do or expect to happen: *I think I will have something to eat after all.* ○ *We could have left our coats at home – it didn't rain after all.* **2** used as a reminder of a fact that is relevant: *Can't I stay up late tonight? After all, there's no school tomorrow!* ○ *You got a fair price for your car. It's six years old, after all.*

again

a,gain and a'gain many times; repeatedly: *I've told him again and again to shut the door but he always leaves it open.*

you can say that again ⇨ say; **now and again/then** ⇨ now; **over again** ⇨ over; **then again = there again** ⇨ there; **there again** ⇨ there; **think again** ⇨ think

against

,as ,against 'sth in contrast with sth: *If you look at sales this year as against those in the same period last year . . ..*

age

,act/,be your 'age (*informal*) stop behaving in a childish way: *Paul, act your age or I won't take you to the cinema again!* (often used as a command)

,come of 'age 1 reach the age when you are considered by the law to be adult: *He will inherit his father's money when he comes of age.* **2** (of an organization) become established: *With more and more people now aware of environmental issues, Green politics has really come of age.*

,under 'age not yet adult, according to the law: *We don't serve alcohol to teenagers who are under age/to under-age teenagers.*

at/to a ripe old age/to the ripe old age of 95, etc ⇨ ripe; **at a tender age** ⇨ tender; **at the tender age of eight, etc = at a tender age** ⇨ tender; **the awkward age** ⇨ awkward; **feel your age** ⇨ feel; **the golden age (of sth)** ⇨ golden; **in this day and age** ⇨ day

ago
many moons ago ⇨ moons

agony
pile on the agony ⇨ pile; **prolong the agony** ⇨ prolong

agree

a,gree to 'differ (of two or more people) allow each other to have different opinions about sth, especially in order to avoid more argument: *Our views on this matter are so different – I think we'll just have to agree to differ (about it).*

I ,couldn't agree (with you) 'more I completely agree (with you): *I couldn't agree with you more about the need to take on extra staff.*

agreement a gentleman's agreement ⇨ gentleman

ahead be ahead of/before/in advance of your time ⇨ time; be, etc ahead of/behind time ⇨ time; be/stay one jump ahead ⇨ jump; be streets ahead ⇨ streets; full steam/speed ahead ⇨ full

aid
what's (all) 'this, etc in aid of? (informal) what is the purpose or cause of this, etc?: What's all this crying in aid of?

air
,in the 'air (of an idea, a feeling, a piece of information, etc) felt to exist (but perhaps not talked about): Spring is in the air. ○ There was a strong feeling of excitement in the air.

(up) in the 'air (of plans, etc) uncertain; not yet decided: I'm hoping to take a holiday this month but my plans are still very much (up) in the air. ○ At the end of the meeting, the matter was left (up) in the air.

,on/,off the 'air (being) broadcast/not (being) broadcast on radio or television: Good-night from all of us here. BBC1 will be on the air again at 7.00 with 'Breakfast News'. ○ 'Going Live' will go off the air for the summer, returning for a new series in the autumn.

as light as air/a feather ⇨ light; a breath of fresh air ⇨ breath; castles in the air/in Spain ⇨ castles; clear the air ⇨ clear; free as air/as a bird ⇨ free; hot air ⇨ hot; in the open air ⇨ open; into thin air ⇨ thin; out of thin air ⇨ thin; walk on air ⇨ walk; with your nose in the air ⇨ nose

airs
,airs and 'graces (disapproving) behaviour which is elegant but unnatural, intended to impress others: Her airs and graces didn't impress her fellow students at all.

,give yourself/,put ,on 'airs behave in a way which shows that you feel you are important: The nice thing about her is that, in spite of being so rich, she doesn't put on any airs.

aisles roll in the aisles ⇨ roll

aitches drop your aitches ⇨ drop

Aladdin
an Aladdin's 'cave a place full of valuable or interesting objects: He kept for his private pleasure an Aladdin's cave of stolen masterpieces.

alarm a false alarm ⇨ false

alec a smart alec ⇨ smart

alert on red alert ⇨ red

alike share and share alike ⇨ share

alive
a,live and 'kicking (informal) still existing and strong or active: The old prejudices were still very much alive and kicking.

skin sb alive ⇨ skin

all
all a'long from the beginning: I've said all along that this would happen. ○ He knew who they were all along but he pretended he didn't.

'all but 1 almost: The snow all but covered the path, making it difficult to walk. ○ The patient was all but dead when the doctor arrived. 2 all (the people or things mentioned) except...: 'Have you done your homework?' 'Yes, all but the last two questions.'

,all 'in 1 (of a price) with nothing extra to pay; inclusive: The holiday cost £250 all in. ○ These are 'all-in prices – room, breakfast, service and tax. 2 (informal, dated) very tired: At the end of the race he was all in.

all in all when everything is considered: All in all the film was a great success, despite the bad publicity.

all of 'sth (of size, weight, distance, etc) at least: 'How old is she?' 'Oh, she must be all of fifty.' (also used ironically to show that the speaker does not consider a size, weight, distance, etc to be great): He never visits his mother and she lives all of three miles away.

and 'all 1 included: They're coming to stay for the weekend, dog and all. 2 (very informal) too: And he stole £5 from me, and all. 3 (informal) and other (connected) things: She doesn't go out much in the evenings now, what with her work and all.

and all that (jazz, rubbish, stuff, etc) (informal) (often used for showing disapproval) and other similar things: He was an intellectual – *read Beckett and Barthes and all that.* ○ *They're always kissing and all that romantic stuff.*

(not) at 'all (used with a negative, in a question or in an *if*-clause) in any way; to any degree: *This isn't at all what I expected.* ○ *Are you hungry at all?* ○ *If you're at all unhappy about marrying him, then don't.*

be all sb can 'do (not) to do sth (*informal*) be very difficult (not) to do sth: *His face looked so funny that it was all she could do not to laugh.*

(not) be/take all day, morning, etc (to do sth) *or* **not have (got) all day, etc** (*informal*) (used as a request to hurry up) (not) take a long time (to do sth): *'Don't take all day shaving,' she shouted to him through the bathroom door.* ○ *Hurry up and choose a book – we haven't got all day.*

be all 'go be (a situation where people are) very active or busy: *The election's on the eighteenth, so it's all go for the next three weeks.*

be ˌall the ˌsame to 'sb *or* (*dated*) **be all 'one to sb** not be important to sb: *If it's all the same to you, I'd prefer to go shopping on my own.*

give sb/get the all-'clear give sb/get a sign that a particular situation is no longer dangerous: *She got the all-clear from the doctor and was sent home from the hospital.* (refers to the signal that is sounded in wartime when a bombing raid is over)

in 'all as a total quantity or number: *We've got six litres of milk in all.* ○ *That's £10.29 in all, please.*

it's/they're ˌall 'yours (used when passing the responsibility for sth/sb or the use of sth, often involving problems or difficulties, to another person): *'There you are, Mr Brown,' she said, taking him into the classroom, 'they're all yours.'*

ˌnot at 'all (used as a polite answer to an expression of thanks): *'Thank you very much. It's very kind of you.' 'Oh, not at all.'*

of ˌall the 'cheek, 'nerve, stupid things to 'do, etc! (*informal*) (used to express annoyance, impatience, etc at what another person has done or said): *Of all the idiots, leaving his car unlocked in the middle of town!* (often used without a noun, especially

to show annoyance): *She said I was fat? Well, of all the . . .!*

of 'all people/places/things chosen from other people/places/things (used to express surprise at a particular person/place/thing that is the most or least likely in the circumstances): *You, of all people, should be sympathetic, having just had a similar accident yourself.* ○ *If it's a rest they need, then why go to Paris of all places?*

that's 'all I need/needed (*informal*) (used when sth bad happens in a situation which is already bad): *The car's broken down? That's all I need!*

after all ⇨ after; **all/just the same** ⇨ same; **for all** ⇨ for; **one and all** ⇨ one

alley a blind alley ⇨ blind

allowances
make allowances for sb not judge sb too strictly because of certain problems or difficulties: *The court was asked to make allowances for the age of the accused.*

alone
let a'lone (follows a negative statement and introduces another negative statement) and most certainly not: *I wouldn't speak to him, let alone trust him or lend him money.* ○ *She didn't even apologize, let alone offer to pay for the damage.*

go it alone ⇨ go; **leave/let sb/sth alone** ⇨ leave; **leave/let well alone** ⇨ well

along
along with sth in addition to sth: *Tobacco is taxed in most countries, along with alcohol.*

be/go along for the ride (*informal*) join a group of people because you are interested in what they are doing, although you don't want to take an active part in it: *Some of the group are not really interested in politics – they're just along for the ride.*

all along ⇨ all; **all along/down the line** ⇨ line; **do sth on/along the way** ⇨ way; **get along/away/on!** ⇨ get; **on/along the lines of sth** ⇨ lines; **on/along the same lines as sth** = **on/along the lines of sth** ⇨ lines; **somewhere, etc along the line** ⇨ line

aloud think aloud ⇨ think

alter change/alter beyond/out of all recognition ⇨ recognition

always it always/never pays to do sth ⇨ pays; once a. . ., always a. . . ⇨ once

amok run amok ⇨ run

amount
any 'amount/'number of sth a large quantity of sth: *There was any amount of food and drink at the party.* ○ *You won't have any difficulty selling your car – there are any number of people who would buy it.*

amount/come to the same thing ⇨ same

anchor weigh anchor ⇨ weigh

and
and 'then some (*especially US*) and even more (than has already been mentioned): *It rained for two hours and then some.*

angels be on the side of the angels ⇨ side

anger do sth more in sorrow than in anger ⇨ sorrow

answer(s)
have (got)/know all the answers be or seem to be more intelligent or know more than others: *He's an economist who thinks he knows all the answers.*

a dusty answer ⇨ dusty

ants
have (got) ants in your pants (*informal*) be restless because you are anxious or excited about sth: *Relax and enjoy yourself – you've really got ants in your pants about something tonight!*

anything
anything 'but certainly not; just the opposite (of): *Ecologists are anything but optimistic about a change in the Government's attitude towards 'green' issues.* ○ *'I suppose the weather in Scotland was terrible.' 'Oh no, anything but.'*

anything 'goes there are no rules about how sb may behave; anything is acceptable: *John always has to wear a suit and tie to the office but where I work anything goes.*

anything like (used with a negative, in a question or in an *if*-clause) **1** in any way similar to: *If the meal's anything like the one we had there, you'll really enjoy it.* ○ *He isn't anything like his brother.* (with positive forms) **nothing like 2** *also* **anywhere near** and, with positive forms, **nowhere near** nearly: *The car isn't anything like/anywhere near as fast as yours.* ○ *This exam's nothing like/nowhere near as easy as last year's.*

as easy, clear, quick, etc as anything (*informal*) extremely easy, clear, quickly, etc: *It was only a small gift but Phil was as pleased as anything with it.*

(as) easy as ABC/anything/pie/falling off a log ⇨ easy; like anything/mad/crazy/billy-o ⇨ like

apart be miles apart ⇨ miles; be poles/worlds apart ⇨ poles; come/fall apart at the seams ⇨ seams

apology
an apology for sth a very poor example of sth: *I'm sorry this is a bit of an apology for lunch – we'll have a proper meal tonight.*

appearances
to all ap'pearances if sth/sb is judged only by what we can see: *The house was, to all appearances, empty.* ○ *Although to all appearances they were the 'ideal couple', in fact they were very unhappy.*

appetite whet sb's appetite ⇨ whet

apple
the ˌapple of sb's 'eye a person, usually a child, whom sb loves very much; a favourite child: *The second child, John, was the apple of his mother's eye.*

upset the/sb's apple-cart ⇨ upset

approach a/the softly-softly approach ⇨ softly

approval
on ap'proval (of goods) not paid for and to be returned, usually within a few days, if the customer decides not to buy them: *I've got it on seven days approval, so if you don't like it I can take it back.*

a seal of approval ⇨ seal

area a grey area ⇨ grey; a no-go area ⇨ no

argument for the sake of argument ⇨ sake

ark

out of the ark (used only of things, not people) extremely old or old-fashioned: *She was using a dictionary that was straight out of the ark.*

arm

keep sb at 'arm's length avoid becoming too friendly with sb: *He's the kind of man who's best kept at arm's length, in my opinion.*

as long as your arm ⇨ long; **chance your arm** ⇨ chance; **the long arm of the law** ⇨ long; **a shot in the arm** ⇨ shot; **twist sb's arm** ⇨ twist; **would give your right arm for sth** ⇨ right

armchair

an armchair critic, traveller, etc a person who knows about a subject only from what they have heard or read and not from personal experience.

armed

armed to the 'teeth (with sth) (*informal*) carrying a lot of weapons or a lot of things needed for a particular purpose: *The tourists got out of the coach, armed to the teeth with cameras, binoculars, and guidebooks.*

armour **a chink in sb's armour** ⇨ chink; **a knight in shining armour** ⇨ knight

arms

up in 'arms (about/over sth) (*informal*) very angry and protesting very strongly (about sth): *Local residents are up in arms over plans to build a new motorway.*

a babe in arms ⇨ babe; **lay down your arms** ⇨ lay; **throw up your hands/arms in horror, despair, etc** ⇨ throw; **with open arms** ⇨ open

around

have been a'round (*informal*) have a wide experience of life; have had many sexual partners: *She's been around a bit so she'll know how to deal with this type of problem.* ○ *He'd had a lot of girlfriends before he met Sue. He'd certainly been around a bit.*

see you around/later! = see you! ⇨ see

arrive **come/arrive on the scene** ⇨ scene

arrow(s) **be, etc straight as an arrow** ⇨ straight; **the slings and arrows** ⇨ slings

arse **lick sb's arse = lick sb's boots** ⇨ lick; **not know your arse from your elbow** ⇨ know

art **have (got) sth down to a fine art** ⇨ fine; **state of the art** ⇨ state

as

as and when whenever; at the moment when: *We'll deal with individual problems as and when they arise.*

as for sb/sth turning to the subject of sb/sth: *I like Sue very much, but as for her boyfriend – I wouldn't care if I never saw him again!*

'as from or (*especially US*) **'as of** (used to indicate the time or date from which something starts): *As from next Monday she'll have a new secretary.* ○ *We shall be at our new address as of mid-June.*

as 'if (used to express anger at or disapproval of a suggestion, an explanation, etc): *As if I really cared!* (can also be used alone when denying a possibility): *'Don't tell Tom I said that, will you?' 'Oh, as if (I would)!'*

as it 'is as the situation is at the moment (often in contrast to what was expected): *I was planning to have this report ready by tomorrow but as it is, it may not be done until Thursday.* ○ *We won't be able to buy a new car this year – we can only just afford a holiday as it is.*

as it 'were also **so to speak** (used to show that this is the speaker's own way of expressing a fact): *Night fell and the city became, as it were, a different place entirely.*

it isn't as if/as though or **it's not as if/as though** (used to show that a particular explanation for sth is not the correct one): *It isn't as if he didn't recognize me! He just walked straight past me as I stood there.*

as/so long as ⇨ long; **as much (as)** ⇨ much; **as of now** ⇨ now; **as such** ⇨ such; **as yet** ⇨ yet

ashes rake over old ashes ⇨ rake; rise from the ashes ⇨ rise

ask

'**ask for trouble/it** (*informal*) behave in a way that is likely to result in problems: *They're asking for trouble, leaving young children alone in the house like that.* ○ *She's really asking for it the way she comes in late every day.* (usually used in the continuous tenses)

I 'ask you! (*informal*) (used to show strong surprise, disbelief, etc): *So they just arrived without telling you they were coming? Well, I ask you!*

if you ask 'me if you want to know my opinion (usually said when an opinion has not been asked for): *If you ask me, Mark shouldn't have bought that car – it just wasn't worth the money.*

ask for/win sb's hand ⇨ hand; **cry/ask for the moon** ⇨ moon

asking

be sb's for the asking be obtained simply by asking (for it): be very easily obtained *If you want any of the furniture, it's yours for the asking.* ○ *Fame and money were hers for the asking in those days.*

asleep be/fall sound asleep ⇨ sound

assured rest assured that ⇨ rest

astray lead sb astray ⇨ lead

atmosphere cut the atmosphere with a knife ⇨ cut

attached no strings attached ⇨ strings

attempt last ditch/stand/attempt/effort ⇨ last

attendance dance attendance on sb ⇨ dance

attention get/have sb's undivided attention ⇨ undivided

avoid

avoid sb/sth like the 'plague (*informal*) avoid sb/sth completely: *It was the sort of restaurant that I would normally have avoided like the plague.*

awakening a rude awakening ⇨ rude

aware be well aware of sth ⇨ well

away get along/away/on! ⇨ get; there's no getting away from it ⇨ getting

awkward

the 'awkward age the period when some young people have difficulties as they approach adult life: *'Gary seems such a quiet boy.' 'Oh, he's just at that awkward age – he'll soon grow out of it.'*

axe

have an 'axe to grind have private, often selfish, reasons for being involved in sth: *Having no particular political axe to grind, he stood for election as an Independent.* (usually used in the negative)

B

babe

a 'babe in 'arms **1** a very young baby not able to walk or crawl. **2** a helpless, inexperienced or innocent person: *He's a babe in arms in financial matters.*

baby

be sb's 'baby (*informal*) be sth that sb has created, is dealing with, etc: *Mary's the lawyer, so the legal problem's her baby.*

be smooth as a baby's bottom = be smooth as silk ⇨ smooth; **leave sb holding the baby** ⇨ leave; **throw the baby out with the bath-water** ⇨ throw; **wet the baby's head** ⇨ wet

back(s)

at/in the back of your mind in your thoughts, but not your main interest or concern: *I think your father knew at the back of* his mind that he was being deceived.

,back and 'forth *or* **backwards and forwards** in one direction and then in the opposite one, repeatedly: *The rope swung back and forth from the branch.* ○ *She travels backwards and forwards between the factory and head office.*

(in) back of sth (*US, informal*) behind sth: *There's a large garden in back of the house.*

the back of beyond (*informal*) a lonely place that is a long way from any town: *That village they've moved to is really in the back of beyond!*

the 'back-room boys (*especially British*) scientists, researchers, etc who do important work but do not have direct contact with the public: *It's thanks to the back-room boys more than to the sales people that the new product is such a success.*

a ,back-seat 'driver (*disapproving*) a passenger who constantly gives a driver unwanted advice and instructions on how to drive; sb who tries to tell the person in charge what to do.

(it's) back to the 'drawing board a new plan must be prepared because an earlier one has failed: *She's refused to consider our offer, so it's back to the drawing board again, I'm afraid.*

,back to 'front with the front part where the back should be: *Your jumper is on back to front.*

,back the wrong 'horse support the person, group etc that later loses a contest or fails to do what was expected: *I certainly backed the wrong horse when I said United would win the Cup Final.* ○ *Many people who had voted for the party in the election were now feeling that they had backed the wrong horse.*

be on sb's 'back (*informal*) annoy or criticize sb a lot: *My new boss is on my back all the time, saying I have to work harder.*

(go) behind sb's back (do sth) without sb knowing, especially because they would not like it: *I feel guilty about going behind his back and complaining to the boss.* ○ *People were often very rude about her behind her back.*

by/through the back door in an indirect or unofficial way: *She has powerful friends, so she got into the diplomatic service by the back door.*

get/put sb's 'back up make sb annoyed: *His silly remarks about her clothes always get her back up.*

get off sb's 'back (*informal*) stop telling sb what to do: *I've done all that already, so why don't you just get off my back?*

get your, etc 'own back (on sb) succeed in getting revenge (against sb): *I got my own back by writing a very rude article about him in the newspaper.*

have (got) your 'back to the wall be in a difficult situation with no easy solution: *Inflation and unemployment have risen this year and the Government has lost a lot of support. The Prime Minister really has his back to the wall now.*

put your 'back into sth work very hard at sth: *We'll get the job finished today if we put our backs into it.*

take a back seat change to a less important role or function: *After forty years in the business, it's time for me to take a back seat and let someone younger take over.*

be/go back to square one ⇨ square; **break your back doing sth/to do sth** ⇨ break; **break the back of sth** ⇨ break; **fed up to the back teeth with sb/sth** ⇨ fed; **get your breath back** ⇨ breath; **give sb/yourself a pat on the back** ⇨ pat; **go back on your word** ⇨ word; **have eyes in the back of your head** ⇨ eyes; **know sth like the back of your hand** ⇨ know; **make a rod for your own back** ⇨ rod; **mind your backs** ⇨ mind; **never/not look back** ⇨ look; **pat sb/yourself on the back = give sb/yourself a pat on the back** ⇨ pat; **pay sth back/return sth with interest** ⇨ interest; **put/turn the clock back** ⇨ clock; **see the back of sb/sth** ⇨ see; **a short back and sides** ⇨ short; **stab sb in the back** ⇨ stab; **turn your back on sb/sth** ⇨ turn; **water off a duck's back** ⇨ water; **way back** ⇨ way; **with one hand tied behind your back** ⇨ hand; **you scratch my back, I'll scratch yours** ⇨ scratch

backside a kick up the backside = a kick in the pants ⇨ kick

backwards
bend/lean over backwards to do sth

try very hard to help or please sb: *We've bent over backwards to help the child, but she refuses to cooperate.*

know sth backwards ⇨ know

bacon **bring home the bacon** ⇨ home; **save your/sb's bacon** ⇨ save

bad

not (so/too) bad (*informal*) quite good: *'How are you feeling today?' 'Not too bad, thanks.'* ○ *Some of his recent books are really not bad.*

(it's) too bad (*informal*) **1** (used to show sympathy or disappointment): *It's too bad you can't come to the party.* **2** (*informal*) (used to show that you are not sympathetic): *I know you don't want me to go. Well, too bad, I'm going!*

bad faith ⇨ faith; **bad/hard/tough luck!** ⇨ luck; **be in a bad way** ⇨ way; **be in good/bad odour** ⇨ odour; **be not bad going = be good going** ⇨ going; **come to a bad/sticky end** ⇨ end; **give sb/sth up as a bad job** ⇨ job; **go from bad to worse** ⇨ worse; **go through, hit, etc a bad/ sticky patch** ⇨ patch; **good/bad form** ⇨ form; **in good/bad repair** ⇨ repair; **leave a nasty/bad taste in the/your mouth** ⇨ leave; **look bad** ⇨ look; **throw good money after bad** ⇨ throw; **with good/bad grace** ⇨ grace

bag

bag and 'baggage with all your belongings: *If you don't pay the rent, you'll be thrown out, bag and baggage.*

a ,bag of 'bones (*informal*) a very thin person or animal: *She refused to eat, until eventually she was a bag of bones.*

in the bag (*informal*) (of a successful result) certain to be achieved: *With a three-goal lead and only ten minutes of the match left to play, victory seemed in the bag.*

be a mixed bag/bunch ⇨ mixed; **a bundle/bag of nerves** ⇨ nerves; **let the cat out of the bag** ⇨ cat; **an old bag** ⇨ old; **she/he couldn't punch her/his way out of a paper bag** ⇨ punch

baggage **bag and baggage** ⇨ bag

bags

bags (I)/(I) bags (*informal*) (used especially by children for claiming the right to have or do sth before anyone else): *Bags I the front seat!* ○ *I bags the biggest one!*

pack your bags ⇨ pack; **three bags full** ⇨ three

bait **rise to the bait** ⇨ rise; **swallow the bait** ⇨ swallow

baker

a baker's 'dozen thirteen.

balance

(be/hang) in the balance be at a point where sth could either develop well or badly; be uncertain: *With the election results due to be announced this afternoon, the future of the party still hangs very much in the balance.*

on 'balance when advantages and disadvantages, successes and failures, etc have been compared: *It has been decided that, on balance, she is the best person for the job despite her lack of experience.*

strike a balance ⇨ strike; **tip the balance/scales** ⇨ tip

ball

the ball is in sb's 'court it is sb's turn to speak, act, etc next: *I've given them a list of the changes that I think are necessary, so the ball's in their court now.*

be on the ball be aware of what is happening and be able to react or deal with it quickly: *For the assistant manager's job we need someone who's really on the ball.*

have (yourself) a 'ball (*informal, especially US*) enjoy yourself very much: *When these exams are finally over, we're going to have a ball.*

set/start/keep the 'ball rolling begin/ continue an activity, discussion etc: *I will set the ball rolling by introducing the first speaker.*

play ball ⇨ play

balloon

when the bal'loon goes up (*informal*) when the trouble or important event begins: *I don't want to be there when the balloon goes up.*

banana **slip on a banana skin** ⇨ slip

bandwagon

climb/jump on the 'bandwagon (*informal*) do sth that others are already doing because it is successful or fashionable: *As soon as their policies became popular all the other parties started to climb on the bandwagon.*

bane

the bane of sb's life/existence a person or thing that makes sb's life unpleasant or unhappy: *That car is always breaking down! It's the bane of my life.*

bang

bang goes sth (*informal*) sth is suddenly gone, finished, lost, etc: *I broke my leg and bang went my chances of playing in the match.*

bang/spot 'on (*informal*) (of an estimate, a description, etc) exactly right: *She was bang on when she called him an idiot – that's just what he is!* ○ *Your sales estimate was spot on. Well done!*

go (off) with a 'bang (*informal*) (of an event, etc) be very successful: *Last night's party really went off with a bang.*

be, etc bang on time = be, etc on time ⇨ time; **knock/bang heads together** ⇨ heads

baptism

a ,baptism of 'fire an unpleasant or frightening first experience of sth: *Her first day in the job was a real baptism of fire because she had to deal with a very difficult case immediately.*

bar

bar none without exception: *This is the best apple pie I've ever tasted, bar none.*

everything but/bar the kitchen sink ⇨ kitchen; **be all over bar the shouting** ⇨ over; **prop up the bar** ⇨ prop

bare

the bare 'bones (of sth) the main or basic facts of a matter: *I had so little time that I could only tell him the bare bones of the story and had to supply the details later.*

bare your soul tell sb your deepest feelings: *Finally she bared her soul to him, saying she had always loved him.*

with your bare hands with your hands only, without any tools or weapons: *He said he'd killed a crocodile with his bare hands!*

lay sth bare ⇨ lay

bargain

into the 'bargain as well; in addition: *She gave us tea and some useful information into the bargain.*

drive a hard bargain ⇨ drive; **strike a bargain** ⇨ strike

bargaining

a 'bargaining counter a special advantage in negotiations, disputes, etc which can be offered in exchange for sth: *The proposed troop reductions were a useful bargaining counter in the disarmament talks.*

barge

not touch sb/sth with a barge-pole ⇨ touch

bark

sb's bark is worse than their bite (*informal*) sb is not really as angry or unkind as they seem: *Don't worry about my father being angry – his bark is worse than his bite.*

bark up the wrong 'tree be mistaken about sth: *The police are barking up the wrong tree if they think I had anything to do with the crime. I wasn't even in the country when it happened!*

barred

no holds barred ⇨ holds

barrel

have (got) sb over a barrel (*informal*) have sb in a position where they are forced to do what you want: *She has us over a barrel – if we don't pay her, we lose everything.*

lock, stock and barrel ⇨ lock; **scrape the barrel** ⇨ scrape

bars

behind 'bars (*informal*) in prison: *Criminals like him ought to be put behind bars for life.*

base

off base (*US, informal*) **1** mistaken: *You're way off base with that guess.* **2** unprepared: *The question caught her off base.*

get to first base ⇨ first

bash

have a bash at (doing) sth (*informal*) make an attempt at sth: *I'm going to have a bash at mending the car.*

bask bathe/bask in reflected glory
⇨ reflected

basket put all your eggs into one
basket ⇨ eggs

bat

like a ,bat out of 'hell (*informal*) very fast:
*If there were a fire, I wouldn't wait to sound the
alarm, I'd be off like a bat out of hell!*

not bat an 'eyelid not seem surprised,
worried, afraid, etc: *She didn't bat an eyelid
when they told her she had lost her job. She just
calmly walked out.*

,off your own 'bat independently,
without the encouragement or help of
others: *Nobody had even tried to persuade Tim
to give up smoking; he did it off his own bat.*

blind as a bat ⇨ blind

bated

with ,bated 'breath hardly able to
breathe because you are very anxious about
sth: *We watched with bated breath as the lion
moved slowly towards him.*

bath throw the baby out with the
bath-water ⇨ throw

bathe bathe/bask in reflected glory
⇨ reflected

bats

have ,bats in the 'belfry (*becoming dated,
informal*) be eccentric or mad.

batteries recharge your batteries
⇨ recharge

battle

do/join battle (with sb) fight, compete
or argue (with sb): *Paul Wilkins will do battle
with Ray Jobson tonight for the British
middleweight boxing championship.* ○ *A group
of local parents have decided to join battle with
the council about their decision to close two of
the town's schools.*

fight a losing battle ⇨ fight; half the
battle ⇨ half; a pitched battle
⇨ pitched; a running battle ⇨ running

bay

hold/keep sb/sth at 'bay prevent sb/sth
from coming too close or attacking: *Vitamin
C helps to keep colds and flu at bay.*

be

the ,be-all and 'end-all (of sth)
(*informal*) the most important thing/person;
the only thing/person that matters: *His
girlfriend is the be-all and end-all of his
existence.* ○ *I'll never be rich, but money isn't
the be-all and end-all, you know.*

,be that as it 'may whether that is true or
not; despite that: *'The film got very good
reviews.' 'Be that as it may, I didn't enjoy it.'*

so be it ⇨ so

beach not the only pebble on the
beach ⇨ pebble

beam

off (the) beam (*informal*) wrong;
incorrect: *No, you're way off beam there.*

broad in the beam ⇨ broad

bean(s)

not (have) a 'bean (*informal, becoming
dated*) (have) no money at all: *'How much
have you saved?' 'Not a bean.'*

full of beans ⇨ full; spill the beans
⇨ spill

bear

bear the brunt of sth suffer most as the
result of an attack, loss, misfortune, etc: *We
all lost money when the business collapsed, but
I bore the brunt of it because I had invested
most.*

bear 'fruit have the desired result; be
successful: *The tireless efforts of campaigners
have finally borne fruit and the prisoners are
due to be released tomorrow.*

like a ,bear with a sore 'head (*informal*)
very bad-tempered: *She's like a bear with a
sore head in the mornings.*

bear/carry your cross ⇨ cross; bear/
keep sb/sth in mind ⇨ mind; bring
pressure to bear (on sb) (to do sth) = put
pressure on sb (to do sth) ⇨ pressure;
grin and bear it ⇨ grin

bearings

get/find your 'bearings find out exactly
where you are, or the details of the situation
you are in, especially when this is new and
unfamiliar: *We got off the bus right in
the centre of town and it took us a moment or
two to get our bearings.* ○ *I've only been in the*

job for a week so I'm still finding my bearings.
lose your bearings ⇨ lose

beast **be no good/use to man or beast**
⇨ man

beat

beat about the 'bush take too long
before saying what you want to say; avoid
saying sth directly: *Don't beat about the bush.*
Tell me exactly what you think is wrong with
my work.

beat sb at their own game be more
successful than sb in their special activity,
sport, etc; defeat sb using their own
methods: *If you thought someone was trying to*
cheat you, would you challenge him or try to
beat him at his own game?

beat your breast (*often ironic*) show that
you know you have done sth wrong and are
sorry for this (often used for suggesting that
you seem too sorry and so are not sincere): *If*
anything happens to the children while you're
out enjoying yourself, don't come beating your
breast to me about it afterwards.

beat the drum (for sb/sth) speak
enthusiastically in support of sb/sth:
Amongst the speakers at the Moscow
conference were many who were eager to beat
the drum for private investment.

beat sb/sth 'hollow beat sb easily in a
contest, etc; be much better than sb/sth: *As a*
cook he beats the professionals hollow.

'beat it (*informal*) (usually used as a
command) go away: *You're not wanted here,*
so beat it.

beat a re'treat go or run away from sb/
sth.

beat 'time show the rhythm of a piece of
music by striking sth, moving your hands,
etc.

,can you 'beat it/'that? (*informal*) (used to
express disbelief, surprise, annoyance, etc):
Can you beat that? He has just broken another
glass.

it ,beats 'me (why, how, etc) (*informal*) I
cannot understand (why, how, etc): *It beats*
me how he can afford a new car on the salary he
earns. ○ *What she does with her time beats me.*

beat/scare the daylights out of sb
⇨ daylights; **beat/knock/kick the hell**
out of sb/sth ⇨ hell; **beat/knock/kick**

the shit out of sb = beat/knock/kick the
hell out of sb ⇨ hell; **your heart misses a**
beat ⇨ heart; **win/beat sb hands down**
⇨ hands

beaten

off the ,beaten 'track far away from
where people normally live or go: *Our house*
is a bit off the beaten track.

beauty

,beauty is in the ,eye of the be'holder
(*saying*) what one person thinks is beautiful
may not seem beautiful to somebody else.

beauty is only skin 'deep (*saying*)
physical appearance is no guide to a
person's character.

the beauty of (doing) sth the advantage
of (doing) sth: *The beauty of (having) a small*
car is that it makes it so much easier to find a
parking space.

get your 'beauty sleep (*humorous*) go to
bed early so that you wake up feeling
healthy and looking attractive: *Look how late*
it is! I won't get my beauty sleep tonight.

beaver **an eager beaver** ⇨ eager

beck

at sb's ,beck and 'call always ready and
required to do exactly what sb asks: *Working*
as a shop assistant means being at the
customers' beck and call all day.

bed

get out of bed on the wrong side be
bad-tempered from the moment when you
get up: *Why is Pete so irritable this morning?*
He must have got out of bed on the wrong side
again!

go to bed with sb have sex with sb: *He*
asked her to go to bed with him.

have ,made your bed and have to 'lie
on it have to accept a difficult or unpleasant
situation that you have caused yourself:
Linda has borrowed more money than she can
ever pay back, but I suppose she's made her bed
and now she's got to lie on it.

take to your 'bed go to bed and stay there
because of illness: *She has taken to her bed*
with a bad bout of flu.

a bed of roses = be all roses ⇨ roses; **die**
in your bed ⇨ die; **reds under the bed**
⇨ reds

bedfellows be/make strange bedfellows ⇨ strange

bee

the ˌbee's 'knees (*informal*) a wonderful person or thing: *He thinks he's the bee's knees* (he has a high opinion of himself).

have (got) a 'bee in your bonnet (*informal*) have an obsession about sth: *Harry's always going around opening windows. He's got a bee in his bonnet about fresh air.*

make a 'bee-line for sb/sth (*informal*) move directly towards sb/sth: *The children made a bee-line for the food the moment they came in.*

a busy bee ⇨ busy

beer small beer ⇨ small

bees the birds and the bees ⇨ birds

beetroot as red as a beetroot ⇨ red

beg

beg the 'question not deal properly with the matter being discussed because you assume that certain facts are true when they have not been proved: *This proposal begs the question of whether a change is needed at all.*

ˌbeg, ˌsteal or 'borrow obtain sth any way you can: *We'll have to beg, steal or borrow enough money to pay the fines.*

beg to differ (*formal*) (usually with *I*) disagree: *I must beg to differ on this. I think you are quite mistaken.*

I beg your pardon 1 (used as a polite way of apologizing for sth you have just said or done): *Did I step on your toe? Oh, I beg your pardon!* 2 (used when you have not heard or understood something) please repeat that. 3 (used to show that you are angry or offended): *I beg your pardon! I'd rather you didn't refer to me as 'that fat man'.*

beggar(s)

beggar beˈlief/deˈscription be too strange and unusual to be believed/described: *Tim left two windows wide open when he went on holiday. His stupidity beggars belief!* ○ *The sight of him half naked and covered with mud and oil beggared description.*

ˌbeggars can't be 'choosers (*informal, saying*) when there is no choice, you have to be satisfied with whatever you can get: *I would have preferred a bed, but beggars can't be choosers so I slept on the sofa.*

if wishes were horses, beggars would/might ride ⇨ wishes

begging

go 'begging (of things) be unwanted: *I'll have that last potato if it's going begging.* (*go* is usually used in continuous tenses)

begin charity begins at home ⇨ charity

beginner

beginner's 'luck good luck or success at the start of learning to do sth.

behold lo and behold ⇨ lo

beholder beauty is in the eye of the beholder ⇨ beauty

being for the time being ⇨ time

belfry have bats in the belfry ⇨ bats

belief beggar belief/description ⇨ beggar

believe

beˌlieve it or 'not it is true, even though it does not sound likely: *Believe it or not, I've just won £10 000 in a competition!* ○ *I am still, believe it or not, very nervous about speaking in public.*

beˌlieve (you) 'me (used for emphasizing a statement, promise, threat, etc): *I'll be seeing her tomorrow, and, believe you me, I'll tell her exactly what I think of her disgusting behaviour.*

if you, they, etc believe ˌthat, you'll, they'll, etc believe 'anything (*informal*) you, they, etc would be very stupid to believe that: *He says he'll pay for your holiday? Well, if you believe that, you'll believe anything!*

I'll believe it/that when I see it (*informal*) (used for expressing doubt that sth will happen or be done): *'He says he's going to give up smoking.' 'I'll believe that when I see it!'*

make believe (that...) pretend (that...): *The journey seemed like an attempt to make believe that the modern world didn't exist.*

not beˌlieve your 'eyes/'ears (usually

used with *can't* or *couldn't*) think that sth you see/hear is very surprising: *I couldn't believe my ears when I heard my name mentioned on the radio.* ○ *I could hardly believe my eyes when I saw the professor arrive dressed as a clown.*

lead sb to believe ⟶ lead

believing

,**seeing is be'lieving** (*saying*) if you actually see sth you can be certain it is true.

bell **clear as a bell** ⟶ clear; **ring a bell** ⟶ ring; **saved by the bell** ⟶ saved

bellyful

have had a bellyful of sb/sth (*informal*) have had too much of sb/sth: *I've had a bellyful of his complaining. If he doesn't stop, I'm leaving.*

belt

below the 'belt (of a comment, attack, etc) unfair and unkind: *Her remarks about his age were a bit below the belt.* (refers to the rule in boxing that forbids blows below the waist)

under your belt already achieved and so making you feel more confident: *With ten years' experience under his belt, Mark was ready to start his own business.* ○ *You'll need to get some qualifications under your belt before you start looking for work.*

tighten your belt ⟶ tighten

bend **bend/lean over backwards to do sth** ⟶ backwards; **bend/stretch the rules** ⟶ rules; **round the bend/twist** ⟶ round

bended

on bended 'knee(s) kneeling to pray or ask for sth: *He went down on bended knee and asked her to marry him.*

beneath **beneath contempt** ⟶ contempt; **beneath sb's dignity** ⟶ dignity

benefit

give sb the benefit of the doubt accept that a person is right or innocent because you cannot prove that they are not: *The old man said that he had put the goods in his bag by mistake and the shopkeeper decided to give him the benefit of the doubt.*

bent

'**bent on (doing) sth** (*informal*) determined to do or have sth: *I advised her against it, but she was bent on taking part in the marathon.* ○ *It is a terrorist organization, bent on destroying the Government.* see also **hell-bent on (doing) sth** ⟶ hell

berth **give sb/sth a wide berth** ⟶ wide

beside **be beside the point** ⟶ point

best

all the 'best (a polite expression used especially when saying goodbye, ending a letter or when drinking with sb) I hope everything goes well for you; good luck: *All the best, then, Maria, and we'll see you in a fortnight.* ○ *Here's wishing you all the best for the coming year.*

at 'best/'worst taking the most/least hopeful or positive view: *Smoking is at best unpleasant and expensive, and at worst lethal.*

at the 'best of times (even) when conditions are good: *This car does not go very fast at the best of times, and with four people in it it will go a lot slower.*

be (all) for the 'best have a good result, though it does not seem good at first: *I was very disappointed when I didn't get the job but now I think it was for the best. I don't think I would have liked it.*

your best bet (*informal*) the best thing for you to do in a particular situation: *Your best bet is to leave the car here and get a bus into town.*

the best of 'both worlds the advantages of two very different situations: *We have the best of both worlds here – it's a peaceful village but we're only twenty minutes from the town centre.*

the best of (British) luck (to sb) *or* **the best of British (to sb)** (*informal, often ironic*) (used to wish sb luck in an activity, especially one in which they are unlikely to be successful): *The four of you are going to live in that tiny flat? The best of British to you!*

look your/its 'best look as attractive, neat, etc as possible: *The garden looks its best when all the flowers are out.*

make the best of sth/things/a bad job do as well as you can in a difficult situation: *It wasn't a very large room, but he made the* *best of it by using space carefully.* ○ *I know the lighting isn't perfect but we'll have to make the best of a bad job and get the best photos we can.*

put your best foot forward go, work, etc as fast as you can: *If we put our best foot forward, we should be there by noon.*

with the 'best of them as well as anybody: *She may be seventy, but she can get up and dance with the best of them!*

with the ˌbest will in the 'world even though you have tried very hard to be fair, generous etc: *He's quite competent, but with the best will in the world, I can't imagine him as head of a large company.*

be past your/its best ⇨ past; **the better/ best part of sth** ⇨ part; **do/try your level best** ⇨ level; **for a/some reason/reasons best known to herself, etc** ⇨ reason; **you, etc had better/best do sth** ⇨ better; **hope for the best** ⇨ hope; **know best** ⇨ know; **the next best thing** ⇨ next; **your Sunday best** ⇨ Sunday

bet

(you can) bet your bottom 'dollar/ your 'life (on sth/that...) (*informal*) (you can) be certain of sth: *You can bet your bottom dollar that he'll forget to come.*

I('ll) bet (that...) (*informal*) I am certain (that...): *I bet he'll get drunk at the party – he always does.* (often used to show that you agree with sb or are not surprised to hear sth: *'I'm furious about what he said to me?' 'I bet (you are)!'*

ˌyou 'bet (*very informal*) certainly: *'Would you like an ice-cream?' 'You bet!'* ○ *'Are you hungry?' 'You bet I am!'*

your best bet ⇨ best; **a safe bet** ⇨ safe

betide   woe betide sb ⇨ woe

bets   hedge your bets ⇨ hedge

better

against your better 'judgement although you know your action, decision, etc is not sensible: *She was persuaded against her better judgement to lend him the money, and now she's regretting it.*

be better 'off be richer, happier, more fortunate, etc: *'You'd be better off with a smaller house, now that your children have left home.'* ○ *Under the new tax regulations I will be*

£17 *a month better off.*

be better off (doing sth) be more sensible (to do sth specified): *You'd be better off resting at home with that cold.*

ˌbetter the ˌdevil you 'know (than the ˌdevil you don't) (*saying*) it is better to deal with sb/sth bad, difficult, etc that is familiar than to make a change and perhaps have to deal with sb/sth worse.

(all) the better for sth made better by (doing) sth; benefiting from sth: *You'll be all the better for (having had) a holiday by the sea.*

ˌbetter ˌlate than 'never (*saying*) it's better to arrive, do sth, etc late than not to arrive, do sth, etc at all: *You were supposed to be here an hour ago, but better late than never, I suppose!*

ˌbetter ˌsafe than 'sorry (*saying*) it is better to be too careful than to do sth careless and have to regret your actions later.

do better to do sth be more sensible to do sth: *You would do better to buy a good-quality radio, even if it is more expensive.*

for ˌbetter or (for) 'worse whether the result is good or bad: *I've decided, for better or for worse, to leave my job.*

get the 'better of sb/sth defeat sb/sth: *She always manages to get the better of me at tennis.* ○ *Eventually, his curiosity got the better of him and he had to take a look in the box.*

go one 'better (than sb/sth) do better (than sb/sth); beat (sb) by improving on what they have done: *I bought a new tennis racket but my sister had to go one better (than me) by buying the most expensive one in the shop.*

you, etc had best/better do sth you, etc should do sth: *You'd better lock the door before you leave: there are lots of thieves about.* ○ *Hadn't you better check to see if the baby is all right?* ○ *'Shall I phone her now?' 'You'd best not. She might be asleep.'*

have seen/known better 'days be in a worse condition than in the past: *That jacket of yours has seen better days – isn't it time you bought a new one?*

so much the 'better/'worse (for sb/ sth) it is better/worse for that reason: *'I seem to have made my curry hotter than usual.' 'So much the better. I love hot curries.'*

your better/other half ⇨ half; **the better/best part of sth** ⇨ part; **half a loaf is better than none/no bread** ⇨ half; **the less/least said, the better** ⇨ said; **not know any better** ⇨ know; **take a turn for the better/worse** ⇨ turn; **think better of sth/doing sth** ⇨ think; **two heads are better than one** ⇨ two

between

between you and me/ourselves (*informal*) as a secret or private matter that nobody else should know about: *Just between you and me, I've heard that the business made a big loss last year.*

in between neither one thing nor another, but having some qualities of both; between two states, kinds, sizes, etc: *'Would you call this dress green or blue?' 'I'd say it was in between.'*

betwixt and between ⇨ betwixt; **few and far between** ⇨ few

beyond

be beyond sb (*informal*) too difficult, amazing, etc to be understood by sb: *Why she decided to marry such a boring man is beyond me.* ○ *Some of the questions in that exam were beyond me, I'm afraid.*

above and beyond sth ⇨ above; **the back of beyond** ⇨ back; **beyond the call of duty** ⇨ call; **not see beyond/past the end of your nose** ⇨ see

bide

bide your time wait for a suitable opportunity to do sth: *She is biding her time until the right job comes along.*

big

Big Brother (is watching you) the state, controlling every aspect of citizens' lives: *We live in a society where all kinds of information about the individual may be stored on computer. Big Brother, if not actually watching you, can quickly check on you if he wants to.* (from the novel 1984 by George Orwell)

a big cheese/wheel (*informal*) an important and influential person in an organization, etc: *His father's a big wheel in the textile industry.*

big deal (*very informal, ironic*) (used for suggesting that sth is not as important or

impressive as sb else thinks it is): *'I've got tickets for next Saturday's football match.' 'Big deal! Who's interested in football anyway?'*

a big fish (in a little pond) an important person (but only in a small community, group, etc): *I would rather stay here in the village and be a big fish in a little pond than go to the city.*

a big noise/shot (*informal*) an important person: *'What does Ian's dad do?' 'Oh, he's a big shot in the City.'*

give sb a big 'hand (*informal*) clap loudly and enthusiastically: *Let's have a big hand, ladies and gentlemen, for our next performer....*

too big for your boots (*informal*) conceited; thinking that you are more important than you really are: *His political rivals had decided that he was getting too big for his boots.*

do sth in a big/small way ⇨ way; **Mr Big** ⇨ Mr; **one big happy family** ⇨ one; **talk big** ⇨ talk; **think big** ⇨ think

bigger

sb's eyes are bigger than their stomach ⇨ eyes; **have other/bigger fish to fry** ⇨ fish

bill

bill and 'coo (*informal*) (of lovers) kiss and whisper lovingly together.

head/top the bill be (listed as) the most important item or performer in a show, play, etc.

a clean bill of health ⇨ clean; **fit the bill** ⇨ fit; **foot the bill** ⇨ foot

bind

bind/tie sb hand and foot ⇨ hand

bird

a ,bird's ,eye 'view (of sth) a good view of sth from high above: *From the church tower you get a bird's eye view of the town.*

the bird has 'flown the person who was being chased or looked for has escaped or gone away: *The police raided the house at dawn, but the bird had flown.*

a bird in the ,hand is worth two in the 'bush (*saying*) it is better to be satisfied with what you have got than to lose it trying to get sth more or better.

a ,bird of 'passage a person who does not stay in a place for very long.

the early bird catches the worm

⇨ early; **free as air/as a bird** ⇨ free; **a home bird** ⇨ home; **a little bird told me** ⇨ little; **a rare bird** ⇨ rare

birds

the birds and the 'bees the basic facts about sex and reproduction, the 'facts of life', as told to children: *Now that Jamie is eleven, isn't it time you told him about the birds and the bees?*

birds of a 'feather (flock to'gether) (*saying*) similar people (spend time together).

(strictly) for the birds (*informal*) not important or interesting.

kill two birds with one stone ⇨ kill

birthday

in/wearing your 'birthday suit (*informal, humorous*) wearing no clothes; naked: *The towel fell off, and there he was in his birthday suit!*

biscuit

take the biscuit/cake (*informal*) be especially surprising, annoying, etc: *Well, that really takes the biscuit! She asks if she can borrow the car, then keeps it for a month!*

bit

bit by 'bit *also* **little by little** a small amount at a time; gradually: *We managed to save the money bit by bit over a period of ten years.* ○ *Little by little, she began to feel better after her illness.*

a bit 'much (*informal*) too much to be acceptable; unreasonable: *Claiming £50 a day for expenses is a bit much, I think.* ○ *Don't you think it's a bit much of him to give me most of the work and then take the afternoon off?*

a bit of all 'right (*very informal*) a very attractive person: *He's a bit of all right, don't you think, Madge?*

a bit of a coward, fool, etc (*informal*) rather cowardly, foolish, etc.

a bit on the 'side (*informal*) a sexual relationship with sb who is not your regular partner: *He's always looking for a bit on the side.*

a bit thick/strong (*informal*) not fair or acceptable: *It's a bit thick of him to expect me to pay every time we go out together.*

do your bit (*informal*) do your share of a task, help a cause, etc: *Everyone is expected to* do their bit to make the business successful. ○ *In re-using this old paper I'm doing my bit for conservation of the rain forests.*

get/take the bit between your 'teeth (*informal*) start doing sth in a determined and enthusiastic way: *Once he gets the bit between his teeth in an argument, no one can stop him.* (the bit is the metal part of the bridle which goes in a horse's mouth and is used to control the horse. If the horse learns to hold the bit between its teeth then it can no longer be controlled by the rider)

not a 'bit (of it) *or* **not one ˌbit** not at all: *I thought she would be glad to see him but not a bit of it – she made some excuse and left as soon as he got here.* ○ *'Do you mind if I borrow the car today?' 'Not one bit. You go ahead.'*

be a bit/rather steep ⇨ steep; **the biter bit** ⇨ biter; **champ at the bit** ⇨ champ; **go a bit far = go too far** ⇨ far; **not a blind bit of notice, difference, etc** ⇨ blind

bitch   a/the son of a bitch ⇨ son

bite

bite the 'bullet (*informal*) realize that you cannot avoid sth unpleasant, and so accept it: *Getting your car repaired is often an expensive business but all you can do is bite the bullet and pay up.*

bite the 'dust (*informal, often humorous*) be killed, defeated, ruined or finished: *Thousands of small businesses will bite the dust if the new tax is introduced.*

bite the hand that 'feeds you be unkind or disloyal to sb who has been kind to you or helpful to you, or who pays your wages: *When you say such nasty things about the organization, you are biting the hand that feeds you.*

bite sb's head off (*informal*) speak to sb angrily without good reason: *It was only a suggestion – there's no need to bite my head off!*

bite your 'lip force yourself not to express the anger, fear, disappointment, etc that you are feeling: *You could tell she thought the criticism was unfair but she bit her lip and said nothing.*

bite your '(finger-)nails (put or press your fingers to your mouth because you) feel very excited, nervous, or afraid. **nail-biting** (*adjective*) very exciting or tense: *What an exciting film that was – real nail-*

biting stuff!

bite off more than you can 'chew (*informal*) attempt to do sth that is too difficult for you or that you do not have enough time to do: *He's promised to get all this work finished by the weekend but I've got a feeling he's bitten off more than he can chew.*

sb's bark is worse than their bite ⇨ bark

biter

the biter 'bit the person who wanted to do harm, cheat sb, etc, has harm done to them, is cheated, etc: *It was a case of the biter bit — she had tried to make him look foolish and ended up being ridiculed herself.*

bites

have/get two bites at/of the 'cherry *or* **have/get a second/another bite at/of the 'cherry** have a second attempt at doing sth, especially sth you have failed to do earlier: *We lost that contract with the German firm last year and we probably won't get two bites at the cherry.*

bits

bits and 'bobs *or* **bits and 'pieces** (*informal*) small things of various kinds; belongings: *The box contained needles and thread and various bits and bobs for sewing.* ○ *She let me store a few bits and pieces in her flat while I was abroad.*

pick, pull, etc sb/sth to 'bits/'pieces criticize sb/sth severely and find as many faults with them/it as you can: *The committee pulled his proposals to bits. They didn't have anything positive at all to say about them.* ○ *As soon as she left the room, everyone started pulling her to pieces.*

thrilled to bits ⇨ thrilled

bitten be bitten by/have the bug ⇨ bug; once bitten, twice shy ⇨ once

bitter

a bitter 'pill (for sb)(to swallow) a thing that is very difficult or unpleasant to accept: *He had been a wealthy man, so having to ask for money must have been a bitter pill to swallow.*

to the bitter 'end right to the end, no matter how long it takes; until everything possible has been done: *Now that we have* begun this project, we must see it through to the bitter end. ○ *We are determined to fight to the bitter end.*

black

black and 'blue covered with bruises: *She was black and blue all over after falling down stairs.*

(in) black and 'white (as) absolutely right or wrong, good or bad, with no grades between them: *My grandmother has very rigid ideas of character and behaviour; she sees everything in black and white.* ○ *It's not a black-and-white issue.*

a black day (for sb) a day when sth sad, unpleasant or disastrous happens (to sb): *It was a black day for this area when the local steel factory closed down.*

a black 'eye dark, bruised skin around the eye caused by an accident, sb hitting you, etc: *How did you get that black eye?*

a black 'look an angry or disapproving expression on sb's face: *She gave me a black look when I suggested she should do the washing-up.*

a black 'mark (against sb) sth that sb has done which makes other people dislike or disapprove of them: *It was definitely a black mark against her that she had not gone to the meeting.*

the black 'sheep (of the family) a person who is considered to have done sth bad, or to be a failure, by their family or the group to which they belong: *Debbie is the black sheep of the family, having left home at seventeen to live with her boyfriend.*

'black spot a place where accidents often happen, especially on a road: *This junction is a well-known accident black spot.*

he, it, etc is not as black as he, it, etc is 'painted he, it, etc is not as bad as people say: *The boss is not as black as she's painted: in fact, I find her quite helpful and friendly.*

in black and 'white in print or writing: *I want to see his statement down in black and white.*

look black ⇨ look; **the pot calling the kettle black** ⇨ pot

blank

a blank 'cheque permission to act as you like (especially to spend money) in a particular task or situation: *Just because I asked you to speak on my behalf, that didn't mean you had a blank cheque to promise anything you liked.* ○ *She was given a blank cheque and told to hire the best singers she could.*

ask, tell, etc sb point blank ⇨ point; **draw a blank** ⇨ draw

blanket a wet blanket ⇨ wet

blast (at) full blast ⇨ full

blaze(s)

blaze a/the 'trail be the first to do sth important or interesting: *As the first female Member of Parliament, she blazed a trail that many others were to follow.*

like blazes ⇨ mad

bleed(s)

bleed sb dry/white (*informal*) take away all sb's money: *He used to be quite wealthy, but his children have bled him dry.*

your heart bleeds for sb ⇨ heart

bless

(God) 'bless you *or* **God bless** (said to sb who has sneezed, or used for expressing thanks or affection): *God bless you, my dear. It's most kind of you to help.*

(God) ,bless your, his, etc 'heart/'soul (used to express affection for sb who has just been mentioned): *Your mother, bless her heart, is the only friend I have.*

blessing(s)

a blessing in dis'guise a thing that seems bad, unpleasant, etc at first but that has advantages in the end: *Not getting that job turned out to be a blessing in disguise, as the firm went out of business only a few months later.*

count your blessings ⇨ count; **a mixed blessing** ⇨ mixed

blind

a ,blind 'alley a course of action which has no useful result in the end: *Our first experiment was a blind alley, but the second one gave us very promising results.*

(as) blind as a 'bat (*informal*) not able to see well: *I'm as blind as a bat without my glasses.*

a ,blind 'date (*informal*) a social meeting between two people who have never met before, often arranged by friends, in the hope that it may lead to a love affair: *A friend of mine set up a blind date for me with his girlfriend's sister.*

blind 'drunk (*informal*) very drunk.

the blind leading the 'blind (*saying*) (an example of) a person with as little ability or knowledge as the person they are trying to help or teach: *I don't know why she asked me to show her how the computer works when I've hardly used it myself. It would be a case of the blind leading the blind!*

a/sb's 'blind spot a small part of a subject that sb does not understand or know anything about: *I'm a real music lover but I have to say that modern jazz is a bit of a blind spot with me.*

blind sb with science deliberately confuse sb with your special knowledge, especially by using difficult or technical words which they do not understand: *Every time I ask her a simple question, she tries to blind me with science.*

not a 'blind bit of notice, difference, etc (*informal*) no notice, difference, etc at all: *She didn't take a blind bit of notice when I asked her to stop. She walked straight past me.*

love is blind ⇨ love; **rob sb blind** ⇨ rob; **swear blind** ⇨ swear; **turn a blind eye** ⇨ turn

blink

on the 'blink (*informal*) (of a machine) not working properly: *Can I watch the film at your house? Our TV's on the blink again.*

block a chip off the old block ⇨ chip; **put/lay your head on the block** ⇨ head

blood

bad blood (between A and B) feelings of hatred or strong dislike: *There has always been bad blood between the two families.*

be out for/after sb's 'blood (*informal*) want to hurt or harm sb, especially as revenge: *They have been after my blood ever since I accidentally damaged their car.*

blood and 'thunder (*informal*) sensational and very dramatic incidents in plays, films, stories, contests, etc: *I don't like blood-and-thunder novels.*

blood is thicker than 'water (*saying*)

your family is more important than other people.

sb's blood is 'up (*informal*) sb feels angry and aggressive: *Normally, he's a quiet man, but when his blood is up he can be very violent.*

have (got) (sb's) 'blood on your hands be responsible for sb's death: *He's a tyrant with the blood of millions of innocent people on his hands.*

in the/sb's blood/genes part of sb's nature and shared by other members of their family: *Both his father and his mother were writers, so literature is in his blood.*

like getting blood out of/from a 'stone (*informal*) (especially of trying to get money from sb) extremely difficult: *Persuading Joe to lend you £10 is like trying to get blood out of a stone.*

make sb's blood 'boil (*informal*) make sb very angry: *Seeing him beating that little dog made my blood boil.*

make sb's blood 'freeze *or* **make sb's 'blood run 'cold** make sb feel horror or extreme fear: *A terrifying scream in the blackness of the night made my blood run cold.*

new/fresh/young blood new members of a group or organization who have fresh ideas, skills, etc and so make the group more efficient: *What this committee really needs is some new blood.*

burst a blood vessel ⇨ burst; **flesh and blood** ⇨ flesh; **have a rush of blood to the head** ⇨ rush; **in cold blood** ⇨ cold; **more than flesh and blood can stand, endure, etc** ⇨ flesh; **your own flesh and blood** ⇨ flesh; **stir sb's/the blood** ⇨ stir; **sweat blood** ⇨ sweat

blot

blot your 'copy-book (*informal*) spoil a previously good record: *He paid back the money he had stolen and wasn't sacked. But he had blotted his copy-book and couldn't hope for promotion.*

a blot on the 'landscape anything, especially an ugly building, that spoils the appearance of a place: *That power station is rather a blot on the landscape.*

blow

at a (single) 'blow *or* **at one 'blow** with a single action or effort; all at once: *By*

stopping all payments to her sons, she made all three of them poor at one blow.

blow away the 'cobwebs (*informal*) make you feel refreshed, especially after you have been indoors for too long: *After sitting around for hours, we went out and had a long walk along the beach to blow away the cobwebs.*

blow your/sb's 'brains out (*informal*) kill yourself/sb by shooting in the head: *He was so depressed about his debts that he wanted to blow his brains out.*

a ,blow-by-,blow ac'count, description, etc an account, description, etc in which all the details of an event are told in the order in which they happened: *He gave us a blow-by-blow account of everything he had done that day.*

blow sb's 'cover (*informal*) discover or reveal the real identity of sb, especially of a spy, etc: *She had been posing as a diplomat, but her cover was blown when she was found sending coded messages to agents.*

blow the 'gaff (*informal*) reveal a secret: *She didn't want anyone to know where she had been, but her husband blew the gaff.*

blow hot and 'cold (*informal*) keep changing your opinions (about sb/sth): *She keeps blowing hot and cold about the job: one day she says it's marvellous, the next she hates it.*

blow 'me! (*informal, becoming dated*) (used for expressing great surprise): *'Isn't that Alice over there?' 'Well, blow me! I thought she was in Japan!'*

blow your/sb's 'mind (*informal, dated*) make you/sb feel extreme pleasure, excitement, etc. **mind-blowing** (*adjective*) *We were stunned by the mind-blowing beauty of the landscape.*

blow your own 'trumpet (*informal*) boast about your own achievements, abilities, etc; praise yourself: *I don't like to blow my own trumpet, but the office was much better run when I was in charge.*

blow sb/sth sky-'high (*informal*) destroy sb/sth completely in an explosion: *The explosives factory was blown sky-high when one of the workers lit a match.*

blow your 'top (*informal*) suddenly become very angry: *My mum blew her top when she found out that I'd damaged her car.*

blow up in sb's face (of a situation, plan, project, etc) end or fail suddenly, with bad results.

blow the whistle (on sb/sth) (*informal*) stop sb doing sth illegal or wrong by telling a person in authority about it: *One of the police officers blew the whistle on his colleagues when he found out they were taking bribes.*

deal sb/sth a blow ⇨ **deal**; **strike a blow for/against sth** ⇨ **strike**

blowed I'm/I'll be damned/blowed if ⇨ **damned**

blows

come to blows begin to hit each other: *They were shouting at each other so much that I thought they would come to blows.*

see which way the wind blows/is blowing ⇨ **see**

blue

sb's blue-eyed boy (*informal, usually disapproving*) the favourite, especially of a person in authority; a person whom sb thinks is perfect: *Bob is certain to be promoted: he's the manager's blue-eyed boy.*

out of the blue suddenly and unexpectedly: *She had no idea that anything was wrong until he announced out of the blue that he wanted a divorce.*

scream, etc blue murder (*informal*) shout, scream, etc very loudly; make a lot of noise or fuss because you disagree very strongly with sth: *Jill will scream blue murder if Ann gets promoted and she doesn't.*

(do sth) till you are blue in the face (*informal*) (do sth) with a lot of effort and for a very long time without success: *You can argue with John till you are blue in the face, he'll never agree with you.*

between the devil and the deep blue sea ⇨ **devil**; **black and blue** ⇨ **black**; **a bolt from the blue** ⇨ **bolt**; **the boys in blue** ⇨ **boys**; **have a pink/blue fit** ⇨ **fit**; **once in a blue moon** ⇨ **once**

bluff call sb's bluff ⇨ **call**

blushes spare sb's blushes ⇨ **spare**

board(s)

above 'board honest and open; not secret: *All my dealings with the company have been* completely above board.

a cross the 'board affecting everything or everyone in a society, organization, etc, equally: *The government claims that standards in education have fallen right across the board.* ○ *The union demanded an across-the-board salary increase.*

board and 'lodging accommodation and food: *I pay £70 a week for board and lodging.*

go by the 'board (of a plan, idea, etc) be abandoned or rejected: *It's certain that our research will go by the board if the government doesn't agree to continue financing it.*

take sth on 'board (*informal*) accept (an idea, suggestion, etc); recognize (a problem, etc): *I hope the committee takes our recommendations on board when coming to a decision.*

back to the drawing board ⇨ **back**; **be stiff as a board** ⇨ **stiff**; **sweep the board** ⇨ **sweep**; **tread the boards** ⇨ **tread**

boat(s) burn your boats/bridges ⇨ **burn**; **in the same boat** ⇨ **same**; **miss the boat** ⇨ **miss**; **push the boat out** ⇨ **push**; **rock the boat** ⇨ **rock**; **when your ship/boat comes in** ⇨ **ship**

Bob

(and) Bob's your 'uncle (*informal*) (often used after explaining how to do sth, solve a problem, etc to stress how easy it is): *To make the alarm go off at the right time, you just press this button, set the clock, and Bob's your uncle!*

bobs bits and bobs ⇨ **bits**

body

body and 'soul physically and mentally; completely: *She devoted herself body and soul to this political cause.* ○ *The company doesn't own me body and soul just because it pays my salary.*

keep body and soul together (*often humorous*) manage to stay alive: *I hardly earn enough to keep body and soul together.*

over my dead body ⇨ **dead**

boggles the mind 'boggles ⇨ **mind**

boil

go off the 'boil go past the time of greatest activity, excitement, etc: *The team were playing brilliantly at the start of the season but* seem to have gone off the boil now.

on the 'boil in a lively or active condition: *Fresh discoveries kept their enthusiasm on the boil.*

bold

be/make so bold (as to do sth) (*very formal*) (used in polite conversation, usually with *I* to make a suggestion or a request) dare, offer or attempt to do sth: *May I make so bold, sir, as to suggest that you try the grilled fish?*

(as) bold as 'brass (*informal*) without seeming ashamed or embarrassed; very cheeky: *He came up to me, bold as brass, and asked me for five pounds.*

bolt

a ,bolt from the 'blue an unexpected, and often unwelcome, event: *She had given us no warning she was going to leave; it came as a complete bolt from the blue.*

bolt upright with your back very straight in an upright position: *The noise woke her suddenly and she sat bolt upright in bed.*

make a 'bolt/'dash for it/sth (*informal*) try to escape or get somewhere quickly: *The prisoners made a bolt for it through an open window.* ○ *We smelt smoke and made a dash for the door.*

shoot your bolt ⇨ shoot

bolted

shut/close the stable door after the horse has bolted ⇨ stable

bolts

the nuts and bolts ⇨ nuts

bombshell

drop a, the, his, her, etc bombshell ⇨ drop

bond

sb's word is their bond ⇨ word

bone

,bone 'idle (*informal*) very lazy.

a bone of con'tention a matter about which there is a lot of disagreement: *The interpretation of this painting has long been a bone of contention among art historians.*

close to/near the 'bone (*informal*) likely to offend or upset sb because, for example, a remark contains elements of truth: *Some of the things she said to him about his failure to find work were a bit close to the bone.*

cut, pare, etc sth to the 'bone reduce

sth to the point where no further reduction is possible: *We have cut the costs of the business to the bone, but they are still too high for us to make any profit.*

have (got) a 'bone to pick with sb (*informal*) have sth that you want to complain to sb about: *Here, I've got a bone to pick with you: why did you tell David that I wasn't at home when he phoned?*

be skin and bone ⇨ skin; **chilled/frozen to the bone/marrow** ⇨ chilled; **(as) dry as a bone** ⇨ dry; **work your fingers to the bone** ⇨ work

bones

make no bones about (doing) sth not hesitate to do sth; be honest and open about sth: *She made no bones about telling him she wanted a pay rise.* ○ *He makes no bones about the fact that he's been in prison.*

a bag of bones ⇨ bag; **the bare bones** ⇨ bare; **feel sth in your bones** ⇨ feel

bonnet

have a bee in your bonnet ⇨ bee

boo

she/he would not say boo to a goose ⇨ say

book

bring sb to 'book (for sth) make sb explain their actions, or punish them: *This is just another of the many crimes for which nobody was ever brought to book.*

by the 'book strictly following the rules or the official way of doing sth: *He insists on doing everything by the book.*

in 'sb's book (*informal*) in sb's opinion; according to sb's judgement: *They took the car away without asking me, and in my book that's theft.*

a closed book ⇨ closed; **an open book** ⇨ open; **read sb like a book** ⇨ read; **take a leaf out of sb's book** ⇨ leaf; **throw the book at sb** ⇨ throw; **use, try, etc every trick in the book** ⇨ trick

books

be in sb's 'good/'bad books (*informal*) have/not have sb's favour or approval: *I'm in his bad books at the moment because I accidentally broke the window.* ○ *'Why are you cleaning her shoes?' 'I'm trying to get into her good books!'*

cook the books ⇨ cook; **a turn up for the book** ⇨ turn

boot

the boot is on the other 'foot (*informal*) a situation is now the opposite of what it was: *She used to be the one who had to obey orders, but the boot is on the other foot now she's been promoted.*

give sb/get the 'boot (*informal*) dismiss sb/be dismissed from a job: *He got the boot for stealing money from the firm.*

put the 'boot in (*informal*) **1** kick sb very hard especially when they are on the ground. **2** say or do sth cruel or unfair to sb, especially when they have already been harmed in some other way: *She was upset about losing her job and then her sister started putting the boot in, telling her she was lazy.*

to boot (*dated*) in addition; as well: *She has a big house, an expensive car, and a holiday villa in Italy to boot.*

boots

be tough as old boots ⇨ tough; **hang up your boots** ⇨ hang; **lick sb's boots** ⇨ lick; **too big for your boots** ⇨ big

bootstraps

pull yourself up by your bootstraps ⇨ pull

bore(d)

bore sb to 'death/to 'tears (*informal*) bore sb very much: *That's not my kind of holiday. I'd be bored to tears lying about on a beach all day.*

bored out of your mind = **out of your mind** ⇨ mind

born

be born with a silver 'spoon in your mouth (*saying*) be born into a very rich family.

born and 'bred born and brought up (in a place): *He's Liverpool born and bred.* ○ *Both my parents were born and bred in London.*

I wasn't born 'yesterday (*informal*) (used when sb is trying to tell you sth that you know is not true) I am not easily deceived: *You don't expect me to believe that, do you? I wasn't born yesterday you know.*

in all my born 'days (*becoming dated, informal*) never in my life (usually used when referring to sth unpleasant): *How dare you say that! I've never been spoken to like that in all my born days!*

there's one born every 'minute (*saying*) (used as a comment on how easily sb has been deceived): *You really believed he would pay you that money back? There's one born every minute!*

not know you are born ⇨ know; **to the manner born** ⇨ manner

borrow(ed)

beg, steal or borrow ⇨ beg; **live on borrowed time** ⇨ live

bosom

in the bosom of sth surrounded or protected by: *He longed to be back safe in the bosom of his family.*

both

you, etc can't have it 'both ways you must choose between two things even though you would like both of them: *You want an interesting job that pays well, and yet one where you don't have many responsibilities. Well, you can't have it both ways.*

the best of both worlds ⇨ best; **burn the candle at both ends** ⇨ burn; **cut both/two ways** ⇨ cut; **have/keep both/your feet on the ground** ⇨ feet; **have a foot in both camps** ⇨ foot; **see both sides** ⇨ see; **take your courage in both hands** ⇨ courage

bothered

can't be bothered (to do sth) (*informal*) not willing to make the effort (to do sth): *I got home late last night and I couldn't be bothered to cook dinner.* ○ *He didn't have an excuse for not coming to the party – he just couldn't be bothered.*

I'm not bothered I don't mind: *'What shall we have for supper tonight?' 'I'm not bothered.'*

hot and bothered ⇨ hot

bottle

have (got), show, etc (a lot of) bottle (*British, very informal*) have, show, etc (a lot of) courage or boldness: *Carol went in and told the boss he wasn't doing his job properly. She's certainly got a lot of bottle!* ○ *The match was very tough and physical and United just didn't have the bottle for it.*

on the 'bottle (*informal*) drinking a lot of alcoholic drinks regularly: *I see he's back on* *the bottle again.*

hit the bottle ⇨ hit

bottom(s)

at bottom basically; in reality: *She seems rather unfriendly, but at bottom I think she is quite kind.*

be/lie at the bottom of sth be the basic cause of sth: *Racist feelings almost certainly lie at the bottom of these recent attacks.*

the ˌbottom drops/falls out of the 'market people no longer want to buy a particular product and so it has to be sold very cheaply: *She invested in coffee, but then the bottom dropped out of the market, and she lost a lot of money.*

the ˌbottom drops/falls out of sb's 'world a person suddenly loses all their happiness, self-confidence, etc: *When his wife left him, the bottom dropped out of his world.*

the ˌbottom 'line (*informal*) the important conclusion, judgement, or result: *We have had some successes this year, but the bottom line is that the business is still losing money.*

bottoms 'up! (*informal*) (used for telling people to finish their drinks)

from the bottom of your 'heart with deep feeling; very sincerely: *I thank you from the bottom of my heart for all your help.*

get to the bottom of sth find the true cause of sth or the solution to sth: *We're determined to get to the bottom of this mystery.*

at the bottom/top of the pile ⇨ pile; **be at rock bottom = reach/hit rock bottom** ⇨ rock; **be smooth as a baby's bottom = be smooth as silk** ⇨ smooth; **bet your bottom dollar/your life** ⇨ bet; **from top to bottom** ⇨ top; **reach/hit rock bottom** ⇨ rock

bound(s)

out of 'bounds (to sb) outside the area sb is allowed to go: *The village is out of bounds to the soldiers in the camp.*

within 'bounds within acceptable limits; under control: *Borrowing money from friends is all right as long as it's kept within bounds.*

bound hand and foot = bind/tie sb hand and foot ⇨ hand; **by/in leaps and bounds** ⇨ leaps; **duty bound** ⇨ duty; **know no bounds** ⇨ know

bow

ˌbow and 'scrape (*disapproving*) behave in a very servile way towards sb: *I will not bow and scrape to him just to get a salary increase.*

another/a second/more than one string to your bow ⇨ string

bowels move your bowels ⇨ move

bows a shot across sb's bows ⇨ shot

boy(s)

the boys in 'blue (*dated, informal*) or (*humorous*) police officers: *If you're not careful, you'll get a visit from the boys in blue!*

ˌboys ˌwill be 'boys (*saying*) you must not criticize boys or men too much for being naughty, noisy, etc as this is a natural way for them to behave.

the back-room boys ⇨ back; **be one of the lads/boys/girls** ⇨ one; **sb's blue-eyed boy** ⇨ blue; **a golden boy** ⇨ golden; **jobs for the boys** ⇨ jobs; **a mother's boy** ⇨ mother; **old boy/girl** ⇨ old; **the old-boy network** ⇨ old; **a whipping boy** ⇨ whipping; **a wide boy** ⇨ wide

box Pandora's box ⇨ Pandora

brain(s)

the 'brain drain the loss of qualified scientists, doctors, engineers, etc to another country, especially one where they are paid more for their work.

brains and/or/versus brawn intelligence and/or/compared with physical strength.

have sb/sth on the brain (*informal*) think and/or talk a lot or too much about sb/sth: *You do nothing but talk about your job; you've got work on the brain!*

blow your/sb's brains out ⇨ blow; **pick sb's brains** ⇨ pick; **rack your brains** ⇨ rack

branch hold out/offer an olive branch ⇨ olive; **root and branch** ⇨ root

brass

get down to brass 'tacks (*informal*) begin to discuss and deal with the really important practical details: *Let's get down to*

brass tacks – how much will it all cost?
bold as brass ⇨ bold; **top brass** ⇨ top

brave

a brave new world (*often ironic*) a new era resulting from great changes, reforms, etc: *She promises us a brave new world of high salaries and good working conditions after the reforms.* (from Shakespeare's play *The Tempest* 'O brave new world, That has such people in't.')

put a brave 'face on sth *or* **put on a brave 'face** try to appear brave or cheerful or to be managing well in a difficult situation, when in fact you are frightened or unhappy: *'How's Mrs O'Brien?' 'She's putting a very brave face on things, but you can see that she's very unhappy.'*

brawn brains and/or versus brawn
⇨ brains

breach step into the breach ⇨ step

bread

sb's ,bread and 'butter the work that sb does which provides them with enough money to live: *He's written one or two novels but journalism is his bread and butter.*

your daily bread ⇨ daily; **half a loaf is better than none/no bread** ⇨ half; **know which side your bread is buttered** ⇨ know

breadline

on the breadline very poor: *Most of the unemployed are on the breadline.*

breadth a hair's breadth ⇨ hair; the length and breadth of sth ⇨ length

break

break your 'back doing sth/to do sth work very hard (to achieve sth): *I've been breaking my back to sell as many books as I can.*

break the back of sth finish the largest or most difficult part of a task: *I won't finish this essay tonight but I'd like to break the back of it before I go to bed.*

,break the 'bank **1** win more money than the funds of the casino, etc. **2** (*informal*) leave sb without any money: *Just lend me £10. That won't break the bank, will it?*

break 'even make neither a profit nor a loss: *In the first year of the business we only*

just managed to break even.

break fresh/new 'ground make a discovery; use new methods, etc: *This group of researchers at the Cavendish is breaking new ground in theoretical physics.* ○ *We're breaking fresh ground with our new freezing methods.*

break sb's 'heart make sb feel extremely unhappy: *That boy is breaking his mother's heart with his wild ways.* ○ *It's a job I would like, but it won't break my heart if I don't get it.* **heartbreak** (*noun*) *He causes his mother nothing but heartbreak.* **heartbreaking** (*adjective*) *a heartbreaking story* **heartbroken** (*adjective*) *We were heartbroken by the news.*

,break the 'ice make a social situation more informal and relaxed by making conversation, introducing people, etc at the beginning: *If you serve drinks as soon as they arrive it will help to break the ice.*

(not) break your 'neck (doing/to do sth) (*informal*) (not) make a great effort: *There's no need to break your neck trying to get here by five. We can wait for you.*

break 'wind (*quite formal*) let gas out from the bowels through the anus.

make a 'break for it (*informal*) try to escape from prison, etc: *Six prisoners shot a guard and made a break for it in a stolen car.*

make or break (*informal*) the thing which decides whether sth succeeds or fails: *This film is make or break for the production company.* ○ *This exhibition will make or break her as an artist.* **make-or-break** (*adjective*) *This is a make-or-break year for us.*

breakfast a dog's breakfast/dinner
⇨ dog

breaking

breaking and entering the act of getting into a building illegally by breaking a window etc: *Although they hadn't stolen anything, they were still found guilty of breaking and entering.*

you can't make an omelette without breaking eggs ⇨ omelette

breaks all hell breaks/is let loose
⇨ hell

breast beat your breast ⇨ beat; make a clean breast of sth ⇨ clean

breath

a breath of fresh air a person or thing that is a welcome and refreshing change: *Having these young people living with us is like a breath of fresh air after years on our own.*

get your 'breath back be able to breathe again properly after running, etc: *She stopped at the top of the stairs to get her breath back.*

out of 'breath not be able to breathe easily after physical effort: *I'm quite out of breath now after running for the bus.*

take sb's 'breath away surprise or amaze sb: *It quite took my breath away when they told me how much money I had won.*
breathtaking (*adjective*) very exciting; spectacular: *a breathtaking view*

under your 'breath in a whisper, so that others cannot hear: *He muttered something under his breath.*

catch your breath ⇨ catch; **don't waste your breath = save your breath** ⇨ save; **hold your 'breath** ⇨ hold; **mention sb/ sth in the same breath** ⇨ mention; **save your breath** ⇨ save; **say, etc sth in the same breath** ⇨ same; **say sth in one breath...and then in the next say... = say, etc sth in the same breath** ⇨ same; **waste your breath** ⇨ waste; **with bated breath** ⇨ bated

breathe

breathe (easily/freely) again no longer need to be afraid, worried, etc: *I was able to breathe easily again once I knew the children were safe.*

breathe down sb's 'neck (*informal*) watch sb too closely, and so make them feel uncomfortable: *I can't work with people breathing down my neck the whole time.*

breathe your 'last (*formal*) die: *Later that night, the King breathed his last.*

(not) breathe a word (about/of sth) (to sb) (not) tell sb sth (especially sth secret): *Please don't breathe a word of this to anyone.*

breathing

a 'breathing-space a time for resting between two periods of effort; pause: *This holiday will give me a bit of breathing-space before I start my new job.*

bred **born and bred** ⇨ born

breeds **familiarity breeds contempt** ⇨ familiarity

breeze **shoot the breeze** ⇨ shoot

brick(s)

make bricks without 'straw try to do a piece of work without the necessary materials, equipment, or information: *I don't know how you expect me to cook dinner when there's hardly any food in the house. You can't make bricks without straw, you know.*

bang, etc your head against a brick wall ⇨ head; **come/be down on sb like a ton of bricks** ⇨ ton; **drop a clanger/brick** ⇨ drop; **like a cat on hot bricks** ⇨ cat; **talk to a brick wall** ⇨ talk

bridge(s)

bridge the gap (between A and B) make it easier to move from one thing to another or for two groups to communicate with each other: *The hostel helps to bridge the gap between prison and life on the outside.*

be water under the bridge ⇨ water; **burn your boats/bridges** ⇨ burn; **cross a bridge when you come to it** ⇨ cross; **a lot of water has passed, etc under the bridge** ⇨ water

brief

in brief in a few words: *I won't give a you a long history of the dispute; in brief, it led to the business closing.* ○ *And now: the news in brief.*

hold no brief for sb/sth ⇨ hold

bright

bright and 'early early in the morning: *You're up bright and early this morning!*

(as) bright as a 'button clever and lively: *That child's as bright as a button!*

bright-eyed and bushy-tailed (*informal*) lively and cheerful; pleased and proud: *She came in to see me, all bright-eyed and bushy-tailed, and announced she was leaving the next day.*

the bright 'lights (*informal*) the big city seen as a centre of entertainment, enjoyment, etc: *Many people from the North are still tempted by the bright lights of London.*

bright 'spark (*informal*) (often used ironically to comment on sb's stupidity) lively and clever: *What bright spark left the front door open all night?*

look on the bright side ⇨ look

British the best of British = the best of (British) luck ⇨ best

broad
broad in the beam (*informal*) having wide hips: *Her waist is quite small, but she's rather broad in the beam.*

in broad 'daylight when it is daylight: *I was mugged in the centre of town in broad daylight.*

it's as ˌbroad as it's 'long (*informal*) there is no real difference between two possible alternatives.

broom a new broom ⇨ new

broth too many cooks spoil the broth ⇨ cooks

brother Big Brother ⇨ big; be sisters/brothers under the skin ⇨ skin

brows knit your brows ⇨ knit

brunt bear the brunt of sth ⇨ bear

brush sweep/brush sth under the carpet ⇨ sweep; tar sb/sth with the same brush ⇨ tar

buck
the buck stops 'here this person, office, etc takes the blame, responsibility, etc for sth and will not pass it on to sb else.

buck up your i'deas (*informal*) start to work harder or more efficiently; become more willing to do things: *He's been late every day for two weeks. He'll have to buck up his ideas if he wants to keep his job.*

pass the buck ⇨ pass

bucket(s) a drop in the ocean/bucket ⇨ drop; kick the bucket ⇨ kick; rain buckets = rain cats and dogs ⇨ rain

bud nip sth in the bud ⇨ nip

bug
be bitten by/have (got) the bug (*informal*) have a sudden strong interest in or enthusiasm for sth: *My mum was never really interested in going abroad until she went to America last year. Now she's been bitten by*

the travel bug and hates staying at home!

be as snug as a bug in a rug ⇨ snug

buggers play silly buggers ⇨ play

build build up/raise sb's hope ⇨ hopes

built Rome wasn't built in a da ⇨ Rome

bulging be bursting/bulging at th seams ⇨ seams

bull
like a bull in a 'china shop very clumsy especially in a situation where you need t be careful: *He was like a bull in a china shop treading on everyone's feet and apologizin constantly.* ○ *The Prime Minister went into th negociations like a bull in a china shop and onl made the relations between the two countrie worse.*

take the bull by the 'horns (*informa* deal with a difficult or dangerous situatio in a direct and brave way: *I decided to take th bull by the horns and ask my bank manager fo a loan.*

a cock-and-bull story ⇨ cock; a red ra to a bull ⇨ red

bullet bite the bullet ⇨ bite

bully
bully for 'sb! (*informal*) well done! (ofte used ironically to show that the speaker i not impressed to hear sth): *'Janet's just won free holiday in Spain.' 'Oh, bully for her! She so rich anyway, she can afford to go awa whenever she wants to.'*

bum a pain in the arse/bum/backsid = a pain (in the neck) ⇨ pain

bump things that go bump in the nigh ⇨ things

bun
have (got) a 'bun in the oven (*dated offensive*) be pregnant.

bunch
a bunch of fives (*dated, informal*) a punch
be a mixed bag/bunch ⇨ mixed; th pick of the bunch ⇨ pick

bundle

not go a bundle on sb/sth (*informal*) not like sb/sth: *I don't go a bundle on that shirt he's wearing.*

a bundle/bag of nerves ⇨ nerves

buried   dead and buried/gone ⇨ dead

burn

burn your 'boats/'bridges do sth that makes it impossible for you to return to a previous situation: *Once you sign this document, you'll have burned your boats, and will have to go ahead with the sale.*

burn the candle at both 'ends exhaust yourself by doing too much, especially by going to bed late and getting up early.

burn the midnight 'oil work or study until very late at night: *Just before the exams, I was burning the midnight oil every night.*

burn your fingers = get your fingers burnt ⇨ fingers; **her, his, etc ears are burning** ⇨ ears; **fiddle while Rome burns** ⇨ fiddle; **get your fingers burnt** ⇨ fingers; **have money to burn** ⇨ money; **money burns a hole in sb's pocket** ⇨ money

burst(ing)

burst a 'blood vessel (*informal*) get very angry and excited: *When I told Dad I had damaged the car, he nearly burst a blood vessel.*

(be) bursting to do sth (*informal*) (be) very eager to do sth: *She was just bursting to tell us the news.* (*I'm bursting* usually means *I need to go to the toilet.*)

be bursting/bulging at the seams ⇨ seams; **be full to bursting = be bursting/bulging at the seams (with sth)** ⇨ seams

bury

bury the 'hatchet (of two people or groups) agree to forget past disagreements and be friends again: *I've said I'm prepared to bury the hatchet, but John says he won't forgive me for what happened.*

bury/hide your head in the sand ⇨ head

bush

bush 'telegraph the spreading of news quickly from one person to another: *Everyone knew about it before it was officially*

announced: *the bush telegraph had been at work again.*

beat about the bush ⇨ beat; **a bird in the hand is worth two in the bush** ⇨ bird

bushel   hide your light under a bushel
⇨ hide

bushy   bright-eyed and bushy-tailed
⇨ bright

business

be (back) in business be working or operating (again) as normal: *Once the switch has been fixed, we will be back in business and can use the machine again.* ○ *It looks as though we're in business: she has agreed to lend us the money.*

be none of sb's business *or* **be no business of sb's** (*informal*) sb has no right to know sth: *'How much do you earn?''That's none of your business.'* ○ *It's no business of yours who I go out with.*

the 'business end (of sth) (*informal*) the part of a tool, weapon, etc that performs its particular function: *Never pick up a knife by the business end.*

get down to 'business start discussing or doing sth seriously, especially after a time of social talk: *Well, it's getting late – perhaps we'd better get down to business.*

go about your 'business be busy with your work, shopping, daily affairs, etc: *He looked out onto the street and watched the people going about their daily business.*

it's business as 'usual things continue normally, despite difficulties or disturbances: *It was business as usual at the theatre yesterday, in spite of all the building work going on.*

like 'nobody's business (*informal*) very fast, very much, very hard, etc: *He's been spending money like nobody's business recently.*

funny business ⇨ funny; **mean business** ⇨ mean; **mind your own business** ⇨ mind; **monkey business** ⇨ monkey

busman

a busman's 'holiday (*informal*) a holiday spent doing the same kind of thing that you do at work.

bust

bust a 'gut (*informal*) make a very great effort: *I'm not going to bust a gut trying to be on time when I know she'll probably be late.*

go 'bust (*informal*) (of a business) fail financially; become bankrupt: *The firm went bust and fifty workers lost their jobs.*

bustle hustle and bustle ⇨ hustle

busy

a ,busy 'bee (*informal*) a cheerful and busy person.

but(s)

,but for 'sb/'sth except for sb/sth; without sb/sth: *But for a brief period after leaving university, he had never been unemployed.* ○ *But for your help, we would not have been able to start up the business.*

nothing but ⇨ nothing; **ifs and/or buts** ⇨ ifs

butter

,butter wouldn't ,melt in her/his 'mouth (*saying*) a person looks very innocent, but probably is not.

sb's bread and butter ⇨ bread; **like a knife through butter** ⇨ knife

buttered know which side your bread is buttered ⇨ know

butterflies

have/get butterflies (in your stomach/tummy) (*informal*) have/get a nervous feeling in your stomach before doing sth: *I always get butterflies (in my stomach) before an interview.*

button bright as a button ⇨ bright

buy

buy 'time delay sth that seems about to happen: *This treatment can buy time for the patient, but will not cure him.*

buy sth for a song = (go) for a song ⇨ song

buzz

give sb a buzz (*informal*) **1** to telephone sb: *I'll give you a buzz before I leave.* **2** provide interest and enjoyment: *If the work gives you a buzz, then you do the job better.*

by

by and 'by (*dated*) after a little time; soon: *Things will be better by and by.*

by the by(e) = by the way ⇨ way; **by far** ⇨ far; **(by) far and away** ⇨ far; **by and large** ⇨ large

bygones

let ,bygones be 'bygones (let us) forget our past quarrels: *This is a ridiculous situation, avoiding each other like this. Why can't we let bygones be bygones?*

byways highways and byways ⇨ highways

C

cackle cut the cackle ⇨ cut

Cain raise Cain/hell ⇨ raise

cake

have your cake and 'eat it (*informal*) (often used with *can't*) enjoy the advantages of two things that cannot exist together: *'I'll have no money at all left after this holiday.' 'But you're having a great time, aren't you? You can't have your cake and eat it!'*

a slice/share of the 'cake a share of the benefits or profits: *Third-world countries are discovering how their natural resources have been exploited by the rest of the world and now they want a bigger slice of the cake.*

the icing on the cake ⇨ icing; **a piece of cake** ⇨ piece; **take the biscuit/cake** ⇨ biscuit

cakes sell/go like hot cakes ⇨ hot

calf kill the fatted calf ⇨ kill

call

(above and) beyond the call of duty
(*formal*) (used for describing a greater degree of courage or effort than is usual or expected in a job, etc): *The young policeman later received an award for bravery beyond the call of duty.*

call sb's 'bluff give sb the chance to do what they are threatening to do, because you believe they will not or cannot do it: *Next time she offers her resignation, they'll call her bluff and accept it.*

call a 'halt (to sth) stop (an activity): *We must call a halt to people leaving work early without permission.*

call it a 'day (*informal*) decide to stop doing sth, especially sth you have been doing for a long time: *We'd painted half the room and were feeling a bit tired so we decided to call it a day.*

call it 'quits (*informal*) decide to end an argument, etc at a point where both sides are equal: *'I know I upset you when I called you a liar but you said some nasty things to me too. Can't we just call it quits and try to forget it?'*

call sb 'names insult sb with rude or unpleasant names: *In the playground, the other children called him names.*

a call of 'nature (*quite formal*) a need to go to the toilet: *He left the meeting to answer a call of nature.*

call sth your 'own claim sth as belonging to you: *At her age she needs a place she can call her own.*

call the 'shots/the 'tune (*informal*) be in control: *Ask Jenny – she's the one who calls the shots around here.*

call a spade a 'spade speak openly and directly about sth unpleasant: *I believe in calling a spade a spade. When a patient's going to die, I say so. Most people prefer to know the truth.*

call sb to account (for/over sth)
(*formal*) make sb explain (a mistake, loss, etc): *His manager called him to account over the missing reports.*

don't call us, we'll call you (*informal*) (used for indicating that the speaker has no interest in meeting sb, taking sth that sb is offering, etc): *I had hoped she might want me to work with her, but her attitude was one of 'don't call us, we'll call you.'*

on 'call (of a doctor, etc) available for duty if needed.

at sb's beck and call ⇨ beck; **bring/call sth into question** ⇨ question; **bring/call/put sth into play** ⇨ play; **bring/call sb/sth to mind** ⇨ mind; **a port of call** ⇨ port

calling
the pot calling the kettle black ⇨ pot

calls
duty calls ⇨ duty; **he who pays the piper calls the tune** ⇨ pays

calm

the calm before the storm (*saying*) a period of unnatural calm before an attack, violent activity, etc: *What the country was experiencing was not peace, but just the calm before another storm.*

camel
be the straw that breaks the camel's back = be the last/final straw ⇨ straw

camps
have a foot in both camps ⇨ foot

can

(be) in the 'can (*informal*) (be) finished and ready for use; (be) already decided or arranged: *I don't need to worry about a grant – my application's been accepted so it's in the can.* (in American English slang, *in the can* can also mean *in prison* or *in the toilet.*)

carry the can ⇨ carry

candle
burn the candle at both ends ⇨ burn; **cannot hold a candle to sb/sth** ⇨ hold; **the game is not worth the candle** ⇨ game

cannon
'cannon fodder large numbers of soldiers who are used in order to win a war, even though most of them are likely to be killed.

cap

go cap in 'hand beg for sth very respectfully: *I've run out of money, but I don't want to go cap in hand to my father.*

if the cap fits (, wear it) (*saying*) if a person feels that a critical remark applies to them, then it does: *'There are too many lazy people in this house.' 'Including me, I suppose?' 'If the cap fits, wear it.'*

a feather in your cap ⇨ feather; **to top/cap/crown it all** ⇨ top

capital

make capital (out) of sth use a situation or event in a way which benefits yourself; exploit sth: *The media made great capital out of his careless remarks in the interview.*

with a capital A, B, C, etc (used for emphasis to mean 'very (great)'): *When I say he's boring, I mean boring with a capital B!*

captain

a captain of 'industry a person who manages a large industrial company.

carbon

a ,carbon 'copy (*informal*) a person or thing that is exactly or extremely like another: *The recent robberies in Leeds are a carbon copy of those that have occurred in Halifax over the last few months.*

cards

keep/hold/play your cards ,close to your 'chest not tell others what you are intending to do: *He keeps his cards pretty close to his chest. I don't know whether he plans to buy the house or not.*

on the cards (*informal*) likely to happen: *With a rail strike on the cards for next week, airline bookings have been unusually high.*

put/lay your 'cards on the table (*informal*) talk honestly and openly about your thoughts and intentions, especially when these have been secret until now: *I think it's time I put my cards on the table; I really can't afford the price you're asking.*

the cards/odds are stacked against sb/sth ⇨ stacked; **a house of cards** ⇨ house

care

care of sb at sb's address: *Write to me care of my sister, because I'll be touring Africa for six months.* (usually written as *c/o* on envelopes)

I, she, they, etc could not care 'less I, etc am not at all interested in, or concerned about, sth: *I couldn't care less if I fail my exams – I don't want to go to university anyway.*

in 'care (of children) living and looked after in an institution owned by the State: *She has been in care ever since her parents died.* ○ *The social worker said that their baby would have to*

be taken into care.

not care a damn, fig, hoot, jot, monkey's, etc (about/for sb/sth) not care at all (about sb/sth): *Steve doesn't care a damn about anybody except himself.* ○ *I don't care a fig for his views. I will do as I like.*

take care (that . . ./to do sth) be careful: *Take care that you don't fall and hurt yourself.* ○ *He took great care not to let his personal problems interfere with the job.*

take care of yourself/sb/sth 1 make sure that you are/sb is safe, well, healthy, etc; look after yourself/sb: *I don't need your help! I can take care of myself quite well, thank you!* ○ *Don't worry about the children while you're away. They'll be taken good care of.* ('Take care' is often used on its own when saying 'goodbye' to sb) **2** be responsible for (dealing with) sb/sth: *Can you take care of the shopping if I do the cooking?* ○ *There's no need for you to pay the bill. It's all taken care of* (it is already done).

cares

for all sb cares (used for suggesting that sb does not care at all): *I could be dead for all she cares.* ○ *For all I care, he can sack me tomorrow.*

who cares? (*informal*) nobody cares; I don't care: *'Who do you think will win the next election?''Who cares?'*

caring

be beyond/past caring (about sth) have reached a stage where you no longer care about or are no longer affected by sth: *She can't hurt him now because he's beyond caring (about) what she says.*

carpet

be on the 'carpet (*informal*) be sent for and criticized, especially by an employer or a superior, because you have done sth wrong: *She is on the carpet for spending too much of the company's money on entertaining guests.*

pull the carpet/rug out from under sb's feet ⇨ pull; **the red carpet** ⇨ red; **sweep/brush sth under the carpet** ⇨ sweep

carrot

the carrot and/or (the) stick reward offered and/or punishment threatened in order to get sb to do sth: *She favoured a carrot-and-stick approach to teaching.*

carry

carry all be'fore you be completely successful in a battle, competition, etc: *In three tournaments since June, this young tennis player has carried all before him, winning easy victories each time.*

carry the can (for sth) (*informal*) accept the responsibility or blame (for sth): *The teachers who were criticized said that they would not carry the can for the faults in the school system.*

carry 'weight be important or able to influence sb: *His opinions carry very little weight with his manager.*

bear/carry your cross ⇨ cross; **carry/take coals to Newcastle** ⇨ coals; **carry/win the day** ⇨ day; **fetch and carry** ⇨ fetch

carte

carte blanche complete freedom to do anything you wish: *The detective was given carte blanche to read any files he liked in his search for the murderer.*

case

a case in 'point a relevant example of sth that has just been discussed: *Many of the students are from Latin America. Carlos is a case in point – he's from Colombia.*

in 'any case whatever may happen or has happened; anyway: *I don't know yet who'll bring it or when, but in any case we'll make sure you get your car back tomorrow.* ○ *My mother came to stay so I couldn't go to the party, but I didn't really want to go in any case.*

(just) in case so as to be prepared for what may or may not happen: *Somebody should stay at home in case John phones.* ○ *'Did John say he would phone?' 'No, but somebody should stay here just in case.'*

in case of sth (*formal*) if sth happens: *In case of fire, leave the building by the nearest exit.*

make out a case (for sth) argue in favour of sth: *In her report, she makes out a case for giving more funds to the health service.*

an open-and-shut case ⇨ open

cash

be strapped for cash ⇨ strapped; **hard cash** ⇨ hard

cast

cast your mind back to sth think about sth in the past: *Cast your mind back to when you were a child.*

cast pearls before swine (*saying*) waste sth valuable on sb who cannot appreciate it.

cast/shed/throw light on sth ⇨ light; **the die is cast** ⇨ die; **draw/cast lots** ⇨ lots; **draw/throw/cast a veil/curtain over sth** ⇨ veil

castles

(build) castles in the 'air/in 'Spain (have) plans, hopes, etc which are unlikely to become reality: *They talked about moving to a little cottage in the country where he would write bestsellers and she could paint, but they knew they were really only building castles in the air.*

cat

(play a) cat-and-'mouse game (with sb) *or* **(play) cat and 'mouse (with sb)** (*informal*) (keep sb) in state of uncertainty, being sometimes kind, sometimes cruel: *She plays a cat-and-mouse game with her boyfriend, telling him he's wonderful one day, and the next saying she doesn't want to see him any more.* (refers to the way a cat plays with, and terrifies, a mouse before it kills it)

(has the) cat got your, his, etc tongue? (*informal*) why don't you say anything?: *What's the matter – cat got your tongue?*

the cat's 'whiskers/py'jamas (*informal, often ironic*) the best person, idea, thing, etc: *She thinks she's the cat's whiskers.*

sb has not (got) a cat in 'hell's chance (*informal*) sb has got no chance at all: *You haven't got a cat in hell's chance of buying a decent car for £500.*

let the 'cat out of the bag (*informal*) make known a secret, usually without realizing what you are doing: *'Who let the cat out of the bag?' 'I'm afraid I did. I thought everybody already knew.'* ○ *Nobody knew she had been offered the job until her husband let the cat out of the bag.*

like a ,cat on hot 'bricks (*informal*) very nervous or restless: *He'll be like a cat on hot* *bricks till he gets his exam results.*

like the ˌcat that got/ate/stole the ˈcream (sometimes used for showing disapproval) very pleased or satisfied: *Ever since she won that prize, she's been like the cat that ate the cream.*

put/set the ˈcat among the pigeons (*informal*) do sth that is likely to cause trouble, annoyance, etc: *She told everyone they would have to cancel their holidays, and that really set the cat among the pigeons.*

when the cat's away the mice will play (*saying*) when the person in charge of children, pupils, or workers is absent, they do as they like, enjoy themselves, or stop working.

curiosity killed the cat ⇨ curiosity; **fight like cat and dog** ⇨ fight; **grin like a Cheshire cat** ⇨ grin; **look what the cat's brought/dragged in** ⇨ look; **no room to swing a cat** ⇨ room

catch

catch your ˈbreath stop breathing for a moment (because of surprise, fear, shock, etc): *The magnificent view made us catch our breath.*

catch your ˈdeath (of cold) (*informal*) get a very bad cold (usually said to emphasize how cold it is): *Don't go out without your coat; you'll catch your death (of cold).*

catch sb's eye attract sb's attention: *I liked all the paintings, but the one that really caught my eye was a Matisse.* ○ *Can you try to catch the waiter's eye?*

catch sb ˈnapping (*informal*) find sb not prepared or not paying attention, and perhaps gain an advantage over them as a result: *Manchester United's defence was caught napping in the final moments of the game when Jones scored his second goal for Liverpool.*

catch sb off their guard happen when sb is not prepared: *The question caught him off his guard and he couldn't answer.* ○ *Businesses had been caught off guard by the sudden rise in interest rates.*

catch sb on the ˈhop (*informal*) find sb in a situation where they are unprepared: *The early start of winter that year caught many farmers on the hop.*

catch sb red-ˈhanded find sb while they are doing sth wrong, committing a crime, etc: *The thief was caught red-handed as she was emptying the till.*

catch the ˈsun get a suntan; become sunburned.

catch sb with their ˈpants/ˈtrousers down (*informal*) find or trap sb when they are unprepared or not paying attention: *After the devastating attack on its military bases, the country was determined not to be caught with its pants down a second time.*

catch/take/tickle sb's fancy ⇨ fancy; **catch/take sb unawares** ⇨ unawares; **the early bird catches the worm** ⇨ early; **(be) a sprat to catch a mackerel** ⇨ sprat

cats rain cats and dogs ⇨ rain

caught be caught/taken short ⇨ short

cause a lost cause ⇨ lost; the root cause ⇨ root; show good cause ⇨ show

caution throw caution to the winds ⇨ throw

cave an Aladdin's cave ⇨ Aladdin

cease wonders will never cease ⇨ wonders

cent not have/not be worth a red cent ⇨ red

centre left, right, and centre ⇨ left

century the turn of the year/century ⇨ turn

ceremony stand on ceremony ⇨ stand

cert a dead cert ⇨ dead

certain

for ˈcertain without doubt: *No one can say for certain how the world's climate is likely to change.*

up to a certain point ⇨ point

chaff separate the wheat from the chaff ⇨ separate

chair on the edge of your chair/seat ⇨ edge

chalk

(like) ˌchalk and ˈcheese or **as different as ˌchalk and ˈcheese** (*informal*) very different: *It's hard to imagine that Mark and John are brothers – they're chalk and cheese.*

not by a long chalk ⇨ long

challenge rise to the occasion/challenge ⇨ rise

champ

ˌchamp at the ˈbit (*informal*) be very impatient when waiting to start sth: *The players were champing at the bit as the start of the match was delayed.*

chance

as ˌchance ˈhas it or **as ˌchance/ˌluck would ˈhave it** as it happens or happened, fortunately or unfortunately: *I'm going to London myself tomorrow, as chance has it, so perhaps we can travel together.* ○ *He asked whether we had a room to let and, as luck would have it, we did.*

ˌchance your ˈarm (*informal*) take a risk (especially when you are unlikely to succeed): *He knew he wasn't likely to win the contest, but decided to chance his arm anyway.*

a chance in a million (*informal*) a very unlikely possibility: *If you lost your ring on the beach, it's a chance in a million that you'd find it again.*

ˈchance would be a fine thing (*informal, often ironic*) I would like to do sth but will not have the opportunity: *'Are you going on holiday this year?' 'Chance would be a fine thing – I can't even afford a day-trip to London!'*

ˈno chance (*informal*) there is no possibility of that: *'Lend us five pounds, will you?' 'No chance!'*

not a ˈdog's chance (*informal*) no chance at all: *He hasn't got a dog's chance of getting that job.*

on the ˈoff chance (*informal*) hoping that sth will happen, even if it is unlikely: *I called at their house on the off chance that they'd let me stay, but they weren't at home.*

take a chance (on sth) do sth without being sure of success: *We took a chance on being able to get tickets on the day of the match, but they were sold out.*

a fat chance ⇨ fat; **a fighting chance** ⇨ fighting; **give sb half a chance** ⇨ half; **sb has not a cat in hell's chance** ⇨ cat; **have an eye to/for the main chance** ⇨ eye; **(not) have a ghost of a chance** ⇨ ghost; **(not) stand a chance** ⇨ stand

chances

(the) chances ˈare (that) (*informal*) it is likely (that): *The chances are (that) he will come if he can finish work on time.*

take ˈchances do risky things: *Take no chances: don't lend money to people you don't know.*

take your ˈchances (*informal*) make as much use as you can of your opportunities: *When the offer of a job in Singapore came, I accepted it. After all, you have to take your chances in life.*

fancy your/sb's chances ⇨ fancy

change(s)

change your mind change your decision or opinion: *He was going to the party but now he's changed his mind and decided to stay in.*

a ˌchange of ˈheart a change in your attitude and feelings, especially becoming kinder, more friendly, etc: *The Government has had a change of heart over the proposed tax reforms and is now prepared to listen to public opinion.*

change ˈplaces (with sb) (of two people, groups, etc) exchange seats, positions, situations, etc: *The Smiths can afford to go on expensive holidays abroad because they haven't got a family to bring up. But I wouldn't want to change places with them.*

ˌchange the ˈsubject start to talk about something different, especially because what was being discussed was embarrassing or difficult to talk about: *'You know I don't like talking about the war. Can't we change the subject?'*

ˌchange your ˈtune (*informal*) change your opinion about or your attitude to sb/sth: *'Parents worry too much about their children,' Tom used to say. But he soon changed his tune when he became a parent himself!*

for a ˈchange for variety; as an improvement on what usually happens: *We usually go to John's family for Christmas but this year we've decided to stay at home for a change.*

change/swap horses in midstream ⇨ horses; **chop and change** ⇨ chop; **a leopard cannot change its spots** ⇨ leopard; **ring the changes** ⇨ ring; **a wind of change** ⇨ wind

chapter

,chapter and 'verse the exact source or words of a quotation, etc: *I can't give you chapter and verse, but I can tell you that the lines she quoted come from a Brecht play.*

a ,chapter of 'accidents a series of small misfortunes or mistakes in a short period of time: *The reorganization of the company has been a chapter of accidents!*

character

in/out of character (of sb's behaviour, etc) of the kind you would/would not expect from them; characteristic/uncharacteristic: *That unpleasant remark she made was quite out of character.* ○ *'I'm sure it was Bill I saw from the bus. He was arguing with a police officer.' 'Well, that's in character, anyway!'*

charge

in charge (of sb/sth) having control or command (of sth): *The teacher in charge of the children has to accompany them on the coach.* ○ *Who's in charge around here?*

take charge (of sth) begin to have control or command: *The Chief Inspector took charge of the investigations into the murder.*

cost/pay/charge the earth ⇨ earth

charity

charity begins at home (*saying*) people should look after their own family before they think about others.

charm   work like a charm ⇨ work

charmed

lead/have a charmed life have a lot of good luck, avoiding accidents or harm.

chase   a wild-goose chase ⇨ wild

cheap

'cheap at the price worth more than the price paid, even though it is expensive: *I know £20 000 is a lot of money, but a superb car like this is cheap at the price.*

go 'cheap (*informal*) be sold at a low price: *These shirts were going cheap, so I bought two.*

on the 'cheap (*informal*) for less than the normal cost (and therefore of poor quality): *He got it on the cheap so I wasn't surprised when it broke after a couple of months.*

cheaply   get   off   lightly/cheaply
⇨ lightly

check

keep/hold sb/sth in check control sb/sth: *The disease is kept in check with drugs.* ○ *It was difficult to hold their enthusiasm in check.*

take a rain check ⇨ rain

cheek(s)

cheek by jowl (with sb/sth) side by side (with sth); very near: *If he had known that he was to find himself seated cheek by jowl with his old enemy he wouldn't have attended the dinner.*

put the roses back in your cheeks ⇨ roses; tongue in cheek ⇨ tongue; turn the other cheek ⇨ turn; with your tongue in your cheek = tongue in cheek ⇨ tongue

cheers   (give) three cheers (for sb/sth)
⇨ three

cheese   a   big   wheel/cheese ⇨ big; chalk and cheese ⇨ chalk; say cheese ⇨ say

cheque   a blank cheque ⇨ blank

cherry   have/get two bites at/of the cherry ⇨ bites; have/get a second/another bite at/of the cherry = have/get two bites at/of the cherry ⇨ bites

Cheshire   grin   like   a   Cheshire   cat
⇨ grin

chest

,get sth off your 'chest (*informal*) say sth that you have wanted to say for a long time and feel better because you have done this: *If something is worrying you, get it off your chest.*

keep/hold/play your cards close to your chest ⇨ cards

put hairs on your chest ⇨ hairs

chestnut   an old chestnut ⇨ old

chew

,chew the 'fat (*informal*) talk about unimportant things; chat: *They sit chewing the fat instead of working.*

bite off more than you can chew ⇨ bite

chicken

be ,no (spring) 'chicken (*informal*) be no longer young: *I'm no spring chicken, but I still like going on long walks.*

a chicken-and-'egg situation a situation in which you do not know which of two connected events is the cause of the other: *Is she unhappy because she gets into debt, or does she get into debt because she's unhappy? I suppose it's a chicken-and-egg situation.*

'chicken-feed (*informal*) a small and unimportant amount of money: *My salary is chicken-feed compared with hers.*

chickens

(your, etc/the) chickens come home to roost after a long time you experience the unpleasant effects of sth bad or stupid that you have done in the past: *For years he avoided paying tax. But now his chickens have come home to roost and he's got a tax bill of £25000.*

not count your chickens ⇨ count

child

'child's play very easy job or task: *Mending the lamp was child's play for an experienced electrician.*

spare the rod and spoil the child ⇨ spare

childhood a/your second childhood ⇨ second

chill send a chill up/down sb's spine ⇨ send

chilled

chilled/frozen to the 'bone/'marrow extremely cold: *We arrived chilled to the marrow, after a long walk through the snow.*

chimney smoke like a chimney ⇨ smoke

chin

keep your 'chin up also (*especially British*) **keep your 'pecker up** (*informal*) stay cheerful in difficult circumstances: *Keep your chin up! Things will get better soon.* (usually used in the imperative. It is

sometimes shortened to 'chin up')

take sth on the chin accept sth bad with courage: *Losing his job after so many years was a great shock, but he took it on the chin.*

china like a bull in a china shop ⇨ bull

China would not (do sth) for all the tea in China ⇨ tea

chink

a chink in sb's 'armour a weakness in sb who is otherwise strong, that might allow other people to defeat, criticize or exploit them: *The one chink in her armour is the lack of a sense of humour. She hates people laughing at her.*

chip

a ,chip off the old 'block (*becoming dated, informal*) a person who is very like one of her/his parents in appearance or character.

have (get) a 'chip on your shoulder be aggressive or too sensitive because you believe that people treat you unfairly, for example because you are not well-educated: *He's got a chip on his shoulder about not having been to university.*

chips

have had your 'chips (*becoming dated, informal*) be dead or defeated.

when the chips are down (*informal*) when the situation is urgent and action must be taken: *Nobody wanted war but when the chips were down and the enemy was ready to attack, everyone volunteered to defend their homeland.*

choice be spoilt/spoiled for choice ⇨ spoilt; **Hobson's choice** ⇨ Hobson; **you pays your money and you takes your choice** ⇨ pays

choose

there's nothing, not much, etc to choose between A and B there is very little difference between A and B: *One of the computers has a larger screen, but otherwise there's not much to choose between them.*

pick and choose ⇨ pick; **pick/choose your moment** ⇨ moment

choosers beggars can't be choosers ⇨ beggars

chop

,chop and 'change (*informal*) change your plans, opinions or methods too often: *I wish he'd make up his mind – I'm tired of all this chopping and changing.*

chord strike a chord ⇨ strike

Christmas a white Christmas ⇨ white

church poor as a church mouse ⇨ poor

circle come/go full circle ⇨ full; go round in circles ⇨ round; square the circle ⇨ square; a vicious circle ⇨ vicious; the wheel has come/turned full circle ⇨ wheel

circumstance force of circumstance ⇨ force

claim stake a/your claim to sb/sth ⇨ stake

clanger drop a clanger/brick ⇨ drop

clap clap/lay/set eyes on sb/sth ⇨ eyes

Clapham the man on the Clapham omnibus = the man in the street ⇨ man

clappers

like the 'clappers (*becoming dated, British, informal*) very fast.

class

be in a class of your/its own *or* **be in a class by yourself/itself** be much better than any others of the same kind: *The winning competitor was in a class by herself.* ○ *For originality, Leo's designs are truly in a class of their own.*

be not in the same league/class/street ⇨ league; **have, etc a touch of class** ⇨ touch

clay feet of clay ⇨ feet

clean

a clean bill of 'health a statement that sb is well or sth is in a satisfactory condition: *The doctor's given her a clean bill of health.*

a clean sheet/slate (in football) a game when the goalkeeper prevents the opposing team from scoring any goals; a new start, with no record of past mistakes: *At the new school, you will start with a clean slate.*

come clean (with sb) (*informal*) tell the truth about sth, especially after lying or keeping it secret: *I'll come clean with you – I've been reading your mail.* ○ *He finally came clean and confessed.*

have clean hands *or* **sb's hands are clean** not be responsible for crime, dishonesty, etc: *After years of corrupt government, we want politicians with clean hands.*

make a clean breast of sth admit fully sth that you have done wrong: *He decided to make a clean breast of it and tell the police.*

make a clean sweep (of sth) (*informal*) **1** remove unwanted things or people: *The Prime Minister is expected to make a clean sweep of the ministers who don't support the new policy.* **2** win all the prizes, etc that are available: *Kenyan athletes made a clean sweep (of the medals) in yesterday's competition.*

keep your nose clean ⇨ nose; **show a clean pair of heels** ⇨ show

cleaners

take sb to the 'cleaners (*informal*) make sb lose a lot of money, often by cheating them: *He's heavily in debt – his ex-wife took him to the cleaners at the time of their divorce.*

clear

clear the 'air remove the causes of disagreement, fear, doubts, etc by talking about them honestly and openly: *Mary had been bad-tempered for days, so, in an attempt to clear the air, I asked her what the matter was.*

(as) clear as a 'bell easily and clearly heard: *'Can you hear me all right?' 'Clear as a bell!'*

(as) clear as 'day easy to see or understand; obvious: *Although it is written on the door as clear as day, people still don't realize that this room is private.*

(as) clear as 'mud (*informal*) not clear at all; very difficult to understand: *The instructions are as clear as mud.*

clear the 'deck(s) get ready for some activity by first dealing with anything not essential to it: *We had been doing some painting in the dining room, so we had to spend some time clearing the decks before our visitors came round in the evening.*

clear your 'throat cough slightly, especially before speaking or to attract sb's attention: *The lawyer stood up, cleared his throat and began to address the jury.*

have (got) a clear 'head be able to think clearly, especially because you have not had any alcohol, drugs, etc: *Don't give me any wine, I must have a clear head for the meeting this afternoon.*

in the 'clear (*informal*) no longer in danger or likely to be blamed, punished, etc: *She told the police that Jim was with her when the burglary happened, so that put him in the clear.*

steer/stay/keep clear (of sb/sth) avoid sb/sth: *I'm trying to lose weight so I have to steer clear of fattening foods.* ○ *It's best to stay clear of the bank at lunchtimes as it gets very busy.*

the coast is clear ➪ coast; **loud and clear** ➪ loud

cleft

be in a cleft 'stick (*informal*) be in a situation where it is difficult to decide what to do, normally because all your options are unpleasant: *I was in a cleft stick – my job was boring but I couldn't move to another firm without losing my company pension.*

clever

a 'clever Dick (*informal*) (used for showing disapproval) a person who is always trying to show that they are cleverer than anyone else: *After I had come back from holiday in Turkey, some clever Dick said he had made the same trip for half the price.* (ironic) *Some clever Dick has parked his car so close to mine I can't get out!*

too clever, etc by half ➪ half

climb **climb/jump on the bandwagon** ➪ bandwagon

clip

clip sb's 'wings limit sb's freedom or power: *The new law was seen as an attempt to clip the wings of the trade unions.*

clock

(work, race, etc) against the 'clock (work, race, etc) very fast and hard in order to finish sth before a certain time: *We were working against the clock to get the report finished before the district manager came round.*

put/turn the 'clock back return to the past; return to old-fashioned ideas, customs, etc: *Sometimes I wish I could turn the clock back to my days as a student.* ○ *These new restrictions on medical research will undoubtedly put the clock back (by) 20 years.*

round the clock ➪ round; **watch the clock** ➪ watch

clockwork

go/run like 'clockwork (of arrangements, etc) proceed without any difficulty or trouble: *The sports day went like clockwork, with every race starting and finishing on time.*

as regular as clockwork ➪ regular

close

at ,close 'quarters from/within a very short distance: *You have to examine the paint at close quarters in order to see the tiny scratches on it.*

close your mind (to sth) be unwilling or unable to consider new ideas, proposals, etc: *His mind is closed to the possibility of reform.*

close 'ranks (of the members of a profession, group, etc) co-operate closely to protect and defend each other: *Although the family quarrelled a good deal among themselves, they quickly closed ranks against any outsider who criticized one of them.*

a ,close shave/'call (*informal*) a situation where a disaster, accident, etc almost happens: *We didn't actually hit the other car, but it was a close shave.*

too close for comfort so near that you become afraid or anxious: *The exams are getting a bit close for comfort.*

be close/dear/near to sb's heart ➪ heart; **be a close-run thing = be a near/close thing** ➪ thing; **be a near/close thing** ➪ thing; **close/shut your eyes to sth** ➪ eyes; **close to/near the bone** ➪ bone; **keep/hold/play your cards close to your chest** ➪ cards; **sail close to the wind** ➪ sail; **shut/close the stable door after the horse has bolted** ➪ stable

closed

be,hind closed 'doors in private; without the public being allowed to attend: *Journalists protested that the trial was being* *held behind closed doors.*

a closed 'book a matter that is past and need not or should not be discussed: *Please let's not talk about her former life, that's all a closed book now.*

a closed 'book (to sb) a subject about which sb knows nothing: *I'm afraid geophysics is rather a closed book to me.*

a closed 'shop a factory, etc where only people belonging to a certain union may work

with your eyes closed/shut ⇨ eyes

closet **a skeleton in the cupboard/ closet** ⇨ skeleton

clothing **a wolf in sheep's clothing** ⇨ wolf

cloud(s)
a (small) cloud on the horizon a sign of trouble or difficulty to come: *Although we are making good profits there is one cloud on the horizon – the government may increase taxes.* see also **on the horizon** ⇨ horizon

every cloud has a silver 'lining (*saying*) there is always something hopeful about even the most difficult or unhappy situation

on cloud 'nine (*informal*) extremely happy: *She's been on cloud nine since she heard the news.*

under a 'cloud (*informal*) suspected of having done sth wrong; in disgrace: *He had been stealing, so he was asked to resign, and he left under a cloud.*

have your head in the clouds ⇨ head

clover
in clover (*informal*) in comfort or luxury: *They were living in clover.*

club **join the club** ⇨ join

clue
not have (got) a clue (*informal*) **1** not know (anything about) sth: *'Who's that woman over there?' 'I'm afraid I haven't a clue.'* ○ *I haven't a clue how to get there.* **2** (*disapproving*) be stupid; lack skill or ability: *It's a waste of time trying to teach him anything: he hasn't got a clue.*

clutch **clutch/grasp at a straw/straws** ⇨ straws

coach **drive a coach and horses through sth** ⇨ drive

coals
(carry/take) coals to 'Newcastle (supply) sth that there is already a lot of: *Exporting wine to France would be like taking coals to Newcastle.* (Newcastle upon Tyne, in the north of England, was once an important coal-mining centre)

haul sb over the coals ⇨ haul

coast
the ,coast is 'clear (*informal*) there is no one around to see or stop what you are doing: *She stuck her head out cautiously, looked left and right to make sure the coast was clear, then ran as fast as she could down the corridor.*

coat **cut your coat according to your cloth** ⇨ cut

cobwebs **blow away the cobwebs** ⇨ blow

cock
a ,cock-and-'bull story (*informal*) a story, excuse or explanation that is so unlikely that no one believes it: *I asked him about his job and he gave me some cock-and-bull story about being so rich he didn't need to work.*

cock a snook at sb/sth (*informal*) **1** make a rude gesture by putting your thumb to your nose **2** do or say sth that shows your lack of respect for sb/sth, especially when you cannot be punished for this: *She cocked a snook at her teachers by going to school with her hair dyed purple.*

go off at ,half 'cock ⇨ half

coffin **a nail in sb's/sth's coffin** ⇨ nail

cog
a cog in the ma'chine/wheel (*informal*) a person who plays a small part in a large organization or plan: *The firm tries hard to make its employees feel that they are not just cogs in the wheel.*

coin
'coin it (in) (*informal*) earn a lot of money: *They must be really coining it at that café on the corner. You can hardly get a seat at any time of day.* (normally used in continuous tenses)

to coin a 'phrase (*often humorous, ironic*)

(used for introducing an expression that you have invented or to apologize for using a well-known idiom or phrase instead of an original one): *Tell him exactly what you think. Don't, to coin a phrase, mince your words.*

the other side of the coin ⇨ other; **toss a coin** ⇨ toss

cold

,cold 'comfort a thing that is intended to make you feel better but which does not: *When you've just had your car stolen, it's cold comfort to be told it happens to somebody every day.*

a ,cold 'fish (*disapproving*) a person who shows little or no emotion, or is unfriendly, reserved, etc.

come in from the 'cold be included in a group, activity, etc that you have had no part in before: *In that year, Spain came in from the cold and became a member of the EC.*

get/have (got) cold 'feet (*informal*) become/be nervous or afraid and no longer want to continue what you intended or have started to do: *She got cold feet a week before the wedding.*

give sb/get the cold 'shoulder treat sb/be treated in a deliberately unfriendly way: *I try to chat to my colleagues during the lunch-hour, but for some reason they have been giving me the cold shoulder.*

in cold 'blood deliberately and calmly, without showing any pity: *The innocent victims were shot in cold blood.* ,cold-'blooded (*adjective*) *a cold-blooded murder*

in the cold light·of day when matters can be looked at calmly and logically: *In the cold light of day, the plans they had made seemed foolish.*

left ,out in the 'cold excluded from a group or an activity; ignored: *Everyone had something to do or somewhere to go. I felt left out in the cold.*

pour/throw cold 'water on sth (*informal*) discourage or try to prevent a plan, etc from being carried out; be unenthusiastic about sth: *I've had lots of ideas about how to improve sales but my manager pours cold water on all my suggestions.*

be in a cold sweat = be in a sweat ⇨ sweat; **your blood runs cold** ⇨ blood;

blow hot and cold ⇨ blow; **go hot and cold** ⇨ hot; **leave sb cold** ⇨ leave

collar **hot under the collar** ⇨ hot

collect **collect/gather your wits** ⇨ wits

colour

off colour (*informal*) unwell: *I'm feeling a bit off colour this morning.*

lend colour to sth ⇨ lend; **see the colour of sb's money** ⇨ see

colours **in glowing terms/colours** ⇨ glowing; **nail your colours to the mast** ⇨ nail; **sb's true colours** ⇨ true; **with flying colours** ⇨ flying

comb **go over/through sth with a fine-tooth comb** ⇨ fine

come

as clever, stupid, etc as they come very clever, stupid, etc: *He's just about as mean as they come. Do you know, he won't even lend me 50p!*

come again? (*informal*) (used for asking sb to repeat sth because you have not heard or understood): *'This is Peter – he's a dermatologist.' 'Come again?' 'A dermatologist – you know, a specialist in skin diseases.'*

,come and 'go exist or be there for a short time and then stop or depart: *Newspapers come and go, and unfortunately the time has now come for this one to close.* ○ *Please feel free to come and go as you please.*

come, 'come or '**come, now** (used for asking sb to act or speak in a sensible or reasonable way): *Come, come! We all know that you were in Manchester the day the crime was committed, so you may as well tell the whole story.*

come ,into your 'own begin to get full recognition for the things that you do well; be seen at your best: *People had always regarded her as a capable politician, but it was only when she became Health Secretary that she really came into her own.*

,come it (with 'sb) (*informal*) try to impress, persuade or deceive sb in the hope of getting their attention, respect, sympathy, etc: *Your leg hurts? Don't come it (with me) – get out there and play with the rest*

comfort

of the team!

come 'off it (*informal*) (used to show that you do not believe sb/sth or that you disagree with sb): *'I can't afford a holiday this year.' 'Come off it, you've got plenty of money.'*

come to 'nothing *or* **not come to 'anything** not have a successful result: *The latest attempt to end the dispute came to nothing. ○ They had a scheme for making a lot of money quickly, but it never came to anything.*

come to 'that *or* **if it comes to 'that** (used when you are going to add sth to what has just been said): *It has been raining all day today. Come to that, it's been raining non-stop since Friday.*

,come what 'may whatever may happen: *My mother taught us always to tell the truth, come what may.*

comfort cold comfort ⇨ cold; **too close for comfort** ⇨ close

comforter a Job's comforter ⇨ Job

comings
,comings and 'goings arrivals and departures; movement of people: *There have been a lot of comings and goings at our neighbour's house this morning.*

command your wish is my command ⇨ wish

common
,common *or* **'garden** ordinary; not unusual: *...a pet shop full of snakes and spiders, and not a common or garden rabbit or hamster in sight!*

have (got) sth in 'common (with sb/ sth) have the same interests, characteristics or experience as sb: *Come and meet my sister. I'm sure you two have got a lot in common. ○ I've got nothing in common with Mark.*

in common with 'sb/'sth together with sb/sth; like sb/sth: *The hospital buildings, in common with many others in this country, are sadly out of date.*

the common/general run ⇨ run.

company
the 'company sb keeps the people with whom sb spends time: *People disapprove of the company he keeps.*

keep sb 'company spend time with sb so that they are not alone: *I've promised to keep my sister company while her husband is away.*

part company ⇨ part; **present company excepted** ⇨ present; **two's company** ⇨ two

compare
beyond com'pare (*formal*) too good, beautiful, etc to be compared with anyone or anything else: *The loveliness of the scene was beyond compare.*

compare 'notes (with sb) exchange ideas, opinions, with sb especially about shared experiences: *We met after the exam to compare notes on how well we had done.*

comparison
there's no com'parison (used when comparing two people or things to emphasize that one is much better, etc): *'Who is the better player, Tom or Anna?' 'Anna is – there's no comparison.'*

compliment(s) fish for compliments ⇨ fish; **return the compliment** ⇨ return

concentrate
,concentrate the 'mind make you consider sth urgently and seriously: *Being informed that one is likely to lose one's job unless one works very much harder concentrates the mind wonderfully.*

conclusion(s) a foregone conclusion ⇨ foregone; **jump to conclusions** ⇨ jump

condition in mint condition ⇨ mint

confidence
take sb into your confidence tell sb your secret plans, problems, etc: *She's the only person I've taken into my confidence about it.*

conjure a name to conjure with ⇨ name

cons all mod cons ⇨ mod; **the pros and cons** ⇨ pros

conscience
in all conscience while being honest or just: *You cannot in all conscience think that is fair pay.*

search your heart/soul/conscience ⇨ search

considered all things considered ⇨ things

conspiracy

a con,spiracy of 'silence an agreement between a group of people who have certain information not to let it be publicly known.

contact lose touch/contact ⇨ lose

contempt

beneath contempt very shameful or disgusting: *Stealing the money was bad enough. Trying to get someone else accused of it was beneath contempt.*

familiarity breeds contempt ⇨ familiarity

content to your heart's content/ desire ⇨ heart

contention a bone of contention ⇨ bone

contradiction

a ,contradiction in 'terms a statement or description containing two words or phrases that contradict each other's meaning: *They call their project 'a peace offensive', which seems to me a contradiction in terms.*

contrary

on the 'contrary quite the opposite (of sth said or suggested); not at all: *'Didn't you find the Smiths rather boring?' 'On the contrary, I enjoyed their company very much.'* ○ *It's not that I don't like him – on the contrary, he seems very pleasant. I just don't think she should marry him.*

to the 'contrary in opposition to, or in contradiction of, sth said or proposed: *Unless you hear from me to the contrary, expect me on Friday at about 6 o'clock.* ○ *She was convinced that John was not capable of murder, in spite of all the evidence to the contrary.*

control control/hold the purse-strings ⇨ purse

converted preach to the converted ⇨ preach

convictions have/lack the courage of your convictions ⇨ courage

coo bill and coo ⇨ bill

cook

,cook the 'books (*informal*) change facts or figures in order to make the situation seem better than it is or to hide the fact that you have stolen money: *The two directors of the company had been cooking the books, a local court heard yesterday.*

,cook sb's 'goose (*informal*) ruin sb's plans or chances of success: *He thought that the police would never find him but when he saw the officer coming towards him he realized that his goose was finally cooked.*

cookie that's the way the cookie crumbles ⇨ way

cooking

what's 'cooking (*informal*) what is being done or planned: *What's cooking in here? You all look very guilty!*

cooks

,too many ,cooks ,spoil the 'broth (*saying*) if too many people try to do sth it will not be done properly.

cool

(as) ,cool as a 'cucumber (*informal*) (of people) very calm, especially when the opposite might be expected, for example on a hot day or in a difficult situation: *Everyone was rushing round trying to get things ready, and he just sat in a deck-chair, cool as a cucumber.*

,cool your 'heels (*informal*) be kept waiting: *The bank manager had asked to see her at four o'clock but she had to sit cooling her heels until almost a quarter to five.*

'cool it behave in a less aggressive or excited way; calm down: *His friends were holding him back and telling him to cool it, but he broke free and punched the barman on the nose.*

keep/lose your cool (*informal*) stay calm/ get angry, excited, etc: *He was very insulting. I really don't know how I managed to keep my cool.*

play it cool ⇨ play

cop

'cop it (*slang*) be punished: *You'll cop it if your father finds out you broke the window!*

not much cop (*slang*) not very good: *'What do you think of the book?' 'It's not much cop, really.'*

it's a fair cop ⇨ fair

copy a carbon copy ⇨ carbon

copybook blot your copybook ⇨ blot

core

to the 'core very much; in every way: *He's a Welshman to the core.* ○ *They believe that our society is rotten to the core* (ie completely bad).

hard core ⇨ hard

corner(s)

corner the market (in sth) become the only supplier of a particular product, so that you control its price and the conditions of sale: *By reducing prices so that the smaller shops can't compete and are forced to close, Bestsave has effectively cornered the market.*

just (a)round the corner very near; soon to happen: *We have been trying to develop the new drug for years, and now that success is just around the corner, the work must not be stopped.*

out of the corner of your eye at the edge of your vision; indirectly: *I just caught sight of him out of the corner of my eye, so I couldn't say exactly what he looked like.*

cut corners ⇨ cut; the four corners of the earth ⇨ four; in a tight corner/spot ⇨ tight; turn the corner ⇨ turn

correctly if my memory serves me right/correctly ⇨ memory

corridors

the corridors of 'power the places where important decisions in government are made.

cost(s)

at 'all costs whatever has to be done, suffered, etc: *He is determined to win at all costs.*

to your 'cost 1 resulting in harm, loss, etc: *The climbers had been advised not to set out until the weather improved – advice which, to their cost, they ignored.* 2 as a result of

suffering harm, loss, etc: *Joanne's not a very reliable person, as I've recently discovered to my cost.*

cost/pay/charge the earth ⇨ earth; count the cost ⇨ count

cotton wrap sb up in cotton wool ⇨ wrap

counsel

keep your own 'counsel (*formal*) keep your thoughts, plans, etc secret: *Try to keep your own counsel when you are with him, or he'll tell everyone what you say.*

count

count your 'blessings realize how lucky you are and not complain: *Stop looking so miserable and count your blessings! At least you've still got a job and somewhere to live.*

count the cost 1 consider carefully what the risks or disadvantages may be before you do sth: *The job was attractive financially, but when I counted the cost in terms of separation from my family and friends, I decided not to take it.* 2 experience the unpleasant consequences of sth, especially a foolish or careless action: *We made a big mistake when we bought that old car, and we're still counting the cost – it breaks down almost every week!*

keep/lose count (of sth) know/not know how many there are of sth: *He's had so many different jobs that I've lost count (of them all).* ○ *Make sure you keep count of all the phone calls you make so you can claim the money back later.*

not count your 'chickens (before they are 'hatched) not be too confident of success until it actually happens: *She said she was certain to be offered a part in the play, but I told her not to count her chickens, as a lot of other people wanted the same part.*

out for the 'count unconscious or in a very deep sleep, either because you have been hit very hard or are very tired: *After a whole day of walking around Paris, I was out for the count!* (refers to the rules in boxing)

counted stand up and be counted ⇨ stand

counter

under the 'counter (of goods bought or

sold in a shop) secretly or illegally: *Before the revolution, such luxuries were only sold under the counter.*

a bargaining counter ⇨ bargaining

country

a country 'cousin (*informal, usually disapproving*) an unsophisticated person from the country who is not used to towns or cities.

go to the 'country (*British*) hold a general election: *The Prime Minister may decide to go to the country in the next few weeks.*

the mother country ⇨ mother

counts **it's the thought that counts** ⇨ thought

courage

have (got)/lack the courage of your con'victions be/not be brave enough to do what you believe to be right: *You say that cruelty to animals is wrong, so why not have the courage of your convictions and join our campaign?*

pluck/summon up (your/the) courage force yourself to be brave: *I had liked her for a long time, and eventually I plucked up the courage to ask her out.*

take your ˌcourage in both 'hands decide to do sth very brave: *I saw him screaming for help far out from the shore, so I took my courage in both hands and swam out to save him.*

Dutch courage ⇨ Dutch

course(s)

a course of action a way of doing, managing, or achieving sth: *What is the best course of action to take?* ○ *Two alternative courses of action are open to us: either we deal with him directly or we get the help of a solicitor.*

run/take its 'course (of a series of events, an illness, etc) develop in the natural or usual way without being changed or stopped: *The doctors agreed to let the illness run its course, rather than prescribe drugs which had little chance of success.* ○ *We must allow justice to take its course.*

as a matter of course ⇨ matter; **be par for the course** ⇨ par; **horses for courses**

⇨ horses; **in due course** ⇨ due; **take/ follow/steer a middle course** ⇨ middle

court

rule/put sth out of 'court make sth not worth considering; completely reject or exclude sth: *The committee ruled any further discussion on the matter out of court.* ○ *My suggestion was ruled out of court because it was too expensive.*

the ball is in sb's court ⇨ ball; **hold court** ⇨ hold; **laugh sb/sth out of court** ⇨ laugh

cousin a country cousin ⇨ country

Coventry send sb to Coventry ⇨ send

cover

cover your tracks be careful not to leave any signs of sth secret or illegal that you have been doing: *He didn't want his wife to know he'd met an old girlfriend so he invented a story to cover his tracks.*

from cover to cover from the beginning to the end of a book, magazine, etc: *I've read the newspaper from cover to cover, but I can't find any mention of yesterday's accident.*

under cover of sth **1** hidden or protected by sth: *They hoped to get into the enemy fortress under cover of darkness.* **2** with a pretence of (doing) sth: *He watched every move under cover of reading a newspaper.*

blow sb's cover ⇨ blow; **cover/hide a multitude of sins** ⇨ multitude

cow(s)

till/until the 'cows come home (*informal*) for a long time, or for ever: *You can talk till the cows come home, but you'll never persuade me to go with you!*

a sacred cow ⇨ sacred

crack

crack a joke tell a joke: *He's always cracking jokes in class.*

the crack of 'dawn (*informal*) very early in the morning: *We'll have to get up at the crack of dawn to be there by 9 am.*

have a 'crack at (doing) sth (*informal*) make an attempt at doing sth: *Why not let me have a crack at fixing the kettle. I'm sure I* *could do better than you!*

a fair crack of the whip ⇨ fair

cracked
not all, etc he, it, etc is cracked 'up to be (*informal*) not be as good, etc as people claim: *The food in this restaurant is not all it's cracked up to be.* ○ *She isn't the brilliant skier that she's been cracked up to be.*

cracking
get cracking (*informal*) start doing sth quickly: *We'll have to get cracking with the painting if we want to be finished by Friday.* ○ *There's an awful lot to do, so let's get cracking.*

cracks paper over the cracks ⇨ paper

cradle
from the ,cradle to the 'grave from birth to death; throughout your whole life: *The new government ministry was formed to look after citizens' social welfare from the cradle to the grave.*

cramp
cramp sb's 'style prevent sb from doing sth freely, or living as they wish: *She thinks that having her parents to stay in her flat will cramp her style.*

cranny every nook and cranny ⇨ nook

craw stick in your throat/craw/gullet ⇨ stick

crawl make your flesh creep/crawl ⇨ flesh; a pub crawl ⇨ pub

crazy
like 'crazy (*informal*) very fast, hard, etc: *run/work like crazy*

cream like the cat that got/ate/stole the cream ⇨ cat

create create/make a scene ⇨ scene; kick up/make/create/raise a stink ⇨ stink

creature
a creature of 'habit a person who always does certain things at certain times: *My grandfather is a real creature of habit – he likes his meals at the same time every day.*

credit
do sb credit *or* **do credit to sb** *or* **be to sb's credit** show sb's good qualities; make sb deserve praise: *The event was arranged with a speed and efficiency that does you credit.* ○ *Their manager, to her credit, was always strongly opposed to the pay cuts.*

have sth to your credit have achieved sth: *At the age of twenty-two he already has several tournament victories to his credit.*

creek
up the 'creek (*informal*) *also* (*very informal*) **up shit creek (without a paddle)** in great difficulty: *Make sure you look after the money and passports – if they get stolen we'll be right up the creek.*

creep(s)
give sb the willies/heebie-jeebies/creeps ⇨ give; **make your flesh creep/crawl** ⇨ flesh

crest
(on) the crest of a 'wave (at) the point of greatest success, wealth, happiness, etc: *He was fortunate to arrive in Hollywood when the film industry was on the crest of a wave.*

cricket
not 'cricket (*dated, British, informal*) not a fair or honourable action or way of behaving.

crocodile
'crocodile tears an insincere show of sadness: *They never visited her when she was ill, but they came to her funeral and wept a few crocodile tears.*

Croesus as rich as Croesus ⇨ rich

crook by hook or by crook ⇨ hook

cropper
come a 'cropper (*British, informal*) **1** fall (to the ground): *Pete came a cropper on his motorbike and ended up in hospital.* **2** fail badly, usually when you are expected to do well: *She's so confident she'll pass her exams without doing any work, but I've got a feeling she's going to come a real cropper.*

cross
be/talk at cross purposes (of two people or groups) misunderstand what the other is referring to or trying to do: *Mary and I spoke*

about Anne for a minute or two before I realized we were talking at cross purposes: *I meant Anne Smith and Mary meant Anne Harris.*

bear/carry your cross suffer the trouble(s) that life brings to you: *We all have our crosses to bear.*

,**cross a ,bridge when you 'come to it** deal with a problem only when it happens and not worry about it before then: *'What will you do if you can't afford to go on holiday next summer?' 'I'll cross that bridge when I come to it.'*

cross sb's mind (of a thought, etc) come into sb's mind for a short time: *He intended to marry her and the thought never crossed his mind that she might refuse.* ○ *It had crossed my mind that I hadn't seen her for a long time so I decided to ring her.* (usually used in negative sentences)

cross my 'heart (and hope to die) (used for emphasizing that you are sincere when making a promise, or that what you say is true): *'Don't tell anyone else about this, will you?' 'Cross my heart, I won't.'*

cross 'swords (with sb) have an argument (with sb): *At the committee meeting, I crossed swords with Professor Smith over her department's overspending.*

cross sb's path = our/their paths cross ⇨ paths; **dot the i's and cross the t's** ⇨ dot; **our/their paths cross** ⇨ paths

crossed

get your 'lines/'wires crossed *or* **have crossed 'lines/'wires** (*informal*) misunderstand each other: *I think we've got our lines crossed somewhere. I said Venice, not Vienna.* ○ *We must have got crossed wires. I thought you were going to drive, not me.*

have/keep your fingers ✶ ,crossed ⇨ fingers 🖐

crossroads

at a 'crossroads at a stage where a decision has to be made: *He's at a crossroads in his career – either he stays in his current job and waits for promotion, or he accepts this new post in Brazil.*

crow

as the 'crow flies (*informal*) (of a distance) measured in a straight line: *From here to the*

village it's five miles as the crow flies, but it's a lot further by road.

crowd

follow/go with the 'crowd (used for showing disapproval) do as everyone else does because you have no ideas of your own: *Dress in the way you like and try not to follow the crowd.*

crown   **to top/cap/crown it all** ⇨ top

cruel

be ,cruel to be 'kind use unpleasant methods because they are necessary to help sb: *I was worried about Katie getting too involved with Steve so I eventually told her about his drug addiction – you've got to be cruel to be kind sometimes.*

crumbles   **that's the way the cookie crumbles** ⇨ way

crunch

if/when it comes to the 'crunch (*informal*) if/when the moment comes when sth must be decided or done or a difficulty can no longer be avoided: *She was always threatening to leave him, but when it came to the crunch she didn't have the courage.*

crust   **the upper crust** ⇨ upper

cry

cry your 'eyes out cry a lot and for a long time: *My son cried his eyes out when we told him we couldn't afford a new bike.*

cry 'wolf repeatedly say there is danger, etc when there is none or ask for help unnecessarily (with the result that people do not think you are telling the truth when there is real danger or when you really need help): *Is the economic future really so bad? Or are the economists just crying wolf?* (from the fable of the shepherd boy who cried 'Wolf!' to make fun of people, so that when a wolf did come, nobody went to help him)

cry/ask for the moon ⇨ moon; **a far cry from sth** ⇨ far; **a hue and cry** ⇨ hue; **in full cry** ⇨ full; **a shoulder to cry on** ⇨ shoulder

crying

for ,crying out 'loud (*informal*) (used to express anger or frustration): *For crying out loud! How many times have I asked you not to* *do that?*

it's no good/use crying over spilt 'milk (*saying*) it is pointless to worry, complain or feel sad about sth which is done and cannot be changed.

cucumber   cool as a cucumber ⇨ cool

cudgels

take up the cudgels for sb/sth *or* **take up the cudgels on behalf of sb/sth** start to defend or support sb/sth: *The local newspapers have taken up the cudgels on behalf of the woman who was unfairly dismissed from her job because she was pregnant.*

cue

(right) on cue just at the appropriate moment: *The bell sounded for the beginning of the lesson, and, right on cue, the teacher walked in.*

take your cue from 'sb be influenced in your actions by what sb else has done: *In designing the car, we took our cue from other designers who aimed to combine low cost with low petrol consumption.*

cuff

off the 'cuff without previous thought or preparation: *I don't know how you can stand up and give an after-dinner speech off the cuff like that.* ○ *an off-the-cuff remark*

cup

(not) be sb's cup of tea (*informal*) (not) be the (kind of) person, thing or activity that you like: *He invited me to the opera but it's not really my cup of tea.*

there's many a slip 'twixt cup and lip ⇨ slip

cupboard

'cupboard love (*informal*) affection shown to sb from whom you hope to get sth: *The dog seems specially fond of her, but it's just cupboard love. She's the one who feeds him.*

a skeleton in the cupboard/closet ⇨ skeleton

curate

(like) the curate's 'egg (, good in parts) sth that has some good things and some bad things about it: *'Is it an interesting book?' 'A bit like the curate's egg, good in parts. The dialogue's often quite amusing.'*

cure   kill or cure ⇨ kill

curiosity

curiosity killed the 'cat (*saying*) (often used in reply to a question that you do not want to answer) don't be nosy: *'Are you two thinking of getting married by any chance?' 'Now, now. Curiosity killed the cat!'*

curl   make sb's hair curl ⇨ hair

curlies   get/have sb by the short and curlies = get/have sb by the short hairs ⇨ short

curry

curry favour (with sb) (*disapproving*) win sb's approval by praise, flattery, etc: *He's always trying to curry favour with the director by telling her how talented she is.*

curtain(s)

be ,curtains for 'sb/'sth (*informal*) cause the death of sb or the end of sth: *It'll be curtains for the business if the bank doesn't give us that loan.*

ring/bring down the curtain (on sth) *or* **ring/bring the curtain down (on sth)** bring an end to sth: *The BBC has finally decided to bring the curtain down on one of its oldest television programmes.*

customer   a tough customer ⇨ tough

cut

be cut 'out for sb/sth *or* **be cut 'out to be sth** (be) well suited in character or ability to sb, a job, profession or activity: *She wasn't a great journalist. She was more cut out for television reporting.* ○ *Why did he join the army? He's really not cut out to be a soldier.*

a cut above sb/sth superior to sb/sth: *This is a cut above the average weekly magazine – it publishes very good articles and short stories.*

cut and dried (of matters, arrangements or opinions) completely decided and unlikely to be changed: *By the end of the evening their plans for carrying out the robbery were cut and dried with nothing, they thought, left to chance.* ○ *The police thought they had a cut-and-dried case.*

cut and 'run (*informal*) make a quick or sudden escape: *She can't rely on Jason – he's the type to cut and run as soon as things get difficult.*

cut and 'thrust the lively exchange of opinions or ideas; competitiveness: *He enjoys the cut and thrust of business.*

(you could) ,cut the ,atmosphere with a 'knife (*informal*) the emotional tension, embarrassment, etc shared by a group of people is very great: *When John came in with his new girlfriend, you could have cut the atmosphere with a knife.*

cut both/two 'ways have an effect both for and against sb/sth: *Banning imports of cars could cut both ways: other countries may ban the import of cars produced here.*

cut the 'cackle (*informal*) stop talking and start working, etc properly; start talking about the important matters.

cut your 'coat ac,cording to your 'cloth (*saying*) not spend more than you can afford.

cut 'corners do things in the easiest, quickest or cheapest way and not in the proper way: *Don't be tempted to cut corners when doing a home decorating job.*

cut a 'dash impress others by your stylish appearance or behaviour: *She cuts quite a dash with her elegant clothes and expensive car.*

cut sb dead pretend not to see sb or not greet sb in order to show your anger, dislike, etc: *Jim has just cut me dead in the street. I'm sure it must be because I criticized his work yesterday.*

cut sb down to size show that sb is less important than they seem or think: *Failing his exams has certainly cut him down to size.*

cut a fine, poor, sorry, etc 'figure have a fine, etc appearance: *In his brand new uniform he cut a fine figure.*

cut the ground from under sb/sb's 'feet do sth which suddenly destroys sb's chances of success in an argument, enterprise, etc: *When he announced that all my figures were out of date, he really cut the ground from under my feet.*

cut it 'fine allow only just enough time to do sth: *Your train leaves in twenty minutes and you're still here! You're cutting it a bit fine, aren't you?*

cut your 'losses stop an unprofitable business, activity, etc before you suffer any further loss, harm, etc: *When our rent went up we decided to cut our losses and shut the shop.*

,cut no 'ice (with sb) not impress or influence sb: *Her aggressive manner may be very useful at work, but it cuts no ice with me.* ○ *Public protests don't cut much ice with this government.*

,cut off your ,nose to ,spite your 'face (*informal*) do sth, for example because you are angry or proud, that is intended to hurt sb else but in fact harms you: *Keeping your class in after school as a punishment is cutting off your nose to spite your face because you have to stay in with them!*

cut sb 'short stop sb speaking: *She was just about to say who had got the job, but I cut her short and asked her to keep it secret.*

cut sth 'short make sth end before the natural time; interrupt sth: *We'll have to cut our stay short, I'm afraid. My husband's father is seriously ill.* ○ *Our conversation was cut short by the arrival of the teacher.*

cut your 'teeth on sth learn or gain experience from sth: *It was a small experimental theatre company and many of today's most successful actors cut their teeth there.*

cut sb to the 'quick hurt sb's feelings; offend sb deeply: *It cut her to the quick to hear him criticizing her family like that.*

cut up rough/nasty (*informal*) behave or react in an angry, bad-tempered or violent way: *I didn't want to ask Jo for a loan, but my landlady had cut up rough when I asked her if she could wait a few more days for the rent.*

to cut a ,long ,story 'short (used when a speaker is not going to describe all the details of sth, only the final result): *...and then the boss told us what had been discussed at the management meeting. Well, to cut a long story short ten people are going to lose their jobs.*

have your work cut out ➪ work; **a short cut** ➪ short

D

dab
be a dab hand at (doing) sth (*British, informal*) be very good at doing sth: *be a dab hand at gardening/carpentry/repairing things*

daddy a sugar daddy ⇨ sugar

daggers
be at daggers drawn (with sb) (be ready to) fight or argue (with sb): *They've been at daggers drawn ever since he borrowed her car and smashed it up.*

look daggers at sb ⇨ look

daily
your daily bread the food or money that you need to live: *Each one of us has to earn our daily bread somehow.*

daisies push up daisies ⇨ push

daisy fresh as a daisy ⇨ fresh

dale up hill and down dale ⇨ hill

damage
what's the damage? (*British, informal*) how much do I need to pay you?: *Thanks for repairing the cooker. What's the damage?*

dammit as near as dammit ⇨ near

damn
damn it (all) (*informal*) (used for expressing anger, annoyance, etc): *I've broken my pen again, damn it!*

damn sb/sth with faint 'praise praise sb/sth so little that you seem to be criticizing them/it.

damned
I'll be damned (*informal*) (used for expressing surprise): *Well, I'll be damned! Isn't that Sarah Parker over there?*

I'm/I'll be damned/blowed if... (*very informal*) I certainly will not, do not, etc: *I'm damned if I will lend any money to that lazy son of mine.* ○ *'Why is she so late?' 'I'll be blowed if I know.'*

damnedest
do/try your 'damnedest (*informal*) try very hard; make a very great effort: *He was doing his damnedest to make me feel uncomfortable so that I would leave.*

damp
a damp 'squib an event, experience, etc that is expected to be interesting or exciting, but is in fact boring or ordinary: *The party turned out to be rather a damp squib.*

damper
put a damper on sth (*informal*) make an event, etc less enjoyable or cheerful: *The news of my father's illness put a bit of a damper on the birthday celebrations.*

damsel
a damsel in distress (*humorous*) a woman who needs help from a man, often to solve a practical problem.

dance
dance attendance on sb do a lot of small jobs in order to please sb: *She always has an assistant dancing attendance on her.*

lead sb a dance ⇨ lead; **make a song and dance about sth** ⇨ song

dare
how 'dare you, she, he, etc (do sth)? (*informal*) (used for expressing anger or shock about sth that sb has done): *How dare you speak to me like that!* ○ *How dare he use my office without permission?*

I dare say I suppose; it seems probable: *I dare say what you say is true, but it's too late to change our plans now.*

dark
a dark 'horse (*informal*) a person who hides their feelings, plans, activities, etc: *You're a dark horse! I had no idea you could play the piano so well.*

keep it/sth dark (from sb) (*informal*) keep sth secret: *I've got a new job but keep it dark, will you?*

a shot in the dark ⇨ shot; **whistle in the dark** ⇨ whistle

darken

not/never darken sb's ˌdoor aˈgain (*dated or humorous*) not/never come to sb's home again because you are very unwelcome: *Go! And never darken my door again!*

dash

dash make a bolt/dash for it/sth ⇨ bolt; **dash/shatter sb's hopes** ⇨ hopes

date

ˌout of ˈdate not modern; not including the latest information: *This atlas is out of date.* ○ *I'm afraid you must have been using an out-of-date catalogue.*

to date up to and including the present time: *To date, we've received 40 bookings for the holiday, so we're doing quite well.*

(be) ˌup to ˈdate 1 possessing the most recent information, ideas, etc about sth/sb: *Are you up to date on what's happening in Iran?* ○ *I'm not really up to date on John and Mary. Are they still together?* ○ *This book on Latin American politics is absolutely up to date.* **2** the most recent, modern or fashionable: *His kitchen is right up to date. He's got all the latest technology in it.*

be past its sell-by date ⇨ past; **blind date** ⇨ blind

daughter

like father/mother, like son/daughter ⇨ father

dawn

the crack of dawn ⇨ crack

day

ˌall day and ˈevery day without change for a long period of time: *I have to be active. I couldn't just sit around all day and every day now I've retired.*

all in a day's ˈwork a normal part of sb's daily activities, job, etc (used especially of events or activities that are considered difficult or unpleasant): *For a nurse, calming the fears of anxious relatives is all in a day's work.*

ˈany day (of the week) (*informal*) (used for showing that you prefer one thing or person to another): *I'd rather have him than his brother any day of the week.*

carry/win the ˈday (*informal*) win a contest, argument, etc; be successful: *It was a difficult match, but the England team finally carried the day.*

day after ˈday for many days, one after the other: *Day after day, she came and waited in his office, until finally he agreed to see her.*

day by ˈday all the time; as the days pass: *Day by day she grew more confident about the job.*

day ˌin, day ˈout every day, without exception: *I drive to work day in, day out, and I'm getting tired of spending so much time travelling.* (*week, month* and *year* can be used in a similar way to *day* in this expression)

the day of ˈreckoning (*formal*) the time when good actions, successes, etc or bad actions, failures, etc will be made known and punished or rewarded: *Tomorrow is the day of reckoning; the accountant will tell me what my profits were and how much tax I will have to pay.*

have had your/its ˈday no longer be as successful, powerful, etc as you once were/it once was: *He used to be one of the world's top soccer players but now, I'm afraid, he's had his day.*

in ˈsb's day/time at the time when sb was alive; when sb was young: *In my grandmother's time, women were expected to stay at home and look after the children.* ○ *In my day, nobody would have spoken to the boss like that.*

in my, his, her, etc ˈday/ˈtime when I, etc was most successful, famous, etc: *He had, in his day, been one of the greatest opera singers in the world.*

in ˈthis day and age at the present time; nowadays: *It's surprising, in this day and age, to discover that there are still many homes which do not have telephones.*

sb is 60, 70, etc ˌif he's a ˈday (*informal*) sb is at least 60, 70, etc years old: *She isn't forty! She's fifty-five if she's a day!*

make sb's ˈday (*informal*) make sb very happy: *Thanks for sending me those flowers. It really made my day!*

not be sb's ˈday (*informal*) be a day when a lot of things go wrong for sb: *First I tore my jacket, then my car broke down. This is definitely not my day!*

ˈsome day at a time in the future: *Some day you will realize what good parents you have.*

ˈthat'll be the ˌday (*ironic*) (used for

saying that sth is unlikely): *'When I'm rich, I'll buy you a new car.' 'That'll be the day!'*

to the 'day exactly: *It is ten years to the day since I first came to this town.*

to this 'day up to now: *To this day I have not been able to find out anything about who my real parents were.*

at the end of the day ⇨ end; **a black day** ⇨ black; **call it a day** ⇨ call; **clear as day** ⇨ clear; **every dog has its day** ⇨ dog; **have a field day** ⇨ field; **happy as the day is long/as a sandboy/as Larry** ⇨ happy; **in the cold light of day** ⇨ cold; **late in the day** ⇨ late; **the light of day** ⇨ light; **live to fight another day** ⇨ live; **name the day** ⇨ name; **night and day** ⇨ night; **the order of the day** ⇨ order; **pass the time of day** ⇨ pass; **the present day** ⇨ present; **put off the evil day** ⇨ evil; **a red-letter day** ⇨ red; **Rome wasn't built in a day** ⇨ Rome; **save the day/situation** ⇨ save; **save it for a rainy day** ⇨ rainy; **till/to/until your dying day** ⇨ dying

daylight

daylight robbery (*informal*) a price or charge that you think is far too high: *£10000 for a useless old car like this? That's daylight robbery!*

in broad daylight ⇨ broad; **see daylight** ⇨ see

daylights

beat/scare the (living) 'daylights out of sb/sth (*informal*) hit sb/sth very hard and repeatedly; frighten sb very much: *They beat the living daylights out of the man who complained about police violence.* ○ *I don't think I'll go to see that new horror film at the cinema. Jane said it scared the daylights out of her.*

days

sb's/sth's days are 'numbered sb has not long left to live; sth will not last much longer: *Now that we are no longer getting any government support, the theatre's days are numbered.*

a ,nine days' 'wonder a person or thing that attracts a lot of attention, but only for a short time: *This new boyfriend of hers is just another nine days' wonder.*

'these days at the present time, as compared with an earlier time; nowadays: *Divorce is getting more and more common these days.*

'those were the days used for talking about a better or happier time in the past: *'They bought the house for £600 in 1930.' 'Ah, those were the days!'*

have seen/known better days ⇨ better; **in all my born days** ⇨ born; **it's early days** ⇨ early; **one of these days** ⇨ one; **one of these fine days** ⇨ one; **one of those days** ⇨ one

dead

dead and buried/gone dead, especially for a long time; long past and forgotten: *Long after I'm dead and gone, you'll still be carrying on the same as you ever were.* ○ *Why bring up old quarrels that have been dead and buried for years?*

(as) dead as a/the 'dodo (*informal*) no longer in existence; very old-fashioned: *Old business practices are as dead as a dodo in the computer age.*

a dead 'cert (*informal*) a person or thing that is certain to win, succeed, etc: *'Would you ever bet money on a horse?' 'No, not unless it was a dead cert.'*

a dead 'duck (*informal*) a plan, idea, etc that has been abandoned or is certain to fail: *They say that the new supermarket is going to be a dead duck because there is no demand for one in this area.*

a dead 'end (*informal*) a point where no more progress can be made: *Lack of further clues meant that the murder investigation came to a dead end.* ○ *He was in a dead-end job with no hope of promotion.*

a dead 'letter an idea, proposal, etc that is no longer valid, useful, etc: *The plans for a new school are a dead letter, now that we know there will be no pupils to attend it.*

a dead 'loss a person or thing that is useless or a complete failure: *This television is a dead loss; the picture fades completely after five minutes.*

(in) the dead of (the) night *or* **at dead of night** in the quietest, darkest hours of the night: *She crept in at dead of night, while they were asleep.*

a dead ringer for sb (*informal*) a person who looks extremely like sb else: *She's a dead* ringer for her mother.

,dead to the 'world (*informal*) fast asleep: *Within two minutes of getting into the bed, I was dead to the world.*

,dead 'wood (*informal*) people or things that are no longer useful or necessary: *The management wants to cut costs by getting rid of all the dead wood in the factory. Fifty workers are to lose their jobs.*

I, he, etc wouldn't be seen 'dead with sb/sth, doing sth, in sth, etc I, he, etc would not do a certain thing because I, etc would feel stupid or embarrassed: *I wouldn't be seen dead in a hat like that.* ○ *She wouldn't be seen dead in a place like this.* ○ *I wouldn't be seen dead with you in those terrible jeans.*

over ,my dead 'body (*informal*) (used for saying that you will do everything possible to stop sth happening): *'They want to use our front garden to widen the road!' 'Over my dead body.'*

drop dead ⇨ drop; **flog a dead horse** ⇨ flog; **kill sth stone dead** ⇨ kill; **wake the dead** ⇨ wake

deaf

(as) deaf as a 'post (*informal*) very deaf: *You'll have to speak louder if you want her to hear you. She's as deaf as a post.*

fall on deaf ears ⇨ fall; **turn a deaf ear to sth** ⇨ turn

deal

deal sb/sth a 'blow *or* **deal a blow to sb/sth** be a shock for sb; make sth fail, etc: *The death of her father dealt her a terrible blow.* ○ *Losing his job dealt a blow to his hopes of buying his own house.*

a raw/rough 'deal unfair treatment: *Many old people feel they are getting a raw deal from the state: they pay money towards a pension all their working life but discover it isn't worth much when they retire.*

big deal ⇨ big; **wheel and deal** ⇨ wheel

dear

dear me *or* **(dear,) oh dear** (used for expressing worry, sympathy, concern, etc): *Dear me! It's started to rain and I've just hung out the washing!*

be close/dear/near to sb's heart ⇨ heart; **for dear life** ⇨ life; **hold sb/sth dear** ⇨ hold; **an old dear** ⇨ old

dearest **nearest and dearest** ⇨ nearest

death

at death's 'door (*often ironic*) so ill that you might die: *Come on, get out of bed. You're not at death's door yet!*

be the death of sb (*often humorous*) cause sb a lot of harm or worry: *You children are so badly behaved! You'll be the death of me one day!*

be ,in at the 'death/'kill be there when sth ends or fails: *I was in at the kill when the Professor finally won the debate against his opponents.*

,do sth to 'death (*informal*) talk or write about a subject, or perform a play, etc so often that it is no longer interesting: *Some people think that the theme of romantic love has been done to death in poetry.*

like death warmed up (*informal*) very unwell or tired: *I feel like death warmed up this morning, but I'm going to go to work anyway.* ○ *You should go home to bed. You look like death warmed up.*

to the death until sb dies or is defeated: *There was a fight to the death between two men armed with knives.*

be tickled to death ⇨ tickled; **bore sb to death/tears** ⇨ bore; **catch your death** ⇨ catch; **dice with death** ⇨ dice; **die the death** ⇨ die; **a fate worse than death** ⇨ fate; **flog sth to death** ⇨ flog; **frighten/scare sb to death/out of their wits** ⇨ frighten; **hang on/hold on like grim death** ⇨ grim; **the kiss of death** ⇨ kiss; **life and/or death** ⇨ life; **sign your own death-warrant** ⇨ sign; **sound the death knell of sth** ⇨ sound; **sudden death** ⇨ sudden; **work yourself to death** ⇨ work; **worry sb to death** ⇨ worry

debt

be in sb's 'debt (*formal*) be very grateful to sb because they have helped you: *When my husband died Ann was the only one prepared to listen to my problems, and I am forever in her debt.*

,get/,run into 'debt begin to owe money: *After she lost her job, she began to run into debt.*

deck

all hands on deck ⇨ hands; **clear the deck(s)** ⇨ clear; **hit the deck** ⇨ hit

deep

deep 'down (*informal*) in your most private thoughts; in reality rather than in appearance: *She's very generous deep down, but this only comes out when you get to know her.* ○ *He seems very confident but deep down I think he's quite shy.*

(in) deep 'water (involved in) very difficult, complicated or dangerous affairs: *She was getting into deep water when she tried to argue that murder is sometimes justified for political reasons.*

jump in/be thrown in at the 'deep end (*informal*) try to do sth difficult without help when you are not prepared or know very little about it: *On the first day of her new teaching job, she was thrown in at the deep end having to teach the most badly-behaved class.* ○ *I didn't know anything about business when I started. I just had to jump in at the deep end.* (refers to the deep end of a swimming pool)

beauty is only skin deep ⇨ beauty; **between the devil and the deep blue sea** ⇨ devil; **still waters run deep** ⇨ still

degree

to the nth de'gree (*informal*) to the greatest possible amount, level, etc; very much: *This book is boring to the nth degree.*

the third degree ⇨ third

degrees

by de'grees little by little; gradually: *The country's economy won't improve straight away, but will only get better by degrees.*

deliver **come up with/deliver/produce the goods** ⇨ goods

delivered **signed, sealed, and delivered** ⇨ signed

delusions

delusions of 'grandeur (*often humorous*) a belief that you are more important than you really are: *He's been suffering from delusions of grandeur ever since he became manager.*

demand

in de'mand wanted by many people; popular: *Beautiful old houses like this one are always in great demand.* ○ *Well-qualified young people with experience in marketing are very much in demand at the moment.*

den

a den of i'niquity/'vice (*often humorous*) a place where people do bad things: *She thinks that just because we sit around smoking and drinking beer the club must be a real den of iniquity.*

beard the lion in his den ⇨ beard

dent

make a dent/hole in sth (*informal*) reduce sth: *Having to pay out unexpectedly for car repairs made a big hole in my savings.* ○ *Being told off in public made quite a dent in his reputation.*

depends

it/that (all) de'pends (*informal*) perhaps; possibly: *'Would you marry him if he asked you to?' 'I might. It all depends.'* ○ *'But is it right to send people to prison?' 'It depends what you mean by right!'*

depth(s)

,in 'depth thoroughly: *The report treats in some depth the subject of homelessness.* **in-depth** (*adjective*) thorough: *an in-depth analysis, discussion, etc*

in the depths of sth at the worst, most unpleasant, etc stage of sth: *in the depths of despair, poverty, depression, etc* ○ *in the depths of winter*

out of your depth (*informal*) in a situation that is too difficult for you to deal with or understand: *When they start talking about economics, I'm out of my depth.*

plumb the depths of sth ⇨ plumb

description **beggar belief/description** ⇨ beggar

deserves **one good turn deserves another** ⇨ turn

designs

have designs on sb/sth (*informal*) intend to take sb/sth for yourself, for example a job or a person whom you find sexually attractive: *Several people have got designs on the office manager's post.* ○ *I think she's got designs on you, Peter.*

desired **leave a lot to be desired** ⇨ leave

devices **leave sb to their own devices** ⇨ leave

devil

be a 'devil (*informal, humorous*) (said as an encouragement to sb to do sth that they are not sure about doing): *Go on, be a devil, Catherine! Buy yourself some new clothes for once!*

between the ,devil and the ,deep blue 'sea (*informal*) in a situation where you have to choose between two things that are equally bad: *In this situation, the government finds itself caught between the devil and the deep blue sea.*

the ,devil looks ,after his 'own (*saying*) bad people often seem to have good luck.

the devil makes work for idle hands (*saying*) people who do not have enough to do often start to do wrong: *She blamed the crimes on the local jobless teenagers. 'The devil makes work for idle hands,' she would say.*

a/the 'devil of a job, nuisance, fellow, etc (*informal, dated*) a difficult, unpleasant, etc example of sth: *We had the devil of a job getting the roots of that tree out of the ground.*

(a/the) devil's 'advocate a person who argues against sth, even though they really agree with it, just to test the arguments for it: *Helen doesn't really think that women shouldn't go out to work. She's just playing (the) devil's advocate.*

(the) devil take the 'hindmost (*saying*) everyone should look after themselves and not care about others: *I like the way people here always queue up. Back home we just push and shove, and the devil take the hindmost!*

like the 'devil (*informal*) very fast, hard, etc: *We had to work like the devil to be finished on time.* ○ *I ran like the devil, but I still missed the bus.*

talk/speak of the 'devil (*saying*) (said when sb who has just been mentioned appears unexpectedly): *'I haven't seen Leo for a while.' 'Well, speak of the devil, here he is!'*

who, what, where, etc the devil (*informal*) (used for showing surprise or annoyance): *Who the devil are you?* ○ *Where the devil have I put my glasses?*

better the devil you know ⇨ better; **hell/the devil to pay** ⇨ pay; **the luck of the devil** ⇨ luck; **needs must** ⇨ needs

diamond a rough diamond ⇨ rough

dice

the 'dice are loaded against sb a person has little chance of succeeding in sth, perhaps for unfair reasons: *If you apply for a job when you're over 40, the dice are loaded against you.* (refers to putting a piece of lead (a very heavy metal) inside a dice so that it always falls in a particular way)

dice with death (*informal*) risk your life by doing sth very dangerous: *Racing drivers dice with death every time they drive in a race.*

Dick a clever Dick ⇨ clever; **every/any Tom, Dick and/or Harry** ⇨ Tom

dicky-bird not say a dicky-bird ⇨ say

die

die the 'death (*informal*) end suddenly and completely; fail: *Our fund-raising appeal died the death when the government failed to support it.* ○ *He died the death as Othello, and never got another role after that.*

die 'hard not be easily changed or removed: *Old habits die hard, and I'm finding it difficult to give up smoking.* ○ *die-hard attitudes* **die-hard** (*noun*) a person who is unwilling to change his or her views.

die in 'harness die while you are still working.

the die is cast (*saying*) a decision has been made, or a risk has been taken, and the situation cannot now be changed: *Once he had invested all his money in the new business, he knew the die had been cast and he could not turn back.*

die laughing (*informal*) laugh until you are exhausted: *His jokes were so funny that I nearly died laughing.*

be, etc straight as a die ⇨ straight; **die/fall/drop like flies** ⇨ flies; **never say die** ⇨ never

differ agree to differ ⇨ agree; **beg to differ** ⇨ beg

difference(s)

make a, some, etc difference (to sb/sth) have an effect (on sb/sth).

with a 'difference (*informal*) (used after nouns) of an unusual kind: *This is a house with a difference: it has a swimming pool in the lounge.*

same difference ⇨ same; **sink your**

differences ⇨ sink; **same difference** ⇨ same; **split the difference** ⇨ split; **there's a world of difference** ⇨ world

different

a different kettle of fish (*informal*) a person or thing that is completely different from sb/sth else previously mentioned: *You may be able to read French well, but speaking it fluently is a different kettle of fish entirely.*

as different as chalk and cheese ⇨ chalk; **know different/otherwise** ⇨ know; **sing a different song/tune** ⇨ sing; **speak/talk the same/ a different language** ⇨ language

dig

,dig your 'heels in (*informal*) refuse to do sth or to change your views: *A number of councils have dug their heels in over the Government's request to reduce spending.*

dig your own grave do sth that will bring harm to yourself: *If you give up your job now, you'll be digging your own grave, because you won't find it easy to get another one.*

dignity

be,neath sb's 'dignity (*often ironic*) seeming so unimportant or unpleasant that sb thinks they are too important to do it: *She considers it beneath her dignity to help with the housework now and again.*

stand on your dignity ⇨ stand

dilemma **the horns of a dilemma** ⇨ horns

dim

take a ,dim 'view of sb/sth think that sb/ sth is bad or wrong; disapprove of sb/sth: *His mother took a very dim view of him staying out until two o'clock in the morning.*

dime

a ,dime a 'dozen (*US informal*) cheap and easy to obtain.

dine **wine and dine** ⇨ wine

dinner(s) **a dog's breakfast/dinner** ⇨ dog **more sth/more often than sb has had hot dinners** ⇨ hot

dint

by dint of sth (*becoming dated*) as a result of (doing) sth; through: *By dint of sheer hard work, she managed to pass all her exams.*

dirt **treat sb like dirt** ⇨ treat

dirty

(give sb/get) a dirty 'look (*informal*) look at sb/be looked at in an angry, or a disapproving way: *She gave me a dirty look when I suggested that she should go and make the beds.*

a dirty old man (*informal, disapproving*) an older man who thinks too much about sex: *Lots of dirty old men stood around looking at pornographic magazines.*

a dirty weekend (*informal, often humorous*) a weekend spent away from home in order to have sex, usually with sb who is not your usual partner: *They went away for a dirty weekend in Brighton.*

a dirty word a thing or idea that sb finds unpleasant or offensive: *Work is a dirty word to these lazy kids.*

do the dirty on sb (*informal*) cheat sb or treat them unfairly: *Mike felt that his fellow students had done the dirty on him by telling the lecturer he'd cheated in the exam.*

talk dirty ⇨ talk; **wash your dirty linen in public** ⇨ wash

disadvantage

put sb/be at a disadvantage make it/ be difficult for sb to succeed: *My lack of experience put me at a disadvantage in comparison with the other candidates for the job.*

disap'pearing

do a disappearing act (*informal*) go away without being seen, especially when sb is looking for you: *Ian always does his disappearing act when I want to ask him to help me.*

disguise **a blessing in disguise** ⇨ blessing

distance

keep your 'distance (from sb/sth) not be too friendly or familiar with sb/sth: *She tends to keep her distance from her neighbours, so none of them know her very well.*

within spitting distance ⇨ spitting

distress **a damsel in distress** ⇨ damsel

district the red-light district ⇨ red

ditch last ditch stand/attempt/effort ⇨ last

ditchwater (as) dull as ditchwater ⇨ dull

dividend a/the peace dividend ⇨ peace

do

could/can do with'out sth (*informal*) not want sth, for example criticism, advice or complaints: *I could do without him telling me what to say all the time.* ○ *I could have done without her ringing me up just as I was about to go out.*

could 'do with sth (*informal*) want or need sth: *I could really do with a coffee.* ○ *You look as if you could do with a good night's sleep.*

do a 'sb (*informal*) do or behave as sb did or would do: *Now don't go and do a Mr. Carpenter on us. He told us he was leaving only three weeks before he went, and it took us months to find a replacement.*

do's and don'ts (*informal*) what to do and what not to do; rules: *This book is a useful guide to the do's and don'ts of choosing and buying your first car.*

'do something for sb/sth (*informal*) make sb/sth look better: *You know, that hat really does something for you!*

have (got)/be to 'do with 'sb/'sth be connected or concerned with sb/sth: *'What do you want to see me about?' 'It's to do with the letter you sent.'* ○ *I'm not sure exactly what he does for a living but I know it's something to do with computers.* ○ *'Where were you last night?' 'Mind your own business! It's got nothing to do with you.'*

how do you 'do? (used as a polite greeting when meeting sb for the first time): *How do you do? May I introduce Mr. Smith, our new sales manager?* (the reply to *how do you do?* is also *how do you do?*)

it/that won't 'do *or* **it/that will never 'do** (*informal*) (it/that is unsatisfactory or unacceptable): *He's spending every afternoon in the park with his friends instead of going to school, and that just won't do!* ○ *I feel very upset but it would never do to show it.*

that will 'do (*informal*) (often said to stop

sb behaving or speaking in a certain way) that is enough: *That will do! I've heard enough of your swearing.*

what did you, etc do with sth? (usually in perfect and simple past tenses) where did you, etc put, lose or hide sth?: *What have you done with my scissors? They were on the kitchen table the last time I saw them.*

be/have nothing to do with sb/sth ⇨ nothing; **do it = do the trick/job** ⇨ trick

dock

put sb in the dock accuse sb of doing sth wrong: *The Government is being put in the dock for failing to warn the public about the flu epidemic.*

doctor

just what the doctor ordered (*saying*) exactly what sb wants or needs: *Ah, a long, cool, refreshing drink! Just what the doctor ordered!*

dodo dead as the dodo ⇨ dead

does

that 'does it (*informal*) (used to show that you will not tolerate sth any longer): *That does it! You've called me a liar once too often. I'm leaving!*

dog

dog eat 'dog (*informal*) fierce competition, with no concern for the harm done or other people's feelings: *In the modern business world, it's dog eat dog in the search for success.*

dog sb's footsteps (of misfortune) seem to follow sb everywhere: *Bad luck seems to have dogged our footsteps from the beginning.*

a dog in the 'manger a person who selfishly stops other people from using or enjoying sth which they cannot use or enjoy themselves. **dog-in-the-manger** (*adjective*) *a dog-in-the-manger attitude*

a dog's breakfast/dinner (*informal*) a very untidy piece of work; a mess: *Don't ask Julie to help you with the decorating – she made a complete dog's breakfast of painting the kitchen!*

a 'dog's life (*informal, often humorous*) a life in which there is not much pleasure or freedom: *It's a dog's life having to do two jobs in order to survive.*

every dog has its 'day (*saying*) (often used to encourage yourself or another person at an unsuccessful time) everybody will, at some time in their life, be successful or lucky.

give a dog a bad 'name (and hang him) (*saying*) when a person already has a bad reputation, it is difficult to change it because others will continue to blame or suspect him or her.

fight like cat and dog ⇨ fight; **the hair of the dog** ⇨ hair; **let the tail wag the dog = the tail is wagging the dog** ⇨ tail; **not a dog's chance** ⇨ chance; **the tail is wagging the dog** ⇨ tail; **teach an old dog new tricks** ⇨ teach; **there's life in the old dog yet** ⇨ life; **top dog** ⇨ top; **work like a dog/slave/Trojan** ⇨ work

doggo **lie doggo** ⇨ lie

doghouse

in the 'doghouse (*informal*) in a situation where sb is angry with you because you have done sth wrong: *I'm in the doghouse with my wife at the moment: I forgot it was her birthday yesterday!*

dogs

go to the 'dogs (*informal*) (often used of a company, organization, country, etc) become less powerful, efficient, etc than before: *Many people think this country's going to the dogs.*

let sleeping dogs lie ⇨ sleeping; **rain cats and dogs** ⇨ rain

doldrums

in the doldrums quiet or depressed: *Property sales have been in the doldrums for some time.* ○ *He was in the doldrums for the whole winter.*

dollar **bet your bottom dollar/your life** ⇨ bet; **the sixty-four thousand dollar question** ⇨ sixty

done

be 'done for (*informal*) be in serious trouble: *The supplies are so low that we will be done for in a few days if help doesn't come soon.* ○ *I think the project is done for – the money's almost gone and we've got no results after three years' hard work.*

be/have 'done with sb/sth no longer do sth or be involved with sb/sth: *I'm fed up with you lot! I'm done with you for ever! ○ Why don't we spend another half hour painting and have done with it.*

done 'in (*informal*) extremely tired: *I feel absolutely done in!*

he, etc has gone/been and done sth (*informal*) (used to express surprise, annoyance, etc at sb's actions): *Someone's gone and locked the door and I haven't got a key! ○ What's he been and done now?*

donkey

'donkey's years (*British, informal*) a very long time: *She's lived in that house for donkey's years.*

the 'donkey work (*informal*) the hard, boring parts of a job: *Why is it always me who has to do the donkey work?*

talk the hind legs off a donkey ⇨ talk

don'ts **do's and don'ts** ⇨ do

doom **a prophet of doom** ⇨ prophet

door

(from) ,door to 'door **1** from the place of departure to your destination: *The whole journey took me four hours from door to door.* **2** from one house, flat, etc to the next: *The church distributes leaflets from door to door.* **door-to-door** (*adjective*) a door-to-door salesman

at death's door ⇨ death; **by/through the back door** ⇨ back; **not/never darken sb's door again** ⇨ darken; **get/have a foot in the door** ⇨ foot; **keep the wolf from the door** ⇨ wolf; **lay sth at sb's door** ⇨ lay; **leave the door open** ⇨ leave; **lie at sb's door = lay sth at sb's door** ⇨ lay; **open the door to/for sb/sth** ⇨ open; **show sb the door** ⇨ show; **shut/close the stable door after the horse has bolted** ⇨ stable; **shut the door on sth** ⇨ shut

doors **behind closed doors** ⇨ close

doorstep

on your/sb's 'doorstep very near your/sb's home: *It's easy to be concerned with problems across the other side of the world and not see the poverty and unhappiness on your doorstep.*

dose give sb a taste/dose of their own
medicine ⇨ medicine

dot

dot the i's and cross the t's pay great
attention to small details in order to
complete sth; be very thorough and careful
in what you do or say: *We reached a broad
agreement on pay, and decided to dot the i's and
cross the t's later.*

on the 'dot (*informal*) at exactly the right
time: *He always finishes work at 4.30 on the
dot.* ○ *She arrived on the dot of 6.00.*

from the year dot ⇨ year

dotted sign on the dotted line ⇨ sign

double

at the 'double *or* (*US*) **on the 'double**
(*informal*) very quickly; immediately: *Go and
get my boots, on the double!* ○ *The boss wants
you to go and see her at the double.*

do a ,double 'take react to sth surprising
or unusual only after a short delay: *I had to
do a double take when she walked in – she looked
exactly like her mother!*

,double 'Dutch (*informal*) language that is
impossible to understand: *I wish someone
would explain this contract in simple English –
it's all double Dutch to me!*

,double 'quick (*informal*) very quick(ly): *If
the machine starts making a hissing noise, then
turn it off double quick.*

doubt

in 'doubt not certain: *The future of the
company is still in doubt.* ○ *If in doubt, call for
an ambulance.*

,no 'doubt probably, almost certainly: *No
doubt you know why I have asked you to come
and see me.* ○ *You will no doubt have already
heard that the chairman has resigned.*

without (a) 'doubt certainly: *This is
without a doubt the finest wine I have ever
drunk.*

beyond/without a shadow of doubt
⇨ shadow; **give sb the benefit of the
doubt** ⇨ benefit; **there isn't a shadow of
a doubt (that)** = beyond/without a
shadow of doubt ⇨ shadow

doubting

a ,doubting 'Thomas a person who will
not believe sth without proof: *Now, for all*
*you doubting Thomases who thought I couldn't
win an important race, here's my medal to
prove it!* (from the Bible)

down

be down to 'sb be the responsibility of sb:
*Our defeat in last week's game is down to the
goalkeeper, who played really badly.*

be down to 'sth have nothing except one
or a few items of the kind mentioned: *I'm
down to my last penny.*

,down and 'out having no home or job
and living on the streets of a city; very poor:
*It must be terrible to be down and out in this
cold weather.* **down-and-out** (*noun*) person
who is down and out: *life among the city's
down-and-outs*

down to 'sb/'sth even including the last
item of a whole list of people or things: *All
were affected by the economic crisis, from the
president down to the poorest citizen.* ○ *She's
thought of everything down to the tiniest
details!*

,down 'tools (*British*) stop work, either at
the end of the day or to go on strike: *The
workers have threatened to down tools as a
protest against the sackings.*

down 'under (*informal*) in or to Australia
and/or New Zealand: *TV stars from down
under*

,down with 'sb/'sth! (shouted as a protest
against sb/sth): *Down with the dictator!*

downhill

downhill all the way (*informal*) very easy
compared with the difficulties that came
before: *I've done three out of the four parts of
the course, so it should be downhill all the way
from now on.*

,go down'hill get worse; deteriorate: *My
work has been going downhill ever since my
divorce.* ○ *This restaurant has definitely gone
downhill since I last came here.*

dozen a baker's dozen ⇨ baker; **a dime
a dozen** ⇨ dime; **it's six of one and half a
dozen of the other** ⇨ six; **talk nineteen
to the dozen** ⇨ nineteen

drabs in/by dribs and drabs ⇨ dribs

drag

drag your 'feet/'heels do sth very slowly
or delay doing sth because you do not want

to do it: *How much longer will the Government go on dragging its feet about whether to invest more money in the railways?*

dragged look what the cat's dragged/brought in ⇨ look

drain

(go) down the 'drain (*informal*) (be) wasted or lost: *He watched his business, which had taken so long to build up, go slowly down the drain.*

the brain drain ⇨ brain; **money down the drain** ⇨ money

draught feel the draught ⇨ feel

draw

draw a 'blank not find sth that you are looking for: *There was no sign of the murder weapon. The police searched every inch of the wood but drew a blank.*

draw in your 'horns spend less money than before: *After making huge losses, the company had to draw in its horns by cancelling some major projects.*

draw the line (at sth) refuse to do or accept sth: *I don't mind cooking dinner for you occasionally, but I draw the line at ironing your shirts!* ○ *He said that he refused to tolerate her lies any longer. The line had to be drawn somewhere.*

draw the short straw be the unlucky person in a group because you are chosen to do sth that nobody wants to do: *You've drawn the short straw, I'm afraid. You're going to have to work on Christmas Day.*

draw/cast lots ⇨ lots; **draw/throw/cast a veil/a curtain over sth** ⇨ veil; **the luck of the draw** ⇨ luck

drawing back to the drawing board ⇨ back

drawn be at daggers drawn ⇨ daggers

dream(s)

not 'dream of (doing) sth (often used with *would*) not even consider (doing) sth under any circumstances: *'Don't tell Gary what I've bought him for his birthday.' 'I wouldn't dream of it.'* ○ *Only a couple of years ago he would never have dreamt of going abroad on his own, and now he's travelling around India!*

work/go like a 'dream (*informal*) work/go very well: *The plan worked like a dream.*

be beyond your wildest dreams ⇨ wildest; **a pipe dream** ⇨ pipe

dressed

dressed to 'kill (*informal*) (especially of a woman) wearing your best clothes, especially clothes that attract attention: *She went to the party dressed to kill.*

dressed up to the nines (*informal, disapproving*) dressed very elaborately, especially to attract attention: *She was dressed up to the nines in her furs and jewellery.*

be mutton dressed as lamb ⇨ mutton

dribs

in ˌdribs and 'drabs (*informal*) in small amounts or numbers: *People started arriving in dribs and drabs from nine o'clock onwards.* ○ *He paid back the money slowly, in dribs and drabs.*

dried cut and dried ⇨ cut

drift lose the drift/thread of sth ⇨ lose

drink

drink like a 'fish (*informal*) regularly drink too much alcohol: *Her husband drinks like a fish.*

drink sb under the 'table (*informal*) drink more alcohol than sb without becoming as drunk as they do: *Believe me, she can drink anyone under the table!*

be meat and drink ⇨ meat; **you can take/lead a horse to water, but you can't make it drink** ⇨ horse; **drive sb to drink** ⇨ drive; **eat, drink and be merry** ⇨ eat; **spike sb's drink** ⇨ spike; **a stiff drink** ⇨ stiff; **the worse for drink** ⇨ worse

drive

drive a coach and horses through sth (*informal*) succeed in avoiding certain rules, conditions, etc in an obvious and important way, without being punished: *The wage increase we've been given is three times the government's limit. We've driven a coach and horses right through their pay policy.*

drive a hard 'bargain make sure that you always gain an advantage in business deals, etc: *I wouldn't do business with Jack,* *he's got the reputation of driving a hard bargain.*

drive sb out of their mind/wits (*informal*) make sb mad, or very nervous or worried: *That noise is driving me out of my mind!*

drive sb to 'drink (*often humorous*) make sb so annoyed, worried, etc that they begin to drink too much alcohol: *A week with those noisy kids is enough to drive anyone to drink!*

drive a wedge between A and B make two people become less friendly or loving towards each other: *The disagreements over money finally drove a wedge between them, and they ended up getting divorced.*

drive/hammer sth home ⇨ home; **drive/send sb up the wall** ⇨ wall

driver back-seat driver ⇨ back

driving

the 'driving force (behind sth) the person or thing that makes sth happen: *She is the driving force behind this new road safety campaign.*

in the 'driving seat managing or controlling sth, for example a business: *With a younger person in the driving seat, we can expect some big changes in the company.*

what are you 'driving at? what are you trying to say or do?: *What are you driving at? Try to explain what you mean more clearly.*

drop

at the ,drop of a 'hat (*informal*) immediately and without hesitating: *He's the sort of person who can sing any song at all at the drop of a hat.*

,drop your 'aitches not pronounce the 'h' sound, especially at the beginning of a word, where it is pronounced in standard English. (This is a feature of certain English accents, for example the London one. It is often mentioned as a typical feature of lower class speech.)

drop a 'clanger/'brick (*informal*) say or do sth that embarrasses or insults sb without realizing it: *I dropped a real clanger when I mentioned the party. He hadn't been invited.*

drop 'dead 1 die very suddenly **2** (*very informal*) (used as a rude way of telling sb to go away): *Drop dead, will you!*

drop a 'hint (to sb) *or* **drop (sb) a hint** suggest sth in an indirect way: *He tried to drop a hint (to them) about it being time to leave, but they didn't seem to take any notice.* ○ *She's dropped me a few hints about what she'd like for her birthday.*

drop a, the, his, her, etc bombshell announce sth that amazes or shocks people: *It was then that he dropped the bombshell – he wasn't planning to come with us.*

a ,drop in the 'ocean/'bucket a very small amount in comparison to the much larger amount that is needed: *£10 million is only a drop in the ocean compared to what is needed to help these people effectively.*

drop sb a line/note (*informal*) write a short letter to sb: *I dropped her a line inviting her to my birthday party.*

fit/ready to drop (*informal*) exhausted: *I feel fit to drop.* ○ *We danced until we were ready to drop.*

let sth 'drop no longer speak, write, etc about sth: *I've heard enough about this subject. Can we let it drop now?*

you could have heard a pin drop ⇨ heard; **die/fall/drop like flies** ⇨ flies; **drop/fall into sb's lap** ⇨ lap

drops the bottom drops/falls out of the market ⇨ bottom; the bottom drops/falls out of sb's world ⇨ bottom; your jaw drops ⇨ jaw; the penny drops ⇨ penny

drown

drown your 'sorrows (*often humorous, informal*) try to forget your problems or a disappointment by drinking alcohol: *Whenever his team lost a match he could be found in the pub afterwards drowning his sorrows.*

drowned

like a drowned 'rat (*informal*) very wet: *She came in from the storm looking like a drowned rat.*

drum beat the drum ⇨ beat

drunk

(as) ,drunk as a 'lord (*informal*) very drunk.

blind drunk ⇨ blind

dry

(as) ,dry as a 'bone very dry.

(as) ,dry as 'dust very boring and tedious: *Her lectures are very useful, but they're dry as dust.*

bleed sb dry/white ⇨ bleed; **high and dry** ⇨ high; **home and dry** ⇨ home

duck

(take to sth) like a ,duck to 'water (be able to do sth) naturally and without any difficulty: *'Do the children like living in the country?' 'They've taken to it like a duck to water/like ducks to water. They've never been happier!'*

be water off a duck's back ⇨ water; **a dead duck** ⇨ dead; **a lame duck** ⇨ lame; **a sitting duck/target** ⇨ sitting

duckling **an ugly duckling** ⇨ ugly

dudgeon **in high dudgeon** ⇨ high

due

give sb their 'due give sb the praise that they deserve: *Helen may not be bright, but to give her her due, her work is always very accurate.*

in ,due 'course at the right time in the future; eventually: *Thank you for your letter applying for the post of manager. We will be in contact with you again in due course.*

with respect ⇨ respect

dull

(as) ,dull as 'ditchwater very boring: *Best seller or not, the book sounds as dull as ditchwater to me.*

dumb **be struck dumb** ⇨ struck

dumps

down in the dumps (*informal*) depressed; miserable: *I've been feeling a bit down in the dumps since I lost my job.*

dust

after/when the dust settles when all the exciting events, changes, etc are over: *When the dust finally began to settle, certain facts about the Prime Minister's resignation started to emerge.*

bite the dust ⇨ bite; **dry as dust** ⇨ dry; **gather dust** ⇨ gather; **like gold dust** ⇨ gold; **not see sb for dust** ⇨ see

Dutch

Dutch courage (*informal*) courage that you get by drinking alcohol: *I was afraid of having to tell my wife about what had happened, so I went to the pub to get some Dutch courage.*

go Dutch (with sb) (*informal*) share the cost of a meal, cinema trip, etc equally with sb else: *She always insists on going Dutch when they go out together.*

double Dutch ⇨ double

duty

duty 'calls I must do sth that cannot be avoided (used especially when you have to stop doing sth pleasant): *Ah, duty calls, I'm afraid – I really must go and finish off those letters.*

beyond the call of duty ⇨ call

dying

be 'dying for sth/to do sth (*informal*) want to have or do sth very much: *I'm dying for a drink.* ○ *She's heard so much about you. She's dying to meet you.*

be 'dying of sth (*informal*) have a very strong feeling of sth, for example hunger or boredom: *We're all dying of curiosity – come on, tell us what happened!* ○ *I'm dying of thirst.*

till/to/until your dying day for as long as you live: *I swear I won't forgive her to my dying day!*

E

eager

an eager ˈbeaver (*informal, often disapproving*) a person who is (too) enthusiastic about work, etc: *She always starts work early and leaves late. She's a real eager beaver.*

eagle

an/sb's ˌeagle ˈeye (*informal*) close attention: *Nothing the workers did escaped the eagle eye of the manager* (he saw everything they did).

ear

go in one ear and out (of) the other (*informal*) (of information, advice, an order, etc) be immediately forgotten or ignored: *He never remembers to do anything I ask. It just goes in one ear and out the other.*

have (got) an ˈear for sth be able to recognize or appreciate sth heard: *He has an ear for the rhythm of Irish speech.* ○ *The child has an ear for music.*

have, get, win, etc sb's ˈear (*formal*) gain the attention of sb important to influence them or get their help: *We will have to gain the ear of the President to win support for our cause.*

keep/have an/your ear close to the ˈground (try to) be well-informed about what is or will be happening: *Jane keeps her ear pretty close to the ground and can tell you what the mood of the staff is.*

out on your ˈear (*informal*) forced to leave a job, home, etc suddenly: *You'll be out on your ear unless your work gets a lot better, my lad.*

give sb/get a thick ear ⇨ thick; **have a word in sb's ear** ⇨ word; **lend an ear** ⇨ lend; **listen with half an ear** ⇨ listen; **make a pig's ear of sth** ⇨ pig; **play by ear** ⇨ play; **play it by ear** ⇨ play; **turn a deaf ear** ⇨ turn; **(send sb away/off) with a flea in their ear** ⇨ flea

early

the ˌearly bird catches the ˈworm (*saying*) you have to get up early or do sth before others in order to be successful.

the early hours the hours from midnight until it gets light: *I was kept awake till the early hours by the noise from the party next door.* ○ *He died in the early hours of Saturday morning.*

it's early ˈdays (yet) it is too soon to be certain about (the results of) sth: *We look forward to the time when Europe will operate as a single economic unit, though of course it's early days yet.*

bright and early ⇨ bright

earn

ˌearn your ˈkeep be useful, helpful, profitable, etc enough to balance any costs that you cause: *Jill more than earns her keep with the help she gives me around the house.* ○ *Though it's expensive to buy and maintain, the new computer is earning its keep as we've been able to reduce the number of staff.*

ears

be all ˈears (*informal*) listen very carefully and with great interest: *Go on, tell me what happened – I'm all ears.*

her/his, etc ears are burning (*informal*) sb thinks or knows that other people have been talking about them: *Jenny's ears must have been burning last night: we talked about her for hours.*

be music to sb's ears ⇨ music; **be wet behind the ears** ⇨ wet; **fall on deaf ears** ⇨ fall; **not believe your eyes/ears** ⇨ believe; **prick up your ears** ⇨ prick; **ring in your head/ears** ⇨ ring; **shut your ears to sth/sb** ⇨ shut; **up to your ears/eyes/eyeballs/neck in sth** ⇨ up; **walls have ears** ⇨ walls

earth

bring sb/come (back) down to ˈearth (with a bang, bump, etc) (make sb) have to deal with sth unpleasant, especially after a time when things seemed to be going well or life was enjoyable: *After such a wonderful holiday, losing all her money certainly brought her back down to earth with a bump.*

cost/pay/charge the 'earth (*informal*) cost/pay/charge a lot of money: *Redecorating your home needn't cost the earth if you use a little imagination.* ○ *They paid the earth to see the Rolling Stones play live.*

how, what, why, etc on 'earth/in the 'world. . . (*informal*) (used with questions to express the speaker's surprise, anger, etc): *How on earth did you know I was coming today when I didn't know myself until the last minute?* ○ *Why on earth would anyone give up such a good job?*

the four corners of the earth ⇨ four; **a heaven on earth** ⇨ heaven; **a hell on earth** ⇨ hell; **like nothing on earth** ⇨ like; **move heaven and earth** ⇨ move; **nothing on earth** ⇨ nothing; **promise the moon/earth** ⇨ promise; **run sb/sth to earth/ground** ⇨ run; **the salt of the earth** ⇨ salt; **the scum of the earth** ⇨ scum; **to the ends of the earth** ⇨ ends; **wipe sth off the face of the earth** ⇨ wipe

earthly

no 'earthly use (*British, informal*) of no use at all; pointless: *It's no earthly use trying to persuade her to tell you the secret. She is determined not to.*

not (have) an 'earthly (chance) (*British, informal*) (have) no chance at all: *You haven't an earthly chance of beating her at tennis – she is one of the best players in the country.* ○ *'Any chance of getting a ticket for the match?' 'Not an earthly, I'm afraid.'*

ease

(stand) at 'ease (a military order to soldiers to) stand in a relaxed position, with the feet apart: *The platoon stood at ease while the officer explained the battle plan.*

put/set sb at (their) ease make sb feel relaxed, not shy, etc: *She looked very nervous when she first arrived so I tried to put her at ease by offering her a drink and chatting to her about the journey.*

ill at ease ⇨ ill; **put/set sb's mind at ease/rest** ⇨ mind

easier

easier said than done (*saying*) it is easier to suggest doing sth than actually to do it: *'All you have to do is climb a ladder and mend the roof.' 'Easier said than done – I'm terrified of heights!'*

easy

(as) easy as ABC/anything/pie/falling off a log (*informal*) very easy: *Try using the new photocopier. It's as easy as pie.*

easy come, easy go (*saying*) something that has been obtained very easily and quickly may be lost or wasted in the same way: *Her parents have given her all the money she wants, but she's always in debt. With her, it's a case of easy come, easy go.*

,easy/,gently/,slowly 'does it (*informal*) (used for telling sb to be careful, calm, etc): *Easy does it! Just lift it a little bit and I think it'll go through the door.*

,easy 'game a person or thing that is easy to attack, criticize, or make a victim: *Car buyers who know nothing about cars are easy game for dishonest dealers.*

,easy 'money money earned for very little work or effort, often by doing sth dishonest: *There's a lot of easy money to be made in this business.*

easy on the eye, ear, etc pleasant to look at, listen to, etc: *When decorating your bedroom, choose colours that are easy on the eye.*

go 'easy on sb (*informal*) not be too strict with sb, especially when they have done sth wrong: *Go easy on the child, she didn't mean to break the window.*

go 'easy on sth do not use too much of sth, speak too much about sth, etc: *Go easy on the spices. I don't like very hot curry.* ○ *When you are talking to Jim, go easy on the subject of marriage – his wife's just left him.*

I'm 'easy (*informal*) (said when you are asked to choose) I do not mind which: *'Tea or coffee?' 'Oh, I'm easy – I'll have whatever you're having.'*

take it/things 'easy (*informal*) go or do sth more slowly; not get angry, excited, etc; relax: *'If you leave at 11 you should be there by midday.' 'I'd rather leave earlier and take it easy.'* ○ *Take it easy, Jenny! There's no need to get so annoyed.* ○ *Bob's still running the business on his own. He really ought to be taking things easy at his age.*

an easy/soft touch ⇨ touch; **free and**

easy ⇨ free; **have an easy time of it** ⇨ time

eat

eat, drink and be merry (*saying*) (said to encourage sb to enjoy life now, while they can, and not to think of the future).

eat your 'heart out be very unhappy because you want sb/sth that you cannot have: *He's eating his heart out for that woman.*

,eat humble 'pie become more respectful or apologetic, especially because your opinions or statements have been proved wrong: *I had to eat humble pie when Harry, who I said would never have any success, got the first prize.*

,eat like a 'horse (*informal*) eat very large quantities of food: *My brother eats like a horse but never puts on any weight.*

eat sb out of ,house and 'home (*informal*) eat all the food that sb has: *She eats us out of house and home every time she comes to stay.*

,eat your 'words be forced to admit that what you have said before was wrong: *Nick told everyone that he'd be picked for the team, but when he wasn't chosen, he had to eat his words.*

I, etc could eat a horse I, etc am very hungry: *What's for dinner? I could eat a horse!*

I'll eat my hat! (*informal*) (used with an *if* clause to express great doubt about the possibility of sth happening, being true, etc): *They're always late – if they get here before eight o'clock, I'll eat my hat.*

he, she, etc won't 'eat you (*informal*) (said to encourage sb to speak to or approach sb who seems frightening): *Come on, Emma, Father Christmas won't eat you! If you go closer, he'll give you a present!*

dog eat dog ⇨ dog; **have your cake and eat it** ⇨ cake

eating

have sb eating out of your hand have sb completely in your control so that they will do whatever you wish: *Once they knew that they could never hope to escape without his help, he had them eating out of his hand.*

what is eating 'sb? (*informal*) why is sb so worried, unhappy, etc?: *You seem a bit quiet today. What's eating you?*

ebb **a low ebb** ⇨ low

edge

have, etc an/the edge on/over sb/sth be slightly better, faster, etc than sb/sth; have an advantage over sb/sth: *Max's design is very good, but I think Paul's has the edge on it.* ○ *Extra training will give our team an edge over the opposition.*

on 'edge nervous, worried or anxious: *Most people feel on edge before exams.*

on the ,edge of your 'seat/'chair tensely watching or listening to an exciting play, story, etc: *The film was so exciting it had me on the edge of my seat right until the last moment.*

on a knife-edge/'razor's edge in a very difficult or dangerous situation where there is a risk of sth disastrous happening: *The future of this company is on a razor's edge.* ○ *He was balanced on a knife-edge between life and death.*

take the 'edge off sth make sth less severe, unpleasant, etc: *He tried to take the edge off the bad news by promising to help them in their difficulties.* ○ *I had a snack before lunch, which took the edge off my appetite.*

set sb's teeth on edge ⇨ set

edgeways **get a word in edgeways** ⇨ word

educated

an educated guess a guess made on the basis of facts, good information, etc, and so probably fairly accurate: *I can't tell you exactly how much the building work will cost, but I can make an educated guess.*

eel **be slippery as an eel** ⇨ slippery

effect

bring/put sth into effect make sth, for example an idea, plan, etc happen: *The government wants to put its new housing policy into immediate effect.*

come/go into effect (of laws, rules, etc) begin to be used, applied, etc: *The winter timetable comes into effect on November 1st.*

in effect in actual practice; in fact: *I earn more than I did last year but because of the new tax laws I am, in effect, worse off.*

of/to no effect not having the result hoped for: *Their warnings were of no effect.* ○

They tried to persuade him to change his mind, but to no effect.

take effect   1 have the intended result: *It will be some time before the painkillers take effect.* **2** (*formal*) start to be valid: *Your promotion takes effect from the end of the month.*

to the effect that... or **to that effect** (used when giving the basic meaning of what sb has said or written, without using their exact words): *A letter was sent to the employees to the effect that the firm would have to close down.* ○ *She told me not to interfere, or words to that effect.*

to good, little, etc effect with a good, etc result: *Her talent as a dancer is shown to considerable effect in this new production.*

with effect from... (*formal*) (used with dates to show when a change will happen): *The Minister has announced a 10p increase in the price of petrol, with effect from 6th April.*

egg

(have) 'egg on your face (*informal*) be made to look foolish: *Let's thi:k this out carefully. I don't want to end up with egg on my face.*

a chicken-and-egg situation ⇨ chicken; **the curate's egg** ⇨ curate; **kill the goose that lays the golden egg/eggs** ⇨ kill

eggs

put all your ,eggs into one 'basket risk all your money, effort, etc on one thing, so that if it is not successful, you have no other chance: *It may be better to invest a small amount of money in several firms rather than putting all your eggs into one basket.*

sure as eggs is eggs ⇨ sure; **teach your grandmother to suck eggs** ⇨ teach; **you can't make an omelette without breaking eggs** ⇨ omelette

eight be/have one over the eight ⇨ one

elbow

at your 'elbow very near; within arm's reach: *I always like to have a dictionary at my elbow to check spellings.*

give sb the 'elbow (*informal*) dismiss or reject sb: *I hear she's finally given her boyfriend the elbow.*

more power to sb's elbow ⇨ power; **not know your arse from your elbow** ⇨ know

elder

an ,elder 'statesman a person who has had an important job in government, business, etc and who, though he may have retired, is still likely to be asked for his opinion and advice.

element

in your 'element doing sth that you enjoy and do well, especially with other similar people: *Jenny is in her element with anything mechanical. She just loves fixing things.*

elephant(s) see pink elephants ⇨ see; **a white elephant** ⇨ white

eleventh

the eleventh hour the moment when it is almost, but not quite, too late to do sth, avoid sth, etc: *Our pianist had fallen ill, and then, at the eleventh hour, when we thought we would have to cancel the performance, Jill offered to replace him.* **eleventh-hour** (*adjective*) *an eleventh-hour decision.*

else

or else   1 (often used as a threat or warning to sb that something unpleasant will happen if they do not do as you say) if not; otherwise: *You'd better clean up this mess, or else!* **2** (used to introduce the second of two possibilities): *I can't get through to Sally. She's out, or else she's decided not to answer the telephone.*

embryo

in embryo still in a very early stage of development: *We have just an editor and a reporter, so you can say that the newspaper exists in embryo.*

empty

on an empty 'stomach without having eaten anything: *If I travel on an empty stomach, I always feel sick.*

end

at the ,end of the 'day when everything has been considered: *At the end of the day we will have to work together, no matter what our disagreements are, so let's talk.*

at the ,end of your 'tether having no

more patience or strength left: *After six hours of hearing the children shout and argue, I was really at the end of my tether.*

be at an end (*formal*) be finished: *Our negotiations are at an end, and we have reached agreement.*

be the end (*informal*) be very annoying; be impossible to tolerate: *Your children really are the end! ○ I'd seen dirty houses before, but theirs was the absolute end!*

come to a bad/sticky end (*informal, becoming dated*) finish in an unpleasant way; finish by having sth unpleasant happen to you, usually because of your own actions: *The neighbours used to shake their heads and say that he'd come to a bad end.*

days, weeks, etc on 'end several days, weeks, etc, one after another: *She stays away from home for days on end. ○ He sits watching TV for hours on end.*

,end it 'all commit suicide: *After years of suffering, she had decided to end it all.*

the ,end of the 'road/'line the point where sb/sth cannot continue: *The workers see the closure of the pit as the end of the line for mining in this area. ○ It's the end of the road for our relationship. We just can't agree about anything any more.*

in the 'end after or in spite of everything that has gone before; finally: *I looked for my keys for hours, and in the end I found them in the car. ○ They tried to get him to confess, and in the end he did.*

keep your 'end up (*British, informal*) stay cheerful or perform well in spite of difficulty: *She managed to keep her end up even though she was suffering from flu. ○ I had trouble keeping my end up in the conversation, because I didn't know anything about the subject.*

no 'end (*informal*) very much: *Your visit pleased her no end.*

no 'end of (*informal*) a lot of: *Mixing with those new friends has done him no end of good. ○ We've had no end of offers of help.*

not be the ,end of the 'world (*informal*) not be a disaster: *It wouldn't be the end of the world if you couldn't get into college. I'm sure you would be able to find a good job anyway.*

not know/not be able to tell one end of sth from the other (*informal*) know absolutely nothing about sth, for example a

machine: *Don't ask me to fix the car. I don't know one end of an engine from another.*

the ,war, ,row, etc to end all 'wars, 'rows, etc *or* **the war, ,row, etc to end them 'all** sth that is the biggest, worst, most unusual, etc of its kind: *Many people said that World War I would be the war to end all wars. ○ (humorous) This is the souvenir to end all souvenirs – you can relive the excitement of the event with this superb video recording.*

at a loose end ⇨ loose; **the be-all and end-all of sth** ⇨ be; **be at your wits' end** ⇨ wits; **be on/at the receiving end** ⇨ receiving; **be at the sharp end** ⇨ sharp; **the business end** ⇨ business; **a dead end** ⇨ dead; **get the wrong end of the stick** ⇨ wrong; **sb's hair stands on end** ⇨ hair; **hear/see the end/the last of sb/sth** ⇨ hear; **jump in/be thrown in at the deep end** ⇨ deep; **light at the end of the tunnel** ⇨ light; **a means to an end** ⇨ means; **not see beyond/past the end of your nose** ⇨ see; **the tail end** ⇨ tail; **the thin end of the wedge** ⇨ thin; **to the bitter end** ⇨ bitter

ends

make (both) ends meet earn enough to pay your living expenses: *Since I lost my job, I'm finding it harder to make ends meet.*

to the ,ends of the 'earth a very great distance: *He would go to the ends of the earth to be with her.*

all's well that ends well ⇨ well; **burn the candle at both ends** ⇨ burn; **odds and ends** ⇨ odds; **the loose ends/ threads** ⇨ loose

enemy

be your own worst enemy ⇨ worst; **would not wish sth on my, etc worst enemy** ⇨ wish

enough

curiously, oddly, strangely, etc enough it is curious, odd, strange, etc: *Funnily enough, I was born on exactly the same day as my wife.*

enough is enough (often used as a warning to sb to stop sth) what has already been said, done, etc is enough: *Enough is enough! I don't mind a joke, but now you've gone too far!*

be man enough ⇨ man; **fair enough** ⇨ fair; **if you throw enough mud, some of it will stick** = **mud sticks** ⇨ mud; **sure enough** ⇨ sure

enter(ing)

enter sb's 'head be thought of by sb; occur to sb: *It never even entered my head that we might fail.*

breaking and entering ⇨ breaking

envy   green with envy ⇨ green

equal

some (people, members, etc) are more equal than others (*saying*) although the members of a society, group, etc appear to be equal, some get better treatment than others: (from the slogan of the pigs in *Animal Farm* by George Orwell: 'All animals are equal but some animals are more equal than others.')

on equal terms = **on the same terms** ⇨ terms; **other/all things being equal** ⇨ things

err

err on the side of 'sth show slightly too much rather than too little of a (usually good) quality: *When I am marking exam papers, I always try to err on the side of generosity* (I give slightly higher marks than the students may deserve).

errand   a fool's errand ⇨ fool

error

the ˌerror of your 'ways what is wrong and should be changed about the kind of life you are leading: *While he was in prison, a social worker and a vicar both visited him in an attempt to make him see the error of his ways.*

by trial and error ⇨ trial

escape

escape sb's 'notice not be noticed by sb: *Has it escaped your notice that your driving licence is no longer valid?*

a narrow escape/squeak ⇨ narrow

essence

of the 'essence absolutely necessary: *Tact is of the essence in dealing with foreign guests.*

eternal   hope springs eternal ⇨ hope

even

get even with sb (*informal*) take your revenge on sb: *I'll get even with him some day for making those nasty remarks about me.*

on an even 'keel progressing calmly and steadily: *After all the troubles of the past weeks, life seems to be getting back on an even keel again.*

break even ⇨ break; **even/much/still less** ⇨ less

event

in the e'vent as it actually happened, contrasted with what was expected: *We all thought he was rather lazy, but in the event he worked very hard and passed his exams.*

in the event of sth if sth happens: (*quite formal*) *The money will be paid to your family in the event of your death.* ○ *In the event of an emergency please call the following number. ...*

a/the happy event ⇨ happy; **be wise after the event** ⇨ wise

events

at 'all events *or* **in 'any event** whatever happens; anyway: *James may arrive this evening or tomorrow morning. In any event, I would like you to meet him at the airport.* ○ *At all events, there will be a change of government.*

turn of events ⇨ turn

ever

ever more (*formal*) more and more: *She grew ever more impatient as time passed.*

ever so/ever such (a) (*informal*) very: *Have you tried one of these sweets? They're ever so nice!* ○ *Thanks ever so much for all your help.* ○ *She plays the piano ever so well.* ○ *He's ever such a nice man.* (some people consider this idiom to be non-standard)

why ever ⇨ why

every   every other ⇨ other

everything

money, winning, etc isn't 'everything money, etc isn't the most important thing: *Work isn't everything. You must learn to relax a bit more.*

everywhere   here, there, and everywhere ⇨ here

evidence

in evidence obviously present; easily seen:

There were very few local people in evidence at the meeting. ○ *What's the matter with John? His sense of humour hasn't been much in evidence recently.*

evil(s)

put off the evil day delay sth unpleasant for as long as possible: *I worried for weeks about how I would tell him the bad news but eventually I couldn't put off the evil day any longer.*

the lesser of two evils ⇨ lesser; **a necessary evil** ⇨ necessary

examined need, etc your head examined ⇨ head

example

make an example of sb punish sb severely for a mistake, crime, etc so that others will be less likely to do wrong: *The judge decided to make an example of the leaders of the riot in order to prevent other disturbances.*

be a shining example ⇨ shining; **set an example** ⇨ set

excepted present company excepted ⇨ present

exception

the exception (that) proves the 'rule (*saying*) if sth is different from or the opposite of a belief or theory, this shows that the belief or theory is true in general: *English people are supposed to be very reserved, but Pete is the exception that proves the rule – he'll chat to anyone!*

take exception to sth be very offended by a remark, accusation, etc: *I take great exception to your suggestion that I did this for the money.*

excuse

excuse me **1** (used before you do or say sth that might annoy sb, or to get sb's attention): *Excuse me, is anybody sitting here?* ○ *Excuse me, could you tell me the time, please?* **2** (used for apologizing or disagreeing with sb or for showing that you are annoyed): *Excuse me, but I think you are mistaken.* ○ *Excuse me, sir, but you can't park there!* **3** (used when you are leaving the room for a short time): *Excuse me a minute, I'll be right back.* **4** (*especially US*) (used

when you have not heard or understood sth) please repeat that **5** (*especially US*) (used for apologizing for something you have done): *Excuse me, did I step on your toe?*

excuse/pardon my French ⇨ French

exhibition

make an exhi'bition of yourself behave in a stupid or embarrassing way that makes people notice you: *She got drunk again and made a real exhibition of herself at the party.*

existence the bane of sb's life/existence ⇨ bane

expecting

be expecting (*informal*) be pregnant: *I hear Sue's expecting.*

expense

at sb's expense **1** paid for by sb: *When Joe is travelling at the firm's expense, he goes first class.* **2** (of jokes, etc) making sb seem foolish: *They all had a good laugh at Pete's expense.*

at the expense of sb/sth causing damage or loss to sb/sth else: *We could lower the price, but only at the expense of quality.*

experience

put sth down to experience accept a failure, loss, etc without too much sadness or anger: *When her second novel was rejected by the publisher, she put it down to experience and began another one.*

extreme(s)

boring, silly, etc in the ex'treme extremely boring, silly, etc: *I must admit, it's puzzling in the extreme just how these books found their way here.*

go to extremes or **carry/take sth to extremes** behave in a way that is not moderate or normal: *She really goes to extremes, spending such huge sums of money on entertaining her friends.* ○ *'You never go out after dark? That's taking being careful to extremes, isn't it?'*

eye

an ,eye for an 'eye (and a ,tooth for a 'tooth) (*saying*) a person who treats sb else badly should be treated in the same way. (from the Bible)

get your 'eye in get to the point in a ball

game (golf, cricket, etc) where you start to judge distances, the speed of the ball, etc, accurately and so start to play well: *The batsman began slowly but once he got his eye in he started to play some very good shots.*

have (got) an eye for sth be good at judging sth: *He has always had an eye for a bargain.*

have (got) your eye on sb/sth watch sb/sth closely; want to have sth: *A house that I'd had my eye on for some time suddenly came up for sale.*

have (got) an eye to/for the main 'chance (*informal*) be good at using opportunities for your own benefit: *She's certainly got an eye for the main chance. Her business has become highly successful.*

keep an/your 'eye on sb/sth take responsibility for sb/sth; make sure that sb/sth is safe: *I keep an eye on how the money is spent.* ○ *Keep an eye on my bag while I go and make a phone call, will you?*

keep an 'eye out (for sb/sth) (*informal*) watch or look carefully (for sb/sth): *Can you keep an eye out for the taxi and let me know when it arrives?*

what the eye doesn't see (the heart doesn't grieve over) (*saying*) if a person does not know about sth that they would normally disapprove of, then it cannot hurt them: *What does it matter if I do use his flat while he's away? What the eye doesn't see. . .!*

with an eye to (doing) sth intending to do sth: *She is doing an interpreters' course with an eye to getting a job abroad.*

would give your eye-'teeth for sth would give anything for sth; want sth very much: *I'd give my eye-teeth to own a car like that.* ○ *He'd give his eye-teeth for a job in television.*

the apple of sb's eye ⇨ apple; **beauty is in the eye of the beholder** ⇨ beauty; **a bird's eye view** ⇨ bird; **a black eye** ⇨ black; **as far as the eye can see** ⇨ far; **catch sb's eye** ⇨ catch; **an/sb's eagle eye** ⇨ eagle; **have a roving eye** ⇨ roving; **hit sb in the eye** ⇨ hit; **in your mind's eye** ⇨ mind; **in the public eye** ⇨ public; **in the twinkling of an eye** ⇨ twinkling; **keep a weather eye on sth/open for sth** ⇨ weather; **look sb in the eye/face** ⇨ look; **the naked eye** ⇨ naked; **one in**

the eye for sb ⇨ one; **open sb's eyes** ⇨ open; **out of the corner of your eye** ⇨ corner; **a private eye** ⇨ private; **see eye to eye** ⇨ see; **there's more to sth than meets the eye** ⇨ meets; **turn a blind eye** ⇨ turn

eyeball

,eyeball to 'eyeball (with sb) (*informal*) standing very close, facing one another, for example in a fight: *The two men stood eyeball to eyeball, shouting insults at each other.*

eyebrow raise an/your eyebrow(s) ⇨ raise

eyelid not bat an eyelid ⇨ bat

eyes

(be able to do sth) with your 'eyes closed/shut (be able to do sth) very easily, especially because you have done it many times before: *She's driven up to Scotland so often that she can do it with her eyes shut.*

be all 'eyes watch with close attention and usually with great interest: *The children were all eyes as, one by one, I took the toys out of the bag.*

before your (very) eyes right in front of you, where you can see sth very clearly: *There, before my very eyes, he took the plane ticket and ripped it into tiny pieces.*

clap/lay/set eyes on sb/sth (*informal*) see sb/sth: *I've no idea who she is. I've never clapped eyes on her before.* ○ *From the moment I set eyes on the house, I knew I could be happy living there.*

close/shut your eyes to sth pretend that you cannot see or do not know sth in order to avoid embarrassment or trouble: *My son has his faults – and I've never closed my eyes to them – but dishonesty isn't one of them.* ○ *The headmaster was accused of shutting his eyes to the way the teacher was being obviously cruel to the children.*

for 'sb's eyes only to be seen only by sb: *This letter is for your eyes only, so keep it locked in your desk.*

have (got) eyes in the back of your 'head (*informal*) seem to be able to see everything and know what is going on: *You have to have eyes in the back of your head to keep control of six lively children.*

in the eyes of 'sb/'sth or **in sb's eyes**
according to sb/sth; in sb's opinion: *You may believe that what you are doing is right, but in the eyes of the law it's a crime.*

keep your eyes open/peeled/skinned (for sb/sth) watch carefully (for sb/sth): *Keep your eyes open, and if you see anything suspicious, call the police immediately.*

make 'eyes at sb (*informal*) look at sb in a way that tries to attract them sexually: *He did nothing all holiday but make eyes at the girls!*

not take your 'eyes off sb/sth not stop looking at sb/sth: *She couldn't take her eyes off the beautiful picture.* (often used with *can/could*)

only have eyes for sb or **have eyes only for sb** be interested in, or in love with a particular person and nobody else: *John has been trying to get Helen to go out with him, but she only has eyes for Chris.*

sb's eyes are bigger than their stomach (*informal, humorous*) sb wants more food than they can really eat: *Can't you finish your food? Your eyes are bigger than your stomach!*

sb's eyes nearly pop out of their head (*informal*) sb has an expression of great surprise on their face: *People's eyes nearly popped out of their heads when they saw a giraffe walking down the High Street.*

through the eyes of sb from the point of view of sb: *You must try to see it through the eyes of the parents, not just from the teacher's point of view.*

with your 'eyes open knowing what you are doing, what to expect, and what the results may be: *If a marriage is to work, both partners must go into it with their eyes open.*

be a sight for sore eyes ⇨ sight; **be up to your ears/eyes/eyeballs/neck in sth** ⇨ up; **cry your eyes/heart out** ⇨ cry; **meet sb's eyes** ⇨ meet; **not believe your eyes/ears** ⇨ believe; **open sb's eyes** ⇨ open; **pull the wool over sb's eyes** ⇨ pull; **the scales fall from sb's eyes** ⇨ scales; **shut your eyes to sth** ⇨ shut

F

face(s)

your face falls you suddenly look disappointed or upset: *He was quite cheerful until we told him the price. Then his face fell.*

face the 'music (*informal*) accept the difficulties, criticism and unpleasant consequences that follow your words or actions: *He's been cheating us out of our money for years and now it's time for him to face the music.*

face to face (with sb/sth) 1 in the presence of sb and close enough to meet, talk, see, etc them: *The two leaders came face to face for the first time in Moscow this morning.* ○ *The programme brought Anna face to face with her father for the first time in her life.* **face-to-face** (*adjective*) *face-to-face discussions, negotiations, etc* **2** in a position where you cannot avoid seeing or doing something about a problem, difficulty, unpleasant fact, etc: *The crisis brought her face to face with a lot of problems she had been*

trying not to think about.

give sth a face-lift improve the appearance of sth, eg a building, room, etc: *We've given our offices a face-lift – new furniture, new lighting and a new carpet.* ○ *The whole street needs a face-lift.* (a face-lift is an operation to lift and tighten the skin on your face in order to make you look younger)

have (got) the face (to do sth) or **have (got) the nerve (to do sth)** (*informal*) dare to do sth which you have no right to do: *I don't know how she's got the face to criticize my designs. She doesn't know anything at all about architecture.* ○ *He had the nerve to ask me for a pay rise after only three weeks in the job.*

in the face of sth even though sth, usually a danger, problem or unpleasant situation, etc exists: *In the face of all the evidence against you, how can you say that you're innocent?* ○ *She married him in the face of opposition from both her parents.* ○ *In the face* *of very dangerous conditions, they managed to rescue all the men from the ship.*

let's 'face it (*informal*) we must accept the unpleasant facts; let's be honest: *Let's face it: we just don't have enough money to buy a new car.* ○ *Let's face it. He married her for her money, not for love.*

make/pull 'faces/a 'face 1 make expressive face movements to show that you do not like sth: *Every time I give him fish for lunch, he makes a face.* ○ *There's no need to pull a face.* **2** make expressive face movements to frighten or amuse people: *The little girl stood outside the restaurant window making faces at everybody.*

on the 'face of it (often used for saying that your first impression of sth may be or was wrong) as sth, eg a situation, a plan, an offer, etc, appears to you when you first look at or consider it: *On the face of it the pay offer looked wonderful, but in fact it wasn't nearly as good as we thought.* ○ *'Well, what do you think of the new plans?' 'On the face of it, they look good but I think we need to look at them more closely.'*

stare/look you in the face (of a fact, an answer, a situation, etc) be obvious but not noticed: *The answer to the problem had been staring her in the face for years but she hadn't seen it.* ○ *'Where's that book?' 'There in front of you, looking you in the face.'* (usually used in continuous tenses)

take sb/sth at (his, its, etc) face value accept that sth is exactly as it first appears: *You can't take everything she says at face value.* ○ *A diplomat learns not to take everything at face value.*

to sb's 'face (say sth) openly, when speaking to sb: *Would you really call her a liar to her face?* ○ *I think he's guilty but I'd never dare say it to his face.*

be not just a pretty face ⇨ pretty; **be written all over sb's face** ⇨ written; **blow up in sb's face** ⇨ blow; **cut off your nose to spite your face** ⇨ cut; **egg on your face** ⇨ egg; **fall flat on your face** ⇨ fall; **fly in the face of sth** ⇨ fly; **a straight face** ⇨ straight; **laugh in sb's face** ⇨ laugh; **laugh on the other side of your face** ⇨ laugh; **a long face** ⇨ long; **look sb in the eye/face** ⇨ look; **lose face** ⇨ lose; **plain as a pikestaff/as the nose on your face** ⇨ plain; **put a brave face on sth** ⇨ brave; **a red face** ⇨ red; **save your/sb's face** ⇨ save; **set your face against sth** ⇨ set; **show your face** ⇨ show; **shut your mouth/trap/face/gob!** ⇨ shut; **a slap in the face** ⇨ slap; **smash sb's face/head in** ⇨ smash; **a straight face** ⇨ straight; **till/until one is blue in the face** ⇨ blue; **wipe sth off the face of the earth** ⇨ wipe; **wipe the/that smile, grin, etc off your/sb's face** ⇨ wipe

fact

a ˌfact of 'life something difficult or unpleasant that cannot be changed and has to be accepted or dealt with: *Taxes are a fact of life. You just have to pay them.* ○ *It is a fact of life that some people are born more intelligent than others.*

in 'fact *or* **in actual 'fact 1** (used for emphasizing that sth is true) really; actually: *This £10 note looks genuine but it is, in actual fact, a fake.* ○ *I thought the lecture would be boring but in actual fact it was very interesting.* **2** (used for introducing more information): *It was cold. In fact, it was freezing.*

as a matter of fact ⇨ matter; **in point of fact** ⇨ point; **the truth/fact of the matter** ⇨ matter

facts

the ˌfacts of 'life the facts about sex, how babies are born, etc, especially when told to children: *When do you think you should tell your children the facts of life?*

hard facts ⇨ hard

fail

without 'fail 1 (used for emphasizing that sth always happens): *She sends me a Christmas card every year without fail.* **2** (used for emphasizing that sth must happen): *You must be here by 8.30 without fail.* ○ *He must remember to take these tablets without fail.*

words fail me ⇨ words

faintest

not have the faintest/foggiest (idea) (*British, informal*) have no idea at all about sth; not know anything at all: *I haven't got the faintest idea what to buy Roger for his* birthday. ○ *'Where are we?''I haven't the foggiest.'*

damn sb/sth with faint praise ⇨ damn

fair

all's fair in love and war (*saying*) normal rules of behaviour do not apply in situations like war and love: *'I told Sarah that John had another girlfriend.' 'But that's not true; he hasn't.' 'I know, but all's fair in love and war.'*

by ˌfair means or 'foul even if unfair methods are used: *He's determined to buy that company by fair means or foul.*

fair and 'square **1** completely and fully: *They were the better team and they beat us fair and square.* **2** directly and with force: *I hit him fair and square on the chin.*

it's a fair 'cop (*informal, dated*) (often used by a person who is caught committing a crime to show that he accepts his arrest by the police as just or fair): *He just said, 'it's a fair cop' and handed the bag to one of the policemen there.*

a fair crack of the 'whip (*informal*) a fair or reasonable opportunity to do sth or to show that you can do sth: *I don't think he was really given a fair crack of the whip. He only had five minutes to present his suggestions.* ○ *We all got a fair crack of the whip. We can't complain.*

fair eˈnough (*informal*) **1** (used for accepting a suggestion, etc): *'I think £200 is a reasonable price.''Fair enough. Can I pay you at the end of the week?'* **2** (used for showing that you think that sth is reasonable): *Letting the students work the machines on their own is fair enough, but they do need some training first.*

fair 'game a person or thing which can be attacked or criticized because he, it, etc deserves it: *In my opinion, all politicians are fair game.* (refers to birds and animals that can be shot or hunted only at certain times of the year)

fair 'play not breaking the rules or cheating; honest or correct behaviour: *We want to see fair play in this competition.* ○ *It may be legal, but it's not fair play.*

fair's 'fair (*informal*) let's be fair: *You may not like her, but fair's fair, she's a good teacher.* ○ *Look, Mike, fair's fair. I've helped you lots of times. Now you can help me.'*

a fair shake (*US, informal*) a fair chance or fair treatment: *This new pay deal means a fair shake for all the workers.*

a/your fair share of sth a usual, expected amount of sth: *We've all paid our fair share except Delia, who's never got any money.*

have more than your fair share of sb/ sth have more than the usual, expected or desired amount of sth: *I've had more than my fair share of problems recently, but now things seem to be getting better again.*

make, etc sth by/with your own fair hand (*humorous*) make, etc sth yourself: *I made this birthday card for you with my own fair hand.*

be set fair ⇨ set; **play fair/straight** ⇨ play

fairy

a/sb's ˌfairy 'godmother a person, perhaps unknown, who helps you unexpectedly when you are in great difficulties: *You'll need a fairy godmother to get you out of your present difficulties.* (the fairy godmother is the magical character in the story of Cinderella who helps Cinderella go to the ball)

faith

bad 'faith **1** lack of trust between two people: *The dispute was the cause of a lot of bad faith and bitterness.* **2** dishonesty: *There were many accusations of bad faith on the part of the government.*

in good 'faith with sincere or genuine intentions (used especially of an action which has bad consequences): *When I recommended Simon for a job in the bank, I did it in good faith. I didn't realize that he had been in trouble with the police.*

pin your faith/hopes on sb/sth ⇨ pin

fall(s)

fall about (laughing/with laughter) (*informal*) laugh in an uncontrollable way: *When he watches Charlie Chaplin films, he falls about laughing. I don't find them funny at all!*

fall between two 'stools not be successful, acceptable, etc because it is neither one thing nor another: *The book falls between two stools. It's neither a love story nor a crime story.*

fall by the 'wayside (*often humorous*) not

be able to continue sth that needs effort, discipline, etc; begin to be dishonest, immoral, etc: *Some 150 people used to go to the church service regularly, but some have fallen by the wayside, and now we have only 120.* (from the Bible. It refers to one of Christ's parables: the seeds that fell on the wayside (the path) did not grow.)

fall 'flat (of sth expected to be amusing, interesting, etc) not have the effect one intends or expects: *I didn't think the comedian was funny at all − most of his jokes fell completely flat.*

fall flat on your face (*informal*) fail completely in an attempt to do sth, especially in a noticeable way: *I thought I would pass my driving test easily but I fell flat on my face.*

fall foul of sb/sth do sth which gets you into trouble with sb/sth: *They fell foul of the law by not paying their taxes. ○ Try not to fall foul of Mr. Jones. He can be very unpleasant.*

fall from grace lose people's approval, eg through a mistake or immoral behaviour: *The government minister fell from grace as a result of the financial scandal.*

fall, etc into sb's 'hands be taken, captured or obtained by sb: *The city has fallen into the hands of the enemy. ○ These documents must not fall into the hands of the wrong people.*

fall on deaf 'ears (of a question, request, etc) be ignored or not noticed: *Our request for more money fell on deaf ears.*

fall on hard 'times become poor: *She has fallen on hard times and hardly has enough money to live on.*

fall 'over yourself to do sth (*informal*) do everything you can for sb because you want to please and impress them: *After he became manager, people were falling over themselves to help him.*

fall short of sth not reach the standard that is necessary or expected; not fulfil hopes, expectations, etc: *Your performance at work has fallen short of what is required in this company*

be/fall prey to sth ⇨ prey; **be/fall sound asleep** ⇨ sound; **be riding for a fall** ⇨ riding; **the bottom drops/falls out of the market** ⇨ bottom; **the bottom drops/falls out of sb's world** ⇨ bottom;

come/fall apart at the seams ⇨ seams; **die/fall/drop like flies** ⇨ flies; **drop/fall into sb's lap** ⇨ lap; **your face falls** ⇨ face; **fall/land on your feet** ⇨ feet; **pride comes before a fall** ⇨ pride; **stand or fall by sth** ⇨ stand

false

a false a'larm a warning of sth, especially sth unpleasant or dangerous, which does not in fact happen: *They thought the packet contained a bomb but it was a false alarm.*

(make) a/one false 'move (*informal*) in an already dangerous or risky situation, (do) sth which makes your position much more dangerous: *She's in a difficult financial situation, and if she makes a false move now she could lose everything. ○ 'One false move and you're dead,' he shouted at the bank clerk.*

(under) false pre'tences by lying about your identity, qualifications, financial or social position, etc: *She was sent to prison for six months for obtaining money under false pretences. ○ He got me there under false pretences. He told me he wanted to discuss a business deal with me, but when I got there, it was a surprise birthday party.*

(make) a false 'start try unsuccessfully to start sth: *After a few false starts, I finally managed to work the fax machine. ○ He made a few false starts early on in his acting career, but then found success with the Royal Shakespeare Company.* (refers to the beginning of a race when sb starts running before the signal has been given)

strike/sound a false note seem wrong, unsuitable, etc in a certain situation: *I really thought his speech at the conference struck a false note. Instead of saying how serious the housing situation was, he kept telling jokes about it.*

ring true/false/hollow ⇨ ring

familiar

have a familiar ring (about/to it) sound familiar: *His complaints have a familiar ring. Others have said exactly the same thing about our designs. ○ The music in the film had a familiar ring to it. I think it was Schumann.*

familiarity

familiarity breeds con'tempt (*saying*) you have little respect, liking, etc for sb/sth that you know too well: *George's father is* regarded by everyone as a great artist, but George doesn't think he is. *Familiarity breeds contempt!*

family

in the family way (*informal*) pregnant.

one big happy family ⇨ **one**; **run in the family** ⇨ **run**

famous

famous last words (*informal, humorous*) (used when you think sb has been too optimistic about sth): *'The journey won't take more than three hours on the high-speed train.''Famous last words! That train is always late!'*(refers to a collection of quotations of the dying words of famous people)

fan   the shit hits the fan ⇨ shit

fancy

catch/take/tickle sb's fancy (*informal*) please or attract sb: *Mary seems afraid some other girl will catch Alan's fancy.* ○ *She saw that the picture had taken my fancy and insisted on giving it to me.*

fancy your/sb's 'chances (*informal*) think (often mistakenly) that you will be successful; be too confident about what you/sb can do: *He fancies his chances as a racing-driver, even though he has hardly ever driven a racing car.* ○ *'Do you think he'll win?' 'No, I don't fancy his chances at all.'*

(just) fancy 'that (*informal*) (used as an expression of surprise): *'He passed all his exams with grade A.' 'Well, fancy that.'*

take a fancy to sb/sth (*informal*) begin to like sb/sth; be attracted by sb/sth: *He's taken quite a fancy to Chinese cooking.* ○ *She's taken a fancy to one of the team.*

a flight of fancy ⇨ **flight**; **footloose and fancy-free** ⇨ **footloose**

far

as/so far as... as much as; to the extent that: *I will help you as far as I am able.* ○ *As far as I'm concerned, the whole matter is no longer my responsibility and is now with the police.*

as far as the eye can see to the horizon: *There was only sand as far as the eye could see.*

by 'far by a very great amount; much: *This is by far the best painting/This is the best painting by far.* ○ *Our holiday this year was better by far than last year's.*

(by) far and a'way (used with superlative adjectives) very much; by a very great amount: *The company has by far and away the biggest share of the car market in this country.* ○ *Her essay is far and away the best.*

far and 'wide everywhere and many places; over a large area: *People come from far and wide to visit the monument.* ○ *The police were searching far and wide for the missing child.*

far be it from me to do sth, but... (*often ironic*) (often used for introducing a criticism or suggestion to sb whose behaviour you disagree with or disapprove of) I know that I have no right to say this but...: *Far be it from me to interfere, but don't you think you've been arguing for long enough?*

a far cry from sth very different from sth: *This house is a far cry from the little flat we used to live in.* ○ *Her designs are a far cry from the eccentric clothes she used to make.*

far from doing sth (used for emphasizing that sth is not what people would expect) rather than doing/being sth: *Far from being grateful for our help, she said we had ruined the evening.*

far 'from it (*informal*) not at all; certainly not: *'Isn't he generous with money?''Far from it! He spends it all on himself.'* ○ *'Are you ready, Alex?' 'Far from it, I'm afraid.'*

far 'gone (*informal*) very drunk, ill, tired, etc: *When we arrived, she was already too far gone to recognize us, and she only lived for a few more hours.* ○ *She seemed quite far gone, even though she'd only had two glasses of wine.*

few and far be'tween very rare or uncommon: *Since her illness, the former Minister's public appearances have been few and far between.* ○ *Houses for sale are few and far between in this part of town.*

go 'far *or* **go a long way** 1 buy much: *Prices are rising all the time, and people find their wages don't go far.* ○ *Five pounds doesn't go a long way these days.* 2 make a positive contribution (to sth): *The government's proposals don't go far enough, and so won't solve the problem.* ○ *This new agreement goes a long way towards satisfying the demands of the workers.* 3 be successful in your professional life: *Linda is an excellent manager. She should go far.* ○ *I always knew he would go a long way in the theatre and his new* *role shows that I was right.* ○ *That boy will go far.*

go as/so far as to do sth do sth, especially something that might be considered surprising, extreme, excessive, etc: *She's a brilliant painter, but I wouldn't go so far as to say she is the best in the country.* ○ *I don't like people smoking but I wouldn't go so far as to forbid it.*

go too far *or* **go a bit far** say or do sth which is considered too extreme or socially unacceptable: *Getting a bit drunk at a party is OK, but arriving completely drunk – that's really going too far.* ○ *You've gone too far this time, Joanna.*

in so far as *or* **insofar as** to the extent that: *In so far as I am a judge of these things, the repair to the car has been done very well.* ○ *It was a good report in so far as it showed what needs to be done.*

not far 'off/'out/'wrong (*informal*) almost correct: *She said she thought it would be sold for £90, and she wasn't far wrong: someone paid £100 for it.* ○ *The original sales estimate was not far off.*

'so far up to this point; up to now: *There haven't been any accidents in this factory so far, and let's hope that none happen in future.*

,so far, so 'good (*informal*) (used when you think that you might have trouble with sth) things have gone well up to now: *'How's the operation going?' 'So far, so good.'*

so near and yet so far ⇨ near

fashion

after a 'fashion (do sth) but not very well: *'Can you skate?' 'Yes, after a fashion.'* ○ *'Have you mended the radio?' 'Yes, after a fashion.'*

parrot-fashion ⇨ parrot

fast

fast and 'furious (of games, amusements, etc) noisy and very active: *Ten minutes before the race, the betting was fast and furious.*

a fast worker (*informal*) a person who wastes no time in gaining an advantage, especially a person who can quickly gain sb's affection: *She's a fast worker! She's only known him for two days, and they've already arranged to go on holiday together!*

in the 'fast lane (*informal*) the exciting and sometimes risky way of life typical of very successful people: *I hear you've just been made chief of the Berlin office, Joan. How's life in the fast lane?* (refers to the outside lane on a motorway)

not so fast (*informal*) (often used for telling sb who may have done sth wrong, etc to stop or wait): *Not so fast, young man! Let me see your ticket!* ○ *'I'm going out to play now, Dad.' 'Not so fast, David. You've got to tidy your room first.'*

hard and fast ⇨ hard; **hold fast to sth** ⇨ hold; **play fast and loose** ⇨ play; **pull a fast one** ⇨ pull; **stick fast** ⇨ stick; **thick and fast** ⇨ thick

fat

a 'fat chance (*informal*) (used when you think that there is no possibility of sth happening): *He said he'd give me a job if I passed my exam with a grade A. A fat chance I have of that!* ○ *'Do you think she'll lend me the money?' 'Fat chance.'*

the fat is in the 'fire (*informal*) something has been said or done that is certain to cause anger, fighting, offended feelings, or other trouble: *The fat's in the fire now. Jim has just told his wife that he has taken a job in another town without mentioning it to her first.*

a 'fat lot of use/help (*informal*) not at all useful/helpful: *A fat lot of use that would be! What a stupid idea.* ○ *He was a fat lot of help, I must say!*

chew the fat ⇨ chew; **live off/on the fat of the land** ⇨ live

fate

a ,fate worse than 'death **1** (*dated*) rape or sexual assault. **2** (*humorous*) a very unpleasant experience: *Go on holiday with the Trumans? You're joking. It would be a fate worse than death.*

tempt fate/providence ⇨ tempt

father

like father/mother, like son/ daughter (*saying*) a child is similar to its father/mother in a particular way: *Young Jim is turning out to be as hard-working as his dad – like father, like son.*

the founding father(s) of sth ⇨ founding; **the mother and father of sth** ⇨ mother; **the wish is father to the thought** ⇨ wish

fatted **kill the fatted calf** ⇨ kill

fault

at fault responsible for doing wrong, making a mistake, etc; to be blamed: *The inquiry will decide who was at fault over the loss of the funds.* ○ *I do not feel that I am at fault. After all, I did not know that I was breaking a rule.*

to a fault (used after an *adjective* describing a good characteristic) (almost) too much; extremely: *John was generous to a fault.*

find fault ⇨ find

favour

be (all) in favour of (doing) sth support or approve an idea, course of action, etc: *As far as Joe's suggestion about saving money is concerned, I'm all in favour of it.* ○ *Some people are in favour of restoring the death penalty for major crimes.* ○ *All those in favour, raise their hands.*

do me a favour **1** (*informal*) (used when asking sb to help you): *Do me a favour, Richard, and lend me £5 till tomorrow, will you?* ○ *Do me a favour and answer the door, will you?* **2** (*very informal*) you can't expect me to believe that: *'It's worth £2000. The man in the antique shop told me.' 'Do me a favour. It's not worth £200.'*

in 'favour (with sb)/out of 'favour (with sb) regarded/not regarded with approval: *I seem to be out of favour with the head of department after my remarks at the meeting.* ○ *He works so hard because he wants to stay in favour with the boss.*

in sb's/sth's favour to sb's advantage: *The court decided in the employee's favour.* ○ *The fact that the dollar is falling is in your favour.*

curry favour ⇨ curry; **without fear or favour** ⇨ fear

fear

for fear of (doing) sth because you do not want sth bad to happen: *I'm not going to put it in the washing machine for fear of spoiling it.*

be/go in fear of your life be afraid all the time that you may be killed, attacked, etc: *After she got involved with the drug dealers, she went in fear of her life.*

in fear and trembling (of sb/sth) feeling very frightened or anxious: *They lived in fear and trembling of being discovered by the police.*

,no 'fear! (*informal*) (used for emphatically saying no to a request or suggestion): *'Who's coming for a midnight swim?' 'No fear! It's much too cold.'* ○ *'Did you see Robert off at the station?' 'At six o'clock in the morning? No fear! I said goodbye to him last night.'*

put the fear of God into/up sb (*informal*) frighten sb very much, especially in order to force them to do as you want: *The first thing that happens when you go into the army is that they put the fear of God into you.*

there's no fear of sth there's no possibility or danger of sth happening: *I've got a new alarm clock so there's no fear of me oversleeping again.* ○ *He's in Morocco so there's no fear of him coming to the party, thank God.*

without ,fear or 'favour (judge, decide sth, etc) in a completely fair way without being influenced by anybody: *The newspaper reprinted the facts, without fear or favour.*

feather

a feather in your cap (*informal*) an achievement, success or honour which you can be proud of: *It's a real feather in his cap to represent Britain in the Olympics.* (from the American Indian custom of giving a feather to sb who had been very brave in battle)

feather your (own) 'nest (*informal, often disapproving*) over a period of time obtain money for yourself dishonestly from your business or a position of responsibility: *He's been feathering his own nest at the expense of the people he was supposed to be helping.*

as light as air/as a feather ⇨ light; **birds of a feather** ⇨ birds; **you could have knocked me down with a feather** ⇨ knocked

feathered

our feathered friends (*informal, humorous*) birds: *We mustn't forget to put out food for our feathered friends during the cold winter months.*

feathers **the feathers/fur/sparks will fly** ⇨ fly; **ruffle sb's feathers** ⇨ ruffle

feature **a redeeming feature** ⇨ redeeming

fed

fed up to the back teeth with sb/sth
(*informal*) depressed, annoyed or bored by
sb/sth: *I'm fed up to the back teeth with
listening to you complaining.*

feeds **bite the hand that feeds you**
⇨ bite

feel

,feel your 'age realize from your physical
condition, opinion, views, etc that you are
getting old: *He's not as energetic as he used to
be – beginning to feel his age, I suppose.* ○
*Listening to this awful pop music really makes
me feel my age.*

feel 'the draught (*informal*) be affected
unpleasantly by economic, social, political,
etc changes around you: *Because of the world
trade recession, a lot of third world countries
are feeling the draught.*

feel 'free (*informal*) (used to give
permission to sb to do sth) you may do as
you want; nobody will object if you do sth:
'May I borrow your bike?' 'Feel free!' ○ *Feel free
to come and go as you like.*

feel sth in your 'bones (*informal*) sense or
suspect sth without really knowing why:
*That's funny – I felt in my bones that there was
something wrong – and now you tell me there's
been an accident.* ○ *'How do you know she's
going to win?' 'I feel it in my bones.'*

feel like (doing) sth want sth/to do sth or
think that you would enjoy (doing) sth: *Do
you know what I feel like? A nice cup of tea!* ○
I'm so tired that I feel like going straight to bed.

feel the 'pinch (*informal*) be under
pressure because you don't have as much
money as you had before: *Schools all over the
country are beginning to feel the pinch after the
government cut back its spending on education.*

feel your ,way do sth in a cautious way
because you are just learning how to do it or
you don't yet have enough information: *I
don't know how they will react to the proposal,
so at the moment I'm still feeling my way.* ○
*He's only been in the job for three months, so
he's still feeling his way.*

feel your'self as healthy, happy, etc feel
you usually feel; feel at ease and able to act
naturally: *I don't feel myself this morning; I
think I'll stay at home.* ○ *She never feels herself
at big parties. She's much more relaxed in a
small group.*

get the feel of sth (*informal*) become
familiar with or get used to sth: *When you're
learning to drive a car, you'll probably find
changing gear difficult, but you'll soon get the
feel of it.* ○ *Once you get the feel of a Ferrari,
you'll never want any other car.*

have a feel for sth (*informal*) be good at
appreciating, judging, etc sth: *A good
politician has to have a feel for what people
want.*

be/feel lost without sb/sth ⇨ lost; **be/
feel out of it/things** ⇨ out; **be/feel sick
at heart** ⇨ sick; **be/feel sorry for sb**
⇨ sorry; **be/feel sorry for yourself**
⇨ sorry; **feel a chill running/going
down your spine = send a chill up/
down sb's spine** ⇨ send; **feel that high =
look/feel small** ⇨ small; **look/feel small**
⇨ small

feelers

put out/have feelers try, in an indirect or
discreet way, to discover what other
people's reaction to sth will be: *They're
putting out feelers about the possibility of
building a new sports complex in Leeds.* (an
insect has feelers (*antennae*) on its head,
which it uses to feel or sense things)

feeling

get/have the feeling feel that sth is true
although you have no direct knowledge or
facts: *I get the feeling that he's got another
girlfriend somewhere.* ○ *Have you ever got the
feeling that you were being watched?*

a/that sinking feeling ⇨ sinking; **that
Monday morning feeling** ⇨ Monday

feelings **have mixed feelings (about
sb/sth)** ⇨ mixed; **no hard feelings**
⇨ hard; **spare sb's feelings** ⇨ spare

feet

at sb's feet respecting and admiring sb,
and so being influenced by them: ○ *He had
the whole of Paris at his feet.*

fall/land on your 'feet (*informal*) be
lucky in finding a good position, job, place to
live, etc, especially when your previous
situation was difficult: *Well, you really fell on
your feet this time, didn't you? A job in Paris, a
large flat, a company car...* (refers to the way a
cat always lands safely)

feet of 'clay surprising weakness(es) in the character of sb who is admired and respected: *Why are people always surprised when they discover that their heroes have feet of clay?* (refers to Nebuchadnezzar's dream in the Bible, when he saw an image with a head of gold and feet of clay)

feet first (*informal*) dead or unconscious: *If you want me to leave this house, you'll have to carry me out feet first* (you'll have to kill me first).

have/keep both/your feet on the 'ground be sensible and realistic; not do foolish, rash or dangerous things: *He is always talking about his big plans to be a great actor. You should tell him to keep his feet on the ground.*

on your 'feet 1 standing up: *Being a shop assistant means that you're on your feet all day long.* 2 (of a business etc) in a strong position again after a period of difficulty, uncertainty, etc: *Only our party's policies will really get the country on its feet again.* ○ *The company seems to be back on its feet now.*

put your 'feet up relax by sitting, or lying down; enjoy a period of rest from work, etc: *After work, I like to have a cup of tea and put my feet up.* ○ *You've worked for this company for 35 years, Jack. Now it's time for you to put your feet up and relax.*

be/get run/rushed off your 'feet be very busy: *In the last few days before Christmas, the sales assistants were rushed off their feet.*

under sb's 'feet annoying sb because you are getting in their way and/or stopping them from working, etc: *It's difficult to do housework with the children under my feet all the time.*

cut the ground from under sb/sb's feet ⇨ cut; **drag your feet/heels** ⇨ drag; **find your feet** ⇨ find; **get/have cold feet** ⇨ cold; **have two left feet** ⇨ left; **have the world at your feet** ⇨ world; **itchy feet** ⇨ itchy; **not let the grass grow under your feet** ⇨ grass; **the patter of tiny feet** ⇨ patter; **pull the carpet/rug out from under sb's feet** ⇨ pull; **six feet under** ⇨ six; **stand on your own two feet** ⇨ stand; **sweep sb off their feet** ⇨ sweep; **take the weight off your feet** ⇨ weight; **think on your feet** ⇨ think; **throw yourself at sb's feet** ⇨ throw; **vote with your feet** ⇨ vote; **walk sb off their feet** ⇨ walk

fell

at one fell swoop with a single action or movement; all at the same time: *Only a foolish politician would promise to lower the rate of inflation and reduce unemployment at one fell swoop.* (refers to the action of a hawk as it swoops down from the sky to kill another bird or an animal)

felt

make your presence felt ⇨ presence

fence

my, her, etc side of the fence ⇨ side; **sit on the fence** ⇨ sit

fetch

fetch and 'carry (for sb) be always doing small jobs for sb; act as if you were sb's servant: *I hate having to fetch and carry for my husband all day. Why doesn't he do more for himself?*

fettle

in fine/good 'fettle healthy and cheerful: *After ten hours' sleep and a good long run, I was in fine fettle.*

fever

at 'fever pitch in a state of great excitement or great activity: *The audience was at fever pitch. I've never seen such excitement at a concert.* ○ *We are working at fever pitch to get the hall ready for the concert at eight.*

few

have a few (too many) (*informal*) drink a lot of alcohol: *Look, he's had a few and he really shouldn't drive home.* ○ *You've had a few too many, Paul. You don't know what you're saying.*

a good few ⇨ good; **a man/woman of few words** ⇨ words; **few and far between** ⇨ far; **precious few/little** ⇨ precious

fiddle

fiddle while Rome burns do nothing or waste your time when you should be dealing with a dangerous or serious situation: *With the world's population* *growing fast and millions getting hungrier every day, the leaders of the rich nations just seem to be fiddling while Rome burns.* (refers to the Emperor Nero during the burning of Rome in AD64)

on the 'fiddle (*informal*) getting money by doing dishonest things, usually at work, for example stealing from your employer, making false claims for expenses, etc: *He was on the fiddle for years and his boss never suspected anything.*

fit as a fiddle ⇨ fit; **play second fiddle** ⇨ play

field

have a 'field day enjoy a time of great excitement or activity: *Whenever this novelist brings out a new book, the critics have a field day, and she is attacked from all sides.* ○ *When the royal family go skiing, press photographers have a field day.*

fight

fight it out continue fighting or arguing until one person wins: *I'm not going to interfere. They can just fight it out between themselves.*

fight like cat and dog (*informal*) argue and quarrel fiercely very often: *They fight like cat and dog, but they are really very fond of each other.*

fight a losing 'battle try without success to achieve or prevent sth: *I'm fighting a losing battle with my weight. I can't lose any.* ○ *The police are fighting a losing battle against car theft.*

fight shy of sb/of (doing) sth avoid sb/(doing) sth; be unwilling to meet sb/do sth: *I tend to fight shy of getting involved in protests, but in this case I feel very strongly that we should complain.* ○ *He fights shy of any real contact with people.*

fight (sb/sth) tooth and 'nail *or* **fight tooth and 'nail for sb/sth** fight in a very determined way: *We fought the government tooth and nail to prevent the new road being built.* ○ *She fought tooth and nail to get the job.*

put up a (good) fight fight or compete bravely against sb/sth stronger than you: *The team put up a good fight but in the end they were beaten.* ○ *She won't accept the decision – she'll put up a fight.*

live to fight another day ⇨ live; **pick a fight/quarrel** ⇨ pick

fighting

a ˌfighting 'chance a slight but real chance of succeeding, avoiding sth etc: *With five minutes of the game left, our team still has a fighting chance of winning.* ○ *Things don't look very hopeful for John Brown in the presidential elections, but he's still in with a fighting chance.*

fighting fit = fit as a fiddle ⇨ fit

figment

a figment of your imagination something which you only imagine: *'Doctor, are you suggesting that the pain is a figment of my imagination?'*

figure

a figure of fun somebody who is often laughed at unkindly by other people: *As a young man he was admired; as an old man he became a figure of fun.*

put a figure on sth give the exact amount or exact value of sth: *'How much is the table worth?' 'It's difficult to put a figure on a table like this, but it is probably worth about £5000.'* ○ *'We're going to invest a great deal of money in our new business.' 'Excuse me, Sir, could you put a figure on that?'*

cut a fine, etc figure ⇨ cut

figures

that figures (*informal*) (used for saying that you are not surprised by a fact that you have just heard because it is what you would expect): *'We're going to need new offices when the company expands next year.' 'That figures.'* ○ *'I think he killed her to get the insurance money.' 'That figures.'*

have a head for figures ⇨ head; **in round figures/numbers** ⇨ round

file

in single/Indian 'file in a line, one person after another: *The whole class walked along behind the teacher in single file.* (refers to the American Indian method of walking in a group; each person walked in the footsteps of the person in front so that they could not be counted by the enemy)

rank and file ⇨ rank

fill

fill sb's shoes satisfactorily replace sb in a

job, function etc: *Mr Carter is retiring and we need a new director to fill his shoes.*

have your fill of sb/sth have had enough of sb/sth: *I've had my fill of Agatha Christie films. I never want to see another one as long as I live.* ○ *She's had her fill of him and his awful temper and she's left him.*

final

be the last/final straw ⇨ straw

find

find fault (with sb/sth) look for faults or mistakes in sb/sth, often so that you can criticize him/it: *He's always finding fault with the children, even when they are doing no wrong.* ○ *I can find no fault with this essay; it's the best I've ever read.*

find your 'feet (*informal*) become used to a new job, new surroundings, etc and start functioning well: *After moving from teaching to industry, it took her a long time to find her feet in a very different job.*

(not) find it in your heart to 'do sth or **(not) find it 'in yourself to ˌdo sth** (not) be able to persuade yourself to do sth: *I can't find it in myself to criticize her work after she's tried so hard.* ○ *I wish you could find it in your heart to forgive her.*

find your tongue (*informal*) finally be able to speak after being too nervous or shy to do so: *He sat silent through the first half of the meeting before he found his tongue.*

take sb/sth as you 'find him/it (often referring to the untidiness of a house, etc) accept sb/sth as he/it is, without criticism or complaint: *The house is in chaos, so when you come you must take us as you find us.*

find/meet your match ⇨ match; **get/find your bearings** ⇨ bearings; **like looking for/trying to find a needle in a haystack** ⇨ needle; **scratch A and you'll find B** ⇨ scratch

finders

ˌfinders 'keepers (*saying*) (often used by children) anyone who finds sth has a right to keep it: *I just found a ten-pound note on the ground. Finders keepers, so it's mine!*

fine

go over/through sth with a fine-'tooth comb (*informal*) search or look at sth very closely or carefully: *I went through the accounts with a fine-tooth comb to see if*

there was any mention of this money. ○ *The police went through his room with a fine-tooth comb.*

have (got) sth down to a fine 'art (*informal, often humorous*) learn through experience how to do sth perfectly: *I found it difficult to organize the timetables at first, but now I've got it down to a fine art.* ○ *She has complaining in restaurants down to a fine art! Head waiters are terrified of her.*

not to put too fine a 'point on it (used when you are about to speak very directly or honestly): *Not to put too fine a point on it, I think you've been a complete idiot.*

be all very fine but... = **be all very well but...** ⇨ well; **chance would be a fine thing** ⇨ chance; **cut it fine** ⇨ cut; **in fine/good fettle** ⇨ fettle

finger

get/pull your 'finger out (*informal*) stop being lazy and inefficient and start to work hard: *I wish the police would get their finger out and solve the crime!* ○ *If you pull your finger out, we might finish on time.*

have a finger in every 'pie (*informal*) be involved in everything that happens: *Jane likes to have a finger in every pie.*

have/keep your finger on the pulse of sth know all that is happening; be aware of new developments etc: *Successful politicians need to keep their finger on the pulse of the voters.* (a doctor takes your pulse by putting his fingers on your wrist and counting your pulse rate)

put your finger on sth (*informal*) say precisely what sth is, what is wrong etc: *I knew something she had said was not true, but I couldn't quite put my finger on it.* ○ *There's something wrong with these statistics but I just can't put my finger on what it is.*

lay a finger on sb/sth ⇨ lay; **lift a finger to do sth** ⇨ lift; **point a/the finger** ⇨ point; **twist sb round your little finger** ⇨ twist

fingers

get your 'fingers burnt or **burn your 'fingers** suffer loss or harm from acting too rashly, optimistically, etc: *She got her fingers burnt when she set up a business and had all her money stolen by her partner.*

have/keep your fingers crossed

(*informal*) hope that sth will be successful; wish sb good luck: *I'm going to give my first lecture tomorrow, so keep your fingers crossed for me, won't you?* ○ *Good luck, Ingrid. Fingers crossed!* (people often cross two fingers when they use this expression)

green fingers ⇨ green; **have your fingers/hand in the till** ⇨ till; **slip through sb's fingers** ⇨ slip; **snap your fingers** ⇨ snap; **tick sth off on your fingers** ⇨ tick; **work your fingers to the bone** ⇨ work

fingertips

have sth at your 'fingertips be so familiar with a subject that you can produce any facts about it easily and quickly: *The Minister was well prepared for the interview. She had all the facts at her fingertips.*

to your fingertips (of a particular type of person) completely; in every way: *He is an artist to his fingertips.* ○ *She's a professional to her fingertips.*

finish

in at the finish be present when sth ends: *I was one of the first people on this project and I certainly want to be in at the finish.*

finishing

the finishing touch(es) the final detail(s) that complete(s) or decorate(s) sth: *We've been putting the finishing touches to the Christmas decorations.*

fire

come/be under 'fire 1 be shot at: *While defending the town we came under fire again last night.* 2 be criticized, insulted, etc: *The government is already under fire over its housing policy.*

add fuel to the fire/flames ⇨ add; **a baptism of fire** ⇨ baptism; **the fat is in the fire** ⇨ fat; **get on like a house on fire** ⇨ house; **hang fire** ⇨ hang; **have many, etc irons in the fire** ⇨ irons; **hold your fire** ⇨ hold; **not/never set the Thames/world on fire** ⇨ set; **open fire** ⇨ open; **out of the frying-pan into the fire** ⇨ frying; **play with fire** ⇨ play; **set sth on fire/set fire to sth** ⇨ set; **there is no smoke without fire** ⇨ smoke

firing

be in the 'firing line be in a position where you are likely to be affected, attacked, criticized, etc: *The newspapers are criticizing the government's policy again, and the Prime Minister is in the firing line.* ○ *In the latest spending cuts, teachers' jobs are again in the firing line.*

firm

be on firm 'ground be sure about one's beliefs, knowledge, etc; be confident: *I don't know a lot about physics, I'm afraid. I'm on firmer ground with mathematics, which I studied at university.*

a firm 'hand strong discipline and control: *What his son needs, if you ask me, is a firm hand!*

stand firm ⇨ stand; **take a firm, etc line** ⇨ line

first

at first glance/sight as things seem at first; judging by first appearances: *At first glance, the exam paper looked fairly difficult, but once I got started I found it quite easy.*

at first hand from your own experience or knowledge, rather than from sb else; directly: *I know at first hand what it is like to be poor; we always had very little money at home.* **first-hand** (*adjective*) *We have a first-hand account of the raid from a witness.*

come 'first be treated as the most important person or thing in sb's life: *His work always came first with Joe, which upset his wife a lot.*

,first and 'foremost before everything else; most importantly: *First and foremost, we must ensure that the children are safe.* ○ *Don't forget, he is first and foremost an actor, not a singer.*

,first and 'last mainly; only : *The book is, first and last, an account of a poet's development.* ○ *I saw him for the first and last time at his father's funeral.*

,first ,come ,first 'served (*saying*) people will be dealt with, seen, etc strictly in the order in which they arrive, apply, etc: *We have 100 tickets for the performance, and they will be distributed on a first come, first served basis. So apply now!*

(in) the first flush of 'youth, en'thusiasm, etc when sth is new or sb is young: *In the first flush of enthusiasm, we were able to get everyone interested in helping.*

○ *By then, he was no longer in the first flush of youth.*

first 'off (*informal*) first of all; to begin with: *First off, we will choose the teams, then we can start the game.*

(give sb, have, etc)(the) first refusal (give sb, etc) the opportunity to buy sth before it is offered for sale to others: *She promised to give me first refusal if she ever decides to sell the grandfather clock.*

‚first things 'first the most important or necessary duties, matters, etc must be dealt with before others: *First things first. We must make sure the electricity is turned off before we start repairing the cooker.*

(be) the 'first/'last (person) to do sth be very willing or likely/unwilling or unlikely to do sth: *I'd be the first person to admit that I'm not perfect.* ○ *Mary is the last person you'd see in a pub – she hates pubs.*

first 'thing (tomorrow, in the morning, etc) at the beginning of the period of time mentioned, before doing anything else: *I always like a cup of tea first thing in the morning.* ○ *Can you lend me some money? I'll pay you back first thing tomorrow.*

get to first base (with sb/sth) *or* **reach/make first base (with sb/sth)** (*especially US, informal*) successfully complete the first stage of sth: *'How are you getting on with that new girlfriend of yours?' 'I haven't even got to first base yet'* (possibly *'I haven't even held her hand or kissed her yet').* ○ *The project hasn't even got to first base yet. Why all this delay?*

of the first order of the best, worst, most extreme, etc type: *It was a scandal of the first order.*

put sb/sth 'first treat sb/sth as the most important person or thing: *A politician should always put the needs of the country first and not his personal ambitions.* ○ *He never put his family first.*

there's a first time for everything (*saying, humorous*) the fact that something has not happened before does not mean that it will never happen: *'The flood water has never reached the house before.' 'Well, there's a first time for everything.'*

feet first ⇨ feet; **love at first sight**

⇨ love; **not know the first thing about sb/sth** ⇨ know; **see sb in 'hell first** ⇨ see

fish

fish for compliments encourage sb indirectly to say nice things about you: *'Well, what do you think of my younger sister?' 'Are you fishing for compliments, Sarah?' 'No, of course not.' 'Well, she's not nearly as beautiful as you.' 'How kind of you to say so.'*

a ‚fish out of 'water (*informal*) a person who feels uncomfortable or embarrassed in unfamiliar surroundings: *Everybody else was dressed in beautiful clothes and I was wearing jeans. I felt like a fish out of water.*

have 'other/'bigger fish to fry (*informal*) have more important, interesting or useful things to do: *He's not interested in reviewing small provincial exhibitions like this one; he's got much bigger fish to fry.* ○ *So you aren't coming out with us tonight? I suppose you've got other fish to fry.*

there are plenty/lots 'more fish in the sea *or* **there are (plenty of) 'other fish in the sea** (*informal*) (often used for comforting sb who is unhappy about losing an opportunity, a boyfriend, etc) there are many other people/things that are as good: *'I'll never love anyone as much again.' 'Look, Julie, there are lots more fish in the sea, you know.'*

a big fish ⇨ big; **a cold fish** ⇨ cold; **a different kettle of fish** ⇨ different; **drink like a fish** ⇨ drink; **an odd fish** ⇨ odd

fist **an iron fist/hand in a velvet glove** ⇨ iron; **make money hand over fist** ⇨ money; **shake your fist** ⇨ shake

fit

(as) ‚fit as a 'fiddle *also* **fighting fit** very healthy and active: *After our walking holiday, we came back feeling fit as a fiddle.*

fit the 'bill (*informal*) be suitable for a purpose: *We need a new sofa for the living-room, and I think this one will fit the bill quite nicely.*

fit (sb) like a 'glove (of a coat, dress, etc) fit the wearer perfectly: *You look wonderful. It fits you like a glove.*

have a pink/blue fit (*informal*) be very angry: *If your mother catches you smoking, she'll have a pink fit.*

have/throw a fit (*informal*) become very excited or angry: *Your father will throw a fit when he sees you've broken another window!*

see/think 'fit (to do sth) (*rather formal*) (often used for showing disapproval) think it is right or acceptable to do sth: *You obviously didn't see fit to inform us of what you were going to do.* ○ *You should warn her about his behaviour if you see fit.*

fit/ready to drop ⇨ drop

fits

in ,fits and 'starts not steadily; often starting and stopping: *'How's the book?' 'Oh, I'm working on it in fits and starts. I sometimes wonder if I'll ever finish it.'* ○ *He made progress in fits and starts at first but now he's improving rapidly.*

if the cap fits ⇨ cap

five(s) **a bunch of fives** ⇨ bunch; **nine to five** ⇨ nine

flag

keep the 'flag flying continue to support an idea, principle, activity, etc which is in danger of disappearing: *They try to keep the flag flying in the British film industry.* ○ *There's only two of us left now to keep the flag flying.*

fly the flag ⇨ fly

flame **an old flame** ⇨ old

flap

be in/get into a flap (*informal*) be in/get into a state of worry or excitement: *Julia's getting into a real flap about her exam.*

flash

a ,flash in the 'pan (*informal*) a success which lasts for a short time and is not likely to be repeated: *He scored a lot of goals early in the season, but hasn't scored any since, so it may have been just a flash in the pan.* (refers to an old type of gun; sometimes the gunpowder exploded with a flash in the 'pan' of the gun instead of firing the shot)

in/like a 'flash (*informal*) very quickly; suddenly: *'Sixty-six!,' she answered in a flash.* ○ *This new liquid will clean your floor in a flash.*

quick as a flash ⇨ quick

flat

and that's flat! (*informal*) (usually used for stressing a refusal, denial, etc) that is my final decision: *I'm not lending you any more money, and that's flat!*

(as) flat as a pancake (*informal*) unusually (and unpleasantly) flat: *There are one or two hills in Norfolk but otherwise the landscape is as flat as a pancake.*

flat 'out (*informal*) **1** as fast as possible; with all the energy, strength, etc you have: *If I worked flat out, I could get all the repairs done today.* **2** lying down, especially because you are ill or exhausted: *He was flat out on the bed.*

in two minutes, ten seconds, etc 'flat (*informal*) (used for emphasizing the speed of sth) in no more than two minutes, etc: *He tidied his room in ten minutes flat.* ○ *She spent nine months writing the first half of the book and then finished it in three months flat.*

fall flat ⇨ fall; **fall flat on your face** ⇨ fall

flavour

flavour of the month (*informal*) a person who is especially popular at the moment: *You know what the newspapers are like. One day you're flavour of the month, the next day you're public enemy number one.* ○ *If I were you, I'd keep quiet at the staff meeting. You're not exactly flavour of the month with the boss at the moment.*

flea

(send sb away/off) with a 'flea in their ear (*informal*) (refuse sb's request) very angrily: *When he came to ask for his job back, we sent him away with a flea in his ear.*

flesh

,flesh and 'blood the human body; the weaknesses, desires, fears, etc that human beings have: *'Why did he do it?' 'Look, he'd been away from home for six months and he was lonely. He's only flesh and blood, you know.'*

in the 'flesh in sb's actual presence; in person: *It's very strange seeing somebody in the flesh after seeing them on television for years.*

make your 'flesh creep/crawl make you feel fear, revulsion or disgust: *This is a film to make your flesh creep.* ○ *The way he looked at me made my flesh crawl.*

more than flesh and blood can stand,

endure, etc too painful, etc to bear: *Sometimes the pain is so bad that it is more than flesh and blood can stand.*

your own ,flesh and 'blood (members of) your own family: *How can I possibly not help him. He's my own flesh and blood, isn't he?*

be a thorn in your flesh/side ⇨ thorn; **go the way of all flesh** ⇨ way; **press the flesh** ⇨ press; **your pound of flesh** ⇨ pound; **the spirit is willing but the flesh is weak** ⇨ spirit

flex

flex your 'muscles show that you are ready and prepared to use your power, abilities, etc: *He's flexing his muscles, waiting for the day he becomes president.* (athletes flex (stretch and tighten) their muscles before a race, fight, match, etc)

flies

die/fall/drop like 'flies die, become ill, etc in large numbers: *During the epidemic people were dropping like flies.*

(there are) no flies on 'sb (*informal*) **1** sb is not stupid and therefore cannot be tricked or deceived easily: *You can't just tell her that you've lost the money; she'll never believe you. There are no flies on Jane, you know.* **2** sb is skilful or clever at doing sth: *There are no flies on Jim. He can persuade anybody to buy a car from him.* (a fly cannot land on sb who is moving fast)

as the crow flies ⇨ crow; **time flies** ⇨ time

flight

a flight of fancy an imaginative but completely unrealistic or impractical idea: *Have you heard about her latest flight of fancy?* ○ *The idea is not just a flight of fancy. It has been done before.*

fling

have a fling (*informal*) **1** enjoy yourself by doing lots of exciting, and perhaps irresponsible, things, especially when it is the last opportunity you will have: *Before I started training, I had one last fling and went with a group of friends to Paris for the weekend.* **2** have a short, not very serious love affair with sb: *'Do you know Sally Taylor?' 'Yes, I know her quite well in fact. We had a bit of a fling a few years ago.'*

fling/sling/throw mud ⇨ mud

flip

flip your 'lid (*informal*) **1** become very angry: *When he saw the damage to his car, he flipped his lid.* **2** go mad; become mentally ill: *After the divorce, she just flipped her lid. She was in hospital for months.*

flit **do a moonlight flit** ⇨ moonlight

flog

,flog a dead 'horse (*informal*) mistakenly continue trying to achieve sth which is impossible: *Pam's flogging a dead horse trying to organize the theatre trip. It's quite obvious that nobody's interested.*

,flog sth to 'death (*informal*) talk or write about or deal with a subject so often that there is no longer any interest in it: *The word 'new' has really been flogged to death in advertisements, and nobody believes it any more.*

flood

,flood the 'market offer for sale large quantities of a product, often at a low price: *Importers flooded the market with cheap toys just before Christmas.*

floodgates **open the floodgates** ⇨ open

floods

be in floods (of tears) (*informal*) be crying a lot: *She was in floods of tears after a row with her family.*

floor

,take the 'floor **1** stand up to talk in a debate, etc: *Next, the chairman asked the treasurer, Ms. Jones, to take the floor.* **2** begin dancing: *A few couples took the floor.*

get, etc in on the ground floor ⇨ ground; **hold the floor** ⇨ hold; **wipe the floor with sb** ⇨ wipe

flotsam

,flotsam and 'jetsam **1** odd items left on the shore by the tide. **2** people considered as a kind of human wreckage: *Under the bridge, you see the flotsam and jetsam of a big city.*

flown the bird has flown ⇨ bird

flush the first flush of youth, etc ⇨ first

fly

the 'feathers/'fur/'sparks will fly (*informal*) there will be anger, annoyance, etc: *The fur will really fly when she tells him he's not allowed to go out tonight.*

fly the flag do sth to show that you support and are proud of your country: *This exhibition of British technology is our way of flying the flag.*

fly in the face of sth ignore or contradict sth: *But such a view flies in the face of all the evidence.* ○ *Your decision is flying in the face of common sense.*

a/the 'fly in the ointment (*informal*) a person or thing that stops a situation, activity, plan, etc from being as good or successful as it could be: *We lead a very happy life here. The only fly in the ointment is that there is too much traffic on our road.*

fly into a 'rage, 'temper, etc suddenly become very angry: *She flies into a rage every time anybody suggests that she should stop working so hard.*

fly a kite (*British, informal*) release a bit of information, etc in order to test public reaction to sth that you plan to do at a later date: *Let's fly a kite. Tell the papers that the government is thinking of raising the school leaving age to 18, and we'll see what the reaction is.* (a kite will tell you which way the wind is blowing)

fly off the 'handle (*informal*) suddenly become very angry: *There's no need to fly off the handle!*

a 'fly on the wall (used when expressing the wish to be somewhere where sth important, secret, amusing, etc is happening) present in a place without being noticed: *I'd love to be a fly on the wall when the committee is discussing the report I wrote!*
fly-on-the-wall (*adjective*) describing a technique of filming real-life situations in which people behave normally, as if they were not being filmed: *Do you remember that fly-on-the-wall documentary about the Thames Valley Police?*

let fly (at sb/sth)(with sth) (*informal*) **1** throw, shoot, etc sth with great force: *He aimed his gun and let fly.* **2** attack sb/

sth: *When I told him that I couldn't find the letter, he let fly at me.* ○ *She let fly at her neighbour with a stream of insults.*

sb would not harm/hurt a 'fly sb is kind and gentle, and would not hurt anyone: *The dog may look very fierce, but he wouldn't hurt a fly.*

go/fly off at a tangent ⇨ tangent; **pigs might/may fly** ⇨ pigs

flying

a 'flying 'visit a very brief visit: *The Prime Minister paid a flying visit to Brussels this afternoon.*

get off to a flying start make a very good, successful start: *She got off to a flying start, gaining several points in the first few minutes.*

with flying colours with great success: *We expect your son to pass the exam with flying colours.* ○ *She came through her French test with flying colours.* (refers to a ship which returns to port after a victory, decorated with flags)

keep the flag flying ⇨ flag

foam

foam at the mouth (*informal*) be extremely angry: *He stood there foaming at the mouth. I've never seen anybody so angry.* (refers to the fact that a mad dog foams at the mouth)

fodder cannon fodder ⇨ cannon

fog

in a fog (*informal*) uncertain and confused: *Thank you for your explanation but I must admit I'm still in a fog over what happened.*

fogy an old fogy ⇨ old

foggiest not have the faintest/foggiest ⇨ faintest

fold return to the fold ⇨ return

follow

follow in sb's 'footsteps do the same job as sb else, especially a parent, has done before; lead a similar life to sb else: *He followed in his mother's footsteps and became a lawyer.*

follow 'suit act or behave in the way that sb else has just done: *One of the oil companies put up the price of petrol today, and the others* *are expected to follow suit.* (playing cards are in four suits: hearts, clubs, diamonds and spades)

follow/go with the crowd ⇨ crowd; **take, follow the line of least resistance** ⇨ line; **take/follow/steer a middle course** ⇨ middle

food

be off your food have no appetite, probably because you are ill or depressed: *She's off her food, she's sleeping very badly and she can't concentrate.*

food for 'thought an event, remark, fact, etc which should be considered very carefully because it is interesting, important, etc: *The lectures were very interesting and gave much food for thought.*

fool

act/play the fool behave in a stupid or playful way to amuse people: *It's impossible to have a decent game of tennis with Frank; he acts the fool the whole time.* ○ *If you played the fool in class a little less and worked a little harder, you could do quite well.*

be ,no 'fool *or* **be ,nobody's 'fool** be a clever person who cannot easily be tricked or cheated by anyone: *You won't be able to cheat her – she's nobody's fool.* ○ *Don't underestimate him. He's no fool.*

a ,fool and his ,money are ,soon 'parted *(saying)* a foolish person usually spends money too quickly and unwisely, or is cheated by others.

a 'fool's errand a journey, task, etc that is a waste of time because it wasn't necessary: *Are you sending me on a fool's errand again? The last time you sent me to get tickets, the play wasn't even on.*

a fool's 'paradise a state of happiness which cannot last because sth which you have not thought of is threatening to destroy it: *You've been living in a fool's paradise. How long do you think we can go on spending our money without earning more?*

make a fool of sb/yourself make sb/yourself appear stupid or ridiculous: *Last time you drank champagne, you made a complete fool of yourself.* ○ *The interviewer made a real fool of me; I just couldn't answer her question.*

,more fool 'you, etc *(informal)* (used as an exclamation) you, etc were very foolish to do sth: *'He's going to give all his money to charity.' 'More fool him! I would keep it all for myself.'* ○ *'I'm not going to accept that job in Vienna.' 'More fool you. You'll never get another chance like that again.'*

(there is) ,no fool like an 'old fool *(saying)* an older person who behaves foolishly appears more foolish than a younger person who does the same thing, because experience should have taught him not to do it: *Fred is going to marry a woman thirty years younger. There's no fool like an old fool.*

fooled

you could have ,fooled 'me! *(informal)* (used for expressing your surprise about a statement, claim, etc): *'He's quite intelligent, you know.' 'You could have fooled me! I've never heard him say anything intelligent at all.'*

fools

fools rush in (where angels fear to tread) *(saying)* people with little experience attempt to do the difficult or dangerous things which more experienced people would not consider doing.

not suffer fools gladly ⇨ suffer

foot

foot the 'bill (for sth) (used of a large amount of money) be responsible for paying for sth: *The local council will have to foot the bill for damage done to the roads during the floods.*

get/have a foot in the door start/have started to be accepted in an organization, group, profession, etc especially when this is difficult: *It's difficult to get your foot in the door as a young actor without any experience.* **foot-in-the-door** *(adjective)* aggressive, foot-in-the-door sales techniques

have a foot in both 'camps *(informal)* be involved with two separate groups, etc that have different ideas: *She works in industry and at a university, so she's got a foot in both camps.*

have one foot in the grave *(humorous, informal)* be so old or ill that you probably will not live much longer: *I may be retired, but that doesn't mean I've got one foot in the grave, you know.*

not/never put/set a foot wrong (*informal*) never make a mistake: *According to her colleagues, she never put a foot wrong.*

on foot walking, in contrast to other ways of travelling: *It'll take you half an hour on foot, or five minutes in the car.*

put your 'foot down (*informal*) **1** go faster in a car, etc by pressing the accelerator down: *If you put your foot down, we might be home by seven o'clock.* **2** use your authority to stop sb doing sth: *When she asked if she could stay out until midnight, I put my foot down and insisted that she come home by eleven.*

put your 'foot in it (*informal*) say or do sth that upsets, offends or embarrasses sb without intending to: *He really put his foot in it when he mentioned the party to her. She hadn't been invited.*

bind/tie sb hand and foot ⇨ hand; **the boot is on the other foot** ⇨ boot; **from head to foot/toe** ⇨ head; **put your best foot forward** ⇨ best; **set foot in/on sth** ⇨ set; **shoot yourself in the foot** ⇨ shoot; **wait on sb hand and foot** ⇨ wait

footloose

footloose and fancy-'free without responsibilities or emotional commitments; free to do what you like: *Here she was, at forty, footloose and fancy-free in New York.*

footsteps **dog sb's footsteps** ⇨ dog; **follow in sb's footsteps** ⇨ follow

for

A for B comparing A with B: *The packets of washing powder are all different sizes, but, weight for weight, this one is the cheapest.* ○ *Man for man, our soldiers are better trained and better equipped than theirs.*

for all **1** in spite of: *For all his qualifications, he isn't really very good at the job.* ○ *For all her claims to be efficient, she is a very slow worker.* **2** (used for saying that the thing you mention does not matter or make any difference): *He can do what he wants, for all I care* (I don't care what he does). ○ *'Where's Peter?' 'For all I know, he may be dead.'*

forbidden

for,bidden 'fruit something that you are not allowed to have, do, etc and for this reason is all the more attractive: *He felt very attracted to his best friend's wife, but admitted that it was partly because she was forbidden fruit.* (refers to the apple in the Bible story of Adam and Eve)

force

bring sth/come into 'force cause a law, rule, etc to become/become valid or take effect: *After the new housing law comes into force, we will find it easier to buy our own home.* ○ *The government says it will bring the new rules into force on July the first.*

force of 'circumstance a situation in which you are forced to do sth by factors beyond your control: *He claimed he turned to crime through force of circumstance. He hadn't been able to find a job and his family was starving.*

force of 'habit a tendency always to do things in a certain way because you have always done them in that way: *I don't know why I check the locks every time I leave the house. It's force of habit, I suppose.*

force sb's 'hand force sb to do sth differently or sooner than planned: *By trying to get the law changed, the opposition party wants to force the government's hand.* (refers to card playing)

force the 'pace make sb do sth more quickly or make sth happen more quickly: *The government is forcing the pace on economic reforms and the public don't like it.* (in a race, if you force the pace, you force the other runners to run as fast as you because you want them to get tired)

a force to be reckoned with a person or thing that must be treated seriously especially as an opponent, obstacle, etc: *The increased size of the country's army means that it is now a force to be reckoned with.* ○ *Be very careful how you deal with her because she's a force to be reckoned with.*

in 'force/'strength (of people) present in large numbers: *The police were out in force to deal with the trouble at the demonstration.* ○ *Party members appeared in strength to welcome the Prime Minister.*

the driving force ⇨ driving; **a show of force** ⇨ show

fore

be/come to the fore be or become prominent, important or well known: *She came very much to the fore during the local campaign against the new bypass.*

forearmed

forewarned is forearmed ⇨ forewarned

foregone

a foregone conclusion a result, consequence or end that is easy to predict: *It's a foregone conclusion that England will win tonight's match.*

forelock

touch/tug your forelock show (too much) respect for a person of a higher rank or status: *This is a democratic country and we don't want people tugging their forelocks.* (in the past people of the lower classes either took off their hats or pulled on their forelocks (the hair above the forehead) to show respect)

foremost

first and foremost ⇨ first

forewarned

fore,warned is fore'armed (*saying*) it is easier to deal with a problem, difficulty, etc if you know about it beforehand: *Jim says that Betty is very angry with me still. Well, forewarned is forearmed, and I'll have to think up an excuse before I see her.*

forgive

for,give and for'get decide to forget a quarrel, insult, etc: *Come on, it's time to forgive and forget.* ○ *Many of his victims find it impossible to forgive and forget.*

form

good/bad form acceptable/unacceptable behaviour as judged by certain rules of politeness, social standards, etc: *I think it was very bad form for Joe to get drunk at the funeral.* ○ *Apparently, good form requires you to wear a hat on these occasions.*

on/off 'form *or* **in (good) 'form** in a good/poor mental or physical state; doing as well/worse than normal: *She had been ill and was off form, so she didn't do so well in the exam.* ○ *He's really on form tonight and is answering all the questions correctly and very quickly.* ○ *The team are in good form this season.*

as a matter of form ⇨ matter; **in the shape/form of sb/sth** ⇨ shape; **on present form** ⇨ present; **true to form** ⇨ true

former

be a shadow of his/its former self ⇨ shadow

fort

hold the 'fort ⇨ hold

forth

and 'so forth *or* **and ,so on '(and so 'forth)** (used to show that a story, list, etc continues in an expected way): *I'm in a bit of a hurry. I've got to pack my bags, find my passport and so on, all before tomorrow morning.*

hold forth ⇨ hold

fortune

fortune smiles on sb a person is lucky and successful: *At first, fortune smiled on him and the business was successful.*

make a fortune make a lot of money: *He made a fortune buying and selling 19th century paintings.*

a hostage to fortune ⇨ hostage; **a small fortune** ⇨ small

forty

forty 'winks (*informal*) a short sleep, especially during the day; a nap: *I managed to get forty winks after lunch.*

forward

put your best foot forward ⇨ best

foul

by fair means or foul ⇨ fair; **fall foul of sb/sth** ⇨ fall

founding

the founding father(s) of sth the people who found or start a country, an organization, a branch of science, etc: *Charles Babbage, the founding father of computer science.* ○ *the founding fathers of the USA*

four(s)

the four corners of the earth the most distant parts of the world: *People come from the four corners of the earth to attend the festival.*

a four-letter word an obscene, offensive word: *Four-letter words used to be banned on radio and television.*

on all 'fours with your knees, toes and hands on the floor: *The ceiling of the tunnel was so low that we had to crawl along on all fours.*

frame

a frame of 'mind a particular way of thinking, mood, etc: *You should ask her for permission when she's in a better frame of mind.* ○ *I wonder what frame of mind he was in when he wrote the letter.*

free

be in/go into free fall be falling/start to fall rapidly: *Share prices are in free fall in Tokyo this morning.* ○ *The value of sterling against the dollar went into free fall as soon as the news was announced.* (from the moment you jump out of a plane until the moment your parachute opens, you are in free fall)

(get, do, etc sth) for 'free 1 without having to pay: *Some children got into the cinema for free by using old tickets.* **2** (used for emphasizing how strongly you feel about sth): *The whole plan is a disaster. I can tell you that for free.*

free and 'easy informal and relaxed: *They had to settle down. Life wasn't free and easy any more.*

(as) free as (the) air/as a bird completely free: *You can't imagine what it's like to feel as free as the air. Nobody who hasn't been in prison can imagine it.*

get, have, etc a free 'hand be given permission or an opportunity to do as you wish in your work, plans, etc: *My boss gives me a free hand in deciding which outside contractor to use.* ○ *She has a free hand in choosing her staff.*

give free 'rein to sth not restrict, limit or control sth: *In a historical novel the author need not keep to the facts, but a history textbook is not the place to give free rein to your imagination.* (refers to giving a horse freedom to go at the speed it wants)

feel free ⇨ feel

freeze make sb's blood freeze ⇨ blood; **chill/freeze sb to the bone/marrow** ⇨ chill

French

excuse/pardon my 'French (*informal, humorous*) (used for apologizing when you

have used or are going to use rude or offensive language): *Ouch, bloody hell! Oops, pardon my French!* ○ *If you'll pardon my French, he's a complete bloody fool.*

take French 'leave leave your work, duty, etc without permission; go away without telling anyone: *I think I might take French leave this afternoon and go to the cinema.*

fresh

(as) fresh as a 'daisy lively or clean and neat: *Even when it's so hot, she looks as fresh as a daisy. How does she do it?*

break fresh/new ground ⇨ break; **a breath of fresh air** ⇨ breath; **new/fresh/young blood** ⇨ blood

Freudian

a Freudian slip a mistake in speaking or writing which shows what you really think or feel about sb/sth: *'I've never loved, I mean I've never stopped loving, my mother.' 'Was that a Freudian slip?'*

friend(s)

a ,friend in 'need (is a ,friend in'deed) (*saying*) a friend who helps you when you are in trouble (is a real friend): *I'll always be grateful to Christine for lending me the money; a friend in need is a friend indeed!*

have friends in high places know people who are in influential and powerful positions and may be able to help you: *Ask Geoff to help with the campaign. He's got friends in high places.*

make 'friends (with sb) become sb's friend: *Roger was new to the district but he soon made friends with other boys of his age.* ○ *She's a very open sort of person and tends to make friends easily.*

what's sth between friends? (used for refusing an offer by a friend to pay or repay you for sth because the amount is small): *'I owe you 50p for that coffee.' 'Don't be silly, Steve, what's 50p between friends?'*

our feathered friends ⇨ feathered

fright

take fright (at sth) be frightened by sth: *The horse took fright as the car passed and galloped off.*

the fright of your life a severe fright or

shock: *I got the fright of my life when I saw the gun pointing at me.* ○ *He gave me the fright of my life when I saw him hanging out of the window.*

frighten
frighten/scare sb to 'death/out of their 'wits *or* **frighten the 'life out of sb** frighten sb very much: *I was frightened to death when I looked out of the window and saw the aircraft's engine on fire.*

frighteners
put the frighteners on (sb) (*informal*) threaten sb so that they will do what you want, for example, not go to the police, etc: *They started putting the frighteners on the witness, sending him threatening letters.*

fringe   the lunatic fringe ⇨ lunatic

fro   to and fro ⇨ to

frog
have a 'frog in your throat (*informal*) not be able to speak clearly because your throat is sore, you want to cough, etc: *She had a frog in her throat, so she had a drink of water before she went on speaking.*

froing   toing and froing ⇨ toing

front
up 'front (*informal*) **1** (of money) paid or promised beforehand; in advance: *Before we can put the musical on, we have to have a million pounds up front.* **2** frank or open: *If that's what they're doing, they ought to be more up front about it.*

back to front ⇨ back

fruit   bear fruit ⇨ bear; forbidden fruit ⇨ forbidden

fruitcake   nutty as a fruitcake ⇨ nutty

fry   have other/bigger fish to fry ⇨ fish; small fry ⇨ small

frying
out of the 'frying-pan (and) into the 'fire (*saying*) out of one situation of danger or difficulty into another (usually worse) one: *It was a case of out of the frying-pan into the fire: she divorced her husband who was an alcoholic and then married another man with the same problem.*

fuel   add fuel to the fire/flames ⇨ add

full
at full 'stretch to the full extent of your powers, abilities, etc: *We've been working at full stretch for weeks to get the hall ready for the conference.*

come/go full 'circle after a long period of changes, return to the position or situation in which sth/you started: ○ *The wheel of fashion has come full circle. I was wearing shoes like that thirty years ago.*

come to a full stop stop unexpectedly before sth is or seems to be finished: *It's a very strange book; you're in the middle of the story and it suddenly comes to a full stop.* ○ *She came to a full stop and seemed unable to continue.*

(at) full 'blast with great noise, power, speed, etc: *Tom had his radio on at full blast – it was deafening.* ○ *The heating was on full blast all day.*

full of 'beans very lively, active and healthy: *Ray is certainly full of beans again after his illness.* (originally used of horses fed on beans)

'full of himself/herself (*informal, disapproving*) feeling successful and rather conceited because of it: *He came to see us next week, very full of himself because he had just been promoted.*

full of the joys of spring very happy, light-hearted and lively: *You look full of the joys of spring this morning.*

full marks (to sb for doing sth) (used for praising sb for being or doing sth): *Full marks to Hannah for being so helpful this morning.* ○ *Full marks, Dominic. You sang that very well.*

full steam/speed ahead with as much speed or energy as possible: *We were working full steam ahead to finish by the end of April.* (refers to the order given on a ship by the captain to the engine room)

full stop (used for showing that you do not intend to explain or add anything) and that is all; I have no more to add: *I don't have to give you any reasons. You can't have a motorbike, full stop.* ○ *I don't like him, full stop.*

(at) full 'tilt/'pelt/'speed with great speed, force, etc: *The police were chasing him so he ran full pelt down the road.* ○ *We drove* *down the road at full speed.*

in full completely; with nothing missing: *I paid the debt in full.* ○ *The programme reported in full on the latest economic crisis.*

in full 'cry noisily and enthusiastically chasing or attacking sth: *The newspapers are in full cry over this new banking scandal.* ○ *The government is having difficulties, and its critics are in full cry again.* (refers to hounds (hunting dogs) chasing a fox)

in full 'swing at the height (of an event, party, election, etc); at its most busy or lively time: *When we arrived at 10 o'clock, the party was already in full swing.* ○ *The tourist season in London is in full swing at the moment.*

in full 'view (of sb) where you can easily be seen (by sb): *The player committed the foul in full view of the referee, and was sent off the field.*

to the 'full as completely or as much as possible: *You'll be able to enjoy life to the full again after your operation.*

be at full/be below full strength ⇨ **strength**; **be full to bursting** = **be bursting/bulging at the seams** ⇨ **seams**; **have your hands full** ⇨ **hands**; **three bags full** ⇨ **three**

fullness

in the fullness of time (*formal*) when (enough) time has passed; eventually: *I knew that, in the fullness of time, somebody with your abilities would emerge and become leader.*

fun

for 'fun *or* **for the fun of it** for the pleasure or enjoyment of sth, not because it's important or serious: *I entered the competition just for fun – I never thought I would win.* ○ *'Why did you say it if you didn't mean it?' 'For the fun of it. I just wanted to see his reaction.'*

fun and 'games (*informal*) **1** lively and playful behaviour: *It's not all fun and games at this school – we make our children work hard as*

well. **2** (*humorous*) trouble: *We had some fun and games putting up those new shelves yesterday.*

in fun to amuse sb, not to upset them: *I'm sorry, darling. I didn't mean to upset you. It was only said in fun.*

make fun of sb/sth *or* **poke fun at sb/sth** make unkind remarks or jokes about sb: *My cousins used to make fun of my strange accent.* ○ *People enjoy making fun of the clothes I wear, though they seem all right to me.* ○ *It's a programme that likes to poke fun at the royal family.*

a figure of fun ⇨ **figure**

funny

'funny business (*informal*) sth that is illegal or disapproved of, for example dishonesty or sexual misbehaviour: *Now, behave yourself! I don't want any of your funny business.* ○ *There's some funny business going on in this company at the moment. We may have to call in the police.*

fur the **feathers/fur/sparks will fly** ⇨ **fly**

furious fast and furious ⇨ **fast**

furniture part of the furniture ⇨ **part**

further nothing could be further from my mind, etc ⇨ **nothing**

fury

like fury (*informal*) with great energy, speed etc: *I worked like fury to get everything done by five o'clock.*

fuse be on/have a short fuse ⇨ **short**

fuss

make a fuss of/over sb/sth pay a lot of attention to sb/sth; show concern, affection etc for sb/sth: *It's sometimes quite pleasant being ill, when people make a fuss of you all the time.*

a fuss about nothing = **a storm in a teacup** ⇨ **storm**

G

gab the gift of the gab ⇨ gift

gaff blow the gaff ⇨ blow

gain
gain ground **1** (of soldiers) move forward in a battle: *Our men began to gain ground, forcing the enemy back towards the river.* **2** (of an idea, development, etc) become more widespread or popular: *Diesel cars seem to be gaining ground because they are cheaper to run.*

gained nothing ventured, nothing gained ⇨ nothing

gallery a rogues' gallery ⇨ rogues

game
sb's (little) game (*informal*) sb's trick, plan or intention: *So that's your little game – getting me moved to a different office and then doing my job for me.*

the ,game is not worth the 'candle (*saying*) sth is not worth the effort needed: *After trying to get permission to build the office for a whole year, we gave up, because the game was just not worth the candle.* (refers to playing cards by candlelight: if the money being gambled was less than the cost of the candle, it was not worth playing the game)

the game is 'up (*informal*) a crime, a secret plan, an activity you disapprove of, etc has been discovered and must stop: *The game is up, Malone. We're arresting you for the murder of Joe Capella.* ○ *The game is up for the Democrats. They'll never win the next election after this scandal.*

give the 'game away (*informal*) (accidentally) reveal your own or another person's secret plan, trick, etc and so spoil it: *Don't laugh when he comes in or you'll give the game away. The birthday present's got to be a surprise.* ○ *He can't keep a secret, so never tell him anything important in case he gives the game away.*

(be/go) on the 'game (*informal*) be/become a prostitute.

be a mug's game ⇨ mug; **beat sb at their**

own game ⇨ beat; **a cat-and-mouse game** ⇨ cat; **easy game** ⇨ easy; **fair game** ⇨ fair; **a game that two can play = two can play at that game** ⇨ two; **name of the game** ⇨ name; **play sb at their own game = play sb's game** ⇨ play; **play the game** ⇨ play; **play the same game = play sb's game** ⇨ play; **two can play at that game** ⇨ two; **a waiting game** ⇨ waiting

games fun and games ⇨ fun

gamut
run the 'gamut of sth experience or describe a range of sth: *This poem runs the gamut of human emotions from despair to joy.*

gander what's sauce for the goose is sauce for the gander ⇨ sauce

gap bridge the gap ⇨ bridge

garden
everything in the garden is lovely (*saying, often ironic*) everything is satisfactory, is going well, or could not be better: *She pretends that everything in the garden is lovely, but I've heard that she is very heavily in debt.*

common or garden ⇨ common; **lead sb up the garden path** ⇨ lead

garters have sb's guts for garters ⇨ guts

gas step on the gas = step on it ⇨ step

gates the pearly gates ⇨ pearly

gather
gather 'dust (of plans, recommendations, etc) be forgotten or ignored: *As usual the report was left to gather dust and not dealt with by the authorities for years.*

collect/gather your wits ⇨ wits

gauntlet
take up the 'gauntlet accept a challenge: *The country needs enormous help to rebuild its economy, and it's time to take up the gauntlet*

93

and do what we can.

run the gauntlet ➪ run; **throw down the gauntlet** ➪ throw

general

in 'general in most cases; usually: *The money is due to come on the first of every month; in general it arrives punctually, but at holiday times it's sometimes late.*

the common/general run ➪ run

gentleman

a gentleman's agreement an agreement, contract, etc in which nothing is written down because both people trust each other not to break it: *'Why don't you tell him you don't want to sell it now?' 'I can't possibly. It was a gentleman's agreement and I must keep to it.'*

gently **easy/gently/slowly does it** ➪ easy

get

get a'long/a'way/'on (with you)! (*informal*) used for expressing surprise, disbelief, annoyance, etc: *Get away with you! You don't expect me to believe that story, do you?*

get a'way from it all go away somewhere on holiday, etc in order to escape from pressures at work, home, city life, etc: *We went walking to get away from it all for a while. ○ Why don't you get away from it all and have a weekend in the country?*

get it (in the neck) (*informal*) be criticized, blamed or punished: *You'll get it when your mother sees all this mess. ○ We'll get it in the neck if we arrive late. They'll say we should have phoned to say we'd been delayed.*

get sb nowhere/not get sb anywhere not help sb make progress: *His job is getting him nowhere. He ought to try and find another one. ○ All these problems with my computer aren't getting me anywhere. I'm weeks behind with my work.*

(not) get somewhere/nowhere/ anywhere (not) make progress: *I'm finally getting somewhere with this radio. It should be mended soon. ○ Are you getting anywhere with that new manager? ○ You'll get nowhere in life if you don't work harder.*

'get there (*informal*) eventually achieve

aims: *Peter is a slow learner, but he gets there in the end.*

be/get on to sb ➪ on; **get sth/it/your act together** ➪ together; **get sth off/get off the ground** ➪ ground; **get your, etc own back** ➪ back; **get with it** ➪ with

getting

be getting 'on **1** (of people) be getting old: *I'm getting on a bit now and I can't walk as well as I used to.* **2** (of the time) be getting late: *It's getting on, so I'd better be off home.*

getting on for... near to or approaching a certain time, number, age, etc: *I've lived here getting on for five years now. ○ She's getting on for 90.*

there's no getting away from it (*informal*) we cannot ignore an important, possibly unpleasant, fact: *There's no getting away from it; this company is not doing as well as it should be. ○ There's no getting away from it. He's a better player than me.*

ghost

give up the 'ghost (*humorous, informal*) **1** (*dated*) die **2** (of a machine, etc) stop functioning because it is so old: *My old typewriter has finally given up the ghost, so I'm getting a word processor.* **3** (of a person) stop making an effort; stop working: *She persuaded me to carry on when I was tempted to give up the ghost.*

(not) have a 'ghost of a chance (of doing sth) (*informal*) have no chance at all (of doing sth): *He doesn't have a ghost of a chance of passing the exam this year.*

gift

the gift of the 'gab (*informal*) the ability to talk fluently for a long time, especially to persuade sb to do sth: *To be a successful sales executive you need the gift of the gab.* ('gab' is possibly from the Irish word for 'mouth'. The Irish have a reputation as good talkers.)

look a gift-horse in the mouth ➪ look

gild

gild the 'lily try to improve sth which is already perfect, and so spoil it: *The dress is perfect. Don't add anything to it at all. It would just be gilding the lily.* (a misquotation from Shakespeare's *King John*: 'to gild refined gold, to paint the lily...is wasteful and ridiculous excess')

gills green about the gills ⇨ green

gilt
  take the gilt off the 'gingerbread spoil sth so that you find it less attractive than before: *He's offered us his villa by the sea for two weeks. The only problem is that we can only have it in February, which rather takes the gilt off the gingerbread.*

gird
  gird (up) your loins (*formal, dated, humorous*) prepare yourself for action, hard work, etc: *There's a lot of hard work to be done before the weekend, so let's gird up our loins and start.*

girl old boy/girl ⇨ old

girls be one of the lads/boys/girls ⇨ one

give
  ,give and 'take be willing to listen to other people's wishes and points of view and to change your demands, if this is necessary: *If we want this marriage to be successful, we both have to learn to give and take.* ,give and 'take (*noun*) *We can't all expect to have exactly what we want. There has to be some give and take.*

  give as good as you get (*informal*) defend yourself very well when you fight or argue with sb: *Don't worry about her. She can give as good as she gets.*

  'give it to sb *or* give sb what 'for attack or punish sb verbally or physically: *The manager will really give it to you when he finds out what you've done.* ○ *If you take my car again without asking me, I'll give you what for.*

  give me sth ('any day/time) (used for saying you like sth much more than the thing just mentioned): *I hate going abroad on holiday. Give me three weeks at the English seaside any day.* ○ *I hate cricket. Give me football any time.*

  give or take (used for giving an approximate time, number, price, etc): *It took us three hours, give or take a few minutes.* ○ *It'll cost about £1000, give or take a bit.*

  give sb the willies/heebie-jeebies/creeps (*very informal*) make sb feel nervous or afraid: *Being alone in the dark gives me the willies.* ○ *She said that spiders gave her the heebie-jeebies.* ○ *He gives me the creeps. He's*

got such strange eyes.

  not give a damn, fig, monkey's, shit, toss, etc (about sb/sth) (*very informal*) not care at all (about sb/sth): *She doesn't give a damn about her father.* ○ *I don't give a shit what Marie thinks. I'll do what I want!* ○ *Nobody gives a monkey's about unemployment any more.*

  give way ⇨ way; hand/give it to sb ⇨ hand

glad
  'glad rags (*informal*) smart clothes worn for a party, etc: *We put our glad rags on and went to the theatre.*

gladly not suffer fools gladly ⇨ suffer

glance at first glance/sight ⇨ first; steal a glance at sb/sth ⇨ steal

glass people who live in glasshouses shouldn't throw stones ⇨ people

glisten all that glitters/glistens/glisters is not gold ⇨ gold

glory bathe/bask in reflected glory ⇨ reflected

glove fit like a glove ⇨ fit; hand in glove ⇨ hand; an iron fist/hand in a velvet glove ⇨ iron

gloves
  the gloves are off (*informal*) in an argument, dispute, etc, stop being gentle with sb and start fighting them with force and determination: *Up to now both sides in the dispute have been cautious, but now the gloves are off and a serious confrontation is expected.* (refers to boxers taking off their gloves)

  handle, treat, etc sb with kid gloves ⇨ kid

glowing
  in glowing terms/colours (describe sb/sth) in a very positive and flattering way: *He describes Manchester in glowing terms. I never realized it was such an interesting place.* ○ *She paints him in glowing colours in this book. I'm sure he wasn't as wonderful as she says.*

glutton
  a glutton for punishment, work, etc (*informal*) sb who seems to like doing

unpleasant or difficult things: *You're going to drive all the way to London and back in a day? You're a glutton for punishment, aren't you?* ○ *She's a glutton for work. She stays late every evening.*

go

as things, people, etc 'go compared to the average thing of that type: *As government statements go, this one was fairly honest.* ○ *As titles for abstract paintings go, 'Field with Figures' is better than most.*

at/in one 'go in one single action; all at the same time: *I don't think I'll be able to solve all the problems at one go.* ○ *He ate the whole cake in one go.*

be on the 'go be busy and active: *I've been on the go all day and I'm exhausted.* ○ *She's always on the go. I wish she would just sit down and relax sometimes.*

go all 'out (for sth/to 'do sth) (*informal*) make a very great effort to get or do sth: *We knew that only one of the firms would get the order for computers and so we went all out to get the contract.* ○ *We must go all out to increase our membership.*

go and do sth (*British, very informal*) (used for expressing anger that sb has done sth): *Why did you go and tell him? It was a secret.* ○ *Look what you've gone and done now! That was my favourite vase.*

'go for it (*informal*) (used for encouraging sb to try and achieve sth difficult or considered difficult): *'He doesn't think it's worth trying to publish my book.' 'Don't listen to him, Jeannie, go for it! How will you ever know unless you try?'*

go it alone (*informal*) do sth, especially sth difficult, without the help or support of others.

have a 'go (at sb) (*informal*) attack, criticize (sb): *She had a go at me last night about crashing the car.* ○ *He's always having a go at me about my spelling.*

have a 'go (at sth/at doing sth) (*informal*) attempt to do, win or achieve sth: *I'm sure I could do better than that. Let me have a go!* ○ *I've got the time, so I'll have a go at the decorating myself.* ○ *I've had a go at mending the radio, but I can't do it.*

have sth on the go (*informal*) be dealing with, working on, etc sth: *She is a very busy*

architect and always has some project on the go. ○ *'Have you got anything interesting on the go at the moment?' 'Yes, I'm working on a programme about the origins of sport.'*

...to go 1 still remaining before sth happens, finishes or is completed: *There's only a few seconds to go before the rocket takes off.* ○ *With only two kilometres to go, Max is still first.* **2** (*especially US, informal*) (of food bought in a restaurant, shop, etc) to be taken away and eaten elsewhere: *We've ordered hamburgers and french fries to go.*

be all go ⇨ all; **be/go/keep on about sth** ⇨ on; **be/go/keep on at sb** ⇨ on; **there you go (again)** ⇨ there; **(and/but/ so) there you go = there it is** ⇨ there

goalposts move the goalposts ⇨ move

goat(s)

act/play the goat (*informal*) deliberately behave in a silly or foolish way: *Stop acting the goat or I'll send you out. I warn you.*

get sb's goat (*informal*) annoy sb very much: *That woman really gets my goat. She does nothing but complain.* ○ *It really gets my goat when people smoke in non-smoking areas.*

separate the sheep from the goats ⇨ separate

gob shut your mouth/trap/face/gob! ⇨ shut

God

(oh) (my) God *or* **good God** *or* **God almighty** (used for expressing anger, surprise, etc; considered offensive by some people): *God almighty! You're not going to wear that terrible old suit to the wedding, are you?* ○ *Oh my God! I've broken my watch again!* ○ *Good God! What on earth have you done to my car?*

God willing (used for expressing your hope that sth will happen): *We've had a lovely holiday and we'll be back again next year, God willing.*

an act of God ⇨ act; **God/goodness/ Heaven knows** ⇨ knows; **God/Heaven help sb** ⇨ help; **honest to God/goodness** ⇨ honest; **in the lap of the gods** ⇨ lap; **put the fear of God into/up sb** ⇨ fear; **thank God!** ⇨ thank; **there but for the**

grace of God ⇨ grace; **work all the hours God sends** ⇨ work

godmother a/sb's **fairy godmother** ⇨ fairy

goes anything **goes** ⇨ anything; **there sb goes = there you go** ⇨ there

going(s)

be good 'going or **be not bad 'going** (*informal*) be good progress: *'It only took me two hours to get to Birmingham.' 'That's good going.'* ○ *'I've written 20 pages today.' 'That's good going.'*

get out, leave, etc while the ,going is 'good leave a situation, organization, etc which is likely to have big problems in the future, before the problems start: *He thinks the company is going to go bankrupt soon, so he's getting out while the going is good.*

have a lot, something, nothing, etc 'going for you have many, some, no, etc achievements, skills, advantages, etc: *As the very intelligent daughter of rich parents, she's got a lot going for her.* ○ *No job, no qualifications, nowhere to live. He doesn't have much going for him, does he?*

comings and goings ⇨ comings; **heavy going** ⇨ heavy; **not know whether you are coming or going** ⇨ know

gold

,all that ,glitters/,glistens/,glisters is not 'gold (*saying*) not everything that seems good, attractive, etc is actually good, etc: *Don't imagine that because they are rich, they are happy. All that glitters is not gold.*

a 'gold mine a very profitable business; a very good source of sth: *That camera shop of his is a real gold mine.*

(as) good as 'gold (of children) very well-behaved: *The children were good as gold. They sat quietly and read all afternoon.*

like 'gold dust very difficult to obtain because everybody wants it/them: *You can't get those new trainers anywhere. They're like gold dust.*

be worth your/its weight in gold ⇨ worth; **have a heart of gold** ⇨ heart; **strike gold** ⇨ strike

golden

the 'golden age (of sth) the period during which sth is best, happiest, or most prosperous: *This book looks back on the golden age of steam engines, and all railway fans will enjoy it immensely.* ○ *Some people think that the reign of Elizabeth the First was a golden age in England.*

a 'golden boy a young man who is very successful and popular: *He had been the golden boy of English cricket.*

a golden 'handshake a large sum of money given to sb when they retire or leave an important job: *The directors will each get a large golden handshake and a pension.*

the golden 'rule the most important rule, principle, etc to remember when you are doing sth: *When you're playing a stroke in golf, the golden rule is to keep your eye on the ball.*

kill the goose that lays the golden egg/ eggs ⇨ kill; **silence is golden** ⇨ silence

gone **dead and buried/gone** ⇨ dead; **far gone** ⇨ far

good

as good as... so close to sth happening that you consider that it has happened: *I thought the car was as good as sold and then the man suddenly decided not to buy it.* ○ *She as good as told me she would come.*

be good for sth **1** be likely to be able to give or provide sth: *I'll ask my aunt if she can help us. She'll be good for a few pounds, I'm sure.* **2** be likely to live, last, etc for a period of time: *This car's probably good for another 20000 miles.*

do 'good be kind and generous to people who need help, for example do voluntary work for a charity: *She tries to do good by visiting prisoners' families.* **do-gooder** (*noun*) (*informal, disapproving*) a person who tries to do good, especially in an unrealistic or interfering way.

do sb 'good benefit sb: *A holiday at the seaside would do you a lot of good.*

for 'good permanently; for ever: *I'm going away for good.* ○ *Today I finished with smoking for good.*

for good or ill (used for reminding sb that they must be responsible for their decisions, actions, etc) whether the effect of an action, fact, etc is good or bad: *Look, for good or ill,* *you chose this profession. You can't just leave it now.*

for your, etc (own) good (of sth unpleasant) so that you will benefit: *I don't like criticizing you but it's for your own good.* ○ *I know you don't want to do all this extra homework, but it's for your own good.*

a good 'few quite a large number: *They've been here a good few years now.*

good for 'you, etc or **good 'on you, etc** (used for saying that you approve of sb's actions, or wish to congratulate them on a particular success): *'I've decided to give up smoking as from tomorrow.' 'Good for you, Philip.'* ○ *'He's saving up his pocket money to buy a football.' 'Good for him.'*

make 'good (*informal*) become rich and successful, especially when you have started your life poor and unknown: *He's a local boy made good.*

make good sth 1 pay for, replace or repair sth that has been damaged or lost: *The suitcase went missing at the airport so the airline have agreed to make good the loss.* ○ *The mechanic explained that they would have to make good the damage to the body of the car before they resprayed it.* **2** do what you promised, threatened, intended, etc to do: *When she became President she made good her promise to promote more women to top jobs.*

to the 'good 1 in profit: *She bought the painting for £250 and then sold it for £550, so she's £300 to the good, lucky woman.* **2** of benefit to sb/sth: *'I'm afraid we've arrived a bit early.' 'Don't worry. It's all to the good. It means we can start the meeting earlier.'*

up to no 'good (*informal*) doing or planning sth naughty, illegal, dishonest, etc: *He doesn't work but he seems to have lots of money. I'm sure he's up to no good.* ○ *Where have those children gone? I'm sure they're up to no good.*

be good going ⇨ going; **be no good/use to man or beast** ⇨ man; **do sb/sth a power/world of good** ⇨ power; **good as gold** ⇨ gold; **good grief!** ⇨ grief; **in good faith** ⇨ faith; **in safe/good hands** ⇨ hands; **so far, so good** ⇨ far

goodbye
kiss/say goodbye to sth or **kiss sth goodbye** (*informal*) give up hope of getting

sth that you want very much: *You'll have to say goodbye to your chances of becoming a doctor if you don't pass the exams.* ○ *After this letter from the bank manager, we can kiss goodbye to our holiday in Australia.*

goodness God/goodness/Heaven knows ⇨ knows; **honest to God/goodness** ⇨ honest

goods
come up with/deliver/produce the 'goods (*informal*) do what you are expected or have promised to do: *You can depend on him to come up with the goods. If he says he's going to do something, he always does it.*

goose cook sb's goose ⇨ cook; **kill the goose that lays the golden egg/eggs** ⇨ kill; **she/he would not say boo to a goose** ⇨ say; **what's sauce for the goose is sauce for the gander** ⇨ sauce; **a wild-goose chase** ⇨ wild

gospel
take sth as/for gospel (truth) believe sth without questioning it or without any real proof: *You can't always take what he says as gospel; she's not the most honest person in the world.* ○ *It would be foolish to take everything in the newspapers for gospel.*

grabs be up for grabs ⇨ up

grace(s)
have the grace to do sth be polite enough to do sth: *Fortunately, she had the grace to apologize as soon as she realized she had offended them.* ○ *He didn't even have the grace to say thank you.*

there but for the grace of God (go I) (*saying*) (used of sb who is in a very unfortunate situation) if circumstances had been different, I might have been in the same situation.

with (a) good/bad grace (do or accept sth unpleasant, unfair, boring, etc) cheerfully and without complaining/unwillingly and in a bad-tempered way: *It is very important in sport to accept defeat with good grace.* ○ *I've never seen anybody do anything with such bad grace.*

airs and graces ⇨ airs **fall from grace** ⇨ fall; **a saving grace** ⇨ saving

grade

make the 'grade (*informal*) reach a high enough standard in an exam, a job, etc: *You'll never make the grade if you don't work hard before the exams.* ○ *Do you think she'll ever make the grade as a journalist?*

grain

(go) against the 'grain be against sb's natural tendencies, instincts or customs: *Voting for the Social Democratic Party goes against the grain with him. He's voted Conservative all his life.* ○ *It goes against the grain for her to spend a lot of money on clothes.* (refers to the grain (direction of the lines) in wood)

grand

a/the ,grand old 'man (of sth) an old man who is very experienced and respected in a particular profession, etc: *At eighty, he is the grand old man of the British film industry.*

grandeur **delusions of grandeur** ⇨ delusions

grandmother **teach your grand-mother to suck eggs** ⇨ teach

granted

take sth for 'granted believe that sth is/will be true, will happen, etc without checking to make sure: *We took it for granted that there would be some rooms available at the hotel but we were wrong.* ○ *He took it for granted that he would get the job, and so he was very surprised when he didn't.*

take sb/sth for 'granted not value sb/sth just because she/he/it is always there: *Your problem is that you take your wife for granted. When was the last time that you told her how much you appreciated her?* ○ *We take so many things for granted these days: electricity, running water, cars....*

grapes **sour grapes** ⇨ sour

grasp

grasp the 'nettle deal with a difficult matter, firmly and with courage: *The government will have to grasp the nettle. If they don't the problem of illegal parking is going to get out of control.*

clutch/grasp at a straw/straws ⇨ straw

grass

the grass is greener on the other 'side (of the fence/hill) (*saying*) things always seem better in another place, job, etc: *She says she would be able to do business better in France, but the grass is always greener on the other side!*

the grass 'roots the ordinary people in an organization, for example a political party or trade union, and not the officials: *The leaders of this union are losing contact with their members. They need to get back in touch with the grass roots.* **grass-roots** (*adjective*) *a grass-roots movement*

not let the grass grow under your feet be very active and do the things that need to be done very quickly: *The new owner didn't let the grass grow under her feet, and immediately started to change the whole layout of the shop.* ○ *'What's your new boss like?' 'Very dynamic: he doesn't let the grass grow under his feet at all.'*

put/turn/send sb out to 'grass (*informal, humorous*) make sb retire from their job because they are too old to be useful: *Old Harry doesn't seem able to remember anything nowadays. Isn't it time he was put out to grass?* (refers to old farm horses, etc which no longer work and stay in the fields all day)

a snake in the grass ⇨ snake

grasshopper **knee-high to a grasshopper** ⇨ knee

grateful **be grateful/thankful for small mercies** ⇨ small

grave **dig your own grave** ⇨ dig; **from the cradle to the grave** ⇨ cradle; **have one foot in the grave** ⇨ foot; **turn in her/his grave** ⇨ turn

gravy

the 'gravy train (*informal*) (of a particular job or situation) an easy way of getting a lot of money and other benefits: *Banking and financial services produce very high earnings, and a lot of people are trying to get onto the gravy train.* ○ *Why do Members of Parliament keep going on foreign tours? It's just a gravy train, as far as I can see.*

grease

grease sb's 'palm (*informal*) give sb money to get information from, influence them, etc; bribe sb.

like greased lightning (*informal*) very fast: *After the phone call, he was out of the door like greased lightning.*

great

be no great shakes (*informal*) be not very good, efficient, suitable, etc: *He's no great shakes as a teacher.* ○ *'What did you think of the film?' 'It's no great shakes.'*

go great guns (usually in the continuous tenses) do sth with energy or vigour; make good progress: *She's half way through the race, and is going great guns.* ○ *He's going great guns on his new book at the moment.*

a good/great many ⇨ many; **great/tall oaks from little acorns grow** ⇨ oaks; **turn sth to great advantage = turn sth to your (own) advantage** ⇨ turn

Greek

be (all) ,Greek to 'sb (*informal*) be too difficult for sb to understand: *This contract is written in such complicated language that it's all Greek to me.*

green

green about the gills (*informal*) looking or feeling as if you are going to vomit, especially at sea; seasick: *You look a bit green about the gills. Go up on deck and get some fresh air.*

the green-eyed monster (*humorous*) jealousy: *In next week's programme we'll be looking at the green-eyed monster, jealousy.* (from Shakespeare's play, *Othello*)

green fingers also (*US*) **a green thumb** (*informal*) skill as a gardener: *I do envy you your green fingers. Your garden always looks so beautiful.*

green with envy very envious: *He was green with envy when he saw their expensive new car.*

give sb/get the green 'light (*informal*) allow sb/be allowed to begin sth: *The council has given the green light for work to begin on the new shopping centre.* ○ *As soon as we get the green light, we'll start advertising for new staff.* (refers to traffic lights)

greener the grass is greener on the other side ⇨ grass

greetings season's greetings ⇨ season

grey

a 'grey area an area of law, policy, etc which is not clear because it does not fall into an existing category: *The question of police evidence in cases like this is a grey area. We will need to consult our lawyers about it.*

'grey matter (*informal*) intelligence or mental powers: *Mark hasn't got much grey matter, but he tries hard.*

(men in) grey suits people such as the managers of a political party, senior civil servants, political advisers, etc who have power but are not known to the public: *It will be the men in grey suits who decide whether the Prime Minister stays or goes.*

grief

come to 'grief be destroyed or ruined; have an accident and hurt yourself: *Many ships have come to grief on these rocks.* ○ *All our plans have come to grief.* ○ *I was riding my bike very fast round that corner when I hit a stone and came to grief over there.*

good grief! (*informal*) (used for expressing surprise or disbelief): *Good grief! You're not going out dressed like that, are you?*

grim

hang on/hold on (to sth) like grim 'death hold on to sth very tight, usually because you are afraid to let go or determined not to let go: *As the horse galloped off, you could see poor Sarah hanging on like grim death.* ○ *The muggers tried to steal my bag, but I held on to it like grim death.*

grin

grin and 'bear it (*informal*) accept sth unpleasant without complaining: *If the holiday is a disaster, you'll just have to grin and bear it.*

grin like a Cheshire cat smile broadly in a foolish or self-satisfied way: *She sat there grinning like a Cheshire cat while we tried to put the tent up.* (refers to the Cheshire cat in Lewis Carroll's story, *Alice in Wonderland*)

grind

grind to a 'halt/'standstill stop slowly:

The machines ground to a halt as the power supply stopped. ○ *All work on the building has ground to a halt because of a shortage of materials.* ○ *Every Friday night traffic grinds to a halt in Hammersmith.* (refers to the way a very large machine stops working)

have an axe to grind ⇨ axe

grindstone keep your nose to the grindstone ⇨ nose

grip
take/get a 'grip/'hold on yourself (*informal*) make an effort to control your feelings, especially in a difficult situation: *I know you're nervous, but you must get a grip on yourself. You're due to go on stage in five minutes.* ○ *Look, Ben, get a grip, will you. If we panic now, we'll be finished.*

lose your grip ⇨ lose

grips
come/get to grips with sb/sth begin to understand or to deal properly with a person, problem, subject, etc: *The government has yet to get to grips with the problem of homelessness.* ○ *I'm trying to get to grips with Russian grammar.*

grist
grist for/to sb's 'mill (of an experience, piece of information, etc) useful to sb: *As a novelist, I feel that any experience, good or bad, is grist to my mill.* (refers to corn which is going to be ground in a mill)

grit
grit your 'teeth not show that you are angry, disappointed, unhappy about doing sth, etc: *When I was a boy, I was forced to have a cold shower every morning. I hated it but I just had to grit my teeth and bear it.* ○ *She shouted at me but I just gritted my teeth and said nothing.*

ground
be, come, get, etc in on the ground 'floor (*informal*) become involved at the beginning of a plan, company, organization, etc and possibly profit from this later: *Reg's investment paid off – he came in on the ground floor and saw the value of his money double in two years.*

get sth off/get off the ground (of a plan, project, etc) get sth started successfully/start

successfully: *By this time next year the new company should be just getting off the ground.* ○ *We're looking for a new manager to help get this project off the ground.*

give/lose 'ground (to sb/sth) allow sb/sth to become more powerful, influential, popular, etc than yourself: *The government has recently lost ground to the opposition, according to the opinion polls.*

go to ground go into hiding in order to escape the police, etc: *He's gone to ground somewhere in Spain, so they'll never get him.* (refers to a fox hiding underground)

hold/stand your 'ground defend and maintain your position in a battle or argument: *In spite of the enemy's fierce attack, we stood our ground and eventually they had to retreat.* ○ *After arguing about future policy for three hours, he was still standing his ground.*

on the 'ground among ordinary people or people closely involved in sth: *Our people on the ground say that there is general dissatisfaction with the party leader.* ○ *And now for some on the ground reaction to the bombings, let's go over to our correspondent in the province.*

be on firm ground ⇨ firm; **break fresh/ new ground** ⇨ break; **cut the ground from under sb/sb's feet** ⇨ cut; **gain ground** ⇨ gain; **a happy hunting ground** ⇨ happy; **have/keep both/your feet on the ground** ⇨ feet; **keep/have an/your ear close to the ground** ⇨ ear; **prepare the ground** ⇨ prepare; **run sb/ sth into the ground** ⇨ run; **run sb/sth to earth/ground** ⇨ run; **shift your ground** ⇨ shift; **suit sb down to the ground** ⇨ suit; **thin on the ground** ⇨ thin

grow great/tall oaks from little acorns grow ⇨ oaks; **money doesn't grow on trees** ⇨ money; **not let the grass grow under your feet** ⇨ grass

growing
'growing pains the problems, difficulties, etc which occur in the early stages of sth: *The troubles that are affecting the three-year-old republic are more than just growing pains.*

guard
be on/off your 'guard be prepared/not be prepared for sth, for example an attack, a danger, a surprise, etc to happen: *We must*

all be on our guard against bomb attacks. ○ *He hit me while I was off my guard.* (refers to sword fighting or fencing)

stand 'guard (over sb/sth) act as a guard: *Two soldiers stood guard over the captured weapons.*

catch sb off guard ⇨ catch; **the old guard** ⇨ old

guess

'anybody's guess (*informal*) nobody knows: *Who will win the match is anybody's guess.*

at a 'guess as a rough estimate: *At a guess, I would say there were about thirty people in the room.*

guess 'what (*informal*) (used to introduce sth surprising or exciting that you want to tell sb): *Guess what, Angela's getting married next month.*

your guess is as good as mine (*informal*) neither of us knows the answer: *'If the government knows how to run the country, why aren't things getting any better?' 'Your guess is as good as mine!'*

an educated guess ⇨ educated; **no prizes for guessing sth** ⇨ prizes

guest

be my 'guest (*informal*) (used for replying to a request) please do as you wish: *'May I look at this book?' 'Be my guest!'* ○ *'Could I switch on the television?' 'Be my guest.'*

gullet stick in your throat/craw/gullet ⇨ stick

gum

by 'gum! (*becoming dated, informal*) (used as an expression of surprise): *By gum! You've grown. You'll be as big as your father soon.*

gum up the 'works (*informal*) make progress or an activity impossible: *The building was going well, but the delay in delivering more bricks has really gummed up the works.* (the works are the moving parts of an engine)

up a 'gum tree (*informal*) in a very difficult or awkward situation: *I've got bills to pay and the bank refuses to lend me any more money. I'm really up a gum tree.* (refers to the opossum which hides up a eucalyptus (gum) tree when it is being hunted)

gun(s)

hold a gun to sb's head/have a gun to your head (*informal*) force sb/be forced to do sth: *He had to sack a hundred workers last week. He didn't want to, but the bank was holding a gun to his head.* ○ *'Why did he go back to his wife?' 'Because he had a gun to his head. She said she would never let him see the children again.'*

go great guns ⇨ great; **jump the gun** ⇨ jump; **spike sb's guns** ⇨ spike; **stick to your guns** ⇨ stick

gut(s)

have (got) the guts (to do sth) (*informal*) have the courage (to do sth): *She didn't have the guts to tell him she was going to live in Australia.* ○ *He'll never agree to sail across the Atlantic with you. He hasn't got the guts.*

have sb's guts for garters (*informal, humorous*) punish sb severely: *She'd have my guts for garters if she knew I'd lent you her car.*

slog/sweat your 'guts out (*informal*) work very hard: *I've slogged my guts out digging this ditch, and I'm completely exhausted.* ○ *You sweat your guts out all your life and what do you get when you retire? Next to nothing.*

bust a gut ⇨ bust; **hate sb's guts** ⇨ hate

gutter

the gutter press popular newspapers which print sensational news stories and scandal: *Somebody must control the gutter press in this country.*

guy

a tough guy ⇨ tough; **a wise guy** ⇨ wise

H

habit

make a 'habit/'practice of sth do sth regularly: *I don't usually make a practice of staying up so late, but there was a film on TV I wanted to watch.*

a creature of habit ⇨ creature; **force of habit** ⇨ force

hackles

make sb's 'hackles rise *or* **raise hackles** make sb angry: *He really makes my hackles rise, that man. He's so rude to everybody.* ○ *Her remarks certainly raised hackles.* (a dog's *hackles* are the hairs on the back if its neck. These hairs often rise when the dog is angry or irritated.)

hair

get in sb's 'hair annoy sb by preventing them from doing sth: *I can do the housework much more quickly when the children aren't getting in my hair all the time.*

the hair of the 'dog (that bit you) (*informal*) an alcoholic drink taken in the morning in order to help cure the unpleasant effects of drinking too much alcohol the night before: *'Why are you drinking whisky at 8 o'clock in the morning?' 'Hair of the dog. I've got the most terrible hangover this morning.'* (in the past, if a person was bitten by a dog, burnt hair from the same dog was used as a protection against infection)

a ˌhair's 'breadth a very small distance or amount: *He escaped death by a hair's breadth. If the other car had been going any faster, he would certainly have been killed.* ○ *She was within a hair's breadth of winning.*

sb's 'hair stands on end (*informal*) sb feels very frightened, nervous or angry: *This is a film which will make your hair stand on end.* ○ *When I first read the report my hair stood on end.*

(not) harm, etc a hair of sb's 'head (not) harm, etc sb in any way at all: *If he harms a hair of my daughter's head, I'll kill him.*

keep your 'hair on *or* **keep your 'shirt on** (*informal*) (used for telling sb who is angry or very excited about sth to keep calm): *Keep your shirt on, Alan. We've got plenty of time to get to the airport.* ○ *Keep your hair on, Mum. You can hardly see the damage.*

let your 'hair down (*informal*) relax completely and enjoy yourself, especially after a period when you have not been able to do so: *It was a great party and we all let our hair down.* ○ *Why don't you let your hair down? Come out with us for a few drinks at the pub.*

make sb's 'hair curl (*informal, humorous*) shock or disturb sb: *The film contained some sex scenes that were enough to make your hair curl.*

not a hair out of place looking very smart, well-dressed, etc: *How does she manage to look so good at the end of a long journey? There's never a hair out of place.*

not turn a hair ⇨ turn; **tear your hair** ⇨ tear

hairs

put 'hairs on your chest (*informal, humorous*) (especially of alcoholic drink) make you feel strong, etc: *This Polish vodka will put hairs on your chest.*

get/have sb by the short hairs ⇨ short; **split hairs** ⇨ split

hale

hale and 'hearty (especially of old people) strong and healthy: *She was still hale and hearty in her nineties.*

half

sth and a 'half (*informal*) (used for emphasizing the size, value, importance, intensity, etc of sth): *That was a meal and a half. I haven't eaten so well for months.*

your better/other 'half (*informal, humorous*) your wife or husband: *I'll have to ask my better half about that.*

give sb half a chance (to do sth) (*informal*) give sb even a small opportunity (to do sth): *Given half a chance, I'd go and work in the USA, but it's so difficult to get a visa.* ○ *If* *you give him half a chance, he'll show how well he can do the job.*

go off at ‚half 'cock (*informal*) start without enough preparation, so that results are unsatisfactory: *Let's not go off at half cock. We must get enough people together before we start the game.*

half the battle (complete, achieve, etc) the most difficult part of sth: *If you manage to keep calm when you're taking your driving test, that's half the battle.*

half the fun, trouble, etc of sth (*informal*) much or a great deal of the enjoyment, etc of sth: *Half the pleasure of coming home is finding out what's been happening while you were away.* ○ *'The team should play better with a new manager.' 'That's half the trouble – everybody expects too much of him.'*

half a loaf is better than none/no bread (*saying*) you should be grateful for sth, even if it is not as good, much, etc as you really wanted; something is better than nothing.

half a minute, tick, second, etc (*informal*) (wait) a very short time: *I'll be with you in half a moment! I've just got to put my coat on.* ○ *Just give me half a tick, will you. I've left the keys upstairs.*

the half of it only some of the facts of a particular situation, not all of them: *The public knows that he's had an affair with his secretary, but that's only the half of it.* ○ *'I hear you've been having trouble with the new managers.' 'You don't know the half of it, Ray. It's been an absolute nightmare.'*

'half the time (*informal*) most of the time: *Do tell me whether you are coming home for lunch or not. I don't know where you are half the time.* ○ *Half the time, I don't understand a word he says.*

have half a mind to 'do sth (*informal*) have a strong desire to do sth, although you probably won't do it: *I've half a mind to tell him what I think of him.* ○ *I've half a mind to sell my car and buy a new one.*

how the 'other half lives the life of people in circumstances very different from your own, especially those much richer or poorer: *You should go and see the homeless in our big cities, then you'd know how the other half lives.* ○ *Look at these photos of houses in*

Hollywood and see how the other half lives.

in 'half the time in a much shorter time than expected: *I don't think much of his work. I could have done the same job in half the time, and much better too.*

no half measures (used for emphasizing that you want sth done as well, fully, etc as possible): *He entertained the visitors very well indeed. There were no half measures: the best food, the best wine, the best silver. . . .*

‚not 'half (*informal*) (used for saying that sth is certainly true, the case, etc): *'Is the film at the Odeon worth seeing, do you think?' 'Yes, not half. It's the best film I've seen for months.'* ○ *'Is it hot out in the garden?' 'Not half. It's much too hot for me.'*

not half as good, nice, etc as sb/sth not nearly as good, nice, etc as sb/sth: *She's not half as nice as her sister.* ○ *His new book isn't half as interesting as his last one.*

too clever, etc by 'half (*informal, disapproving*) much too clever, etc: *That boy is too charming by half – he can get you to do anything he wants.* ○ *I don't like her at all – she's too clever by half.*

listen with half an ear ⇨ listen; **it's six of one and half a dozen of the other** ⇨ six

halfway

a ‚halfway 'house **1** (for people leaving prison, a psychiatric hospital, etc) a place where you can stay for a period of time, under supervision, before you find a more suitable place to live: *We're opening several halfway houses for people who've been in this hospital.* **2** a compromise between two plans, wishes, etc: *We really wanted to build a completely new hospital, but we didn't have the money, so this extension is a kind of halfway house.*

meet sb halfway ⇨ meet

hallmarks

have all the hallmarks of sth/sb have all the characteristics or typical features of sth/sb: *The burglary had all the hallmarks of a professional job.* (refers to the marks on gold and silver objects which tell you where and when they were made)

halt **call a halt** ⇨ call; **grind to a halt/ standstill** ⇨ grind

halved a trouble shared is a trouble halved ⇨ trouble

halves

do nothing/not do anything by 'halves do sth as well, completely, enthusiastically, etc as you can: *She does nothing by halves. When she decided to write a book, it was 1000 pages long.*

go 'halves with sb (*informal*) share the total cost of sth equally with sb else: *If you drive me up to Manchester, we'll go halves on the petrol.*

hammer

go/be at sb/sth ,hammer and 'tongs (*informal*) do sth, especially argue with sb, in a very vigorous and forceful way: *The boss went at me hammer and tongs. I've never seen him so angry.* ○ *The couple in the flat upstairs are always at each other hammer and tongs.* (refers to the noise made by a blacksmith at work)

go/come under the 'hammer be offered for sale at an auction: *The house and all its contents are to come under the hammer next Thursday.* (the auctioneer hits the table with a hammer to show that he has accepted the highest offer)

drive/hammer sth home ⇨ home

hammering

give sb/get a hammering (*informal*) beat sb/be beaten severely or easily; punish sb/be punished hard: *Real Madrid gave Milan a hammering in the European Cup.* ○ *When I was small, I once stole some money from my mother. I got a real hammering when she found out.*

hand

ask for/win sb's hand (*dated*) ask for/get permission to marry sb: *'Did John ask your father for your hand?' 'No. Nobody does that any more, do they?'*

at 'hand near in place or time: *Some people think that the end of the world is at hand.* ○ *It's a very convenient place to live. We've got everything at hand – shops, schools, and a library.*

bind/tie sb hand and 'foot remove or restrict sb's freedom of action or movement: *Staying at home to look after a sick parent often means that a person is tied hand and foot.* ○ *I can* do nothing to help you because I'm bound hand and foot by my present contract.

by 'hand 1 (of a letter, etc) to be sent by personal messenger rather than through the postal service 2 made/done without using machinery: *Several local farmers still milk their cows by hand.* ○ *These wine glasses were made by hand.*

get out of 'hand become uncontrollable: *How can we stop increases in wages and prices getting out of hand?* ○ *The student teacher saw that the class was getting completely out of hand, so he had to ask for help.*

give sb a 'hand (with sth) help sb (to do sth): *I can't lift this piano on my own. Can you give me a hand, John?* ○ *Could you give me a hand with these suitcases please?* also **need a hand (with sth)** need help (to do sth): *Do you need a hand (with the washing-up)?*

go hand in 'hand (with sth) be closely connected (with sth): *Poverty tends to go hand in hand with disease, and raising people's incomes usually helps to improve their health.* ○ *A bad economic situation and rising crime go hand in hand.*

'hand/'give it to sb (*informal*) (usually with must/have (got) to) admit, perhaps unwillingly, that you admire sb for their skill, achievements, determination, etc: *You have to hand it to him; he certainly knows how to play tennis.* ○ *To be honest, I didn't think she could cook, but I have to hand it to her. Tonight's meal was fantastic.*

,hand in 'glove (with sb) very closely associated with sb, usually in sth dishonest: *The terrorists are working hand in glove with the drug smugglers.* ○ *They are hand in glove with the secret police.*

,hand in 'hand (of people) holding each other's hand, usually as a sign of affection: *The lovers walked along the river bank, hand in hand.*

hand sb sth on a plate (*informal*) give sb sth without them having to make any effort to get it: *She was handed the job on a plate. Somebody just telephoned her one afternoon and asked her if she'd like to work for the BBC.* ○ *Nobody's going to just hand you a contract on a plate.*

,hand to 'hand (of fighting) using your hands, fists, etc: *Soldiers are trained to fight hand to hand.* **hand-to-hand** (*adjective*)

There are reports of hand-to-hand fighting outside the city.

have/take a hand in (doing) sth be involved in (doing) sth, especially sth bad, wrong, etc: *We think all three of you had a hand in planning the robbery. So, come on, confess.* ○ *I'm sure he had a hand in creating this problem.*

in 'hand 1 (of a task, matter, etc) now being dealt with, thought about, discussed, etc: *Let's stop talking about other subjects and get back to the matter in hand.* **2** still to be used, played, spent, etc; remaining: *The two teams have an equal number of points, but Liverpool still has a game in hand.* ○ *The club still has money in hand for the improvements.*

keep your 'hand in practise a skill occasionally, so that you do not lose it: *The director likes to teach a class occasionally, just to keep her hand in.*

lift/raise a 'hand against sb threaten to hit sb: *She never raised a hand against her son because she didn't believe in hitting children.*

on either/every hand on both/all sides; in every direction: *We were surrounded on every hand by dancing couples.*

on 'hand near and available; present: *We have to have a doctor on hand in case of emergency.* ○ *In an international hotel like this, you can have fax machines and computers, as well as secretaries and interpreters, on hand.*

on (the) one hand…on the other (hand) (used to show two different aspects of the same situation): *On the one hand, it's very cheap living here. On the other, it costs a lot to get home!*

out of 'hand immediately and without further thought or consideration: *They rejected my suggestion out of hand.*

put your ˌhand in(to) your 'pocket spend or give money: *One of our colleagues is retiring, so I expect they'll want us to put our hands into our pockets for a present.* ○ *He's one of the meanest men I know. He never puts his hand in his pocket for anything.*

show/reveal your 'hand do sth which reveals your intentions, plans, etc: *In court a good lawyer does not reveal his hand too soon.* (refers to showing your cards in card playing)

ˌtake sb/sth in 'hand begin to control or look after sb/sth, especially in order to make improvements in their behaviour, their performance, etc: *That child is very badly behaved; someone should take her in hand.* ○ *The new manager hopes to take the organization in hand, because in recent months it has been in chaos.*

to 'hand (have sth) with or near you; (be) readily available: *I don't seem to have my diary to hand at the moment – can I ring you back and make an appointment?* ○ *She had all the necessary information to hand.*

with one hand tied behind your back (*informal*) **1** unable to use your full powers: *The government has one hand tied behind its back in these negotiations.* **2** very easily; with little effort: *She could run the restaurant with one hand tied behind her back.*

with your hand on your heart speaking very honestly and sincerely: *I can tell you with my hand on my heart that I never took any money out of your purse.* ○ *How can you stand there with your hand on your heart and tell me that you have never been unfaithful to me?*

at first hand ⇨ **first**; **be a dab hand at sth** ⇨ **dab**; **a bird in the hand is worth two in the bush** ⇨ **bird**; **bite the hand that feeds you** ⇨ **bite**; **a firm hand** ⇨ **firm**; **force sb's hand** ⇨ **force**; **give sb a big hand** ⇨ **big**; **go cap in hand** ⇨ **cap**; **get, have, etc a free hand** ⇨ **free**; **have sb eating out of your hand** ⇨ **eating**; **have your fingers/hand in the till** ⇨ **till**; **have sb in the palm of your hand** ⇨ **palm**; **a helping hand** ⇨ **helping**; **hold sb's hand** ⇨ **hold**; **an iron fist/hand in a velvet glove** ⇨ **iron**; **know sth like the back of your hand** ⇨ **know**; **the left hand does not know what the right hand is doing** ⇨ **left**; **lend a hand** ⇨ **lend**; **make, etc sth by/with your own fair hand** ⇨ **fair**; **make money hand over fist** ⇨ **money**; **an old hand at sth** ⇨ **old**; **ready to hand** ⇨ **ready**; **your right-hand man** ⇨ **right**; **rule with a rod of iron/with an iron hand** ⇨ **rule**; **shake sb by the hand = shake hands** ⇨ **shake**; **sleight of hand** ⇨ **sleight**; **strengthen your hand** ⇨ **strengthen**; **throw your hand in** ⇨ **throw**; **try your hand** ⇨ **try**; **the upper hand** ⇨ **upper**; **wait on sb**

hand and foot ⇨ wait; **the whip hand** ⇨ whip

handle

get a handle on sb/sth (*informal*) become familiar with and so understand sb/sth: *I can't really get a handle on the situation here. What's happening?*

fly off the handle ⇨ fly; **too hot to handle = (too) hot for sb** ⇨ hot

hands

all ˌhands to the ˈpump *or* **all ˌhands on ˈdeck** (*saying, humorous*) everybody helps or must help, especially in an emergency: *When the kitchen staff became ill, it was all hands to the pump and even the manager did some cooking.* ○ *There are 30 people coming to dinner tonight, so it's all hands on deck.* (a *hand* is a sailor)

get/lay your ˈhands on sb (used mostly in threats) catch sb who has done sth wrong: *Just wait until I get my hands on the person who stole my bike!*

get/lay your hands on ˈsth obtain sth that you want or need very much: *Do you know where I can get my hands on a Russian dictionary? I need to check a translation.* ○ *I would buy a new car if only I could lay my hands on the money.*

sb's hands are tied sb cannot do sth because of certain responsibilities, duties, rules, etc: *I'm afraid my hands are tied. I can't allow anyone to bring visitors to the club. It's against the rules.*

(keep your) ˌhands ˈoff sb/sth do not touch, harm, etc sb/sth; do not criticize sb/sth: *There was a demonstration against the Government's education policy, with banners reading 'Hands off our schools!'* ○ *Those cakes are for tea, so hands off!* ○ *Keep your hands off my tools, please.*

have (got) your ˈhands full be very busy: *I've got my hands full looking after four children.* ○ *You look as if you've got your hands full today. Would you like me to help you?*

in sb's ˈhands in the control of sb or sb's responsibility: *I'll leave the matter entirely in your hands.* ○ *The future of the industry now lies in the hands of the Government.*

in safe/good ˈhands well cared for by a responsible person or organization, and unlikely to be harmed or damaged: *When the child is with my mother, I know she's in good hands.* ○ *It's a good hospital. I'm sure he's in safe hands.*

many hands make light work (*saying*) a task is done easily if a lot of people share the work.

off sb's ˈhands no longer the responsibility of sb: *Now that the children are off my hands, I've got more time for other things.*

on sb's ˈhands 1 (of work, etc) to do: *I've got a lot of work on my hands at the moment.* **2** for which/whom sb is responsible: *I've got the neighbour's children on my hands this afternoon.*

on your hands and knees with your knees, toes and hands on the ground: *The tunnel was so low in places that we had to crawl along on our hands and knees.* ○ *She was down on her hands and knees looking for her earring.*

ˌout of sb's ˈhands no longer in the control of or the responsibility of sb: *I'm afraid the matter is now out of my hands. You'll have to write to the Area Manager.*

take sth/sb off sb's hands take sth away from sb who no longer wants it or take a responsibility from sb who needs a rest: *I wish somebody would take this old table off my hands. I haven't room for it.* ○ *Look, you and Tony relax at the weekend, and I'll take the children off your hands for a couple of days.*

win/beat sb ˌhands ˈdown win/beat sb very easily: *England won the match hands down. The score was five nil.*

with your bare hands ⇨ bare; **the devil makes work for idle hands** ⇨ devil; **fall, etc into sb's hands** ⇨ fall; **have blood on your hands** ⇨ blood; **have clean hands** ⇨ clean; **have time on your hands** ⇨ time; **play right into sb's hands** ⇨ play; **be putty in sb's hands** ⇨ putty; **shake hands** ⇨ shake; **a show of hands** ⇨ show; **take your courage in both hands** ⇨ courage; **take the law into your own hands** ⇨ law; **take your life in your hands** ⇨ life; **take matters into your own hands** ⇨ matters; **throw up your hands/arms in horror, despair, etc** ⇨ throw; **tie sb's hands/sb's hands are tied** ⇨ tie; **wash your hands of sb/sth** ⇨ wash; **wring your hands** ⇨ wring

handshake a golden handshake
⇨ golden

handy
,come in 'handy/'useful (*informal*) be useful when needed: *Those sacks will come in handy for putting the garden rubbish in.* ○ *The money my aunt gave me will come in handy to pay for my music lessons.*

hang
can go hang (*informal*) (used for saying that you do not care about sb/sth or about what happens to sb/sth): *I don't care what the film critic of the Washington Post says about my film. As far as I'm concerned, he can just go hang.*

get the hang of sth (*informal*) learn or begin to understand how to do, use, etc sth: *I haven't yet got the hang of how to use the coffee-making machine.* ○ *It took him a long time to get the hang of all the irregular verbs.*

hang by a 'thread be in a very uncertain situation: *After the operation, his life hung by a thread for several hours.* ○ *The future of this company hangs by a thread. Unless we get two or three big orders by the end of the month, we are finished.*

hang 'fire delay or be delayed: *We'll have to hang fire on that decision, I'm afraid.* (refers to a gun which does not fire immediately)

hang your head (in/for shame) look or feel embarrassed or ashamed: *When I think of how I behaved, I have to hang my head in shame.* ○ *The thief hung his head as he was led away through the crowd.*

hang loose (*very informal, especially US*) relax and don't worry; keep calm and in control: *'What shall I do about Tony?' 'Just hang loose. Give him time to sort out his problems.'*

hang on 'in there (*very informal, especially US*) (used for encouraging sb to continue trying to achieve sth): *'I'll never get a job in the BBC.' 'Look, just hang on in there. I'm sure there'll be something soon.'*

hang on sb's 'words/every 'word listen to what sb says with great attention: *The professor was talking to a group of students, who hung on her every word.*

hang over sb's head *or* hang over sb (of a possible problem, etc) worry sb: *With the threat of job losses hanging over their heads,*

the staff are all very worried. ○ *She can't enjoy herself with all these financial problems hanging over her head.* (refers to the sword of Damocles)

hang up your boots retire from playing football, etc: *At the age of 38 he decided it was time to hang up his boots.*

hang/hold on like grim death ⇨ grim; a peg to hang sth on ⇨ peg

hanged
you may/might as well be hanged/hung for a ,sheep as (for) a 'lamb if you are going to be punished for doing sth wrong whether it is a big or small thing, you may as well do the big thing: *I'm already late but I'll stay and have another drink. May as well be hanged for a sheep as for a lamb.* (in the past people were hanged for stealing sheep)

hangs a question mark hangs over sb/sth ⇨ question; time hangs/lies heavy ⇨ time

ha'porth spoil the ship for a ha'porth/ha'penny-worth of tar ⇨ spoil

happen accidents will happen ⇨ accidents

happens
as it happens 1 by chance: *'Has anybody got a pair of scissors?' 'Yes, as it happens. I've got some in my bag.'* 2 (used for giving emphasis to a statement): *'You don't know anything about car engines, Joan.' 'Well, as it happens, I do. I did an evening course in car maintenance last year.'* ○ *'Do you like her?' 'No, as it happens, I don't.'*

happy
(as) happy as the day is 'long/as a 'sandboy/as 'Larry (*informal*) very happy: *Grandpa's as happy as a sandboy helping the children to fly their kites.*

a/the happy event (*humorous*) the birth of a baby: *'When's the happy event, then?' 'At the end of July.'*

a happy 'hunting ground 1 (*humorous*) a very good place to find what you want: *The Sunday antique market is a happy hunting ground for collectors.*

a/the happy 'medium a sensible balance between two extremes: *I like to know my colleagues well, but not too well. The sort of*

friendship I have with them now is a happy
medium. ○ In life generally we should try to find
the happy medium. Extreme solutions to
problems always lead to difficulties.

many happy re'turns (of the day)
(becoming dated) (used as a greeting to sb on
their birthday) happy birthday: Here's your
present. Many happy returns!

one big happy family ⇨ one

hard

as hard as 'nails (of a person) not
sensitive or sympathetic: She doesn't care
what happens to anybody. She's as hard as
nails.

be hard 'at it be working hard: She's been
hard at it all day. ○ When I left at six, he was
still hard at it.

be hard on sb 1 treat, criticize or
punish sb too severely: Don't be too hard on
little Emma. She didn't intend to break the
cup. **2** be unfair to sb; be unfortunate for
sb: It's hard on the doctors and nurses who have
to work on Christmas Day.

be hard 'up (informal) have very little
money: In those days we were so hard up that
meat was a real luxury.

do/learn sth the 'hard way learn sth
from experience, especially when this is
unpleasant: I learned the hard way not to trust
door-to-door salesmen. ○ Why do you always
do everything the hard way?

,hard and 'fast (of rules, etc) that cannot
be changed: These regulations are not hard and
fast. They can be changed by general consent. ○
hard and fast regulations, guidelines, etc

hard 'cash real money, not shares,
cheques, etc: How much is it worth in hard
cash?

(the) 'hard core 1 a small group of the
most active, loyal or committed members of
a larger group: We can always depend on a
hard core of about 20 members. **hard-core**
(adjective) a hard-core political
activist **2** pornography of an extreme
kind: **hard-core** (adjective) hard-core sex
magazines

hard 'done by (informal) unfairly treated: I
think you've been hard done by – you've had to
work twice as long as anyone else.

hard 'facts the real or true facts of a
situation, etc: I'm not interested in your

opinion. I want hard facts. ○ This is a newspaper
which deals in hard facts, not rumours.

a hard 'luck story a story of misfortune
which sb tells you because they want your
sympathy, money, etc: He stopped me in the
street and told me a long hard luck story about
his wife leaving him. All he really wanted was
some money for a drink. ○ Don't give me any of
your hard luck stories, John. I don't believe
them.

hard of 'hearing unable to hear well;
rather deaf: He's become rather hard of
hearing. ○ The television programme has
subtitles for the hard of hearing.

hard 'put (to it) to do sth or **hard
'pressed to do sth** able to do sth only with
great difficulty: I'd be hard put to name all the
countries in the world.

the 'hard stuff (informal) strong alcoholic
drinks like whisky, brandy, etc: a drop of the
hard stuff

make hard 'work of sth make sth more
difficult, complicated, etc than it should be: I
don't know why he's making such hard work of
his maths homework. It's really quite easy.

no hard 'feelings (used for saying that
you would still like to be friendly with sb you
have just beaten in a fight, competition,
argument, etc): When he heard that he had
won the contract, he turned to his competitor
and said, 'No hard feelings, I hope.'

too much like hard work so difficult,
tiring, etc that you do not want to do it: This
job is a bit too much like hard work for me. I'm
going to look for something easier.

bad/hard/tough luck! ⇨ luck; **die hard**
⇨ die; **drive a hard bargain** ⇨ drive; **fall
on hard times** ⇨ fall; **hard/hot on sb's
heels** ⇨ heels; **a hard/tough nut** ⇨ nut;
hit sb/sth hard ⇨ hit; **play hard to get**
⇨ play

harden

harden your heart against sb/sth no
longer be emotionally affected by sb/sth
because of your anger, bitterness, etc,
towards them/it: Doctors have to harden their
hearts against the suffering they see every day.

hare
mad as a March hare ⇨ mad; **run
with the hare and hunt with the
hounds** ⇨ run

harm

,not come to (any) 'harm or come to ,no 'harm not be injured, badly treated or damaged, etc: *The child will come to no harm if she stays there.*

out of harm's way in a place where sb/sth cannot cause or suffer injury, accident, loss, etc: *Most people think that dangerous criminals should be locked up out of harm's way.* ○ *You should put these glasses out of harm's way. They're much too valuable to use every day.*

sb would not harm/hurt a fly ⇨ fly

harness die in harness ⇨ die

Harry every/any Tom, Dick and/or Harry ⇨ Tom

hash make a mess/hash of sth/doing sth ⇨ mess

haste

more haste, less speed (*saying*) if you try to do sth quickly, you are more likely to make mistakes and so take a longer time than necessary.

marry in haste ⇨ marry; post haste ⇨ post

hat

,keep sth under your 'hat (*informal*) keep sth secret: *I'm going to apply for another job, but keep it under your hat for a while, will you?*

pick, etc sth out of a hat (*informal*) choose sb/sth completely by chance: *We couldn't decide where to go on holiday so we just picked a place out of a hat.*

take your 'hat off to sb *or* your 'hat goes ,off to sb (*informal*) (used for expressing admiration for what sb has done): *I take my hat off to the doctors and nurses of the hospital. They were magnificent.* ○ *My hat goes off to you. That's the best fish soup I've ever tasted.*

at the drop of a hat ⇨ drop; I'll eat my hat! ⇨ eat; old hat ⇨ old; pass the hat round ⇨ pass

hatch

,down the 'hatch (*informal*) (said before you drink alcohol): *He raised his glass, said, 'Down the hatch!' and then drank it all at once.*

hatchet bury the hatchet ⇨ bury

hate

,hate sb's 'guts (*informal*) dislike sb very much: *Don't invite that man to the party. I hate his guts.*

hatter mad as a hatter ⇨ mad

haul

,haul sb over the 'coals (*informal*) criticize sb very strongly for sth they have done: *I was hauled over the coals for being late.*

a long haul ⇨ long

have

and what 'have you (*informal*) similar people, things, places, etc: *If you add up the cost of petrol, oil, insurance, repairs and what have you, running a car certainly isn't cheap.*

have (got) sth 'coming (to you) (*informal*) be about to experience sth unpleasant, especially if you deserve it: *He's got a shock coming to him when he takes the exams and sees how difficult they are.* ○ *He thinks he can break all the rules; but, believe me, he's got it coming to him one day.*

have 'had it (*informal*) 1 (of sth) no longer work or function properly; fail: *This television's had it; we'll have to get a new one.* ○ *The company's had it, I'm afraid.* 2 (of sb) die or be about to die: *He's had it, I'm afraid.* 3 miss the opportunity to do sth: *We've had it. We'll never be able to get tickets this late.* 4 be unwilling to continue a relationship with sb or continue using sth: *I've had it with them. They make promises all the time, but they never keep them.*

have (got) it 'in you (to do sth) have the unexpected ability, determination, courage, etc to do sth: *She managed to finish the crossword all on her own! I didn't know she had it in her!* ○ *He stood up and gave a brilliant speech to 1000 people. I didn't know he had it in him.*

have it 'in for sb (*informal*) want to harm or cause trouble for sb because you have had a bad experience with them: *She's had it in for those boys ever since they damaged her roses.* ○ *The government has had it in for the trade unions for years.*

have (got) it made (*informal*) (be certain to) be successful; be in a very comfortable or advantageous situation: *With his brains and energy, he's got it made.* ○ *A good job, a beautiful house, lovely children: she's really got it made.*

have it 'off/a'way with sb (*very informal, offensive*) have sex with sb.

have it 'out with sb have a serious discussion with sb in order to end a disagreement, quarrel, etc: *You must stop ignoring Fred because of what he said, and have it out with him.*

'have it that... say that...; claim that...: *Rumour has it that you're going to retire. Is that true?* ○ *She will have it that her brother is a better athlete than you, but I don't believe her.*

have (got) what it takes to do sth (*informal*) have the ability, character, intelligence, etc that is needed for sth: *I enjoy painting, but I know I haven't got what it takes to be an artist.*

have/be to do with sb/sth ⇨ do; **let sb have it** ⇨ let

haves

the haves and the have-nots the rich people and the poor people: *You can see the haves and the have-nots in this city – the millionaires in their huge houses and the homeless sleeping in cardboard boxes.*

havoc

play/wreak havoc with sth cause damage, destruction or disorder with sth: *The terrible storms wreaked havoc with electricity supplies, because so many power lines were down.*

haw

hum/hem and haw = um and aah ⇨ um

hawk

watch sb/sth like a hawk ⇨ watch

hay

make hay while the 'sun shines (*saying*) make the best use of opportunities and favourable conditions while they last: *Opportunities for starting your own business will never be better, so make hay while the sun shines and go and see your bank manager today.*

haystack

like looking for/trying to find a needle in a haystack ⇨ needle

haywire

go haywire (*informal*) go out of control; start functioning or behaving in a

strange way: *My printer's gone haywire. It keeps stopping and starting.*

head

above/over sb's 'head too difficult for sb to understand: *It was clear from the expression on his face that the lecture went completely over his head.*

bang, etc your head against a brick 'wall (*informal*) try for a long time to achieve sth, persuade sb to do sth, etc without success: *I realized they weren't even listening to my protests. I was just banging my head against a brick wall.* ○ *Why do you go on asking him to help? You're banging your head against a brick wall.*

bring sth/come to a 'head cause sth to reach/reach a crisis point or state where action must be taken urgently: *Matters came to a head yesterday when an emergency meeting was called to demand the directors' resignation.* ○ *Her recent public remarks about company policy have brought matters to a head.*

bury/hide your head in the sand refuse to deal with unpleasant realities, possible dangers, etc by pretending they do not exist: *Stop burying your head in the sand, Tim. Stop pretending that everything is all right.* (refers to the ostrich, which buries its head in the sand when it is in danger)

do sth/go ,over sb's 'head do sth without telling the people who have a right to know: *He gets angry when you go over his head and talk to his boss.*

from ,head to 'foot/'toe all over your body; completely: *She was dressed from head to foot in white.* ○ *He was covered from head to foot in mud.*

get your 'head down (*informal*) **1** work or study hard: *If you want to pass that French exam, you'll have to get your head down.* **2** go to bed and sleep: *It's time to get our heads down; we have to be up early tomorrow morning.*

get your 'head round sth (*informal*) understand sth difficult, often with a lot of effort: *The plan is so complicated – I'm still trying to get my head round it.*

get sth into your/sb's (thick) head (*informal*) succeed in understanding or in making sb understand sth fully: *When are you going to get it into your head that you don't*

need to worry about money? You're rich now. ○
*I can't get it into my thick head that I'm free to
do what I want now.* ○ *I'm trying to get it into
his thick head that he's got to go.*

get/take it into your head that...
(*informal*) understand or believe sth, often
wrongly: *Somehow she's taken it into her head
that her husband is trying to poison her.*

give sb their 'head give sb the freedom to
do what they want: *We must give the new art
teacher her head, so that she has the freedom to
do things differently.* (refers to allowing a
horse to go as fast as it likes when you are
riding it)

go to sb's 'head **1** (of alcohol) make sb
feel a bit drunk: *I can't drink more than two
pints of beer – it goes to my head.* **2** (of
success, fame, praise, etc) give sb a false
sense of their importance, abilities, etc;
make sb behave in a conceited, arrogant
way, etc: *Just because you've become a film
actor, don't let it go to your head!*

have a (good) head for figures be good
at arithmetic, calculations, etc: *If you want
to be successful in business, you must have a
good head for figures.*

have a (good) head for heights be able
to stand on a high place without feeling ill or
afraid: *I won't go up the church tower with
you. I've no head for heights.*

have (got) your head in the clouds
(*informal*) not be realistic because you are
always thinking of your own hopes, ideas,
dreams, etc: *He wants us to start a business
together but it would never work. He's got his
head in the clouds half the time.*

**have your 'head screwed on (the
right way)** (*informal*) be sensible: *You can
certainly trust Ann with your money. She's got
her head screwed on the right way.*

head and 'shoulders above sb/sth
very much better, greater, etc than sb/sth:
*He's head and shoulders above the other
candidates.*

head over 'heels (in love) completely (in
love): *He's head over heels in love with her.*

sb's 'head rolls sb is dismissed from their
job or position because they have made a big
mistake: *When the spy scandal was exposed,
many said that heads should roll in the
government.* ○ *Have you seen this article about*

police corruption? Heads will roll, I'm sure.

keep your 'head think clearly and remain
calm: *If there is a robbery, you should try to
keep your head and do as you are told.*

keep your head above water succeed in
staying out of debt; manage to deal with
tasks, responsibilities, etc: *The company had
great difficulty keeping its head above water
during the economic crisis.* ○ *I don't know how
she manages to keep her head above water. She
has so much to do.*

keep your 'head down (*informal*)
1 avoid being noticed or being seen in
public: *She's so unpopular with the voters that
the Prime Minister has told her to keep her head
down until after the election.* ○ *In the army you
soon learn to keep your head down and stay out
of trouble.* **2** work very hard: *He kept his
head down for weeks before the entrance exam.*

laugh, scream, etc your 'head off
laugh, scream, etc in an extreme way: *They
were laughing their heads off at his absurd
jokes.*

(not) make head (n)or 'tail of sth
(*informal*) (used mostly in negative
sentences or in questions) (not) understand
sth at all: *I can't make head or tail of this
picture – is it upside down?*

need, want, etc your 'head examined
(*informal*) (used for saying that sb is
behaving in a mad or stupid way): *She spent
£300 on a pair of shoes? She needs her head
examined.*

on sb's head 'be it (often used for
warning sb) somebody is alone responsible
for the results of their action or decision: *You
refuse to go to your own daughter's wedding?
On your head be it!* ○ *On his own head be it if he
decides to leave university early.*

put your head in the lion's mouth
deliberately put yourself in a dangerous or
risky situation: *So I put my head in the lion's
mouth and asked my boss for a pay rise.*

put/lay your head on the block risk
defeat, failure, etc; put yourself in a situation
where you might be blamed, criticized, etc:
*The government laid its head on the block and
said that if it loses this vote in Parliament
tonight it will call an election.* ○ *I'm prepared to
put my head on the block and promise that the
new building will be ready by the end of the
year.* (refers to a person being beheaded.)

put sth out of your 'head stop thinking about or wanting sth: *I am not going to let you go to the party, so put that idea out of your head.*

rear/raise its (ugly) head (used of sth considered unpleasant) appear again after being hidden or forgotten: *Political corruption has reared its ugly head again.* ○ *Famine has raised its ugly head again in many parts of the world.*

stand/turn sth on its 'head 1 turn sth upside down **2** completely change sth; reverse sth: *He stood the argument on its head, saying that the plan wouldn't save money and would, in fact, cost more.*

take it into your head to do sth suddenly decide to do sth: *She's taken it into her head to give all her books away.*

be soft in the head ⇨ soft; **bite sb's head off** ⇨ bite; **do sth standing on your head** ⇨ standing; **enter sb's head** ⇨ enter; **sb's eyes nearly pop out of their head** ⇨ eyes; **hang your head** ⇨ hang; **hang over sb's head** ⇨ hang; **harm, etc a hair on sb's head** ⇨ hair; **have a clear head** ⇨ clear; **have eyes in the back of your head** ⇨ eyes; **have a rush of blood to the head** ⇨ rush; **head/top the bill** ⇨ bill; **hit the nail on the head** ⇨ hit; **hold a gun to sb's head** ⇨ gun; **hold your head up high** ⇨ hold; **keep a level head** ⇨ level; **knock sth on the head** ⇨ knock; **like a bear with a sore head** ⇨ bear; **lose your head** ⇨ lose; **need/want sth like a hole in the head** ⇨ hole; **off the top of your head** ⇨ top; **a price on sb's head** ⇨ price; **put ideas in sb's head = give sb ideas** ⇨ ideas; **ring in your head/ears** ⇨ ring; **a roof over your head** ⇨ roof; **scratch your head** ⇨ scratch; **shake your head** ⇨ shake; **smash sb's face/head in** ⇨ smash; **talk your head off** ⇨ talk; **talk through the back of your head** ⇨ talk

headlines

hit the 'headlines (*informal*) attract a great deal of attention from the news media: *His reputation has suffered a lot since the scandal over his love affair hit the headlines.*

heads

heads or tails (used when sb tosses a coin in the air to decide who will win, do, etc sth):

'Let's toss for it. Heads or tails?' 'Heads, please.' 'Heads it is. You win.'

knock/bang 'heads together (*informal*) (expresses irritation at other people's stupid quarrels) force people to stop quarrelling: *I'd like to bang those stupid politicians' heads together.*

put our/your/their 'heads together (*informal*) cooperate to solve a problem, etc: *If we all put our heads together, we might find a way to solve the problem.*

two heads are better than one ⇨ two

health   a clean bill of health ⇨ clean

hear

can't hear yourself think (*informal*) there is so much noise around you that you cannot concentrate: *Can you turn the volume down? I can't hear myself think in here.*

hear, hear! (called out, usually at a public meeting, etc to express agreement and approval): *'It is the wish of this government that both unemployment and inflation be reduced to acceptable levels.' 'Hear, hear!'*

hear/see the end/the last of sb/sth (often used with not, never, etc) (often of sb who you do not like, or sth which bores or irritates you) hear/see sb/sth for the last time: *We'll never hear the end of her visit to Buckingham Palace.* ○ *He says he's not going to come back to England, but I'm sure we haven't seen the last of him.*

will/would not hear of sth not allow sth to happen: *'May I pay for the phone call?' 'Don't be silly! I wouldn't hear of it!'* ○ *He won't hear of his daughter becoming a policewoman. He thinks it's much too dangerous.*

heard

you could have heard a 'pin drop it was extremely quiet: *As the Minister told Parliament of the crisis you could have heard a pin drop.*

hearing   hard of hearing ⇨ hard

heart

at 'heart (used for saying what sb is really like) really; in fact: *He seems strict but he's a very kind man at heart.*

be close/dear/near to sb's 'heart be a person or thing that sb is very fond of, concerned about, interested in, etc: *The*

113

campaign to keep our local hospital open is very close to my heart.

by 'heart (learn sth) so that you can remember it perfectly: *There was a time when I knew the poem (off) by heart.*

do sb's heart 'good make sb feel happy, more cheerful, hopeful, etc: *It did my heart good to see him looking so well.*

(come) (straight) from the heart (be) genuine and sincere: *The letter comes straight from the heart. He means every word of it.*

have a 'heart (*informal*) (used for asking sb to be sympathetic or kind): *'We'll work until midnight.' 'Have a heart, Joe. Can't we stop earlier than that?'*

have a heart of 'gold have a very kind and helpful nature, even though it's not always obvious: *I know he's often bad-tempered but really, you know, he's got a heart of gold.*

have a heart of 'stone be hard, unfeeling, cruel, etc: *Don't ask her to give any money to the fund; she's got a heart of stone.*

(your) heart and 'soul (with) all your enthusiasm, energy, sincerity, etc: *She puts her heart and soul into the job.* ○ *A dancer must throw herself heart and soul into the performance.*

your heart 'bleeds for sb (*informal, often ironic*) you feel great pity or sympathy for sb: *'I have to get up at 6 o'clock tomorrow!' 'Oh, my heart bleeds for you – I have to do that every day!'*

your heart goes out to sb you feel great pity or sympathy for sb: *My heart goes out to all those who lost relatives in the disaster.*

your heart is in your 'mouth (*informal*) you feel very anxious or afraid: *My heart was in my mouth as I waited to hear whether the jury would find me guilty or not guilty.*

sb's 'heart is in the right place sb is really a kind, generous person with the right values in life even though they do not always appear to be so: *I know she is often bad-tempered, but basically her heart is in the right place.*

sb's heart is not in it sb does not give all their enthusiasm, interest and energy to sth: *He agreed to write the book for a large sum of money, but his heart wasn't in it, and it was never finished.*

your heart misses a beat sudden fear or other strong emotion makes it seem as if your heart has stopped beating for a short time: *For a moment she thought she saw the dead man's face looking in through the window and her heart missed a beat.*

the 'heart of the matter the most central and important part of a situation, problem, etc: *And now we come to the heart of the matter. Who is going to pay for all this?*

your heart sinks suddenly you feel sad, disappointed or afraid: *My heart sank when I realized I would have to walk home in the rain.*

heart to 'heart (talk, etc) honestly and openly about a private matter: *My mother and I talked heart to heart about my problems.* **heart-to-heart** (*noun*) *We had a heart-to-heart last night and I think we finally understand each other now.*

in your 'heart of 'hearts in your deepest feelings or thoughts: *I know in my heart of hearts that you're right, but I still find it difficult to accept.* (from Shakespeare's play *Hamlet*)

a man, woman, etc after your own 'heart a person you particularly like because they have the same interests, opinions, etc as you: *He's a man after my own heart. We get on very well.*

not have the heart (to do sth) not be able or willing to do sth which could hurt sb else: *I didn't have the heart to take the money from him – it was all he had.*

take sth to 'heart **1** be very upset or offended by sb's criticism: *Her review of your book is stupid. Don't take it so much to heart.* **2** pay great attention (to sb's suggestions, etc): *I'm pleased to see that they have taken my suggestions to heart and followed my advice.*

to your heart's con'tent as much or as long as you want: *On holiday I'll be able to read to my heart's content.*

with all my, her, etc heart (used for emphasizing how strongly you feel about sth): *She hoped with all her heart that she would never have to see him again.* ○ *I love you with all my heart.*

with a heavy/sinking heart with a feeling of sadness or fear: *It was with a heavy heart that he left the school for the last time.*

be/feel sick at heart ⇨ sick; be, stay, etc young at heart ⇨ young; bless your, etc heart/soul ⇨ bless; break sb's heart ⇨ break; a change of heart ⇨ change; cross my heart ⇨ cross; eat your heart out ⇨ eat; find it in your heart to do sth ⇨ find; from the bottom of your heart ⇨ bottom; harden your heart against sb/sth ⇨ harden; home is where the heart is ⇨ home; lose heart ⇨ lose; lose your heart ⇨ lose; open your heart ⇨ open; pour out your heart ⇨ pour; search your heart/soul/conscience ⇨ search; set your heart/mind on sth/doing sth ⇨ set; strike fear, terror, etc into sb/sb's heart ⇨ strike; wear your heart on your sleeve ⇨ wear; with a light heart ⇨ light; with your hand on your heart ⇨ hand

heartstrings tug at sb's heartstrings ⇨ tug

hearty hale and hearty ⇨ hale

heat

in the ‚heat of the 'moment (of a decision, action, remark, etc which you now regret) while in a state of strong emotion or excitement: *I must apologize for the rude things I said yesterday in the heat of the moment.*

take the heat out of sth make a situation less tense, emotional, dangerous, etc: *The police tried to take the heat out of the situation by withdrawing for a while.*

turn on the heat ⇨ turn

heaven

a heaven on earth a place or situation where everything is perfect: *The island is a real heaven on earth.*

be in seventh heaven ⇨ seventh; **God/Heaven help sb** ⇨ help; **God/goodness/Heaven knows** ⇨ know; **manna from heaven** ⇨ manna; **move heaven and earth** ⇨ move; **smell/stink to high heaven** ⇨ high

heavens

(good) Heavens! or **Heavens above!** (used as a mild expression of shock, surprise, etc): *Good Heavens! What have you done to your hair?*

the heavens open (*informal*) it suddenly begins to rain very heavily: *We were walking back from the bus stop when the heavens opened.*

heavy

‚heavy 'going boring, tiring, difficult, etc: *I do find her novels very heavy going.* o *The last part of the journey was very heavy going because of the muddy paths.* (refers to the condition of a race course)

make heavy 'weather of (doing) sth make sth seem more difficult than it really is: *You're making very heavy weather of repairing that bike. What's the problem?*

time hangs/lies heavy ⇨ time; **with a heavy/sinking heart** ⇨ heart

hedge

‚hedge your 'bets (*informal*) try to reduce the risk of losing your money, being wrong about sth, etc by choosing two or more courses of action at the same time: *She's invested her money in two quite different businesses, so she's hedging her bets.* (refers to putting money on more than one horse in a race)

heebie-jeebies give sb the willies/heebie-jeebies/creeps ⇨ give

heel

bring sb to 'heel/come to 'heel make sb obey/obey or keep the rules: *He'll soon come to heel if I start to get nasty with him.* o *Tell him you'll leave him if he does it again. That'll bring him to heel, I'm sure.* (refers to making a dog obey you)

‚down at 'heel (of sb's appearance) looking poor: *Since he lost his job, he has begun to look rather down at heel.* (refers to the worn heels of old shoes)

under sb's heel completely in sb's control; dominated by sb: *For years, the country was under the heel of a dictator.*

an/sb's Achilles heel ⇨ Achilles; **turn on your heel** ⇨ turn

heels

at/on sb's 'heels following closely behind sb: *Every day she walks past my house, with her little black dog at her heels.*

hard/hot on sb's 'heels following sb closely because you want to catch them:

Jane has the most points in the championship at the moment, but there are some others hard on her heels. ○ *The police are hard on his heels.*

take to your 'heels run away very quickly: *The burglars took to their heels when they heard the police arrive.*

cool your heels ⇨ cool; **dig your heels in** ⇨ dig; **drag your feet/heels** ⇨ drag; **head over heels** ⇨ head; **kick your heels** ⇨ kick; **show a clean pair of heels** ⇨ show

heights **have a head for heights** ⇨ head

hell

all 'hell breaks/is let loose (*informal*) there is suddenly an angry, noisy reaction to sth; suddenly everything becomes confused, chaotic, noisy, etc: *When soldiers fired shots into the crowd, all hell broke loose.* ○ *All hell broke loose when they heard that their pay had been cut.*

beat/knock/kick the 'hell out of sb/ sth (*informal*) **beat/knock/kick the 'shit out of sb/sth** (*very informal, offensive*) beat, etc sb/sth very hard: *If the crowd had managed to get hold of the robber, they would have beaten hell out of him.* ○ *The police knocked hell out of him for no reason at all. It was a scandal.* ○ *They said they'd kick the shit out of him if he told the police.*

be hell-bent on (doing) sth be absolutely determined to do sth stupid, dangerous, etc: *Have you seen how fast he drives that car? I'd say he was hell-bent on killing himself.*

come ,hell or high 'water (*informal*) whatever the difficulties or opposition may be: *Come hell or high water, we've got to reach the injured men tonight.*

for the 'hell of it (*informal*) (often of things done against the law, normal rules, etc) just for fun, with no particular reason: *The youths had nothing to do so they went round breaking windows just for the hell of it.*

get the hell 'out of here/there (*very informal*) get out of or leave a place very quickly: *Here come the police. Let's get the hell out of here.* ○ *Get the hell out of here and don't come back.*

give sb 'hell (*informal*) make sb's life very unpleasant; shout at sb angrily because they have done sth wrong: *Her back is giving her hell at the moment; she's in pain the whole time.* ○ *His mother gave him hell for coming home so late.*

go to hell (*very informal, offensive*) go away; stop saying, doing, etc sth annoying: *He wanted to come back but she told him to go to hell.* ○ *'Why don't you answer my question, Jim?' 'Oh, go to hell, will you. I'm tired of your stupid questions.'*

hell for 'leather (*informal*) with the greatest possible speed, energy, etc: *I saw a man going hell for leather down the street, with two policemen running after him.*

a/the/one hell of a... (*informal*) sb/sth that is very bad, good, unusual, impressive, etc: *We had a hell of a good time at the night club.* ○ *I had one hell of a hangover the next morning.* (also written *a helluva*, especially in informal US English)

a hell on earth a place or situation that is extremely bad or unpleasant: *Life for the ordinary soldiers was hell on earth.*

like 'hell (*informal*) **1** very hard, very much, very fast, etc in an effort to achieve, etc sth: *I had to run like hell to catch the bus.* **2** (used for saying no emphatically to a suggestion, idea, etc): *'He thinks you're going to lend him your car this weekend.' 'Like hell I am.'*

to hell with sb/sth (*informal*) I don't care about sb/sth; I've had enough of sb/sth: *To hell with this stupid car. I'm going to buy a new one.*

what the hell! (*very informal*) it doesn't matter; I don't care: *'Do you want a cigarette?' 'No, thanks, I've given up. Oh, what the hell! Yes, I will have one, after all.'*

sb has not got a cat in hell's chance ⇨ cat; **hell/the devil to pay** ⇨ pay; **like a bat out of hell** ⇨ bat; **not have a hope in hell** ⇨ hope; **play hell with sb/sth** ⇨ play; **raise Cain/hell** ⇨ raise; **the road to hell is paved with good intentions** ⇨ road; **scare the hell out of sb** ⇨ scare; **see sb in hell first** ⇨ see; **sure as hell** ⇨ sure

helm

at the 'helm/'tiller in control of an organization, etc: *The company began to make profits again with the new managing director at* *the helm.* (refers to the person steering a ship)

take (over) the helm take control of an organization, etc from another person: *When Mr Davies retired, his daughter took the helm.*

help

can't help (doing) sth not be able to avoid or resist doing sth: *A kleptomaniac is a person who can't help stealing things.* ○ *'I'm sorry, I can't help it,' he said bursting into tears.* ○ *He's a bit of a fool, but you can't help liking him.*

God/Heaven 'help sb (*often humorous*) (used for expressing sympathy with sb): *'The Italian team have just been knocked out of the World Cup by Colombia.' 'God help them when they get back home.'*

not if 'I can help it (used for saying you do not want sth to happen): *'Your daughter told me that she wants to leave school when she's 16.' 'Not if I can help it.'*

so 'help me (God) (used when making a serious promise, threat, etc): *I'll catch the man who did this to my son, so help me God.* ○ *I'll kill him, so help me.* (in a British law court a witness swears to 'tell the truth, the whole truth and nothing but the truth, so help me God')

a fat lot of use/help ⇨ fat

helping

a ,helping 'hand help: *The new charity tries to offer a helping hand to young people who have become addicted to drugs.* ○ *A helping hand is very welcome at the moment.*

here

,here and 'now 1 at this moment; immediately: *I'm afraid I can't tell you the answer here and now. I'll find out for you later.* **2** the present situation: *Don't worry so much about the future. Concentrate more on the here and now.*

,here and 'there to or in various places: *Here and there in the crowd I saw people I recognized.*

here goes or **here we go** (said before you begin to do sth dangerous, exciting, difficult, etc): *It's time for me to start the final race. Well, here goes!* ○ *Is everybody ready? OK, here goes. Turn on the electricity and let's see what*

happens.

,here, there, and 'everywhere in, to or from many different places: *The letters came from here, there, and everywhere.* ○ *We searched here, there, and everywhere, but couldn't find the document they wanted.*

here's to 'sb/'sth! (used for wishing sb/sth success, happiness, etc, especially when drinking a toast to sb/sth): *Here's to the happy couple! May they have a long and happy marriage!* ○ *What a wonderful meal. Here's to the cook!* ○ *Here's to the success of the project!*

here we go a'gain (often used for expressing anger or annoyance that sth is happening again): *Here we go again! They're digging up the road – it's the third time this year.* ○ *Here we go again. Another train cancelled. This is getting ridiculous.*

have had it up to here ⇨ up; **look here!** ⇨ look; **neither here nor there** ⇨ neither; **same here** ⇨ same; **take it from here/there** ⇨ take

herring **a red herring** ⇨ red

hesitates

he who hesitates (is lost) (*saying*) if you delay in doing sth you may lose a good opportunity: *You should have applied for that job. I'm sure you would have got it. Remember, he who hesitates . . . .*

hide

hide your ,light under a 'bushel not show your abilities or achievements to other people because you are modest: *We didn't know you could play the guitar! You've been hiding your light under a bushel all this time!* (from the Bible)

bury/hide your head in the sand ⇨ head; **cover/hide a multitude of sins** ⇨ multitude; **have a hide/skin like a rhinoceros** ⇨ rhinoceros

hiding

be on a ,hiding to 'nothing (*informal*) have no hope of succeeding, whatever happens: *The Government is on a hiding to nothing in these elections.*

high

as high as a 'kite (*informal*) in an excited state especially because of drugs, alcohol, etc: *He was as high as a kite when they came to* *arrest him.*

be for the 'high jump (*informal*) be about to be punished, criticized, dismissed, etc: *When your father sees your school report, you'll be for the high jump.*

be/get on your ˌhigh 'horse be annoyed because you think that sb has not treated you with enough respect: *When they suggested that she might have made a mistake, she got on her high horse and asked them how they dared question her ability.*

ˌhigh and 'dry abandoned or left in a very difficult situation: *When the travel company went bankrupt, many holidaymakers were left high and dry abroad or waiting at the airport.* (refers to boats left on the beach after the tide has gone out)

ˌhigh and 'low (search, etc for sth) in every possible place; everywhere: *I've been hunting high and low for that pen, where did you find it?*

ˌhigh and 'mighty (*informal*) conceited and arrogant: *He's too high and mighty to mix with ordinary people like us!*

high jinks (*informal*) a lot of fun and amusement: *They got up to all sorts of high jinks on the trip.*

the 'high spot of sth the best, most interesting, entertaining, etc part of sth: *The high spot of our holiday was the visit to Rome.*

high 'water mark (*rather formal*) the highest stage of achievement: *This was the high water mark of the ancient Egyptian civilization.*

in ˌhigh 'dudgeon full of anger and resentment because sb has hurt or upset you: *After being refused entry to the club, he went off in high dudgeon.*

on the high seas in international waters; on a part of the sea which does not belong to any country: *What happens if a crime is committed on the high seas?*

smell/stink to high 'heaven (*informal*) **1** have a very strong and unpleasant smell: *When was the last time you cleaned the dog kennel? It stinks to high heaven.* **2** give the impression of being illegal, corrupt, etc: *This whole deal stinks to high heaven. I'm sure somebody was bribed.*

be in high/low spirits ⇨ spirits; **come hell or high water** ⇨ hell; **feel that high**

= **look/feel small** ⇨ small; **have friends in high places** ⇨ friends; **hold your head up** ⇨ hold; **it is high/about time** ⇨ time; **knee-high to a grasshopper** ⇨ knee; **riding high** ⇨ riding; **set your sights high/low** ⇨ set; **take on, etc a high/low profile** ⇨ profile

highly **speak highly of sb** ⇨ speak; **think highly of sb/sth** ⇨ think

highways
highways and byways (on/along) all the roads, large and small, of a country, area, etc: *She travelled the highways and byways of Scotland collecting folk songs and traditions.*

hill(s)
over the 'hill (*informal*) no longer young; past your best: *Some people think if you're 30, you're over the hill!*

up ˌhill and down 'dale to or from many places; everywhere: *They cycled up hill and down dale, glad to be away from the city.*

old as the hills ⇨ old

hilt
to the 'hilt (support, etc sb) completely: *I will support you to the hilt on this.* (refers to a sword in its scabbard (container) as far as it will go, ie as far as the hilt (handle))

hind
talk the hind legs off a donkey ⇨ talk

hindmost
the devil take the hindmost ⇨ devil

hint
take a 'hint understand what sb has suggested indirectly and act accordingly: *She yawned and said, 'Goodness, it's late.' 'OK,' said Pete, 'I can take a hint. I'll be going home now.'*

drop a hint ⇨ drop

history
go down in/make 'history (of people) be remembered for a long time because you do sth very important; (of events, actions, etc) be remembered for a long time because of its importance: *Roger Bannister made history as the first man to run a mile in less than four minutes.* ○ *This battle will go down in history as one of our most important victories.*

hit

,hit and 'miss *or* **,hit or 'miss** not properly planned; unsystematic: *The advertisements were rather hit and miss and not based on proper market research.* ○ *They use rather hit-and-miss techniques for selecting new staff.*

hit and run a road accident in which a driver leaves the place where the accident happened without stopping to give help, leave his name, etc: *a hit-and-run accident/ driver*

hit the 'bottle (*informal*) regularly drink too much: *She managed to resist alcohol for a year, then hit the bottle again when her husband died.* ○ *He's really hitting the bottle at the moment.*

hit the 'deck (*informal*) **1** lie down on the ground very suddenly to avoid gunfire, danger, etc; fall to the ground: *When we heard the shooting we hit the deck.* ○ *The champion landed another heavy punch and the challenger hit the deck for the third time.* **2** get out of bed: *Come on! It's time to hit the deck.*

hit sb/sth 'hard affect sb/sth very badly: *Small businesses have again been hard hit by the increase in interest rates.* ○ *The death of her daughter hit her very hard.* (in the passive, we usually say 'hard hit by' instead of 'hit hard by')

hit the 'sack (*informal*) go to bed: *I think it's time to hit the sack.*

hit sb in the 'eye (*informal*) be very obvious or striking: *The strange mixture of colours hits you in the eye as soon as you enter the room.*

hit it 'off (with sb) (*informal*) quickly form or have a good relationship with sb: *I met a girl at the party, and she and I hit it off straight away* (or *we hit it off straight away*).

hit the 'jackpot suddenly win, earn, etc a lot of money; suddenly be very successful: *She's hit the jackpot with her latest book – it has sold millions.* (refers to the card game called poker)

a 'hit list (*informal*) a list of people that gangsters, terrorists, etc want to kill or that a person wants to harm: *The terrorists have drawn up a hit list of about 50 politicians.* ○ *Be careful how you speak to her because I think you're on her hit list.*

hit the nail on the 'head (*informal*) give a perfect description, explanation or interpretation of a situation: *'So you want to move to another department.' 'You've hit the nail on the head. That's exactly what I want.'*

hit the 'road (*especially US*) **hit the 'trail** (*informal*) begin a journey: *Well, we'd better hit the road, we've a long way to go.*

hit the 'roof (*informal*) suddenly become very angry: *Every time I mention Patricia, Sam hits the roof.*

make a (big, etc) hit with sb impress sb very favourably: *You've made quite a hit with my mother. She really likes you.*

hit the headlines ⇨ headlines; **hit/ strike home** ⇨ home; **hit/touch a nerve** ⇨ nerve; **reach/hit rock-bottom** ⇨ rock; **a smash hit** ⇨ smash

hitch   thumb/hitch a lift ⇨ lift

hitched

get hitched (*informal*) get married: *They got hitched last year without telling anybody about it.*

hither

,hither and 'thither in many different directions: *When you look down at the square, you see all the people hurrying hither and thither.*

Hobson

,Hobson's 'choice the choice of taking what is offered or nothing at all, in reality no choice at all: *It's Hobson's choice really, as this is the only room we have empty at the moment.* (refers to a seventeenth century Cambridge man, Tobias Hobson, who hired out horses; he would only offer his clients the horse nearest the stable door)

hock

in hock (*informal*) owing money: *I'm in hock for about £5 000.*

hog   go the whole hog ⇨ whole

hoist

be hoist with your own pe'tard be caught in the trap that you were preparing for another person. (from Shakespeare's play, *Hamlet*)

hold

cannot hold a candle to sb/sth

(*informal*) be very inferior to sb/sth; be not good, etc enough to be compared to sb/sth: *She is a good player, but she can't hold a candle to a champion like Jane.*

get hold of sb/sth obtain sth; reach or contact sb: *Do you know where I can get hold of a telephone directory for France? ○ I spent all morning on the phone trying to get hold of the manager.*

hold your 'breath **1** stop breathing for a short time, for example because you're afraid of or very anxious about sth: *I held my breath as the car skidded towards me.* **2** wait very anxiously for news, a result, etc: '*When will you hear about your university application?' 'Not till next week. I'm holding my breath until then.'* **3** (*informal*) **don't hold your breath** (used for telling sb that it's not worth waiting for sth): *We'll let you know if there's any work for you, but don't hold your breath.*

hold 'court (*often disapproving*) (of an important person or sb who thinks they are important) talk to a group of less important people, who pay attention in the same way as courtiers would to a king or queen: *There was Professor Johnson, holding court as usual in the students' coffee bar.*

hold sb/sth 'dear (*rather formal*) feel sb/sth is of great value: *He mocked the ideas they held dear.*

hold fast to sth refuse to stop believing in (a theory, principle, religion, etc): *She knew that whatever happened in her life, she would hold fast to her religious beliefs.*

hold your 'fire delay or stop shooting for a while; stop attacking sb: *Hold your fire! I think they're going to surrender. ○ She told the journalists to hold their fire. If they didn't listen to her, how would they know what she thought.*

hold the 'floor speak at a public meeting, etc for a long time, often stopping others from speaking: *The American delegation held the floor for three quarters of an hour, putting forward their proposals.*

hold the 'fort (*informal*) be in charge or taking care of sth while the person usually responsible is absent: *I'm going abroad for a few weeks, and Kathy will hold the fort while I'm away.*

hold 'forth (about/on sth) (*disapproving*) speak to other people for a long time, especially in a very confident or pompous way: *The politician held forth on the importance of living in a society free from social injustice. ○ He's a real bore. He's always holding forth about something or other.*

hold good/true be or remain true, valid, correct, etc: *This principle holds true in every case. ○ Will your promise hold good even if you don't get the money?*

hold sb's 'hand give sb help, comfort, support, etc in a difficult situation: *Industry cannot expect the government to hold its hand every time it has problems. ○ This is Jane's first day in the office, so I've asked Mary to hold her hand a bit.*

hold your 'head up (high) not feel ashamed, guilty or embarrassed about sth: *After this scandal, he will never be able to hold his head up high again.*

hold your 'horses (*informal, becoming dated*) (used for asking sb to stop for a moment, speak more slowly, etc): '*Hold your horses! We haven't finished the last question yet.'*

'hold it (*informal*) wait a moment: *Hold it a second! I just have to make sure the doors are locked.*

hold your 'own **1** manage to do sth satisfactorily or well enough, compared to other people: *There was a lot of competition but she managed to hold her own.* **2** manage to resist attack, illness, etc: '*How's your father?' 'He's holding his own, but only just. We'll just have to hope and pray that he'll get better soon.'*

hold no brief for sb/sth (*formal*) not be in favour of or support sb/sth, for example a cause, an idea, etc: *I hold no brief for long prison sentences but this terrible crime really deserves one.*

hold 'sway (over sb/sth) (of a person, movement, idea, etc) have power, control or great influence over sb/sth: *After many years during which the right wing held sway, the socialists formed a government. ○ These ideas held sway for most of the century.*

hold sb to 'ransom **1** hold sb as a prisoner until money has been paid for their release **2** try to force sb to do what you want by using threats: *The government said that the workers were holding the country to ransom by demanding a ten per cent pay rise.*

,hold your 'tongue say nothing; stay silent: *We don't want anyone to know what's happened, so you'd better hold your tongue – do you understand? ○ I didn't want to start another argument, so I held my tongue.*

hold 'water (*informal*) (of a theory, etc) remain true even when examined closely: *Your argument just doesn't hold water.*

on hold (of plans, etc) no further action for the moment: *We can't find the money, so all our plans are on hold at the moment.* ○ *We'll have to put the decision on hold until we get more details about the economic situation.*

control/hold   the   purse-strings ⇨ purse; **hang on/hold on like grim death** ⇨ grim; **have/hold the aces** ⇨ aces; **hold/keep sb/sth at bay** ⇨ bay; **hold/stand your ground** ⇨ ground; **hold a gun to sb's head/have a gun to your head** ⇨ gun; **hold out/offer an olive branch** ⇨ olive; **keep/hold/play your cards close to your chest** ⇨ cards; **keep/hold sb/sth in check** ⇨ check; **take/get a grip/hold on yourself** ⇨ grip

holding

there is no holding/stopping sb a person cannot be prevented from doing sth because of their enthusiasm, energy, determination, etc: *There was no holding him once he started talking about his life in India.* ○ *You know Hannah. Once she's decided to do something there's no holding her.*

leave sb holding the baby ⇨ leave

holds

(with) no holds barred (of fighting, competition, etc) with no or very few rules or restrictions: *This started off as a very clean election campaign, but now it's no holds barred.* **no-holds-barred** (*adjective*) *a no-holds-barred row over the latest political scandal* (refers to wrestling without strict rules)

hole

need/want sth like (you need/want) a hole in the head (*informal*) definitely not need/want sth at all: *I had to get home before midnight, and just then I needed a flat tyre like a hole in the head.*

make a dent/hole in sth ⇨ dent; **money burns a hole in sb's pocket** ⇨ money

holes   pick holes ⇨ pick

holiday   a busman's holiday ⇨ busman

hollow   beat   sb/sth   hollow ⇨ beat; **ring true/false/hollow** ⇨ ring

holy

holy of holies (*often humorous*) a special place which only certain people can enter: *This room is the holy of holies. It contains the most valuable books in the world.* ○ *The boss invited me into his holy of holies this morning. What a fantastic office he's got!* (refers to the inner part of the Jewish temple which only the chief priest can enter)

home

at home   1 (feeling) comfortable or relaxed, as if you are in your own home: *I like the village. I feel at home here.* ○ *Come in and make yourself at home while I finish cooking the dinner.* **2** (of a sports event) at your own ground, club, etc: *We're at home to Oxford United on Saturday, and the week after we're away to Luton.* **3** (of a subject, topic of conversation, etc) know about and feel confident discussing it: *I'm not really at home with seventeenth-century literature. I specialize in the nineteenth century.*

bring home the 'bacon (*informal*) be successful in sth; be the person who earns money for a family, organization, etc: *The firm wants very much to get this contract, and we're expecting you to bring home the bacon.* ○ *He's the one who brings home the bacon.*

bring sth 'home to sb make sb realize sth important fully: *This documentary brought home the tragedy of the poor to many people.* ○ *Visiting that hospital for the mentally ill really brought home to me how sad some people's lives are.*

come 'home (to sb) become fully clear or understood: *The danger of the situation we were in suddenly came home to me.*

drive/hammer sth home (to sb) make sure that sb understands sth completely, for example by repeating it often: *The instructor tried to drive home to us the need for safety precautions before diving.* ○ *Police used statistics to hammer home their warning about car theft.*

hit/strike home   1 (of a punch, a blow, an arrow, a bullet, etc) hit sb/sth where you intended; hit its target: *The punch hit home and Ferguson fell to the floor.* **2** (of an insult, a remark, criticism, etc) affect or hurt sb in the intended way; make sb really understand sth: *His criticism of my work struck home. I knew he was right.* ○ *My remarks last week obviously hit home because he has not been late for work since.*

home and 'dry in a safe or good position because you have successfully completed or won sth: *When we've won four out of six games, we'll know that we're home and dry.* ○ *All they have to do is sign the contract and then we'll be home and dry.*

a 'home bird a person who spends most of the time at home because they are happiest there: *Sheila's a home bird really. She likes to spend her free time around the house.*

a ,home from 'home a place where you feel as comfortable, happy, etc as in your own home: *They used to stay in their father's flat in Brighton every holiday. It was a real home from home.*

home is where the heart is (*saying*) a home is where the people you love are: *When I ask him if he's happy travelling around the world all the time, he just says, 'Home is where the heart is. If my wife and children are with me, then I'm happy.'*

a ,home 'truth an honest criticism of a person said directly to them: *It's time someone told you a few home truths, my boy!*

on the ,home 'straight/'stretch approaching the end of a task, project, course, etc: *Ten exams done and two more to do. You're on the home straight now.* ○ *I never thought the prison sentence would end, but I feel I'm on the home straight now.* (refers to the last part of a horse race when the horses are approaching the finishing line)

who's 'sb when she's/he's at ,home (*informal, humorous*) (used for asking who the person that has just been mentioned is): *'Shirley Hughes wants to meet you.' 'Who's she when she's at home?'*

be nothing, etc to write home about ⇨ write; **be sb's spiritual home** ⇨ spiritual; **charity begins at home** ⇨ charity; **chickens come home to roost** ⇨ chickens; **eat sb out of house and home** ⇨ eat; **press sth home** ⇨ press; **ram sth home** ⇨ ram; **romp home/in** ⇨ romp; **till/until the cows come home** ⇨ cows

homework

do your homework (on sth) find out the facts, details, etc of a subject in preparation for a meeting, speech, article, etc: *He had just not done his homework for the meeting. He couldn't answer our questions.*

honest

honest to 'God/'goodness (*informal*) (used for emphasizing the truth of what you are saying): *I didn't do it – honest to God!* **honest-to-goodness** (*adjective*) *This book is an honest-to-goodness attempt to describe life as a political leader.*

make an honest 'woman of sb (*humorous*) marry a woman with whom you have been having a sexual relationship: *When are you going to make an honest woman of her, Peter?*

honesty

in all 'honesty speaking honestly: *I can't in all honesty say that I've had much experience of this kind of work, but I'm willing to try it.*

honeymoon

a/the 'honeymoon period a period of time at the beginning of sth, for example a relationship, a job, a period in government, etc, when everybody is pleased with you and there appear to be no problems: *The honeymoon period is over now for the new President.* (refers to the period just after a couple gets married)

honour(s)

do the 'honours (*often humorous, informal*) act as the host; pour drinks for guests: *Harry, could you do the honours? Tom and Angela both want gin and tonic.* ○ *His father was ill, so Charles did the honours.*

word of honour ⇨ word

hook

by ,hook or by 'crook (of sth difficult) by any method, whether it is honest or not: *Don't worry – we'll have the money ready by 4 o'clock, by hook or by crook.*

get sb off the hook (*informal*) help sb to avoid punishment, etc: *You're going to need a very clever lawyer to get you off the hook this time.*

,hook, line, and 'sinker (accept or believe sth) completely, either because you have been deceived or you believe things too easily: *Are you telling me that you swallowed his absurd lies hook, line, and sinker?* (refers to items used for fishing)

let sb off the 'hook (*informal*) allow sb to escape from a difficult situation or punishment: *We'll let you off the hook this time, but if you make any more mistakes like that, you'll lose your job.* ○ *There won't be enough time for me to read my report to the committee, so that's let me off the hook.* (refers to a fish escaping after it has been caught)

hop **catch sb on the hop** ⇨ catch

hope

,hope against 'hope (that...) continue to hope that sth will happen, etc, even if this seems useless or foolish: *It was a couple of days since the earthquake, but the family were still hoping against hope that their son was safe.*

,hope for the 'best hope that everything will go well, even if there are doubts that it will: *There is nothing more the doctors can do for her. All we can do now is hope for the best.*

hope springs eternal human beings never stop hoping: *She's sure that he'll come back to her one day. I'm not so sure, but hope springs eternal.* (from *An Essay on Man* by Alexander Pope)

not have a hope in hell (*informal*) not have any chance at all: *You haven't got a hope in hell of winning the race – you're far too slow!*

not a hope or **some hope(s)!** (*informal*) there is no or little chance of sth happening: *Some hope of your becoming manager – you're far too lazy!* ○ *'Your dad will lend you the money, I'm sure.' 'Not a hope.'*

the one/a ray of hope ⇨ ray

hopes

build up/raise sb's hopes make sb feel optimistic or hopeful about sth: *Don't raise her hopes too much. She may not win.*

dash/shatter sb's hopes destroy sb's hopes of doing or getting sth: *Any remaining hopes that the museum would be built this year were dashed yesterday when the council announced its plans to spend less money on the arts.* ○ *His poor performance in the exam shattered his hopes of becoming a lawyer.*

pin your faith/hopes on sb/sth ⇨ pin

hopping

hopping 'mad (about/over sth) (*informal*) extremely angry about sth: *Anne was hopping mad about the sales figures.*

horizon

on the ho'rizon soon to happen: *The change of government means that there are new developments on the horizon.*

a cloud on the horizon ⇨ cloud

horns

(on) the horns of a di'lemma (in) a situation in which you must choose between two actions which are equally unsatisfactory, unpleasant, dangerous, etc: *I'm really on the horns of a dilemma. I need the car but I can't afford it.*

draw in your horns ⇨ draw; **lock horns with sb** ⇨ lock; **take the bull by the horns** ⇨ bull

hornet

a 'hornet's nest a lot of trouble: *When Charles got the manager's job, it stirred up a real hornet's nest, because everyone was angry about his fast promotion.* (a hornet is a flying insect, rather like a bee, which stings)

horse

you can ,take/,lead a horse to ,water, but you ,can't make it 'drink (*saying*) you can give sb the opportunity to do sth, but you cannot force them to do it if they do not want to.

(straight) from the horse's 'mouth (*informal*) (of information, etc) directly from the person who really knows because they are closely connected with its source: *'How do you know he's leaving?' 'I got it straight from the horse's mouth. He told me himself.'*

back the wrong horse ⇨ back; **be/get on your high horse** ⇨ high; **a dark horse** ⇨ dark; **eat like a horse** ⇨ eat; **flog a dead horse** ⇨ flog; **I, etc could eat a horse** ⇨ eat; **(not) look a gift-horse in the mouth** ⇨ look; **a one-horse race** ⇨ one; **a one-horse town** ⇨ one; **shut/close the stable door after the horse has bolted** ⇨ stable

horses

change/swap horses in mid'stream change your opinion or plans while in the middle of doing sth; suddenly transfer your loyalty from one person or group to another: *'I don't believe in changing horses in midstream,'* he said. *'Give this policy a chance before you think of changing it.'*

horses for courses people or things should only be used for the purpose for which they are most suitable: *He's not the right kind of ambassador for Moscow. Johnson would be much better. It's a question of horses for courses.* (refers to the fact that horses race better on a track that suits them)

drive a coach and horses through sth ⇨ drive; **hold your horses** ⇨ hold; **if wishes were horses, beggars would/might ride** ⇨ wishes; **wild horses couldn't/wouldn't drag sb there, etc** ⇨ wild

hostage

a hostage to fortune an action which may cause you great trouble in the future: *Are you really sure you want to know who your real mother is? It may be taking a hostage to fortune, you know.*

hot

hot air (*informal*) impressive but worthless or empty promises: *Don't believe anything she says. It's all hot air.*

go hot and cold (all over) (*informal*) suddenly feel very worried, upset or frightened when you remember sth very unpleasant: *I go hot and cold all over when I think of that train accident. It was so terrible.* ○ *When I think how stupid I was that day, I still go hot and cold with embarrassment.*

(all) hot and 'bothered (*informal*) worried and upset: *Officials at the Defence Ministry are getting all hot and bothered about secrets getting out.*

(too) hot for sb *or* **too hot to handle** (*informal*) (too) difficult, dangerous, etc for sb: *When the scandal became public, things got too hot for the Minister and she resigned.* ○ *The newspapers daren't print the story; it is just too hot to handle.*

a 'hot line (to sb) a special telephone line to an important person, such as a president, etc which is used in emergencies: *The President of the United States spoke on the hot line with the Prime Minister about the crisis.*

a hot po'tato (*informal*) a very sensitive matter that is difficult or embarrassing to deal with: *The minister's resignation is a political hot potato.*

in the 'hot seat (*informal*) a position of responsibility in which you must deal with difficult questions, criticism or attacks: *Our radio phone-in today is on transport, and the Minister of Transport will be in the hot seat, ready to answer your questions.*

a 'hot spot (*informal*) a country or area where there is or will be war, riots, etc: *As a journalist, I get sent to one hot spot after another.*

hot 'stuff (*informal*) **1** sb/sth of very high quality: *He's really hot stuff as a tennis player.* **2** a sexually attractive person; (of a film, book, etc) sexually very explicit: *She seems to think he's really hot stuff.* ○ *His new book is really hot stuff.*

hot under the 'collar (*informal*) annoyed, embarrassed or excited: *He gets very hot under the collar if people disagree with him.*

in hot 'water (*informal*) in trouble: *She got into hot water for being late.* ○ *The new clerk was in hot water because she forgot to ask for a receipt for the money.* ○ *This sort of behaviour will land him in hot water.*

make it hot for sb (*informal*) make a situation very difficult or uncomfortable for sb: *If you insist on staying here, I can make it very hot for you.*

more sth/more often than sb has had hot dinners (*informal, often humorous*) (used for emphasizing how much/many or how often sb has done sth): *He's won more medals than you've had hot dinners.* ○ *She's been to France more often than you've had hot dinners.*

not so/too hot (*informal*) not very well, healthy, etc; not very good: *'How do you feel today?' 'Not so hot.'* ○ *Her work's not too hot, is it? I thought she'd be better than this!*

sell/go like hot 'cakes (*informal*) be sold quickly in great quantities: *The band's latest record is selling like hot cakes.*

blow hot and cold ⇨ blow; **hard/hot on sb's heels** ⇨ heels; **in hot pursuit** ⇨ pursuit; **like a cat on hot bricks** ⇨ cat; **strike while the iron is hot** ⇨ strike

hounds run with the hare and hunt with the hounds ⇨ run

hour

in your hour of need (often humorous) when you really need help: *Where were you in my hour of need? Sitting in the pub with your friends.*

on the 'hour/half-'hour at exactly 5 o'clock, 6 o'clock, etc/ 5.30, 6.30, etc: *Buses leave here for Oxford on the hour.*

the eleventh hour ⇨ eleventh

hours

,after 'hours after the period during which a shop, pub, etc is open: *Pubs are not allowed to sell drinks after hours.*

at 'all hours at any time during the night or day; all the time: *He comes here at all hours, sometimes in the middle of the night.*

till/until all hours until very late at night or early next morning: *She sat up till all hours trying to finish her essay.*

the early hours ⇨ early; **the small hours** ⇨ small; **work all the hours God sends** ⇨ work

house

bring the 'house down (informal) make an audience laugh, applaud or cheer loudly: *Their act brought the house down when they played in London.* ○ *'Did he sing well?' 'He brought the house down!'*

get on like a 'house on fire (informal) quickly develop a very friendly relationship with sb: *I was worried about introducing my boyfriend to my parents, but they got on like a house on fire.*

a house of cards a plan, project, system, etc that is or seems likely to fail or collapse: *His plans collapsed like a house of cards when he was told he hadn't won the scholarship.*

on the 'house (especially of alcoholic drinks) given to a customer free by the hotel, restaurant, bar, etc: *Drinks are on the house tonight!*

put/set your (own) 'house in order (often used of sb, an organization, etc that has criticized another person or organization) arrange your own affairs efficiently: *A government minister warned the newspaper industry to put its own house in order before it started to tell other industries how they should be run.*

eat sb out of house and home ⇨ eat; **a halfway house** ⇨ halfway; **in the doghouse** ⇨ doghouse; **open house** ⇨ open; **set up house** ⇨ set

household

a ,household 'word/'name a word/name that is extremely well known: *The business she founded made her into a household name.* ○ *MacDonald's is a household name.*

houseroom

not give sb/sth 'houseroom not want sb/sth in your house because you dislike or do not approve of sb/sth; completely reject sb/sth: *I wouldn't give that ugly old furniture houseroom.* ○ *I wouldn't give any of these theories houseroom.*

houses

be safe as houses ⇨ safe; **people who live in glasshouses shouldn't throw stones** ⇨ people

housetops

shout, etc sth from the 'housetops/'rooftops (informal) tell sth to everyone: *Don't shout it from the housetops, will you? I want to keep it a secret just between us for a while.* ○ *If you tell her it's secret, she'll announce it from the rooftops. Don't trust her.*

how

how/what about sb/sth? **1** (used for making a suggestion or offer): *You look cold. How about a nice hot drink?* ○ *How about going to see a film this evening?* **2** (used for asking sb's opinion about sb/sth): *What about our team winning again last night, eh?* ○ *I like her. How about you?* ○ *What about the wine? Do you like it?* **3** (used for introducing sb/sth into a conversation or reminding sb of sb/sth): *I know she's very happy now, but what about him?* ○ *'I've never been to Spain before.' 'What about the conference you went to in Madrid?'*

how/what about that, (then)! (informal) (used for expressing surprise, praise, great respect, etc): *'Have you heard Jane's been offered a film part in Hollywood?' 'Well, how about that, then!'*

how come? (informal) (used for expressing surprise, annoyance, etc) why is that? why is it that...: *'They've decided not to buy the house.' 'How come? I thought they definitely* *wanted it.'* ○ *How come I earn so little and you earn so much when we're doing the same job?*

how's this/that for a. . .? (*informal*) (used for asking for sb's reaction to sth): *'How's that for a surprise present?' 'It looks wonderful. Thank you!'* ○ *'Well, how's that for bad hotel service?' 'Unbelievable.'*

how stupid, lazy, etc can you, etc 'get? (used for expressing surprise at sb's stupidity, laziness, etc): *Sport on all four television channels at the same time. How stupid can they get?* ○ *She spent £200 on a pair of shoes? How ridiculous can you get?*

any old how ⇨ **old**

hue

a ,hue and 'cry loud opposition, protest, etc: *There was a great hue and cry among the parents when it was announced that the school was to close.* ○ *If the government raises taxes too much, there'll be a real hue and cry.* (refers to a medieval law 'hu et cri' whereby the public had to chase and catch a criminal)

huff

,huff and 'puff 1 breathe heavily, while making a great physical effort: *They huffed and puffed as they carried the sofa upstairs.* **2** show irritation, anger, etc in an obvious way: *She huffed and puffed about the loss of the documents, but nobody paid any attention to her.*

hum ,hum/,hem and 'haw = um and aah ⇨ **um**

human the milk of human kindness ⇨ **milk**

humble eat humble pie ⇨ **eat**

hump

give sb/get the 'hump (*British, informal*) annoy sb/become annoyed, angry, etc: *She gets the hump when people don't listen to her.* ○ *That stupid man in the sales department really gives me the hump.*

over the 'hump (*informal*) past the largest, worst or most difficult part of a job, illness, etc: *I'll be over the hump when I've done this exam – then there'll be just two left.*

hundred

a hundred/thousand/million and one (things, etc to do, etc) (*informal*) very many or too many (things to do, people to see, etc): *I'm so busy – I've got lectures to prepare, a book to finish, and a hundred and one letters to write – I just don't know where to start.* ○ *She's always got a thousand and one excuses for everything.*

it's a hundred, etc to one that sth/sb will (not) do sth it is almost certain that sth/sb will (not) do sth: *It's a hundred to one that the train will be late.* ○ *It's a hundred to one that she'll be before us. She always is.*

not a hundred/thousand/million miles away/from here (*humorous*) (used for identifying sb/sth indirectly) very close to this place: *The person I'm talking about is not a hundred miles from here, but I'm not in a position to say who he is.* ○ *We're talking about a car factory not a hundred miles from here.*

a/one hundred per 'cent completely: *I agree with you one hundred per cent.*

ninety-nine times out of a hundred = nine times out of ten ⇨ **nine**

hunt run with the hare and hunt with the hounds ⇨ **run**

hunting a happy hunting ground ⇨ **happy**

hurt

it won't/wouldn't hurt sb to do sth (*informal, often ironic*) it will/would be better for sb to do sth; it would be a good idea for sb to do sth: *It wouldn't hurt her to walk instead of going in the car all the time.* ○ *It won't hurt you to work a bit harder for your exam.*

sb would not harm/hurt a fly ⇨ **fly**

hustle

hustle and bustle busy and excited activity: *I can't concentrate on my work with all this hustle and bustle going on around me.* ○ *I love the hustle and bustle of big cities.*

Hyde a Jekyll and Hyde ⇨ **Jekyll**

I

ice

put sth on ice decide to take no action on sth for a period of time; postpone sth: *They have put the plans for the new hospital on ice because of the economic situation.* ○ *My plans for going to the USA are on ice.*

be skating on thin ice ⇨ skating; **break the ice** ⇨ break; **cut no ice** ⇨ cut

iceberg **be the tip of the iceberg** ⇨ tip

icing

the icing on the cake something attractive, but not necessary, which is added to sth already very good: *The meal was perfect, the wonderful view from the restaurant the icing on the cake.*

idea

get the i'dea (*informal*) understand sth when it has been explained to you: *'Do you understand how it works now?' 'Yes, I think I've got the idea. Thanks for showing me.'*

have no i'dea not know sth; not know how to do sth: *I've no idea what time it is.* ○ *Don't ask him to mend it; he's got no idea about cars.*

the (very) idea! (*informal*) (used to express surprise or disapproval at the way sb behaves): *She expected me to pay for everything. The idea!*

run away with the idea/notion ⇨ run

ideas

give sb i'deas *or* **put i'deas in sb's head** suggest to sb that they could do something that they had never thought of before. This may be something difficult or impossible: *'Don't keep telling him about your adventures in Africa. You're giving him ideas.'*

buck up your ideas ⇨ buck

idle **bone idle** ⇨ bone; **the devil makes work for idle hands** ⇨ devil

if(s)

if ˌI were 'you (used to introduce a suggestion or a piece of advice) if I were in the same situation as you: *If I were you, I wouldn't buy that car. You can see it's been in*

an accident.

if 'only (used to express a wish that something had happened or would happen): *If only she'd done what I told her, she wouldn't be in this trouble.* ○ *If only you would let me explain.*

ˌifs and/or 'buts (often used in the negative; used to stop sb arguing, protesting or making excuses when you tell them to do sth): *I want this work finished by Friday and no ifs and buts.*

it isn't as if/as though ⇨ as; **what if?** ⇨ what

ill

ˌill at 'ease nervous, especially in a social situation: *He always feels ill at ease at parties.* ○ *She looked very ill at ease during her speech.*

it's an ˌill 'wind (that blows nobody any good) (*saying*) in every disaster or misfortune there is always somebody who gains or profits from it: *The fire destroyed half the village. For the builders business has never been better. It's an ill wind. . . .*

for good or ill ⇨ good; **speak ill of sb** ⇨ speak; **wish sb/sth well/ill** ⇨ wish

image

be the (very/spitting) image of sb/sth (*informal*) look exactly like sb/sth: *She's the spitting image of her mother.*

the living image of sb ⇨ living

imagination **a figment of your imagination** ⇨ figment; **by no stretch of the imagination** ⇨ stretch

immemorial **from/since time immemorial** ⇨ time

impression

be under the impression that... believe, usually wrongly, that. . .: *I was under the impression that you were coming tomorrow, not today.*

in

anything/nothing/something in it for sb (*informal*) some/no advantage,

127

especially financial, to sb: *He wanted to know more about the business but I told him there was nothing in it for him.*

be 'in for sth 1 be about to get or experience sth unpleasant, for example a shock, a surprise, trouble, bad weather, etc: *He'll be in for a big surprise when he opens that letter.* ○ *I think we're in for trouble with the new boss.* **2** be taking part in sth, for example, a competition; be trying to get sth, for example, a job: *I'm in for both the 100 metres race and the long jump.* ○ *I hope Jan gets that professorship she's in for.*

,in and 'out of sth (going) in and out of places all the time: *I've been in and out of the travel agency all this week, trying to arrange my holiday.* ○ *After the accident, he was in and out of hospital for a couple of years.*

'in on sth (*informal*) knowing about sth; included in sth: *I'd like to be in on this project if you'll have me.* ○ *She wants to get in on what the others are doing.* ○ *Shall we let him in on the secret?*

keep (well) 'in with sb be friendly with sb, not because you like them, but because they may be useful to you: *If you want to do well in this company, keep well in with the boss.*

something, anything, nothing, etc 'in it some, any, no truth in what is being said: *'Is there anything in the story that he is leaving the company?' 'No, I'm sure there's nothing in it.'* ○ *'Yes, I think there's something in it.'*

have it in you ⇨ have; **have it in for sb** ⇨ have

inch

every inch a/the leader, man, film star, etc a leader, star, etc in every way; completely a leader, star, etc: *She was every inch a leader.* ○ *He looked every inch the romantic hero.* ○ *That horse looks every inch a winner.*

,give sb an 'inch (and they will ,take a 'yard/'mile) (*saying*) if you say yes to sb for a small request, they will want much more: *I said Joe could borrow my car occasionally, and then he started to borrow it every night! Give him an inch!*

within an inch of (doing) sth very near/close to (doing) sth: *I came within an inch of death in that car accident.* ○ *They came within an inch of winning the match.*

Indian

an ,Indian 'summer 1 a period of unusually dry, sunny, warm weather in the autumn: *We had a splendid Indian summer last October.* **2** a period of success or happiness near the end of sb's life: *He made his best films in his seventies; it was for him a real Indian summer.*

in single/Indian file ⇨ file

industry
a captain of industry ⇨ captain

influence
under the 'influence (*formal or humorous*) (used of sb driving a car) drunk: *She was fined £500 for driving while under the influence.*

information
be a mine of information ⇨ mine

iniquity
a den of iniquity/vice ⇨ den

initiative
do sth on your own i'nitiative do sth which is your own idea, not a suggestion or order from another person: *Did you ask him to organize a meeting, or did he do it on his own initiative?*

take the initiative lead people by being the first to act in a situation: *France took the initiative in the peace talks.* ○ *California took the initiative in banning smoking in public places.*

injury
do sb/yourself an 'injury (*often humorous*) hurt yourself physically: *I nearly did myself an injury carrying those heavy suitcases.*

add insult to injury ⇨ add

inner
the ,inner 'man/'woman 1 your mind or soul: *Prayer is good for the inner man.* **2** (*humorous*) your appetite: *It's time to do something for the inner man; let's look for a restaurant.*

innings
a good 'innings (*British, informal*) (often used of sb who is at the end of their life or who has just died) a long life; a long and successful period in your life: *I've enjoyed my life. I've had a good innings.* ○ *He's had a good*

innings but now it's time for him to retire and let someone younger be director.

inroads
make inroads in/into sth **1** reduce the amount of sth: *Repairs to the house had made deep inroads into their savings.* **2** advance successfully into a new area: *Doctors are making great inroads in the fight against cancer.* ○ *Their products are already making inroads in these new markets.*

ins
the ins and outs of sth all the details of sth, which are often difficult to understand: *It would take me a long time to explain all the ins and outs of the English education system.* ○ *I don't know all the ins and outs of the case.*

inside
on the in'side working in an organization and possessing secret information about it: *Someone on the inside must have passed on the information to the bank robbers.*

know sb/sth inside out ➪ know; **turn sth inside out/upside down** ➪ turn

instance
for 'instance as an example: *Some of my books have sold well. My most recent one, for instance, sold 100 000 copies.*

instant not for a/one minute/moment/second/instant ➪ minute

insult add insult to injury ➪ add

intents
to all intents (and purposes) in almost every important way: *The fighting has stopped, so to all intents and purposes, the war is over.*

intentions the road to hell is paved with good intentions ➪ road

interest
pay sth back/return sth with interest react to the harm sb has done you by doing sth even worse to them: *Peter pushed his sister, so she paid him back with interest by kicking him hard.* (interest is the extra money you receive when you lend money)

have a vested interest ➪ vested

invention necessity is the mother of invention ➪ necessity

Irish the luck of the Irish = the luck of the devil ➪ luck

iron(s)
an ,iron 'fist/,hand in a ,velvet 'glove harsh treatment of sb that is hidden behind a gentle manner: *The president ruled his country by using an iron fist in a velvet glove.*

have many, etc irons in the fire have many, etc different plans, projects, etc at the same time, often with the hope that at least one will be successful: *She's got several irons in the fire: her television work, her film work and her writing.*

rule with a rod of iron/with an iron hand ➪ rule; **strike while the iron is hot** ➪ strike

issue
(the point, etc) at issue (used when you want people to concentrate on a particular thing) the point, etc that it is important to discuss: *The point at issue here is his honesty, not the quality of his work.*

make an issue (out) of sth behave as if sth is more serious or important than it really is: *'Look, it's not important who did it. Let's not make an issue out of it.'*

take issue with sb/sth (*formal*) disagree and argue with sb about sth: *I'd like to take issue with you about what you just said.*

itch the seven-year itch ➪ seven

itchy
itchy feet (*informal*) a desire to travel, move house, change your job, etc: *He never stays in a job long. He gets itchy feet after two or three years.*

ivory
an ,ivory 'tower a way of life in which people avoid the unpleasant realities of life: *Just because I'm a writer, it doesn't mean I live in an ivory tower. I have to earn a living like anyone else.* ○ *What do professors and academics sitting in their ivory towers know about the real world?*

J

jack

a jack of 'all trades a person who can do many different kinds of work, but perhaps not very well: *He repairs cars, he paints houses, he makes furniture. He's a real jack of all trades.* (often in the phrase 'jack of all trades and master of none')

all work and no play ⇨ work; **before you, etc can/could say Jack Robinson** ⇨ say; **I'm all right, Jack** ⇨ right

jackpot   hit the jackpot ⇨ hit

jam   be money for jam = be money for old rope ⇨ money

Jane   a plain Jane ⇨ plain

jaw

your 'jaw drops your mouth opens because you are very surprised: *When they told her that she had won a million pounds, her jaw dropped in amazement.*

Jekyll

a Jekyll and 'Hyde a person with two separate personalities or ways of behaving, one good, pleasant, etc and one evil, unpleasant, etc: *He's a real Jekyll and Hyde. At home he shouts at his wife and children all the time; at work he's always charming and friendly.* (from a story by R.L.Stevenson, *Dr Jekyll and Mr Hyde*)

jelly   shake like a jelly/leaf ⇨ shake

jet

the 'jet set (*informal*) the group of very rich, luxury-loving, and fashionable people who travel a lot, either on business or for pleasure: *She's really joined the jet set now, skiing in St.Moritz, winter holidays in Barbados, shopping in Paris.* ... **'jet-setter** (*noun*) a person who belongs to the jet set: *His job takes him to New York, San Francisco, Tokyo, Rome and Madrid. He's a real jet-setter.*

jetsam   flotsam and jetsam ⇨ flotsam

jinks   high jinks ⇨ high

Job

a Job's 'comforter (*becoming dated*) a person who is sympathetic but says things which make you feel even more unhappy than you are already: *Ann came to see me when I was in hospital. She was a real Job's comforter! She told me about somebody who had the same operation as me, and then died a month later.* (a reference to the story of Job in the Bible)

the patience of Job ⇨ patience

job(s)

do the 'job/'trick (*informal*) do what is needed or wanted: *These pills should do the job. You'll feel better in no time.* ○ *I tried many different ways to stop smoking; acupuncture finally did the trick.*

give sb/sth up as a bad 'job decide that it is impossible to do sth or to change sb and then stop trying to do it: *'Are you still studying Japanese?' 'No, I gave it up as a bad job. It was far too difficult for me!'* ○ *The teacher gave her up as a bad job when she said that she didn't want to go to university.*

(it's) a good 'job/'thing (*informal*) (it's) lucky: *It's a good job he was here. We couldn't have moved the piano without him.* ○ *It's a good job my luggage was insured.*

(and) a ,good job/thing 'too (*informal*) (used to show that you are pleased to hear some news, especially if you have been waiting for it for a long time): *'They've cut the price of petrol.' 'And a good thing too.'* ○ *'I've given up smoking.' 'And a good job too.'*

have a job (doing sth) find it difficult to do sth: *I had a job getting to work on time this morning. The traffic was terrible.* ○ *'I'm going to try and repair this radio.' 'You'll have a job.'*

jobs for the 'boys (*informal, disapproving*) (giving) good jobs, positions or contracts to people only or mainly because they are friends, relatives or supporters: *The city officials here are completely corrupt. It's jobs for the boys.*

just the 'job/'ticket (*informal*) exactly what is wanted or needed.

on the job (*informal*)   **1** (while) actually working, and not drinking coffee, talking, wasting time, etc: *I've been on the job all day, and I feel exhausted.* ○ *At work we can smoke in the canteen or the corridor, but not on the job.*   **2** (*very informal, humorous*) having sex.

lie down on the job ⇨ lie; **make the best of sth/things/a bad job** ⇨ best; **odd jobs** ⇨ odd; **a put-up job** ⇨ put

jog

jog sb's memory help sb to remember sth: *So you don't remember Mary Woodson? Well, here's a photograph of you with her at Brighton which might jog your memory.*

join

join the 'club (said as a reply to someone who tells you their bad news when you are or have been in the same situation yourself; an expression of sympathy): *'I failed the exam again!' 'Join the club! Pete, Sarah and I have as well, so don't worry!'*

do/join battle ⇨ battle

joint   **put sb's nose out of joint** ⇨ nose

joke

be/get/go beyond a 'joke be no longer funny; be serious: *This has got beyond a joke! Open this door and let me out at once!* ○ *The state of the roads in this country is beyond a joke.*

be no 'joke be serious or difficult: *Trying to find a job nowadays is no joke.* ○ *It's no joke living on such a small income.*

take a 'joke find a joke or trick which is played on you amusing and accept it: *He didn't think it was funny at all when we put that pin on his chair. He really can't take a joke, can he?*

crack a joke ⇨ crack; **a practical joke** ⇨ practical

joking

you must be 'joking! (*informal*) (used to show that you don't believe sth, or that you find sth ridiculous): *'The boss wants us to work late again.' 'What? You must be joking!'* ○ *'It's the best film I've ever seen.' 'You must be joking!'*

Joneses

keep up with the Joneses (*informal,* disapproving) try to have a standard of living as high as your neighbours, especially by buying what they buy, for example a new car, new kitchen equipment, etc: *First the Smiths got a swimming pool, and now their neighbours, the Sinclairs, are building one. It's silly the way people always have to keep up with the Joneses.*

jot

not one/a jot (or tittle) (*informal*) (used both as a noun and adverb) not even the smallest amount: *There's not a jot of truth in the story.* ○ *It seems that his divorce has not affected him one jot.*

jowl   **cheek by jowl** ⇨ cheek

joy(s)

(get/have) no joy (from sb) (*informal*) (get/have) no success or luck in getting sth you want: *I tried to find that record but no joy.* ○ *'I've just been fishing.' 'Any joy?' 'Yes, I caught a big one.'* ○ *You won't get any joy from her. She doesn't give money to any kind of charity.*

full of the joys of spring ⇨ full; **sb's pride and joy** ⇨ pride

judgement   **against your better judgement** ⇨ better; **pass judgement** ⇨ pass; **sit in judgement** ⇨ sit; **a value judgement** ⇨ value

juice   **let sb stew in their own juice** ⇨ stew

jump

be/stay one jump ahead of sb/sth be/ stay slightly ahead of sb, either because you can guess, or you know, what they are going to do next or because you are better at seeing how a situation will develop: *For years he has managed to stay one jump ahead of the police.* ○ *People who are successful in business are always one jump ahead of their competitors.*

go (and) jump in a/the lake (*very informal, offensive*) (a very direct way to tell sb who is annoying you to go away or stop doing something): *I'm sick of you and your stupid questions. Go and jump in the lake!* ○ *She made me so angry that I told her to go jump in a lake.*

jump down sb's 'throat (*informal*) react

to sth that sb has said or done by suddenly speaking to them angrily: *He asked her a very simple question and she jumped down his throat. He couldn't believe it.* ○ *'It's not my fault. Don't jump down my throat.'*

jump the ˈgun (*informal*) do sth before the right time: *They jumped the gun by building the garage before they got permission from the town council.* (refers to an athlete in a race who starts running before the starter has fired the gun)

jump the ˈlights (*informal*) drive on when the traffic lights are red: *A policeman stopped us for jumping the lights.*

jump out of your ˈskin (*informal*) make a quick, sudden movement because sth, for example a loud noise or sb touching you from behind, has frightened you: *When I heard the explosion, I nearly jumped out of my skin.* ○ *She nearly jumped out of her skin when somebody banged on the door in the middle of the night.*

jump the ˈqueue (*British informal*) take a place in a queue in front of people who were there before you: *I get very angry with people who jump the queue.*

jump ˈship (of a sailor) leave a ship without permission before the end of the voyage: *Two of the sailors jumped ship in New York.*

jump to conˈclusions *or* **jump to the conˈclusion that...** decide too quickly that sth is true without knowing all the facts: *She wasn't wearing a wedding ring, and he had jumped to the conclusion that she wasn't married.* ○ *Don't go jumping to conclusions. You don't know yet what he said.*

jump to it (*informal*) (used by sb with more authority than you to tell you to do sth immediately) do it now; hurry up: *You have got ten minutes to clean this room. Now jump to it.* ○ *Jump to it, will you. We haven't got much time.*

be for the high jump ⇨ high; **climb/ jump on the bandwagon** ⇨ bandwagon; **jump in/be thrown in at the deep end** ⇨ deep; **take a running jump** ⇨ running

jungle **the law of the jungle** ⇨ law

jury
the jury is/are (still) out (on sth)

people have not yet decided if sth is good or bad: *No one knows whether the government's housing policy is popular or not. The jury is still out on that until the next election.* ○ *Was Mrs Thatcher a good Prime Minister? The jury is still out on that question.* (In the English system of law, 12 members of the public are chosen for a jury and have to decide if a person is guilty or not. They leave the courtroom to discuss the case and make their decision in secret.)

just
just about (*informal*) **1** almost; nearly: *I've just about finished my essay.* ○ *'Do you feel all right?' 'Yes, I suppose so, just about.'* **2** approximately; about: *The company has lost just about a million pounds this year.* ○ *It was just about midnight when they arrived.*

just like ˈthat suddenly and unexpectedly: *She announced that she was leaving her job at the end of this week, just like that.*

ˌjust ˈso 1 as it should be; with everything in its proper place or with everything done properly: *He likes his office to be just so, with everything in its place.* **2** (*British formal, becoming dated*) yes, I agree: *'This must never happen again.' 'Just so.'*

all/just the same ⇨ same; **be just the thing** ⇨ thing; **be not just a pretty face** ⇨ pretty; **just the job/ticket** ⇨ job; **just my, etc luck** ⇨ luck; **just think** ⇨ think; **just this once** ⇨ once; **just what the doctor ordered** ⇨ doctor; **that's just it** ⇨ that

justice
ˌdo sb/sth ˈjustice say or do sth which shows that you know or recognize the true value of sb/sth; show the true value of sth: *They were not hungry and couldn't do justice to her excellent cooking.* ○ *This photograph doesn't do him justice; he's much more handsome than that really.*

ˌdo yourself ˈjustice show how skilled, talented, clever, etc you are: *She's a very good painter, but in her recent work she has not done herself justice.* ○ *He didn't do himself justice in the match. He hadn't trained hard enough.*

poetic justice ⇨ poetic; **rough justice** ⇨ rough

K

keel on an even keel ⇨ even

keen

(as) ,keen as 'mustard (*informal*) very eager and enthusiastic: *She's as keen as mustard. She gets here first in the morning and she's the last to leave work in the evening.*

be mad keen ⇨ mad

keep

,keep it 'up (often used in the imperative) continue doing sth as well as you are already doing it: *Well done! Keep it up and maybe you'll win again next year.* ○ *They've done well so far. I wonder how long they can keep it up.*

keep yourself to your'self (used to describe a person who does not mix very much with neighbours, colleagues, etc and does not talk about personal affairs): *My neighbour keeps himself to himself. We smile and say 'good morning', but that's all.*

keep sth to yourself not tell other people about sth: *I don't want John to know about this, so keep it to yourself.*

earn your keep ⇨ earn; **keep in with sb** ⇨ in

keepers

finders keepers ⇨ finders

keeping

in/out of keeping with sth suited/unsuited to sth: *The furniture should be in keeping with the style of the house.* ○ *Her remarks were out of keeping with the formality of the occasion.*

keeps

for 'keeps (*informal*) permanently; for ever: *'Are you really giving me this beautiful ring?' 'Yes, it's yours. For keeps.'*

ken

beyond/outside your ken (*dated*) not within your knowledge or understanding: *Such things are beyond my ken.*

kettle

a different kettle of fish ⇨ different; **the pot calling the kettle black** ⇨ pot

key under lock and key ⇨ lock

kick

get a kick from/out of sth (*informal*) get a feeling of excitement, enjoyment, etc out of sth: *She got a real kick from seeing her photo in the newspaper.*

,kick against the 'pricks harm yourself by protesting when it is useless to do so: *People in prison learn very quickly not to kick against the pricks. If they complain, the prison officers make their lives very difficult.*

,kick the 'bucket (*British, very informal, humorous*) die: *He got married for the first time when he was 85 and a week later he kicked the bucket.*

,kick your 'heels (*informal*) have nothing to do while you are waiting for sth: *I've been kicking my heels here for an hour, waiting for the passport office to open.*

a kick in the pants *or* **a kick up the backside** (*very informal*) something (a shock, strong criticism, etc) which will make sb try harder, start behaving more sensibly, etc: *What he needs is a good kick up the backside. Then he'd do some work.*

kick sb in the teeth (*informal*) do sth to discourage or disappoint sb when they need and expect your help: *The workers feel they've been kicked in the teeth by their employers. They have met all their orders this year but are still being made redundant.* **a kick in the teeth** *I expected to get that job. It was a real kick in the teeth when I didn't.*

,kick over the 'traces do things which show that you do not accept the rules or control of sb in authority, for example your parents: *She smokes, she drinks, she takes drugs. She's really kicking over the traces. Her parents don't know what to do with her.*

kick up a 'fuss, 'row, etc (*informal*) complain very noisily and loudly about sth: *He kicked up a real fuss about the slow service in the restaurant.* ○ *Every time her newspaper arrives late, she kicks up a fuss.*

,kick sb up'stairs promote sb to a higher but less powerful job or position because you want to put sb better or more suitable in their present job, etc: *They couldn't sack him, so they kicked him upstairs onto the board of directors, where he could do less damage.*

'**kick yourself** (*informal*) be angry with yourself for sth you have done or not done: *'Buy it. It's a real bargain. You'll kick yourself if you don't.'* ○ *I told John that Susan was really lazy. Then somebody told me that she was a good friend of his. I could have kicked myself for being so stupid.*

beat/knock/kick the hell out of sb ⇨ hell; **kick up/make/create/raise a stink** ⇨ stink

kicking **alive and kicking** ⇨ alive

kicks

for 'kicks (*informal*) (especially of crime or violence) done for excitement and pleasure: *They destroyed the telephone boxes just for kicks.* ○ *'Why did he steal the car?' 'Just for kicks. He was bored.'*

kid

handle, treat, etc sb with kid 'gloves treat sb very carefully and gently because you don't want to upset them or make them angry: *She is so easily upset that I feel I have to treat her with kid gloves all the time.*

a whizz kid ⇨ whizz

kidding

,no 'kidding **1** (*informal*) (used to emphasize that what you are saying is true) I'm serious; I'm not joking. **2** (*informal*) (to express surprise, sometimes ironic): *'You're soaking wet.' 'No kidding.'*

kids

'**kids' stuff** something very easy: *'What did you think of the maths exam?' 'Kids' stuff. It was really easy.'*

kill(ed)

,**kill the fatted 'calf** welcome home sb who has been away for a long time by having a big celebration. (refers to the story of the prodigal son in the Bible, whose father arranged a banquet when he returned to his family)

,**kill the ,goose that ,lays the ,golden 'egg/eggs** (*saying*) destroy the thing that provides you with money, success, etc either because you don't realize what you are

doing or because you are greedy: *By trying to stop people smoking, the government may be killing the goose that lays the golden eggs, because it makes millions of pounds from the tax on cigarettes.* (from a traditional story)

,**kill or 'cure** extreme action which will either be a complete success or a complete failure: *This new chemical will either clean the painting perfectly or it will damage it badly. It's kill or cure.*

kill sth stone dead (*informal*) completely destroy sth; end sth: *This has killed my chances of promotion in this company stone dead.*

kill 'time, a couple of 'hours, etc or **have time, a couple of hours, etc to kill** do sth to help pass the time while you are waiting for sth: *'What did you do at the airport when your plane was late?' 'We killed time by playing cards and doing crosswords.'* ○ *I had two hours to kill before the train left, so I went to see a film.*

kill ,two ,birds with ,one 'stone manage to achieve two aims by doing one thing: *If we have to go to Manchester for the meeting, then let's visit Auntie Joan on the way there. We can kill two birds with one stone.*

,**kill sb with 'kindness** harm sb by being too kind to them, usually without realizing what you are doing: *The patient needs lots of exercise. Don't let him stay in bed – you'll kill him with kindness.*

kill yourself (laughing) (*informal*) laugh a lot because you find something very funny: *It was a very funny film. We killed ourselves laughing from beginning to end.*

kill yourself doing sth (*informal*) (usually in negative sentences) make a very great effort to do sth: *It would be good to leave at 7 o'clock, but don't kill yourself getting here by then. We can leave a bit later if we need to.* ○ *I nearly killed myself finishing the report in time for this meeting.*

be in at the death/kill ⇨ death; **curiosity killed the cat** ⇨ curiosity; **dressed to kill** ⇨ dressed

killing

,**make a 'killing** make a lot of money quickly, especially in business or on the stock market: *He was clever. He invested a lot* *of money in property. When prices went up, he made a killing.*

kin **kith and kin** ⇨ kith; **next of kin** ⇨ next

kind

in kind **1** (of payment) in the form of goods or services, not money: *People in the country used to pay the doctor in kind with meat, vegetables, eggs and things like that.* **2** do the same thing to sb as they have done to you, usually something unpleasant: *If they attack our troops, we will retaliate in kind.*

kind/sort of (*informal*) (used with adjectives, adverbs and verbs when something is difficult to describe or when the word you use is not exactly what you mean): *My new dress is sort of green.* ○ *He said it sort of nervously.* ○ *She kind of smiled at me.* (sometimes spelt *kinda* or *sorta*, especially when used in a song, poem, etc)

(two) of a kind (*often disapproving*) (two) people or things with similar characteristics: *Uncle Fred and your father are two of a kind; football and beer, that's all they are interested in.* ○ *He always uses the same style of photography and similar music so all his films are very much of a kind.*

of a kind/sort (*informal*) (used after a noun) of poor quality; not what he/she/it should be: *He is a poet of a kind.* ○ *They gave us meat of a kind; we could hardly eat it.*

be cruel to be kind ⇨ cruel; **nothing of the kind/sort** ⇨ nothing

kindly

not take kindly to sb/sth find it difficult to accept sb's suggestions, criticisms, opinions, behaviour: *I don't take kindly to criticism from him.* ○ *She didn't take kindly to my suggestion.* ○

kindness **kill sb with kindness** ⇨ kill; **the milk of human kindness** ⇨ milk

king

a ˌking's ˈransom a very high price: *This antique silver dish is worth a king's ransom.* (in the past, if a king was captured in a war, his country would pay a ransom for his release)

the uncrowned king/queen (of sth) ⇨ uncrowned

kingdom

blow, send, etc sb to kingdom ˈcome (*very informal*) kill sb, especially with a gun, a bomb or other very violent methods: *'If you try to call the police, I'll blow you to kingdom come.'*

till/until kingdom ˈcome (*informal*) (often used when you feel that you are wasting your time) for a long time, for ever: *You can dig here until kingdom come, but you will never find water.*

kiss

the kiss of ˈdeath (*informal*) an action or event which is certain to make a person, organization, plan, etc fail although it is meant to be favourable: *When the chairman said he had every confidence in me, I knew it was the kiss of death. Two weeks later I was looking for another job.*

the kiss of ˈlife **1** the method of restarting sb's breathing by blowing air into their lungs through the mouth; mouth-to-mouth resuscitation: *He gave the child the kiss of life, but unfortunately it was too late.* **2** any thing or action that saves an organization, business, etc: *This loan is the kiss of life that our company needs.*

kiss sth goodbye = kiss/say goodbye to sth ⇨ goodbye; **kiss/say goodbye to sth** ⇨ goodbye

kitchen

everything but/bar the kitchen ˈsink (*informal, humorous*) many more things than are necessary: *She was only staying for a few days, but she brought everything with her bar the kitchen sink!*

kite **as high as a kite** ⇨ high; **fly a kite** ⇨ fly

kith

kith and kin (*formal*) (with singular or plural verb) friends, relatives and people of your country: *He has returned to live in Italy. There he will be surrounded by his kith and kin.*

kittens

have ˈkittens (*British, informal, humorous*) be nervous and anxious, especially when you are waiting for news of sth: *Your mother's having kittens. She hasn't heard anything from John for three weeks.*

knee(s)

bring sb/sth to his/its 'knees defeat, but not completely destroy sb/sth; weaken sb/sth greatly: *The economic crisis brought the company to its knees.* ○ *The banking scandal brought the government to its knees.*

sb's knees are knocking (*informal*) feel great nervousness or fear: *It was the first time I'd ever spoken in public, and my knees were knocking!*

knee-high to a 'grasshopper (*informal, humorous*) (of a child) very young and small: *I remember the first time I saw you. You were knee-high to a grasshopper – and look at you now!*

on your 'knees **1** kneeling down: *He was on his knees praying.* ○ *She was on her knees looking for the coin.* **2** defeated; weakened greatly: *The country's economy is on its knees.* **3** (*informal*) very tired, exhausted: *After my first day in the new job, I was on my knees.*

the bee's knees ⇨ bee; **be/go weak at the knees** ⇨ weak; **on bended knee(s)** ⇨ bended; **on your hands and knees** ⇨ hands

knell **sound the death knell of sth** ⇨ sound

knickers

get/have your 'knickers in a twist (*British, informal*) react too strongly to a difficult situation by getting angry, upset, confused, etc: *Don't get your knickers in a twist! It's not the end of the world.* ○ *The boss is getting his knickers in a twist about the sales figures.*

knife

get your knife into sb *or* **have your knife in sb** (*informal*) harm and continue to harm sb (usually not physically) whom you consider your enemy: *He's had his knife into me for months, and every time I make a mistake, he tells my boss.*

like a knife through butter (cut/go) easily through sth hard: *It went through the metal door like a knife through butter.*

turn/twist the knife in the wound deliberately remind sb of sth they are already upset about, and so upset them even more: *After the divorce, her friend turned the*

knife in the wound by saying she had always thought that the marriage wouldn't last. ○ *'All right. I know I was stupid. You don't have to twist the knife.'*

cut the atmosphere with a knife ⇨ cut; **on a knife-edge/razor's edge** ⇨ edge

knight

a knight in shining armour (*often humorous*) a person who arrives to help you when you are in trouble or danger: *My car broke down at the roundabout. Luckily, a knight in shining armour stopped to help me.*

knit

knit your 'brows frown: *She knitted her brows, trying to think how she could have spent so much that week.*

knives

the knives are out (for sb) many people are criticizing sb, saying that they should stop doing sth, resign from their job, etc: *The knives are out for the Prime Minister. People are demanding his resignation.*

knock(ed)

you could have knocked me, etc down with a 'feather (*informal*) (used when telling sb about a very surprising experience) I was very surprised: *When they told me how much the painting was worth, you could have knocked me down with a feather!*

knock it 'off (*very informal*) (often used as a command) stop doing sth, esp making a noise: *Knock it off, will you? I'm trying to work.*

knock sb off their 'perch/'pedestal show that sb does not deserve to be admired so much: *This new book really knocks him off his pedestal.*

knock sth on the head (*informal*) put an end to a project, by showing that it is impossible, unrealistic or incorrect: *The increase in prices has knocked our plan to buy a house on the head.* ○ *These statistics knock your theory on the head, I'm afraid.*

knock sb 'sideways (*informal*) shock or amaze sb very much: *His wife's death has really knocked him sideways.*

knock 'spots off sb/sth (*informal*) be very much better than sb/sth else: *This book knocks spots of all the other books on Napoleon.* ○ *You'll knock spots off her. You're a much* *better player.*

knock the stuffing out of sb (*informal*) make sb feel weak, mentally and/or physically: *When his wife left him, it seemed to knock the stuffing out of him.* o *This flu has really knocked the stuffing out of me.*

beat/knock/kick the hell out of sb/sth ⇨ hell; **get/knock/lick sb/sth into shape** ⇨ shape; **knock/bang heads together** ⇨ heads; **knock on wood = touch wood** ⇨ touch

knocking sb's **knees are knocking** ⇨ knees

knot(s) at a **rate of knots** ⇨ rate; **get tied in knots = tie yourself in knots** ⇨ tie; **tie the knot** ⇨ tie; **tie sb up in knots** ⇨ tie; **tie yourself in knots** ⇨ tie

knotted

get 'knotted/'stuffed (*very informal, offensive*) (used for expressing anger at sb): *John's neighbour started complaining about the noise again, so he told her to get stuffed.*

know

before you know where you are before you have time to realize that sth has happened: *Before I knew where I was, my handbag had been snatched and the thief was running away with it.* o *Air travel is fantastic. You get on a plane in London, in the rain, and before you know where you are, you're sitting on a beach in the sun.*

in the 'know (*informal*) having information or knowledge that most other people do not have: *Only a few of us were in the know about the date of the wedding. We didn't want the press to find out.* o *People in the know say that this is the best Spanish wine you can buy.*

know sth 'backwards (*informal*) know sth (a subject, a book, the law, etc) very well: *He knows the play backwards.* o *She knows the history of Scotland backwards.*

know 'best know what should be done in a situation because you have knowledge and/or experience: *'I want to get up.'' But the doctor said you were to stay in bed, and he knows best.'* o *Everyone said that I shouldn't go there alone but I thought I knew best.*

know sb by sight recognize sb and know who they are, without having spoken to

them: *I haven't actually met Dr. Galston, but I know him by sight of course.*

know 'different/'otherwise (*informal*) have more information about sth: *People thought she was depressed about her husband's death, but I knew different.*

know sb/sth inside 'out know sb/sth very well: *You've read that book so often that you must know it inside out by now.* o *She knows me inside out. I can't hide anything from her.*

know sth like the back of your 'hand know a place very well: *As a taxi-driver, you have to know the city like the back of your hand.*

know no 'bounds (usually with abstract nouns) be without limits; be very great: *His generosity knows no bounds.*

know your own 'mind know what you want or like: *At 25 you are old enough to know your own mind and make these decisions for yourself.*

know the 'score (*informal*) know the true situation, especially if this is bad: *'Look, I know the score, but I'm still prepared to try.'*

know your 'stuff (*informal*) know everything that you should know about a job, a subject, etc: *I was very impressed by the lawyer. He really knows his stuff.*

know a thing or two (about sb/sth) (*informal*) (often used ironically) know a lot about sb/sth from your own experience: *After ten years as a teacher, I know a thing or two about how children learn.* o *'How much do you know about computers?' 'Oh, I know a thing or two.'* also **can/could teach/tell sb a thing or two (about sth)** be able to help sb, or teach sb how to do sth, because you have more experience: *He thinks he knows a lot about farming, but old Bert could teach him a thing or two.*

know sth very/perfectly well (used when you wish to indicate that the person you are speaking to already knows sth you have just said or are about to say.): *You know very well that smoking is forbidden in this room.* o *You know perfectly well what I am referring to.*

know your way about/around (sth) be familiar with a place, with how things are done etc; be experienced: *I'd used the library before, so I knew my way around and found the* book quite quickly.

know what you are 'doing/a'bout
(*informal*) have experience of doing sth and
therefore understand it fully: *'I'm worried
about David using that machine.' 'Don't worry.
He knows what he's doing.'*

know what you are 'talking about
(*informal*) have good knowledge of sth; be an
expert on sth: *I really enjoyed that lecture. She
certainly knows what she is talking about.* ○
*That history teacher doesn't know what he is
talking about. He makes a lot of mistakes.*

know what is good for you know what
is necessary for you to do to be successful,
etc; know how to avoid trouble: *If you know
what's good for you, young man, you'll talk to
nobody about what you've seen here tonight.*

know what it is to be/do sth have
personal experience of being/doing sth: *I
know what it is to be a mother, so believe me
when I say it is very hard work.*

know what's 'what (*informal*) know all
that needs to be known in a particular
situation or in general: *Ask Ann. She knows
what's what. She's been here for years.*

know where you are/stand know what
your position is; know what sb expects of
you: *I don't know where I stand with him. I
don't know what he feels about me.* ○ *'Has she
talked to you about your chances of promotion?
Do you know where you stand?'*

know where you are going know
clearly what you want to achieve (in life, in
your job, etc): *He knows exactly where he is
going. He wants to be president.*

**know which side your 'bread is
buttered** (*informal*) know what to do in
order to gain advantages, stay in a
favourable situation, etc: *I'm sure Ray will
make a special effort to please the new
supervisor – after all, he knows which side his
bread is buttered!*

not know any 'better not behave well,
politely, etc because you have never learned
how to: *You can't blame him for his bad table
manners; he doesn't know any better.*

not know you are born (*informal*) not
realize how easy your life or situation is
compared to other people's: *We complain
about our health service here, but really we
don't know we're born. Some countries have far*

worse services than ours.

not know your arse from your 'elbow
(*very informal, offensive*) know nothing or
very little; be incompetent: *Don't ask him to
organize it! He doesn't know his arse from his
elbow!*

not know the first 'thing about sb/sth
(*informal*) know nothing at all about sb/sth:
*I don't know the first thing about Chinese
history.*

not know sb from 'Adam (*informal*) not
know who sb is: *This man came into the office
and he said that he knew me. I didn't know him
from Adam. It was very embarrassing.*

not know the 'meaning of the word
(*disapproving*) not have enough experience
of sth to understand what it really is; not be
capable of really understanding sth: *Love?
He doesn't know the meaning of the word.* ○
*They talk about justice, but they don't know the
meaning of the word.*

not know what you are missing not
realize how good, amusing, interesting, etc
sth is because you have never tried it: *'Why
don't you come windsurfing at the weekend?'
'Thanks, but I'm not really interested in it.' 'Oh,
come on. You don't know what you're missing.'*

not know what to 'do with yourself
not know how to spend your time: *I hardly
know what to do with myself when the children
go back to school. I have so much free time.*

**not know whether you are coming or
going** (*informal*) be confused about what
you are doing, because you are doing too
many things at the same time: *I've got so
much work to do that I don't know whether I'm
coming or going.*

not know which way to look *or* **not
know where to look** (*informal*) not know
how to react or behave in an embarrassing
situation: *When a half-naked woman walked
into the room, nobody knew where to look.*

not know which way to turn *or* **not
know where to turn** not know what to
do, where to get help, etc in a difficult
situation or crisis: *I've got so many problems
at the moment that I don't know which way to
turn.* ○ *She didn't know where to turn for help
when her daughter started taking drugs.*

**(well) what do you 'know (about
'that)?** (*informal*) (used for expressing

surprise, usually pleasant, when sb tells you some interesting news): *'Dave tells me he's getting married to Jane next month.' 'Well, what do you know?'*

you know (*informal*) **1** (used to remind sb of sth you have told them before): *You know I bought a new bag. Well, someone stole it last night.* **2** (used to emphasize sth): *'Do you love me?' 'You know I do.'* **3** (used when you are trying to explain sth more clearly): *He's, you know, strange. It's hard to explain what I mean.*

,you know as well as 'I do (used when you are trying to convince sb) it is obvious: *You know as well as I do that if she finds out, she'll stop us going.*

better the devil you know ⇨ better; **have/know all the answers** ⇨ answers; **I know what = I/I'll tell you what** ⇨ tell; **not want to know** ⇨ want; **show sb/ learn/know the ropes** ⇨ ropes; **you never know** ⇨ never

knowing
there is no knowing/saying/telling...

it is impossible to know/say/tell: *There is no telling what he may do when he gets angry.* ○ *There's no saying what will happen.*

knowledge have a working knowledge of sth ⇨ working

known for a/some reason/reasons best known to herself, etc ⇨ reason; **have seen/known better days** ⇨ better

knows
God/goodness/Heaven knows 1 (*informal*) I don't know; no one knows: *'What's going to happen next?' 'God knows.'* **2** (used for adding emphasis to a statement, opinion etc): *God knows how he manages to survive on such a small salary.* ○ *I'm no gardening expert, goodness knows!*

Lord knows! ⇨ Lord

knuckles give, get, etc a rap over the knuckles ⇨ rap; **rap sb over the knuckles = give, get, etc a rap over the knuckles** ⇨ rap

L

labour
a ,labour of 'love work that you do for your own pleasure and satisfaction, not for money or profit: *This tablecloth is a real labour of love. It took her years to make it.*

'labour the point continue to repeat or explain sth that is already clear: *I think you've said enough – there's no need to labour the point.*

lack
not for lack/want of trying, being told, etc not because you haven't tried, etc: *He's had no success in finding a job, though not for want of trying.*

have/lack the courage of your convictions ⇨ courage

ladder the top of the tree/ladder ⇨ top

ladies
a 'ladies' man a man who likes the

company of women and is successful with them: *Jim had always been a bit of a ladies' man, but he didn't get married until he was 45.*

lads be one of the lads/boys/girls ⇨ one

lake go jump in a/the lake ⇨ jump

lamb
as/like a lamb to the slaughter (do sth or go somewhere) without protesting, probably because you do not realize that you are in danger: *When the war started, thousands of young men went off to fight, like lambs to the slaughter.*

be mutton dressed as lamb ⇨ mutton; **sb may/might as well be hanged/hung for a sheep as a lamb** ⇨ hanged

lame
a ,lame 'duck (*informal*) a person or an organization that is in serious difficulties

and needs help in order to survive: *My uncle is a bit of a lame duck. The family has to help him all the time.* ○ *The shipping industry had become a lame duck.*

land

in the land of the 'living (*humorous*) alive: *Nice to see you. I'm glad to see that you're still in the land of the living.*

fall/land on your feet ⇨ feet; **live off/on the fat of the land** ⇨ live; **the promised land** ⇨ promised; **spy out the land** ⇨ spy

landscape a blot on the landscape ⇨ blot

lane in the fast lane ⇨ fast; **take sb/go down memory lane** ⇨ memory

language

speak/talk the same/a different language share/not share ideas, experiences, opinions, etc, that make real communication or understanding possible: *Unions and managers are at last beginning to speak the same language.* ○ *Artists and scientists simply talk a different language.*

strong language/words ⇨ strong

lap

drop/fall into sb's lap (*informal*) be obtained without any effort: *You won't find a job by waiting for it to fall into your lap. You'll have to go out and find one!*

in the lap of the 'gods (the success of something is) uncertain because it depends on luck or on things beyond your control: *I don't know what's going to happen. It's in the lap of the gods now. All we can do is wait.*

in the lap of 'luxury in conditions of great comfort and luxury: *I really enjoyed living in the lap of luxury for a couple of weeks. It was a wonderful hotel.*

the last lap ⇨ last

large

at 'large 1 (after a noun) as a whole, in general: *The public at large does not know enough about AIDS.* **2** (of an escaped criminal or dangerous animal) free: *A lion has escaped and is at large in north London.*

by and 'large generally speaking; taking everything into consideration: *By and large,* schools are good in this country.

(as) large as 'life (used of sb who is seen in person, often unexpectedly): *I thought she'd left the country, but there she was, large as life, in the supermarket!*

in great/large measure ⇨ measure; **in large part** ⇨ part; **loom large** ⇨ loom

larger

larger than 'life very impressive but seeming slightly unreal: *He's one of those larger than life characters.*

lark

be up/,rise with the 'lark get up early in the morning: *She was up with the lark this morning.*

Larry

(as) happy as the day is long/as a sandboy/as Larry ⇨ happy

last

at (long) 'last at the end of a period of waiting, trying etc; finally: *At long last she's got a job in a theatre in Manchester.*

at the last 'minute/'moment as late as possible; almost too late: *Why do you always have to arrive at the last moment?* **last-minute** (*adjective*) *last-minute changes of plan, decisions, preparations, etc*

have the last 'laugh (*informal*) be successful at sth in the end, even though other people thought that this was not possible: *When he invented this machine, everybody laughed at it, but he's sold 10 000 of them. He certainly had the last laugh.*

have, etc the last 'word make the final point in a discussion or argument: *She always likes to have the last word in any argument.*

last but not least *or* **last but by no means least** (used to say that the last person or thing on a list, etc is as important as the others): *He thanked everyone by name for their help: Mr. Watkins for preparing the food, Ms Smith for the flowers, Ms Jackson for her speech, and last, but by no means least, Mr Jones for arranging the seats.*

a ,last-,ditch 'stand/at'tempt/'effort a final attempt to avoid defeat: *They are making a last-ditch stand to save the company.* ○ *This is a last-ditch attempt to stop the strike.*

the last 'lap the final part of sth, for

example your studies, a journey, which has taken a long time: *Her medical studies finish next year. She's on the last lap now.* ○ *They are on the last lap of their journey round the world.* (a lap is a single circuit of a running track)

(as) a last re'sort a thing you decide to do when everything else has failed: *Nobody wanted to lend me the money. As a last resort I asked my brother-in-law, and luckily he was able to help me.*

last 'thing (at night) immediately before going to bed or to sleep: *Last thing at night they always had a cup of hot chocolate.*

the last 'word (in sth) the most recent, most fashionable, etc of its type: *The advertisers say that this new car is the last word in luxury.* ○ *This is the last word in computer technology.*

your last 'word (on/about sth) my, her, etc final decision or statement about sth: '*Will you take £900?*' '*No, £1 000 and that's my last word.*' ○ '*That's my last word on the matter.*'

on your/its last legs (*informal*) (of people) about to die; very tired, exhausted; (of a thing, organization) about to stop functioning, for example, because it is old: *He was on his last legs and would never paint another picture.* ○ *This photocopier is on its last legs.*

be the last/final straw ➪ straw; **breathe your last** ➪ breathe; **famous last words** ➪ famous; **first and last** ➪ first; **the first/last to do sth** ➪ first; **he who laughs last laughs longest** ➪ laughs; **hear/see the end/the last of sb/sth** ➪ hear; **a week last Monday, etc** ➪ week

late

of late (*formal*) recently: *He has been feeling rather unwell of late. He ought to see the doctor.*

late in the 'day (do sth) later than you should: *It's a bit late in the day to tell me that. I've already bought the tickets.*

better late than never ➪ better

later

see you around/later = **see you!** ➪ see; **sooner or later** ➪ sooner

laugh

for a laugh *or* **for laughs** for fun and amusement: '*Why did you hide her glasses?*' '*Oh, just for a laugh.*' ○ *We all went swimming at 2am just for a laugh.*

laugh in sb's 'face (*informal*) openly show your low opinion of sb when they ask for sth, or say sth that you find silly or ridiculous: *When I made my suggestion at the meeting, everybody just laughed in my face.*

laugh on the other side of your face (*informal*) (said rudely and unkindly) your happiness or satisfaction with something changes to unhappiness or disappointment, which you deserve: *If you think you've tricked me, then you're wrong! You'll soon be laughing on the other side of your face!*

laugh sb/sth out of 'court (*informal*) refuse, in an unpleasant way, to consider seriously sb's suggestion, opinion, etc because you think it's stupid: *When she suggested trying the new treatment, they laughed her out of court.*

laugh up your 'sleeve (at sb/sth) be secretly amused by sth: *Only he knew the whole story about the money. He must have been laughing up his sleeve all through the meeting.*

have the last laugh ➪ last; **raise a laugh/smile** ➪ raise

laughing

be 'laughing (*informal*) be in a fortunate position; have no worries: *If you earn that huge amount in your new job, you'll be laughing!*

no laughing 'matter something which is too serious to joke about: *Trying to find a job at the moment is no laughing matter.* ○ *This is no laughing matter. The situation is very serious.*

die laughing ➪ die

laughs

he who laughs last laughs 'longest (*saying*) (often used to warn sb that they should not be too confident of their success) do not be too proud of your present success; in the end another person may be more successful than you: *You think just because you've won this game, that means you're the best player. Well, wait until the championship. Remember, he who laughs last laughs longest.*

laurels

laurels look to your laurels ➪ look; **rest on your laurels** ➪ rest

law

have the 'law on sb (*very informal*) (often used as a threat) report sb to the police: *'If you have one more noisy party, I'll have the law on you.'*

law and 'order a situation in which most people in a country respect and obey the law; public order: *There has been a breakdown in law and order in some parts of the country.* ○ *It's the job of the police to maintain law and order.* ○ *The President praised the forces of law and order* (= the police and the army).

the law of the 'jungle a situation where there are no rules of civilized behaviour; a state of fierce competition in which the strongest win and the weakest are not protected: *The police daren't go into certain parts of the city. It's the law of the jungle in there.* ○ *In this business it's the law of the jungle.*

a law unto him'self/her'self a person who does what he/she wants, even when this is against the rules and customs of a group or society in general: *That man is a law unto himself. He comes to work when he likes, he goes home when he likes and when he's here he doesn't do what he's supposed to do.*

take the law into your own 'hands take action personally against sb who, in your opinion, has broken the law or done sth wrong instead of calling the police: *I knew who had stolen my car, so I took the law into my own hands. I went to his house and beat him up. The police arrested both of us!*

lay down the law ⇨ lay; **the letter of the law** ⇨ letter; **the long arm of the law** ⇨ long; **Parkinson's law** ⇨ Parkinson; **possession is nine points/tenths/parts of the law** ⇨ possession; **sb's word is law** ⇨ word

lay(s)

lay sth at sb's door blame sb for sth: *The failure of the talks cannot be laid at the government's door.* **lie at sb's door** (of the responsibility for a mistake, etc) belong to sb: *The main problem is the design of the building and the responsibility for that lies clearly at the architect's door.*

lay sth 'bare reveal sth which has never been seen before: *She laid bare her feelings for him.* ○ *The report lays bare the shocking housing conditions in this city.*

lay down your 'arms stop fighting in a war etc: *Tell your men to lay down their arms –the war's over.*

lay down the 'law (*informal*) (used for showing disapproval) give sb orders and express your opinions in an unpleasant, aggressive way, often when you have no right to do so: *He came in here this morning and started laying down the law about all kinds of things. Who does he think he is?*

lay down your 'life (for sb/sth) (*formal*) die for (your country, a cause etc): *Thousands of young men laid down their lives in the war so that we could live in freedom.*

lay a 'finger on sb/sth (*informal*) (usually in negative sentences) harm sb/sth by touching, etc him/it: *If you lay a finger on her, I'll call the police.* ○ *'Who broke the video camera?' 'Not me, I didn't lay a finger on it, I promise.'*

lay/pile it 'on (thick/with a trowel) say that sth is much better or much worse than it really is because you want to impress sb: *He told her that she was his favourite author, that she wrote the most beautiful English, and that she deserved the Nobel Prize for literature. He really laid it on with a trowel.* ○ *The headteacher shouted at me for ages about my poor work. He really piled it on.*

,lay it on the 'line (*informal*) tell sb sth in an honest, direct and forceful way: *She laid it on the line. She told us that we would fail the exam unless we worked harder.*

lay sb 'low (*informal*) (of an illness) cause sb to go to bed or be unable to work normally: *That flu laid her low for a couple of weeks.*

lay sb to 'rest (*formal*) bury sb: *He was laid to rest in Westminster Abbey, with other great English poets.*

lay sth to 'rest put an end to sth (a story, a rumour, a belief, a theory, etc): *The rumour about the Prime Minister and that journalist has finally been laid to rest.*

lay sth 'waste *or* **lay 'waste to sth** (*formal*) destroy everything, especially in a war: *As the army retreated, it laid waste to thousands of acres of farmland.*

clap/lay/set eyes on sb/sth ⇨ eyes; **get/lay your hands on sb** ⇨ hands; **get/lay your hands on sth** ⇨ hands; **kill the**

goose that lays the golden egg ⇨ kill;
put/lay your cards on the table ⇨ cards;
put/lay your head on the block ⇨ head

lead

give a 'lead (on sth) give people
encouragement to do sth by doing it yourself
first: *The government should give a lead on
protection of the environment.*

lead sb astray encourage sb to behave in a
silly or criminal way: *Small children are easily
led astray by older children.* ○ *He's a weak
character, who's easily led astray.*

lead sb to believe (that...) make sb think
sth is true, often wrongly: *I was led to believe
that I didn't need a visa to enter the country,
and now it appears that I do.* ○ *She led me to
believe that she was a student, but she wasn't.*

lead sb up the garden 'path (*informal*)
cause sb to believe sth that is not true;
deceive sb: *I think you're just leading us up the
garden path – now, come on, tell us the truth!* ○
*He had led her up the garden path, telling her he
wasn't married.*

lead the 'way   1 go in front of sb in order
to show them the way: *She led the way to the
conference hall.*   **2** be the first to do or
develop sth: *The United States was leading the
way in space research.*

**you can take/lead a horse to water, but
you can't make it drink** ⇨ horse; **lead/
live the life of Reilly/Riley** ⇨ life; **swing
the lead** ⇨ swing

leading

a ,leading 'light (in/of sth) an important
and respected member of a group, an
organization, a profession, etc: *Mr Harris is a
leading light in the local business community.*

a ,leading 'question a question carefully
formed to obtain the answer that the
questioner wants to hear: *That's a leading
question.* ○ *Lawyers are experts on leading
questions. You have to be very careful when you
answer them.*

the blind leading the blind ⇨ blind

leaf

take a leaf out of sb's 'book follow sb's
example because you admire them and their
way of doing sth: *If you're having difficulty
with the children, take a leaf out of Sandra's
book. She knows how to control them.*

shake like a jelly/leaf ⇨ shake; **turn
over a new leaf** ⇨ turn

league

**be not in the same league/class/
street** (*informal*) be of a much lower
standard than sb/sth: *He was a good painter,
but not in the same league as Picasso.* ○ *We're
not in the same class as the Swiss ski team.
They're the best in the world.*

leak   spring a leak ⇨ spring

lean   bend/lean over backwards to do
sth ⇨ backwards

leap(s)

by/in ,leaps and 'bounds in large
amounts or very quickly: *My knowledge of
German increased by leaps and bounds when I
lived in Germany for a year.* ○ *Production is
going up by leaps and bounds.*

come/spring/leap to mind ⇨ mind; **look
before you leap** ⇨ look; **a quantum leap**
⇨ quantum

learn

learn your 'lesson learn sth from your
(unfortunate) experiences in the past: *I used
to carry a lot of money on me, until one day my
bag was stolen. Since then, I've learned my
lesson.*

do/learn sth the hard way ⇨ hard;
show   sb/learn/know   the   ropes
⇨ ropes; **live and learn** ⇨ live

lease   a new lease of life ⇨ new

leash   strain at the leash ⇨ strain

least

at least   **1** (of a number) not less than:
*There were at least 70 000 people at the
concert.*   **2** the minimum sb should do: *I
know it's difficult for him to telephone me, but
he could at least write.* ○ *You could at least
apologize.*   **3** (used for talking about the
only advantage or good point of sb/sth): *This
car is slow, it uses a lot of petrol, but at least it
doesn't break down.*   **4** (used to show you
are not completely sure of sth): *It's true. At
least, I think so.*

(,not) in the 'least (used in negative
sentences, questions and *if*-clauses) (not) at
all: *She wasn't in the least afraid.* ○ *If you are in
the least worried about it, then ask for help.*

the (very) least you can do the minimum you should do: *The least you can do is apologize.* ○ *'Thank you so much for helping me.' 'Well, it was the least I could do.'*

not least especially: *There are a lot of complaints about the new road, not least because of the noise.*

last but not least ⇨ last; **the less/least said, the better** ⇨ said; **take/follow the line of least resistance** ⇨ line; **to say the least** ⇨ say

leather **hell for leather** ⇨ hell

leave

leave/let sb/sth a'lone/'be not take, touch, disturb, etc sb/sth: *Please leave those books alone. I don't want anybody to touch them.* ○ *She's working, so let her be!*

leave a bad/nasty 'taste in the/your mouth (of an experience) make you feel angry, bitter, or disgusted: *The idea that the money had been stolen from her sick mother left a nasty taste in the mouth.* ○ *When you see someone being treated so unkindly, it leaves a bad taste in your mouth.*

leave sb 'cold not interest, excite, move or impress sb: *Classical music leaves me absolutely cold, but I love rock.* ○ *His kind of humour just leaves me cold.*

leave the 'door open (for/on sth) allow sb to continue discussions, negotiations, etc if they wish: *The management were intelligent enough to leave the door open for further negotiations with the union.*

leave sb holding the 'baby (informal) leave sb to take the responsibility or blame for sth: *It's always the same. We all agree to do something, then you all say you're too busy to arrange it, and I am left holding the baby.*

leave sb in the 'lurch (informal) leave sb who is in a difficult situation and needs your help: *You can't resign now and leave us all in the lurch. It wouldn't be fair.*

leave it at 'that (informal) say or do no more about sth: *We talked about it for a few minutes, I made a few suggestions, and we left it at that.*

leave a lot, much, etc to be de'sired be not good enough: *Your standard of work has gone down. In fact, it leaves a great deal to be desired.* ○ *The acting in some of those early films left much to be desired.*

leave no stone un'turned try everything possible to find or obtain sth: *We must leave no stone unturned in our search for peace.* ○ *The police left no stone unturned in their efforts to find the little girl.*

leave of absence (formal) permission to be absent from work for a certain period of time: *Several of my colleagues have had leave of absence to go on training courses.*

leave sb/sth standing (informal) be much better than sb/sth: *In maths and science she leaves the others standing.* ○ *This dictionary leaves the others standing.*

leave sb 'to it (informal) allow sb to continue doing sth on their own, without your help: *Oh well, we'll leave you to it, Derek – you seem to be managing very well by yourself.*

leave sb to their own de'vices leave sb to do something without your help, or to spend their time as they like: *I've explained everything to him. Now I'm leaving him to his own devices, and we'll see how he manages.* ○ *The children were usually left to their own devices in the summer holidays.*

leave word (with sb) leave a message with sb: *He left word with his secretary where to contact him if necessary.*

take it or leave it **1** (used to end a discussion about an offer to buy, sell, etc) accept this offer or refuse it – I am not going to change my mind. **2** (informal) (with can, not used in the negative) not feel strongly about sth; not mind sth: *'Do you like Indian food?''I can take it or leave it.'*

take ˌleave of your 'senses (informal, humorous) behave as if you are mad: *You want £25 000 for it? Have you taken leave of your senses?* ○ *I think my aunt has taken leave of her senses. She wants to make a will leaving all her money to a dogs' home.*

keep/leave your options open ⇨ options; **leave/make your/its mark** ⇨ mark; **leave/put sth on one side** ⇨ side; **leave/let well alone** ⇨ well; **take French leave** ⇨ French

left

have two left 'feet (informal) be unable to dance, run, etc well because you are clumsy: *I'm a hopeless dancer. I've got two left* *feet.*

the left hand does not know what the right hand is doing (*informal*) one part of an organization, group, etc does not know what another part is doing: *First I got a letter from them saying they couldn't return my money, and then the next day they sent me a cheque. Obviously the left hand doesn't know what the right is doing.*

,left, right, and 'centre (*informal*) in or from all directions: *He was shouting orders left, right, and centre.* ○ *She was criticized left, right, and centre for her views on education.*

leg

give sb a 'leg up   1 (*informal*) help sb climb up or onto sth, for example, a horse or a wall: *I gave him a leg up.*   **2** (*informal*) help sb, usually by giving them money: *His father gave him a leg up when he was starting his business.*

not have a ,leg to 'stand on (*informal*) not be able to prove what you say: *He claims he wasn't there, but four people saw him, so he doesn't have a leg to stand on.*

pull sb's leg ⇨ pull

legend

a living 'legend *or* **a legend in your own 'lifetime** a person who has become famous while still alive: *Her 30-year study of chimpanzees made her a living legend.*

legs have, etc your tail between your legs ⇨ tail; **on your/its last legs** ⇨ last; **stretch your legs** ⇨ stretch; **talk the hind legs off a donkey** ⇨ talk

leisure

at your leisure *or* **at leisure** without needing to hurry, at a convenient time for you: *Holidays are wonderful; you can do everything at leisure.* ○ *I'm not going to read this report now; I'll read it later at my leisure.*

lend

lend 'colour to sth make sth seem probable: *The tracks outside the house lend colour to her claim that somebody tried to break in last night.*

lend an 'ear (to sb/sth) (*becoming dated*) listen to what sb is telling you: *He's a good friend. He's always ready to lend a sympathetic ear.*

lend a 'hand (with sth) help (to do sth): *I saw two men pushing a broken-down car along the road so I stopped to lend a hand.* ○ *She stayed with us for three weeks and didn't once lend a hand with the washing-up!*

lend your name to sth allow your name to be used publicly by an organization, campaigners, etc: *Famous actors sometimes lend their names to political causes.*

length(s)

at length   1 (*formal*) after a long time: *There was a long silence and when, at length, she spoke, he could hardly hear her.*   **2** in great detail and taking a long time: *She talked at length about her work in hospitals.*

go to any, great, etc 'lengths (to do sth) try very hard (to do sth); do whatever is necessary: *She went to great lengths to find this book.* ○ *They were prepared to go to any lengths to find their son.*

the length and breadth of sth everywhere in an area: *I've travelled the length and breadth of Britain, but I've never seen such beautiful scenery as here.*

keep sb at arm's length ⇨ arm

leopard

a leopard cannot change its spots (*saying*) a person's character does not change: *A dictator is unlikely to become a good leader in a democracy. A leopard cannot change its spots.*

less

even/much/still less (follows a negative statement and introduces another negative statement, for emphasis) and certainly not: *I don't want even to see her, much less speak to her.* ○ *I don't like beer, even less do I like warm, weak English beer.*

in less than 'no time (*informal*) in very little time; very quickly: *She started learning Chinese last year and in less than no time she could hold a conversation in it.*

the less/least said, the better ⇨ said; **more haste, less speed** ⇨ haste; **more or less** ⇨ more;   **not   care   less** ⇨ care; **nothing less than** ⇨ nothing

lesser

the ,lesser of two 'evils the better of two things that are both bad: *Neither candidate* *seemed capable of governing the country. People voted for him as the lesser of two evils.*

lesson **learn your lesson** ⇨ learn; **an object lesson** ⇨ object; **teach sb a lesson** ⇨ teach

let

let sb/sth go *or* **let go of sb/sth** stop holding sb/sth: *Let go of me.* ○ *Don't let go of my hand, or you'll get lost.*

,let yourself 'go behave more freely than usual; relax: *The students really let themselves go at the party after their exams.*

,let yourself/sth 'go not look after your appearance, your house, garden, etc: *He has really let himself go since his wife died.* ○ *When I'm so busy, I just have to let the garden go.*

let sb 'have it (*very informal*) punish sb or speak to them very angrily: *She annoyed me so much that I let her have it.* ○ *Dad will let you have it when he sees that broken window.*

let it 'go (at that) say or do nothing more about sth: *I could have disagreed with him, but I let it go at that. I don't like arguments.* ○ *The police spoke firmly to the boy about the damage and then let it go at that.*

letter

the ,letter of the 'law the exact meaning of a law, agreement, etc; a strict interpretation of the law: *We must keep to the letter of the law.*

to the letter with attention to every detail; exactly: *I followed your instructions to the letter.*

a dead letter ⇨ dead; **a four-letter word** ⇨ four; **an open letter** ⇨ open; **a poison-pen letter** ⇨ poison; **a red-letter day** ⇨ red

level

do/try your level best try as hard as you can: *I'll do my level best to be there by ten o'clock, but I can't promise anything.*

keep a level head remain calm and sensible, even in difficult situations: *She managed to keep a level head when all the others panicked.* **level-headed** (*adjective*) *Nurses need to be level-headed.*

,level 'pegging making progress at the same rate as another person or group: *There's ten minutes left, and the teams are still level pegging.*

on the 'level (*informal*) honest; genuine; sincere: *I promise you that he's on the level. He's never been involved in anything criminal.*

sink to sb's level ⇨ sink

liberties

take liberties (with sb/sth) be more free with sb/sth than you should be: *The translator has taken too many liberties with this. The original meaning is lost.* ○ *She uses our telephone without asking. She's really taking liberties.* ○ *She's not the sort of woman people would take liberties with.*

liberty

at liberty (to do sth) (*formal*) having permission to do sth: *You are at liberty to leave, if you wish.*

take the liberty of doing sth (*formal*) do sth without permission: *I have taken the liberty of giving your address to a friend who is visiting London. I hope you don't mind.*

licence **poetic licence** ⇨ poetic

lick

lick sb's 'boots (*informal*) *or* **lick sb's arse** (*offensive*) behave towards sb in power in a very humble way, doing everything you can to please them: *It makes me very angry when I see Andrew licking Mr Smith's boots all the time.*

a lick of paint a coat of fresh paint: *All this house needs is a good clean and a lick of paint.*

lick your 'wounds comfort yourself after sth painful or disappointing has happened to you: *'He heard this morning that he hasn't got the job.' 'Where is he?' 'Licking his wounds somewhere, probably.'*

get/knock/lick sb/sth into shape ⇨ shape

lid

keep/put the 'lid on sth (*informal*) try to make sure that people don't do sth or find out about sth: *The government wants to keep the lid on discussion of tax reforms at the moment.*

lift, blow, etc the 'lid off sth (*informal*) reveal a scandal to the public: *The story in today's paper really lifts the lid off the use of drugs in horse racing.*

put the (tin) 'lid on sth (*informal*) bring

to an end an activity, your hopes, plans, etc: *I've got a place at an American university but I can't afford to go, so that's put the lid on that.* ○ *It rained and rained, so that put the tin lid on our plans for a picnic in the park.*

lie

give the 'lie to sth (*rather formal*) show that a statement, etc is false or inaccurate: *These statistics give the lie to the government's claim that inflation is under control.*

lie 'doggo (*informal*) be very still or hide somewhere so that you will not be found: *I lay doggo in the shed while the police searched the house for me.*

lie down on the 'job (*informal*) not do a job properly: *I'm not going to employ anybody here who lies down on the job. I only want people who work hard.*

lie in state (of the body of a king, queen, political leader, etc) be placed for people to see before it is buried: *Before the funeral, Churchill's body lay in state in Westminster Abbey.*

lie in 'store (for sb) (of events, etc) be waiting to happen (to sb): *I wonder what lies in store for us in our new life in California.*

lie in 'wait hide and wait for sb so that you can attack them: *The police think the murderer must have been lying in wait for her.*

lie 'low (*informal*) hide or keep quiet for a short time: *The thieves lay low for a few days in a farmhouse, then tried to leave the country with the money.*

lie through your 'teeth (*informal*) tell very obvious lies without being embarrassed: *He was lying through his teeth when he said he had been given the money.*

lie your way into/out of sth get yourself into/out of a situation by telling lies: *I lied my way into the concert by claiming to be a journalist.* ○ *'How is he going to lie his way out of that?' 'He can't. Too many people already know the truth.'*

have made your bed and have to lie on it ⇨ bed; **let sleeping dogs lie** ⇨ sleeping; **lie at sb's door = lay sth at sb's door** ⇨ lay; **a white lie** ⇨ white

lies

a pack of lies ⇨ pack; **there is/lies the rub** ⇨ rub; **time hangs/lies heavy** ⇨ time; **a tissue of lies** ⇨ tissue

life

bring sb/sth to 'life make sb/sth more lively, interesting or attractive: *It was only her performance that brought the film to life.* ○ *If you put two or three lamps in here, it would really bring the room to life.* ○

for dear 'life *or* **for your 'life** because you are in danger: *Run for your life! A tiger has escaped from the circus!* ○ *They were clinging for dear life to the edge of the rock.*

lead/live the life of 'Reilly/'Riley (*informal*) have a comfortable and enjoyable life without any worries: *He inherited a lot of money and since then he has been living the life of Riley.*

(a matter of) life and/or death (*informal*) sth very important that affects the success or failure or survival of sth: *It's hardly a life or death decision whether we go by bus or take the train, is it?* ○ *We need that business deal, it's a matter of life or death to the company.*

life and 'limb death or injury which results from doing sth dangerous: *Fire fighters risk life and limb daily in their work.* ○ *The magician said there was no danger to life and limb, but one spectator fainted.*

the life and soul of the party (*informal*) very cheerful or enthusiastic: *People always expect Jane to be the life and soul of the party.*

make sb's life a misery make sb's life unpleasant or difficult: *Ever since he joined the company he's made my life a misery.* ○ *Her arthritis makes her life a misery; she's in constant pain.*

not for the 'life of me, etc (used for saying emphatically that you cannot do sth): *I couldn't for the life of me remember his first name.* ○ *He couldn't for the life of him understand why she was so annoyed with him.*

not on your life (*informal*) (used for emphasis when saying no to a suggestion, request, etc) definitely not; never: *Go out and miss the football match on TV? Not on your life!* ○ *Lend him £50? Not on your life.*

take sb's 'life (*formal*) kill sb: *In my opinion, the state does not have the right to take a person's life*

take your life in your 'hands (*sometimes humorous*) risk being killed, injured, attacked, etc: *You take your life in* *your hands if you let him drive.* ○ *The reason that his photos are so good is because he takes his life in his hands to get them.*

take your own life (*quite formal*) kill yourself; commit suicide: *His children died in a house fire and shortly afterwards he took his own life.*

that's 'life (used as an exclamation when sth disappointing, unfair, etc has happened) life is not fair, and we must accept that: *Some people are born intelligent and some people are not. That's life.*

there's life in the old dog 'yet (*humorous*) a person is old but is still active, energetic, adventurous, etc: *At 70 he's decided to go round the world. There's life in the old dog yet!* ○ *I'm not too old to enjoy myself! There's life in the old dog yet, you know.*

this is the life! (used when you are in an ideal situation and very happy): *Sunshine, a swimming pool and champagne. This is the life!*

to the life (of a painting, sculpture, description, etc) exactly like the person/thing painted, etc: *This new portrait really is Prince Charles to the life.* ○ *When I read her description of him, I could see him again so clearly. It was him to the life.*

what a life! (used as an exclamation when you think your life is very difficult or unpleasant): *Three hours travelling to work in a crowded train every day. What a life!* ○ *Cooking, cleaning, ironing seven days a week. What a life!*

where there's life (, there's hope) (*saying*) in a terrible situation you must not give up hope because there is always a chance that it will improve: *The doctors are doing all they can to save her. Where there's life, there's hope.*

at my, etc time of life ⇨ time; **the bane of sb's life/existence** ⇨ bane; **be/go in fear of your life** ⇨ fear; **can/could not do sth to save your life** ⇨ save; **a dog's life** ⇨ dog; **a fact of life** ⇨ fact; **the facts of life** ⇨ facts; **from every walk/all walks of life** ⇨ walk; **the fright of your life** ⇨ fright; **frighten the life out of sb** = **frighten/scare sb to death/out of their wits** ⇨ frighten; **have the time of your life** ⇨ time; **the kiss of life** ⇨ kiss; **large as life** ⇨ large; **larger than life** ⇨ larger; **lay down your life** ⇨ lay; **lead/have a**

charmed life ⇨ charmed; **lose your life** ⇨ lose; **loss of life** = **lose your life** ⇨ lose; **a new lease of life** ⇨ new; **in the prime of life** ⇨ prime; **in real life** ⇨ real; **see life** ⇨ see; **a slice of life** ⇨ slice; **spring to life/action** ⇨ spring; **such is life** ⇨ such; **that's the story of my life** ⇨ story; **variety is the spice of life** ⇨ variety; **you can bet your bottom dollar/your life** ⇨ bet

lifetime **a living legend/a legend in your own lifetime** ⇨ legend

lift

(not) lift a 'finger to do sth (*informal*) (not) make any effort at all to do sth, especially to help sb: *He didn't lift a finger to help me when I was in trouble.* ○ *She does all the work in the house. Nobody else lifts a finger.*

thumb/hitch a lift stand by the side of the road with your thumb out because you want a motorist to stop and take you somewhere: *We thumbed a lift to Liverpool. We only had to wait half an hour before somebody stopped.*

give sth a face-lift ⇨ face; **lift/raise a hand against sb** ⇨ hand; **raise/lift the roof** ⇨ roof

light

as light as 'air/a 'feather weighing very little; very light: *I love this jacket; it's really warm but it's as light as a feather.* ○ *Her sponge cakes are as light as air.*

be/go out like a 'light (*informal*) fall asleep very quickly or suddenly lose consciousness: *She went out like a light after an exhausting day at work.* ○ *One minute she was talking and laughing and the next minute she was out like a light. It was very frightening.*

bring sth to 'light show information, evidence, etc: *The police investigation brought to light evidence of more than one crime.* ○ *Recently discovered documents have brought new information to light about Shakespeare's early life.*

cast/shed/throw (new) 'light on sth by adding new information about it make sth clearer and easier to understand: *This book sheds new light on the role of the CIA.* ○ *'Can you throw any light on the matter?'*

come to 'light become known; be

revealed: *It recently came to light that he'd been in trouble with the police before.*

in the 'light of sth (*rather formal*) taking some new information into consideration: *In the light of what you have just told me, I am prepared to increase your loan to £5000.*

(see) the light of 'day be thought of or discovered by sb or become known to a lot of people at a particular time: *It was then that the idea of a European parliament first saw the light of day.*

(see the) light at the end of the 'tunnel (see) the possibility of success, happiness, etc in the future especially after a long period of difficulty: *The question about the search for a cure for AIDS is whether there is any light at the end of the tunnel? ○ Business has been bad recently, but I think we're beginning to see some light at the end of the tunnel.*

make 'light of sth treat sth or behave as if sth is less serious, important etc than it really is: *She was in great pain but she always made light of it. ○ They made light of their difficulties but it was obvious that things were going badly.*

make light 'work of sth (*informal*) do sth very easily; defeat sb very easily: *She made light work of that translation. ○ They made light work of their match against Manchester United and won the championship.*

with a light heart with a feeling of happiness or relief: *She left the doctor's with a light heart. There was nothing seriously wrong with her after all.* **light-hearted** (*adjective*) (of sb) cheerful and happy; (of sth) amusing, not serious: *The programme is a light-hearted look at the tourist industry.*

be all sweetness and light ⇨ sweetness; **give sb/get the green light** ⇨ green; **hide your light under a bushel** ⇨ hide; **in the cold light of day** ⇨ cold; **a leading light** ⇨ leading; **many hands make light work** ⇨ hands; **the red-light district** ⇨ red; **see the light** ⇨ see; **travel light** ⇨ travel

lightly

get off 'lightly (*informal*) be lucky and escape serious injury/punishment or trouble: *Only two years in prison for stealing all that money? I think he got off very lightly.*

lightning

at/with 'lightning speed very fast: *The lecturer talked at lightning speed. ○ They're a very efficient company. They reply to your letters with lightning speed.*

lightning never strikes twice (in the same place) (*saying*) a misfortune is not likely to happen twice to the same people or in the same place.

like greased lightning ⇨ greased

lights **the bright lights** ⇨ bright; **jump the lights** ⇨ jump; **shoot the lights** ⇨ shoot

like

and the 'like (*informal*) and similar people or things: *Professional people include lawyers, doctors, architects and the like.*

anything/something/nothing like that anything, etc of that kind: *Do you do aerobics or play tennis, or anything like that? ○ She's an expert in the preservation of paper or something like that. ○ No, there's nothing like that available yet.*

as 'like(ly) as not (*informal*) quite/very probably: *As like as not, he'll be late. He usually is.*

as like as two 'peas (in a pod) (*informal*) very similar in appearance: *I had never met his brother before but I recognized him immediately because they are as like as two peas.*

I like your 'nerve, 'cheek, etc or **I like 'that!** (*informal, ironic*) (used for saying that you think sb's behaviour is very unreasonable or unfair): *She crashed into my car and now she wants me to pay for her car to be repaired. Well I like her nerve! ○ 'He wants me to do his work for him while he goes to a cricket match! Well, I like that!'*

like anything/mad/crazy/billy-o (*informal*) very much or very enthusiastically: *My head hurt like anything. ○ They worked like crazy to get it finished on time.*

like it or 'lump it (*informal*) whether willingly or unwillingly: *There's no milk, so we're having black coffee, like it or lump it.*

like nothing on earth very ill or unattractive: *After two hours in that tiny boat I felt like nothing on earth. ○ I hadn't slept for*

48 hours. I must have looked like nothing on earth.

anything like ⇨ anything; **nothing like** ⇨ nothing

likely

a 'likely story (*informal, humorous, ironic*) (used for showing that you don't believe what sb has said): *They said they'd found the wallet on the ground outside the pub; a likely story!*

not (bloody, etc) 'likely (*informal*) (used for emphatically saying no to a request, suggestion, etc) definitely not: *'Sign a blank cheque for you? Not bloody likely!'*

as like(ly) as not ⇨ like

likes

the likes of sb (*informal*) people like sb: *Champagne isn't for the likes of you and me. Beer's more our style.*

lily   **gild the lily** ⇨ gild

limb

out on a limb (*informal*) in a risky or difficult position because you are saying or doing sth which does not have the support of other people: *When he started that company, he really went out on a limb. It might have been a disaster.* ○ *I seem to be out on a limb here. Does nobody agree with my idea?*

life and limb ⇨ life; **tear sb limb from limb** ⇨ tear

limbo

in 'limbo in a state of uncertainty or between two states: *We're in limbo at the moment because we've finished our work in this country and now we're waiting for our next contract.* ○ *Our plans for buying a flat in Spain are in limbo at the moment.*

limelight

out of/in the 'limelight receiving no/a lot of public attention: *If you are married to a Prime Minister, you are always in the limelight.* (in theatres, lime used to be burnt in front of the stage to give a bright light)

limit(s)

(be) the (absolute) 'limit (be) a very annoying person or thing: *'You're the limit, Michael. I've been waiting for you for over two hours. Where on earth have you been?'* ○ *The*

trains on this line are the absolute limit. They are never on time.

within 'limits   1 to a certain extent; not completely: *'Do you support what he says?' 'Yes, within limits!'*   **2** as long as it is reasonable; to a reasonable degree: *I will do anything I can to help you, within limits, of course.*

the sky's the limit ⇨ sky

line

all along/down the line *or* **right down the line** (*informal*) completely; at every stage: *We've had problems with this software all along the line. It was a complete waste of money.* ○ *He supported their campaign right down the line.*

bring sb/sth into 'line (make sb/sth) behave, function, etc in the same way as other people, organizations, etc: *He's a very clever child but he's naughty. I feel that he needs bringing into line a bit.* ○ *We're trying to bring our production methods more into line with our Japanese competitors.*

in 'line for sth likely to get sth: *She's in line for the top job at the Ministry.* ○ *If he thinks I'm going to lend him my new car, he's in line for a surprise.*

(be) in/out of 'line with sb/sth be in agreement/disagreement with sth: *Her views on education are quite out of line with the official view.* ○ *The changes being made are in line with the new policy.*

line your/sb's 'pocket(s) (*informal*) make a lot of money dishonestly, especially by stealing it from your employer: *He'd been lining his pockets for years before it was discovered.* ○ *We thought he was giving our money to the Church Building Fund and he was busy lining his pockets.*

on the line (of a job, your career, reputation, etc) at risk: *If I don't get enough contracts this month, my job will be on the line.* ○ *By making such a strange film, he has really put his reputation on the line.* ○ *You're putting your career on the line, you know. If you don't produce the results you've promised nobody will employ you again.*

somewhere, etc along the 'line at some particular moment or stage during sth: *With an idiot like him to advise you, it was certain that you would get into trouble somewhere* along the line. ○ 'How did it happen?' 'I don't know. I just know that somewhere along the line we stopped loving each other.'

take a firm, etc 'line (on sth) act in a firm, decisive way when you are dealing with a problem: *They've taken a strong line on the sale of guns to the public.*

take/follow the line of least re'sistance when you have a choice between two or more courses of action, choose the one which causes you the least trouble: *He married her only because she threatened to kill herself if he didn't. He took the line of least resistance, and now he regrets it.* ○ *You'll never get anywhere in life if you always take the line of least resistance.*

be in the firing line ⇨ firing; **the bottom line** ⇨ bottom; **draw the line** ⇨ draw; **drop sb a line/note** ⇨ drop; **the end of the road/line** ⇨ end; **hook, line, and sinker** ⇨ hook; **a hot line** ⇨ hot; **lay it on the line** ⇨ lay; **the party line** ⇨ party; **sign on the dotted line** ⇨ sign; **step out of line** ⇨ step; **toe the line** ⇨ toe

lines

on/along the 'lines of sth *or* **on/along the same 'lines as sth** **1** similar to sth; in a similar way, style, etc to sth: *I'm looking for a silver teapot, something along the lines of this one here.* **2** (used for giving a summary of sth you have read or heard): *'What did he say in his defence?' 'Something along the lines of his being so drunk that he didn't realize what he was doing.'*

get your lines/wires crossed ⇨ crossed; **have crossed lines/wires = get your lines/wires crossed** ⇨ crossed; **read between the lines** ⇨ read

lining **every cloud has a silver lining** ⇨ cloud

lion(s)

the 'lion's share (of sth) the largest part of sth that is being shared: *The lion's share of the awards have gone to American films again.* (from one of Aesop's fables)

put your head in the lion's mouth ⇨ head; **throw sb to the wolves/lions** ⇨ throw

lip(s)

my, etc lips are sealed (*informal,* *humorous*) I, etc promise not to tell your secret: *Don't worry. I won't tell anybody. My lips are sealed.*

bite your lip ⇨ bite; **pay lip-service to sth** ⇨ pay; **a stiff upper lip** ⇨ stiff; **there's many a slip 'twixt cup and lip** ⇨ slip

list **a hit list** ⇨ hit; **a list as long as your arm** ⇨ long

listen

listen with half an ear not listen with one's full attention: *I was watching television and listening with half an ear to what he was telling me.*

little

a little 'bird told me (that...) (*informal,* *humorous*) I have heard about sth but I don't want to say who told me: *A little bird told me that you might be applying for another job. Is that true?* ○ *'Who told you I was getting married?' 'Oh, a little bird.'*

,little by 'little making progress, but slowly; gradually: *Her English is improving little by little.* ○ *Little by little she began to feel better.*

make 'little of sth **1** treat sth as unimportant or less important than expected: *She made little of all the problems in the department and said everything was all right.* **2** hardly understand sth: *I read the article on the relationship between physics and art, but I'm afraid I could make little of it.*

be little/nothing short of sth ⇨ short; **great oaks from little acorns grow** ⇨ oaks; **more than a little/bit drunk, excited, etc** ⇨ more; **precious few/little** ⇨ precious

live

live and 'learn **1** learn through your mistakes or experience: *I left my bike unlocked for five minutes and it was stolen. You live and learn I suppose.* **2** (used for expressing surprise at sth new which you have just heard, read, etc): *It says in this book that the Romans were the first to have a state postal service. Well, you live and learn, don't you?*

live and 'let live (*saying*) allow people with different customs, habits, ideas to yours to live as they wish; be tolerant of people who don't live like you: *If we could all* *live and let live a little more, the world would be a much happier place.*

live beyond/within your 'means live on more/less money than you have or earn: *They seemed wealthy but they were living well beyond their means.* ○ *I find it very hard to live within my means.*

live by/on your 'wits survive financially by being clever and perhaps dishonest (usually because you don't have a regular job): *Any refugee will tell you that you soon learn how to live by your wits.* (here *wits* means 'brains')

live it 'up (*informal*) have a very enjoyable time, often spending a lot of money: *Since his retirement he has been living it up in the south of France.* ○ *We are very careful with our money, but for two weeks a year while we're on holiday, we really live it up.*

live off/on the ,fat of the 'land (*informal*) (often used for expressing disapproval) have plenty of money to spend on the best food, drink, entertainment, etc: *Money was no problem then. We were living off the fat of the land in those days.* ○ *It's always the same: the rich live off the fat of the land and complain that the poor are lazy.*

live on ,borrowed 'time (of a person who is seriously ill) live longer than the doctors expected: *The doctors say he's living on borrowed time.*

live to ,fight another 'day (*informal, humorous*) have another chance to win because you were only just defeated in a contest, etc: *She only just lost the election, so she lives to fight another day.*

live to tell the tale (*informal, often humorous*) survive a terrible experience: *Only one man out of fifteen lived to tell the tale.* ○ *It will be a terrible ordeal, but I expect you'll live to tell the tale!*

live up to your, etc/its reputation be as good, bad, etc as people say: *The restaurant lived up to its reputation. We had a wonderful meal.* ○ *I'm afraid that he lived up to his reputation. He got more and more drunk, and finally went to sleep under the table.*

a live 'wire (*informal*) a lively and enthusiastic person: *You must invite her to your party, she's a real live wire.* ○ *We need a live wire like him in this department. Let's give him the job.*

lead/live the life of Reilly/Riley ➪ life; **people who live in glasshouses shouldn't throw stones** ➪ people

lively **look lively/sharp** ➪ look

lives **how the other half lives** ➪ half

living

be ,living 'proof of sth show sth is true simply by being alive or existing: *He plays tennis, golf, runs, swims and cycles. He's living proof that a heart attack doesn't mean the end of an active life.*

in/within ,living 'memory that can be remembered by people who are alive now: *These are the worst floods within living memory.*

the living image of sb physically very similar to sb: *She's the living image of her mother.*

in the land of the living ➪ land; **a living legend/a legend in your own lifetime** ➪ legend; **the world owes you a living** ➪ world

lo

,lo and be'hold (*humorous, often ironic*) (used when telling a story to introduce sb's unexpected appearance): *I walked into the pub and, lo and behold, there was my boss with his secretary.*

load

get a load of 'this (*very informal*) (used for drawing attention to some surprising information you are going to give sb) listen to this: *Get a load of this. They want to build a new road right across here.*

a load of (old) rubbish, cobblers, etc (*informal*) nonsense; worthless: *His explanation was a load of cobblers.* ○ *Don't bother to watch that film. It's a load of old rubbish.*

(take) a load/weight off sb's mind ➪ mind

loaded **the dice are loaded against sb** ➪ dice

loaf **half a loaf is better than none/no bread** ➪ half; **use your loaf** ➪ use

lock

,lock 'horns with sb argue or fight with

sb: *The lawyers did not want to lock horns with the judge.* (refers to fighting with horns or antlers between animals such as bulls, stags, etc)

,lock, stock, and 'barrel including everything; completely: *They were emigrating so they were selling everything they had, lock, stock and barrel.* (the lock, stock and barrel are the three main parts of a rifle)

under ,lock and 'key locked up in prison, in a safe, etc: *The escaped prisoners are now safely under lock and key.* ○ *The exam papers must be kept under lock and key until half an hour before the exam.*

lodging board and lodging ⇨ board

log easy as ABC/anything/pie/falling off a log ⇨ easy; sleep like a log/top ⇨ sleep

loggerheads

at loggerheads (with sb) disagreeing or arguing very strongly (with sb): *The students are at loggerheads with the college over the price of food in the canteen.* ○ *Management and staff are at loggerheads over the plan.*

loins gird your loins ⇨ gird

lone

a lone 'wolf a person who chooses to work, live, be, etc alone: *In the police force he had the reputation of being something of a lone wolf.*

long

as/so long as on condition that: *As long as you tidy your room first, you can go out to play.* ○ *I'll lend you my car so long as you promise to take great care of it.*

(a list) as long as your arm (*informal*) (of a list) with many things to do, buy, etc on it: *I've got a list as long as your arm of things I need to buy for the party.*

(not) by a 'long chalk (*informal*) (not) by a considerable amount: *'Do you think she's ready to take First Certificate?' 'No, not by a long chalk.'* ○ *He's the fastest runner in the school by a long chalk.*

have come a long way have made good progress and achieved a lot: *The manager has come a long way since she joined the company as a messenger.*

in the 'long run in the end; when you take everything over a period of time into consideration: *I know buying your own house is a big expense at the beginning but in the long run it is cheaper than paying rent.* ○ *I thought gas heating would be cheaper but in the long run it isn't.*

the long and the short of it the basic fact of a situation, etc is: *The examiners discussed your paper for at least an hour. I'm afraid the long and the short of it is that you have failed.* ○ *The long and the short of it is that we haven't got enough money to employ another cleaner.*

the long arm of the law the ability of the police and the legal system to find criminals and punish them: *You have to be a very clever criminal to escape the long arm of the law.*

a long 'face a sad or disappointed look on your face: *I asked him if he wanted to go out to the cinema but he pulled a long face and said no.*

a long 'haul (*informal*) a long and difficult task or journey: *It's been a long haul doing the degree part time, but the effort has been worth it.* ○ *They started on the long haul back to the camp.*

(be) ,long in the 'tooth (*informal, usually humorous*) old: *I'm a bit long in the tooth for all-night parties.*

a 'long shot (*informal*) an attempt or a guess which you don't expect to be successful but which is worth trying: *Try ringing him at home. It's a long shot, I know, but he might just be there.* ○ *'Are you going to apply for the manager's job?' 'I think I will. It's a long shot, I know, but it's worth a try.'*

long time no 'see (*informal*) (used when you greet sb you have not seen for a long time: *Well, hello! Long time no see.*

(be) not long for this world (*dated*) likely to die soon: *She looked extremely ill and I fear she's not long for this world.*

so long (for now) (*informal*) goodbye until we next meet: *So long for now. I'll see you on Thursday.*

take a long (hard) 'look at sth think about a problem or possibility very carefully: *After taking a long hard look at the cost of employing an extra person, we decided against it.* ○ *We need to take a long look at the plan before we decide.*

take the 'long view think about the possible future effects of sth rather than its immediate effects: *You always have to take the long view when you are thinking about spending money on education.* ○ *If we really want to save the planet, we must take the long view in our energy policy.*

at (long) last ⇨ last; **go a long way = go far** ⇨ far; **happy as the day is long/as a sandboy/as Larry** ⇨ happy; **in the long/medium/short term** ⇨ term; **it's as broad as it's long** ⇨ broad; **to cut a long story short** ⇨ cut

longest **he who laughs last laughs longest** ⇨ laughs

look

be 'sb's (own) lookout (*British, informal*) be sb's problem because they are responsible for causing it: *If he wants to invest all his money in one company, that's his lookout.* ○ *It's my own lookout if I fail this exam.*

be on the lookout for sb/sth be searching for sb/sth: *We're always on the lookout for good computer programmers.* ○ *I'm on the lookout for a good book on German history.*

by/from the look(s) of it/things (*informal*) judging from the way things seem to be: *From the look of it, there's going to be another war.* ○ *By the looks of things, we're going to be late.*

look bad *or* **not look good** **1** (of behaviour) give a bad impression: *It will look bad if you don't go to your own mother's funeral.* ○ *It doesn't look good if you forget people's names.* **2** suggest probable failure, problems, etc: *Things don't look good for the economy at the moment.*

look before you 'leap (*saying*) before you decide to do sth think carefully about the possible risks and effects: *I know you don't like this job but don't just accept the first job offered to you. Remember to look before you leap.*

look black show no signs of hope or improvement: *I know things look black at the moment but I'm sure you'll get a job soon.*

look 'daggers at sb look at sb very angrily but not say anything: *He looked daggers at her across the room when she mentioned his divorce.*

look down your 'nose (at sb) (*informal*) treat sb with little respect because you feel superior to them: *Why do you always look down your nose at people who don't speak with the same accent as you?* ○ *She looked down her nose at my family.*

(not) look a ˌgift-horse in the 'mouth (*informal*) (not) find sth wrong with sth given to you free: *He didn't want to accept the offer of a free holiday but I told him not to look a gift-horse in the mouth.* (the usual way to judge the age of a horse is to look at its teeth)

ˌlook 'here! (used when you are going to say sth important to sb and you are annoyed or angry): *Look here, I've been waiting to be served for half an hour. The service here is terrible.* ○ *Look here, I paid a lot of money for this car. I didn't expect it to break down after a month.*

(be unable to) look sb in the 'eye(s)/ 'face (be unable to) look at sb directly (because you feel embarrassed, ashamed, etc): *I knew he was telling a lie because he wouldn't look me in the eye when he spoke to me.*

look lively/sharp (*informal*) do sth quickly; hurry up: *Come on, look lively or we won't get to the station in time.*

look on the 'bright side be optimistic in spite of problems, difficulties, etc: *I know it's inconvenient to be without a car, but look on the bright side – at least you'll save money on petrol.*

look the other 'way ignore sb/sth deliberately: *We only had three tickets but the woman at the door looked the other way and let all four of us in.* ○ *The university authorities know there is a lot of drug-taking among students, but they just look the other way.*

look the part look like a particular type of professional person, character in a play, etc: *I think Tim Evans should play Robin Hood. He really looks the part.* ○ *He's a funny kind of bank manager; he doesn't look the part at all.*

look a sight (*informal*) be ugly or messy: *She looked a real sight. A yellow hat, pink dress, black stockings, blue shoes.* ○ *Your bedroom looks a sight. Go and tidy it.*

look to your laurels do sth to protect your good position or reputation from competition by others: *He thinks he's the best at maths in the class but there's a new girl who* *is very good. He's going to have to look to his laurels.*

look sb up and 'down (*informal*) openly look at sb from head to foot in a way that embarrasses them: *When I started working there, I could feel people looking me up and down and wondering what I was like.*

look what the 'cat's dragged in (*informal, humorous*) (an expression used when sb who looks very dirty, untidy or wet comes into a room): *'Look what the cat's dragged in!' shouted his brothers as he came into the room soaking wet from the storm.*

(not) look your'self (*informal*) (not) look as healthy as you normally do: *She wasn't looking herself at all yesterday.* ○ *He looks more himself this morning. His temperature's come right down.*

never/not look 'back (*informal*) (after a change of career, etc) become very successful: *She hasn't looked back since she started her own business five years ago.* ○ *He moved to New York and never looked back.*

not be much to 'look at (*informal*) not be very attractive: *The boat is not much to look at but it's easy to sail.* ○ *He's not much to look at, but he's got a great sense of humour.*

not get/have a 'look-in (*informal*) not get the chance to do sth you want because of other people who are better or more determined than you: *There are already too many good players, so I never get a look-in when they're choosing the team.*

to look at sb/sth *or* **by the look of sb/ sth** (*informal*) judging from the way sb/sth appears: *To look at him, you wouldn't think he was the richest person in the country.* ○ *To look at them, you'd never imagine that they tasted so delicious.*

be/look past it ⇨ past; **a black look** ⇨ black; **a dirty look** ⇨ dirty; **look/feel small** ⇨ small; **not know which way to look** ⇨ know; **stare/look you in the face** ⇨ face; **take a long look at sth** ⇨ long

looking **like looking for a needle in a haystack** ⇨ needle

looks **the devil looks after his own** ⇨ devil

loom
loom large (of an important problem,

event, etc) approach and seem worrying or frightening: *With the local elections looming large, the Conservative party is beginning to look nervous.* ○ *In your last year of school, public exams loom very large in your mind.*

loose
at a loose 'end having nothing to do; not knowing what to do: *I'm at a bit of a loose end this afternoon. Do you fancy a game of tennis?*

the loose 'ends/'threads the minor details of sth which have still not been dealt with or explained: *We've almost finished the report. There are just a few loose ends to tie up and then it'll be ready.* ○ *It's a very unsatisfactory detective story. You know who committed the murder, but there are far too many loose ends.*

(be) on the 'loose **1** (of an escaped prisoner, animal, etc) (be) free: *There are ten prisoners on the loose.* **2** (be) enjoying a period of freedom from your normal life or usual rules or restrictions: *Her boyfriend's on the loose in Paris this weekend, but she doesn't seem to mind.*

all hell breaks/is let loose ⇨ hell; **hang loose** ⇨ hang; **have a screw loose** ⇨ screw; **play fast and loose** ⇨ play; **tear loose** ⇨ tear

lord
'Lord knows nobody can guess: *She comes and goes as she pleases. Lord knows when we'll see her again.*

drunk as a lord ⇨ drunk

lose
lose your 'bearings become lost or suddenly confused: *The old man seemed to have lost his bearings for a moment.*

lose the 'drift/'thread of sth be unable to follow a story, discussion, etc because you cannot understand the relationship between events, facts, etc: *I had to go out in the middle of the film and when I came back I found I'd lost the thread entirely.* ○ *When they started talking about artificial intelligence, I completely lost the drift of the argument.*

lose 'face lose the respect of other people because you have been defeated: *The government can't agree to the changes without losing face.* **a loss of face** (*noun*) *This gives him an opportunity to change his mind without* *loss of face.* (the opposite is 'save face')

lose your 'grip (on sth) (*informal*) be unable to control or do sth as well as you did before: *She's definitely made some bad decisions recently. I think she's losing her grip.*

lose your 'head (*informal*) stop thinking clearly; panic: *It's a very frightening situation, but we mustn't lose our heads.*

lose 'heart become discouraged: *The revolutionaries lost heart after their leader was killed.*

lose your 'heart (to sb/sth) (*often humorous*) fall in love (with sb/sth): *She lost her heart to a waiter in New York, together with her credit card, savings and car keys.* ○ *I've quite lost my heart to those little kittens of yours. Can we take one home?*

lose your 'life (*rather formal*) be killed: *Sixty people lost their lives in the air crash.* **loss of life** (*noun*) *Fortunately there was no loss of life in the battle.*

lose your 'marbles (*informal*) become mad or mentally confused: *They say the old man has lost his marbles because of the strange things he has been saying, but I'm not so sure.*

lose your 'rag (*informal*) become very angry and behave in an uncontrolled way: *He really lost his rag when the children broke another window with their ball.*

lose your 'shirt (*informal*) lose all or a lot of your money by betting money on horses, investing stupidly, etc: *'How did you two get on at the races?' 'I won £80 and Paul lost his shirt.'*

lose 'sight of sb/sth (of a purpose, aim, etc) forget about sth because you are concentrating on sth else: *The government seem to have lost sight of their aims and are now just trying to survive.*

lose your 'touch lose the skill or ability to do sth which you used to do very well: *I don't know what's happened to her playing. She seems to have lost her touch.* ○ *He's not as good a salesman as he used to be. He's losing his touch.*

lose 'touch/'contact (with sb/sth) not write/speak to sb or hear/read about sb/sth as you did in the past: *She lost touch with most of her old friends when she moved to London.*

not lose any sleep over sb/sth *or* **lose no sleep over sb/sth** (*informal*) not worry a lot about sb/sth: *The business does have problems at present but it's nothing I'm going to lose any sleep over.*

give/lose ground ⇨ ground; **keep/lose your cool** ⇨ cool; **keep/lose count** ⇨ count; **keep/lose your temper** ⇨ temper; **keep/lose track** ⇨ track; **lose/waste no time** ⇨ time; **there's no time to lose** ⇨ time

losing **fight a losing battle** ⇨ fight

loss(es)

at a 'loss (*informal*) uncertain about what to do or how to do sth, etc: *We're at a loss to know what to do with all this food from the party yesterday.* ○ *I was completely at a loss. I couldn't understand the instructions.*

at a loss for words unable to say anything: *He's never at a loss for words, in fact it's difficult sometimes to stop him talking.* ○ *I was completely at a loss for words. I had never been spoken to like that in the whole of my life.*

a dead loss ⇨ dead; **cut your losses** ⇨ cut

lost

all is not 'lost (*saying*) there is still a chance that you may succeed, survive, etc: *The baby is very ill, but all it not lost yet.* ○ *I know business looks very bad, but all is not lost.*

be lost on sb be wasted or have no effect on sb because they don't understand or appreciate sth: *I'm afraid that joke is lost on me.* ○ *Good writing is lost on him. He's just not interested in literature.*

be/feel 'lost without sb/sth (*informal*) feel unable to work or live without sb/sth: *I left my watch at home and I feel lost without it.* ○ *I'm completely lost without my diary.*

get 'lost! (*very informal*) go away!: *I told him to get lost, but it makes no difference, he just keeps following me around.*

give sb/sth up for 'lost (*informal*) stop looking for sb/sth because you no longer expect to find them/it: *The fishermen had been given up for lost in the storm but they have now arrived safely back.*

a lost cause an ambition, project or aim which seems certain to end in failure, perhaps because not enough people support it: *For many years he supported the* development of the electric car, but he now thinks it's a lost cause. ○ Trying to help him to improve his pronunciation is a lost cause.

there's no love lost between them ⇨ love

lot **have a lot of time for sb/sth** ⇨ time; **have a lot on/don't have much/a lot on** ⇨ on; **take a lot out of sb = take it out of sb** ⇨ take; **there's a lot to be said for sth** ⇨ said; **throw in your lot with sb** ⇨ throw

lots

draw/cast lots decide who is going to do sth by giving each person a piece of paper or a stick so that the person who has the paper with a mark on or the shortest stick is chosen: They drew lots to see who should speak to the parents.

there are plenty/lots more fish in the sea ⇨ fish

loud

loud and clear (informal) said in a very clear voice or expressed very clearly: The message of the book is loud and clear: smoking kills. ○ He let us know loud and clear that he would not accept students arriving late for his lectures.

for crying out loud ⇨ crying; **think out loud = think aloud** ⇨ think

louder **actions speak louder than words** ⇨ actions

love

(do sth) (just) for 'love/for the 'love of sth without payment or other reward, because you like the work or the person you are working for: She works in the museum during the summer but she doesn't get paid. She helps for the love of it.

for the love of 'God, etc (informal) (used for showing surprise, disappointment, frustration, anger, etc): For the love of God, Jeff, you can't stay here: half the police in the country are looking for you. ○ For the love of God, shut up. I'm trying to finish this essay.

love at first 'sight falling in love with sb the first time you meet them: I never really believed in love at first sight until I met you.

love is blind (saying) when you are in love with sb, you cannot see their faults.

make love (to sb) have sex (with sb): They made love all night long.

not for love (n)or money (informal) (used for saying that you are unable to do sth): The show is sold out. You can't get a ticket for love nor money.

there's no 'love lost between sb and sb/them (informal) they dislike each other greatly: They may have been the best of friends when they were younger but there's no love lost between them now.

all's fair in love and war ⇨ fair; **cupboard love** ⇨ cupboard; **a labour of love** ⇨ labour

lovely **everything in the garden is lovely** ⇨ garden

low

be/run 'low (on sth) not have much of sth left: We're running low on petrol! Do you think we will have enough to get home?

give sb/get the 'low-down (on sb/sth) (informal) give sb/get confidential information on sb/sth: Can you give me the low-down on this deal with the Bank of China?

(at) a low 'ebb not as good, strong, successful, etc as usual: Business confidence is at a low ebb at the moment. ○ Our family fortunes are at a bit of a low ebb. (refers to a very low tide, when the sea is a long way from the land)

be in high/low spirits/ ⇨ spirits; **high and low** ⇨ high; **keep, etc a high/low profile** ⇨ profile; **lay sb low** ⇨ lay; **lie low** ⇨ lie; **set your sights high/low** ⇨ set; **stoop so low** ⇨ stoop

lower **raise/lower your sights** ⇨ sights

luck

as luck would 'have it (sometimes ironic) fortunately/unfortunately: She had just the qualifications they wanted, and as luck would have it, they happened to have a job they could offer her immediately. ○ I was driving home from the party and, as luck would have it, I was stopped by the police.

bad/hard/tough luck! (sometimes ironic) (used for expressing sympathy with sb who has just failed to do sth, etc): 'I didn't get the job in Cardiff. I heard this morning.' 'Bad luck, Jim. I'm sure you'll get the next one.' ○ 'Jim's *crashed his new motorbike.' 'That's his tough luck. He shouldn't drive so fast.'*

be down on your luck (*informal*) be temporarily in an unfortunate situation, especially experiencing money problems: *He employed a retired soldier who was down on his luck to tidy up the garden.*

just my, etc luck (*informal*) my, etc typical bad luck: *I wanted the steak but there wasn't any left. Just my luck! ○ They sold the last tickets to the people in front of us. Just our luck.*

your 'luck is in *or* **you're in 'luck** you are lucky at the moment: *I knew my luck was in today when all the traffic lights were green on my way to work. And now I've found that money I lost.*

the luck of the devil *or* **the luck of the Irish** extraordinary good luck, perhaps not deserved: *You need the luck of the devil to get a seat on the train in the rush hour. ○ It was the luck of the Irish that saved him.*

the ,luck of the 'draw the result of chance only: *Some teachers get a job near home, others are sent hundreds of miles away. It's the luck of the draw.*

no such luck (*informal*) unfortunately not: *I thought I might finish early today, but no such luck.*

beginner's luck ⇨ beginner; **the best of luck** ⇨ best; **chance your arm/luck** ⇨ chance; **a hard luck story** ⇨ hard; **push your luck** ⇨ push; **take pot luck** ⇨ pot; **try your luck** ⇨ try; **worse luck** ⇨ worse

lucky

'you'll, etc be lucky *or* **'you, etc should be so lucky** (*informal*) what you expect or hope for is unlikely to happen: *You were hoping I'd come and collect you from the airport after midnight? You'll be lucky! Try a taxi! ○ 'Come and see us if you are ever in Australia.' 'I should be so lucky.'*

strike lucky ⇨ strike; **thank your lucky stars** ⇨ thank

lump

a lump in your throat a tight feeling in your throat caused by a strong emotion: *I didn't cry but I did have a lump in my throat.*

like it or lump it ⇨ like

lunatic

the lunatic 'fringe (*disapproving*) members of an organization or group who are more extreme than the others; extreme groups: *It's the lunatic fringe of the Animal Liberation Front which smashes the windows of butchers' shops, not ordinary members like us.*

lurch   leave sb in the lurch ⇨ leave

luxury   in the lap of luxury ⇨ lap

lying

take sth lying down (*informal*) accept sth which is unfair without complaining or protesting about it; accept a defeat easily: *I'm not going to take this stupid decision lying down. If necessary, I'll take the Council to court. ○ She's the kind of person who won't take defeat lying down.*

M

machine   a cog in the machine/wheel ⇨ cog

mackerel   a sprat to catch a mackerel ⇨ sprat

mad

be mad keen (on sb/sth) (*informal*) be very interested in or enthusiastic about sb/sth: *She's been mad keen on African music ever since she came back from Zimbabwe last year. ○*

He's mad keen on getting into the army.

(as) mad as a 'hatter (*informal*) mad. (mercury used to be used in making hats and fumes from mercury can cause brain damage. In *Alice in Wonderland* by Lewis Carrol one of the characters is called the Mad Hatter.)

(as) mad as a March 'hare (*informal*) mad. (in the spring hares do a strange leaping dance in the fields)

be/go **stark raving mad** ⇨ stark;
hopping mad ⇨ hopping; **like anything/
mad/crazy/billy-o** ⇨ like

madness there's **method in sb's
madness** ⇨ method

main

in the 'main mostly; on the whole: *In the
main, the students did well in the exam.*

have an eye to/for the main chance
⇨ eye

majority the silent **majority** ⇨ silent

make

make 'do (with sth) or **make (sth) 'do**
use sth, although it is not really satisfactory
or adequate: *I didn't have time to go to the
shops today so I suppose we'll have to make do
with what is left from yesterday's meal.* ○ *I
really need a large frying pan but if you haven't
got one I'll have to make do with that small one.*

make a 'go of (doing) sth (*informal*) try
very hard to make sth successful: *He was
determined to make a go of his second marriage.*

'make it (*informal*) **1** be successful in
your job: *She's a very good dancer but I'm not
sure she'll make it as a professional.* ○ *He wants
to be a professor by the time he's 30. Do you
think he'll make it?* **2** succeed in reaching
a place: *The train leaves in ten minutes. Hurry
up or we won't make it.* ○ *I don't think we'll
make it before dark.* **3** survive after an
illness, accident, etc: *'Do you think she'll
make it, doctor?' 'It's really too soon to say.'*

on the 'make (*disapproving, informal*) **1** be
trying openly to become successful, rich,
etc: *Bill Johnson? Now, there's a young man on
the make. Success at any price – that's what he
wants.* **2** be trying to find a sexual
partner: *It was one of those terrible parties
where half the men were on the make and the
other half were really boring.*

make good ⇨ good; **make good sth**
⇨ good; **make the most of sth** ⇨ most;
make much of sth ⇨ much; **make
nothing of sth** ⇨ nothing

maker meet your **maker** ⇨ meet

making

be the making of sb/sth be the reason
that sb/sth succeeds or develops well: *It was
only a small part on a TV show, but it was the
making of her.* ○ *Those two years of hard work
were the making of him.*

(be) in the 'making (be) developing into
sth or being made: *He's very good at public
speaking – I think he's a politician in the
making.*

(be) of your own making (used about a
problem or difficulty) (be) caused by you:
*The problem is of your own making, so don't try
to blame anyone else.*

makings

have the makings of sth (of a person)
have the necessary qualities or character to
become sth: *She's got the makings of a good
tennis player, but she needs to practise much
harder.* ○ *Their new show has got the makings
of a hit.*

man

be 'man enough (to do sth) be brave
enough (to do sth): *He won't fight – he's not
man enough!*

be sb's man/woman (*quite informal*) be
the best person to choose to do a job: *If you
need a good music teacher, she's your woman.* ○
If you need a driver, then I'm your man.

be no good/use to man or beast
(*informal*) be completely useless: *Since the
Chernobyl disaster the land round here has been
no use to man or beast.*

it's every ,man for him'self (*saying*) you
must think about your own interests, safety,
etc first, before the interests, etc of other
people: *In business, it's every man for himself.*

the ,man in the 'street or **the man on
the ,Clapham 'omnibus** (*British*) the
average, ordinary person, especially the
average voter: *You have to explain it in terms
that the man in the street would understand.* ○
*That won't convince the man on the Clapham
omnibus.*

the ,man of the 'match the man who
plays the best in a game of football, cricket,
etc.

a ,man of 'straw a weak or cowardly
person: *You don't need to be frightened of him;
he's a man of straw.*

to a man all do sth: *To a man, they all agreed.*

you can't keep a good man down
(*saying*) a person who is determined or
wants sth very much will succeed: *He failed*

his driving test twice, but passed on the third try – you can't keep a good man down!

be a man/woman of his/her word ⇨ word; **be a/the poor man's sb/sth** ⇨ poor; **be twice the man/woman** ⇨ twice; **a dirty old man** ⇨ dirty; **every man has his price** ⇨ price; **a/the grand old man** ⇨ grand; **the inner man/woman** ⇨ inner; **a ladies' man** ⇨ ladies; **a man/woman of few words** ⇨ words; **a man/woman of (many) parts** ⇨ parts; **a man/woman of the world** ⇨ world; **a marked man** ⇨ marked; **the odd man/one out** ⇨ odd; **old man** ⇨ old; **your right-hand man** ⇨ right

manger a dog in the manger ⇨ dog

manna
manna from heaven something unexpected, eg a gift of money, which comes to help you when you are in difficulties: *That cheque for £1000 from my aunt came like manna from heaven. I had three or four big bills to pay.* (from the Bible; *manna* was the food the Israelites found in the desert)

manner
in a manner of speaking if you think about it in a certain way: *'Are they married?' 'In a manner of speaking – they've lived together for 15 years.'*

(as if) to the manner born as if a job, a social position, etc were completely natural to you: *He rides round in a Rolls Royce as if to the manner born.*

many
a good/great many very many; a lot: *A good many people think she's right.* ○ *There are a great many places in the world I'd like to visit.*

'many's the time (used for emphasizing how often sth happens/happened): *Many's the time we've sat at this table talking until two or three o'clock in the morning.*

have one too many ⇨ one

map
(be) off the 'map (be) far away from other places; (be) remote: *It's a little house in the country, a bit off the map.*

put sb/sth on the 'map make sb/sth famous or important: *Her performance in her*

first film really put her on the map. ○ *The newspaper story put the village on the map.*

marbles lose your marbles ⇨ lose

march quick march ⇨ quick; **steal a march on sb** ⇨ steal

March mad as a March hare ⇨ mad

marching
give sb their 'marching orders (*informal, often humorous*) tell sb to leave a job, a relationship, etc: *He kept arriving late, so he was given his marching orders.* ○ *When she found out he was seeing another woman, she gave him his marching orders.* also **get your marching orders** be told to leave.

mark(ed)
be ,quick/ ,slow off the 'mark be quick/slow to do sth or understand sth: *You have to be quick off the mark when you answer a newspaper advertisement for a flat.* ○ *Jenny was rather slow off the mark, and they had to explain the joke to her.*

leave/make your/its mark (on sth/sb) do sth important, that has a lasting effect or makes a lasting impression (on sth/sb): *As Minister for Education, he left his mark on British politics.* ○ *War has made its mark on the country.* ○ *Her two unhappy marriages have left their mark* (have made her an unhappy person).

,make your 'mark become famous because you are very good at sth: *He's an actor who has made his mark in films.*

mark my words (often used for introducing a warning) listen carefully to what I am saying: *He'll be back, mark my words! He never stays away for long.*

mark 'time stay in one situation, job, etc, not making any progress, but waiting for an opportunity to do so: *'What are you doing at the moment?' 'I'm just marking time until somebody offers me a better job.'* (refers to soldiers marching on one spot)

a marked 'man a man who is in danger of being killed by his enemies: *When they discovered he was a spy, he was a marked man.*

not be ,up to the 'mark not be of a high enough standard: *His English and History are very good, but his maths is not up to the mark at all.* ○ *I don't think we should promote her. She's* *just not up to the mark.*

be/fall wide of the mark ➪ wide; **be way off the mark = be/fall wide of the mark** ➪ wide; **a black mark** ➪ black; **high water mark** ➪ high; **near the mark** ➪ near; **overshoot the mark** ➪ overshoot; **overstep the mark** ➪ overstep; **a question mark hangs over sb/sth** ➪ question; **toe the mark = toe the line** ➪ toe

market

(be) in the market for sth (*informal*) (be) interested in buying sth: *I'm not in the market for a car as expensive as that.* ○ *Do you know anyone in the market for some stereo equipment?*

on the 'market be available for sale: *This computer isn't on the market yet. You should be able to buy one early next year.* also **come on (to) the market** be offered for sale: *This house only came on the market yesterday.* also **put/bring sth on (to) the market** offer sth for sale: *We're putting a new range of cosmetics on the market next month.*

the bottom drops/falls out of the market ➪ bottom; **corner the market** ➪ corner; **flood the market** ➪ flood; **price sth/yourself out of the market** ➪ price

marks

on your ,marks, get ,set, 'go! (said by a person who is starting an athletics race): *He raised the starting gun. 'On your marks, get set, go!' he shouted, and fired into the air.*

full marks ➪ full

marrow **chilled/frozen to the bone/marrow** ➪ chilled

marry

marry in haste (, repent at leisure) (*saying*) people who marry quickly, without really getting to know each other, will discover later that they have made a mistake.

marry money (*informal*) marry a rich person: *His sister married money – she lives in Bermuda now.*

mass

be a mass of sth be full of or covered with sth: *The garden was a mass of flowers.*

mast **nail your colours to the mast** ➪ nail

master **a past master** ➪ past

match

be no match for sb/sth not be as good, etc as sb/sth; not be able to compete successfully against sb/sth: *He's no match for Karpov. Karpov's much the better player.* ○ *We are no match for the Japanese when it comes to cameras.*

find/meet your match (in sb) meet sb who is as good at doing sth as you are, and perhaps better: *He thought he could beat anyone, but he's finally found his match.* ○ *As a saleswoman, she's met her match in Lorna.*

the man of the match ➪ man; **a slanging match** ➪ slanging

matter

(do sth) as a matter of 'course (do sth) as a regular habit, or as a normal way of behaving: *Before making any important decision, I discuss it with my wife as a matter of course.* ○ *As a matter of course, you should go to the dentist once a year.*

as a matter of 'fact (used when you are telling sb sth interesting, new or important): *I'm going home early today. As a matter of fact, it's my birthday.* ○ *I don't agree, as a matter of fact.*

(do sth) as a matter of 'form (do sth) because it is polite, or because it is the correct way to do sth; do sth as a formality: *We knew everyone agreed, but we had a vote as a matter of form.* ○ *I need your signature, just as a matter of form.*

be the matter (with sb/sth) be the reason for unhappiness, pain, problems, etc (for/with sb/sth): *What's the matter, Gail? You look ill.* ○ *John's been very quiet recently. I wonder if there's anything the matter with him.* ○ *Don't worry, there's nothing the matter.* ○ *There's something the matter with this radio. It's stopped working.* ○ *There's nothing the matter with a drink in the pub occasionally* (it is not wrong or harmful).

be (all) a matter of sth/doing sth depend on sth/doing sth: *Success in business is all a matter of experience.* ○ *Doing anything well is a matter of practice.*

be a matter of o'pinion be sth which

people disagree about: *'She's a great singer.'* *'That's a matter of opinion (I do not agree).'*

for 'that matter (used to say that the second thing mentioned is just as important or true as the first thing): *Don't shout at your mother like that – or at anyone else, for that matter.* ○ *She thought that TV – and cinema too, for that matter, – was bad for children.*

a matter of 'days, 'miles, 'pounds, etc a certain number of days, etc (used especially when this number is small): *Don't worry, it'll only be a matter of hours before he gets back.* ○ *It will only cost us a matter of a few pounds.* ○ *Travelling by boat could take us a matter of weeks.*

no matter who, what, where, when, etc whoever, whatever, wherever, whenever; it doesn't matter who, what, etc: *Don't open the door, no matter who comes.* ○ *No matter what he says, don't trust him.* ○ *I'll find her, no matter where she's hiding.*

the 'truth/'fact of the matter (used when you want to show you are being honest, or when you are telling sb sth unusual or surprising) the truth: *I didn't take anything, and that's the truth of the matter.* ○ *The fact of the matter is that they only got married so she could stay in the country.*

grey matter ⇨ grey; **the heart of the matter** ⇨ heart; **it is only, etc a matter/question of time** ⇨ time; **mind over matter** ⇨ mind; **no laughing matter** ⇨ laughing

matters

take matters into your own hands do sth yourself, because you are tired of waiting for sb else to do it: *The police were doing nothing about finding my car, so I decided to take matters into my own hands and look for it myself.*

not mince matters ⇨ mince

maybe

that's as 'may be/'maybe (but. . .) (used for saying that a particular fact does not change your opinion about sth) that may be true (but. . .): *'That dress cost £800.' 'That's as may be, I still don't like it.'*

McCoy **the real thing/McCoy** ⇨ real

meal

make a 'meal (out) of sth (*informal*) do sth with more effort and care than it really needs; treat sth as more serious than it really is: *Just write her a short note – don't make a meal of it.* ○ *It's only a small mistake. There's no need to make such a meal out of it, is there?*

a square meal ⇨ square

mean

be no mean 'sth be a thing of a very high quality; be a very good example of sth: *This is no mean whisky, Jock. Where did you get it?* ○ *Cycling around France at the age of 75 is no mean achievement.*

I mean (to say) (an expression which introduces an emphatic comment or question on what the speaker has just said): *I blame the parents. I mean, would you allow a 13-year-old to stay out until 2 o'clock in the morning?*

mean 'business be serious about what you plan to do; be determined: *He means business. If we try to escape, he'll shoot us.* ○ *I'm not joking. This time I mean business.*

'mean well (often used of sb who has upset or offended you) have good intentions: *Your father means well, I know, but I wish he'd stop telling us what to do.* ○ *'She's always suggesting ways I could improve my cooking. I know she means well but it really gets on my nerves.'* **well-meaning** (*adjective*) *She's very well-meaning, but she only makes the situation worse.*

be/mean nothing to sb ⇨ nothing; **be/mean the world to sb** ⇨ world; **what's that supposed to mean?** ⇨ supposed

meaning

get sb's meaning (*informal*) understand what sb is really saying: *I get your meaning. You don't need to say any more.*

not know the meaning of the word ⇨ know

means

by 'all means (*quite formal*) (used for giving permission to sb, or for saying yes to a request) yes, of course; certainly: *'Can I smoke?' 'By all means.'* ○ *'Do you think I could borrow this dictionary?' 'Yes, by all means.'*

by 'no (manner of) means or **not by 'any (manner of) means** (*quite formal*) in no way at all; definitely not: *She is by no means poor, believe me. She only pretends to be.*

○ *He hasn't won yet, not by any manner of means.*

(be) a ˌmeans to an ˈend a thing you do only in order to achieve or obtain another thing: *He saw his marriage simply as a means to an end – he was only interested in his wife's money.*

by fair means or foul ➪ fair; **last but by no means least = last but not least** ➪ last; **live beyond/within your means** ➪ live; **ways and means** ➪ ways

meantime

in the ˈmeantime in the time between two things happening: *In five minutes, there's the news: in the meantime, here's some music.* ○ *The bus doesn't leave until six o'clock. In the meantime we can go and have a coffee.*

measure(s)

beyond ˈmeasure (*formal*) very great; very greatly: *His relief was beyond measure.* ○ *It has improved beyond measure.*

(do sth) for good ˈmeasure do, etc sth extra in order to make certain that everything is all right, safe, etc: *Put a couple more spoonfuls of tea in the pot for good measure. There's nothing worse than weak tea.* ○ *I've put new locks on all the doors, and just for good measure, I've put locks on all the downstairs windows too.*

in great, large, etc ˈmeasure (*quite formal*) to a great extent or degree: *His success is in great measure the result of good luck.* ○ *You are in large measure responsible for all our problems.*

make sth to ˈmeasure make a piece of clothing especially for sb, by taking personal measurements: *All his shirts are made to measure.* **made-to-measure** (*adjective*) *a made-to-measure suit*

no half measures ➪ half

meat

be meat and ˈdrink (to sb) (*quite informal*) be sth that a person enjoys very much or is very interested in: *Stories about the royal family are meat and drink to journalists.*

medicine

give sb a taste/dose of their own ˈmedicine treat sb in the same unpleasant, unkind, impolite, etc way that they have

treated you: *Give her a dose of her own medicine and make her wait for you. Then maybe she won't be so slow next time.*

take your ˈmedicine (like a ˈman) (*usually humorous*) accept sth unpleasant, for example, punishment, without protesting or complaining: *He really hates shopping, but he goes anyway and takes his medicine like a man.*

medium

a/the happy medium ➪ happy; **in the long/medium/short term** ➪ term

meet

meet the/your ˈeye(s) (*rather formal*) be seen: *A strange sight met our eyes.*

meet sb's ˈeyes look straight at sb because you realize that they are looking at you: *She was afraid to meet my eyes because she knew what I was thinking.*

meet sb halfˈway (*of two people, etc*) be willing to accept some of the demands, suggestions, etc of the other person in order to be able to reach an agreement: *I can't agree to all your suggestions, but I am prepared to meet you halfway.*

meet your ˈmaker (*usually humorous*) die: *The car was out of control. There was nothing I could do except prepare to meet my maker!*

ˈmeet your Waterˈloo be finally defeated: *She can usually beat anyone at chess, but I think with Kathy she's met her Waterloo.* (refers to the Battle of Waterloo in 1815, in which Napoleon was finally defeated and taken prisoner)

find/meet your match ➪ match; **make ends meet** ➪ ends; **I'm pleased to meet you** ➪ pleased

meeting

a meeting of ˈminds people thinking in the same way about sth; a special understanding between people: *I think there will be a meeting of minds on this subject.* ○ *The discussions were a failure. There was no meeting of minds.*

meets

there's more to sth than meets the eye a thing is more complicated, difficult, interesting, etc, than it appears: *Sailing isn't easy – there's more to it than meets the eye.* ○

Colleagues felt that there was more to his resignation than met the eye.

melt butter wouldn't melt in sb's mouth ⇨ butter

memory

if my memory serves me right/ correctly *or* **if memory serves** if I remember correctly: *I first went to Canada in June 1982, if my memory serves me right.* ○ *It was 1983, if memory serves.*

(do sth) in memory of sb (do sth) to remember sb who is dead, especially to show love and respect: *He goes to France every year in memory of his late wife, who was French.* ○ *Monuments were built in memory of those who died.*

take sb/go down memory lane *or* **take a trip down memory lane** (make sb) remember pleasant things that happened a long time ago: *We'll be going down memory lane this evening when Mary Smithson talks about her 50 years in film-making.* ○ *Reading those letters took me down memory lane.* ○ *The book of old photos is a real trip down memory lane.*

have a mind/memory like a sieve ⇨ sieve; **in/within living memory** ⇨ living; **jog sb's memory** ⇨ jog; **refresh sb's/your memory** ⇨ refresh; **slip sb's memory/mind** ⇨ slip

men be all things to all men ⇨ things

mend

be on the 'mend (*informal*) be getting better after an illness or injury: *Jan's been very ill, but she's on the mend now.*

make do and mend mend, repair or make things yourself instead of buying them: *Anybody who has lived through a war knows how to make do and mend.*

mend your 'ways improve your behaviour, way of living, etc: *If Richard doesn't mend his ways, they'll throw him out of college.*

mental

make a mental note of sth/to do sth make an effort to remember sth (without writing it down): *I must make a mental note to order more wood.* ○ *She made a mental note of the car's registration number.*

mention

don't 'mention it (used as a polite reply when a person thanks you): *'Thanks – that's very kind of you!' 'Don't mention it.'*

mention sb/sth in the same breath compare a person or thing with another much better person or thing: *How can you mention Mozart and the Beatles in the same breath?*

not to mention sth (used for introducing an additional important piece of information) as well as sth: *He's got a house in London and a cottage in the country, not to mention the villa in Spain.* ○ *The food was marvellous. Not to mention the wine, which was first class.*

mercies be grateful/thankful for small mercies ⇨ small

mercy

mercy (be) at the mercy of sb/sth be completely dependent on and defenceless against the power, will, etc of sb/sth: *Small businessmen are completely at the mercy of the banks these days.* ○ *a little ship at the mercy of the storm* **have (got) sb at your mercy** *I've got you at my mercy now. What shall I do with you?*

throw yourself on sb's mercy ⇨ throw

merry

make merry (of a group of people) enjoy themselves very much drinking, talking, dancing, etc: *There was a group of rugby players making merry in the bar last night until 2 o'clock.* **merrymaking** (*noun*) *There was a lot of merrymaking in this town when Leeds won the cup final.*

the more the merrier (*saying*) the more people there are, the better it is: *Bring as many friends as you like. The more the merrier.*

eat, drink and be merry ⇨ eat

mess

make a mess/hash of sth/doing sth (*informal*) do sth very badly: *We tried making some wine, but we made a mess of it* (it did not taste good). ○ *I made a complete hash of the whole exam.*

message

get the 'message (*British, informal*) understand what sb means, even if they do not say it directly: *She said she was too busy to* *see me – I got the message, and didn't ask her again.*

messing

no messing (*very informal*) (used to show that you are telling the truth, or to ask sb if they are telling the truth): *That's the honest truth! No messing!* ○ *Are you sure? No messing?*

method

there's method in sb's madness although sb's actions seem strange, illogical, etc, there is a good reason for them: *'Why do you always read your newspaper backwards?' 'Ah, there's method in my madness – the back pages are where the sport is.'* (from Shakespeare's *Hamlet*)

mettle

be on, show, prove, etc your 'mettle (be prepared) to do the best work that you can or perform as well as you can in a particular situation: *When the boss comes round, I want you all to show your mettle.* ○ *He'll have to be on his mettle if he wants to win the next race.* also **put sb on their 'mettle** make sb do the best work they can, or perform as well as they can: *The school inspection is going to put the teachers on their mettle.*

mice

when the cat's away, the mice will play ⇨ cat

mickey

take the mickey/mick (out of sb/sth) (*very informal*) make fun of sb/sth: *Are you taking the mickey?* ○ *People are always trying to take the mickey out of him because of his funny accent.*

Midas

(have) the 'Midas touch be very successful in making money: *Stephanie has the Midas touch – she makes lots of money whatever she does.* (refers to King Midas in Greek legend, whose touch turned everything to gold)

middle

(be/live) in the middle of 'nowhere (*informal*) (be/live) somewhere very far from a town, village, other people, etc: *They own a small farm in the middle of nowhere.* ○ *The house isn't easy to find – it's in the middle of nowhere.*

take/follow/steer a middle 'course follow a plan that is halfway between two opposing plans; compromise: *Kate wanted to stay for the rest of the week, and I wanted to leave straight away: in the end we followed a middle course and stayed a couple of days.* ○ *In politics you often have to steer a middle course.*

pig/piggy in the middle ⇨ pig; **split sth down the middle** ⇨ split

midnight
burn the midnight oil ⇨ burn

midstream

stop, pause, etc in midstream suddenly stop doing sth, especially talking, to do sth else: *The speaker stopped in midstream, coughed, then started up again.* ○ *She interrupted him in midstream.*

change/swap horses in midstream ⇨ horses

might

might is 'right (*saying*) having the power to do sth gives you the right to do it: *Their foreign policy is based on the principle that 'might is right'.*

mightier
the pen is mightier than the sword ⇨ pen

mighty
high and mighty ⇨ high

mildly

put it 'mildly (used for showing that you could have said sth much stronger or more critical, etc): *He was annoyed, to put it mildly* (he was very angry). ○ *'She said you didn't like it.' 'That's putting it mildly – it's hideous!'*

mile

can/could tell/see (sth) a 'mile off (*informal*) see or know (sth) very easily because it's so obvious: *She's lying: you can tell a mile off.* ○ *You could see they were tourists a mile off.*

stand/stick out a 'mile (*informal*) be easy to see or notice; be obvious: *He's not telling the truth – it stands out a mile.* ○ *It sticks out a mile that they're having problems.*

a miss is as good as a mile ⇨ miss; **run a mile** ⇨ run

miles

be 'miles apart (of two sides in an

argument, dispute, etc) not at all close to reaching agreement: *The Government and the trade unions are still miles apart in this dispute.* ○ *We're miles apart on our understanding of the problem.*

be 'miles away (*informal*) not hear or notice what is happening around you because you are thinking or day-dreaming about sth completely different: *When I ask him a question in class, he just looks at me. He's always miles away.* ○ *'What do you think of Anne's idea, Dan?' 'Sorry, I was miles away. What idea is that?'*

(be/live) miles from 'anywhere/ 'nowhere (be/live) far away from a town, village, other houses, etc: *The car broke down when they were miles from anywhere.* ○ *They live in the country, miles from nowhere.*

milk

the milk of human kindness kind feelings: *There's not much of the milk of human kindness in him. I've never known such a hard man.*

it's no good/use crying over spilt milk ⇨ crying

mill

put sb/go through the 'mill (*quite informal*) (make sb) experience sth difficult or painful: *It was a very difficult interview. They really put me through the mill.* ○ *She's been through the mill this year. First she lost her job and then her house was burgled.*

grist for/to sb's mill ⇨ grist

million a chance in a million ⇨ chance; a hundred/thousand/ million and one ⇨ hundred; not a hundred/thousand/million miles away from here ⇨ miles; one, etc in a million ⇨ one

millstone

be a millstone around sb's 'neck sth which limits your freedom or makes you worry: *The house is a millstone round my neck.* ○ *Some of his colleagues on the right wing are a millstone round the Prime Minister's neck.*

mince

not 'mince matters *or* **not mince your 'words** speak openly or directly; say what you think, even though you may offend sb: *I*

won't mince matters: I think it's a stupid idea.* ○ *Sir John, never a man to mince his words, said in a TV interview that the government had lied.*

mincemeat

make 'mincemeat of sb/sth (*informal*) defeat sb completely in a fight, argument, etc; completely destroy sb's argument, theory, etc: *France made mincemeat of Portugal, beating them 5 goals to nil.* ○ *The professor made mincemeat of the speaker at the conference.*

mind

be all in the mind not be true or real; imagined: *She's not really ill; it's all in the mind.*

be of one/like mind *or* **be of the same mind** (*quite formal*) agree about sth: *Doctors are of one mind on the dangers of smoking.* ○ *My husband and I aren't always of the same mind about politics.*

bear/keep sb/sth in 'mind not forget about sb/sth: *We'll bear you in mind if a job becomes available.* ○ *I'll keep your advice in mind.* ○ *You ought to bear in mind that the tickets are usually sold very quickly.*

bring/call sb/sth to mind remind you of sb/sth: *His performance brings to mind Olivier's Hamlet.* ○ *Her paintings bring to mind hot summer days in Provence.*

come/spring/leap to 'mind think of sth quickly and effortlessly: *'Have you any suggestions?' 'Nothing springs to mind, I'm afraid.'* ○ *Just say whatever comes to mind – it doesn't matter.*

do you 'mind? 1 (used for asking permission or making a suggestion to do sth): *Do you mind if I smoke?* ○ *Do you mind if we discuss this later?* **2** (*ironic*) (used for showing your disapproval of sb's bad manners): *This man pushed into me without apologizing so I turned round and said, 'Do you mind?' and he looked very embarrassed.*

don't mind 'me 1 (used when you apologize for disturbing a meeting, lesson, meal, etc and you ask the people there to ignore you): *Don't mind me. Please carry on with your supper.* **2** (used ironically for showing your anger at not being included in sth or being asked about sth): *What's the matter with Joanna this morning? I opened the window in the office and she said, 'Don't mind* me, will you,' in a really unpleasant voice.

give your 'mind to sth concentrate on sth; think hard about sth: *He hadn't really been giving his mind to the problem.* ○ *I'm sure you'll learn it if you give your mind to it.*

go over sth in your mind think very carefully about sth that happened to you: *I go over that terrible moment in my mind every day.*

have (got) a ˌgood ˌmind to 'do sth would very much like to do sth but probably will not do it, perhaps because it would be unwise: *I've a good mind to give up this stupid job.* ○ *I've a good mind to write to my member of parliament about this new tax.*

have (got) sth in mind *or* **have (got) it in mind to do sth** plan or intend to do sth: *What do you have in mind for dinner tonight?* ○ *We've got it in mind to go to Spain this year.* ○ *How long have you had it in mind?*

have (got) sb/sth in mind (for sth) be planning to ask sb to do a job, or use sth to do a job: *I need a secretary, but I haven't got anyone in mind.* ○ *I've got a picture by Hockney in mind for the front cover of the book.*

have (got) a mind of your 'own 1 be able to make decisions, form opinions, etc without help from anyone else: *She certainly doesn't need your advice; she's got a mind of her own, that girl.* **2** (of machines, etc) behave in an unpredictable way: *This photocopier has a mind of its own. If I ask for ten copies it does one; if I ask for five, it does 15.*

have your mind on other 'things not be concentrating on sth because you are thinking about other things: *'He's made mistake after mistake today. What's the matter with him?' 'He's got his mind on other things. Family problems mainly.'*

have a mind to do sth want to do or achieve sth: *He could pass the exam easily, if he really had a mind to.* ○ *I have a mind to find out the truth behind all this.*

have sth on your 'mind be worried about sth; be thinking a lot about a problem, etc: *His daughter's very ill, so he's got a lot on his mind just now.* also **be on your 'mind** *She asked me if there was anything on my mind.*

I don't mind if I 'do (*informal*) (used when accepting an offer, for example of a drink) Yes, please: *'Another pint, Gary?' 'I don't mind*

if I do.'

I wouldn't mind I'd (quite) like: *I wouldn't mind a gin and tonic.* ○ *I wouldn't mind living abroad for a few years. What about you?*

in your mind's 'eye as a picture in your mind or in your imagination: *I can see his face quite clearly in my mind's eye.* ○ *Try to picture in your mind's eye the scene in parliament that day.*

(take) a load/weight off sb's mind (cause sb to feel) great relief, because a problem has been solved: *Selling the house was an enormous weight off my mind.* ○ *'I've finished all my essays.' 'I bet that's a load off your mind.'* ○ *It took a load off my mind when the doctor said there was nothing wrong with me.*

make up your 'mind decide: *I've made up my mind to be a doctor.* ○ *She's finally made her mind up.* ○ *My mind is made up and nothing will change it.*

the mind 'boggles (at sth) (*informal*) you find it difficult to imagine sth because it is so amazing, strange or complicated: *The mind boggles at the thought of a boxer dressed up as a fairy.* **mind-boggling** (*adjective*) *Distances in space are mind-boggling.*

mind how you go (*informal*) **1** (used to tell sb to be careful): *Mind how you go with that knife – it's very sharp!* **2** (used when saying goodbye to sb): *Goodbye then! Mind how you go!*

(keep) your mind on sth think about sth; concentrate on sth: *I'll write her a letter later. I can't keep my mind on anything today.* ○ *Your mind's not on your work today, is it?*

ˌmind over 'matter the influence of the mind on the body; the power to change things by thinking: *'How does he manage to work when he's so ill?' 'Mind over matter.'*

mind 'you 1 (used for introducing a statement which adds to, explains or contrasts with sth just said): *It's a fantastic restaurant. Expensive, mind you.* ○ *It's an excellent book. Mind you, it's difficult to read.* ○ *She's a very unpleasant woman, in my opinion. But a very good doctor, mind you.* **2** (used after a word you want to emphasize): *When we were children, we used to walk, walk mind you, 5 miles to and from school every day.*

mind your backs! (*informal*) (used to tell

people to move out of your way, for example when you are carrying something): *Mind your backs! I'm coming through!*

,mind your own 'business **1** (*rather offensive*) (used when refusing to answer a question) it does not concern you: *'Who was the girl I saw you with last night?' 'Mind your own business!'* **2** not get involved in the life, affairs, business, etc of other people: *I don't ask questions about where she gets her money. I just mind my own business.* ○ *I was sitting in a café minding my own business when a man came up to me and hit me in the face.*

mind your Ps and Qs (*informal*) be careful how you behave; remember to be polite: *Sally's got very strict ideas about how her children should behave, so mind your Ps and Qs.* (p=please, q=(than)kyou)

out of your mind **1** mad: *You want to go on a parachuting holiday? Are you out of your mind?* **2** confused and upset because of worry, illness, etc: *She's out of her mind with worry.* **bored, etc out of your mind** (*informal*) very bored, etc: *'What was the lecture like?' 'I was bored out of my mind.'*

put you in mind of sb/sth (*quite formal*) remind you of sb/sth: *Her way of speaking puts me in mind of my mother.* ○ *That music always puts me in mind of holidays in Turkey.*

put sth out of your mind try to stop thinking about sth upsetting or worrying: *Let's put the problems with the bank out of our minds and try to enjoy ourselves a bit. There's no point worrying all the time.*

put/set sb's 'mind at ease/rest do or say sth to sb which stops them worrying about sth: *If you'd phoned me it would have put my mind at ease. I had absolutely no idea where you were.* ○ *He was nervous about meeting my parents, so I tried to set his mind at rest.*

put/set/turn your mind to sth give all your effort and attention to (achieving) sth: *You could be a very good writer if you put your mind to it.* ○ *He can turn his mind to the detail if he has to.*

take sb's mind off sth prevent sb from thinking about sth that worries or upsets them: *I went out to see a film to try to take my mind off my problems.* ○ *We're trying to take his mind off things a bit.*

to 'my mind in my opinion: *To my mind, his earlier works are better.*

turn sth over in your mind think about sth, for example an offer, a plan, etc, very carefully before you make a decision: *I've been turning over the job offer in my mind all weekend. I really don't know what to do.*

with sth in mind for a particular reason: *He wrote the book with his son in mind (for his son).* ○ *I went out for a drive, with no particular destination in mind.*

at/in the back of your mind ⇨ back; **be/ get stoned out of your mind** ⇨ stoned; **be of the same mind** ⇨ same; **blow your/sb's mind** ⇨ blow; **cast your mind back to sth** ⇨ cast; **change your mind** ⇨ change; **concentrate the mind** ⇨ concentrate; **drive sb out of their mind/wits** ⇨ drive; **a frame of mind** ⇨ frame; **give sb a piece of your mind** ⇨ piece; **have got/keep an open mind** ⇨ open; **have half a mind to do sth** ⇨ half; **have a mind/memory like a sieve** ⇨ sieve; **have a one-track mind** ⇨ one; **in your right mind** ⇨ right; **know your own mind** ⇨ know; **mind/ watch your step** ⇨ step; **never mind** ⇨ never; **never mind (doing) sth** ⇨ never; **out of sight, out of mind** ⇨ sight; **peace of mind** ⇨ peace; **a practical, etc turn of mind** ⇨ turn; **presence of mind** ⇨ presence; **prey on sb's mind** ⇨ prey; **read sb's mind/ thoughts** ⇨ read; **set your heart/mind on sth/doing sth** ⇨ set; **slip sb's memory/mind** ⇨ slip; **speak your mind** ⇨ speak; **stick in your mind** ⇨ stick; **weigh on your mind** ⇨ weigh

minds **be in two minds about sth/ doing sth** ⇨ two; **a meeting of minds** ⇨ meeting

mine
be a mine of information (about/on sth) be a person who knows a lot about sth or a thing which contains a lot of useful information: *My grandmother was a mine of information on the family's history.* ○ *People criticize television, but for children it's a mine of information.*

a gold mine ⇨ gold

mint
in mint condition in such good condition that it looks brand new, although it is not:

The books were 30 years old but they were in mint condition. ○ *My bicycle isn't exactly in mint condition so I really can't ask much for it: £50 at the most.* (the mint is the factory where money is manufactured)

make, etc a mint (of money) (*informal*) make a lot of money: *They've made a mint of money with their new range of travel books.* ○ *You can earn a mint selling ice-cream on the beach in July and August.*

minute

be, etc ,up to the 'minute (*informal*) following the latest fashion; containing or giving the most recent information: *She's a tremendous follower of fashion. Everything she wears is up to the minute.* ○ *Our reporters will keep you up to the minute with the latest developments in California.*

,not for a/one 'minute/'moment/' second/'instant (*informal*) not at all; definitely not: *I didn't think for a minute that he was married.* ○ *Not for one instant would I ever consider going there on holiday again.*

at the last minute/moment ⇨ last; **there's one born every minute** ⇨ born

miracle work/do wonders/miracles ⇨ work

mischief

,do sb/yourself a 'mischief (*informal or humorous*) hurt sb/yourself: *You could do yourself a mischief wearing such tight trousers!*

make 'mischief deliberately do or say sth that annoys or upsets sb; make trouble for sb: *She told those lies because she was jealous and wanted to make mischief.*

miserable
be miserable/ugly as sin ⇨ sin

misery

put sb/sth out of her/his/its 'misery 1 kill an animal which is badly injured or very ill in order to end its suffering: *You can't let a horse go on suffering such terrible pain. Put it out of its misery, for God's sake.* **2** tell sb what they have been waiting anxiously to hear: *You can't keep telling him to wait for your answer. Put him out of his misery and tell him now.*

make sb's life a misery ⇨ life

miss(es)

give sth/sb a 'miss (*informal*) decide not to do, etc sth: *She usually goes to a yoga class on Mondays, but last week she gave it a miss.* ○ *I think I'll give the pudding a miss. I've eaten so much.*

,miss the 'boat (*informal*) lose the opportunity to do or get sth because you do not act quickly enough: *I'm afraid we've missed the boat; all the tickets for Saturday's performance have been sold.* ○ *We should have bought a house last year. Prices are much higher now. It looks as if we've missed the boat.*

a ,miss is as ,good as a 'mile (*saying*) there is really no difference between only just failing in sth and failing in it badly because the result is still the same: *What's the difference between failing an exam with 35% or 10%? Absolutely nothing; a miss is as good as a mile.*

not miss a 'trick *or* **not 'miss much** (*informal*) be very aware of things happening around you; be very alert or observant: *I'm sure Julie knows your secret – she never misses a trick!* ○ *How did he know it was the right time to sell his IBM shares? He doesn't miss a trick, does he?*

your heart misses a beat ⇨ heart; **hit and miss** ⇨ hit; **a near miss** ⇨ near; **not know what you are missing** ⇨ know

mistake
and 'no mistake! (*informal*) (used for emphasizing the truth of a statement) without any doubt: *It was a disaster, and no mistake!*

mistaking
there's no mistaking sb/sth sb/sth is easy to recognize; sth is obvious: *There's no mistaking her voice – she's got a very strong French accent.* ○ *There's no mistaking the new mood of optimism in the country.*

mixed

be a ,mixed 'bag/'bunch (*informal*) a group of people or things of different types or of different abilities: *The entries to the competition were a real mixed bag; some excellent, some awful.* ○ *This year's students are rather a mixed bunch.*

have (got) ,mixed 'feelings (about sb/ sth) have both positive and negative feelings (about sb/sth): *I've got mixed feelings* about leaving college – it's great to finish my studies, but I'm rather worried about finding a job. ○ I've got mixed feelings about our new boss. She's very pleasant but I don't think she's a very good organizer.

a ˌmixed ˈblessing sth good, pleasant, fortunate, etc which also has disadvantages: Living in such a beautiful old castle is something of a mixed blessing. Just think of the heating bills, for example.

mockery

make a mockery of sth make sth seem worthless or foolish: The imprisonment of these men makes a mockery of British justice. ○ This decision makes a mockery of the government's economic policy.

mod

(with) all mod ˈcons (of a house, caravan, etc) equipped with running water, bath, toilet, cooker, fridge, etc: We want a camp-site with all mod cons. ○ From the outside it looks really primitive but inside it's got all mod cons – even a washing machine. (a short form of 'modern conveniences')

Mohammed **if the mountain will not come to Mohammed, Mohammed must go to the mountain** ⇨ mountain

molehill **make a mountain out of a molehill** ⇨ mountain

moment(s)

at the ˈmoment now; at the present time: 'The number is engaged at the moment.' 'OK, I'll phone again later.' ○ I'm unemployed at the moment.

have your/its ˈmoments have periods of success, excitement, joy, etc in your otherwise ordinary and uninteresting life; have parts which are more interesting or exciting than the rest: My job's rather boring most of the time but it does have its moments. ○ 'What did you think of the film'. 'Well, it had its moments but on the whole it wasn't very good.'

the ˌmoment of ˈtruth a time when sb's/sth's true value, qualities, feelings, etc are revealed by her/his/its behaviour and reactions in a difficult and testing situation: The moment of truth for this country is approaching. We will have to decide whether we are really Europeans or not. ○ He asked her if she still loved him. It was a moment of truth.

pick/choose your moment (sometimes ironic) carefully choose the right time to do sth: I wanted to make sure she agreed, so I picked my moment, when she was in a good mood. ○ You told her you wanted a divorce two days after her operation! Well, you really picked your moment, didn't you?

the woman, man, etc of the ˈmoment the person most admired and talked about at a particular time: The man of the moment is the Secretary General of the United Nations because he seems to have stopped a very dangerous situation developing. ○ This is the woman of the moment. The first Olympic gold medalist in gymnastics in this country.

at the last minute/moment ⇨ last; **at a moment's notice = at short notice** ⇨ short; **for the moment/present = for the time being** ⇨ time; **in the heat of the moment** ⇨ heat; **a moment of weakness = a weak moment** ⇨ weak; **not for a/one minute/moment/second/instant** ⇨ minute; **on the spur of the moment** ⇨ spur; **a weak moment** ⇨ weak

Monday

that Monday ˈmorning feeling a feeling of depression because you have to go back to work after the weekend: Since I started this job, I never have that awful Monday morning feeling.

money

be in the ˈmoney (informal) have a lot of money: I'll be in the money if I get this job.

be ˈmade of money be rich; have a lot of money: I can't afford that! I'm not made of money, you know! ○ Why do people always think that lawyers are made of money?

be money for old ˈrope or **be money for ˈjam** (informal) be money that is earned with very little effort: All I have to do in my job is answer the phone occasionally – it's money for old rope.

for ˈmy money (informal) in my opinion: For my money, Alec's idea is better than John's. ○ English apples are the best, for my money.

get/have your ˈmoney's-worth get good value for the money you have spent: What an exciting final it was! The crowd certainly got it's money's-worth. ○ I don't feel I've had my money's-worth. The film was only an hour long.

have (got) money to 'burn (*informal*) have so much money that you can spend as much as you like: *I was staying at the Ritz – I had money to burn in those days!* ○ *He's got money to burn. He's just spent £4 000 on a picture of Mickey Mouse.*

have (got) more money than sense have a lot of money, and spend it in a silly, wasteful way: ○ *Collectors with more money than sense pay thousands of pounds for them.*

make money hand over fist (*informal*) earn a lot of money: *Some of these tennis players are making money hand over fist.*

money burns a hole in sb's pocket (*informal*) a person spends money very quickly and carelessly: *She can't wait to spend her prize money: it's burning a hole in her pocket.* ○ *He gets paid on Friday and by Monday he's spent it all. Money just burns a hole in his pocket.*

money doesn't grow on trees (*saying*) (often used for explaining why you are not going to give sb, for example a child, some money) the amount of money we have is limited by what we earn; you don't get money for doing nothing: *'Dad, I've seen a really nice tennis racquet in town. It's only £60.' 'I haven't got £60 for a tennis racquet, Alice. Money doesn't grow on trees, you know.'*

money down the drain (*informal*) a waste of money: *All her expensive education will just be money down the drain if she gets a job in a café.* ○ *He argued that any further spending on the project would be just pouring money down the drain.*

money 'talks (*saying*) if you have a lot of money you can persuade people to do things, get special treatment, have more power, etc: *Of course he'll get what he wants. Money talks, doesn't it?*

put money into sth invest money in sth: *I'd advise you to put money into land.* ○ *The Government should put more money into the film industry.* ○ *She put the money into stocks and shares.*

put (your) money on sb/sth 1 bet that a horse, dog, etc will win a race: *Put your money on Second Wind for the 3.30.* **2** (*informal*) be certain that sb will do sth, or that sth will happen: *I'd put money on him passing that exam.* ○ *I wouldn't put any money on that car lasting much longer.*

put your money where your 'mouth is (*informal*) show that you really mean what you say, by actually doing sth, giving money, etc rather than just talking about it: *The government talks about helping disabled people, but doesn't put its money where its mouth is.* ○ *You think she'll win? Come on, then, put your money where your mouth is (have a bet with me).*

easy money ⇨ easy; **a fool and his money are soon parted** ⇨ fool; **a good run for your money** ⇨ run; **marry money** ⇨ marry; **not for love or money** ⇨ love; **pin money** ⇨ pin; **rolling in it/ money** ⇨ rolling; **see the colour of sb's money** ⇨ see; **throw good money after bad** ⇨ throw; **throw your money about/ around** ⇨ throw; **throw money at sth** ⇨ throw; **time is money** ⇨ time; **you pays your money and you takes your choice** ⇨ pays

monkey

make a monkey out of sb (*informal*) make sb look stupid or foolish: *No one makes a monkey out of me.* ○ *Are you trying to make a monkey out of me? Telling me it costs £20 when I know it only costs £15.*

'monkey business (*informal*) dishonest or unacceptable behaviour, mischievous tricks, which may annoy some people: *There's money missing from the office and it's not the first time it's happened. I think there's some monkey business going on.* ○ *That's enough monkey business. Let's get down to more serious matters. This is, after all, a meeting, not a party.*

monster
the green-eyed monster ⇨ green

month
(not for/in) a month of 'Sundays (*informal, mainly British*) (not for) a very long time; maybe never: *'Do you think she'll be able to sell the house at that price?' 'Not in a month of Sundays. It's far too much.'*

flavour of the month ⇨ flavour

mood
be in the mood for sth/doing sth *or* **be in the mood to do sth** have a strong desire to do sth; feel like doing sth: *I'm in the mood for going out and having a good time.* ○

moon

She said she wasn't in the mood to dance. also **be in no mood for sth/doing sth** *or* **be in no mood to do sth** not want to do sth; not feel like doing sth.

moon

be over the 'moon (*informal*) be very happy and excited: *'How does it feel to have won the championship?' 'I'm over the moon, Jimmy.'*

cry/ask for the moon *or* **want the moon** (*informal*) want or ask for sth you cannot get, or sth that will not be given to you: *Is it asking for the moon to hope for peace in this country? ○ I don't want the moon; I just want him to listen to me for once.*

once in a blue moon ⇨ once; **promise the moon/earth** ⇨ promise

moonlight

do a moonlight 'flit (*British informal*) leave the place you have been living in quickly and secretly, usually to avoid paying your debts, rent, etc: *When I called to get the money she owed me, I found she'd done a moonlight flit.*

moons

many 'moons ago (*usually humorous*) a very long time ago: *Many moons ago, when I was young. . . .*

moot

be a moot 'point be a subject that people disagree about; be an uncertain or undecided matter: *It's a moot point whether women or men make better drivers.*

Mop a Mrs Mop ⇨ Mrs

moral

(give sb) ,moral sup'port (give sb) your friendship, encouragement, approval, etc rather than financial or practical help: *Will you stay and give me some moral support while I explain to him why I'm late? ○ Your moral support alone isn't enough. We need money to buy guns to defend ourselves with.*

more

be more than glad, ready, etc (to do sth) be very glad, etc (to do sth): *If you ever want to borrow the car, I'll be more than happy to lend it to you. ○ The project's made very good*

progress – I'm more than satisfied.

more like (used to disagree with what a person has just said, and give the true amount, situation, etc): *'How many people were there – about 40?' 'No, more like 20.' 'We need another bottle.' 'Another two, more like.' ○ A failure? More like a disaster!*

,more or 'less **1** almost: *I've more or less finished reading the book. ○ She's finished, more or less.* **2** roughly; approximately: *I earn £20 000 a year, more or less.*

more than a little drunk, excited, etc quite or very drunk, etc: *Peter was more than a little disappointed not to be chosen for the team. ○ I was more than a little surprised to see it still there two days later.*

ever more ⇨ ever; **what's more** ⇨ what

morning

the morning 'after (the night be'fore) (*informal*) the effects of drinking too much alcohol the evening before; a hangover: *I always feel terrible the morning after.*

morning, noon, and night repeatedly or constantly: *When Sally was a baby she used to cry morning, noon and night. ○ 'Morning, noon and night we have to put up with the neighbour's dog barking! I wish they would do something to keep it quiet.'*

that Monday morning feeling ⇨ Monday

moss a rolling stone gathers no moss ⇨ rolling

most

at (the) most not more than this amount; as a maximum: *I'll be away for a week, or perhaps ten days at the most. ○ At the most I might earn £250 a night. ○ There were 50 people there at the very most.*

make the most of sth get as much good as you can out of sth: *The meeting finished early so I decided to make the most of being in London and do some shopping. ○ The opportunity won't come again so make the most of it now.*

make the most of yourself, himself, etc look as attractive as possible: *She's a pretty girl but she doesn't make the most of herself.*

mother

be mother (*informal*) pour the tea: *The tea's ready. Shall I be mother?*

the mother and father of sth (*informal*) (of sth unpleasant) a very impressive, etc example of sth: *There was the mother and father of a storm that night. It lasted for hours.* ○ *The mother and father of all battles is being fought outside Tripoli this morning.*

the 'mother country the country where you or your parents, grandparents, etc were born: *The café was a meeting place for the immigrants, a welcome reminder of the tastes of the mother country.*

a 'mother's boy or **'mummy's boy** a boy or man who is thought to be too weak because he is influenced and controlled by his mother: *She always makes sure he wears a scarf – he's a real mother's boy.* ○ *He's a bit of a mummy's boy really. He ought to leave home and become a bit more independent.*

your ˌmother 'tongue the language you first learned to speak as a child; your native language: *She was born in Singapore, but her mother tongue is French.*

like father/mother, like son/daughter ⇨ father; **necessity is the mother of invention** ⇨ necessity

motion(s)

go through the motions (of doing sth) do sth but with no enthusiasm, commitment or real effort: *He went through the motions of welcoming her friends, but then quickly left the room.* ○ *She's not really interested in the subject – she's just going through the motions.*

put/set sth in 'motion or **set the wheels in 'motion** or **start the wheels turning** do what is necessary to make a start on a (large) project, plan, meeting, etc: *The Government wants to put the new reforms in motion before the election.* ○ *It's time to set the wheels in motion for our election campaign.* ○ *It will be many years before we see any results, but at least we know that the wheels are turning.* (refers to starting a large and complicated piece of machinery)

mountain(s)

if the mountain will not come to Mohammed, Mohammed must go to the mountain (*saying*) if a person cannot or refuses to come and see you, you must go and see them: *He's refused to fly to the USA to see the Defence Secretary, so it's a case of if the mountain will not come to Mohammed.* (from a story about the prophet Mohammed)

make a mountain out of a 'molehill make a small or unimportant problem seem much more serious than it really is: *It's not such a big problem! You're making a mountain out of a molehill.*

move mountains = move heaven and earth (to do sth) ⇨ move

mouse **(play) cat and mouse/a cat-and-mouse game with sb** ⇨ cat; **quiet as a mouse** ⇨ quiet

mouth

down in the mouth (*informal*) unhappy or depressed: *Why is she looking so down in the mouth?*

keep your 'mouth shut (*informal, often offensive*) not say anything, especially about sth secret: *They told him to keep his mouth shut about the robbery.*

make sb's mouth water (of food) make sb feel hungry; make sb very eager to do or have sth: *The smell of your cooking is making my mouth water.* ○ *The sight of all that money made his mouth water.* **mouthwatering** (*adjective*) a mouthwatering smell

be born with a silver spoon in your mouth ⇨ born; **butter wouldn't melt in sb's mouth** ⇨ butter; **by word of mouth** ⇨ word; **foam at the mouth** ⇨ foam; **from the horse's mouth** ⇨ horse; **have a plum in your mouth** ⇨ plum; **your heart is in your mouth** ⇨ heart; **leave a bad/nasty taste in the/your mouth** ⇨ leave; **look a gift-horse in the mouth** ⇨ look; **open your mouth** ⇨ open; **put your head in the lion's mouth** ⇨ head; **put your money where your mouth is** ⇨ money; **put words in sb's mouth** ⇨ words; **shoot your mouth off** ⇨ shoot; **shut sb's mouth** ⇨ shut; **shut your mouth/trap/face/gob!** ⇨ shut; **take the words out of sb's mouth** ⇨ words

move(s)

get a 'move on (*informal*) hurry; do sth faster: *You'd better get a move on or you'll be late.*

make a 'move **1** (*informal*) leave one place in order to go to another: *It's getting late. I think it's time we made a move.* ○ *I've been in this job far too long already; it's time I made a move.* **2** (in business negotiations, etc) do sth which will be noticed or responded to by the other people involved: *We're waiting to see what our competitors will do before we make a move.* (refers to the game of chess)

move your bowels (*formal*) excrete when you go to the toilet: *The doctor asked me if I'd moved my bowels today.*

move the 'goalposts (*British*) change the rules without warning; change the terms of an informal arrangement without warning: *Originally the competition was for amateurs only but they've suddenly moved the goalposts and said that professional photographers can take part in it as well. I don't think that's fair.* ○ *You said you'd give me £5 if I cleaned all the windows. Now you say I've got to clean the car as well. That's what I call moving the goalposts, Dad.*

move heaven and 'earth (to do sth) *or* **move 'mountains (to do sth)** do everything you can in order to help sb, achieve sth, etc: *His friends moved heaven and earth to free him from prison.* ○ *Faith can move mountains* (achieve the impossible).

not move a muscle (of a person) stay very still, without moving: *The patient didn't move a muscle for weeks.*

on the 'move **1** moving or travelling from one place to another: *The army is on the move at last.* ○ *It is important for patients to keep on the move while they are recovering.* ○ *The economy was on the move again after years of depression.*

as/if/when the spirit moves you ⇨ spirit; **a/one false move** ⇨ false

moving

get 'moving hurry; start to increase, make progress, etc: *It's late: we ought to get moving.* ○ *The tourist trade gets moving around June.*

get sth 'moving make sth start working well: *The new management really got the business moving.*

the moving spirit the person who begins and leads a group, for example a political party, a group of artists, etc: *He was one of the moving spirits in the establishment of the United Nations.*

Mr

Mr Big (*informal*) (often used for showing disapproval) the most important person in a group, area, etc: *Harry Turner, considered the local Mr Big of the criminal underworld, was found dead today at his home in Wandsworth.*

Mrs

a Mrs Mop (*informal*) a woman who cleans houses or offices as a job; a charlady: *I'm not your Mrs Mop, you know! Do it yourself!*

much

as much (as) the same (as): *Please help me – you know I'd do as much for you.* ○ *I thought as much* (that's what I expected).

be ,much of a 'muchness (*informal*) especially of people or things which are not very good, etc; be very similar: *It's hard to choose between them – they're all much of a muchness.* ○ *All the restaurants round here are much of a muchness.*

make much of sb/sth (*rather formal*) treat sb/sth as important: *They made much of the fact that she was the first woman pilot to fly a jumbo jet.*

much as/though (used for contrasting two statements) even though: *Much as I'd like to stay, I really must leave now.* ○ *He agreed, much though he disliked the idea of selling the business.*

not be much of a sth not be a good sth: *You're not much of a help, standing there with your hands in your pockets.* ○ *I'm not much of a cook.* ○ *It wasn't much of a speech really.*

not up to much (*quite informal*) not very good: *His French isn't up to much but his German is excellent.* ○ *The weather wasn't up to much but we still had a good time.*

be not so much sth as sth ⇨ so; **(not) so much as sth/doing sth** ⇨ so; **so much for sb/sth** ⇨ so

muchness **be much of a muchness** ⇨ much

mud

fling/sling/throw 'mud (at sb) (*informal*) try to damage sb's reputation by telling other people bad things about them: *Just before an election, politicians really start to* sling mud at each other. **'mud-slinging** (noun) *There's too much mud-slinging by irresponsible journalists.*

,mud 'sticks *also* **if you throw enough mud, some of it will stick** (saying) people remember and believe the bad things they hear about other people, even if they are shown to be false.

clear as mud ⇨ clear; **sb's name is mud** ⇨ name

muddy
muddy the waters make sth which seemed clear and easy to understand before seem much less clear now: *The recent research findings have muddied the waters considerably. Nuclear scientists are now having to re-examine all their existing theories.* ○ *They're just muddying the waters with all this new information. They're trying to confuse the tax authorities.*

mug
be a 'mug's game (especially British, informal) an activity which brings little or no benefit to you: *Don't start smoking – it's a mug's game.* ○ *The money's terrible in this job – it's a real mug's game.* (mug means 'fool')

mule
be (as) ,stubborn as a 'mule be very obstinate: *If you tell her what to do, she won't do it because she's as stubborn as a mule. Why not just suggest it to her?*

multitude
cover/hide a multitude of sins (often humorous) (used to say that sth is not as good as it looks, sounds, etc): *The term 'abstract art' covers a multitude of sins.* ○ *A coat of paint can hide a multitude of sins.*

mum
keep mum (informal) say nothing about a secret; stay silent: *I just kept mum when she asked me where Ben was. She'd be furious if she*

knew. ○ *Please will everyone keep mum about Saturday. We want to give them a real surprise.*

mum's the 'word! (informal) (used for telling sb to keep a secret or for telling sb that you will keep a secret): *'Nobody must mention this project outside the office. I hope that's clear.' 'We understand, John. Mum's the word!'*

mummy
mummy's boy = **a mother's boy** ⇨ mother

murder
get away with 'murder (informal, often humorous) do sth wrong without being punished, criticized, etc: *His latest book is rubbish! He seems to think that because he's a famous author he can get away with murder!* ○ *She lets the students get away with murder.*

scream, etc blue murder ⇨ blue

murmur
(do sth) with,out a 'murmur (do sth) without complaining: *She paid the extra money for the holiday without a murmur.*

muscle(s)
flex your muscles ⇨ flex; **not move a muscle** ⇨ move

music
be (like) music to sb's 'ears (quite informal) (of information, etc) be sth that is pleasant to hear: *The news that she'd finally left was like music to my ears.* ○ *The bell at the end of the lesson is always music to my ears.*

face the music ⇨ face

mustard
keen as mustard ⇨ keen

muster
pass muster ⇨ pass

mutton
be mutton dressed (up) as 'lamb (used for showing disapproval) be an older person, usually a woman, who dresses like a younger person: *Have you seen her? Mutton dressed as lamb. Somebody should remind her that she's 55, not 25.*

N

nail(s)

nail your colours to the 'mast show clearly which side you support: *It's time to nail our colours to the mast and condemn this policy.* (in a battle at sea, nailing your colours to the mast showed your intention to continue fighting and not to surrender)

a nail in sb's/sth's 'coffin something, especially one of a series of things, which makes the failure or destruction of sth more likely: *If we don't succeed with this campaign, it'll be the final nail in our coffin.* ○ *The increase in petrol prices drove another nail into the company's coffin.* ○ *The new tax is another nail in the coffin of the British film industry.*

as hard as nails ⇨ hard; **bite your nails** ⇨ bite; **fight tooth and nail** ⇨ fight; **hit the nail on the head** ⇨ hit

naked

the naked eye without the help of a microscope, telescope, etc: *Bacteria are invisible to the naked eye.*

the naked truth the truth, which may be unpleasant: *If you want the naked truth about it, he will certainly give it to you!*

name

(not) have sth to your 'name (*informal*) (not) possess sth: *I've only got two dresses to my name.* ○ *She didn't have a penny to her name when she arrived here.*

in the name of 1 by the power or authority of sb/sth: *In the name of the law, I order you to open this door.* ○ *They ordered the men to stop shooting in the name of the Revolutionary Council.* 2 (used for appealing to sb's respect for sb/sth): *In the name of God, stop fighting.* ○ *I'm asking you, in the name of love, to stop meeting that woman.* 3 (of tickets, a restaurant table, etc) reserved for sb: *The reservation was made in the name of Brown.*

make a 'name for yourself *or* **make your 'name** become successful and well known because of your skill in doing sth very well: *She quickly made a name for herself as one of the best brain surgeons in the country.* ○ *He made his name in the theatre and then moved into films.*

name the day choose the date for a wedding: *They are engaged but they haven't named the day yet.*

sb's name is 'mud (*informal*) people dislike or are angry with sb, though perhaps only for a short time, because of sth that they have done: *Your name will be mud at home if you don't write to your family soon.* ○ *My name is mud at the moment. It's all because I forgot to book our holidays in time.*

name 'names state publicly the names of people who are guilty or accused of making serious mistakes, committing crimes, etc: *If the newspapers really know the people responsible for these terrible crimes, then they should name names.* ○ *I won't name names, but there are some people in this room who have broken several of the club's rules. I shall speak to them individually later.*

the name of the game (*informal*) the thing that is considered central, essential, really important, etc in a particular situation: *Survival is the name of the game when you're in the jungle.* ○ *In the art world good publicity is the name of the game, not talent.*

a name to 'conjure with 1 the name of a well-known, very respected and admired person, group or thing in a particular field: *My great grandfather went to school with Charlie Chaplin – now there's a name to conjure with!* 2 (*humorous*) (used when you mention a name that is difficult to remember or pronounce): *The soup was called chlodnik – now there's a name to conjure with!*

put a name to sth/sb know or remember what sth/sb is called: *I know that plant but I can't put a name to it for the moment.* ○ *I know the face but I can't put a name to it.*

take sb's name in vain talk about sb in a rude or disrespectful way, especially when they are not there; use the name of God disrespectfully, especially by swearing: *Don't worry about what he says about me; he's always taking my name in vain.* ○ *I get very upset when people take God's name in vain.* (refers to one of the Ten Commandments in the Bible)

you 'name it, sb's ˌgot it (*informal*) sb has everything you can think of: *He's got an amazing collection of jazz records; you name it,* *he's got it.*

give a dog a bad name ⇨ dog; **a household word/name** ⇨ household; **lend your name to sth** ⇨ lend; **a rose by any other name** ⇨ rose; **worthy of the name** ⇨ worthy

nameless

somebody, who will/shall remain/be nameless (*humorous*) (used when the people listening to you already know who you are talking about, or used if you don't wish to embarrass somebody by mentioning their name) I won't mention their name: *Somebody, who will remain nameless, actually managed to drink two bottles of champagne!*

names   call sb names ⇨ call

napping   catch sb napping ⇨ catch

narrow

a narrow escape/squeak a situation where sb only just avoids injury, danger or failure: *We had a narrow escape on the way here. The wind blew a tree down just in front of us. We could have been killed.*

keep to, etc the straight and narrow ⇨ straight

nasty

a 'nasty piece of work (*informal*) a very unpleasant and dangerous person: *Keep away from Bill Smith; he's a very nasty piece of work.* ○ *The factory manager was a nasty piece of work. We were all terrified of him.*

cut up rough/nasty ⇨ cut; **leave a bad/nasty taste in the/your mouth** ⇨ leave

native

go 'native (*informal, often humorous*) adopt all the customs of a country which you visit or go to live in: *She was one of a number of artists who had emigrated before the war and gone native.* ○ *If you want to go native, come on one of our Explore Holidays.*

nature

in the nature of things (*rather formal*) (used for saying that sth that happens is normal in a particular situation and not at all surprising): *Don't worry about it. It's in the nature of things for children to argue with their parents when they're teenagers.* ○ *In the nature of things, people who have power don't like*

losing it.

be second nature ⇨ second; **a call of nature** ⇨ call

near

as near as dammit *or* **as near as makes no difference** (*informal*) very nearly; so nearly sth or so like sth that you can consider it the same: *The bill for the meal was £100, as near as dammit.* ○ *Here's some paint to cover that scratch on the car. It's not an exact match but it's as near as makes no difference.*

near the mark almost correct or accurate: *She thinks it will take six months to complete the job, but I think eight would be nearer the mark.* ○ *The estimate of the total cost had been pretty near the mark, in fact.*

a near miss a situation in which an accident, usually involving two moving objects, is only just avoided: *There was another near miss this afternoon just over Heathrow Airport. A jumbo nearly hit a small private plane.* ○ *He drove like a maniac. We had one near miss after another.*

so ˌnear and ˌyet so 'far (used to describe a situation in which sb is very near to success, but finally fails): *He came second in the piano competition, only one point behind the winner. So near and yet so far.*

be close/dear/near to sb's heart ⇨ heart; **be a near/close thing** ⇨ thing; **a close run thing** = **be a near/close thing** ⇨ thing; **close to/near the bone** ⇨ bone; **nowhere near** ⇨ nowhere

nearest

ˌnearest and 'dearest (*often humorous, sometimes ironic*) the people you love most, that is, your closest relations: father, mother, wife, husband, sisters, etc: *Plane crashes only become real when your nearest and dearest are involved.* ○ *She usually spends Christmas with her nearest and dearest and then leaves as soon as she can.*

nearly   pretty well / much / nearly ⇨ pretty

necessary

a necessary evil a thing that is unpleasant or even harmful, but which must be accepted because it brings some benefit: *Injections against tropical illnesses are* a necessary evil when you are planning to travel to that part of the world. ○ I suppose the security services are a necessary evil. We don't like what they do, but the country needs them.

necessity

ne,cessity is the ,mother of in'vention (*saying*) a very difficult new problem forces people to think of, design, produce, etc a solution to it: *'So how did you manage to open the bottle?' 'I used a bit of wire and a stick. Necessity is the mother of invention, as the saying goes.'*

make a virtue of necessity ⇨ virtue

neck

be in sth up to your neck (*informal*) be deeply involved in sth, especially sth dangerous or criminal: *He says he knows nothing about the drug smuggling, but the police are sure he's in it up to his neck.*

in your, etc/this ,neck of the 'woods (*informal*) in a particular area or part of the country: *Hi, Jim! What are you doing in this neck of the woods? ○ Not much happens in our neck of the woods. It's very quiet.*

,neck and 'neck (in a race, competition, etc) level with each other: *With another 100 metres to go, Jones and Saville are neck and neck. ○ For a long time they were neck and neck in the race to discover the first really effective AIDS vaccine.*

be a millstone around sb's neck ⇨ millstone; **be up to your ears/eyes/ eyeballs/neck in sth** ⇨ up; **(not) break your neck** ⇨ break; **breathe down sb's neck** ⇨ breathe; **by the scruff of sb's/the neck** ⇨ scruff; **risk your neck** ⇨ risk; **save sb's/your neck/skin** ⇨ save; **stick your neck out** ⇨ stick; **wring sb's neck** ⇨ wring

need

if need(s) be if it is necessary: *We should have enough money, but if need be, we can cash one of our traveller's cheques. ○ Give him a tablet now to relieve the pain; you can give him two more in three hours if needs be.*

a friend in need ⇨ friend; **in your hour of need** ⇨ hour; **that's all I need/needed** ⇨ all

needle(s)

like looking for/trying to find a

,needle in a 'haystack very difficult to find: *We'll never find the quotation if you don't even know what part of the book it comes from. It's like looking for a needle in a haystack.*

have pins and needles ⇨ pins

needless

,needless to 'say as you would expect: *Needless to say, the students who had studied mathematics before did better in the statistics exam. ○ He got home from the party the next morning. Needless to say, his parents were furious.*

needs

needs 'must (when the devil drives) (*saying*) in certain situations it is necessary for you to do sth you don't like or enjoy: *I would rather go to the beach than sit here studying for my exams, but needs must I suppose.*

neither

neither here nor there not important because it is not connected with the subject being discussed; irrelevant: *The fact that she's the managing director's daughter is neither here nor there. The fact is, she's the most suitable person for the job. ○ I'm not interested in what Jack thinks of the plan. His opinion is neither here nor there.*

nelly

not on your nelly (*British, very informal*) definitely not!: *'You want me to swap my car for yours? Not on your nelly.'*

nerve

have (got) a nerve (*informal*) behave in a rude, disrespectful way towards sb: *He used your car without asking you first? He's got a nerve. ○ She had a nerve, arriving half an hour late for the meeting.* also **what a nerve!** (used as an exclamation): *She borrowed my new bicycle without asking. What a nerve!*

hit/touch a (raw) 'nerve say sth which upsets sb because they are very sensitive about that subject: *You touched a raw nerve when you talked to the manager about the need for better communications within the company.*

have the nerve = have the face ⇨ face; **strain every nerve/sinew** ⇨ strain

nerves

a bundle/bag of 'nerves (*informal*) a

person who is very frightened, worried or nervous about sth: *She was a bundle of nerves at the start of the interview but she became more confident later.* ○ *He's a bag of nerves. He needs a holiday.*

get on sb's 'nerves (*informal*) annoy sb a lot: *He really gets on my nerves the way he only ever talks about his job and his car.* ○ *The noise is getting on my nerves.* ○ *By the end of the week, they were all getting on each other's nerves.*

have (got) nerves of 'steel be not easily frightened in a difficult or dangerous situation: *She won't be frightened of doing it. She's got nerves of steel.* ○ *You need nerves of steel to speculate in foreign currencies.*

a war of nerves ⇨ war

nest

a 'nest egg a sum of money saved for the future: *She has a nice little nest egg which she intends to use for travelling round the world one day.*

feather your nest ⇨ feather; **a hornet's nest** ⇨ hornet

net spread your net wide ⇨ spread

nettle grasp the nettle ⇨ grasp

network the old boy network ⇨ old

never

never 'mind (used to make sb feel better when sth bad but not too serious has happened) don't worry about it: *You left your umbrella on the train? Never mind, it's stopped raining.* ○ *You failed your driving test did you? Never mind, they say the best drivers always fail the first time.*

never mind (doing) sth (used to tell sb to stop doing or saying sth) stop, or don't start, doing sth: *Never mind the washing-up — we haven't got time.* ○ *Never mind saying how sorry you are, who's going to pay for the damage you've done?*

never say 'die (*saying*) do not stop trying or hoping for sth.

never you 'mind (*informal*) do not ask about sth, because I will not tell you: *'How much did you pay for it?' 'Never you mind.'* ○ *Never you mind why I want it, just give it to me.*

you never know (with sb/sth) you cannot be sure (about the behaviour of sb/sth or the quality of sth): *Don't throw away those old stamps. You never know, they might be valuable one day.* ○ *You can depend on local wine, but you never know with the imported stuff.* ○ *You never know with him; one day he's smiling and laughing. The next day he won't speak to anybody.*

well I never ⇨ well

new

be a ,new one on 'me be a story, joke or piece of information that you haven't heard before and which you may find a bit difficult to believe: *Butter that always stays soft — that's a new one on me.* ○ *No, I've never heard that one before. It's a new one on me.*

a new 'broom (sweeps clean) (*saying*) a person who starts a new job at the head of an organization, department, etc usually make a lot of changes in order to make it more efficient, etc: *The new managing director is clearly a new broom. He's already got rid of ten members of staff and now he's looking at our working methods.*

a new lease of life a chance for sb/sth to live/last longer; a chance to get more enjoyment and satisfaction out of life: *The successful heart operation gave him a new lease of life.* ○ *The outside of the town hall has just been cleaned and it's given the old place a new lease of life.*

break fresh/new ground ⇨ break; **new/ fresh/young blood** ⇨ blood; **ring out the old and ring in the new** ⇨ ring; **teach an old dog new tricks** ⇨ teach

Newcastle coals to Newcastle ⇨ coals

news

no news is 'good news (*saying*) if there were bad news you would hear it, so if you haven't heard anything that means everything must be all right: *He's been in the mountains for a week without ringing us. I just hope no news is good news.*

newt pissed as a newt ⇨ pissed

next

as good, well, etc as the 'next person as good/well etc as most other people: *I can swim as well as the next person, but I can't compete with her; she's an Olympic champion.*

the next best thing the best alternative or substitute for a thing that you can't have: *I couldn't find any more of that Italian ice cream but this is the next best thing in my opinion.*

(your) next of 'kin (*formal*) (often used in official forms/documents) your closest relative: *The hospital need to contact her next of kin – she is very ill indeed.*

the 'next thing (I knew) (*informal*) (used when sb tells a story and wants to say that sth happened suddenly or surprisingly): *I was just walking down the road and then the next thing I knew someone was pointing a gun at my face.* ○ *I heard a terrible explosion and the next thing I knew, I was lying in a hospital bed.*

(in) next to 'no time *or* **in no time (at all)** (*informal*) very quickly: *The meal was ready in next to no time.* ○ *This machine develops films in no time at all. You'll get them back within the hour.*

next to 'nothing a very small amount; almost nothing: *He knows a great deal about flowers but next to nothing about trees and shrubs.* ○ *He was able to buy the neighbouring farm for next to nothing.*

the 'next world (according to some religious beliefs) the place you go to when you die: *She had had a difficult life but she was convinced her reward would come in the next world.*

nice

nice and peaceful, comfortable, warm, etc pleasantly or agreeably peaceful, comfortable, warm, etc: *Sit by the fire. It's nice and warm there.* ○ *We want to go on holiday somewhere nice and peaceful.* ○ *Drink your coffee while it's nice and hot.*

nice work (if you can get it) (*informal, humorous*) (used for saying how lucky a person is to have such a pleasant and well-paid job): *She has to see all the latest films as part of her job. Nice work if you can get it.*

nick

in good, bad, etc 'nick (*informal*) in good/bad condition or health: *When I last saw him he looked in pretty good nick.* ○ *She wants to sell the bike, but she won't get very much for it because it's in terrible nick.*

in the nick of 'time (*informal*) at the last possible moment; just in time: *He got to the railway station in the nick of time.* ○ *He*
remembered in the nick of time that his passport was in his coat pocket.*

night

make a night of it (*informal*) decide to spend the whole evening doing sth enjoyable: *They met old friends in the pub after work and decided to make a night of it by going to a restaurant and then to a nightclub.*

night and 'day all the time; without stopping: *She worked night and day on the computer program until it was finished.*

a 'night owl (*informal*) somebody who feels more lively at night and usually goes to bed very late: *She's a night owl and has always done her best work after midnight.*

be ships that pass in the night ⇨ ships; **the dead of night** ⇨ dead; **it will be all right on the night** ⇨ right; **like a thief in the night** ⇨ thief; **morning, noon, and night** ⇨ morning; **a night on the town/on the tiles** = go, etc on the town ⇨ town; **a one-night stand** ⇨ one; **spend the night with sb/together** ⇨ spend; **things that go bump in the night** ⇨ things

nine(s)

a nine days' 'wonder (often used to show your disapproval of sb/sth) a person or thing that attracts a lot of attention, but only for a short time: *The satellite that landed in their garden made the family a bit of a nine days' wonder, but no one remembers their name now.*

nine times out of ten *or* **ninety-nine times out of a hundred** almost always: *Ninety-nine times out of a hundred she's right about people but this time she was wrong.* ○ *Nine times out of ten our opponents will beat us. We just hope this is the one in ten.*

nine to 'five normal office working hours: *After years working nine to five in a boring job, he set off to sail round the world.* ○ *She'd had a typical nine-to-five job in the civil service before she worked in the theatre.*

dressed up to the nines ⇨ dressed; **on cloud nine** ⇨ cloud; **possession is nine points/tenths/parts of the law** ⇨ possession; **a stitch in time saves nine** ⇨ stitch

nineteen

talk, etc nineteen to the dozen

(*informal*) talk a lot and very fast, usually in an informal conversation: *An hour later they were still sitting there talking nineteen to the dozen.*

ninepins

,go down like 'ninepins (*informal*) (of large numbers of people) become ill, be killed or die at the same time; (of businesses, etc) go bankrupt, etc: *In last year's flu epidemic both children and teachers at this school were going down like ninepins.* ○ *As the enemy advanced, men and horses went down like ninepins.* ○ *Small businesses are going down like ninepins at the moment.* (in the game of 'ninepins' you roll a ball towards a group of nine wooden skittles in order to knock down as many of them as possible)

ninety

ninety-nine times out of a hundred = nine times out of ten ⇨ nine

nip

nip sth in the bud stop sth in its early stages because you think it is dangerous to let it develop: *I do not want drugs in this school. It's essential that we nip the problem in the bud so I want a meeting with all the parents next week.* ○ *The scheme to allow all pensioners a free travel pass was nipped in the bud by the government, who said it would cost too much.*

nitty

get down to the nitty-'gritty (*informal*) start discussing the basic, especially the practical aspects of a matter/decision: *We've talked about our hopes and ambitions but let's get down to the nitty-gritty now and see what it's possible to do with the money available.* ○ *We talked for an hour without really getting down to the nitty-gritty of the problem.*

no

no 'go (*informal*) also (US) no dice (*very informal*) impossible; unsuccessful: *I asked him if I could have an extra week's holiday, but it was no go.* ○ *'Could you lend me your car this weekend, Mike?' 'No dice, I'm afraid. I need it myself.'*

a no-go area a part of a town or country which the police or army do not enter because it would be too dangerous or politically unwise to do so: *Several parts of the city have become no-go areas for the police.*

nod

give sb the 'nod (*informal*) give sb permission to do sth; tell sb that you are willing or ready for sth to happen: *Just give me the nod when you've decided, and I'll make all the necessary arrangements.*

a nod is as good as a wink (to a blind man) (*saying*) (used for telling the speaker that it is unnecessary to explain sth further because you have already understood): *'Charlie, I've invited Marianna to dinner tomorrow night. What time will you be coming home?' 'Don't worry, a nod is as good as a wink, Bill. I'll be back very late.'*

on the 'nod (*British, quite informal*) (of a matter being discussed by a committee, etc) agreed to by all the members of the group, so that a vote or further discussion is unnecessary: *The decision to increase bus fares went through on the nod.* (refers to nodding to show agreement with sb/sth)

nodding

have a nodding acquaintance with sb/sth know sb slightly/know a little about sth: *I have a nodding acquaintance with some members of the committee.* ○ *You need at least a nodding acquaintance with the rules of chess to understand the book.*

be on 'nodding terms with sb know sb not terribly well, but well enough to say 'hello' when you meet them.

noise(s)

make a (lot of) noise about sth (*informal*) talk or complain about sth a lot: *People are making more noise these days about pollution.* ○ *The unions are making a lot of noise about the new legislation.*

make noises (*informal*) show that you are interested in (doing) sth, but not in a direct way: *The government has been making noises about listening to the public but it still hasn't changed any of its policies.* ○ *She hasn't exactly said that she wants to change her job but she has been making noises in that direction.*

make the right noises ⇨ right; a big noise/shot ⇨ big

none

have/want none of it/that *or* not have/want any (of it/that) (*informal*) refuse to do, become involved in, accept or agree to sth: *She wants me to work late again this week but I'm having none of it. I've told her I won't do it.* ○ *He asked her to lend him £50 until he got paid but she wasn't having any of that.* ○ *The management has offered a 3% pay rise and an extra day's holiday but the workers want none of it. They're demanding a 10% increase.* ○ *The new secretary wants to modernize the office but the boss isn't having any.*

none other than sb (used for emphasizing that it was surprising to find sb in a particular situation): *And who do you think was responsible for the mistake? None other than the director himself!*

none too clever, happy, quickly, etc not at all clever, quickly, etc: *The driver was none too pleased about having to leave so early.* ○ *Her chances of winning are none too good, I'm afraid.*

bar none ⇨ bar; **be none the wiser/no wiser** ⇨ wiser; **none too soon** ⇨ soon; **none the worse for sth** ⇨ worse

nook

(in) every nook and cranny everywhere; all parts of a place: *I've looked in every nook and cranny but I can't find it.* ○ *She knows every nook and cranny of Oxford, so she's the perfect guide.*

noon morning, noon, and night ⇨ morning

normal as per usual/normal ⇨ per

nose

get up sb's nose (*very informal*) (of a person) annoy sb: *It gets right up my nose, the way they keep telling you how successful they are.*

have a nose for sth (*informal*) have a natural ability in finding or recognizing sth: *Don't worry about your money, he'll invest it wisely. He's got a nose for that sort of thing.* ○ *She seems to have a nose for good restaurants.*

have your nose in a book, magazine, etc (*informal*) be reading sth with great concentration and as a result not notice or care what is happening around you: *She's always got her nose in a book.*

keep your 'nose clean (*informal*) do nothing that will get you into trouble with the police or other authorities: *After he came out of prison, he was determined to keep his nose*

clean. ○ *She was in a lot of trouble at school last year. They told her that she'd have to keep her nose clean if she wanted to stay there.*

keep your nose out of sth (*informal*) not interfere in sth that does not concern you: *Keep your nose out of my business affairs, will you. They're nothing to do with you.*

keep your ,nose to the 'grindstone (*informal*) continue to work very hard: *Keep your nose to the grindstone and you should pass the exam easily.* (a grindstone is a machine used for grinding, sharpening and polishing knives and tools)

poke/stick your nose in/into sth (*informal*) interfere in the affairs or business of other people: *She's always sticking her nose into other people's affairs. It's really annoying.* ○ *What happens in this department does not concern him. Why does he have to poke his nose into everything all the time?*

put sb's 'nose out of joint (*informal*) offend or upset sb by spoiling their plans, hopes, etc; make sb feel insecure: *The problem for first children is that their noses get put out of joint when a new baby comes along. They're often terribly jealous.* ○ *The new teacher speaks much better German than he does. That's going to put his nose out of joint.*

(right) under sb's nose (*informal*) **1** (often used of sth which sb is having difficulty in finding) right in front of sb so that it can easily be seen: *'Where are the car keys?' 'There, right under your nose.'* ○ *I'm always looking for things which are right under my nose.* **2** (often used to talk about sth bad that happens over a period of time, but which nobody has noticed) in your presence: *Stealing from the kitchen has been going on right under their noses for years.*

with your 'nose in the air (used for showing disapproval) looking and feeling very superior to other people: *I hate the way she walks round with her nose in the air. She thinks she's better than us just because her family is rich.* ○ *He sat with his nose in the air and never bothered to speak to anybody.*

be no skin off sb's nose ⇨ skin; **cut off your nose to spite your face** ⇨ cut; **look down your nose** ⇨ look; **not see beyond/past the end of your nose** ⇨ see; **pay through the nose** ⇨ pay; **plain as a pikestaff/plain as the nose on**

your face ⇨ plain; **powder your nose** ⇨ powder; **rub sb's nose in it** ⇨ rub; **thumb your nose at sb/sth** ⇨ thumb; **turn your nose up at sth** ⇨ turn

nosy

a Nosy 'Parker (*British informal*) (used to show disapproval) a person who is very curious about other people's private lives: *Our next door neighbour is a real Nosy Parker.*

not

(and) not before time this should have happened a long time ago: *Julia's been promoted, and not before time, considering the amount of work she does.*

note(s)

of note important or famous: *The old theatre is one of the town's few buildings of note.*

take note of sth notice and think about or remember sth: *Well, Ms Brown, I have taken note of everything you have told me, and I'll give you my answer next week.* ○ *I'd like everyone to take note of the changes I've made to the timetable.*

compare notes ⇨ compare; **drop sb a line/note** ⇨ drop; **make a mental note of sth/to do sth** ⇨ mental; **strike/sound a false note** ⇨ false

nothing(s)

be/have nothing to 'do with sb/sth 1 have no connection with sb/sth: *I'm absolutely sure that the stars have nothing to do with our personalities.* ○ *Wynne-Williams Ltd is nothing to do with Owen Wynne-Williams. It's a completely different company.* **2** avoid or refuse contact with sb/sth: *She wants to have nothing to do with drugs, thank God.* ○ *She will have absolutely nothing to do with that organization. She doesn't approve of it.*

be/mean 'nothing to sb (*informal*) not be important for sb; not be a person that sb loves: *Why should he go to the funeral? The dead man was nothing to him.* ○ *The danger was nothing to them.*

for 'nothing 1 without paying; free: *We got into the concert for nothing because my uncle works there.* ○ *They were giving packets of sweets away for nothing at the supermarket this morning.* **2** (do sth) and not achieve what you wanted; (do sth) for no reason or

purpose: *All that hard work for nothing!* ○ *When I got to Berlin, he had already left. I had made the journey for nothing.*

make nothing 'of sth treat sth as easy or unimportant: *I know that she lost a lot of money on that property deal, but when I asked her about it, she made nothing of it at all.* ○ *He made nothing of it – pretended he didn't mind.*

not for nothing do, will, etc I, etc do sth (used for emphasizing that there is a good reason for sth): *Not for nothing do people call this beer the best in the world. It's absolutely wonderful.*

nothing 'but only: *Nothing but the freshest vegetables are used in our restaurant.*

nothing could be further from my mind, the truth, etc (used for replying to sb who tells you what you are thinking at a particular moment) the thing just mentioned is an opinion, wish, etc that I definitely do not have, agree with, think true, etc: *'You must be thinking how dreadful I look.' 'Nothing could be further from my mind. You're as beautiful as you always were.'* ○ *They expected the richest people to be the most generous. Nothing could be further from the truth.*

nothing if not sth (*informal*) (used for emphasis) very; very much a particular type of person: *She's nothing if not fair.* ○ *Her work is nothing if not original.*

(there's) nothing 'in it 1 (*informal*) (used to talk about a contest where the competitors are level and it is hard to say who will win): *Right up to the end of the match, there was nothing in it. Either team could have won.* **2** (of a rumour, report, story, etc) there's no truth in it: *There was a rumour that he was about to resign, but apparently there's nothing in it.*

nothing is sacred (often used by sb to complain that people don't respect traditions, ideas, values, etc as much as they should): *They've introduced a new tune for the national anthem. Is nothing sacred?*

nothing less than (used for emphasis) very; completely: *Their defeat was nothing less than amazing.* ○ *Her survival was nothing less than a miracle.*

nothing 'like (*informal*) not; not at all like sth: *It's nothing like as bad as he said.* ○ *We've sold nothing like enough books to make a profit.*

nothing 'more than (used for emphasis) only: *The injury is not serious; it's nothing more than a sprained ankle.*

nothing of the 'kind/'sort (*informal*) not at all as sb said or as you expected: *The brochure said it would be a beginners' course but it's nothing of the sort.* ○ *I said nothing of the kind. She completely misunderstood me.*

nothing on earth (*informal*) absolutely nothing: *Nothing on earth would make me tell anyone our secret.*

nothing succeeds like success (*saying*) success encourages you and often leads to more success: *The first task the students do should be one they are likely to do successfully. This is because nothing succeeds like success.*

nothing ventured, nothing gained (*saying*) if you don't try, you won't succeed; if you don't take risks, you won't achieve anything: *Business is not good but she's still going to open another shop. Nothing ventured, nothing gained, I suppose.* ○ *Go on. Apply for it. You know what they say: nothing ventured, nothing gained.*

there's nothing 'for it (but to do sth) there is only one possible action in a particular situation: *When the river flooded, there was nothing for it but to move everything upstairs.* ○ *There was nothing for it but to try to swim to the shore.*

there's nothing 'to it (*informal*) it is easy to do: *It's not difficult to use. All you have to do is pull these two switches and it starts. You see, there's nothing to it!* ○ *I finished the work very quickly. There was nothing to it really.*

like nothing on earth ⇨ like; **sweet nothings** ⇨ sweet

notice at short notice ⇨ short; **escape sb's notice** ⇨ escape

now

,any minute, day, time, etc 'now in the next few minutes, days, etc: *The taxi will be here any minute now.*

as of now from now on; from this moment on: *As of now, smoking is forbidden in this house.*

it's now or 'never you must do sth now because you won't get another opportunity to do it: *If we don't climb it now, we never will. It's now or never.*

(every) now and again/then occasionally: *We see each other every now and again.* ○ *She sat by the window, peering out now and then to see if they were coming.* ○ *'How often do you go to the cinema?' 'Now and then. Not often.'*

now, now (*informal*) **1** (used for comforting sb who is upset): *Now, now darling. What's the matter? Stop crying and tell me what's happened.* **2** (used for introducing a friendly warning or criticism): *Now, now, that's no way to speak to your father!*

'now then 1 (used for getting sb's attention before you start to tell them or ask sth): *Now then, let's begin the next exercise.* ○ *Now then, lads, what's going on here?* **2** (used when you are trying to remember sth): *The capital of Cuba? Now then, let me think. ... Havana, that's it, isn't it?*

nowhere

nowhere near not nearly: *The bus was nowhere near full.* ○ *The test was nowhere near as difficult as I expected.*

nowhere to be found impossible to find: *They searched the house but the necklace was nowhere to be found.*

(be/live) in the middle of nowhere ⇨ middle

nude

in the nude wearing no clothes; naked: *It's a painting of the Duchess of Alba in the nude.* ○ *People sunbathe in the nude on the rock above the creek.*

null

null and 'void (*formal*) (of a legal agreement) no longer effective or valid: *The contract was declared null and void.*

number

have (got) sb's number (*informal*) really understand what type of person sb is, especially their faults, weaknesses, bad intentions, etc: *Don't worry. I've got his number. I shall be very careful in any business do with him.* ○ *You can't fool me, you know. I've got your number.*

sb's (lucky) 'number comes up (*informal*) sb is very lucky in a competition etc: *If my lucky number comes up, we'll have a holiday in Venice.*

sb's number is 'up (*informal*) sb is about to die or experience sth very unpleasant: *There's no point worrying about getting killed in a plane crash. When your number's up, your number's up.* ○ *The police have got the evidence they need to arrest him, so it looks as if his number's up.*

number one (*informal*) **1** (often used for showing disapproval) yourself: *She doesn't care about other people and their problems. She just looks after number one.* ○ *Take care of number one and forget everybody else. That's his philosophy of life.* **2** the boss of an organization, etc: *We're looking for a new number one for our factory in Swindon.*

sb's number two (*informal*) sb's deputy or assistant: *Brian Jones is the new number two at the ministry.*

any amount/number of sth ⇨ amount; **your opposite number** ⇨ opposite

numbered sb's/sth's days are numbered ⇨ days

numbers

by 'numbers sth done easily but without imagination; following instructions: *I'm not a great cook. I just do it by numbers.* ○ *I once got a painting by numbers set for Christmas.*

in round figures/numbers ⇨ round; **there's safety in numbers** ⇨ safety; **weight of numbers** ⇨ weight

nut

do your nut (*very informal*) be very angry

or worried: *He'll do his nut when he sees all that mess.* ○ *She's doing her nut because she hasn't heard from her son for weeks. She's sure that something terrible must have happened.*

a hard/tough nut (to crack) (*informal*) a very difficult problem to solve; a very difficult person to deal with: *Persuading drivers to leave their cars at home and use public transport will be a very tough nut to crack.* ○ *You'll find it difficult to make him change his mind. He's a tough nut.*

nuts

the nuts and 'bolts (*informal*) the most important and practical details of sth: *If we look at the nuts and bolts of the plan, what problems can we see?* ○ *He worked there for two years, long enough to learn the nuts and bolts of the business.*

nutshell

(put sth) in a nutshell (*informal*) (express sth) in a very few words; very briefly: *Unemployment is rising, prices are increasing, in a nutshell the economy is in trouble.* ○ *'Do you like your new son-in-law?' 'To put it in a nutshell, no.'*

nutty

nutty as a 'fruitcake (*informal, humorous*) mad: *He's as nutty as a fruitcake. Do you know what he did yesterday? He had lunch out in the garden in the pouring rain.*

O

oaks

great/tall oaks from little acorns grow (*saying*) large and successful organizations, enterprises, etc sometimes begin in a very small or modest way. (an oak is a large tree and the acorn is its fruit)

oar

put/stick your 'oar in (*informal*) interfere in the affairs of other people: *This project is nothing to do with Dave. Why does he keep trying to stick his oar in all the time?*

oats

get your oats (*very informal, British*) have sex regularly: *'What's the matter with you, John? Not getting your oats?'*

sow your wild oats ⇨ sow

object

money, expense, etc is no object there is no need to worry about the amount of money, etc either because there is enough or it has no importance: *Choose whatever you like from the menu. It's your birthday so money is no object.* ○ *He was ready to travel anywhere.*

Distance was no object.

an object lesson a very clear and instructive example of sth: *It was an object lesson in how not to make a speech. He did absolutely everything wrong.*

occasion(s)

have occasion to do sth (*rather formal*) have a reason or need to do sth: *If you ever have occasion to visit Zurich, you will always be welcome to stay with us.*

on occasion(s) sometimes; not very often: *I don't smoke cigarettes but I like to smoke a cigar on occasion.*

ocean **a drop in the ocean/bucket** ⇨ drop

odd

an ˌodd ˈfish (*informal*) a strange person: *He's an odd fish. He's got a lot of very strange ideas.*

odd jobs various small, practical tasks, repairs, etc in the home, often done for other people: *I've got some odd jobs to do around the house; the bedroom door needs to be painted and the wall light fixed.* **odd job man** (*noun*) a person who is employed to do odd jobs.

the odd man/one out **1** the person who remained without a partner, group, team, etc at the end of a selection process, usually because the number of people is odd (see note): *That's the problem with 13 people in a group. If you need to work in pairs, there's always an odd man out.* **2** a person who is different from other people in a group: *Tom is nearly always the odd man out. He never wants to do what we want to do, or go where we want to go.* ○ *Why do you always have to be the odd one out, Ben?* ('odd' numbers are 1, 3, 5, 7, etc and 'even' numbers 2, 4, 6, 8, etc)

odds

against (all) the odds in spite of great difficulties or problems; although it seemed impossible: *Against all the odds this little-known man succeeded in becoming President.* ○ *It's a romantic story of love surviving against all the odds.*

be at odds (with sb/sth) (about/over sth) **1** not be in agreement (with sb) (about sth): *I'm at odds with her on the question of nuclear energy.* **2** (of two things) not match or correspond to each other: *His colourful and confident way of dressing is strangely at odds with his shy personality.*

make no odds (to sb/sth) (*informal*) make no difference: *It makes no odds to me what you decide to do.*

odds and ends different small objects of little value either used for decoration or put away in a drawer, etc because you have no use for them: *She's got all kinds of interesting odds and ends on her desk.*

odds and sods (*very informal*) (usually shows disapproval) people: *It was a very strange party. There were all sorts of odds and sods there.*

the odds ˈare (that...) or **(it's) odds-ˈon (that...)** it is very likely that: *I don't think we can come. The odds are that we won't be able to get a babysitter – not on Christmas Eve.* ○ *It was odds-on that they would decide to get married, so no one was surprised.*

the odds are against sth/sb doing sth sth is very unlikely: *The odds are against them winning, I'm afraid.* ○ *The odds are against her because she's less experienced than the other applicants.*

over the odds (*informal*) more than the usual price: *He paid over the odds for that bike and now he's regretting it.*

what's the odds (*informal*) what difference does it make? what does it matter?: *Work this weekend or next weekend? What's the odds? You get the same money.* ○ *Fail five exams or fail six? What's the odds?*

the cards/odds are stacked against sb/sth ⇨ stacked

odour

be in good/bad odour (with sb) (*rather formal*) (of a person) be approved of/disapproved of by sb: *He's in rather bad odour with his boss at the moment.*

offer **hold out/offer an olive branch** ⇨ olive

offing

in the offing likely or about to happen soon: *There's a pay rise in the offing, I hear.*

often

every so often occasionally: *She pays*

someone to do the gardening every so often.

(as) often as not or **more often than not** frequently; usually: *As often as not I watch TV after dinner.*

oil

be no 'oil painting (*informal*) (usually of a person) not be good-looking or attractive: *He's no oil painting but he's a marvellous actor.*

oil the wheels (*often disapproving*) make it easier to get or do sth, especially by using personal contacts, influence, or by giving people money: *He doesn't worry about bureaucratic procedures because he knows just where to oil the wheels.*

burn the midnight oil ⇨ burn; **pour oil on troubled waters** ⇨ pour

ointment a/the fly in the ointment ⇨ fly

OK

be doing OK/okay (*informal*) be successful; be making a lot of money: *'How's business?' 'We're doing OK thanks.'* ○ *They're doing more than okay with those new restaurants. They're making a fortune.*

give sb/get the OK (*informal*) give sb/ receive approval or permission: *We're waiting for the Ministry to give us the OK, and then we can go ahead with production.* ○ *They can't start until they've got the OK.*

old

'any old how carelessly; untidily: *You can't just dress any old how for such an important occasion.*

'any old thing, time, place, etc it doesn't matter which thing, when, where, etc: *Come on, let's go out now – you can do the housework any old time.* ○ *We can't have any old person looking after the kids – it has to be someone reliable.*

for old times' sake because of pleasant memories of things you did together in the past: *I saw John Smith today. I hadn't seen him for years. We had a drink together for old times' sake.* ○ *I lent him the money for old times' sake.*

of the 'old school following old methods, standards, etc: *He's one of the old school, a teacher who believes in discipline and politeness.*

(as) old as the hills (*informal*) very old;

ancient: *That joke's as old as the hills!*

an old bag (*disapproving, offensive*) an annoying and unpleasant woman: *Some old bag came in here complaining that we'd charged her too much.*

old boy/girl (*informal*) **1** an older man/ woman: *There's a nice old boy living next door.* **2** a former pupil of a school: *He's one of our most famous old boys.* ○ *We have an Old Girls' Reunion every five years.*

the old boy network (*British, disapproving*) an informal system of contacts, used to obtain jobs, information, contracts, etc, between upper class men who have been educated at the same private schools or universities.

an old chestnut (*informal*) a joke or story that has often been repeated and as a result is no longer amusing: *'He told us all about the police arresting him for climbing into his own house' 'Oh no, not that old chestnut again.'*

an old dear (*informal*) an old lady: *And then this old dear came in looking very ill, so I asked the doctor to see her before the other patients.*

an old flame (*informal*) a person you were once in love with; a former boyfriend or girlfriend: *My mother has an old flame who sends her a bottle of perfume once a year.*

an old fogy (*usually disapproving*) (usually of an older person) a person with very old fashioned or traditional views, opinions, etc: *I'm not such an old fogy that I can't remember what it was like to be a student.* (a young person with old fashioned views, style of dress, etc is sometimes called a 'young fogy') *He's one of the young fogies who write for the 'Spectator'.*

the old guard the original or older members of a group, etc, whose traditional ideas and ways of working are being replaced: *The old guard in European politics is being challenged by fresh new ideas.*

an old hand at (doing) sth a person who is very experienced at (doing) sth: *Pete's an old hand at negotiating our contracts – he's been at the firm nearly twenty years, so he knows all the procedures.*

old hat (*informal*) not new or original; out of date: *This is supposed to be a new method of learning English, but frankly, it's old hat.*

an old maid (*disapproving*) an old,

unmarried woman, especially one who is rather fussy.

old man (*informal*)   **1** father: *I go to see my old man every month. He's 77 now, you know.*   **2** husband: *Ask your old man if he can mend it.*

the old school tie (*British, disapproving*) an informal system in which upper class men educated at the same school help each other with jobs, contracts, etc in their adult lives: *People say that the bank is run on the old school tie system.*

an old 'wives' tale a traditional piece of advice or an old belief which is now often thought to be nonsense or foolish: *When you're expecting a baby, people tell you all sorts of old wives' tales.*

old woman (*very informal*)   **1** wife: *Give your old woman a surprise and take her out for a nice meal.*   **2** (*informal, disapproving*) a man who worries about silly little things: *My boss is a real old woman. He gets so annoyed if I make even the smallest mistake.*

at/to a ripe old age/to the ripe old age of 95, etc ⇨ ripe; **be money for old rope** ⇨ money; **a chip off the old block** ⇨ chip; **a dirty old man** ⇨ dirty; **a/the grand old man** ⇨ grand; **it's the same old story** ⇨ story; **no fool like an old fool** ⇨ fool; **poor old sb/sth** ⇨ poor; **ring out the old and ring in the new** ⇨ ring; **teach an old dog new tricks** ⇨ teach; **there's life in the old dog yet** ⇨ life; **be tough as old boots** ⇨ tough

olive

hold out/offer an 'olive branch (to sb) show that you want to make peace with sb following a quarrel, fight, etc: *After their argument, he was the first one to hold out an olive branch.* (the olive branch is an ancient symbol of peace)

omelette

you can't make an omelette without breaking eggs (*saying*) you cannot make an important change in sth without causing problems for sb: *I know that all these changes in the car industry are painful to many people, but you can't make an omelette without breaking eggs.*

omnibus **the man on the Clapham omnibus** = **the man in the street** ⇨ man

on

be (just) not 'on (*informal*) be not a good or an acceptable way to behave: *He told her that using his bike without asking just wasn't on.* ○ *It's not on – you should know better.*

be/go/keep 'on about sth (*informal*) keep talking about the same thing so that people become bored or irritated: *'What's she on about now?' 'Her problems with her daughter-in-law.'* ○ *Don't keep on about your terrible holiday. It's so boring.*

be/keep/go 'on at sb (to do sth) (*informal*) keep criticizing sb or telling them what to do, etc: *He keeps on at her all the time about her smoking.*

be/get 'on to sb **1** have started to discover or uncover sb's secret, a crime, etc: *The police are on to you. You'd better try and leave the country.* ○ *How did the journalists get on to him?* **2** be talking to sb in order to get information from them or to try and get their help or co-operation: *I've just been on to the local council about all the rubbish in the street.*

be 'on to sth be discovering sth important or very interesting: *Researchers at the Hammersmith Hospital in London appear to be on to an important new discovery in biochemistry.*

have (got) a lot on/don't have much/a lot on be busy/not busy: *I'm sorry I can't come with you, but I've got a lot on at the moment.* ○ *I haven't got much on next week, so I might be able to spend some time with the kids.*

have sth on sb have information about sb which is proof of their criminal activities or which would embarrass them if you told other people: *The police have got nothing on him at all. For the moment he's quite safe.* ○ *The press have got something on him and his secretary, but for the moment they're keeping quiet.*

on and off *or* **off and on** not regularly; not continuously: *It rained on and off during the night.*

on and 'on without stopping or finishing: *The road seemed to go on and on.* ○ *The band played on and on, repeating the same tunes.*

you're on! (*informal*) **1** (used for showing that you agree to sb's good, interesting, etc suggestion): *'You pay for the wine and I'll pay for the food.' 'You're* *on.'* **2** used for accepting a bet from sb: *'I bet you £5 that England beat Scotland.' 'You're on.'*

once

,all at 'once suddenly: *All at once it began to rain.*

at 'once **1** immediately: *I'm afraid there's a bomb scare; I must ask you to leave the building at once.* **2** at the same time: *Don't all speak at once! ○ I'm not superwoman, you know. I can't do a hundred things at once.*

(just) for 'once (used for emphasizing how unusual it is for sb/sth to do sth or for sth to happen): *For once he was early. ○ Try and get here on time for once, will you?*

give sb/sth the once-'over (*informal*) quickly inspect or examine sb/sth: *The landlord gave the house the once-over today to check if anything was broken or missing.*

just this once on this occasion, only and as an exception to normal rules, routine, behaviour, etc: *'Can I stay up till 11, Dad?' 'Well just this once, as it's your birthday.'*

once a...always a... in certain respects people do not change, although circumstances change: *He can't resist explaining things in detail. Once a teacher, always a teacher.*

,once and for 'all finally and definitely: *I've decided once and for all that this city is not the place for me.*

,once ,bitten, ,twice 'shy (*saying*) if something has gone wrong once, you are very careful not to let sth similar happen again: *'Will she marry again, do you think?' 'I doubt it – once bitten, twice shy.'*

,once in a blue 'moon very rarely: *Sue's daughter only visits her once in a blue moon.*

,once in a 'while occasionally: *We go to the theatre once in a while, but there's not much worth seeing.*

,once upon a 'time a long time ago (often used to begin children's fairy stories): *Once upon a time in a faraway land there lived a princess in a big castle.*

one

you, etc are a one! (*very informal, humorous*) (used for showing surprise or amusement at sb's daring or unconventional behaviour): *'She's just about*

to marry for the fifth time.' 'Ooh, she is a one, isn't she?'

be at 'one (with sb/sth) (*formal*) agree completely (with sb): *Both political parties are at one on the question of foreign imports.*

be one for (doing) sth (*informal*) be a person who likes (doing) sth very much: *They live in the country and they're great ones for long walks. ○ She's not one for staying up late – she likes to be in bed by eleven.*

be one of the lads/boys/girls (*informal*) be a member of a group of friends of the same sex and a similar age, who meet regularly to enjoy themselves: *His wife doesn't understand that he likes being one of the lads from time to time. ○ She's never really been one of the girls. She much prefers the company of men.*

be/have one over the eight (*informal*) be slightly drunk: *From the way he was walking it was obvious he'd had one over the eight.*

be/have (got) one 'up on sb (*informal*) be in a better position than sb; have an advantage over sb: *Joyce likes to be one up on her neighbours. ○ Why do you always have to be one up on everybody else?*

I/you, etc...for one (used for emphasis): *'Who is definitely coming to the meeting?' 'Well, Mr Davies is, for one, and I'm almost sure Jill is too.'*

for 'one thing, ... (, and for another, ...) one reason is..., and another reason is...: *You ought to stop smoking, you know. For one thing, you're damaging your health, and for another, you can't afford it!*

(you've, he's, etc) got it in 'one (*informal*) used when sb understands or gets the right answer immediately: *'You know, I don't think this job really suits me.' 'So you're thinking of leaving. Is that it?' 'Yes, Dick, you've got it in one.'*

go one 'better (than sb/sth) do sth better than sb else; improve on sth: *We went to Greece for our holidays, but our neighbours had to go one better. They went to Jamaica.*

have ,one too 'many (*informal*) drink too much alcohol: *I think David's had one too many. He can hardly stand up.*

have (got) a ,one-track 'mind think only about one thing, especially sex: *James will always bring sex into a conversation if he* can. *He's got a one-track mind.*

one and all everybody in a particular group: *Happy Christmas, one and all.*

the ˌone and 'only (used for emphasis) unique: *That was the one and only James Brown, with 'Try me'.* ○ *Going to France is the one and only time I've been out of the country.*

ˌone and the 'same (used for emphasis) the same; identical: *In some countries, the police and the army are one and the same thing.*

one big happy family (*informal, sometimes ironic*) a group of people who live or work together happily and without disagreements: *We were always together. We were like one big happy family.* ○ *'Is your office a happy place to work in?' 'Oh sure, we're just one big happy family. Everybody hates everybody else.'*

'one by 'one one after another: *She read all of Agatha Christie's novels one by one.* ○ *One by one the guests were leaving.*

'one day at some time in the future or in the past: *One day I'd like to go to China.* ○ *One day we decided to go to the seaside.*

a one-horse race a competition, etc in which the result is clear even before it starts because one competitor is much better, etc than the others: *The presidential elections are going to be a one-horse race this time.*

a one-horse town (*informal*) a small, boring town where nothing happens: *The President likes to remind people that he grew up in a small one-horse town in the Midwest.*

one in the eye for sb (*informal*) an unpleasant surprise for sb who may, in your opinion, deserve it: *The police took away his driving licence? Well, that's one in the eye for him, isn't it.*

one, etc in a 'million a person or thing that is very rare, very unlikely or the best: *It's an opportunity in a million, and we shouldn't waste it.* ○ *I think there's about a one-in-a-million chance of winning.* ○ *My secretary's one in a million.*

a ˌone-night 'stand 1 (*informal*) a situation where two people have sex with each other on one night only and never again: *She thought it was true love, but for him it was only a one-night stand.* **2** (*becoming dated*) one performance, concert, etc in a town, given by an orchestra, theatre company, etc which is travelling round from town to town: *He left the band because he got tired of one-night stands. It's not much fun moving from place to place all the time.*

'one of these days at some unspecified time in the future: *It's been nice talking to you. We must meet up again one of these days.*

'one of these (fine) days (used especially in warnings) soon: *One of these (fine) days you'll find that you have no friends left, and who'll help you then?*

(just) one of those 'days a day on which unpleasant things happen: *It's been one of those days. I lost my keys and then I fell over running for the bus.*

a ˌone-'off 1 a unique object or an event that happens only once: *'This plate is a one-off produced by Minton in 1898.'* ○ *'Are they going to do another concert in the church this year?' 'I don't think so. It was just a one-off.'* **2** (*informal, humorous*) a person who is quite unlike other people: *There'll never be another Charlie Chaplin. He was a one-off.*

(what with) ˌone thing and a'nother (because of) several different events, tasks, duties, etc: *What with one thing and another I haven't had time to sit down all day.*

one up to sb (used for showing approval of what sb has done) well done; congratulations: *One up to the BBC for showing so many foreign films.*

(in) ˌone way and a'nother/the 'other *or* **(in) ˌone way or a'nother/the 'other** in various different ways now considered together: *One way and another we had a very good time when we were students.*

with one voice (*becoming dated*) (of a group of people) in complete agreement: *It's very rare to find the unions and management speaking with one voice, but on the question of safety at work there is total agreement.*

be all one to sb = **be all the same to sb** ⇨ **all**

only

only to do sth (used to show that sth happened immediately after sth else, especially when this is disappointing, surprising, etc): *I arrived at the museum only to find that it was closed for the day.* ○ *She tried to be friendly to him, only to be shouted at by him again.*

only too glad, ready, etc (to do sth) extremely glad, ready, etc: *If you want any advice, I'd be only too willing to give it.* ○ *'Can you help me with this homework?' 'Only too glad.'*

only too well (used for saying emphatically that you already know about sb/sth or have already experienced sth unpleasant, etc): *'Do you know Alex Humber?' 'Only too well. He's not one of my favourite people, I'm afraid.'*

for sb's eyes only ⇨ eyes; **if only** ⇨ if; **the one and only** ⇨ one; **only have eyes for sb** ⇨ eyes

open

be open to sth be willing to consider sth: *We are open to any suggestions you care to make.*

have got/keep an open 'mind (on/ about sth) be willing to change your opinion (on/about sth): *I've still got an open mind on the question of nuclear defence.* **open- minded** (*adjective*)

(out) in(to) the 'open (of a piece of information) no longer secret or confidential and now known by a lot of people: *The whole banking scandal came into the open after somebody found some confidential documents on a train.*

in the open 'air outside; not indoors: *In summer I think it's nice to eat in the open air.* **open-air** (*adjective*) *an open-air swimming pool*

an open-and-shut case (of a legal case, crime, etc) so clear or simple that it can be dealt with or solved very easily and quickly: *It's an open-and-shut case. His fingerprints were on the gun and he can't prove where he was that night.*

an open 'book a person whose behaviour, attitudes, thoughts, etc are very easy to understand, either because you know them very well or because they are very open and honest: *After living with him for 20 years, he's an open book to me.* ○ *His life is an open book. He has no secrets.*

open the door to/for sb/sth provide sb with the chance or opportunity to do sth new, interesting, etc: *Going to university opened the door to a whole new world for her.*

open sb's eyes (to sth) make sb aware of

sth they didn't already know or understand: *The trip to China really opened the Minister's eyes.* ○ *He opened my eyes to the beauty of poetry.* **an eye-opener** (*noun*) *The film on police methods was a real eye-opener for me.*

open fire (on sb/sth) start shooting (at sb/sth): *The officer gave the order to open fire on the enemy.*

open the floodgates (to sth) remove the restrictions or controls which for a long time have prevented a lot of people from doing sth they want to do; do sth which allows sb to express feelings which have been kept under control for a long time: *Political changes in eastern Europe opened the floodgates to thousands of people who wished to emigrate.* ○ *The discussion sessions allow people to open the floodgates to their deepest fears.*

open your 'heart (to sb) tell sb about your feelings, problems or worries: *She longed to be able to open her heart to someone who would understand.*

(keep) open 'house be willing to receive guests in your home at any time, and give them food, drink, etc: *They kept open house. Whenever you visited them, the house was always full of guests. Everybody was welcome.*

an ,open 'letter a letter containing a protest, piece of advice, etc to a well-known person, which is published in a newspaper: *In an open letter to the Prime Minister, six famous authors attacked the government's policy on the arts.*

open your (big) mouth (*very informal*) say sth when you should not: *Why do you always have to open your big mouth? Can't you just keep quiet sometimes?*

an open 'question *or* **open to 'question** a matter that cannot be decided easily or that people hold several different views on: *Whether private schools give children a better education is open to question.* ○ *It's an open question whether meat is bad for you.*

an open 'secret a fact that is supposed to be a secret but that everybody knows: *It's an open secret that they're getting married.*

open 'sesame! (*humorous*) a magic word which allows you to go into a place which is normally closed or very difficult to get into: *The bank had just closed but I banged on the door and – open sesame – they let me in!* (refers to 'Ali Baba and the Forty Thieves', one of the stories in *The Thousand and One Nights*. The words *open sesame* open the door of the thieves' cave)

with open 'arms with enthusiasm; eagerly: *Don't expect her to welcome you with open arms, will you. She's still very angry with you.*

be wide open ⇨ wide; **keep your eyes open/peeled/skinned** ⇨ eyes; **the heavens open** ⇨ heavens; **keep/leave your options open** ⇨ options; **leave the door open** ⇨ leave; **wide open** ⇨ wide; **with your eyes open** ⇨ eyes

openers

for 'openers (*US, informal*) to begin with; for a start: *For openers, I don't think his work is very original.*

opinion

be of the opinion that... (*formal*) think or believe that...: *I'm firmly of the opinion that smoking should be banned in all public places.*

be a matter of opinion ⇨ matter

opportunity a window of opportunity ⇨ window

opposite

your ,opposite 'number a person who holds the same position as you in another country, organization, company, etc: *The American Secretary of State will tomorrow meet his Russian opposite number.* ○ *She's my opposite number in IBM.*

option(s)

keep/leave (all) your 'options open delay choosing between several different plans because it will be better for you to decide later: *Doing business with him is sometimes quite stressful. He likes to keep all his options open until the very last minute.*

a soft option ⇨ soft

order

in order 1 as it should be: *I checked that everything was in order.* ○ *If the documents are not in order, the house cannot be sold.* 2 allowed or permitted: *Remarks like that are definitely not in order at a meeting like this, Mr. Smyth.*

in the order of (*formal*) (of an amount)

about; approximately: *They own a business worth in the order of fifteen million pounds.* ○ *We employ in the order of 4000 people in this factory.*

on order requested from a shop, factory, etc but not yet received: *We've got 1000 envelopes on order. They should be here later this week.*

the order of the day what is normally done, etc or should be done in a particular situation; the usual attitudes, beliefs, etc of a particular group of people: *Dinner jackets and evening dresses are the order of the day at these parties.* ○ *Among some groups of young people these days violence and racism seem to be the order of the day.*

,out of 'order 1 (of a machine, etc) broken or not working properly: *The phone is out of order again.* ○ *There was a notice on the toilet door saying 'out of order'.* 2 (of behaviour, remarks, etc) not acceptable in a particular situation: *Your remarks were completely out of order at a meeting like that.*

be a tall order ⇨ tall; **in working order** ⇨ working; **law and order** ⇨ law; **of the first order** ⇨ first; **the pecking order** ⇨ pecking; **put/set your house in order** ⇨ house

ordered just what the doctor ordered ⇨ doctor

orders

be under orders (to do sth) have been ordered or commanded (to do sth): *Prisoners of war were under orders to reveal only their name, rank and number.*

give sb their marching orders ⇨ marching

ordinary

out of the ordinary unusual; strange: *His new book is certainly out of the ordinary. I've never read anything like it before.*

other

every other (person/thing) every second (person/thing): *We go abroad for our holidays every other year.* ○ *I buy milk every other day.*

the other day/morning/evening/afternoon/night only a few days ago: *The other evening we went for a drive in the country.*

the other side of the 'coin the other
aspect of the situation; a different or opposite
way of looking at a situation: *Third World
countries receive a lot of money from developed
countries; but the other side of the coin is that
they have to spend this money on expensive
imports, and that's a big problem for their
economies.*

'somebody/'something or other (used
when you don't think it's necessary to be
more precise about sb/sth, or for showing
that the person/thing mentioned does not
have much importance or value in your
opinion): *'What did you have for pudding?'
'Oh, something or other covered with cream.'* ○
*'Where's your pen?' 'Oh, I lent it to someone or
other at work and he forgot to give it back.'*

otherwise **know different/otherwise**
⇨ know

out(s)

be/feel 'out of it/things not be/feel part
of a group, conversation, activity, etc: *I
didn't know anybody at the party so I felt a bit
out of it really.*

be (all) out to do sth *or* **be (all) out for
sth** want or plan to do or get sth: *I think he's
out to kill me.* ○ *I'm not interested in a few
thousand pounds. I'm out for a million!*

,out and a'bout (of sb who has been ill) out
of the house and beginning to live an
ordinary life again: *I saw Mrs Neve in the
village this morning. I was pleased to see her out
and about again.*

'out and out complete; absolute: *He agreed
with us on a couple of points, so the meeting
wasn't an out and out failure.* ○ *Tony's an out
and out liar.*

'out with it! (used to make sb tell you sth
they are hiding, or hesitating to tell you):
Come on, out with it! I want to know the truth!

the ins and outs of sth ⇨ ins

outside

at the outside (of an amount, number,
etc) at the most: *I doubt if this factory makes
more than 500 cars a year at the very outside.*

the outside world *or* **the world
outside** the rest of the world; somewhere
where you are in contact with or have the
normal way of life of most people: *Some
tribes in the Amazon have still no contact with*

the outside world. ○ *After 15 years in a
monastery, he got a job in the outside world. It
was quite a shock for him.*

beyond/outside your ken ⇨ ken

oven **have a bun in the oven** ⇨ bun

over

be all over ,bar the 'shouting (of a
performance, contest, etc) be finished or
decided, with only the audience's reaction
or the official announcement to follow: *Now
that the first few election results have been
declared, it's really all over bar the shouting.*

be all 'over sb (*informal*) be too friendly or
affectionate towards sb: *He was all over her at
the party – he must have heard how rich she
was!*

be all over the office, town, etc (of a
piece of information or news) be/become
known by everyone in a place: *The news was
all over the village within minutes.*

be over and done with (often used of sth
unpleasant, upsetting, etc) be completely
finished: *Well I'm glad that's over and done
with. I was so nervous. I've never spoken in
front of so many people before.*

be ,sb all 'over (*informal*) be typical of sb: *It
was an unkind thing to say, but that's John all
over!*

(all) over a'gain once more; for a second
time: *I'm not sure if I could stand seeing the film
over again.* ○ *He told me the work was so bad
that I would have to do it all over again.*

,over and a'bove in addition to sth: *Higher
safety standards are needed over and above the
ones already in place.*

,over and ,over (a'gain) many times;
repeatedly: *Her doctor warned her over and
over again to stop smoking.*

overboard

go 'overboard (about/for sb/sth)
(*informal*) **1** do much more than is
necessary: *I told her just to cook a simple meal
but she went completely overboard.* **2** fall
deeply in love (with sb): *He doesn't just like
her. He's gone completely overboard about her.*

throw sth overboard ⇨ throw

overdo

over'do it/things do too much: *He rather
overdid it last Saturday playing football, and*

now he's aching all over. ○ *I've been overdoing things a bit recently. I really need a holiday.*

overdrive
go, etc into 'overdrive begin to work much harder, increase production, etc: *Production at the factory has shifted into overdrive in an attempt to meet the new orders on time.*

overstay
outstay/overstay your welcome ⇨ welcome

overstep
overstep the 'mark go beyond the limit of what is polite or acceptable: *I don't mind him being friendly, but when he tried to kiss me he was really overstepping the mark.*

overshoot
overshoot the 'mark make a mistake when you are judging the amount, etc of sth: *He overshot the mark by about £3 million.*

overtures
make overtures (to sb) try to become friendly with sb; try to start a relationship with a group of people, company, etc: *On my first day at work everyone made friendly overtures.* ○ *If we want to stay in business I think we ought to start making overtures to the bank manager!*

owes
the world owes you a living ⇨ world

owl
a night owl ⇨ night

own
on your, etc 'own alone; without help or supervision: *Why are you sitting all on your own?* ○ *She made it all on her own.*

come into your own ⇨ come; **get your, etc own back** ⇨ back; **hold your own** ⇨ hold

oyster
the world is your oyster ⇨ world

P

pace
do sth at your own 'pace do sth at the speed you prefer: *When you are learning a language at home, you can work at your own pace.*

keep pace (with sb/sth) 1 move, progress or develop at the same speed or rate as sb/sth: *In this business we have to keep pace with our foreign competitors.* ○ *He isn't really keeping pace with the other children in his class.* **2** keep informed about sth which is changing very fast: *I find it difficult to keep pace with all the political changes that are taking place.*

put sb/sth through her/his/its 'paces (*informal*) test sb's/sth's ability to do sth by making her/him/it show how well she/he/it can actually perform certain actions, tasks, etc: *We watched the trainer putting the police dog through its paces.* ○ *They're putting the new machinery through its paces.* ○ *We really put our young officers through their paces on this training course.* **go through her/his/its paces** *We watched the trainee waiters going through their paces.* (refers to judging the performance of a horse, for example before you decide to buy it)

at a snail's pace ⇨ snail; **force the pace** ⇨ force; **set the pace** ⇨ set; **stand the pace** ⇨ stand

pack(ed)
pack your 'bags (*informal*) prepare to leave a place you have been living in because of a disagreement, etc: *He hadn't paid any rent for three months so she told him to pack his bags.*

pack it 'in (*informal*) stop doing sth: *Your guitar playing is getting on my nerves. Pack it in, will you?* ○ *I didn't like my last job so I packed it in.*

a pack of lies (*informal*) a lot of lies told at the same time: *The police discovered that her story was a pack of lies.* ○ *He told me a pack of lies when I asked him about previous jobs.*

pack a (hard, etc) 'punch (*informal*) **1** be able to hit very hard: *He's a boxer who packs a nasty punch!* **2** be very powerful or strong: *Don't drink too much of his home-made beer; it packs quite a punch!*

pack them in *also* **pack the house** attract a large audience; fill a theatre, hall, etc: *This group's been playing for twenty years but they're still packing them in.* ○ *The city orchestra always plays to packed houses.*

packed (together) like sardines (*informal*) (of people) very close together because there isn't enough space: *On the tube in the rush hour the passengers are packed like sardines.* (small fish called sardines are sold packed in tins)

packet

make, lose, spend, etc a 'packet (*informal*) make, etc a large amount of money: *He went to the USA and made a packet in office property.* ○ *We spent a packet on our holiday in London; everything was so expensive.*

packing send sb packing ⇨ send

paid

a (fully) ˌpaid-up 'member, etc (used for emphasis) a person who has paid the money necessary to become a member of a group, etc; a strong and enthusiastic supporter of a group, etc: *The society has got over 10000 paid-up members.* ○ *He is a fully paid-up supporter of the right wing of the Conservative Party.*

put 'paid to sth make it impossible for sth to happen or continue: *Her poor exam results have put paid to any chance she had of getting into medical school.*

pain

on/under pain of death, imprisonment, etc (*sometimes humorous*) with the threat of being killed/put in prison, etc if you do not obey a command, order, law, etc: *They were forbidden on pain of death to talk to the other prisoners.* ○ *She ordered us to be here tomorrow at exactly 3 o'clock on pain of death. It's going to be a very important meeting.*

a pain (in the neck) (*informal*) *or* **a pain (in the arse/bum/backside)** (*very informal*) a person or thing that you find annoying: *Writing letters is a real pain in the neck.* ○ *Her boyfriend is a real pain; he never*

stops talking. (when describing a person this idiom is rather offensive)

pains

be at (great) pains to do sth show that you are very eager to do sth well, carefully, properly, etc: *The manager was at great pains to point out that no-one would lose their job after reorganization.* ○ *She was at pains to make us feel welcome in her country.*

for your pains (used for expressing disappointment or dissatisfaction with the response given by other people to your hard work, great efforts, etc): *I helped them in the shop for a week, and all I got for my pains was a box of chocolates.*

take (great) 'pains with sth/to do sth *or* **go to great pains 'to do sth** make a great effort to do sth well, carefully, properly, etc: *It looks easy but in fact he went to great pains to achieve that particular effect in his paintings.* ○ *She takes great pains with the flower arrangements.*

growing pains ⇨ growing; **spare no expense/pains/trouble (to do sth/in doing sth)** ⇨ spare

paint

paint a terrible, depressing, etc picture (of sth) (usually used with adjectives expressing a negative quality) describe sth in a way which makes it seem terrible, etc: *You paint a depressing picture of your childhood!* ○ *People who don't like students paint the worst possible picture of their behaviour.* ○ *His book paints a very gloomy picture of the British economy.*

paint the town 'red (*informal*) celebrate sth by going out with other people to bars, discos, restaurants, etc and having a very good time: *It was the end of term and students decided to celebrate by painting the town red.*

a lick of paint ⇨ lick; **he, etc is not as black as he, etc is painted** ⇨ black

painting be no oil painting ⇨ oil

pair show a clean pair of heels ⇨ show

pale

beˌyond the 'pale (of sb's behaviour) considered socially unacceptable *Her behaviour towards her employees is completely beyond the pale. She treats them like servants.*

(In the fourteenth century, the part of Ireland that was under English rule was called the 'Pale'. The area outside this was 'beyond the pale'. From the Latin – 'palum', a wooden stake)

palm

have (got) sb in the ˌpalm of your ˈhand have sb completely under your control or influence: *Her boyfriend will do anything for her; she's got him in the palm of her hand.*

grease sb's palm ⇨ grease

pan a flash in the pan ⇨ flash

pancake flat as a pancake ⇨ flat

Pandora

Pandora's ˈbox a source of great trouble and suffering, although this may not be obvious at the beginning: *The publication of the diaries opened up a real Pandora's box.* (refers to the Greek myth of Pandora, the first woman on earth. Zeus gave her a box that she was forbidden to open, and when she opened it, all the evils flew out of it into the world.)

panic

ˈpanic stations (*informal*) a state of confused activity; a state of panic: *At the moment it's panic stations in the office because we're preparing for the president's visit next week.*

pants

scare, bore, etc the ˈpants off sb (*informal*) scare, bore, etc sb very much: *He would creep up behind people and scare the pants off them.* ○ *He was clearly boring the pants off his audience.*

catch sb with their pants/trousers down ⇨ catch; **have ants in your pants** ⇨ ants; **a kick in the pants** ⇨ kick

paper

on paper considering sth from what is written down about it, rather than what is actually true in practice; in theory: *This idea looks very good on paper, but I'm not sure that it's very practical.*

paper over the cracks try to hide a big difficulty or problem, etc either by behaving as if everything is all right or by taking action which will only improve the situation temporarily, rather than solve the fundamental problems: *These new prison reforms are just papering over the cracks. What we need is a fundamental change in the prison system.* (refers to putting wallpaper on a wall in order to hide the cracks in the plaster)

a ˌpaper ˈtiger a person or thing that is less strong, powerful, dangerous than she/he/it appears: *He claimed that the enemies of his party were paper tigers and not to be feared.*

she/he couldn't punch her/his way out of a paper bag ⇨ punch; **not be worth the paper it's written on** ⇨ worth; **put pen to paper** ⇨ pen

par

be below/under ˈpar below/under the usual standard, quality, etc; not as healthy as usual: *I've been feeling rather below par recently and I think it's time I took a holiday.* ○ *His performance at the concert was well below par.*

be on a ˈpar with sb/sth be equal to sb/sth; be at the same level as sb/sth (in importance, rank, value, etc): *He doesn't think his salary is on a par with his position in the company.* ○ *As actors, I would say they were on a par.*

be (about) ˌpar for the ˈcourse (*informal*) be normal; be what you would expect to happen: *'The food on this plane is terrible.' 'Well, that's about par for the course.'*

be up to/above ˈpar of an acceptable standard, quality, etc; better than the usual standard, quality, etc: *His driving was well up to par and he won the race easily.* ○ *Her research is just not up to par. We can't recommend her for a grant.* ○ *You don't need to worry. Your work is well above par.*

paradise a fool's paradise ⇨ fool

paragon

a paragon of ˈvirtue a person who is without faults; a completely perfect, virtuous person: *Unfortunately we can't expect all policemen to be paragons of virtue.*

parcel be part and parcel of sth ⇨ part

pardon

ˌpardon ˌme for ˈbreathing, etc

(*informal*) (used ironically when you consider that sb has spoken to you unnecessarily rudely) please forgive me: '*This is a meeting for women only, so get out and mind your own business.' 'Oh, pardon me for existing!'* ○ *'I'm not interested in your opinion, thank you.' 'Oh, pardon me for breathing.'*

I beg your pardon ⇨ beg; **excuse/ pardon my French** ⇨ French

Parker a **Nosy Parker** ⇨ nosy

Parkinson's law

'**Parkinson's law** the amount of work you have increases to fill the amount of time you have to do it: *Why do we need so many people in public administration? They're just wasting public money. It's Parkinson's law, that's what it is.* (the title of a book by C. Northcote Parkinson about inefficient administration)

parrot

(learn, repeat, etc sth) '**parrot- fashion** (learn, repeat, etc sth) without understanding the meaning: *When we were at school we used to learn history parrot- fashion; all I can remember now is the dates.* (you can teach a parrot to repeat what you say)

sick as a parrot ⇨ sick

part(ed)

be part and ,parcel of 'sth be a necessary or inevitable part of sth: *Long hours spent planning lessons are part and parcel of a teacher's job.*

the better/best part of sth for most of sth: *I worked at the camp for the better part of the summer.* ○ *He had lived there for the best part of fifty years.*

for the 'most part mainly; on the whole; generally: *I agree with you for the most part but there are a few details I'd like to discuss further.*

for 'my (own) part (*rather formal*) as far as I am concerned: *For my part I don't care whether the England team wins or not.*

in large part *or* **in no small part** to a large extent: *The speech was in large part an attack on the Prime Minister.* ○ *She was in no small part responsible for the success of this company and we mustn't forget that.*

on sb's part (*rather formal*) *or* **on the part of sb** (of an action) done, made or performed by sb: *The argument started because of an angry remark on his part.* ○ *If you want to go camping, son, there'd be no objection on our part.*

part 'company (with sb/sth) 1 leave sb; separate and go in different directions: *We walked down into town together and then parted company at the station.* ○ *They've finally parted company after a long, unhappy marriage.* 2 disagree with sb: *I'm afraid I have to part company with you on the question of nuclear energy.* 3 (*humorous*) come apart; separate: *In the high winds the sail and the boat parted company.*

part of the furniture (*informal*) sb who has worked or been in a particular place for such a long time that people hardly notice them: *The librarian had been there so long he seemed like part of the furniture.*

take sth in good 'part not be annoyed or upset when sb criticizes or teases you: *They played a trick on her by putting a horrible plastic spider in her bed, but she took it in good part.* ○ *He took my criticism in good part.*

take 'part be one of a group of people doing sth together; participate: *He's taking part in a golf competition this weekend.* ○ *She never takes part in any village activities.*

take sb's 'part (*formal*) defend or support what sb has said or done, especially in an argument: *Personally I take Emma's part on this matter.* ○ *He never takes my part in an argument.*

a fool and his money are soon parted ⇨ fool; **look the part** ⇨ look; **play a/your part** ⇨ play

Parthian a **Parthian shot** = a **parting shot** ⇨ parting

parting

the parting of the ways 1 the place where two or more people who have been travelling together separate and take different routes: *We travelled to India together, and in Delhi it was the parting of the ways. Ray went on to China and I went on to Australia.* 2 the time when two or more people who have been working, living, etc together separate and begin a new period in their lives: *After university it was the parting* of the ways. We all went to live in different parts of the country and gradually lost touch. (from the Bible)

a parting 'shot or **a Parthian 'shot** a remark or action, often unkind or provocative, that somebody makes just as they are leaving: As Jim walked out of the door, his parting shot was, 'I never want to see any of you again.'(the Parthians used to fire arrows at the enemy as they were retreating from battle)

parts

round/in these parts in this area: We don't see many tourists round these parts. ○ What are the food specialities in these parts?

a woman/man of (many) 'parts (formal) a person who can do many different things well: Winston Churchill was a man of many parts: a great leader, a very clever politician, a good writer and a competent painter.

possession is nine points/tenths/parts of the law ⇨ possession

party

be (a) 'party to sth (rather formal) take part in a (secret) plan, agreement, etc, and therefore be partly responsible for it: 'Were you a party to this, Anna?' 'No, Mrs Jones, I was away on holiday at the time.' ○ How many people were party to the plan?

the ,party 'line the beliefs or policies of a political party: Ministers in the government are expected to follow the party line. ○ She has gone against the party line again. ○ No one seems to know exactly what the party line is on this issue.

your 'party piece the same song, poem, trick, etc that you often do in order to entertain people at parties: His party piece is to stand on his head and recite the 'to be or not to be' speech from 'Hamlet'.

the party's over a period of freedom, enjoyment, very good fortune, etc has now come to an end and life is about to return to normal: We've had a good time while the manager's been away, but now the party's over.

the life and soul of the party ⇨ life

pass

(things) come to a (pretty) 'pass (used for expressing surprise, disappointment, shock, etc at the way a difficult or unfortunate situation has developed or arisen): Things have come to a pretty pass when mothers are forced to beg for money in order to feed their children.

let sth pass ignore or pay no attention to sth that sb says or does because you think it's better not to argue about or criticize it: He started saying terrible things about my mother again but I let it pass. It only makes things worse if I say something.

make a 'pass at sb make a direct approach to sb you are interested in sexually: He can't resist making a pass at every woman he meets.

,pass the 'buck (informal) refuse to accept responsibility for a mistake, accident, important decision, etc and try to get another person, organization, etc to accept responsibility for it instead: The same thing happens after every disaster. All the officials and ministries involved just try to pass the buck. **buck-passing** (noun) The public is tired of all this political buck-passing. They just want to know who was responsible for the decision to build the power station here. also **the buck stops here** (used for telling sb that you are prepared to accept responsibility for sth): We don't try to escape our responsibilities. The buck stops here.

pass the 'hat round or **pass round the 'hat** (informal) collect money from people, for example to buy sb a present or to show your appreciation of sb's performance: Anthony had his car radio stolen, so his friends passed the hat round and bought him a new one.

pass 'judgement (on/about sb/sth) give your opinion about sb/sth especially if this is critical: Don't be too quick to pass judgement, you're not perfect yourself, you know.

pass 'muster be good enough; be acceptable: I didn't think Charlie's parents would like me, but evidently I pass muster.

pass the/your time (doing sth) spend your time (doing sth), often while you are waiting for sth else: They told each other jokes to pass the time while they waited for the next train. ○ We passed our time planning the next production.

pass the time of 'day greet sb and have a short conversation with them about unimportant things like the weather, etc: *I don't know any of the neighbours very well, only just enough to pass the the time of day.*

pass 'water (*formal*) urinate: *The patient was having difficulty in passing water.*

be ships that pass in the night ⇨ ships

passage a bird of passage ⇨ bird

passing
in passing speak very briefly about sb/sth while you are speaking about another matter: *'What did the minister say about educational reform?' 'Not very much. He just mentioned it in passing.'* ○ *Could I just say in passing that. . .?*

past
be past your/its best be no longer as strong, fresh, young, beautiful, etc as before *What do you mean, somebody over 35 is past their best? That's nonsense.*

be past its 'sell-by date (*informal*) no longer useful or valued: *His ideas on economics are well past their sell-by date, in my opinion.* (refers to the date which is written on food packaging)

be/look 'past it (*informal*) (of a person) be too old to do sth as well as they used to in the past; (of a thing) be no longer in good condition or functioning well because of its age: *He might look past it, but I bet he can run faster than you.* ○ *Those shoes are a bit past it, aren't they? You need a new pair.*

I wouldn't put it 'past her/him, etc (to do sth) I think she, etc is quite capable of doing sth surprising, unusual, etc: *'Do you think he'd ever steal from his friends?' 'I wouldn't put it past him.'*

a ,past 'master (in/of/at sth) (*disapproving*) a person who is very good at doing sth: *He's a past master at making other people feel guilty.*

not see beyond/past the end of your nose ⇨ see

pasting
give sb/get a pasting (*informal*) **1** beat sb/be beaten very easily: *Our team was given a real pasting on Saturday. We lost 10-0.* ○ *The Social Democrats got a real pasting at the local elections.* **2** criticize sb/be criticized very severely: *His new film got a pasting in the*

newspaper yesterday. ○ *She gave me a real pasting for handing in my essay a week late.*

pasture
put sb out to pasture (*informal*) ask sb to leave a job because they are getting old; make sb retire: *Isn't it time some of these politicians were put out to pasture?*

pat
give sb/yourself a ,pat on the 'back *or* **pat sb/yourself on the 'back (for doing sth)** congratulate or praise sb/yourself: *I think we should give James a pat on the back for working so hard.* ○ *I feel I'm entitled to pat myself on the back for having everything ready in time.* also **get, deserve, etc a ,pat on the 'back**

have/know/get sth off 'pat know or have learned sth so well that you can repeat it at any time: *I'm afraid I haven't got the answer off pat.* ○ *She's got all our names and telephone numbers off pat.*

patch
go through, hit, etc a 'bad/'sticky patch come to a difficult time in your business, marriage, etc: *We've struck a bad patch in our marriage.* ○ *High inflation meant that her business went through a sticky patch.*

not be a 'patch on sb/sth be not nearly as good as sb/sth: *The film isn't a patch on the book.*

path(s)
our/their paths cross we/they meet by chance: *Our paths crossed several times during the war and then after that, we never met again.*
cross sb's path *He never crossed my path, thank God. He was the last person in the world I wanted to meet.*

lead sb up the garden path ⇨ lead; **the primrose path** ⇨ primrose; **smooth the path/way** ⇨ smooth

patience
the patience of 'Job very great patience: *You need the patience of Job to deal with customers like that.* (from the Bible)

patter
the patter of tiny 'feet (*humorous*) (the sound of) young children around you in your home; a baby: *She's not interested in*

having children but her husband longs for the patter of tiny feet.

Paul rob Peter to pay Paul ⇨ rob

pause

give sb pause (for thought) make sb stop and think about sth, maybe stopping them from doing sth they had intended to do: *His remarks on the conditions in our prisons gave me pause for thought. Until that moment I'd never realized things were so bad.*

a pregnant pause/silence ⇨ pregnant

pave(d)

,pave the 'way (for sb/sth) make the arrival of sb/sth easier; prepare for sb/sth: *Babbage's early work on calculating machines in the nineteenth century paved the way for the development of computers.*

the road to hell is paved with good intentions ⇨ road

pay

be in sb's/sth's pay *or* **be in the pay of sb/sth** be receiving money secretly from a rival company, government, the secret police, etc in exchange for information, services, etc: *He's been in the pay of our rivals for the last ten years.*

'hell/the 'devil to pay (*informal*) a lot of trouble: *There'll be hell to pay when your father sees that broken window.*

pay 'dividends be advantageous, beneficial or useful at a later date: *Learning a foreign language will always pay dividends.* ○ *Hard work while you're young pays dividends later.* (if you invest in a company, the money you receive as your share of the profit is called a *dividend*)

pay 'lip-service to sth pretend to support or agree with an ideal, movement, etc: *The government just pays lip-service to the cause of human rights.* ○ *He doesn't really believe in women's liberation. He just pays lip-service to it because he doesn't want to appear old-fashioned.*

pay the 'price for doing sth *or* **pay the 'penalty for sth/doing sth** suffer or be disadvantaged as a result of getting sth you really want: *She insisted on marrying him against everybody's advice, and now she's paid the penalty. She's terribly unhappy.* ○ *I'm really paying the price for all that whisky I*

drank last night. I've never had such a headache.

pay your re'spects (to sb) (*formal*) show respect for sb by visiting them, attending their funeral, etc: *At the funeral the whole neighbourhood came out to pay their respects (to him).*

pay through the 'nose (for sth) (*informal*) pay a very high price for sth: *Why pay through the nose? Come to Smith's for cars at prices you can afford!*

pay 'tribute to sb/sth show that you respect or admire sb/sth: *Members of the musical profession paid tribute to the late Leonard Bernstein.*

pay sb/sth a visit *or* **pay a visit to sb/sth** visit sb/sth

pay your/its (own) 'way (of a person, group, etc) have or make enough money to support yourself/itself: *While she was a student she had to work as a waitress in order to pay her way.* ○ *The local theatre doesn't get a grant from the Arts Council so it has to pay its own way.*

cost/pay/charge the earth ⇨ earth; **rob Peter to pay Paul** ⇨ rob; **pay sth back/return sth with interest** ⇨ interest

pays

he who pays the piper calls the tune (*saying*) the person who provides the money for sth has the right to say how it should be spent; the person with power makes the decisions: *The Rockefeller Foundation helps the project financially; and they have the right to say 'no' to any part of it which they don't agree with. He who pays the piper. That's the way it works.* ○ *In this strike it's the ordinary union members who are calling the tune, not the union leaders.* (both parts of this idiom can be used separately)

it always/never pays to do sth it is always/never advisable to do sth: *It always pays to get good professional advice.* ○ *It never pays to cheat in exams because you will always be discovered eventually.*

you ,pays your ,money and you ,takes your 'choice (*saying*) you should make your own choice because your opinion is as good as anyone else's: *'I can't decide whether to buy this textbook – it is well written but it's* *rather short.' 'Well, you pays your money and you takes your choice.'*

peace

be at peace **1** not be fighting against sb: *In 1945 the western world was once again at peace.* **2** be calm and contented: *Since he stopped drinking, he's much more at peace with himself than he used to be.* **3** (of sb who has recently died) no longer suffering: *We have to comfort ourselves with the knowledge that she's at peace now.*

keep the 'peace **1** prevent people from fighting, arguing, etc: *The United Nations is sending in troops to keep the peace.* ○ *If I'm at home I can keep the peace; if I'm not, they fight all day long.* **2** (formal) not create a disturbance in a public place: *The court ordered him to keep the peace.*

make your peace with sb end an argument, quarrel, etc with sb, for example by apologizing to them: *He made his peace with his mother just before she died.*

peace and 'quiet a period of calm, silence, etc, especially after noise, stress, etc: *Why don't you all go out and play in the garden? Your mother needs a bit of peace and quiet.*

a/the peace dividend money that governments save by not buying weapons: *The Health Service should benefit from the peace dividend.*

peace of 'mind freedom from worry, anxiety, guilt, etc: *He seemed to find peace of mind in the last few weeks of his life.*

pearls

pearls of 'wisdom (humorous or ironic) good advice; wise remarks: *They all gathered round her, hoping for some of her pearls of wisdom.*

cast pearls before swine ⇨ cast

pearly

the pearly 'gates (humorous, informal) the gates of heaven: *What's going to happen when I get to those pearly gates?*

peas as like as two peas/as peas in a pod ⇨ like

pebble

not the 'only pebble on the beach (informal, disapproving) (used for criticizing sb who is being selfish) not the only person who is important or who should be considered: *'She thinks she should be chosen to go to the meeting in Paris.' 'She's not the only pebble on the beach, you know.'*

pecker keep your pecker up = keep your chin up ⇨ chin

pecking

the 'pecking order (informal) the way a group is organized, with some members being more important or powerful than others; the hierarchy: *You don't get a company car unless you're pretty high up in the pecking order.* (this expression was first used by a scientist in the 1920s studying groups of birds; he noticed there was a hierarchy when birds were feeding)

pedestal

put/set/place sb on a 'pedestal admire sb so much that you are unable to see their faults: *Don't try to put her on a pedestal, she's as guilty as the rest of them!*

knock sb off their perch/pedestal ⇨ knock

peeled keep your eyes open/peeled/skinned for sb/sth ⇨ eyes

Peeping

a 'Peeping 'Tom (disapproving) a person who likes to watch people secretly, especially when they are undressing: *You often get Peeping Toms outside nurses' homes and student residences.* (In 1040 in the English town of Coventry, the wife of the local leader, Lady Godiva, rode through the streets completely naked in an attempt to make her husband change his mind about imposing high taxes on the people. In the legend, only one man, Tom, watched her and he was struck blind.)

peg

bring/take sb 'down a peg (or two) (informal) make sb realize that they are not as important, wonderful, talented, etc as they think: *He didn't win first prize after all. That'll bring him down a peg or two.* ○ *It's time that somebody took that woman down a peg or two. She behaves as if she were the queen.*

off the 'peg (of a suit, etc) ready to wear; not made specially to fit one person: *He couldn't afford a made-to-measure suit, so he* *bought one off the peg.*

a peg to hang sth on *or* **a peg on which to hang sth** an event, occasion, subject of discussion, etc which is used by sb to express opinions or ideas about sth else: *The professor makes any subject a peg on which to hang his political views.*

be a square peg ⇨ square

pegging level pegging ⇨ level

pelt full tilt/pelt/speed ⇨ full

pen
the ˌpen is ˌmightier than the ˈsword (*saying*) writers and thinkers have a greater effect on history and human affairs than soldiers and wars.

put ˌpen to ˈpaper (*formal*) write sth, for example a letter.

a slip of the tongue/pen ⇨ slip

penalty pay the penalty for sth/doing sth = pay the price for doing sth ⇨ pay

pennies not have two pennies/two ha'pennies to rub together ⇨ two

penny
be two/ten a ˈpenny be very cheap or very common: *In the small towns on the coast, lobsters are two a penny.* ○ *Finding a job will be difficult. History teachers are ten a penny at the moment.*

ˌin for a ˈpenny, ˌin for a ˈpound (*saying*) once you have decided to start doing sth, you may as well do it as well as you can, even if this means spending a lot of time, energy, money, etc: *The new carpet made everything else look so old that it was a case of in for a penny, in for a pound, and we put up new wallpaper and curtains as well!*

not have a penny to your name (*informal*) have no money; be very poor: *Everyone thought he was rich, but when he died we found out he didn't have a penny to his name.*

the ˈpenny drops (*informal*) suddenly understand the meaning or significance of sth, for example a joke: *She never understands jokes. It usually takes about half an hour for the penny to drop.* ○ *There was a long silence on the stage, and then the penny finally dropped – it was my turn to speak. I felt so stupid.*

a ˌpenny for your ˈthoughts *or* **a penny for them** (*informal*) (said to sb who is thinking deeply) tell me what you are thinking about: *A penny for your thoughts, Hugh! You haven't said anything all evening!*

spend a penny ⇨ spend; **turn up like a bad penny** ⇨ turn

people
people who live in glass ˈhouses shouldn't throw stones (*saying*) you shouldn't criticize other people for faults that you have yourself: *'He said you weren't a hundred per cent honest in business.' 'Oh, did he? Well tell him from me that people in glasshouses shouldn't throw stones. He'll know what I mean.'*

pep
a ˈpep talk (*informal*) a talk by sb to give people confidence or encouragement: *Just before the exams, our teacher gave us all a pep talk.*

per
as per ˈusual/ˈnormal (*informal*) in the usual or normal manner: *'What time is the lesson?' 'Thursday at 3, as per usual.'* ○ *'Is he in a bad mood this morning?' 'Yes, as per normal.'*

a hundred per cent ⇨ hundred

perch knock sb off their perch/ pedestal ⇨ knock

perfect practice makes perfect ⇨ practice

perfectly know sth very/perfectly well ⇨ know

peril
at your peril (often used as a warning) at the risk of serious danger: *People who go climbing in winter do so at their own peril.* ○ *You go in Mike's car at your peril. He's a terrible driver.*

period a/the honeymoon period ⇨ honeymoon

perish
ˌperish the ˈthought! (*often humorous, informal*) I hope it will not happen; may it never happen *'A picnic is a good idea but what if it rains?' 'Perish the thought!'*

person

about/on your 'person (*formal*) carried with you, for instance in a pocket or bag: *The defendant had 100 grams of heroin on his person.*

in 'person personally; physically present: *I'm sorry, I won't be able to come in person, but I'm sending my assistant.*

as good, etc as the next person ➪ next

personally

take sth personally feel personally offended by sb's general remark, etc: *I was talking about people having smelly socks, and I'm afraid Tim took it personally.* ○ *Look, don't take this personally, Jan, but there are several people in this office who are not working hard enough.*

perspective

put, get sth in/out of per'spective be able/not be able to see or understand the relative importance of certain events, facts, etc: *When you're depressed, it's very easy to get things out of perspective. Everything worries you.* ○ *Let's try and put your present problems in perspective, and then perhaps you'll see that things are not as bad as you think.*

petard **be hoist with your own petard**
➪ hoist

Pete

for Pete's 'sake (used as an exclamation of annoyance or impatience): *For Pete's sake, what are you doing in that bathroom? You've been in there for nearly an hour.*

Peter **rob Peter to pay Paul** ➪ rob

phone **be on the telephone/phone**
➪ telephone

phrase **to coin a phrase** ➪ coin; **a turn of phrase** ➪ turn

pick

pick and 'choose take time and care to choose sth you really want: *There are so few jobs in banking at the moment that you're not really in a position to pick and choose. You must accept any job offered to you.*

pick sb's 'brains ask sb who knows a lot about a particular subject for information or ideas: *I need some help with my homework. Can I pick your brains?*

pick a 'fight/'quarrel (with sb) deliberately start a fight or argument (with sb): *Why do you always pick a fight with boys smaller than you?* ○ *At work he's always picking quarrels.*

pick 'holes (in sth) (*informal*) criticize sth or find fault with sth, for example a plan, reason, argument, etc: *It's easy for you to pick holes in my explanation, but have you got a better one?*

the pick of the 'bunch (*informal*) the best example of a group of people or things: *This Australian wine is the pick of the bunch.*

pick sb's 'pocket steal money or other things from sb's pocket without them realizing: *I can't find my wallet. I think somebody's picked my pocket!* ○ *If she's not careful she'll get her pocket picked.*
pickpocket (*noun*) a person who picks pockets: *Be careful of pickpockets when you're on the underground in London.*

pick up the 'pieces do what you can to get your life, a situation, etc back to normal after a disaster, shock, etc: *After his son was killed in a car accident, it took him a long time to pick up the pieces.* ○ *It's always the same with her husband. He upsets everyone and then leaves his wife to pick up the pieces.*

pick up 'speed go faster: *The train began to pick up speed.*

pick up the tab (*informal*) pay the bill, especially for a group of people in a restaurant, etc: *Her father picked up the tab for all the champagne at the wedding.*

pick up the threads start sth, for example an activity, relationship, career, again after a break: *It's not easy for women returning to work to pick up the threads of their earlier careers.*

take/have your 'pick (of sth) choose whatever you like: *With that much money you can have your pick of any car in the showroom.* ○ *There's ham, cheese or egg sandwiches. Take your pick!*

get up/pick up steam ➪ steam; **have a bone to pick with sb** ➪ bone; **pick/choose your moment** ➪ moment

pickle

in a real, etc 'pickle (*informal*) in a difficult situation; in a mess: *'How's work?' 'Things are in a real pickle at the moment, I'm* *afraid. My assistant's left and I'm completely lost without him!'*

picnic

be no 'picnic (*informal*) be difficult or unpleasant: *Living with someone like her is no picnic, believe me.*

picture

be the picture of health, happiness, etc be completely or extremely healthy, etc: *She's the picture of happiness in this photo.* ○ *He's the picture of misery, isn't he? Look at him standing there in the rain.*

get the picture (*informal*) understand sth: *I get the picture – you want me to keep it a secret.*

put sb in the 'picture give sb the information they need in order to understand a particular situation, etc: *Before you start work, let me put you in the picture about the way the office is run.*

paint a terrible, depressing, etc picture ⇨ paint; **pretty as a picture** ⇨ pretty; **a/one side of the story/picture** ⇨ side

pie

,pie in the 'sky (*informal*) ideas that are not practical; false hopes or promises: *Most voters know that the big promises which politicians make before an election are just pie in the sky.* ○ *He says he's going to make a film in Hollywood, but I think it's all pie in the sky.*

easy as ABC/anything/pie/falling off a log ⇨ easy; **eat humble pie** ⇨ eat; **have a finger in every pie** ⇨ finger

piece

give sb a piece of your 'mind (*informal*) angrily tell sb your true opinion of them; criticize sb angrily: *If he doesn't turn that music down soon, I'm going to give him a piece of my mind.* also **get a piece of sb's mind**

in one 'piece not hurt or harmed, especially after being in danger or in an accident: *You ought to thank God you came through that crash in one piece.* ○ *'Are you all right, Richard?' 'Yes, thanks. I'm still in one piece, I think. I've torn my trousers, that's all.'*

(all) of a piece (with sth) possessing the same character or qualities; consistent (with sth): *When you see a lot of his paintings together, you feel that his work is all of a piece.* ○ *The pews, the pulpit and the altar are of a piece*

with the simple elegance of the church itself.

,piece by 'piece one part at a time: *He took his motorcycle apart piece by piece, cleaned it, and put it back together.*

a piece of 'cake (*informal*) also **a piece of 'piss** (*very informal, offensive*) (of a task, etc) very easy to do: *After climbing mountains in the Swiss Alps, going up English hills is a piece of cake.* ○ *Taking the photo would be a piece of piss with the new lens he'd got.*

a nasty piece of work ⇨ nasty; **your party piece** ⇨ party; **say your piece** ⇨ say; **the villain of the piece** ⇨ villain

pieces

go (all) to 'pieces (*informal*) after a terrible shock, etc, become so upset or nervous that you can no longer lead your life normally: *After he lost his job he just seemed to go to pieces.*

bits and pieces = bits and bobs ⇨ bits; **pick, pull, etc sb/sth to 'bits/pieces** ⇨ bits; **pick up the pieces** ⇨ pick; **tear sb/sth to shreds/pieces** ⇨ tear

pig

make a pig's 'ear (out) of sth (*informal*) do sth very badly: *He made a pig's ear of his geography exam.* ○ *I can't understand how anybody could be such a bad cook. She makes a real pig's ear of everything.*

make a 'pig of yourself (*informal*) eat and drink too much; be greedy: *She always makes such a pig of herself.*

(be) pig/piggy in the 'middle (*informal*) be unwillingly caught in the middle of an argument, quarrel, etc between two people or groups: *Her parents hated each other and she was always pig in the middle in their quarrels.* (refers to a children's game where two children throw a ball to each other, and a third child in the middle tries to catch it)

(buy) a pig in a 'poke (*informal*) buy or pay for sth without seeing it or examining it carefully first. (refers to an old market trick of putting a rat in a bag and selling it as a young pig)

'pig it (*informal*) live or behave in a dirty way: *'Where does he live?' 'He pigs it in a bedsitter in Camden.'*

sweat like a pig ⇨ sweat

pigeon(s)

that's (not) 'my pigeon (*informal*) that's (not) my responsibility: *Somebody will have to write a report on training for the manager, but it's not my pigeon.*

put/set the cat among the pigeons ⇨ cat

piggy pig/piggy in the middle ⇨ pig

pigs

,pigs might/may 'fly (*saying*) wonderful and impossible things might happen (used when you do not believe sth will happen): *'You might get into the football team if you practise hard.' 'Yes, and pigs might fly!'*

pikestaff plain as a pikestaff/plain as the nose on your face ⇨ plain

pile

at the bottom/top of the pile (*informal*) in a low/high position in society: *You've no idea what life at the bottom of the pile is like, have you? When do you ever talk to ordinary people?*

make a/your 'pile (*informal*) make a lot of money: *If you want to make a pile, don't go into the restaurant business.*

pile on the 'agony (*informal*) **1** make sth unpleasant sound much worse than it really is in order to gain sympathy from other people: *He always piles on the agony when he has a cold; you'd think he was dying.* **2** make sb feel even worse about an unpleasant situation: *This bad result just piles on the agony for poor Oxford United. If they lose their next match, they'll be going down to the second division.*

lay/pile it on ⇨ lay

pill

be on the pill be taking regularly a pill that will stop you getting pregnant: *When I went to see the doctor, he asked me if I was on the pill.*

sugar/sweeten the 'pill make sth that is unpleasant, for example bad news, seem less unpleasant: *He tried to sweeten the pill by telling her she'd only be in hospital a few days.*

a bitter pill ⇨ bitter

pillar

a pillar of so'ciety, etc a person who is respected in society, etc; a person of importance: *I couldn't believe that a pillar of the community like him had been caught stealing from his employer.*

rush, go, etc from ,pillar to 'post continually rush from one place or person to another in a way which you find stressful, frustrating, etc: *European members of parliament have to run from pillar to post between meetings at home and abroad.*

a pillar/tower of strength ⇨ strength

pillow

'pillow talk (*informal*) a conversation in bed between lovers or husband and wife when promises may be made which should not be taken too seriously or secrets may be revealed: *'He said he'd never been so deeply in love in the whole of his life.' 'That was just pillow talk.'* ○ *'How did he find out about that?' 'Pillow talk, probably.'*

pin

pin your faith/hopes on sb/sth put your trust in sb/sth; hope for sb/sth: *He's pinning his faith on the revival of the economy.* ○ *The idea that he'll be out of prison in five years is all she's got to pin her hopes on.*

'pin money (*informal*) money earned from a part-time job, used for luxuries, etc: *She teaches a little French now and then, just for pin money.*

clean as a new pin ⇨ clean; **you could have heard a pin drop** ⇨ heard

pinch

at a 'pinch/'push (*informal*) possible if you try very hard or if it is absolutely necessary: *We usually only accept 55 guests but at a pinch, we could take 60.*

take sth with a pinch of 'salt (*informal*) do not believe everything sb says: *She told me she knew a lot of people in the government, but I took that with a pinch of salt.* ○ *I take everything he says with a large pinch of salt.*

feel the pinch ⇨ feel

pink

(be) in the pink (of condition/health) (*informal*) (be) in very good health or excellent physical condition: *The dog that won the competition was in the pink of condition.*

be tickled pink ⇨ tickled; **have a pink/ blue fit** ⇨ fit; **see pink elephants** ⇨ see

pins
have (got) ,pins and 'needles get an unpleasant prickling sensation in your arm or leg when it has been in the same position for a long time: *The best thing to do when you have pins and needles in your leg is to stamp your foot on the floor several times.*

on your pins (*informal, becoming dated*) (often used about old people) on your legs; when standing up or walking *He's not as steady on his pins as he used to be. I worry about him going out.*

for two pins ⇨ two

pint
put/pour/get a quart into a pint pot ⇨ quart

pip
pip sb at the 'post just beat sb in the final stages of a race, competition, etc: *We thought we'd won the contract, but we were pipped at the post by a rival company.* ○ *I was winning the race until Tina came up very fast behind me and pipped me at the post.*

pipe
a 'pipe dream a hope, belief, plan, etc that will probably never come true: *She's got this pipe dream about being a pop star.* (refers to smoking opium)

put 'that in your pipe and smoke it (*informal*) (used after telling sb angrily an unpleasant fact or truth which they must accept): *I'm not giving you any more money to spend on that car. So put that in your pipe and smoke it!*

pipeline
in the 'pipeline already being considered, planned, prepared or developed, but not yet ready: *We've an interesting new database program in the pipeline. It should be on sale early next year.*

piper **he who pays the piper calls the tune** ⇨ pays

piss
take the 'piss (out of sb/sth) (*very informal, offensive*) make fun of sb/sth: *He told me he thought I had a fantastic singing voice, but I think he was taking the piss* (he was

only joking). ○ *Are you taking the piss out of me?*

a piece of piss = a piece of cake ⇨ piece

pissed
(as) pissed as a 'newt (*very informal, offensive*) very drunk.

pit
pit your wits (against sb/sth) compete with sb/sth in a test of intelligence or knowledge: *He's pitting his wits against the computer chess game.*

pitch **at fever pitch** ⇨ fever

pitched
a pitched battle an angry dispute; a violent confrontation or riot: *The residents are involved in a pitched battle with the council over the plans to build new houses in the village.* ○ *There was a pitched battle earlier today in Trafalgar Square between the police and demonstrators. Two hundred people were injured, ten seriously.*

pits
be the pits (*very informal*) be very bad; be the worst kind of sth: *The teaching at this school is the pits.* ○ *This newspaper is really the pits.*

pity
more's the 'pity unfortunately: *He can't read and he doesn't want to learn, more's the pity.*

place
all 'over the place 1 everywhere: *In my job I have to travel all over the place.* 2 left everywhere in a messy or untidy way: *In London there's litter all over the place.* ○ *There were books and papers all over the place.* 3 (of a person) very confused, emotionally unstable, etc: *She's all over the place at the moment. It's really worrying.*

(not) be sb's place to do sth not have the right to do sth, for example to criticize sb, suggest sth, etc: *'Why didn't you tell him?' 'It wasn't my place to.'* ○ *He told his secretary that it wasn't her place to question what he said.*

fall, drop, slide, etc into 'place 1 because of a new piece of information, the relationship between several events, facts, etc suddenly becomes clear: *When I found out that he was Lucy's uncle, then everything fell into place.* ○ *When we got the final result of our experiment, everything dropped into place.* **2** (of a complex situation) finally reach a satisfactory conclusion: *Last year everything was so difficult; then John changed his job, I started work, the children moved school and everything finally fell into place.*

in the 'first, etc place 1 (used for introducing your reasons, points, etc in an argument or explanation) firstly, etc: *In the first place it's not your car; and in the second you're not old enough to drive it. Is that clear?* **2** right at the beginning (of a discussion, etc): *'We've decided it's too expensive for us to buy.' 'That's exactly what I said in the first place, if you remember.'*

in place prepared and ready: *Everything seems to be in place for a successful peace conference.*

out of 'place 1 unsuitable in a particular place or position; incongruous: *That beautiful piano looks completely out of place in this tiny room.* ○ *I feel quite out of place at a smart party like this.* **2** (of sb's behaviour, a remark, etc) not socially acceptable in a particular situation: *Your silly remarks were completely out of place at such an important meeting.*

a place in the sun (of a person) a very favourable position, especially in your professional life: *When he was offered a professorship at Caltech, he felt that he had finally found his place in the sun.*

put sb in their 'place remind sb forcefully of their real position in society or at work: *That young man needs putting in his place. He behaves as if he were the manager here.*

take 'place (*rather formal*) happen: *The meeting will take place at eight o'clock.* ○ *Some strange things had taken place in that old castle.*

take sb's place or **take the place of sb** do sth which another person was doing before; replace sb: *Miss Jones has left the school and this term her place has been taken by Mr Carter.* ○ *I was ill so Bill took my place at the meeting.*

sb's heart is in the right place ⟹ heart; **not a hair out of place** ⟹ hair; **pride of place** ⟹ pride; **put/set/place sb on a pedestal** ⟹ pedestal; **put/place a**

premium on sth ⟹ premium; **put yourself in sb's shoes/place** ⟹ shoes

places

'go places (*informal*) be successful or likely to be successful in your life or job: *If you're young, energetic and want to go places, write to this address and we'll send you a job application form.*

change places ⟹ change; **have friends in high places** ⟹ friends

plague **avoid sb/sth like the plague** ⟹ avoid

plain

be (all) ,plain 'sailing (sth) that progresses or is done without any difficulty: *Life with him isn't all plain sailing, you know.* ○ *She answered the first question well and from then on it was all plain sailing.*

(as) plain as a pikestaff/plain as the nose on your face (*informal*) easy to see or understand; obvious: *It's as plain as a pikestaff; this government is ruining the economy.* ○ *You can't miss the sign, it's right there, as plain as the nose on your face.*

a plain 'Jane (*disapproving*) a girl or woman who is not very pretty or attractive.

planks **be thick as two short planks** ⟹ thick

plant **plant/sow the seeds of sth** ⟹ seeds

plate

have (got) enough, a lot, etc on my, your, etc 'plate (*informal*) have got enough/a lot of things, etc to do or be responsible for: *I can't help you next week, I've got too much on my plate.* ○ *She's got a lot on her plate at the moment; that's why she looks so worried all the time.*

hand sb sth on a plate ⟹ hand

play

bring/call/put sth into 'play make sth begin to work or operate; involve sth in sth: *The exercise brings many skills into play.* ○ *This latest decision calls many new factors into play.*

come into 'play (begin to) operate or be active; have an effect or influence: *It's time for the first part of our plan to come into play.* ○ *A lot of different factors came into play in* *making this decision.*

in/out of 'play (used in sport) (of the ball in football, etc) in/out of a position where it can be played according to the rules: *The defender kicked the ball out of play.* ○ *The ball's in play, so play on.*

make great, much, etc 'play of/with/ about sth put a lot of emphasis on; behave as if sth is very important: *The English love of gardening is something he makes great play of in his latest book.* ○ *He always makes great play of the fact that he went to a famous school.*

make a 'play for sb/sth make a well-planned attempt to get sth you really want: *He was making a play for a top government position.* ○ *If you want to make a play for her, send her flowers.*

play 'ball (with sb) (informal) do what others want you to do; co-operate (with other people): *We need their help, but will they play ball?* ○ *So he won't play ball, eh? He'll soon realize he can't manage without us.*

play (sth) by 'ear play (music) which you have heard or remembered but which you have not seen written down: *She can't read music, so she plays all the tunes by ear.*

play your 'cards right (informal) act carefully and intelligently in the hope of getting sth you want: *If you play your cards right you could get promotion in a year or two.*

play 'fair/'straight (with sb) act honestly and fairly: *I don't think it's playing fair to blame her for other people's mistakes.*

play fast and 'loose (with sb/sth) (informal) keep changing your feelings or attitudes towards sb and as a result upset or disturb them: *If he plays fast and loose with my daughter's feelings, I'll make sure he regrets it.* ○ *If you start playing fast and loose with your political allies, you'll soon get into trouble.*

play for 'time try to delay sth or prevent sth from happening now because you think there will be an advantage to you if you act later: *If I can play for time a bit longer, they might lower their price.*

play the 'game act honestly and fairly; act with regard to other people's feelings: *'That's the third time this week you've gone home early leaving me to finish all your work. You're not playing the game, Alan.'* ○ *You can't break your promise to her like that. It's not playing the game.*

play sb's game *or* **play the same game (as sb)** *or* **play sb at their own game** use the same methods or tactics as a competitor, opponent, enemy, etc: *The Socialists are playing the Conservatives' game when they criticize unions in order to gain middle-class votes.* ○ *Safeway started cutting its food prices, so Asda decided to play them at their own game by cutting prices even more.*

play hard to 'get (informal) pretend not to be interested in sb/sth in order to increase sb's interest in or desire for you: *She's playing hard to get, but I'm sure she really wants to go out with me.* ○ *My advice is, play hard to get for a while and they might offer you more money.*

play (merry) 'hell with sb/sth disturb, upset or trouble sb/sth very much: *These storms play merry hell with our TV reception.*

play it by 'ear (informal) decide how to act in a situation as it happens or develops rather than by planning in advance: *You can't really prepare for the questions the interviewer will ask – you'll just have to play it by ear, I'm afraid.*

play it cool (informal) not appear excited, worried, angry, etc: *If you play it cool and don't seem too interested, he might lower the price.* ○ *He was shouting at me, but I played it cool – I didn't want him to see how angry I was.*

play it straight *or* **play a straight bat** deal with a situation in an honest and straightforward way: *'Do you think we should try and hide this from the newspapers?' 'No, play it straight; I'm sure the public will see our point of view.'* (refers to a way of holding a cricket bat)

a play on 'words a joke or amusing use of words which depends on using words that sound either the same or similar but which have different meanings; a pun: *When Elvis Presley had his hair cut off in the army he said, 'Hair today and gone tomorrow'. It was a play on words. The usual expression is 'here today and gone tomorrow.'*

play a/your part (in sth) be involved in sth; be a reason for sth happening: *You too can play a part in the defence of your country.* ○ *Arguments within the party played a part in the downfall of the government.*

play right into sb's 'hands without realizing it, do sth which will put an enemy, rival, competitor, etc in a position of advantage or power over you: *The thieves played right into the hands of the law by trying to sell stolen property to a police informer.*

play (it) 'safe avoid danger; act safely, even if another course of action should be more successful: *I know all these locks seem unnecessary but I believe it's always better to play safe.*

play second 'fiddle have a lower or less important position than another person: *She wants to be the boss, not play second fiddle to somebody less dynamic than she is.* (*fiddle* is an informal word for 'violin')

play 'silly buggers (with sth) (*very informal, offensive*) act foolishly or irresponsibly: *Stop playing silly buggers and answer the question.*

play to the 'gallery act in a way which amuses and is appreciated by ordinary people, rather than by more educated and sophisticated people, because you think the support of the ordinary people is more important to your cause, career, etc: *The most popular and successful politicians in our history have always known how to play to the gallery.* (the gallery is traditionally the part of the theatre where the cheapest seats are)

play 'truant or (*informal*) **play 'hookey** be absent from school, work, etc without reason or permission: *Is she off school because she's ill, or is she playing truant?*

play with 'fire take unnecessary and dangerous risks: *Be very careful, Mike. You are playing with fire. If they discover who you really are, they'll kill you.* ○ *I know he's wonderful but he's married. You're playing with fire.*

act/play the fool ⇨ fool; **act/play the goat** ⇨ goat; **all work and no play** ⇨ work; **child's play** ⇨ child; **play/wreak havoc with sth** ⇨ havoc; **the state of play** ⇨ state; **two can play at that game** ⇨ two; **when the cat's away the mice will play** ⇨ cat

please(d)

(as) ,pleased as 'Punch very pleased; delighted: *My brother was as pleased as Punch when he passed his driving test.* (refers to Mr Punch in the traditional puppet play *Punch and Judy*)

I'm (very) pleased to 'meet you (*formal*) (said when you are meeting sb for the first time, often as you shake hands): *'John, this is Dr Savary.' 'I'm pleased to meet you.'*

please/suit yourself ⇨ yourself

pleasure

have had the 'pleasure (*formal*) have been introduced to sb before: *'Tony, have you met Angela Evans?' 'No, I don't think I've had the pleasure.'*

it's a 'pleasure (used after sb thanks you for doing sth to help them): *'Thanks for coming to help us.' 'It's a pleasure.'*

with pleasure (*rather formal*) (used for accepting an offer, invitation, etc or for saying that you are willing to do what sb has requested): *'Would you like to come and have lunch on Sunday?' 'With pleasure. I'd love to come.'*

pledge

sign/take the 'pledge (*usually humorous*) promise never to drink alcohol: *He hasn't been much fun since he took the pledge.* (refers to the anti-drinking campaigns in the nineteenth century when people signed a promise never to drink alcohol)

plenty
there are plenty/lots more fish in the sea ⇨ fish

plot

the plot 'thickens (*humorous*) (used when the events in a story, etc or a situation in real life are getting more complicated, more puzzling and more interesting)

pluck
pluck/summon up courage ⇨ courage

plum

have a plum in your mouth (*British, disapproving*) speak with an upper-class accent: *She speaks as if she's got a plum in her mouth.*

plumb

plumb the 'depths of sth reach the lowest or most extreme point of sth: *When his friend was killed, he plumbed the depths of despair.* ○ *This book plumbs the depths of depravity.*

plunge
take the 'plunge (*informal*) decide to do

sth new, difficult or risky, especially after thinking about it for some time: *After working for twenty years he's decided to take the plunge and go back to college.* (refers to diving into cold water)

pocket(s)

be ,in/,out of 'pocket have more/less money at the end of a financial transaction than you expected to have; make/lose money in a transaction: *I paid the bill in the restaurant and then everybody paid me their share of the bill later, but for some reason I was still £10 out of pocket.* ○ *Even after paying the extra fee, we were still £100 in pocket.*

in sb's 'pocket (*informal*) be in sb's control, under sb's influence, etc: *The gang have got hundreds of policemen in New York in their pockets. ○ She makes all the decisions, not him. He's completely in her pocket.*

out of your own pocket with your own money: *He paid for the trip out of his own pocket.*

line your/sb's pockets ⇨ line; **money burns a hole in sb's pocket** ⇨ money; **pick sb's pocket** ⇨ pick; **pocket/ swallow your pride** ⇨ pride; **put your hand into your pocket** ⇨ hand

poetic

poetic 'justice a punishment or reward that is deserved

poetic 'licence (*often ironic*) freedom from the normal rules of grammar, vocabulary, accuracy, etc, typical of poetry: *He was using poetic licence when he described this room as 'large, modern and comfortable'.*

point

ask, tell, etc sb point 'blank ask, tell, etc sb very directly, and perhaps rudely: *I told him point blank that we no longer wanted him to work for us. ○ She asked me point blank why I didn't like her.*

be beside the 'point be of no importance to the matter being discussed; be not relevant *His political interests are beside the point. All I want to know about him is whether he can do the job properly.*

be on the point of doing sth be about to do sth: *I was on the point of posting the letter when I saw it didn't have a stamp on it.*

be to the 'point 1 be relevant to the matter being discussed: *The editor cut out a few sentences that weren't strictly to the point.* **2** well expressed in a few words: *It's a good advertisement because it's absolutely to the point. ○ The speech was short and to the point.*

come/get (straight) to the 'point talk about the most important problem, matter, etc immediately rather than have a general conversation first: *Stop avoiding the issue and come to the point! ○ Let me get straight to the point. I don't think you'll pass unless you work harder.*

get the 'point (of sth) understand sb's explanation: *You haven't got the point of what I'm trying to say. ○ Oh, I see. I get the point.*

have (got) a 'point (there) have made a good suggestion; have a good idea: *He's got a point there; if you sell the house now you'll lose money, so why not wait till next year? ○ I think animal rights campaigners have a point when they say that a lot of animal testing is unnecessary.*

if/when it ,comes to the 'point if/when the time comes when you have to do or decide sth: *I'm not frightened of flying, but when it comes to the point I'd rather travel by train.*

in point of 'fact (used for correcting or adding an extra piece of information to sth that has just been said) actually: *'Picasso painted this picture in 1935' 'In point of fact, Joanna, he painted it in 1934.' ○ I'll visit you next time I come to Berlin. In point of fact, I'm supposed to be going to Berlin next month; so why don't I come and see you then?*

make your 'point explain your opinion fully; tell sb exactly what you mean: *They were all talking so loudly I didn't get a chance to make my point. ○ Look, I think you've made your point, Mr Davies. Perhaps we should hear somebody else's opinion.*

make a point of doing sth make sure you do sth; make an effort to do sth because you think it's the correct way to do things: *I always make a point of locking up at night. ○ She always makes a point of thanking all the staff before she leaves.*

(be) more to the 'point (be) more important or relevant to the subject being discussed than what has already been mentioned: *'Drink driving is against the law* *and, more to the point, extremely dangerous.*

point a/the 'finger (at sb) say you think sb is responsible for sth; accuse sb: *'Who pointed the finger at him in the end?' 'I think it was his wife.'*

(get to, reach, etc) the ˌpoint of ˌno reˈturn (get to, etc) the point in a journey, process, activity, etc where you cannot or should not go back to where you started: *We've invested so much in the project that we simply must finish it. We've reached the point of no return.*

a ˌpoint of 'view **1** sb's opinion about sb/sth: *I don't agree with her, but she has the right to her point of view.* **2** one way of looking at or judging sth: *From the businessman's point of view these new hourly flights to Paris are just what is needed.*

point the 'way (to/towards sth) show how things will develop in future: *These new high-speed trains are pointing the way to a new age of European travel.*

take sb's 'point understand and accept the truth of what sb has said, especially during an argument, discussion, etc: *'Look, Jane. I know a lot more about physics than you, so why do you keep disagreeing with what I say?''Point taken, Kate.'* ○ *I take your point, Simon, but I don't think it's as simple as you think.*

to the point of 'sth/of . . .ing to such an extent that a stronger description could be used: *The restaurant staff were unhelpful to the point of rudeness.* ○ *His remarks were unkind to the point of being cruel.*

up to a (certain) 'point to some extent; not completely: *I'm willing to help you up to a point, but after that you'll have to look after yourself.* ○ *I agree with you up to a point, but not completely.*

be a moot point ⟹ moot; **be your strong point/suit** ⟹ strong; **a case in point** ⟹ case; **saturation point** ⟹ saturation; **labour the point** ⟹ labour; **not to put too fine a point on it** ⟹ fine; **score a point/points off/over/against** ⟹ score; **a sore point** ⟹ sore; **stretch a point** ⟹ stretch

points
have (got) your 'good, 'plus, etc points have (got) some good qualities or

aspects: *Europe has its good points, but I prefer the Eastern way of life.* ○ *She often seems rather unfriendly, but I suppose she's got her good points.*

possession is nine points/tenths/parts of the law ⟹ possession

poison
a ˌpoison-'pen letter an unsigned letter which says very unpleasant or threatening things: *Most politicians get poison-pen letters, sometimes threatening their lives.*

poke **a pig in a poke** ⟹ pig; **poke fun at sb/sth = make fun of sb/sth** ⟹ fun; **poke/stick your nose in/into sth** ⟹ nose

poker **be stiff as a poker** ⟹ stiff

pole(s)
be 'poles/'worlds apart be completely unlike one another; hold opinions or positions which are very far apart: *Politically, the two leaders are poles apart.* ○ *After hours of discussion and negotiation, they're still poles apart.*

be up the pole (*very informal*) **1** be mad, crazy, etc: *My neighbour's really up the pole. I can hear him singing and shouting night after night.* **2** in trouble or difficulties: *The whole industry is up the pole at the moment. Nobody knows what its future will be.*

polish **spit and polish** ⟹ spit

poor
(as) poor as a church 'mouse very poor: *She was as poor as a church mouse, living on a tiny pension.* (refers to the fact that there is usually no food in a church)

be a/the poor man's sb/sth be sb/sth that is a cheap or inferior replacement for sb/sth: *Try some of this sparkling white wine – the poor man's champagne.*

poor old sb/sth (*informal*) (used to express sympathy): *Poor old Mrs Kirk's just gone into hospital again.* ○ *She sat down to rest her poor old legs.*

a poor relation sb/sth with less importance, respect or power than others: *At the peace conference, our country was treated very much as the poor relation.*

in good/poor spirits = be in high/low

spirits ⇨ spirits; **take a dim/poor view of sb/sth** ⇨ view

pop
pop the 'question (*humorous*) ask sb to marry you

sb's eyes nearly pop out of their head ⇨ eyes

porridge
do porridge (*British, informal*) be in prison serving a sentence: *He's doing porridge again.*

port
any port in a 'storm (*saying*) when you are in trouble you will accept help, etc that would be unacceptable otherwise: *When he went to work there he had been unemployed for a year. It was a case of any port in a storm.*

a ,port of 'call a place where you stop for a short time before continuing your journey: *Our first port of call this morning is the baker's.* (refers to ports where ships stop for a short time during a voyage)

pose **strike a pose** ⇨ strike

positive **proof positive** ⇨ proof; **think positive** ⇨ think

possessed
what (ever) possessed sb to do sth? why did sb do sth bad, stupid, unexpected, etc?: *'She drove straight to the airport and got on the first plane.' 'What possessed her to do that?'*(refers to sb being possessed by an evil spirit)

possession
possession is nine points/tenths/ parts of the 'law (*saying*) if you already have or control sth, it is difficult for sb else to take it away from you, even if they have the legal right to it.

take possession (of sth) (*formal*) become the owner of sth: *He couldn't pay his taxes, so the government took possession of his property.*

post
post 'haste (*becoming dated*) with great speed: *He wants that report post haste, so hurry up with it.*

deaf as a post ⇨ deaf; **pip sb at the post** ⇨ pip; **rush, etc from pillar to post** ⇨ pillar

posted
keep sb 'posted (on/of/about sth) (*informal*) keep sb informed: *There are no jobs available at the moment, but I'll keep you posted.* ○ *He said he'd keep me posted of his movements.*

pot
go (all) to 'pot (*informal*) gradually get worse until it is very bad, completely spoilt, ruined, etc: *Under this government the country's gone to pot.* ○ *She used to write very nicely, but her handwriting's really gone to pot recently.*

the ,pot calling the kettle 'black (*saying*) a person criticizing sb for a fault which they also have: *'You haven't done any work all morning!' 'Neither have you! Talk about the pot calling the kettle black!'*(when cooking was done over a fire, cooking utensils were blackened by the smoke)

take ,pot 'luck (*informal*) **1** take a chance when you are choosing sth, rather than make a careful or informed choice: *'Did somebody recommend the hotel to you?' 'No, we just took pot luck. It was the first hotel in the brochure.'* **2** (of an unexpected guest in sb's home) eat the ordinary family meal rather than sth specially prepared for a guest: *'Come and have supper with us this evening if you don't mind taking pot luck.'*

put/pour/get a quart into a pint pot ⇨ quart; **a watched pot never boils** ⇨ watched

potato **a hot potato** ⇨ hot

pound
(take, demand, etc) your pound of 'flesh (demand, insist on) sth you have a right to, even when this is morally unacceptable because of the harm and suffering it will cause: *They want their pound of flesh; they want every penny we owe them by next Monday.* ○ *I didn't realize working here was going to be such hard work. They really demand their pound of flesh, don't they?* (from Shakespeare's *The Merchant of Venice*)

in for a penny, in for a pound ⇨ penny

pour(s)
pour oil on troubled 'waters try to end an argument, quarrel, etc by speaking calmly to the people involved; take action

which will calm a tense or dangerous situation: *There's going to be big trouble in this prison unless somebody pours oil on troubled waters fast.* ○ *He was always having rows with his son and his wife's attempts to pour oil on troubled waters usually made things worse.*

pour out your heart (to sb) tell sb all about your troubles, feelings, etc: *When I asked her what was the matter, she burst into tears and poured out her heart to me.*

pour scorn on sb/sth say that sb/sth is bad, stupid, worthless, etc; speak with contempt about sb/sth: *She poured scorn on his plans to get rich quick.*

it never rains but it pours ⟹ rains; **pour/throw cold water on sth** ⟹ cold; **put/pour/get a quart into a pint pot** ⟹ quart

powder

(go to) powder your nose (*humorous*) go to the ladies' toilet: *I'm just going to powder my nose and I'll be with you in a minute.*

power(s)

be the power behind the 'throne be the person who really controls a family, business, country, etc, even though people think sb else controls it: *It's not the president who makes the important decisions; his wife is the real power behind the throne.*

do sb/sth a 'power/'world of good (*informal*) do sb/sth a lot of good; benefit sb/sth: *She's under a lot of stress at work, and a few days at the seaside would do her a power of good.*

more power to sb's 'elbow (*informal*) (used to show approval and support for what sb is doing) good luck to sb: *'He's so angry at his train being late every morning that he's decided to make an official complaint to British Rail.' 'Good for him. More power to his elbow.'*

the ,powers that 'be (*humorous*) the people who control a country, organization, etc: *It's the powers that be that decide things. We just have to live with their decisions.* (from the Bible)

the corridors of power ⟹ corridors

practical

for (all) 'practical purposes in actual fact; in reality: *Your daughter does so little work at school, Mrs Brown, that for all practical purposes she might as well not be here at all.*

(play) a ,practical 'joke (on sb) play a trick on sb which involves using an object, physical action, etc: *They put a frog in his bed as a practical joke.* **a ,practical 'joker** (*noun*) a person who plays practical jokes.

practice

,in/,out of 'practice having practised/having not practised a skill regularly for a period of time: *I've got to keep in practice if I'm to win this race.* ○ *I haven't played the piano for a while so I'm a bit out of practice.*

in practice in reality; in fact; in a real or normal situation: *The pilot is there to fly the plane, but in practice it flies itself most of the time.* ○ *In theory it should work very well, but in practice it doesn't.*

,practice makes 'perfect (*saying*) if you practise a skill regularly, you will eventually be very good at it: *If you want to learn a language, speak it as much as you can. Practice makes perfect!*

put sth into 'practice actually do or carry out sth which was only planned or talked about, etc before: *It's not always easy to put your ideas into practice.*

make a habit/practice of sth ⟹ habit; **sharp practice** ⟹ sharp

practise

,practise what you 'preach (*saying*) live or act the way you advise others to live or act: *He's always telling me to go on a diet, but he doesn't practise what he preaches.*

praise(s)

praise sb/sth to the 'skies praise sb/sth very much; say sb/sth is very good, beautiful, etc: *She's always praising you to the skies: she says she's never had such a good assistant before.*

damn sb/sth with faint praise ⟹ damn; **sing sb's/sth's praises** ⟹ sing

preach

preach to the con'verted tell people to support a view or idea when they already support it: *Why do they keep telling us about the importance of women in industry? They're* *preaching to the converted here.*

practise what you preach ⇨ practise

precious

precious few/little (*informal*) very few/ little: *There are precious few places in Basingstoke where you can get really good Indian food.* ○ *Look, darling, don't ask me for any more pocket money this month. We've got precious little money for anything at the moment.*

pregnant

a pregnant 'pause/'silence a pause/ silence in which everyone is waiting or listening for sth, or a moment of silence which is full of meaning: *'How do you plead? Guilty or not guilty?' the judge asked. There was a pregnant pause. 'Not guilty,' he replied.*

premium

at a 'premium having great value or importance; difficult or expensive to buy, find, obtain, etc: *During a war, ordinary foods like bread or meat are often at a premium.* ○ *Good mathematics teachers are always at a premium in this country.*

put/place a premium on sth consider sth very important or valuable: *This company puts a high premium on the loyalty of its employees.*

prepare

prepare the ground (for sth) do something which makes it possible or easier for sth to happen: *By making her his deputy, the chairman was preparing the ground for her to replace him after he retired.* ○ *The meeting was to prepare the ground for next week's peace talks.*

presence

make your presence 'felt do sth which makes people notice your importance, strength, abilities, etc: *In the first half of the match the Scottish team really made their presence felt.* ○ *The demonstrators made their presence felt by shouting and waving banners.*

presence of 'mind the ability to act quickly and intelligently in a difficult situation: *A little girl from Leeds showed remarkable presence of mind yesterday when she saved her brothers from a fire in their home.* ○ *Unfortunately, he didn't have the presence of mind to report it to the police.*

present

at present now; at the moment: *How many people are living in this house at present?*

make a 'present of sth (to sb) make it easy for sb to take or steal sth from you, or to gain an advantage over you, because you have been careless: *Before you go out, lock all the doors and windows. Don't make a present of your property (to thieves).* ○ *Leeds United played terribly in the first half, constantly making a present of the ball to their opponents.*

on 'present form judging by sb/sth's present performance or behaviour; as things are at the moment: *On present form I'd say he should win easily.* ○ *A watercolour by Durant could sell for well over a million on present form.*

present company ex'cepted or **excepting present 'company** (used as a polite remark to show that the criticisms you are making are not directed at the people you are talking to): *My feeling is that the people in this part of the country, present company excepted of course, are rather unfriendly.*

the ,present 'day modern times; now: *These customs have continued right up to the present day.* **present-day** (*adjective*) Present-day attitudes to women are different.

for the moment/present = **for the time being** ⇨ time; **no time like the present** ⇨ time

press

get/have a good, bad, etc 'press get/ have good, etc things said about you in the newspapers, on television, etc: *The Royal Family's been getting a good press recently, for a change.* ○ *Zoos have been getting a bad press over the last few years.*

press (home) your ad'vantage make good use of an advantageous position: *Once they realized that the management was so weak, the union leaders pressed home their advantage and asked for another three days' holiday.*

press the flesh (of a politician) shake hands with members of the public in order to persuade them to vote for you.

press sth 'home make a point in an argument or discussion with force: *She kept pressing home the point that more money should be spent on education.*

press sb/sth into 'service use sb/sth because she/he/it is needed urgently or because you haven't or can't find anyone/anything more suitable: *Before an election the political parties press all kinds of people into service delivering leaflets, writing envelopes, etc.* (refers to the 'press gangs' in the eighteenth century who forced young men to join the navy)

the gutter press ⇨ gutter

pressed

be pressed/pushed for time, money, space, etc have very little time, etc: *I'm going to be very pressed for cash unless I get paid soon.* ○ *I'll have to do those letters tomorrow; I'm a bit pushed for time this afternoon.*

hard pressed to do sth = hard put to do sth ⇨ hard

pressure

put 'pressure on sb (to do sth) *or* **bring 'pressure to bear (on sb) (to do sth)** try to force, lead or persuade sb to do sth: *The landlord is putting pressure on us to move out.* ○ *If the ministry won't listen, we'll have to bring some more pressure to bear.*

pretences **false pretences** ⇨ false

pretty

be not just a pretty 'face (*informal, often humorous*) (often used after a person praises you or tells you that you have good qualities) be intelligent, capable, etc as well as attractive: *'I hear you passed all your exams.' 'Yes, I'm not just a pretty face, you know.'*

not a pretty 'sight (*informal*) a very unpleasant or shocking sight: *When he stepped out of that boxing ring, he wasn't a pretty sight, I can tell you.*

(as) pretty as a 'picture very pretty

pretty well/much/nearly (*informal*) almost; just about: *This nightclub is pretty much the best this town can offer.* ○ *I'm pretty well disgusted by your behaviour.* ○ *It's worth pretty nearly a hundred thousand pounds.*

be sitting pretty ⇨ sitting

preview **a sneak preview** ⇨ sneak

prey

be/fall 'prey to sth be worried or troubled by sth; be destroyed by sth: *He was often prey to doubt and despair.* ○ *Thousands of small businesses are falling prey to high interest rates.*

prey on sb's 'mind worry or trouble sb very much: *The death of his father is really preying on his mind at the moment. He thinks it was his fault.*

price

at 'any price without considering how much it might cost or how many unpleasant things you might have to do (to achieve sth): *Victory at any price.* ○ *Be elected president at any price; that's his aim.*

at a 'price (get sth) only by paying a high price, by spending a lot of time, effort, etc: *Accommodation is available in central London but at a price!* ○ *He knew he could be a successful businessman, but at a price – he'd hardly ever see his family.*

beyond/without 'price so valuable that it cannot be bought; priceless: *The Crown Jewels are without price.* ○ *These paintings are almost beyond price.*

every man has his price (*saying*) everybody can be persuaded to do sth against their moral principles if you offer them enough money.

not at 'any price not at all; in no circumstances; never: *'What about joining the army?' 'Not at any price. That's the last thing I want to do.'*

a 'price on sb's head a reward for finding or killing a criminal: *In the Wild West there were cowboys who used to hunt down any man with a price on his head.*

price sth/yourself out of the 'market demand such a high price for sth that no one wants to buy it: *If you charge so much, you'll price yourself out of the market.*

put a 'price on sth give the value of sth in money: *Any businessman will tell you it's hard to put a price on public confidence.* ○ *I've never seen a gun like this before, so I'm afraid I can't put a price on it.*

what price 'sth. . .? (used for expressing feelings of disappointment, cynicism, etc at the failure or destruction of sth you value) what is sth worth now?: *What price the freedom of the press now, after all these new* *restrictions?*

cheap at the price ⇨ cheap; **pay the price for doing sth** ⇨ pay

prick(s)

,prick up your 'ears start to listen carefully: *'And the winner is . . .' He pricked his ears up. '. . . Michael Poole.'*(refers to the way dogs, horses and other animals listen with attention)

kick against the pricks ⇨ kick

pride

sb's pride and 'joy sb/sth that sb is very proud and pleased to have: *That car's his pride and joy.* ○ *His granddaughter is his real pride and joy.*

pride comes before a 'fall (*saying*) if you are too proud or confident, sth may happen which will make you look foolish: *Remember, John, pride comes before a fall. Don't go round talking about your success in business all the time.*

(give sth) pride of 'place the best or most important position: *All the entries in the flower show are good, but pride of place must go to Cynthia Jones's roses.* ○ *Sally gave her award pride of place on the mantelpiece.*

take pride in sb/sth be proud of sb/sth; consider sth to be worth doing well: *She takes a lot of pride in running such a successful business.*

swallow your pride ⇨ swallow

prim

prim and 'proper (of a person) very correctly behaved and easily shocked by any immoral behaviour: *Don't invite her to the party. She's so prim and proper.*

prime

in the prime of (your) 'life at the age when you're feeling the strongest, healthiest, most able, etc: *He was struck down in the prime of his life by a heart attack.* ○ *What do you mean, I'm old? I'm still in the prime of life.*

prime the pump give sb, an organization, etc financial help in order to support a project, business, etc when it is beginning: *The government should really prime the pump in new high technology projects. That's the only*

way they'll be able to survive in the curre economic climate. **pump-priming** (*noun*)

primrose

the primrose 'path (to rui destruction, etc) an easy and pleasurab way of life, which may lead to disaster: *If followed your advice we'd all be walking do the primrose path to ruin.* (fro Shakespeare's play, *Hamlet*)

principle

in principle **1** according to the gener principles or theory: *In principle it shou work in all different types of climate, but haven't actually tried it out abroad yet.* **2** general but not necessarily in detail: *principle I agree with you, but I'm not sure th it's the most effective solution to the problem*

on principle because of your beliefs ideas about how people should behave: *I l meat, but I don't eat it on principle.*

print(ed)

get into print have your work printed a published (for the first time): *If you want get into print, you have to know the rig people.*

in/out of 'print (of a book or autho being/no longer being regularly printed published; available/not available bookshops: *Eliot has stayed in print since s was first published.* ○ *His books are no longer print.* ○ *Shakespeare and the Bible will never out of print.*

the printed 'word stories, articles, e printed in a book, magazine, newspape etc.

the small print ⇨ small

priorities

get your pri'orities right/wrong do get things in the right order of importance. *you think enjoying yourself is more importa then it's clear that you've got your prioriti wrong.* ○ *The country has got its priorities rig – it has invested in industry to achieve econom success.*

private

a ,private 'eye (*informal*) a priva detective: *They hired a private eye to look more evidence.*

private 'parts the external sex organs o man or woman.

prizes

(there are) no prizes for guessing sth (*informal*) (it is) not difficult to guess or find the answer to sth: *No prizes for guessing who does all the work round here.*

probability

in ‚all proba'bility very probably: *The changes were, in all probability, made before 1600.*

problem

no 'problem (*informal*) (used for saying that you can do sth or are willing to do sth for sb): *'Can you be here at 5.30 tomorrow morning?' 'No problem.'*

process

in the 'process (of doing sth) **1** while doing sth: *In the process of cleaning the furniture, I found six pound coins.* ○ *He was supposed to be cutting my hair, but he nearly cut off my ear in the process.* **2** in the middle of doing sth: *We're still in the process of trying to find somewhere to live.*

prodigal

the prodigal 'son (*often humorous*) a person who leaves home as a young man, lives an immoral life of luxury and leisure, then regrets it and returns to his family, who welcome him home: *All the family went to the airport to welcome home the prodigal son.* (from the Bible)

produce come up with/deliver/produce the goods ⇨ goods

profile

in profile (of a face) seen from the side: *In profile he's got a nose like an eagle!*

take on, keep, adopt, etc a ‚high/‚low 'profile attract/do not attract other people's interest, attention, etc: *In the run-up to the elections all three candidates maintained a high profile.* ○ *If I were you, I'd try and keep a low profile until she's forgotten about the whole thing.*

prolong

prolong the 'agony make an unpleasant situation last longer than is necessary: *Don't prolong the agony. Just say yes or no, and then I'll know where I stand.*

promise(d)

the promised 'land a place or situation in which people expect to find happiness, wealth, freedom etc: *For millions of people in Europe the USA was seen as the promised land.* ○ *The Prime Minister's speech seemed to suggest that we had already reached the promised land.* (from the Bible)

promise (sb) the 'moon/'earth (*informal*) make very big or impossible promises that you are unlikely to keep: *He promised her the moon, but after ten years of marriage they hardly had enough to live on.*

promises

sb/sth promises 'well sb/sth seems likely to do well in future: *The new trainee promises well.* ○ *The harvest promises well this year.*

proof

the proof of the 'pudding (is in the 'eating) (*saying*) you can only say sth is a success after it has actually been tried out or used: *I know you didn't think it was a very good product, but just look at the fantastic sales figures. That's the proof of the pudding.*

proof 'positive definite or convincing proof: *It's proof positive of her belief in the company that she's investing her own money in it.*

be living proof of sth ⇨ living

prop

‚prop up the 'bar (*informal*) (of sb who visits a particular pub or bar very frequently) be sitting at the bar drinking: *'Where's Paul?' 'Propping up the bar in the King's Head, as usual.'*

proper prim and proper ⇨ prim

property be public property ⇨ public

prophet

a ‚prophet of 'doom a person who always expects the worst to happen, especially when considering the future of the world: *Various prophets of doom have suggested that standards in education are worse than ever.*

proportion

out of (all) proportion (to sth) greater or more important, serious, etc than it really is or should be: *When you're really depressed, it's very easy to get things out of proportion.* ○

The punishment is out of all proportion to the crime.

pros

the pros and 'cons (of sth) the arguments for and against sth; the advantages and disadvantages (of sth): *Your idea is interesting, but let's look carefully at its pros and cons before we take any decisions.* (from the Latin *pro*=for, *contra*=against)

protest

under 'protest unwillingly because you think something is unfair: *The new contract was accepted, but only under protest.*

proud

do sb 'proud (*informal*) look after a guest very well, especially by serving good food, etc: *We spent Christmas with them and they really did us proud.*

proves

the exception proves the rule
⇨ exception

providence

tempt fate/providence
⇨ tempt

prowl

be/go on the 'prowl (of animals) move around quietly while hunting for food; (of people) be moving around quietly because you are trying to catch sb or intending to commit a crime: *Our cats go on the prowl at night, and then they sleep here all day.* ○ *Look out for burglars on the prowl. If you see anything suspicious, call the police immediately.*

pub

a 'pub crawl (*British, informal*) an evening spent drinking in one pub after another: *We went on a pub crawl last night.*

public

be ,public 'property be known or talked about by everyone: *When you're famous, you become public property.* ○ *His affair with that Scottish girl is now public property.*

go 'public 1 (of a company) sell shares to the public: *We're hoping to go public early next year.* **2** make a public statement about a private matter because you think this is the right thing to do: *He decided to go public about his alcoholism in order to warn other athletes of the dangers.*

in the public 'eye well known because you are often seen on television or in newspapers: *The royal family are always in the public eye.*

wash your dirty linen in public ⇨ wash

pudding

the proof of the pudding
⇨ proof

puff

huff and puff ⇨ huff

pull

pull the ,carpet/,rug out from under sb's 'feet (*informal*) take the help, support or confidence away from sb suddenly: *I was just about to invite her to come on holiday with me when she pulled the rug out from under my feet by telling me she's getting married next month.* ○ *The bank's pulled the carpet out from under his feet, unfortunately. It looks as if he'll have to sell the business.*

pull a 'fast one (on sb) (*informal*) tell lies or cheat sb to get their money, possessions, etc; deceive sb: *Don't try to pull a fast one on me. I'm not stupid, you know.*

pull sb's 'leg (*informal*) tell sb sth which is not true, as a joke: *'You came first! You've won the prize!' 'Really? Or are you just pulling my leg?'*

pull no 'punches (*informal*) attack or criticize sb as hard or as much as you can: *The review pulled no punches. The critic wrote that it was the most boring play he'd ever seen in his life.* ○ *I don't believe in pulling punches. If they're wrong, let's say so.*

pull the 'other one (– it's got bells on!) (*humorous, saying*) (used when you think that sb is telling you sth untrue as a joke (ie pulling your leg) I don't believe you!: *'I've been offered a job in New York.' 'Pull the other one! 'No, really!'*

pull out all the 'stops (*informal*) do everything you can to make sth successful: *We'll have to pull out all the stops to get this order ready by the end of the week.* (refers to pulling out all the stops on an organ when you want to make the music very loud)

pull the 'plug on sth (*informal*) destroy or bring an end to sth, for example sb's plans, a project, etc: *The banks are threatening to pull the plug on the project.* ○ *They've pulled the plug on that new comedy programme on Channel Four.*

pull 'rank (on sb) make unfair use of your senior position, authority, etc in an organization, etc: *The Junior Minister had waited for an hour to see the Prime Minister but, just as he was about to go in, the Foreign Secretary pulled rank on him and said he had to see the PM about something very urgent.* (refers to ranks in the army, etc)

pull your 'socks up (*informal*) work harder, be more determined, etc: *You really must pull your socks up if you want to beat Jackie in the competition.*

pull 'strings (for sb) (*informal*) use friends in high positions at work, in society, etc to get sth you want (for sb), for example a job, a visa, etc: *She doesn't want me to pull any strings for her; she says she prefers to be offered a place on her own merit.* ○ *His uncle in the BBC can pull strings for him.*

pull the strings (secretly) control the actions of other people: *I don't understand this situation at all. I want to know exactly who is pulling the strings.* (refers to the strings which are attached to puppets, marionettes, etc)

pull yourself 'together bring your feelings under control and start acting normally; stop feeling sorry for yourself: *I know she's upset but it's time for her to pull herself together and stop crying.*

pull yourself up by your (own) 'bootstraps (*informal*) improve or regain your previous position by your own efforts, without any help: *She started life as a shop assistant and she's now a senior executive. Nobody helped her; she pulled herself up by her own bootstraps.*

pull your 'weight do your fair share of the work: *If everyone pulls their weight we're going to get this prize with no trouble at all.*

pull the 'wool over sb's eyes (*informal*) deceive sb; hide the truth from sb: *It's no use you trying to pull the wool over my eyes; you've been taking drugs, haven't you?*

bring/pull sb up short ⇨ short; **get/pull your finger out** ⇨ finger; **make/pull faces/a face** ⇨ face; **pull sb/sth to bits/pieces** ⇨ bits

pulse **have/keep your finger on the pulse of sth** ⇨ finger

pump **all hands to the pump** ⇨ hands; **prime the pump** ⇨ prime

punch(es)
she/he couldn't punch her/his way out of a paper bag (*humorous, informal*) she/he is so weak, timid, etc that she/he would never dare react forcefully to sth: *You don't need to worry about what Jim would do; he couldn't punch his way out of a paper bag.*

pack a punch ⇨ pack; **pleased as Punch** ⇨ pleased; **pull no punches** ⇨ pull

pure
pure and 'simple and nothing else: *They are terrorists, pure and simple, and must be punished.* **purely and simply** (*adverb*) *I am basing my opinion purely and simply on the facts of the case.*

purpose(s)
(do sth) on 'purpose (do sth) deliberately: *He took the worst jobs he could find on purpose, and then wrote a book about his experiences.* ○ *Don't shout at me like that. I didn't break it on purpose.*

to little/good/some/no 'purpose (*formal*) with little, etc result or effect: *Another meeting was held, to little purpose.* ○ *She had used the profits to good purpose.* ○ *She called after them to no purpose. They had gone.*

accidentally on purpose ⇨ accidentally; **for practical purposes** ⇨ practical; **serve the purpose** ⇨ serve

purse
control/hold the 'purse-strings (*informal*) be the person who controls the amount of money spent and the way in which it is spent: *In this organization, I'm the one who controls the purse-strings, and you must come to me if you want any more money.*

pursuit
in hot pur'suit (of sb/sth) chasing sb; trying to catch sb: *He grabbed the jewels and ran off, with the shopkeeper in hot pursuit.*

push
give sb/get the 'push (*British, informal*) **1** tell sb/be told to leave your job: *He was stealing from the firm so the manager gave him the push.* ○ *The company is in trouble. Who will be the next to get the push?* **2** end a relationship with sb/be rejected by sb you

have had a relationship with: *His girlfriend gave him the push and he's a bit upset.* ○ *Why is it always me that gets the push? What's wrong with me?*

if/when push comes to 'shove (*informal*) if/when a situation demands action or becomes desperate: *I don't want to work away from home, but if push comes to shove, I might have to.*

push the 'boat out (*informal*) spend a lot of money on food, drinks, etc when celebrating a special occasion: *They really pushed the boat out for their daughter's wedding.*

push your 'luck (*informal*) (often used in a warning to sb) take a risk which will only be successful if your present good luck continues; behave in a way that annoys or provokes sb: *You've already got a good pay-rise. Now don't push your luck by asking for more holidays.* ○ *Look, boys, I told you ten minutes ago to leave. Just don't push your luck. Get out of here now or I'm calling the police.*

push up (the) 'daisies (*informal, humorous*) be dead: *I'll be pushing up daisies by the time that happens.* (a daisy is a small white flower that often grows in grass)

at a pinch/push ⇨ pinch; **be pressed/pushed for time, etc** ⇨ pressed

pushing
pushing 40, 50, etc (*informal*) nearly 40, etc years old: *My grandmother's pushing eighty but she's as fit as ever.*

put
put it 'on (*informal*) pretend that you are

hurt, angry, etc: *She's not really scared. She's only putting it on.*

put it 'there! (used for offering your hand to sb you admire, wish to congratulate or to sb you have just completed a deal with) shake my hand.

put one 'over on sb (*informal*) tell lies or cheat sb to get their money, possessions, etc; deceive sb: *'Don't believe a word he says. He's just trying to put one over on you.'*

put sb 'through it force sb to do sth difficult or unpleasant: *During the training they really put you through it; I was exhausted*

a 'put-up ,job (*informal*) something that is planned to trick or deceive sb: *The whole thing was a put-up job. He set fire to the shop himself so that he could claim insurance money*

putty
be putty in sb's 'hands (*informal*) be willing to do anything sb wants or tells you to do: *As soon as she starts crying, I'm putty in her hands.* (putty is a soft flexible substance used for fixing glass in windows)

pyjamas the cat's whiskers/pyjamas ⇨ cat

Pyrrhic
a Pyrrhic victory a victory which is achieved at too high a price and therefore not worth having: *It was a Pyrrhic victory. They won the strike but then most of them lost their jobs.* (refers to the battle of Heraclea in 280BC when Pyrrhus, King of Epirus, defeated the Romans but lost all his best officers and men)

Q

quandary
in a quandary uncertain about what to do in a particular situation: *She's in a bit of a quandary about which job to accept. They're both interesting and well-paid, so it's difficult to choose.*

quantity an unknown quantity ⇨ unknown

quantum
a quantum leap a sudden very large

increase, advance or improvement in sth: *This latest research represents a quantum leap in our understanding of the universe.* ○ *The quantum leap in writing technology came with the introduction of micro-computers.*

quarrel pick a fight/quarrel ⇨ pick

quart
put/pour/get a ,quart into a pint 'pot try to do sth impossible, especially to try to

put sth into a space which is too small for it: *30 people in this small room! You can't put a quart into a pint pot you know.* (a pint is 0.568 and a quart 1.136 litres)

quarters   at close quarters ⇨ close

queen
'**queen it over sb** behave in a haughty manner towards sb you have authority over: *She sits in her office queening it over all the junior staff.*

question
beyond/without 'question without any doubt: *She is without question the best student in the class.* ○ *The view is, beyond question, the most spectacular in the whole area.*

bring/call sth into 'question make it necessary for sth to be reconsidered because there are now doubts about it: *Scandals like this call into question the honesty of the police.* ○ *The high number of accidents has brought government policy on industrial safety into question.*

it's a 'question of sth it concerns sth; it is really about sth: *It's not a question of money; it's much more a question of principle.* ○ *If it's a question of paying you a bit more, then I think we can consider that.*

out of the question impossible and so not worth considering: *An expensive holiday is out of the question this year.*

the person/thing in question (*formal*) the person/thing being discussed: *The money in question doesn't belong to you; it belongs to your sister.*

a 'question mark hangs over sb/ sth *or* **there is a 'question mark (hanging) over sb/sth** there is some doubt about sb/sth: *A question mark hangs over the future of this club.* ○ *There's a question mark over his loyalty to the company.*

there is some/no question of sth/ doing sth there is some/no possibility of sth/doing sth: *I'm afraid there is no question of you leaving work early this afternoon.* ○ *Apparently there is some question of our getting three days' extra holiday this year. I hope we do.*

(do sth) without question do sth without arguing or complaining about it: *I expect officers to obey my orders without question.*

beg the question ⇨ beg; **it is only, etc a matter/a question of time** ⇨ time; **a leading question** ⇨ leading; **an open question** ⇨ open; **pop the question** ⇨ pop; **the sixty-four thousand dollar question** ⇨ sixty; **a vexed question** ⇨ vexed

queue   jump the queue ⇨ jump

quick
quick as a 'flash (*informal*) very fast or suddenly: *Quick as a flash he replied that he had never seen it before.* ○ *When the cat appeared, the bird flew away, quick as a flash.*

quick march (used for telling sb to walk quicker): *Come on. Quick march or we'll never get the bus.* (**quick march** is a command given to soldiers)

a 'quick one (*informal*) a drink, usually alcoholic, which you have a short time before doing sth else: *Have you got time for a quick one before your train goes?*

be quick/slow off the mark ⇨ mark; **be quick/slow on the uptake** ⇨ uptake; **cut sb to the quick** ⇨ cut; **double quick** ⇨ double

quids
quids in (*informal*) be in a very favourable and profitable situation: *I've just received three cheques so we're quids in at the moment.*

quiet
on the quiet (*informal*) without people knowing about it; secretly or confidentially: *As well as this job, he's been working somewhere else on the quiet.* ○ *Well, just on the quiet, she's actually leaving her job next month. Don't tell anyone, will you?*

(as) quiet as a 'mouse (*informal*) (of a person) saying very little or making very little noise: *He's quiet as a mouse in class.* ○ *Be as quiet as a mouse when you go upstairs; the baby is asleep up there.*

peace and quiet ⇨ peace

quite
quite a/some sb/sth (*informal*) (used to show that you think sb/sth is impressive, unusual, remarkable, etc): *That's quite some swimming pool you've got there. I've never seen one so large in a private garden.*

quite the best, the worst, etc (*informal*) absolutely the best/worst: *It was quite the worst film I've ever seen.*

quite 'so (*rather formal*) used for agreeing with what sb has just said: *'It's a very interesting book.' 'Quite so. That's why I wanted you to read it.'*

quite some 'time quite a long time: *Quite some time has passed since I last saw my brother.*

be not quite there = be not all there ⇨ there

quits

be 'quits (with sb) (*informal*) **1** be in a position in which neither of two people owe each other money any more: *If I give you this £10, then we're quits, aren't we.* **2** have done sth unpleasant to sb who did sth unpleasant to you: *He crashed my motorbike last year and now I've crashed his car, so we're quits.*

call it quits ⇨ call

quote

'quote (unquote) (used by a speaker to show that they are using sb else's words and perhaps that they don't agree with them): *This quote novel of the century unquote is probably the most boring book I've ever read.*

R

race a one-horse race ⇨ one; **the rat race** ⇨ rat

rack

go to rack and 'ruin because of neglect, gradually decay and so become unfit to live in, use, etc: *The house has gone to rack and ruin over the last few years.* ○ *The country is going to rack and ruin under this government.*

(be) on the 'rack (be) in a state of anxiety, stress, pain, etc.

rack your 'brains (*informal*) try very hard to think of sth or remember sth: *I've been racking my brains all day (trying) to remember his name.*

rag

the 'rag trade (*British, informal*) the business of designing, making and selling clothes: *He's worked in the rag trade all his life.*

lose your rag ⇨ lose; **a red rag to a bull** ⇨ red

rage

all the 'rage (*informal, becoming dated*) very popular or fashionable: *Short skirts are all the rage at the moment.*

rags

from rags to riches (*informal*) from being very poor to being very rich in a short period of time: *She went from rags to riches in less* than five years. **rags to riches** (*adjective*) *It was a real rags-to-riches story.*

glad rags ⇨ glad

rails

go off the 'rails (*British, informal*) start behaving in a way which shocks or upsets other people: *Away from the routine of army life some of the ex-soldiers go completely off the rails.* (refers to a train leaving the rails)

rain

come ,rain, come 'shine *or* **(come) rain or shine** (*informal*) whatever the weather is like; whatever happens: *They met in the park, come rain or shine, every Saturday morning for twenty years.*

rain cats and dogs *or* **rain 'buckets** (*informal*) (often used in the continuous form to describe what is happening now) rain very heavily: *We can't possibly play golf today. It's raining cats and dogs out there.* ○ *It's been raining buckets all morning.*

take a 'rain check (on sth) (*especially US, informal*) (used for refusing an invitation and indicating that you will accept the same invitation later): *'Would you like to try that new restaurant in the city with live jazz tonight?' 'I'm afraid I'm busy tonight, but can I take a rain-check on it?'*

as right as rain ⇨ right

rains

it never rains but it pours (*saying*) when one thing goes wrong, so do others: *It never rains but it pours! First, I found that the car had been stolen and then discovered I had lost the keys to my flat.* ○

rainy

save, keep, etc it for a rainy day (*informal*) save money or things for a time in the future when you might need them: *'Don't spend it all at once,' his aunt said to her. 'Save some of it for a rainy day.'*

raise

raise Cain/hell (*informal*) complain or protest noisily and angrily, often as a way of getting sth you want: *He'll raise hell if we don't finish on time.* **hell-raiser** (*noun*) a violent and destructive person

raise an/your eyebrow(s) (at sth) show surprise or disapproval (by raising your eyebrows): *Eyebrows were raised when he arrived at the wedding in a track suit.* **raised eyebrows** (*noun*) *When he said he was leaving his wife and children, there were a lot of raised eyebrows.*

raise a laugh/smile do or say sth that makes other people laugh/smile: *If the speeches are not going well, ask Paula to speak; she can always raise a laugh.* ○ *His jokes didn't even raise a smile. It was embarrassing.*

raise sb's spirits make sb happier: *Good weather always raises her spirits.*

raise the temperature (*informal*) make the situation more likely to end in conflict; increase the differences between two sides and as a result increase the danger: *The government's refusal to take part in the talks is likely to raise the temperature in the dispute.*

raise your voice speak in a louder voice, often because you are angry: *Don't raise your voice at me. It wasn't my fault.*

raise a voice against sb/sth say publicly that you do not agree with sb's actions/plans/policies, etc: *He was the only person to raise his voice against the plan.*

build up/raise sb's hopes ⇨ hopes; **kick up/make/create/raise a stink** ⇨ stink; **lift/raise a hand against sb** ⇨ hand; **raise hackles = make sb's hackles rise** ⇨ hackles; **raise/lift the roof** ⇨ roof;

raise/lower your sights ⇨ sights; **rear/raise its (ugly) head** ⇨ head

rake

rake over the ashes/the past discuss with sb unpleasant things that happened between you in the past: *When they met each other again, ten years after the divorce, they both tried hard not to rake over the past.*

as thin as a rake ⇨ thin

ram

ram sth home (*informal*) force sb to understand sth important: *The terrible injuries I saw in that accident really rammed home for me the importance of wearing seat belts.*

rampage

go/be on the rampage run round the streets causing damage to shops, cars, etc: *After their team lost, some of the crowd went on the rampage through the town.*

rank(s)

(the) rank and file (the) ordinary members of a group/organization especially a trade union, political party, etc: *I can see that you are happy with the plan but what will the rank and file think?* **rank and file** (*adjective*) *The rank and file members don't elect the leader.* (refers to ordinary soldiers, not officers)

rise/come up through the ranks after starting your career at the bottom or low down in an organization, finally reach a high position in it because of your experience and abilities: *The new managing director has come up through the ranks, which is quite unusual these days.* (refers to the armed forces where some ordinary soldiers, etc may become officers if they have the right qualities)

close ranks ⇨ close; **pull rank** ⇨ pull

ransom

hold sb to ransom ⇨ hold; **a king's ransom** ⇨ king

rant

rant and rave (*informal*) complain or protest about sth in a wild, excited way: *He stood there for about twenty minutes ranting and raving about the colour of the new paint.*

rap

give, get, etc a ˌrap over the ˈknuckles or **ˌrap sb over the ˈknuckles** (*informal*) criticize sb/be criticized for doing sth wrong: *He got rapped over the knuckles for spending too much money on his business lunches.*

take the rap (for sb) (*informal*) be blamed/punished, perhaps for sth you did not do: *Why should I take the rap for something you did?*

raptures

be in/go into ˈraptures (about/over sb/sth) be extremely enthusiastic about sb/sth you like: *Each time I mention your name, he goes into raptures about you.*

rare

a ˌrare ˈbird a person or thing that is unusual, often because she/he/it has two very different interests/qualities: *Jill is a very rare bird, a good politician and an excellent listener.* (a translation of the Latin idiom 'rara avis')

raring

raring to go (*informal*) very keen to begin sth: *At the start of the project we were raring to go but unfortunately we've lost a lot of our early enthusiasm.*

rat

the ˈrat race intense competition for success in jobs, business, etc, typical of a big city: *Paul got caught up in the rat race and was never at home. His wife got fed up with it. That's why they divorced.*

like a drowned rat ⇨ drowned; **smell a rat** ⇨ smell

rate

at ˈany rate **1** (used for indication that what you have just said is not as relevant or important as what you are going to say) in any case; anyway: *'How did your interview go?' 'It was a complete failure. I talked too much and I'm sure they didn't like me. At any rate, I didn't get the job.'* **2** at least: *He said he'd be here on the 5th; at any rate, I think he said the 5th.*

at a rate of ˈknots (*informal*) very fast: *You must have been going at a rate of knots to have finished already.* (refers to the speed of a boat, which is measured in knots)

at ˈthis/ˈthat rate if the situation continues as it is: *The traffic's terrible. At this rate we'll never get to the airport on time.*

rather

rather you, etc than me or **sooner you, etc than me** (*especially British*) (used for saying that you are pleased that you don't have to do a difficult or unpleasant thing): *'She works every weekend.' 'Rather her than me.'*

be a bit/rather steep ⇨ steep

rave   rant and rave ⇨ rant

raving   be/go stark raving mad ⇨ stark

raw

in the ˈraw in an uncivilized or uncontrolled state: *If you want to see life in the raw, get a job as a policeman.*

a raw/rough deal ⇨ deal

ray

the one/a ray of ˈhope the one small sign of improvement in a difficult situation: *They've actually stopped fighting, so perhaps there's a ray of hope after all.* ○ *Our one ray of hope is my father. He might be able to lend us the money.*

a ray of ˈsunshine (*informal*) a person or thing that makes sb's life happier: *She calls her granddaughter her 'little ray of sunshine'.*

razor   on a knife-edge/razor's edge ⇨ edge

razzle

be/go out on the ˈrazzle (*informal*) enjoy yourself very much by going out to pubs, restaurants, etc drinking alcohol and eating: *It's a long time since I went out on the razzle, but your birthday will be a wonderful excuse.*

reach

reach for the ˈstars be very ambitious: *She decided very early that she was going to be a banker and was going to reach for the stars and get to the top.*

reach/hit rock-bottom ⇨ rock

read

ˌread between the ˈlines find or look for a hidden or extra meaning in sth a person says or writes, usually their real feelings about sth: *Reading between the lines, it was obvious that he was feeling lonely.*

,read sb like a 'book (*informal*) understand sb so well that you can guess what they will say or do before they say or do it: *She found that after living with him for a year or more, she could read him like a book.*

,read sb's 'mind/'thoughts (*informal*) (often used in the negative) understand what sb is thinking, feeling, planning, etc: *I can't read your mind! If you don't tell me what's worrying you, I can't help you.*

read the 'riot act tell sb forcefully and angrily that you will punish them if they do not stop behaving badly; be angry with sb who has behaved badly: *The headmaster came in and read the riot act. He said he would keep us in after school if there was one more complaint about us.* ○ *My dad read us the riot act when we broke the kitchen window. He was furious.* (In 1715 the Riot Act was passed in Parliament. Groups of more than twelve people were not allowed to meet in public. If they did, an official came to read them the Riot Act, which ordered them to stop the meeting.)

,take sth/it as 'read consider that sth does not need discussing because everybody already knows, understands, or agrees about it: *Can I take is as read that we all agree on this matter?* (from an expression used in committees. At the start of each meeting the committee must agree that the minutes (notes) of the last meeting are a correct record. To save time the members are asked if the minutes can be taken as read.)

ready

at the 'ready prepared for immediate action or use: *Cameras and microphones at the ready, they waited for the new President to appear.*

ready to hand easy to reach or get: *Surgeons need their instruments ready to hand during an operation.*

ready when 'you are (used for indicating to sb that you are ready and are waiting for them to do sth, for example begin to speak): *'When would you like me to begin?' 'Ready when you are.'*

fit/ready to drop ⇨ drop; **rough and ready** ⇨ rough

real

for real 1 (*informal*) (do sth) which is real rather than imagined, practised or talked about, etc: *You might think that killing somebody in a war is easy; but when you do it for real, it's a terrible experience.* ○ *He's joked about committing suicide in the past, but this time I think it's for real.* **2** (*informal*) genuine: *Are these diamonds for real? ○ Do you think this offer of a free holiday is for real?*

in real 'life not the life people have in books, films, plays, etc: *She plays the role of an alcoholic in this play, but in real life she doesn't drink at all.*

the real 'thing/Mc'Coy (*informal*) the original and therefore the best type of sth; the best example of sth: *'What kind of whisky is this?' 'This is the real thing. You can't buy better whisky than this.'* ○ *This apple pie is the real McCoy. I haven't eaten one like this for years.*

reality

in re'ality (used to point out a difference between two claims, beliefs or perceptions of sth) in actual fact: *He thought the painting was worth a million, but in reality it was worth only a few hundred pounds.*

rear

bring up the rear 1 be the last person or group to appear in a line or procession: *The President led the way out of the courtyard, followed by senior ministers of government. Junior ministers brought up the rear.* **2** finish last in a race or competition: *Smith finished in 2nd place, Warren in 3rd, with poor Davis bringing up the rear in 12th place.*

rear/raise its head ⇨ head

reason

for a/some reason/reasons best known to herself/himself (*humorous*) for a reason or reasons which other people find hard to understand: *For reasons best known to himself, he wears three pairs of socks.*

within 'reason on the condition that it is sensible or reasonable: *She wanted it repaired immediately and said she would pay what we asked, within reason.*

it stands to reason ⇨ stands; **neither/no/without rhyme (n)or reason** ⇨ rhyme; **see sense/reason** ⇨ see

rebound

on the 'rebound (begin a new romantic relationship with sb) while or because you are still unhappy about another relationship which has just ended: *She married John on the rebound from Geoff. I knew it wouldn't last.*

receiving

be on/at the re'ceiving end (of sth) receive sth, usually unpleasant, for example criticism, unkind remarks, unpleasant behaviour, etc: *He's been on the receiving end of a lot of criticism recently.*

recharge

recharge your batteries (*informal*) rest for a while to get more energy (for the next period of activity): *You've been working too much. What you need is a good holiday to recharge your batteries.*

reckoned   a force to be reckoned with
⇨ force

reckoning   the day of reckoning
⇨ day

recognition

change/alter, etc beyond/out of all recognition change such a lot that people don't recognize you/it, etc: *I went back to Birmingham after 20 years; it had changed beyond all recognition.* ○ *She had changed beyond all recognition since I last saw her.*

record

be/go on 'record *or* **put sth on 'record** say sth publicly (perhaps in a newspaper) so that what you say is written down: *He is on record as saying that he never wanted to become President, but now he's fighting for the job.*

(just) for the 'record so that the facts should be recorded or remembered correctly: *I'd like to make it clear, just for the record, that I disagree with the committee's decision.*

off the 'record (of information, opinions, etc) given unofficially: *If the minister speaks to a journalist off the record, the journalist is not allowed to quote the minister's name in the newspaper.* **off-the-record** (*adjective*) *It was an off-the-record remark and you shouldn't have attached my name to it in your article.*

on 'record officially noted or written down: *It was the warmest day on record.*

put/set the 'record straight (*informal*) give a correct version, explanation of events, facts, etc because you think sb has made a mistake: *Let's put the record straight – we don't owe you £5000. You owe us £5000.*

a track record ⇨ track

red

as red as a 'beetroot (*informal*) with red cheeks, because you feel angry or embarrassed: *I could feel myself turning as red as a beetroot when she said that my work had been chosen for the prize.*

in the 'red (*informal*) in debt: *At this time of year we are usually in the red.* (in bank accounts, an amount owed used to be written in red figures, not black)

not have a red 'cent (*US, informal*) have no money: *I wish I could come skiing with you, but I haven't got a red cent at the moment.*

on red alert in a state of complete readiness to deal with an emergency, for example the beginning of a war, a terrorist attack, an accident, etc: *If there's an underground accident in London, all the big hospitals are immediately put on red alert.*

the red 'carpet a very special welcome given to an important visitor: *When I went to my girlfriend's house for the first time, her family really put out the red carpet for me.* **red-carpet** (*adjective*) *It was an unofficial visit so the queen didn't get the usual red-carpet treatment.* (a red carpet is sometimes used on official visits by royalty, presidents, etc)

a red 'face (*informal*) embarrassment: *There are going to be a lot of red faces at the bank when they discover how easily we stole the money.*

a red 'herring a fact, etc which sb introduces into a discussion because they want to take people's attention away from the main point: *Look, the situation in French agriculture is just a red herring. We're here to discuss British agriculture, not French.* (the strong fishy smell of herring was sometimes used to confuse dogs which were following the scent (smell) of an animal)

a red-'letter day (*informal*) a very special day which is remembered because sth important or good happened: *Today was a red letter day. We heard we had won a free holiday in Japan.* (from the custom of printing

Sundays and religious days (holidays) in red on calendars)

the red-'light district part of a city where prostitutes work and sex shops are found.

(like) a red rag to a 'bull (*informal*) certain to make a particular person very angry or even violent: *Don't mention anything about religion to your uncle. It's like a red rag to a bull.* (refers to the belief that bulls do not like the colour red)

red 'tape unnecessarily complicated bureaucratic procedures which people find very annoying: *Do you know how much red tape you have to go through if you want to import a car?* (legal documents are sometimes tied up with red ribbon or tape)

catch sb red-handed ⇨ catch; **paint the town red** ⇨ paint; **see red** ⇨ see

redeeming
a redeeming feature sth good or positive about sb/sth that is otherwise bad: *Her one redeeming feature is her generosity.* ○ *The one redeeming feature of the hotel was the swimming pool. Apart from that, it was the worst hotel I've ever stayed in.*

reds
reds under the bed (*becoming dated, humorous*) the fear or belief that there are communist secret agents everywhere, who are working to defeat capitalist countries: *During the 1950s in the USA there were reds under the bed stories in every newspaper.*

reflected
bathe/bask in reflected glory get attention and fame not because of sth you have done but through the success of sb else connected to you: *She wasn't happy to bathe in the reflected glory of her daughter's success, she wanted to succeed on her own.*

reflection
a sad, poor, etc reflection on sth a thing which damages/weakens sb's/sth's reputation: *His performance in the exams was a sad reflection on his expensive education.*

refresh
refresh sb's/your memory remind sb/yourself of sth that you have forgotten: *Refresh my memory will you? How many children have you got?* ○ *Before I interviewed*

him, I read his book again just to refresh my memory.

refusal **first refusal** ⇨ first

regards
as regards sb/sth (*formal*) about or concerning sb/sth: *As regards the method of payment, a decision will be made after the contract has been signed.*

region
in the 'region of approximately: *The house should sell for something in the region of £100000*

regular
as regular as clockwork very regularly; happening at the same time in the same way; reliable: *She arrives at work on her bicycle at 8.45 every day, as regular as clockwork.*

Reilly **lead/live the life of Reilly/Riley** ⇨ life

rein **give free rein to do sth** ⇨ free; **keep a tight rein on sb/sth** ⇨ tight

relation **a poor relation** ⇨ poor

remain **be/keep/stay/remain in the swim** ⇨ swim; **somebody, who will/shall remain/be nameless** ⇨ nameless

remember
something to re'member sb by (*informal*) a punishment, for example, a beating: *If I ever catch you stealing my apples again, I'll give you something to remember me by.*

repair
beyond repair impossible to repair: *The engine was damaged beyond repair.*

in good/bad re'pair *or* **in a good/bad state of re'pair** in good/bad, etc condition: *The house is in a terrible state of repair.* ○ *If it were in a better state of repair, it would be worth quite a lot of money.*

reputation **live up to your, etc/its reputation** ⇨ live

resistance **take/follow the line of least resistance** ⇨ line

resort . **a last resort** ⇨ last

respect(s)

in re'spect of (*formal*) (used especially when talking about the cost of sth or a period of time) concerning: *Large increases can now be expected in respect of gas and electricity prices.*

with (all) (due) respect (*quite formal*) (often used before you politely criticize or disagree with sb): *With all due respect, Mrs Brown, don't you think you are being a bit old-fashioned?* ○ *With respect sir, I think that your information may be wrong.*

with respect to 'sth (*formal*) (often used in business letters, especially at the beginning) concerning sth; with reference to sth: *With respect to your enquiry about the new pension scheme, I have pleasure in enclosing our leaflet.*

pay your respects ⇨ pay

rest

for the 'rest (*formal*) as far as other less important matters are concerned: *The most important thing in life is to do your duty. For the rest I care nothing.*

(why don't you) give it a 'rest! (*informal*) (used by sb when they are annoyed by sb else's actions) stop doing sth: *Give it a rest will you! That's the third time you've criticized my driving this morning.*

rest assured that be completely certain or confident that. . .: *You can rest assured that we will do everything we can to get your money back.*

,rest on your 'laurels be satisfied with the success(es) you have already gained and so no longer try to improve your position, etc: *I know you got a very good degree from Oxford but what are you going to do with your life now? You can't rest on your laurels for ever, you know.* (laurel leaves were used in Roman times to make a crown for the winner of a race or competition)

lay sb to rest ⇨ lay; **lay sth to rest** ⇨ lay; **put/set sb's mind at ease/rest** ⇨ mind

retreat   **beat a retreat** ⇨ beat

return

in return (for sth) in exchange for sth; as payment or reward: *What will you give me in return for this information?*

return the compliment do or say the same pleasant thing that sb else has done or said to you: *Thanks for a lovely meal. We'll try and return the compliment very soon.*

return to the 'fold come back to a group or community (especially a religious or political society): *She left the party 10 years ago but has recently returned to the fold.* (refers to the comparison in the Bible between the lost sheep which returns to the fold and the sinner who repents)

pay sth back/return sth with interest ⇨ interest; **the point of no return** ⇨ point

returns   many happy returns ⇨ happy

reveal   show/reveal your hand ⇨ hand

revert

revert to type return to the way you would expect sb to behave when you remember their family, sex, work, history, etc: *She was a student revolutionary for a while but now she's reverted to type. I saw her in a Mercedes the other day.*

reward   virtue is its own reward ⇨ virtue

rhyme

neither/no/without rhyme (n)or reason no sense or logic: *There is neither rhyme nor reason in his actions.* ○ *Changes were being made without rhyme or reason.*

rhinoceros

have a hide/skin like a rhi'noceros (*informal*) be tough and not easily offended; have no fear of criticism from others: *Say what you like about him, he won't care; he's got a skin like a rhinoceros.*

rich

as rich as Croesus (*informal*) extremely wealthy: (Croesus was a very rich king in Lydia, Asia Minor in the sixth century BC)

that's 'rich (*informal*) (used to show surprise and amusement at sb's words or actions): *'She says you're the best assistant she has ever had.' 'That's rich. She never stops criticizing me.'*

be stinking rich ⇨ stinking; **strike it rich** ⇨ strike

riches   from rags to riches ⇨ rags

ride

let sth ride (*informal*) take no further immediate action: *The manager knows who is leaving work early, but he's decided to let it ride for the moment.*

ride 'roughshod over sb/sth treat sb/sb's feelings, ideas, protests, etc with no respect at all because you do not consider them important: *The local authority rode roughshod over the protests of parents and closed down the school.*

take sb for a ride (*informal*) cheat or deceive sb: *If you've paid £6000 for that car you've been taken for a ride!*

be/go along for the ride ⇨ along; **ride out/weather the storm** ⇨ storm; **a rough ride** ⇨ rough

riding

be riding for a fall behave in a way which will cause problems for you later: *He's riding for a fall if he keeps talking to the boss so rudely.*

riding 'high being very successful: *The government are riding high in the opinion polls at the moment.*

right

all 'right 1 (used as a way of agreeing to do sth): *'Could you post this letter for me, please?' 'Yes, all right.'* **2** (of a person) in good health; safe(ly): *I had flu last week but I'm all right now.* ○ *Did you get home all right on Saturday night?* (on its own, *all right* can be used in answer to the question *'How are you?'*): *'How are you, Dave?' 'Oh, all right, thanks – how are you?'* (as a question it can also be a greeting): *'All right?' 'Yes, thanks – and you?'* **3** (of a thing) not damaged; in working order: *The car has been all right since its service.* **4** (only just) good/well enough: *The wine's all right but it's not as good as the last bottle.* **5** (used at the end of a statement, promise or threat) certainly: *He pretended to be looking the other way but he saw me all right.* ○ *'... and tell her we're very annoyed.' 'I'll tell her all right!'* **6** *also* **right** (*informal*) (used to join parts of an explanation) have you understood so far?: *Turn left at the end of the road and go straight on at the traffic lights. All right? Then turn left again after the pub....* **7** (used at the beginning of a sentence to show that you are annoyed or impatient): *All right, all right,*

there's no need to get so cross with me!

as of 'right *or* **by 'right** (*formal*) according to the law: *The house is hers as of right but it is not clear who owns the furniture and paintings.*

as right as 'rain (*informal*) in good health or condition: *You'll need lots of fresh air and rest and you'll soon be feeling right as rain again.*

be all right (by/with sb) be convenient (for sb); be allowed: *'Yes, thank you, I will stay the night if it's all right with you.'* ○ *Is it all right to park here?*

be in the 'right be in a legally or morally correct position (in a particular situation): *The problem with Kate is that she always thinks she's in the right. She will never accept that sometimes she is in the wrong.*

do 'right by sb (*informal*) treat sb fairly: *The factory will close but the company have promised to do right by the workforce and find jobs for those who want them.*

get sth 'right/'straight understand sth clearly and correctly: *Have I got this right? You want me to jump off the bridge and onto a moving train? Never!* ○ *Let's get one thing straight. I'm the boss and I tell you what to do.*

I'm all right, Jack (*saying*) (said of another person's attitudes or behaviour) selfish; not caring about other people: *He has a typical 'I'm all right, Jack' attitude – as long as he's doing well he doesn't care about anyone else.*

in your own 'right because of your own skills, qualifications, work, etc and not because of other people: *She is the daughter of a world-famous actor but this prize will make her famous in her own right.*

in your right mind (*informal*) sane; not mad: *Nobody in their right mind would buy a second-hand car without driving it first.*

it's/that's all right (used as a response to sb thanking you or apologizing): *'Thank you so much for the flowers.' 'Oh, that's all right.'* ○ *'I'm sorry I didn't call you yesterday.' 'Oh, it's all right – I'd forgotten all about it.'*

it's ,all right for 'some (used to express envy at another person's good fortune): *Jane's going to Paris next week – it's all right for some, isn't it?*

it will ,be all ,right on the 'night

(*catchphrase*) (used when preparations for an important event are not going well) problems will be solved before the event takes place.

make (all) the right noises (*informal*) behave as if you support or agree with sth, usually because it is fashionable or to your advantage to do so: *A lot of the doctors are making the right noises about the reforms to the health service, but I'm not sure that they actually agree with them.*

put sth 'right correct sth; repair or mend sth: *There seems to be a mistake in my hotel bill. I wonder if you could put it right, please.* ○ *There's nothing seriously wrong with your television. I can put it right in ten minutes.*

put/set sb 'right **1** tell sb the truth about sth because they misunderstood sth or have incorrect information: *She was telling everybody that I'd written the report so I soon put her right.* **2** make sb feel better: *These tablets should put you right soon.*

put things right do sth to improve a difficult situation or correct a mistake: *The firm is inefficient. A good director could put things right very quickly.*

right (you are)! (*informal*) yes, I will: *'Two teas, please.' 'Right you are!'*

right/straight away immediately; without any delay: *They asked him to start right away.*

your right-hand man (*informal*) an assistant whom you trust with everything: *'I'd like to introduce you to Peter Davies, my right-hand man. He will help you when I am away.'*

too 'right/'true (*informal*) (used for showing that you completely agree with sth/sb): *Too right! This is the worst team we've had for years.*

would ‚give your right 'arm for sth (*informal*) want sth very much: *I'd give my right arm to own a horse like that.*

be on the right/wrong side of 40, 50, etc ⇨ side; **be on the right/wrong track** ⇨ track; **a bit of all right** ⇨ bit; **get your priorities right/wrong** ⇨ priorities; **get/keep on the right/wrong side of sb** ⇨ side; **sb's heart is in the right place** ⇨ heart; **if my memory serves me right/**

correctly ⇨ memory; **the left hand does not know what the right hand is doing** ⇨ left; **left, right, and centre** ⇨ left; **might is right** ⇨ might; **play right into sb's hands** ⇨ play; **right down the line = all along/down the line** ⇨ line; **see sb right** ⇨ see; **serve sb right** ⇨ serve

rights

by rights according to what should happen or what you would expect: *By rights I should be feeling sorry for shouting at her, but I don't.*

put/set sth to rights correct a situation, etc which is unjust or unfair: *As a young politician, she wanted to put the world to rights.*

(be) within your 'rights have the moral or legal rights(s) (to do sth): *They were acting perfectly within their rights when they refused to let you into their house.*

Riley
lead/live the life of Reilly/Riley ⇨ life

ring(s)

ring a 'bell (*informal*) sound familiar; help you remember sth, but not completely: *That name rings a bell but I can't remember exactly where I've read it before.*

ring the 'changes (on sth) arrange or do things differently for the sake of variety: *I'm pleased to see that they're ringing the changes in the staff canteen. The new menus are much more interesting.*

ring in your 'head/'ears a sound or sb's words which make a very strong lasting impression on you: *Years later, the applause at the Berlin Wall concert was still ringing in her ears.*

‚ring out the ‚old (year) and ‚ring in the 'new celebrate the end of one year and the start of the next one.

ring 'true/'false/'hollow seem true/false/insincere: *What you've said about Jim just doesn't ring true. Are we talking about the same person?* ○ *His apology after killing six people rings a little hollow.*

have a familiar ring ⇨ familiar; **ring/bring down the curtain** ⇨ curtain; **run rings round sb/sth** ⇨ run

ringer
a dead ringer for sb ⇨ dead

ringside

have a ringside 'seat/'view (*informal*) be in a very good position to see sth happen: *My flat overlooks the central square, so I had a ringside view of the demonstration.*

riot
read the riot act ⇨ read; **run riot** ⇨ run

rip
let sth 'rip (*informal*) allow a car, boat, etc to go as fast as it can: *There's a straight road ahead. Let it rip!*

let rip (at sb) (with sth) (*informal*) speak, etc with force, angrily or passionately: *When her husband came home drunk again, she really let rip at him.* ○ *He let rip at me with a stream of abuse.* ○ *In the last song, the singer really let rip.*

ripe
at/to a 'ripe old age/to the ripe old age of '95, etc at/to a very old age: *My grandmother lived to a ripe old age.* ○ *My uncle was still driving a car at the ripe old age of 93.*

the time is ripe ⇨ time

rise
rise and 'shine (*British, informal, humorous*) (used for telling sb to get out of bed in the morning): *Rise and shine, everyone, we've a long way to travel today.*

rise from the ashes from a situation of destruction and ruin, become great again: *If you ask people for an example of something rising from the ashes, they usually say Germany or Japan after the Second World War.* (refers to the story of the phoenix, a mythological bird which burns to death and then 'rises from the ashes' to be born again)

rise to the 'bait act or react to sth in exactly the way another person wants you to: *I knew he was trying to get me angry, but I didn't rise to the bait.* (refers to catching fish: a fisherman uses bait to attract fish to his hook)

rise to the oc'casion/'challenge, etc do sth successfully in a difficult situation/emergency: *When the main singer became ill, Cathy had to take her place. Everyone thought she rose to the occasion magnificently.* ○ *This company must be prepared to rise to the challenge of a rapidly changing market.*

take the rise out of sb try to annoy sb by

making fun of her/him: *She used to take the rise out of him by mimicking his foreign accent.*

be up/rise with the lark ⇨ lark; **make sb's hackles rise** ⇨ hackles; **rise/come up through the ranks** ⇨ ranks

risk
risk your 'neck (*informal*) take a big risk by doing sth dangerous, stupid, etc: *I'm not going to risk my neck complaining about the boss.*

river
sell sb down the river ⇨ sell

road
be off the 'road (of a car) need to be repaired and therefore impossible to use: *We'll have to go by bus. My car's off the road at the moment.*

on the road to re'covery, suc'cess, 'stardom, etc on the way to achieving sth desirable: *The operation was a success and the patient is now well on the road to recovery.* ○ *After many years struggling to get their company started, they are now firmly on the road to success.*

on the road to 'ruin, di'saster, de'struction, etc following a course of action that leads to ruin, etc: *I don't know whether it was losing his job or alcohol that set him on the road to ruin.* ○ *Is Europe on the road to disaster?*

the road to hell is paved with good intentions (*saying*) it's not enough to intend to do good things, behave better, etc; you must actually do them, be better, etc: (Christians believe that after death good people go to heaven and bad people to hell)

the end of the road/line ⇨ end; **get/keep the show on the road** ⇨ show; **hit the road** ⇨ hit

roaring
do a roaring 'trade (*informal*) sell sth very quickly or do a lot of business: *Toy shops do a roaring trade just before Christmas.*

a roaring suc'cess a very great success: *The musicians were such a roaring success that they have been asked to stay for an extra week.* ○ *His films have not exactly been a roaring success, have they?*

rob
rob sb 'blind (*informal*) get a lot of money

from sb by deceiving them or charging them too much for sth: *The investment consultant robbed his clients blind. He was taking about 25% of their profits.*

rob Peter to pay Paul take money from one area and spend it in another: *Government spending on education has not increased. Some areas have improved, but only as a result of robbing Peter to pay Paul.*

robbery daylight robbery ⇨ daylight

robin a round robin ⇨ round

Robinson before you can/could say Jack Robinson ⇨ say

rock
reach/hit rock-'bottom also **be at rock bottom** 1 (of prices, demand for goods, etc) at the very lowest point: *Demand for new cars is at rock bottom. This month's sales figures are the lowest in ten years.* 2 (of people) very depressed or demoralized: *I really hit rock bottom after my marriage broke up. That's when I started to drink heavily.* ○ *Morale is at rock bottom in the police force.* **rock-bottom** (*adjective*) *For rock-bottom prices, come to McArthur's Furniture Store.*

rock the 'boat (*informal*) do sth that might upset sb/sth, cause problems or change the balance of a situation in some way: *Politicians who are prepared to rock the boat are popular with newspapers but not with their parties.*

rocker
off your rocker (*informal*) mad; behaving as if you were mad: *Spend a thousand pounds on a dress! Are you off your rocker?*

rocket
give sb a 'rocket (*informal*) criticize sb very strongly for doing sth wrong: *His boss gave him a rocket for losing the contract.*

rocks
on the 'rocks 1 in danger of failing or being destroyed: *Their marriage is on the rocks.* ○ *The economy of this country is on the rocks. Something must be done before it's too late.* (refers to a ship which has hit the rocks) 2 (of an alcoholic drink) served with ice: *'How would you like your whisky?' 'On the rocks, please.'*

rod
make a rod for your own 'back do sth which is likely to cause problems for yourself, especially in the future: *I think she's making a rod for her own back by not telling him she's in love with someone else. When he finds out, there'll be trouble.*

rule with a rod of iron/with an iron hand ⇨ rule; **spare the rod and spoil the child** ⇨ spare

rogues
a rogues' 'gallery (*informal, humorous*) a selection of police photos of criminals; photos of people you would not trust: *Have you seen these photos of the new government? What a rogues' gallery!*

roll
roll in the 'aisles (*informal*) (of an audience) laugh uncontrollably: *The comedian was very good indeed. He had the audience rolling in the aisles.*

roll 'on (the day) (*informal*) (used for saying you are looking forward impatiently to a particular day, season, event, etc): *Roll on spring! I hate the winter.*

roll up your 'sleeves (*informal*) get ready for hard work: *We've just moved into a bigger house and there's a lot to do. I guess we'll just have to roll up our sleeves and get on with it.*

rolled
(all) rolled into 'one (*informal*) several qualities/things combined in one place, person, object, etc: *It's a penknife, scissors, corkscrew all rolled into one.* ○ *He's a writer, scientist and journalist rolled into one.*

rolling
(be) 'rolling in it/money (*informal*) (be) very rich: *She's been the managing director of the company for 10 years, so she must be rolling in it by now.*

a rolling stone (gathers no 'moss) (*saying*) a person who moves from place to place, job to job, etc and so does not have a lot of money, possessions, and friends but is free from responsibilities.

rolls sb's head rolls ⇨ head

Rome
Rome wasn't built in a day (*saying*) it takes time, patience, and hard work to do a

difficult or important job: *She asked me why the film wasn't yet finished so I reminded her that Rome wasn't built in a day.*

when in 'Rome (do as the Romans do) (*saying*) follow the example of other people and act as they do especially if you are a stranger or new to a place or situation: *I don't take taxis usually but it seemed to be what everyone did in the city; so I said to myself 'when in Rome'.*

fiddle while Rome burns ⇨ fiddle

romp

romp home/in (*informal*) win easily, especially in a race, election, etc: *The Queen's horse romped home in the first race.* ○ *The Democratic Party romped home in the recent elections.*

roof

go through the 'roof (*informal*) **1** become very angry: *He went through the roof when I told him I'd lost the money.* **2** (of prices, numbers) rise very high very quickly: *Prices have gone through the roof since the oil crisis began.*

raise/lift the 'roof *or* **bring the 'roof down** (*informal*) (of a large group of people) make a very loud noise, for example by shouting or singing: *The audience raised the roof when the band played their favourite song.* ○ *The crowd brought the roof down when the home team scored. I had never ever heard such cheering.*

a roof over your head (*informal*) a place to live in; a house: *Everyone needs a roof over their heads but thousands remain homeless.*

under one/the same 'roof (*informal*) in the same house, etc: *There were three generations of the family living under one roof.*

hit the roof ⇨ hit; **shout, etc sth from the housetops/rooftops** ⇨ housetops

room

no room to swing a 'cat (of a room) very small; not big enough: *In most modern student accommodation there's not enough room to swing a cat.* ○ *I'd love a bigger kitchen. There isn't room to swing a cat in this one.* (refers to a special kind of whip, the cat-o'-nine-tails, which was used to punish sailors)

roost chickens come home to roost ⇨ chickens; **rule the roost** ⇨ rule

root

get to the 'root of sth be able to see or do sth about the main cause (of a problem, etc): *We must get to the root of the drugs problem.*

,root and 'branch (destroy, remove, etc) complete(ly); thorough(ly): *The independence movement has been destroyed root and branch.* (from the Bible)

the root cause (of sth) (of a problem, etc) the main or fundamental cause: *Poverty is the root cause of most of the crime in the city.*

take 'root become firmly established: *His ideas on education never really took root; they were just too extreme.*

rooted

rooted to the spot unable to move for a moment because you are shocked or surprised: *She stood there rooted to the spot when she saw the dead body.*

roots

put down (new) 'roots go to live in a place and gradually become part of a local community: *We've moved around a lot because of my job and it seems to get more difficult to put down new roots each time.*

the grass roots ⇨ grass

rope(s)

give sb enough rope (and she'll/he'll hang herself/himself) (*saying*) deliberately give sb enough freedom for them to make a mistake and get into trouble: *I'm going to give John enough rope to hang himself. Then the police will be forced to take some action, and we might be able to get some professional help for him.*

on the ropes (*informal*) near to collapse or defeat: *The company is on the ropes; unless the bank extends their loan, it's finished.* (refers to a boxer in the ring)

show sb/learn/know the 'ropes (*informal*) explain to sb/learn/know how to do a particular job, task, etc correctly: *It will take me a couple of weeks to learn the ropes but after that I should be fine.* ○ *Mrs Brian will show you the ropes.* (refers to a sailor learning the different ropes for the sails of a ship)

be money for old rope ⇨ money

rose(s)

be all 'roses *or* **be roses, roses all the**

way or **a bed of roses** (*informal*) be easy, comfortable or pleasant: *Being a film star isn't all roses, you know.* ○ *Don't expect married life to be a bed of roses, because it's not.*

everything's coming up roses (*informal*) everything is happening as well as or better than you hoped: *She's had a very unhappy time recently but everything seems to be coming up roses for her now.*

look at, see, etc sth through rose-tinted/rose-coloured spectacles, etc notice only the pleasant things in life and think things are better than they really are; be too optimistic: *She is convinced the company will make a big profit but then she does tend to see things through rose-tinted spectacles.*

put the roses back in your cheeks make you look healthier because you are not so pale: *A week with your grandma in the country will put the roses back in your cheeks.*

a rose by any other 'name (would smell as 'sweet) (*saying*) what is important is what people or things are, not what they are called. (from Shakespeare's *Romeo and Juliet*)

rot

the rot sets 'in a situation starts to get worse: *The rot really set in when the team's best player left the club last year.*

stop the rot ⇨ stop

rough

,rough and 'ready 1 simple or basic, usually because it has been made, done, etc quickly or cheaply: *I can give you a rough and ready estimate of the cost of the work now and a more detailed estimate later.* **2** (of sb) not very well-mannered; unsophisticated: *His rough and ready approach annoyed some of the customers.*

rough-and-'tumble 1 a noisy but not serious fight: *The toddlers often join in the rough-and-tumble of the older children's games.* **2** competitive struggle: *In the rough-and-tumble of politics you can't trust anyone.*

a rough 'diamond somebody who may not be polite or have good manners but is basically kind and good

rough justice punishment or rewards given without enough care so that people feel they have been unfairly treated: *The pensioners complained that they had received rough justice from the government when their claim for an increase in benefits was rejected without discussion.*

(give sb, have, etc) a rough ride (*informal*) (give sb/get) unpleasant treatment or questioning: *The minister was given a rough ride in parliament over government cuts in education.* ○ *The Prime Minister has had a rough ride from the popular press recently.*

take the ,rough with the 'smooth accept the unpleasant part of sth as well as the pleasant.

cut up rough/nasty ⇨ cut; **a raw/rough deal** ⇨ deal; **sleep rough** ⇨ sleep

roughshod

ride roughshod over sb/sth ⇨ ride

round

go round in 'circles keep making the same points without making progress in a discussion, argument, etc: *This discussion is going round and round in circles. Let's make a decision.*

in round 'figures/'numbers approximately, to the nearest 10, 100 or 1000: *In round figures, how much do you think the work will cost?*

(drive sb/be/go) round the bend/ twist (*informal*) (make sb/be/become) mad or very frustrated: *He practises the same tune all day; it drives me round the bend.* ○ *I'm going round the twist trying to repair this machine. Nothing I do seems to work.*

round the clock for twenty four hours without stopping: *The police watched the house round the clock but no one went in or came out.* **round-the-clock** (*adjective*) *Her mother needs round-the-clock care and attention.*

a round robin a letter of protest, dissatisfaction, etc which is signed by many people in such a way that no single person can be blamed or punished for sending it: *Did you sign that round robin that was sent to the manager this week?*

all year round ⇨ year; **get your head round sth** ⇨ head; **just (a)round the corner** ⇨ corner; **pass the hat round** ⇨ pass; **round/in these parts** ⇨ parts;

stand a round ⇨ stand; **turn round and do sth** ⇨ turn

roundabouts swings and roundabouts ⇨ swings

rounds

do the 'rounds go from place to place or from person to person: *We did the rounds of the local pubs but he wasn't in any of them.*

go the 'rounds be passed from person to person: *News of her resignation soon went the rounds and it wasn't long before another company offered her work.* ○ *This cold seems to be going the rounds at the moment.*

roving

have a roving 'eye be always looking for a chance to start a new love affair or get sth that you want: *Be careful of Brian. He's got a roving eye.*

row

in a 'row (of a number of events, etc) happening one after another; consecutively: *We've won five matches in a row.*

rub

rub sb's 'nose in it *or* **rub it in** (*informal*) continue reminding sb about a mistake they have made or an unpleasant truth: *She's always rubbing my nose in it. She's never forgiven me for not getting that job in London.* ○ *I know I made the wrong decision, but there's no need to rub it in, is there?*

rub 'salt into the wound/into sb's wounds make sb who is already feeling upset, angry, etc about sth feel even worse: *She was already upset about not getting the job, but the fact that they gave it to one of her own trainees really rubbed salt into the wound.*

rub 'shoulders (with sb) (*informal*) meet and talk (to rich, famous, etc people): *I used to rub shoulders with some very wealthy people when I worked in banking.*

rub sb up the wrong 'way (*informal*) annoy sb a lot: *She's a very good lawyer but she does sometimes rub clients up the wrong way.*

there is/lies the 'rub that is the main difficulty: *To get a job you need somewhere to live and there's the rub. I have nowhere to live and so I can't get a job.* (from Shakespeare's *Hamlet*)

not have two pennies to rub together ⇨ two

rude

a rude awakening (*rather formal*) a sudden, unexpected discovery of an unpleasant fact, truth, etc: *If he thinks that the exam's going to be easy, he's going to get a rude awakening.*

ruffle

ruffle sb's 'feathers (*informal*) annoy sb by doing sth that upsets and disturbs them: *All this talk in the newspapers of an election has clearly ruffled the government's feathers.*

rug be as snug as a bug in a rug ⇨ snug; **pull the carpet/rug out from under sb's feet** ⇨ pull

ruin(s)

in 'ruins badly damaged or affected by sth: *The city was in ruins at the end of the war.* ○ *Their life was in ruins after the death of their only child.*

go to rack and ruin ⇨ rack

rule(s)

as a (general) 'rule usually: *It's lucky for you that I'm still awake. As a rule I'm in bed by eleven.*

bend/stretch the rules allow sb to break the rules to some extent because you think there is a good reason: *We don't normally employ people over 50, but in your case we're prepared to stretch the rules a little.*

make it a rule to do sth always do sth because you think it is a good idea or the right thing to do: *I make it a rule to invite all my students to a party at my house once a year.*

a rule of 'thumb a quick, practical, but not exact, way of measuring or calculating sth: *As a rule of thumb you need a litre of paint to every 12 square metres of wall.* (refers to the old practice of using your thumb to measure things)

rule the 'roost (*informal*) be the person who controls a group, family, community, etc: *It is a family firm where the owner's mother rules the roost.*

rule (sb/sth) with a rod of 'iron/with an iron 'hand (*informal*) govern (sb/sth) in a very strong or harsh way: *They ruled the country with an iron hand and anybody who* *protested was arrested.*

the exception proves the rule ⇨ exception; **the golden rule** ⇨ golden; **rule/put sth out of court** ⇨ court

run

the common/general 'run (of sth) the average or usual type (of sth) *The play is better than the general run of television comedies.*

give sb/get/have the run of sth (*informal*) allow sb/be allowed to use freely a house, etc that belongs to another person: *He was very kind and let us have the run of his house while he was at work.*

a good run for your money (*informal*) **1** more than enough, but not total, satisfaction or pleasure from sth; good value for sth: *I've had a good run for my money as director of this company, but now I think it's time someone younger took on my job.* **2** strong and satisfying competition, opposition, etc: *They may not beat your team but they'll certainly give you a good run for your money.*

have a run-in with sb (*informal*) have an argument or quarrel with sb: *She had a run-in with her son's teacher this morning. She doesn't think he gives the children enough homework.*

on the 'run 1 (of an escaped prisoner, criminal, etc) be running away or hiding from the police: *Four prisoners escaped from Brixton Prison this morning. Three of them were caught but one of them is still on the run.* **2** (of an enemy, opponent, etc) being defeated or retreating: *Liverpool have got Manchester United on the run.* ○ *The rebels are on the run now. Victory is ours.* **3** be very busy or active: *She's been on the run all day. It's not surprising she's tired.*

run a'mok behave in a wild or uncontrolled way: *The crowd ran amok through the city streets when they heard their leaders had been killed.*

run a'way with the idea/notion (*informal*) wrongly believe sth false or unrealistic because you haven't thought about it sensibly: *Don't run away with the idea that you're going to be famous just because you've appeared once on television.*

(try to) run before you can 'walk (*informal*) try to do sth that is very difficult before you have succeeded in doing sth easy: *The important thing about cooking is not to try and run before you can walk. Get the basics right first and the rest will follow.*

'run for it (*informal*) run away from danger very quickly: *Run for it. There's a bomb in here.*

run the 'gauntlet be attacked or criticized by many people at the same time: *The Prime Minister's car had to run the gauntlet of a large group of protesters outside the conference hall.* (refers to an old army punishment where a man was forced to run between two lines of soldiers who hit him)

run in the family (of a physical characteristic or moral quality) be sth that many members of a family have: *He was never going to live long because heart disease runs in both families.* ○ *Good looks run in the family.*

run sb/sth into the 'ground wear sb/sth out completely; exhaust sb: *In just one year, she managed to run her new car into the ground.* ○ *These children are running me into the ground.*

run a 'mile (from sb/sth) (*informal*) try to avoid sb or escape from doing sth: *She likes him but she'd run a mile if he proposed to her.*

run out of 'steam (*informal*) lose the energy, enthusiasm, etc that you had before: *His presidential campaign began well but ran out of steam after a couple of months.* (refers to a steam engine)

run 'riot get out of control: *They allow their children to run riot – it's not surprising that the house is always in such a mess.* ○ *His imagination ran riot as he thought about what he would do if he had a million pounds.*

run 'rings (a)round sb/sth (*informal*) do sth very well and so make your opponent look foolish: *I don't want to compete against her in the debate, she'll run rings around me.*

run short of only have a small amount of sth left and need more: *We're running short of butter. Can you get some more today?*

run the show (*sometimes disapproving*) be in control of a plan, project, organization, etc: *Why does Sheila always have to run the show? There are plenty of other people who could organize the event just as well as her.*

run a tight ship run an organization in a strict and efficient way: *The boss runs a very tight ship and everybody is expected to work very hard.* (refers to the captain of a ship)

run sb/sth to 'earth/'ground (*informal*) find sb/sth after a long, difficult search: *I spent years looking for the stolen picture but eventually ran it to ground in London.* ○ *The escaped prisoner was run to ground within a couple of days.*

run to 'fat (of people) begin to get fat: *After he stopped playing football he quickly ran to fat.*

run 'wild (*informal*) grow or behave in an uncontrolled way: *Their parents believed in letting the children run wild when they were young and it doesn't seem to have done them any harm.* ○ *I just let the roses run wild in this part of the garden.*

run with the hare and hunt with the hounds try to remain friendly with both sides in a quarrel.

be/run low ⇨ low; **be/get run/rushed off your feet** ⇨ feet; **cut and run** ⇨ cut; **get/run into debt** ⇨ debt; **get/have/run a temperature** ⇨ temperature; **go/run to seed** ⇨ seed; **hit and run** ⇨ hit; **in the long run** ⇨ long; **make sb's blood run cold** ⇨ blood; **run the gamut of sth** ⇨ gamut; **run/take its course** ⇨ course; **still waters run deep** ⇨ still; **a trial run** ⇨ trial

runner

do a runner (*very informal*) leave or escape from sb/a place, often after doing sth wrong: *He stole all the money in the office and did a runner.* ○ *'What happened to his wife?' 'She did a runner. Nobody's seen her for months.'*

running

come running come very quickly and eagerly because you want sth very much or you want to please sb very much: *He expects his wife to come running every time he wants something.*

in/out of the 'running have some/no chance of succeeding or achieving sth: *She's definitely in the running for a prize.* ○ *He's out of the running for the Paris job now.*

make the 'running lead or be very active in sth, which other people must then follow or join: *In the field of electronics, it's the Japanese who are making the running.* (refers to the person in a race who, by running faster than the others, determines the speed of the race)

a running battle an argument, dispute, etc which continues over a long period of time: *There's been a running battle between John and his neighbour for years about the garden fence.*

take a running 'jump (*very informal*) (tell sb angrily to) go away: *He asked me if I would sell him the painting for £5. I told him to take a running jump.*

in running order = in working order ⇨ working

runs **a chill runs/goes down sb's spine = send a chill up/down sb's spine** ⇨ send; **a shiver runs down sb's spine = send a shiver up/down sb's spine** ⇨ send

rush(ed)

have a rush of blood to the head (*humorous*) because of a strong emotion, suddenly (decide to) do sth foolish or dangerous: *'Why did you buy that vase? It was a crazy thing to do.' 'I don't know. It was so beautiful. I just had a rush of blood to the head and wrote a cheque.'*

be/get run/rushed off your feet ⇨ feet; **fools rush in** ⇨ fools

rut

in a 'rut in a fixed, rather boring way of doing things: *I suddenly realized one day that I'd been in a rut for years: same job, same flat, same friends, same holiday every year. So I got a new job doing something quite different and I'm much happier now.* (refers to a wheel which gets stuck in a rut in a road)

S

sack

give sb/get the sack (*informal*) tell sb/be told to leave a job especially because their/your work is poor or they/you have done something wrong: *If you don't work harder you'll get the sack.* ○ *She gave him the sack because he was always drunk.*

hit the sack ⇨ hit

sacred

a sacred 'cow a person, belief or institution that a group of people greatly respect and never criticize: *The National Health Service is a political sacred cow. No one likes to criticize it.* (in the Hindu religion, cows are respected and never harmed)

nothing is sacred ⇨ nothing

saddle

be in the 'saddle be in a position of responsibility and control in an organization: *It's too early to say if she is a good manager. She hasn't been in the saddle for very long.*

safe

be (as) safe as 'houses (*informal*) be very safe or secure; not be dangerous: *Investing your money with us is as safe as houses.*

,safe and 'sound safe; not hurt or harmed: *The police found the missing children safe and sound, thank God.*

a safe 'bet (*informal*) something that is likely to be right or successful: *If you want a cheap holiday with lots of sunshine, then Spain is a safe bet.*

to be on the 'safe side to be careful or prepared; just in case sth unpleasant or unexpected happens: *I'll just go and check whether the gas is off, just to be on the safe side.* ○ *You'd better take an umbrella, to be on the safe side.*

better safe than sorry ⇨ better; **in safe/good hands** ⇨ hands; **play safe** ⇨ play

safety

there's ,safety in 'numbers (*saying*) it's safer for a group of people to do something which could be dangerous for one person alone: *We decided there was safety in numbers, so we asked everyone in the office to sign our letter of complaint.*

said

the less/least said, the better (*saying*) it is better in a difficult situation to say nothing or very little (because you might make it worse): *He's very angry and she's very upset. Don't say anything about cars or accidents. Remember, the less said, the better.*

there's a lot to be said for sth *also* **sth has a lot to be said for it** sth has a lot of advantages or good qualities: *There's a lot to be said for eating sensibly.* ○ *There's not a lot to be said for this book; in fact, it's the worst book I've ever read.*

when all is said and done when all the facts are considered: *She doesn't have a lot of experience but, when all is said and done, she's the best person for the job.*

you 'said it! (*informal*) I agree completely; that is very true: *'That was the most boring lecture I've ever heard.' 'You said it!'*

easier said than done ⇨ easier; **no sooner said than done** ⇨ sooner

sail

sail close to the 'wind behave in a way that is almost illegal or socially unacceptable: *Isn't he sailing a bit close to the wind, driving without car tax and a licence?* ○ *She's been late for work three times this week; she's been sailing very close to the wind.*

sailing be plain sailing ⇨ plain

sails take the wind out of sb's sails ⇨ wind

sake

do sth for its own sake do sth because you are interested in it, and not because you could gain from doing it: *I'm not learning Arabic for any special reason. I'm doing it for its own sake. I enjoy it.*

for God's, Heaven's, pity's, etc sake...! (used to express anger, impatience or irritation): *For God's sake try and control yourself!*

for the sake of argument as a starting point for a discussion; to discuss things in theory only: *For the sake of argument, let's say that prices continue to rise by 20 per cent a year.*

for old times' sake ⇨ old; **for Pete's sake** ⇨ Pete

salt

the salt of the 'earth (a) good, honest, and dependable person/people. (from the Bible)

rub salt into the wound/into sb's wounds ⇨ rub; **take sth with a pinch of salt** ⇨ pinch; **worth your salt** ⇨ worth

same

,all/,just the 'same anyway; in spite of this; nevertheless: *I don't want a lift, but thanks all the same.* ○ *'You don't need a raincoat! The weather's fine!' 'All the same, I think I'll wear one; you never know.'*

amount/come to the same 'thing it doesn't matter how something happens or is done, the result in the end is the same: *Whether it was your fault or his fault, it still amounts to the same thing. My car is ruined.*

be of the same 'mind (as sb) (about/on sb/sth) agree with sb about sth: *I am afraid that he and I are not of the same mind on this matter.* ○ *They seem to be of the same mind about most things.*

by the same token (used for introducing a fact or statement which follows logically from what you have just said) as well; also: *He hates teachers and by the same token he thinks that all school work is a waste of time.*

in the same boat (*informal*) in the same difficult position or situation as another person or people: *None of us could do the maths exam, so we're all in the same boat.*

same difference (used to show that you accept sb's correction of what you have just said, but you feel that the difference between the two statements is not important or relevant): *'She's divorced from her husband.' 'No she's not, she's only separated.' 'Same difference.'*

,same 'here (*informal*) I agree; so am, do, have, etc I: *'I thought it was a terrible film.' 'Same here.'*

the ,same to 'you (used to wish sb what they have just wished you; as a reply to an insult (used especially by children): *'A very happy New Year' 'And the same to you.'* ○ *'Stupid idiot.' 'Same to you.'*

say, etc sth in the same breath *or* **say,** etc sth in one breath...and then in the next say...** say sth which appears to be the opposite of what you have just said: *He told me that my work had improved and then in the same breath he told me that I was lazy.*

be all the same to sb ⇨ all; **by the same token** ⇨ token; **it's the same old story** ⇨ story; **mention sb/sth in the same breath** ⇨ mention; **on/along the same lines as sth = on/along the lines of sth** ⇨ lines; **on the same terms** ⇨ terms; **one and the same** ⇨ one; **play the same game = play sb's game** ⇨ play; **tar sb/sth with the same brush** ⇨ tar; **under one/the same roof** ⇨ roof

sand **bury/hide your head in the sand** ⇨ head

sandboy **(as) happy as the day is long/as a sandboy/as Larry** ⇨ happy

sardines **packed like sardines** ⇨ packed

saturation

(get to, reach, etc) satu'ration point so full that you cannot add any more: *The refugee camps have reached saturation point.*

sauce

what's ,sauce for the ,goose is ,sauce for the 'gander (*saying*) if one partner (in a marriage or relationship) can behave in a certain way, then the other partner should also be allowed to behave in this way: *If she can go out with her friends, why can't I? What's sauce for the goose is sauce for the gander.* (a gander is a male goose)

sausage

not a sausage (*very informal*) (used for emphasis) nothing at all: *There's nothing in here. Not a sausage!*

save

can/could not do sth to save your life (*informal*) cannot do sth at all or can only do sth very badly: *He can't cook to save his life.*

save your/sb's 'bacon (*informal*) rescue yourself/sb from a difficult or dangerous situation: *Thank you for helping me with my exam preparation. You really saved my bacon.*

save your 'breath *or* **don't waste your breath** (*informal*) don't waste your time speaking to sb because they will not listen to your comments, advice, suggestions, etc: *Save your breath. He never listens to anybody.* (from the saying 'save your breath to cool your porridge')

save the 'day/situ'ation do sth that changes probable failure into success: *Jones saved the day for England with a last-minute goal.*

save (your/sb's) 'face do sth in order to keep the respect of other people: *The announcement was an attempt by the government to save face.* (the opposite is 'lose face') **face-saving** (*adjective*) *a face-saving operation* ○ *face-saving measures*

save sb's/your (own) 'neck/'skin (*informal*) save sb or yourself from a dangerous or unpleasant situation: *Don't rely on him for help, he's only interested in saving his own skin.*

saved

(be) saved by the bell (be) saved from a difficult, embarrassing, etc situation at the last moment (often used as an exclamation): *Saved by the bell! He was just asking me why my essay was two weeks late when you came in.* (refers to the bell that marks the end of a round in a boxing match)

saves a stitch in time saves nine ⇨ stitch

saving

a saving 'grace a quality which prevents sb/sth from being completely bad: *She can be difficult at times. Her saving grace is her sense of humour.*

saw

he, they, etc saw you coming (*informal*) he, they, etc knew that you were innocent or stupid and decided to lie to you or cheat you: *'I paid £500 for it, and it doesn't work!' 'They must have seen you coming.'*

say

as they say *or* **as the saying goes** (often used before or after a saying or idiom): *We can kill two birds with one stone, as they say.* ○ *He was, as the saying goes, as mad as a hatter.*

before you, etc can/could say Jack Robinson (*informal*) very quickly or suddenly.

have your say give your opinion: *You've*

had your say, now let me have mine.

have (got) something/nothing to 'say for yourself 1 be able/unable to explain your actions: *I've asked him what he was doing here in the middle of the night, but he's got nothing to say for himself. Let's call the police.* 2 be able/unable to hold a conversation or express your opinions: *She seems very nice but she's got nothing to say for herself.*

'I'll say! (*becoming dated*) (used to agree very emphatically) yes indeed; absolutely!: *'Is his dog dangerous?' 'I'll say! It nearly bit my hand off!'*

I say (used to attract sb's attention when you want to tell them sth): *I say, our train leaves in twenty minutes. We must hurry.*

never say 'die (*saying*) do not stop trying or hoping for sth.

not say a dicky-bird (*informal*) say nothing: *Don't look at me! I didn't say a dicky-bird.* (*dicky-bird* is Cockney rhyming slang for 'word')

not to say (used to suggest that you could, with good reason, use a stronger adjective or adverb to describe sth/sb): *He is very difficult, not to say impossible, to understand.*

say cheese! (used by a photographer) smile, please!

say no 'more it's not necessary for sb to continue speaking because you already understand the situation: *'He's only 21, and he's marrying a rich old lady of 65.' 'Say no more!'*

say your piece (*informal*) say sth that you have prepared in advance, for example a complaint or request: *Well, I went to see the boss this morning and I said my piece about our working conditions. He wasn't very happy about it.*

say 'when tell sb when to stop giving or pouring you sth, for example milk in your tea or coffee.

(just) say the 'word (used to show that you are willing and ready to do something immediately sb asks): *If you need any help, just say the word.*

she/he would not say boo to a goose (*informal*) sb is very shy and afraid of upsetting or annoying people: *How could he ever succeed in politics? He wouldn't say* *boo to a goose.*

to say the (very) 'least (used to say that you are using the least strong way of saying sth): *I'm not very happy with his work, to say the least.*

to say nothing of sth and also; not forgetting: *She is an expert in Chinese, to say nothing of speaking several European languages.*

what would/do you say to 'sth? (used to make a suggestion or offer) would you like sth/to do sth?: *'What would you say to a weekend in Paris?'*

you can say 'that again! (*informal*) I agree completely! I know that already!: *'She's the most boring person I've ever met.' 'You can say that again.'*

you don't 'say! 1 (used to show interest or surprise in what sb is saying) is that really true?: *'My brother's an astronaut, you know.' 'You don't say!'* **2** (*ironic*) *'I was in the Scouts for six years.' 'You don't say'* (I'm not interested).

I dare say ⇨ dare; **kiss/say goodbye to sth** ⇨ goodbye; **needless to say** ⇨ needless; **not/never have a good word to say for/about sb/sth** ⇨ word; **suffice it to say** ⇨ suffice

saying

it goes without 'saying (that...) it is obvious, already known or natural (that...): *Of course I'll visit you in hospital. It goes without saying!* **that goes without saying** *'You realize that this is a very responsible job, don't you?' 'Yes, that goes without saying.'*

it's/that's not saying much, etc (used to show that what you have just said is not particularly remarkable or impressive): *It rains less in London than in Edinburgh, but that's not saying much* (it rains quite a lot in London).

there is no knowing/saying/telling... ⇨ knowing

says

it, etc says a 'lot, 'much, etc about/for sb/sth (that...) something reveals a lot, etc about sb's/sth's qualities, personality, etc: *It says much about the quality of the instruments that many of them are still in use today.* ○ *The kind of car you drive says a great*

deal about you.

what/whatever sb says goes (*informal*) when a certain person in authority gives an order, this order must be obeyed: *Don't argue with me. I'm the boss here and what I say goes.*

scales **tip the balance/scales** ⇨ tip

scarce

make yourself 'scarce (*informal*) leave the place you are in in order to avoid an embarrassing or difficult situation: *I could see they wanted to be alone, so I made myself scarce.*

scare

scare the 'hell out of sb (*informal*) frighten sb very much: *The sight of a man with a gun scared the hell out of her.*

beat/scare the daylights out of sb/sth ⇨ daylights; **frighten/scare sb to death/out of their wits** ⇨ frighten

scene

be (not) sb's scene (*informal*) be (not) the kind of place, activity, etc that sb likes or feels comfortable with: *The holiday wasn't really our scene. Most of the people were much older than us and there wasn't any night-life.* ○ *This is more like my scene; plenty of music, drinking and dancing.*

come/arrive on the 'scene arrive in/at a place, probably to change the existing situation: *John and I were really happy together, and then she came on the scene.* ○ *When the police arrived on the scene, it was too late.*

create/make a scene complain noisily, behave badly, etc especially in a public place: *Jan refused to buy any beer, so Roger made a scene in the supermarket.* ○ *Please don't create a scene in public.*

set the scene/stage ⇨ set

scenes

behind the 'scenes (of discussions, arrangements, preparations, negotiations, etc) not seen by the public: *The general public knows very little about what happens behind the scenes in politics.* **behind-the-scenes** (*adjective*) *There was a lot of behind-the-scenes activity at the peace conference.* (refers to the parts of the stage in a theatre which the audience cannot see)

scent

be on the scent (of sb/sth) have information that will lead you to sb/sth: *The police are on the scent of the criminals.* (animals, for example dogs, follow the scent (=smell) of other animals, especially when hunting)

put/throw sb off the 'scent give sb false information to prevent them from finding out or knowing sth: *I threw the police off the scent by pretending I was in Mexico City on the day of the murder.*

scheme

the 'scheme of things the way the world and other things are or seem to be organized: *Low-paid workers like us don't have a very important place in the scheme of things.*

school

a school of 'thought theories or opinions held by certain groups of people: *There are two schools of thought on this matter.*

of the old school ⇨ old; **the old school tie** ⇨ old; **tell tales out of school** ⇨ tell

science   blind sb with science ⇨ blind

score

on 'that/'this score regarding that/this subject: *The accommodation is excellent so I don't think we've got any problems on that score.*

score a point/points off/over/against sb defeat sb in an argument; say sth that makes sb appear stupid: *Why don't you try to solve the problem instead of scoring points over each other?* ○ *I don't like David. He's always trying to score points off everybody.*

have a score/an account to settle with sb = settle a score ⇨ settle

scorn   pour scorn on sb/sth ⇨ pour

scrape

scrape (up) an ac'quaintance with sb (*informal*) try to become friends with sb because they might be useful to you.

scrape (the bottom of) the 'barrel use things or people of a low quality because all the good ones have already been used: *Television is terrible at the moment, it's nothing but old films. They're really scraping the barrel,*

aren't they?

bow and scrape ⇨ bow

scratch

do sth from 'scratch do sth from the beginning, not using any work done earlier: *The fire destroyed all the plans. Now we'll have to start again from scratch.*

scratch A and you'll find B (used to generalize about certain types of people) carefully consider or examine sb/sth and you will find that they are different from their outside appearance: *Scratch a senator from Texas and you'll find a cowboy.*

you scratch 'my back and ,I'll scratch 'yours (*saying*) if you do me a favour, I'll do one for you in return. **back-scratching** (*noun*) *There is too much back-scratching in local politics in this town.*

scratch your 'head not know the answer to sth; be puzzled by sth, sometimes scratching or rubbing your head at the same time: *We're all scratching our heads for an answer to the problem.*

(only) scratch (at) the 'surface (of sth) look at or deal with a subject, problem, etc, but only briefly and not fully enough; deal with sth superficially: *The government report only scratches the surface of the problem.*

up to 'scratch to the good standard that is expected or needed: *The level of safety in our power stations must be brought up to scratch.* ○ *If he doesn't come up to scratch, get rid of him.* (from boxing – the line in the ring which the boxers have to come to when they start to fight is called the 'scratch')

screen   the silver screen ⇨ silver; the small screen ⇨ small

screw(ed)

have a 'screw loose be a bit mad: *He dresses his cats up in little coats for the winter. Sometimes I think he must have a screw loose.*

have your head screwed on ⇨ head; **a turn of the screw** ⇨ turn

screws

put the 'screws on (sb) (*informal*) use force or threats to make sb do sth, especially to pay a debt: *The electricity company is really putting the screws on. We've got a week to pay before our supply is cut off!* (refers to *thumbscrews* which were used as an instrument of torture)

scrounge

be/go on the 'scrounge (for sth) (*informal*) ask sb for money, food, etc without doing any work for it or paying for it: *She's always on the scrounge for cigarettes. Why doesn't she buy her own?*

scruff

by the scruff of sb's/the 'neck (hold sb or an animal) by the back of the neck: *The barman took her by the scruff of the neck and threw her out.*

scum

the scum of the earth a group of people thought to be worthless, evil or completely without good qualities. (*scum* is a layer of dirt on the surface of water)

sea

all, completely, etc at 'sea confused; not organized: *We're still completely at sea trying to understand the new regulations.*

between the devil and the deep blue sea ⇨ devil; **there are plenty/lots more fish in the sea** ⇨ fish

seal

a ,seal of ap'proval the formal support or approval of a person or organization: *Our project has the director's seal of approval.*

set the seal on sth ⇨ set

sealed **my, etc lips are sealed** ⇨ lips; **signed, sealed, and delivered** ⇨ signed

seams

be bursting/bulging at the 'seams (with sth) *or* **be full to bursting (with sth)** be very or too full (of sth): *All of our hospitals are bursting at the seams; we must build new ones urgently.*

come/fall apart at the seams (*informal*) begin to fail or collapse: *The Government's economic policy is falling apart at the seams.* ○ *After only six months, their marriage has come apart at the seams.*

seamy

the 'seamy side (of life, etc) the unpleasant, dishonest, etc aspects (of life, etc), for example crime, prostitution, poverty, drugs, etc: *It's well known that the*

world of entertainment has its seamy side: drug abuse, corruption, alcoholism.

search

search your 'heart/'soul/'conscience (*formal*) think carefully about your feelings or your reasons for doing sth: *If I searched my heart I'd probably find that I don't always tell the truth.* **heart-searching, soul-searching** (*nouns*) *His divorce forced him to do a lot of soul-searching.*

,search 'me I don't know; I've no idea: *'What's the capital of Queensland?' 'Search me!'*

seas **on the high seas** ⇨ high

season

,in/,out of 'season 1 (of fruit, vegetables, fish, etc) available/unavailable in shops because it is the right/wrong time of year for them: *Peaches are in season at the moment.* **2** during the most/least popular time of year for holidays: *Hotels are much cheaper out of season.* **3** during the time of year when you can/cannot hunt animals: *You can't shoot ducks out of season.*

(the) season's 'greetings (used as a written greeting at Christmas especially on Christmas cards)

the silly season ⇨ silly

seat **have a ringside seat/view** ⇨ ringside; **in the driving seat** ⇨ driving; **in the hot seat** ⇨ hot; **on the edge of your seat/chair** ⇨ edge; **take a back seat** ⇨ back

second

be second 'nature (to sb) do sth automatically, without thinking about it, because you have done it for so long or so often: *It took a while to learn to drive, but now it's second nature (to me).*

be ,second ,only to 'sb/'sth be in a position where only one person or thing is better, more important, etc: *As a pianist, he was second only to Rubinstein.*

get your second 'wind find energy, strength or enthusiasm after feeling tired or after a period when you produce little: *After midnight, the dancers seemed to get their second wind and went on till dawn.* (from running; after feeling out of breath at the beginning of a race, you later find it easier to breathe)

have second 'thoughts change your opinion about sth; have doubts about sth: *We were going to go to Italy, but we had second thoughts and came here.* ○ *I usually vote Conservative, but I'm having second thoughts this time.*

on 'second thoughts (used when you want to change what you have said or decided): *On second thoughts, I won't have a beer, I'll have a whisky.*

a/your second 'childhood a period in life, especially in old age, when you sometimes act childishly, forget things, etc: *I have to feed her and dress her. She's really in her second childhood.*

second 'sight the special ability to know what will happen in the future or what is happening somewhere else: *Sometimes I think I've got second sight because my dreams always seem to come true.*

second to 'none very good; as good as the best: *This airline's safety record is second to none.*

another/a second/more than one string ⇨ string; **have/get a second/another bite at/of the cherry = have/get two bites at/of the cherry** ⇨ bite; **not for a/one minute/moment/second/instant** ⇨ minute; **play second fiddle** ⇨ play; **a split second** ⇨ split

secrecy **swear sb to secrecy** ⇨ swear

secret **an open secret** ⇨ open; **top secret** ⇨ top; **a trade secret** ⇨ trade

see

not see beyond/past the end of your nose not notice anything apart from what you are doing at present: *I'm so busy with running the office day to day that I can't see beyond the end of my nose.*

not see sb for dust (*informal*) not see sb because they have left a place very quickly: *If I ever win a lot of money, you won't see me for dust. I'll be on the next plane for New York.*

not see the wood for the 'trees (*informal*) not have a clear understanding of a situation because you are only looking at small aspects of it and not considering the situation as a whole: *The situation in the Middle East is so complex that many peace negotiators are unable to see the wood for the trees.*

(be glad, etc to) see the 'back of sb/sth (*informal*) (be happy to) see sb/sth that you do not like go or leave: *I thought we'd never see the back of that stupid woman.* ○ *This year's been awful, I'll be glad to see the back of it.*

see both sides (of the question, etc) understand why one person or group has an opinion, and why a different person or group disagrees with it: *When people are in politics, it's difficult for them to see both sides of a question.*

see the colour of sb's 'money (*informal*) make sure that sb has enough money to pay you, especially if you think they might not have it: *I want to see the colour of his money before I start doing such a dangerous job for him.*

see daylight see signs that your problems will end soon: *Sometimes you have so many problems that it's hard to see daylight.*

(not) see eye to 'eye (with sb) (about/on/over sth) (not) have the same opinion or attitude as sb else (about a particular issue, problem, etc): *My boss and I don't see eye to eye over the question of finance.*

see for your'self see or experience sth yourself so that you will believe it is true: *'Don't you believe she's here? Well, come in and see for yourself.'*

see sb in 'hell first (*informal*) (used when you emphatically reject sb's suggestion): *You want me to invite that woman to this house? I'll see her in hell first.*

see life see and experience different ways of living, for example by travelling, working with many different kinds of people, etc: *She's done many different jobs all over the world. She's seen life, that's for sure.* ○ *He's certainly seen a bit of life.*

see the 'light **1** understand or accept sth after you have spent a lot of time thinking about it: *I think he's finally seen the light and is going to retire while he's still able to enjoy himself.* **2** change what you believe as a result of a religious experience: *She was an atheist but now she says she's seen the light.*

see a lot, nothing, etc of sb often, never, etc see sb socially: *'Do you see much of Jennifer these days?' 'No, but I see a great deal of her sister.'*

see pink elephants (*informal*) see things that are not really there, because you are drunk.

see 'red (*informal*) suddenly become very angry: *Cruelty to animals makes him see red.*

see sb (all) right (*informal*) make sure that sb is treated correctly, paid properly for sth they have done, etc: *If I die, then the company will see my wife right.*

(make sb) see 'sense/'reason (cause sb to) begin to act and think more reasonably than before: *Ah, you've given up smoking! I'm glad you've seen sense at last.* ○ *It's time somebody made him see reason.*

see service 1 be in the army, navy or air force: *He saw service in Korea and later in Vietnam.* 2 be used: *This new type of engine won't see service until next year.*

see the sights visit the famous places in a city, country, etc: *We spent our first day in London seeing the sights.* **sightseeing, sightseer** (*nouns*) *There are always sightseers outside Buckingham Palace.*

see 'stars (*informal*) see small bright lights for a few moments, for example after being hit on the head: *There was a bang. I saw stars, and the next thing I knew, I was lying on the kitchen floor.*

'see things (*informal*) see things that are not really there; have hallucinations: *Some people start to see things if they take drugs or drink heavily.* ○ *So it was you that brought that snake into the house! I thought I was seeing things.*

'see to it (that) make certain (that): *I want you to see to it that she never comes in here again.* ○ *This report must be sent to Head Office immediately. Would you see to it for me?*

see your way (clear) to doing sth (*informal*) (in a request or answer to a request) be able to help or to do sth: *Could you see your way clear to lending me £10 until next week?*

see which way the 'wind blows/is blowing see what most people think, or what is likely to happen before you decide how to act yourself: *Most politicians are careful to see which way the wind's blowing before they make up their minds.*

see the world travel, live or work in many different parts of the world: *A lot of students take a year off after university to travel and see the world.*

see you! *or* **see you a'round/'later!** *or* **(I'll) be 'seeing you!** (*informal*) (used to say goodbye to sb whom you expect to see again soon)

so I see! (used to show that you are not pleased with the present situation) you do not need to tell me about that because it is obvious: *'I'm afraid I'm a bit late this morning.' 'So I see.'*

as far as the eye can see ⇨ far; **can/could tell/see a mile off** ⇨ mile; **hear/see the end/the last of sb/sth** ⇨ hear; **I'll believe it/that when I see it** ⇨ believe; **long time no see** ⇨ long; **see/think fit** ⇨ fit; **wait and see** ⇨ wait; **what the eye doesn't see** ⇨ eye

seed(s)

go/run to seed (*informal*) (of a person) become untidy or dirty because you no longer care about your appearance, etc: *I was very surprised when I saw her. She has really run to seed.* (in a plant, when the flower dies seeds form)

plant/sow the seeds of sth start a process which will develop into sth large, important etc: *What first planted the seeds of doubt in your mind?* ○ *The seeds of conflict were sown when oil was discovered on the border between the two countries.*

seeing

seeing as/that (*informal*) because; considering that; since: *Seeing as we're both going the same way, can I give you a lift?*

seeing is believing (*saying*) if you see sth, you can be sure it really exists: *He might be telling the truth about the spaceship, but seeing is believing, I always say.*

seen

when you've seen, heard, etc ,one, you've seen, heard, etc them 'all (*saying*) they are all more or less the same: *I don't like science fiction novels much. When you've read one, you've read them all.*

have seen/known better days ⇨ better; **I, he, etc wouldn't be seen dead with sb/sth, doing sth, in sth, etc** ⇨ dead

self be a shadow of your/its former self ⇨ shadow

sell

sell sb down the 'river (*informal*) act very unfairly to sb who trusts you; betray sb: *The workers thought that their own leaders had sold them down the river.* (from the days of slavery in the US. A slave who was sold to a plantation owner further down the Mississippi would experience harsher conditions than before)

sell sb 'short cheat sb by giving them less than they have paid for: *He sold us short! We paid for a kilo of mushrooms and only got three-quarters!*

sell yourself/sb/sth 'short describe yourself/sb/sth as being less good, valuable, etc than you, etc really are: *Don't sell yourself short when you go for an interview.* ○ *It was a great idea, but you sold it short.*

sell your 'soul (*informal, often humorous*) do something morally or legally wrong in order to get sth you want very much: *He'd sell his soul to get that job.* (refers to selling your soul to the devil in exchange for power, money, etc)

be past its sell-by date ⇨ past; **sell/go like hot cakes** ⇨ hot

send(s)

send a chill up/down sb's spine *or* **a chill runs/goes down sb's spine** *or* **feel a chill running/going down your spine** cause sb to feel horror and fear: *The picture sent a chill up my spine.* ○ *When I read the details of the murder, a chill ran down my spine.* **spine-chilling** (*adjective*) *a spine-chilling horror novel*

send sb 'packing (*informal*) tell sb rudely to go away because they are annoying or disturbing you; dismiss sb from a job: *He wanted to borrow money off me, but I sent him packing.* ○ *They caught him stealing company property and he was sent packing.*

send a shiver up/down sb's spine *or* **a shiver runs down sb's spine** cause sb to feel excitement or anxiety: *This piece of music sends shivers down my spine.* ○ *When I heard all those people shouting and cheering, a shiver ran down my spine.*

send sb to 'Coventry (of a group of people) not talk to sb in order to punish them for sth, for example, not being loyal to the group: *Joe Evans worked all through the strike, so when the strike was over, the other workers sent him to Coventry.* (Coventry is a town in the centre of England. It is said that people there did not like soldiers and refused to talk to any who were sent to the town)

drive/send sb up the wall ⇨ wall; **put/turn/send sb out to grass** ⇨ grass; **work all the hours God sends** ⇨ work

sense

in 'no sense emphatically; not at all: *In no sense do I agree with this suggestion.*

in a 'sense *or* **in 'one sense** considered in one way, rather than in other ways: *In a sense we are all responsible for the problem of starvation in the world.*

knock, beat, etc some sense into sb (*informal*) do something to make sb behave more sensibly, etc: *I wish somebody would knock some sense into our politicians.*

make 'sense 1 be understandable; have a clear meaning: *This sentence doesn't make sense; there's no verb.* **2** be sensible or practical: *It makes sense to buy a house now because prices will certainly go up soon.*

make sense of sth understand sth that is difficult or not very clear: *I don't understand these instructions. Can you make any sense of them?*

have more money than sense ⇨ money; **see sense/reason** ⇨ see; **a sixth sense** ⇨ sixth

senses

come to your 'senses 1 stop behaving unreasonably or stupidly: *At last he has come to his senses. He now understands that a restaurant in this part of town will never succeed.* **2** wake up from being unconscious: *When I came to my senses I found myself in a hospital bed.* also **bring sb to her/his 'senses** do sth to stop sb behaving unreasonably or stupidly.

take leave of your senses ⇨ leave

separate

go your separate ways (of two or more people) stop seeing each other socially, because you are living in different places, doing different jobs, etc: *After school we went our separate ways.*

separate the sheep from the 'goats separate the good people from the bad people: *The exams at the end of the first year usually separate the sheep from the goats.* (from the Bible)

separate the ‚wheat from the 'chaff separate people or things of a better quality from those of a lower quality: *When all the applications came in, our first job was to separate the wheat from the chaff.*

seriously

take sb/sth seriously regard or treat sth as important or serious: *We told him he was in danger but he didn't take us seriously.*

seriousness

in all 'seriousness seriously; not jokingly: *Surely you're not telling me, in all seriousness, that you want to work in a factory for the rest of your life!*

serve

serve the 'purpose (of doing sth) *or* **serve a, his, its, etc 'purpose** *or* **serve his, its, etc 'turn** be useful for a particular purpose or period of time; good or useful enough for sb: *It's not a very good radio, but it serves its purpose.* ○ *He used his friends and then abandoned them when they had served their turn.*

serve sb 'right (*informal*) (often used to comment on the silly or unwise behaviour of sb) be a just punishment for sb: *After the way you've treated her, it will serve you right if she never speaks to you again!* ○ *I told you the dog would bite if you teased it. It serves you right.*

do/serve time ➪ time; **first come, first served** ➪ first; **if my memory serves me right/correctly** ➪ memory

service

be at sb's service (*formal*) be ready to help sb: *If you need to know anything else, I'm at your service.*

be of service (to sb) (*formal*) be helpful (to sb): *If I can be of service, please let me know.*

press sb/sth into service ➪ press; **see service** ➪ see; **a skeleton crew/staff/service** ➪ skeleton

sesame open sesame! ➪ open

set

be (all) 'set (for sth/to do sth) be ready or prepared to do sth: *They were all set to go*

out when the phone rang. ○ *The team looks set for another easy win.*

be (dead) 'set against sth/doing sth not agree to a plan, proposal, etc: *I've tried to persuade him to move house, but he's dead set against it.* ○ *She's not very well, but she's set against going to the doctor.*

be set 'fair 1 (of weather) good and with no sign of change: *The weather forecast says the weather is set fair for the rest of the week.* **2** likely to be successful: *They are set fair to win the championship.*

be set in your 'ways be unable or unwilling to change your behaviour, habits or ideas, usually because you are old: *He's too set in his ways to agree to a holiday on a boat.*

be (dead) set on (doing) 'sth intending or determined to do sth: *The President thought that some of his ministers were set on overthrowing him.* ○ *She's dead set on leaving her husband.*

not/never set the 'Thames/'world on fire never do anything exciting, extraordinary or wonderful: *He's good, but he will never set the Thames on fire. He's not dynamic enough.*

set (sb) a (good, bad, etc) example show a (good, etc) standard of work or behaviour for others to follow or copy: *You shouldn't use bad language in front of your children; it sets a bad example.* ○ *She sets us all an example* (= a good example).

set your face against sth be strongly opposed to sth and refuse to change your opinion: *She's set her face against selling her land.*

set sth on fire/set fire to sth 1 cause sth to start burning, because you want to destroy or damage it: *Three youths were accused of setting the house on fire.* **2** make sb/sth very interested or excited: *Her new book has really set the literary critics on fire.*

set foot in/on sth arrive at a place; enter a place: *Neil Armstrong was the first man to set foot on the moon, in July 1969.* ○ *She's been complaining from the moment she set foot in this hotel.*

set your heart/mind on sth/doing sth *or* **have your heart/mind set on sth/doing sth** want sth very much; want to do or achieve sth very much: *When she was a small girl, her heart was set on a horse of her own.* ○ *He set his mind on becoming a doctor.* ○ *I have my heart set on a new guitar.*

,set the 'pace do sth at a speed which other people must follow if they want to be successful; lead by being better, cleverer, more original, etc than other people: *Jones set the pace in the 5000 metres.* ○ *This completely new style of bicycle has really set the pace for the rest of the industry.* **pace-setter** (*noun*) *Richard Rogers is a pace-setter in modern architecture.* (from athletics; one person in a running race sets the pace for the other runners by running faster than them)

set the seal on sth be the highest or best thing to happen in a successful career, project, etc: *His Nobel prize set the seal on a brilliant academic career in physics.*

set the 'scene/'stage (for sth) 1 describe in detail a place or situation where something important is going to happen: *Before the Queen arrived at the Houses of Parliament, the radio commentator set the scene for the listeners by describing the building, the people, the customs, etc.* **2** create the conditions in which an event, for example a war, might take place: *With so many economic and political problems, the scene was set for another war.*

set your sights high/low be ambitious/ not ambitious; expect a lot/not much from your life: *If you set your sights high, you could do anything.*

set your sights on sth/doing sth *or* **have your sights set on sth/doing sth** try to achieve or get sth: *She's set her sights on winning an Olympic gold.* ○ *He has his sights on owning the biggest property company in the USA.* (from shooting; you use the sights on a gun to help you hit the target)

set (no, great, little, etc) store by sth think that sth has (no, great, little, etc) importance or value: *She sets little store by what her husband says.* ○ *Why do people set such great store by their horoscopes?*

set sb's 'teeth on edge 1 (of an unpleasant noise, for example, chalk on a blackboard) make sb feel physically uncomfortable. **2** annoy sb; make sb feel

tense: *It sets my teeth on edge when I hear him talking to his mother so rudely.*

set the tone (of/for sth) create or establish a general feeling or atmosphere among a group of people (about a particular subject): *His very clever and very funny speech set the tone for the rest of the evening.*

set up 'house (with sb/together) start to live with sb (rather than with your parents): *They didn't have much money, so they set up house in an old caravan.*

set up 'shop start a business (in a particular place): *He worked as a writer for several years, then set up shop as a small publisher.* ○ *The young lawyer set up shop in a new office in the centre of town.* (used to describe any business, not just a shop)

clap/lay/set eyes on sb/sth ⇨ eyes; **go/ set to work** ⇨ work; **the jet set** ⇨ jet; **not/never put/set a foot wrong** ⇨ foot; **on your marks, get set, go!** ⇨ marks; **put/set sb at ease** ⇨ ease; **put/set the cat among the pigeons** ⇨ cat; **put/set your house in order** ⇨ house; **put/set sth in motion** ⇨ motion; **put/set sb's mind at ease/rest** ⇨ mind; **put/set/ place sb on a pedestal** ⇨ pedestal; **put/ set the record straight** ⇨ record; **put/ set sb right** ⇨ right; **put/set sth to rights** ⇨ rights; **put/set/turn your mind to sth** ⇨ mind; **the rot sets in** ⇨ rot; **set/start/ keep the ball rolling** ⇨ ball; **set tongues wagging = tongues wag** ⇨ tongues; **set the wheels in motion = put/set sth in motion** ⇨ motion

settle(s)

settle a(n old) 'score (with sb) *or* **settle your/an ac'count (with sb)** hurt, attack or get angry with sb because they have behaved badly towards you; get revenge: *Before he left the school, he wanted to settle an old score with one of his teachers.* also **have (got) a score/an account to settle with sb** want to hurt or harm sb because they have hurt or harmed you in the past: *I've got a score to settle with him after the terrible things he said about my girlfriend.*

after/when the dust settles ⇨ dust

seven(s)

the seven-year itch (*informal*) the wish

for a new sexual partner because you are bored with your husband or wife: *He's started looking at all the women in the office. It must be the seven-year itch.*

be at sixes and sevens ⇨ sixes

seventh

be in (your) seventh heaven be extremely happy: *When she has all her grandchildren around her, she is in seventh heaven.* (from the belief that God and the highest class of angels live in the seventh heaven)

shade

put sb/sth in the 'shade (*informal*) be much better or more successful than sb/sth: *The new player really puts the rest of the team in the shade.*

shadow

be a shadow of your/its former 'self be less strong, healthy or energetic than before: *He'd been ill for some time, and he looked a shadow of his former self.* ○ *As a politician she is a shadow of her former self.*

beyond/without a shadow of (a) doubt *or* **there isn't a shadow of a doubt (that)** there is no doubt at all (that); absolutely certainly: *He's innocent beyond a shadow of doubt.* ○ *There isn't the tiniest shadow of doubt in my mind about the safety of the system.*

shaggy

a shaggy-'dog story (*informal*) a long, complicated story or joke, which has no proper ending and is not very funny.

shake(s)

shake your 'fist (at sb) hold up your fist at sb because you are angry: *He got out of the car shaking his fist in anger at the driver in the car behind.*

shake 'hands (with sb) *or* **shake sb's 'hand** *or* **shake sb by the 'hand** take hold of sb's hand and move it up and down when meeting, saying goodbye, congratulating sb or making peace or an agreement.

shake your 'head move your head from side to side to show you mean 'no', or to show refusal, disagreement, disappointment or sympathy.

shake like a jelly/leaf *or* **shake in your shoes** (*informal*) shake or tremble with fear; be very afraid or nervous: *Before I went into the exam room I was shaking like a leaf.*

shake (hands) on it/sth shake hands with sb to show that you have made an agreement, deal, etc: *'OK, I'll let the car go for £5 000.' 'Do you want to shake on it?'* ○ *'Let's shake on it.'*

a fair shake ⇨ fair; **be no great shakes** ⇨ great

shame

put sb/sth to 'shame something very good makes sb/sth appear less good than before: *This new stereo puts our old one to shame.*

'shame on you! (an exclamation said to sb who has behaved badly or done sth they should be ashamed of): *Shame on you for forgetting your mother's birthday!*

shape

be in (good, bad, etc) 'shape (of a person) be in good, etc health or physical condition; (of a thing) be well, etc organized or in good condition: *He's in good shape for a man of his age.* ○ *The economy's in very bad shape and is likely to get worse.*

be out of 'shape (of a person) be unfit: *I hadn't been training and was out of shape.*

be the ‚shape of ‚things to 'come *or* **be a ‚taste of ‚things to 'come** be a sign or example of how things are likely to be in the future: *These new sixth generation computers are the shape of things to come.* ○ *Telephones with television screens: this is the shape of things to come.*

get (yourself) (back) into 'shape take exercise, etc, to become fit and healthy (again): *After she had the baby, she started swimming every day, to get back into shape.*

get/knock/lick sb/sth into 'shape make sb/sth more orderly or organized; improve sb/sth: *Do you think you can lick this company into shape?*

in 'any shape (or form) of any kind: *I hate green vegetables in any shape or form.*

in the shape/form of sb/sth (follows a general word and introduces a particular example of it; sometimes used humorously or ironically): *There was entertainment on the ship, in the form of a disco and a cinema.* ○ *Help arrived in the shape of a policeman.*

take 'shape develop to a point where you can see what sth will finally be like: *After months of discussion, a peace agreement is gradually taking shape.* ○ *An idea for a new book started to take shape in his mind.*

shapes

come in all shapes and sizes are of many different forms or types: *Pasta comes in all shapes and sizes.* ○ *The containers come in all shapes and sizes.*

share(d)

share and share a'like (*saying*) share things equally: *Children must learn to share and share alike.*

a/your fair share of sth ⇨ fair; **have more than your fair share of sb/sth** ⇨ fair; **the lion's share** ⇨ lion; **a slice/ share of the cake** ⇨ cake; **a trouble shared is a trouble halved** ⇨ trouble

sharp

be (at) the 'sharp end (of sth) (*informal*) be (doing) the most difficult or risky job or activity: *As head of the school, I'm at the sharp end if there are complaints.*

have (got) a sharp tongue (*informal*) (of a person) often speak in an unkind or unpleasant way: *You've got to be careful of her, she's got a sharp tongue.* **sharp-tongued** (*adjective*) *a sharp-tongued old man*

sharp 'practice clever but dishonest methods of business, etc: *There's a lot of sharp practice in the second-hand car business.*

look lively/sharp ⇨ look

shatter dash/shatter sb's hopes ⇨ hopes

shed cast/shed/throw light on sth ⇨ light

sheep

do sth/be like 'sheep do sth because other people are doing it rather than take your own decisions: *If John says that something must be done, they do it. They just follow his orders like sheep.*

black sheep ⇨ black; **sb may/might as well be hanged/hung for a sheep as a**

lamb ⇨ hanged; **separate the sheep from the goats** ⇨ separate; **a wolf in sheep's clothing** ⇨ wolf

sheet a clean sheet/slate ⇨ clean; white as a sheet/ghost ⇨ white

shelf

buy, get, etc sth off the shelf buy, etc sth which is not made specially for sb, and is found in an ordinary shop: *Did they buy the computer system off the shelf or was it designed specially for them?*

on the 'shelf 1 (usually used about a woman) unmarried and unlikely to marry because you are no longer young: *Some women used to think they were on the shelf if they weren't married at 30.* **2** neglected because you are no longer useful: *Unemployed people often feel they've been left on the shelf.*

shell

come out of your 'shell (*informal*) speak and behave less shyly or more confidently: *When Anna first joined the club, it took her a long time to come out of her shell.* also **bring sb out of their 'shell**

go, retreat, withdraw, etc into your 'shell become more shy and less confident with other people: *If you ask him about his family, he goes into his shell.*

shift

shift your 'ground change your opinion or position during an argument: *He's shifted his ground a bit; he still believes in the death penalty, but now only for murderers.*

shine

take a shine to sb/sth (*informal*) like sb/ sth immediately: *You're in luck; the manager's taken a shine to you and the job is yours.*

come rain, come shine ⇨ rain; **make hay while the sun shines** ⇨ hay; **rise and shine** ⇨ rise

shining

be a shining example (of sb/sth) *or* **be a shining light** be a very good example of sb/sth, which other people can follow or copy: *Their friends think Phillip and Joan are a shining example of a happily married couple.* ○ *His books on grammar are a shining light in a* *very difficult and confused field.*

a knight in shining armour ⇨ knight

ship(s)

be (like) ,ships that ,pass in the 'night (*informal*) (of people) meet briefly, by chance, and perhaps for the only time in their lives: *We met on holiday in Spain, and we fell in love. But we both knew that it was just ships that pass in the night.*

when your 'ship/'boat comes in (*informal*) when you are suddenly successful or have a lot of money: *Perhaps, when our ship comes in, we'll be able to buy that flat in Paris.*

jump ship ⇨ jump; **run a tight ship** ⇨ run; **spoil the ship for a ha'porth /ha'penny-worth of tar** ⇨ spoil

shirt

put your 'shirt on sth (*informal*) bet a lot or all of your money in a horse-race, etc; invest all your money in sth: *I've put my shirt on Diamond Lady in the 10.15.* ○ *I've put my shirt on the future of this company.*

lose your shirt ⇨ lose; **a stuffed shirt** ⇨ stuffed

shit

be in the 'shit (*very informal, offensive*) be in a lot of trouble.

(when) the shit hits the fan (*very informal*) (when) things reach a crisis point or there is trouble for sb: *When the committee finds out what actually happened, the shit will really hit the fan.*

beat/knock/kick the shit out of sb = beat/knock/kick the hell out of sb ⇨ hell

shiver(s)

give sb/get the shivers (*informal*) make sb feel fear and horror: *That old portrait gives me the shivers.* ○ *I get the shivers every time I hear his name.*

send a shiver up/down sb's spine ⇨ send

shoes

be in sb's shoes (*informal*) be in sb's position: *I'd leave that job immediately if I were in his shoes.*

put yourself in sb's shoes/place consider what you would do or feel if you

were in the position of sb else: *Put yourself in his shoes! If your mother had just died, how would you feel?*

fill sb's shoes ⇨ fill; **shake in your shoes = shake like a jelly/leaf** ⇨ shake; **step into sb's shoes** ⇨ step

shoestring

(do sth) on a 'shoestring (do sth) with very little money: *The Government is trying to run the Defence Department on a shoestring.*

shoot

shoot your bolt make a final attempt to do something, especially if this attempt comes too early to be successful: *In an argument it's important not to shoot your bolt too soon. Keep one or two good points for the end.* (refers to shooting an arrow from a crossbow)

shoot the 'breeze (*especially US, informal*) talk in a friendly, informal way; chat.

shoot sb/sth down (in flames) (*informal*) successfully attack sb's ideas, suggestions, opinions, etc: *I thought it was a brilliant idea, but she shot it down in flames.*

shoot the lights (*informal*) go through red traffic lights: *In this city people shoot the lights all the time.*

shoot your 'mouth off **1** talk publicly or carelessly about things which should be secret: *This is a secret. Please don't shoot your mouth off to everyone about it.* **2** talk loudly and boastfully: *Mark is always shooting his mouth off about all the girls he knows.*

shoot yourself in the foot (*informal*) do/ say sth stupid which is against your own interests: *You'd better prepare your argument carefully; you don't want to shoot yourself in the foot.*

shop

all 'over the shop (*informal*) everywhere: *I've been looking for you all over the shop. Where have you been?* ○ *Since you explained about idioms to me, I keep seeing them all over the shop.*

a closed shop ⇨ closed; **like a bull in a china shop** ⇨ bull; **set up shop** ⇨ set; **shut up shop** ⇨ shut; **talk shop** ⇨ talk

short

at (very) short notice *or* **at a moment's notice** with very little warning; without much time to prepare: *In this job you have to be able to work weekends at short notice.*

be caught/taken 'short (*informal*) suddenly need to go to the toilet in a place where it is difficult to find one.

be in ,short sup'ply not be enough of sth; be scarce: *Good mathematics teachers are always in short supply.* ○ *During the war, many things were in short supply.*

be ,little/,nothing ,short of 'sth (used for emphasizing the truth of a statement) (nearly) the same as sth: *The way she behaves is little short of ridiculous.* ○ *This book is nothing short of pornographic.*

be on/have a short 'fuse (*informal*) be likely to get angry easily, because you are tired, stressed, etc: *Your father's having trouble at work, so his temper's on a short fuse today.* ○ *Be careful what you say to the director. She has a very short fuse.*

be ,short and 'sweet (*informal*) last for a short time, but still be good or pleasant; be good because it is short: *The patient is very tired, so make your visit short and sweet.* ○ *The chairman promised to make the introduction short and sweet.*

be short of sth not have enough of sth: *I'm a bit short of money at the moment.*

bring/pull sb up 'short make sb stop what they are doing because sth attracts their attention or because they suddenly realize sth: *His criticism of my work pulled me up short because I thought he was pleased with it.*

for 'short as a shorter way of saying sth: *Her name's Joanna, but her friends call her 'Jo' for short.*

get/have sb by the short 'hairs *or* **get/have sb by the short and 'curlies** (*very informal*) get/have sb in a position where they must agree to what you want: *We can't go on strike because the boss will simply hire new men. He's got us by the short and curlies.*

give sb/sth short 'shrift *or* **get short 'shrift** treat unsympathetically and pay little attention to a complaint, suggestion, request, etc or the person making it; receive this treatment: *Mrs Jones gave my suggestion very short shrift. I was quite surprised.* ○ *When Ann complained about the toilets, she got very* short shrift.

go short (of sth) not have as much of sth as you need: *Give the boy some pocket money. I don't want him to go short.*

in 'short in a few words; briefly: *This picture has been badly damaged, and besides, it's not signed: in short, it's worthless.*

make short work of sth/sb do or finish sth very quickly; defeat sb very easily: *The children certainly made short work of the chocolate biscuits!* ○ *The champion made very short work of the challenger in the title fight.*

a short back and sides a conventional haircut for men where the hair is cut very short around the ears and above the neck, like an army haircut.

a 'short ,cut (to sth) **1** a shorter way to go to a place: *I usually take a short cut behind the post office to get to college.* **2** a way of doing sth more quickly or easily: *Producing a quality wine takes years – there are really no short cuts.*

win, lose, etc by a short 'head win, etc but by only a little. (from horse racing)

be thick as two short planks ⇨ thick; **cut sb short** ⇨ cut; **cut sth short** ⇨ cut; **draw the short straw** ⇨ draw; **fall short of sth** ⇨ fall; **in the long/medium/short term** ⇨ term; **the long and the short of it** ⇨ long; **run short of** ⇨ run; **sell sb short** ⇨ sell; **sell yourself/sb/sth short** ⇨ sell; **stop short** ⇨ stop; **to cut a long story short** ⇨ cut

shot

be (all) shot (to pieces) (*informal*) be destroyed or in very bad condition: *All my dreams were shot to pieces when I heard the news.* ○ *This engine's totally shot; I'll have to get a new one.*

get/be 'shot of sb/sth (*informal*) get rid of sb/sth that you don't want or like or which has given you trouble: *It's time we got shot of this car; it's falling apart.*

(do sth) like a 'shot (do sth) immediately or quickly, without hesitating: *I'd be off like a shot if he offered me a job abroad.* ○ *If she wanted him, he'd go back to her like a shot.*

(fire) a (warning) shot across sb's bows do sth to warn an enemy, competitor, etc that you will take further action against them, if necessary: *The minister's speech on*

Friday was a shot across the bows of the banks.
If they don't change their policies, he will
change the law. (refers to encounters
between ships of hostile nations. One ship
might fire a warning shot at another, not in
order to hit it, but to warn it to move)

a shot in the 'arm (*informal*) a thing that
gives sb/sth new energy, help or
encouragement or provides a quick solution
to a problem: *The discovery of gas reserves was
a much-needed shot in the arm for the economy.*
(refers to an injection of a drug)

a shot in the 'dark a complete guess
because you have very little or no
information about the real answer.

a big noise/shot ⇨ big; **a long shot**
⇨ long; **a Parthian shot** = **a parting
shot** ⇨ parting

shotgun

a ,shotgun 'wedding (*informal*) a
marriage which takes place because the
woman is pregnant. (refers to the father of
the woman, who threatens to shoot the
man unless he marries her)

shots call the shots/the tune ⇨ call

shoulder(s)

**be, stand, act, etc shoulder to
'shoulder (with sb)** be, etc supporting sb
or in agreement with sb: *We fought shoulder
to shoulder to defend our country.* ○ *I stand
shoulder to shoulder with Julia on this
important issue.*

a shoulder to cry on a person who listens
to your troubles and offers sympathy and
kindness: *When you're depressed, you need a
shoulder to cry on.*

give sb/get the cold shoulder ⇨ cold;
have a chip on your shoulder ⇨ chip;
head and shoulders above sb/sth
⇨ head; **rub shoulders** ⇨ rub; **tell, etc
sb straight from the shoulder** ⇨ straight

shout be nothing, not much, etc to
shout about = be nothing, not much,
etc to write home about ⇨ write

shouting be all over bar the shouting
⇨ over

shove if/when push comes to shove
⇨ push

show

be on 'show be shown or displayed, often
for sale: *A couple of the new models are on show
at the BMW garage.* ○ *At English weddings the
gifts given by the guests are often on show.*

do sth/be for 'show do sth/be done to
attract attention or admiration, and for no
other purpose: *That expensive computer is just
for show; he doesn't really know how to use it.* ○
*She doesn't really like whisky; she just drinks it
for show.*

get/keep the show on the road start/
continue doing sth, usually sth that needs a
lot of organization: *Come on! You'll all have to
help if we're going to get the show on the road.*

**have (got) something, nothing, little,
etc to show for sth** have or produce sth,
etc as a result of your efforts, work, etc:
*Students who fail the final exam have nothing
to show for years of hard work.*

it (just/only) goes to 'show (that...)
(used to say that sth is an example of a
general truth or principle): *He had all his
money stolen? It just goes to show you should
always lock your doors.*

**put on a good, poor, wonderful, etc
show** make a good, etc attempt at doing
sth, especially in spite of difficulties:
*Considering that the children had no help, they
put on a marvellous show.*

show (sb) a clean pair of 'heels
(*informal, often humorous*) run away; get
ahead of sb in a competition: *They ran after
her, but she showed them a clean pair of heels.* ○
*As makers of quality hi-fi, they've shown the
rest of the industry a clean pair of heels.*

show sb the 'door (*informal*) tell sb to
leave because of an argument or bad
behaviour: *If she spoke to me like that, I'd
show her the door!*

show your 'face be in or go to a place,
especially when you are not welcome: *After
what happened yesterday, I don't know how
you dare show your face here.* ○ *If he ever shows
his face in here again, there'll be trouble.*

**show good cause (why.../for doing
sth)** (*informal*) give a good reason (why sth
happened): *Can you show good cause for your
accusation?* ○ *She could show no good cause for
being in the office in the middle of the night.*

a show of 'force an act which clearly

shows your power or gives a warning to people not to act against you: *The government sent in tanks as a show of force, and the rebels left the town.*

a show of 'hands a method of voting in which each person shows her/his opinion by raising her/his hand: *If you like, we can settle this debate with a show of hands.*

show your teeth do sth that shows that you are able to act fiercely and powerfully in a situation, if it is necessary: *Up until now, the police have been very patient with the strikers, but today they really showed their teeth.*

run the show ⇨ run; **show sb/learn/ know the ropes** ⇨ ropes; **show/reveal your hand** ⇨ hand; **steal the show** ⇨ steal

shreds **tear sb/sth to shreds/pieces** ⇨ tear

shrift **give sb/sth short shrift** ⇨ short

shrinking

a ‚shrinking 'violet (*humorous*) a shy, timid, easily frightened person: *I can't imagine why a dynamic young woman like her is marrying a shrinking violet like him.*

shudder

I shudder to think (how, what, etc. . .) (*informal, often humorous*) (sometimes used as an exclamation) I am afraid to think or ask myself about sth, because the answer might be terrible or unpleasant: *I shudder to think when he last had a bath.* ○ *'How much more work is there?' 'I shudder to think!'*

shufti

take/have a shufti (at sb/sth) (*informal*) have a (quick) look (at sb/sth): *I don't mind having a shufti at the bike, but I can't afford to buy it.*

shut

shut the door on sth refuse to consider an idea, plan, etc: *I think this company should remain open to ideas and not shut the door on change.*

shut your ears to sth/sb refuse to listen to sth/sb; ignore sb/sth: *The government has shut its ears to our protests.*

shut your eyes to sth refuse to see or take notice of sth; pretend that you do not know

about sth, for example sth which is criminal or embarrassing: *We have all shut our eyes to his faults, but he has many.* ○ *Politicians seemed to be shutting their eyes to corruption in the police force.*

shut sb's 'mouth stop sb from saying sth, especially from revealing a secret: *His employers tried to shut his mouth by offering him money, but he told the story to the newspapers anyway.*

shut your ‚mouth/'trap/'face/'gob! (*very informal, offensive*) stop speaking: *'Shut your face', Roger said, 'or I'll kick you out.'* ○ *Why can't you learn to keep your big mouth shut?* (*trap* and *gob* mean 'mouth')

shut up 'shop close a business forever, or for the night, etc: *The family had run a small grocer's for years, but when the old man died they decided to shut up shop.* ○ *It's 6 o'clock; time to shut up shop and go home.*

keep your mouth shut ⇨ mouth; **an open-and-shut case** ⇨ open; **shut/close the stable door after the horse has bolted** ⇨ stable; **with your eyes closed/ shut** ⇨ eyes

shy **fight shy of sb/of sth** ⇨ fight; **once bitten, twice shy** ⇨ once

sick

be/feel sick at 'heart be very unhappy, afraid, disappointed or doubtful: *When I realized the accident was my fault, I felt sick at heart.*

be off sick not be at work or school because you are ill: *He broke his arm and was off sick for a fortnight.*

make sb 'sick (*informal*) disgust, anger or upset sb: *You make me sick, lying around in front of the TV all day!* ○ *Half a million pounds for the director of the bank! It makes you sick.*

(as) sick as a 'parrot (*informal, humorous*) very disappointed.

sick (and tired) of sb/sth *or* **sick to death of sb/sth** (*informal*) bored or annoyed by sb or by sth which has happened too often or which has continued too long: *I'm sick and tired of hearing you complaining all day long.* ○ *I'm sick to death of the bus service in this town.*

sick to your 'stomach (*US, informal*) disgusted or angry: *I feel sick to my stomach* *every time I think about the way that child was punished.*

side

be (a bit, a little, etc) on the 'cold, 'small, etc side be rather or too cold, etc: *These boots are a bit on the big side, but they're quite comfortable.* ○ *It's a bit on the cold side this morning.*

be on the ,right/,wrong side of '40, '50, etc (*informal, often humorous*) be younger/older than forty, etc: *'How old is she?' 'On the wrong side of forty, I'd say.'*

be on the side of the angels having correct moral principles and behaving correctly: *The policemen in Scobie's crime novels are not always on the side of the angels.*

come down/out on the side of sb/sth decide, especially after careful consideration, to choose or support sb/sth: *After much discussion, they finally came down on the side of nuclear energy.* ○ *In the argument that followed, my father came down firmly on my side.*

get/keep on the right/wrong side of sb try to please sb and not annoy them/ annoy sb and make them dislike you: *She got on the wrong side of her boss after criticizing him in a meeting.*

leave/put sth on one 'side put sth in a separate place so that you can deal with it later: *After you've taken the bread out of the oven, leave it on one side to cool.*

let the 'side down (*informal*) behave in a way that disappoints or brings shame to your family, friends, team, etc: *Everyone in the sales team has increased their sales except you. You're letting the side down badly.*

(do sth) on the 'side 1 (do sth) in addition to your main job: *He's a teacher but he does some journalism on the side.* **2** (*informal*) (do sth) secretly: *Her husband doesn't know it, but she's got a boyfriend on the side.*

my, her, the other, the same, etc side of the fence my, her, the opposite, same, etc point of view or position in an argument: *The former allies are now on opposite sides of the fence.* ○ *Make up your mind – which side of the fence are you on?*

,side by 'side (with sb/sth) 1 close together; supporting each other: *The two*

dogs lay side by side on the floor. ○ *Party members fought side by side with trade unionists for a change in the law.*

a/one side of the story/picture only one way of looking at a situation: *There are two sides to this story, and you've only heard Jim's.* ○ *This programme on AIDS only shows one side of the picture.*

take sb to one 'side take sb away from a group of people in order to speak to them in private: *She took me to one side to explain why she hadn't given me the job.*

be a thorn in your flesh/side ⇨ thorn; **a bit on the side** ⇨ bit; **err on the side of sth** ⇨ err; **get out of bed on the wrong side** ⇨ bed; **the grass is greener on the other side** ⇨ grass; **know which side your bread is buttered** ⇨ know; **laugh on the other side of your face** ⇨ laugh; **let the side down** ⇨ let; **look on the bright side** ⇨ look; **the other side of the coin** ⇨ other; **the seamy side** ⇨ seamy; **time is on sb's side** ⇨ time; **to be on the safe side** ⇨ safe; **the wrong side of the tracks** ⇨ wrong

sidelines

on the 'sidelines (watching what is happening while) not taking an active part; waiting to take an active part in sth, eg politics: *The Prime Minister's husband talked about what it was like on the sidelines of political life.* ○ *He is waiting on the sidelines for a chance to re-enter politics.*

sides

from/on all sides or **from/on every side** from every direction: *People from all sides are criticizing him.*

take 'sides or **take sb's side** support one person or group in an argument or quarrel: *I refuse to take sides in this argument. It's nothing to do with me.* ○ *Whenever we quarrel, you always take Carole's side.*

see both sides ⇨ see; **a short back and sides** ⇨ short; **split your sides** ⇨ split

sideways   knock sb sideways ⇨ knock

sieve

have (got) a mind/memory like a sieve (*informal*) forget things easily or quickly: *I'm terribly sorry I didn't remember your birthday – I've got a memory like a sieve.*

sight

be in/within sight **1** be close enough to be seen: *In fine weather the mountains are just within sight.* **2** likely to happen, almost a reality: *Prison reform is now within sight.* ○ *The end of our problems is in sight at last.*

be a ˌsight for sore ˈeyes (*informal*) be a person or thing that you are happy to see; be welcome or much needed.

do sth on ˈsight do or feel sth immediately you see sb/sth: *She complained constantly about the hotel, which she hated on sight.* ○ *The soldiers were ordered to shoot on sight.*

keep sight of sb/sth *or* **keep sb/sth in sight** **1** stay in a position where you can see sb/sth: *If you keep the church tower in sight, you won't get lost.* **2** remain aware of sth; not forget sth: *It's important to keep sight of the fact that you have a very small chance of winning.*

ˌout of ˌsight, ˌout of ˈmind (*saying*) we often forget about a person if they are not present or cannot be seen.

a (damn, bloody, etc) sight ˈbetter, ˈworse, ˈbigger, etc (than sb/sth) (*informal*) a lot better, etc (than sb/sth): *Life would be a sight easier if we could afford a car!* ○ *A car as big as this uses a damn sight more petrol.*

a (damn, bloody, etc) sight too ˈgood, too ˈmuch, too ˈsmall, etc (*informal*) far too good, etc: *There's a damn sight too much rubbish on TV.*

at first glance/sight ⇨ first; **know sb by sight** ⇨ know; **look a sight** ⇨ look; **lose sight of sb/sth** ⇨ lose; **love at first sight** ⇨ love; **not a pretty sight** ⇨ pretty; **second sight** ⇨ second

sights

raise/lower your ˈsights increase/reduce your hopes and ambitions: *You should raise your sights and apply for the director's job.* ○ *Some women feel that staying at home and having a family means lowering their sights.*

see the sights ⇨ see; **set your sights high/low** ⇨ set; **set your sights on sth/doing sth** ⇨ set

sign

(be) a ˌsign of the ˈtimes something that shows the way the world is changing: *Seventy per cent of last year's graduates are still unemployed – a sign of the times, I'm afraid.*

sign on the dotted ˈline sign your name at the bottom of a contract and so agree to a deal, etc: *The house isn't mine until I've signed on the dotted line.*

sign your own ˈdeath warrant do sth that results in your own death, defeat or failure: *By refusing to play pop music this new radio station is signing its own death warrant.*

sign/take the pledge ⇨ pledge

signed

signed, sealed, and delivered (of a written agreement) properly completed and signed (and given to sb): *At the Paris conference they hope to have a treaty signed, sealed and delivered by Tuesday.*

silence

ˌsilence is ˈgolden (*saying*) it is sometimes best not to say anything in a difficult or dangerous situation. (the complete saying is 'speech is silver, silence is golden')

a conspiracy of silence ⇨ conspiracy; **a pregnant pause/silence** ⇨ pregnant

silent

the ˌsilent maˈjority the great majority of a population, who support the ruling political party and the established system of law, morals, etc. Because they do not protest or demonstrate, the news media do not report their views or opinions: *The government is appealing to the silent majority to support its foreign policy.* (the US President, Richard Nixon, used this phrase during the Vietnam War)

silk **be smooth as silk** ⇨ smooth

silly

the ˈsilly season the period in the late summer when silly or trivial stories appear in the news, because people are still on holiday and fewer important things happen.

play silly buggers ⇨ play

silver

the silver ˈscreen (*dated*) the film industry: *the heroes and heroines of the silver screen*

be born with a silver spoon in your

mouth ⇨ born; **every cloud has a silver lining** ⇨ cloud; **a silver/smooth tongue** ⇨ tongue

simple pure and simple ⇨ pure

sin

be (as) miserable/ugly as 'sin (said of another person) be very miserable or bad-tempered/very ugly: *He arrived at the party looking as miserable as sin.* ○ *Some babies are as ugly as sin at that age.*

sincerely

Yours sincerely (used before you sign your name in a formal letter)

sinew strain every nerve/sinew ⇨ strain

sing

sing a different 'song/'tune (be forced to) change your opinion: *Anne says she wants to have a large family but she'll soon sing a different tune when she's had one or two children!*

sing sb's/sth's 'praises (*informal*) praise sb/sth very much, enthusiastically; say that sb/sth is very good: *Both her grandsons are doctors, and she never stops singing their praises.* ○ *One day he's singing your praises; the next day he's telling you you're stupid.*

single in single/Indian file ⇨ file

sink

sink your 'differences agree with sb to forget or ignore your past quarrels or arguments: *The two groups sank their political differences and joined together to beat the ruling party.*

,sink or 'swim (*saying*) either succeed without help from other people, or fail: *The government refused to give the company any help, and just left it to sink or swim.*

sink to sb's level stop behaving well and begin to behave badly, especially in an argument or fight, because other people are behaving in this way: *Use words, not violence, or you'll just be sinking to their level.*

everything but/bar the kitchen sink ⇨ kitchen; **sink, vanish, etc without trace** ⇨ trace

sinker hook, line, and sinker ⇨ hook

sinking

(have/get) a/that 'sinking feeling (have/get) a feeling that sth bad has happened/is going to happen: *Most people know that sinking feeling you get when a bill arrives in the post.*

with a heavy/sinking heart ⇨ heart

sinks your heart sinks ⇨ heart

sins

(do/be sth) for your sins (*humorous*) be/do sth as a punishment: *'I hear you are going to be the new manager.' 'Yes, for my sins.'*

cover/hide a multitude of sins ⇨ multitude

sisters be sisters/brothers under the skin ⇨ skin

sit

sit in 'judgement (on/over sb) judge or decide if sb is wrong or right, even if you have no right to do so: *What gives you the right to sit in judgement over us?*

sit on the 'fence avoid deciding between two sides of an argument, discussion, quarrel, etc: *You must say if you support me or not. You can't sit on the fence all your life.* ○ *Politicians cannot sit on the fence. People expect them to have clear ideas.* **fence-sitter** (*noun*) an undecided person.

sit 'tight not move; not change your position, in the hope that your present difficulties will be solved or go away: *If your car breaks down on the motorway, sit tight and wait for the police.* ○ *In a period of economic recession businessmen have to sit tight and hope for better times in the future.*

sitting

be ,sitting 'pretty (*informal*) be rich, successful or in a pleasant situation: *If you make £50 000 profit when you sell this house, you'll be sitting pretty.*

do sth in/at one sitting do sth in one continuous period of activity or session, without getting up from your chair: *You can have as much salad as you like, but you must eat it at one sitting. You can't get up and take some more.*

a ,sitting 'duck/'target an easy target; sth that is very easy to attack or criticize: *It's* *always easy to attack teachers; they're just sitting ducks.*

sure as I'm standing/sitting here = sure as eggs is eggs ⇨ sure

situation(s)

situations vacant jobs available (used in newspapers to show that details of jobs on offer are below): *the 'situations vacant' column*

a chicken-and-egg situation ⇨ chicken; **save the day/situation** ⇨ save

six

it's six of one and half a dozen of the other (*saying*) (of two people or things) they are equally to blame; there is no difference between them: *Patrick said John started the fight, but I think it was probably six of one and half a dozen of the other.* ○ *I've tried both ways of getting to Oxford and as far as I can see it's six of one and half a dozen of the other* (they both take the same time).

knock/hit sb/sth for six (*informal*) **1** (often of sth unpleasant) greatly surprise sb: *It really hit me for six to find that my father had written about me in his book.* **2** destroy completely a plan, idea, suggestion; knock sb/sth over/down: *The stock market crash has knocked the economy for six.* ○ *Toby took a step backwards and knocked the video camera for six.* (refers to six runs in the game of cricket)

six feet under (*informal, humorous*) dead (and buried in the ground): *By then, all the witnesses were six feet under.*

sixes

be at ‚sixes and 'sevens be in a state of disorder and confusion: *I'm completely at sixes and sevens this week. My secretary's ill, I've got a report to write, and we're moving offices.*

sixth

a sixth sense knowing or sensing sth, for example danger, the thoughts of other people, by intuition: *A kind of sixth sense told her that there was someone else in the room, and she turned round quickly.*

sixty

the sixty-four thousand dollar question a very important question which it is difficult or impossible to answer: *The sixty-four thousand dollar question for modern astronomy is 'Is there life elsewhere in the universe?'* (from a popular US radio quiz programme)

size(s)

that's about the 'size of it *or* **that's about 'it** that is a good or fair description of the situation: *'So you're leaving university just to go to India?' 'Yes, that's just about the size of it.'*

come in all shapes and sizes ⇨ shapes; **cut sb down to size** ⇨ cut

skates

get/put your 'skates on (*informal*) hurry up: *If you don't put your skates on, you'll be late for work.*

skating

be skating on ‚thin 'ice be in a risky or dangerous situation: *They were skating on very thin ice, publishing the election result before it had been confirmed.*

skeleton

a skeleton crew/staff/service the minimum number of staff necessary to run an organization or service, for example at night or during a public holiday: *Over Christmas we have a skeleton staff to deal with emergencies.*

a skeleton in the 'cupboard/'closet an embarrassing secret or scandal in your own past or your family's past which is kept hidden.

skids

on the skids moving towards disaster; declining: *It was clear months ago that the firm was on the skids.*

put the skids under sb/sth (*informal*) make sb/sth fail; stop sb/sth doing sth: *Unfortunately the government's put the skids under the hospital building programme.*

skies

praise sb/sth to the skies ⇨ praise

skin

be no skin off 'sb's nose (*informal*) not matter to sb: *It's no skin off my nose if the price of cigarettes goes up. I don't smoke.*

be (all) sisters/brothers under the skin be women/men with similar feelings, despite outside appearances such as skin colour, beauty, dress, etc: *Actors and politicians are brothers under the skin. They both need public approval.*

be (nothing but/all/just) skin and 'bone(s) (*informal*) be very or too thin: *After two years in prison, he was nothing but skin and bone.*

do sth by the ˌskin of your 'teeth (*informal*) only just do sth; nearly fail to do sth: *We thought we'd miss the plane, but we caught it by the skin of our teeth.*

get under sb's 'skin (*informal*) attract or disturb sb: *I've tried to forget her, but I know that I've got her under my skin.* ○ *He gets under his opponents' skins and they make stupid mistakes.* (from a song by Cole Porter)

skin sb alive punish sb very severely (said as a threat or warning): *Your mother would skin you alive if she knew you'd started smoking!*

(have) a thin/thick 'skin (*informal*) be sensitive/insensitive to criticism or unkind remarks: *He's got rather a thin skin for a politician. He'll have to learn to take the odd unkind remark.* ○ *A traffic warden needs a thick skin.* **thin-skinned, thick-skinned** (*adjectives*)

be/get soaked to the skin ⇨ soaked; **beauty is only skin-deep** ⇨ beauty; **have a hide/skin like a rhinoceros** ⇨ rhinoceros; **jump out of your skin** ⇨ jump; **save sb's/your neck/skin** ⇨ save; **slip on a banana skin** ⇨ slip

skinned **keep your eyes open/peeled/skinned** ⇨ eyes

sky

the sky's the limit (*saying*) there is no limit or end to sth, especially sb's success or progress: *For an ambitious young woman in this business, the sky's the limit.*

blow sb/sth sky-high ⇨ blow; **pie in the sky** ⇨ pie

slanging

a 'slanging match (*informal*) a noisy, angry argument: *It started as a peaceful discussion, but it ended as a real slanging match.*

slap

(a bit of) slap and 'tickle (*British, humorous, becoming dated*) cuddling and kissing.

a slap in the 'face an unexpected rude refusal or rejection: *The bank refused to lend her any more money; it was a real slap in the face for her.*

a slap on the 'wrist a small punishment or warning: *I got a slap on the wrist from my secretary today for leaving the office so untidy.*

slate

(put sth) on the 'slate (*informal*) put sth on your account (in a shop, a pub, etc) to be paid for later.

a clean sheet/slate ⇨ clean; **wipe the slate clean** ⇨ wipe

slaughter **as/like a lamb to the slaughter** ⇨ lamb

slave

be a slave to/of sth be a person whose life is completely controlled by sth, for example a habit, a job, an interest, etc: *She's a slave to fashion; she's always buying new clothes.*

work like a dog/slave/Trojan ⇨ work

sleep

ˌgo to 'sleep (of your leg, arm, hand, etc) be unable to feel anything in your leg, etc because it has been in a particular position for a long time.

not sleep a 'wink *or* **not get a wink of sleep** not sleep at all: *I didn't sleep a wink last night because I was worrying about my driving test.*

put sb/sth to 'sleep **1** give sb drugs or an anaesthetic before an operation to make them unconscious: *Before the operation we'll put you to sleep; so don't worry, you won't feel a thing.* **2** (of a sick, old or injured animal) kill painlessly by using drugs: *She took her old dog to the vet and he put it to sleep.*

sleep like a 'log/'top (*informal*) sleep very well; sleep without waking: *After our long walk yesterday, I slept like a log.*

sleep on it not make a decision until the following day so that you can have more time to think about it: *If you aren't sure what to do, sleep on it and give us your decision tomorrow.*

sleep 'rough sleep outside in the streets because you have no home or money: *Hundreds of people sleep rough in central London.*

sleep 'tight! (*informal*) (said to sb, usually a child, who is going to bed or in bed) sleep well!: *Goodnight, Pat, sleep tight!*

get your beauty sleep ⇨ beauty; **not lose any sleep over sb/sth** ⇨ lose

sleeping

let sleeping dogs 'lie (*saying*) do not disturb a situation which could cause trouble: *Everything seems to be all right between them now. I was very careful about what I said. It's better to let sleeping dogs lie.*

sleeve(s)

have (got) sth up your sleeve (*informal*) have a good idea, plan or piece of information which you are not telling anybody about now, but which you intend to use when the time is right: *John was smiling to himself all through the meeting; I'm sure he's got something up his sleeve.* **have (got) an ace/trick up your sleeve** have an idea or plan which you are keeping secret and can use if you need to (especially in order to gain an advantage over sb): *They think they've won the contract but we've still got a couple of aces up our sleeve.*

laugh up your sleeve ⇨ laugh; **roll up your sleeves** ⇨ roll; **wear your heart on your sleeve** ⇨ wear

sleight

sleight of 'hand 1 something done with very quick and skilful movements of the hand(s) so that other people cannot see what really happened. **2** skilful use of facts or statistics to give people the wrong impression of sth or to make them believe sth which is not true: *We now realize that much of Burt's research was presented with a statistical sleight of hand.*

slice

a slice of life a story, play or film that shows aspects of ordinary life: *In this book Dickens shows us a slice of nineteenth century London life.*

a slice/share of the cake ⇨ cake

slightest

not in the 'slightest not at all; not in the least: *Flying doesn't worry me in the slightest.*

sling(s)

the slings and arrows (of sth) the problems and difficulties (of sth): *As a politician you have to deal with the slings and arrows of criticism from the newspapers.* (from Shakespeare's *Hamlet*, 'the slings and arrows of outrageous fortune')

fling/sling/throw mud ⇨ mud

slip

give sb the 'slip (*informal*) get away from sb who is following you: *The police were chasing us but we managed to give them the slip.*

slip sb's memory/mind forget about sth or forget to do sth: *I was supposed to go to the dentist today, but it completely slipped my mind.*

a slip of the 'tongue/'pen a small mistake when speaking or writing: *Did I say North Street? Sorry, that was a slip of the tongue; I meant South Street.*

slip on a ba'nana skin (*informal*) (usually of a public figure, especially a politician) make a stupid mistake: *The new minister slipped on a banana skin before he had been in the job a week.*

slip through sb's 'fingers (of an opportunity, money, etc) escape or be missed: *I wouldn't let a wonderful opportunity like this slip through your fingers if I were you.*

there's ,many a ,slip ,twixt ,cup and 'lip (*saying*) (of plans, hopes, etc) nothing is completely certain until it happens because things can easily go wrong.

a Freudian slip ⇨ Freudian

slippery

be (as) slippery as an 'eel (*informal*) be a dishonest person who is good at not answering questions, etc.

the slippery 'slope a situation or way of behaving that could quickly lead to danger, disaster, failure, etc: *My mother thinks that even a small drink is the start of the slippery slope towards being an alcoholic.*

slipping

be 'slipping (*informal*) (of sb's behaviour or

performance) not as good, tidy, efficient, etc as usual; not be up to sb's usual high standard: *You're slipping, Edwina: this essay is full of spelling mistakes.* ○ *This record isn't as good as his last one; I think he's slipping.*

slog

slog/slug it 'out (*informal*) (of people, organizations, competitors, etc) fight sb very hard until one person, etc finally wins: *The boxers slugged it out to the finish.* ○ *The two teams slogged it out for second place.*

slouch

be no slouch at sth/doing sth (*informal*) be good at sth/doing sth: *He's no slouch in the kitchen; you should try his spaghetti bolognese.*

slow be quick/slow off the mark ⇨ mark; **be quick/slow on the uptake** ⇨ uptake

slowly

slowly but surely (used for describing definite but slow progress in sth): *Attitudes to women at work are changing slowly but surely.*

easy/gently/slowly does it ⇨ easy

slug slog/slug it out ⇨ slog

slum

slum it (*informal, often humorous*) live in worse conditions than you do usually: *We're slumming it tonight. No champagne, just ordinary table wine.*

sly

do sth on the 'sly do sth secretly: *She didn't seem to have much appetite for dinner. I wonder if she's been eating chocolates on the sly?*

small

be grateful/thankful for small 'mercies be happy that a bad situation is not even worse: *The thieves took the TV and stereo but didn't take the silver, so let's be thankful for small mercies.*

it's a small world (*saying*) (used when you meet or hear about sb you know, in an unexpected place)

look/feel 'small *or* **feel 'that high** (when using 'feel that high' the speaker often uses their thumb and finger to indicate sth small) feel stupid, embarrassed or ridiculous in front of other people: *'Why did*

you tell everyone that I'd failed all my school exams? I felt so small.' ○ *Mrs Jones made him feel that high when she criticized his work in front of everybody.*

,small 'beer something that has little importance or value: *Jacob earns about £25 000, but that's small beer compared with his brother's salary.*

a ,small 'fortune a lot of money: *This house cost hardly anything when we bought it, but now it's worth a small fortune.*

small fry (*informal*) people, groups or businesses that are not considered to be important or powerful: *These local companies are only small fry compared to the huge multinationals.*

the 'small hours the first few hours after midnight: *We stayed up talking into the small hours.* ○ *I woke in the small hours of the morning and couldn't get back to sleep.*

the small 'print the parts of a written agreement or legal contract that are printed in very small letters, but which may contain important information: *Make sure that you read the small print before you sign.*

the small 'screen (the) television: *Cinema films reach the small screen very quickly these days.*

(make) 'small talk (take part in) polite conversation about unimportant things: *Maria introduced me to her parents, and we sat there making small talk for a while.*

in no small part = in large part ⇨ part; **the still small voice** ⇨ still

smart

a 'smart alec (*informal, disapproving*) a person who tries to show that they are cleverer than everybody else: *Some smart alec wrote in to say that the last edition of the newspaper contained 37 printing errors.*

smash

smash sb's face/head in (*British, very informal*) hit sb very hard in the face/head: *Give me the money or I'll smash your head in.*

a smash hit (*informal*) (of a record, play or film) very popular and a great success: *Still at number one it's The Rubber Band, with their smash hit, 'Love me'.* ○ *Up to now actress Donna May has been in 15 Broadway smash hits.*

smell

smell a 'rat (*informal*) think or suspect that sth is wrong or that sb is trying to deceive you: *She says that the business is making a lot of money, but I smell a rat somewhere. The figures are too good.*

smell/stink to high heaven ⇨ high

smile(s)

be all 'smiles be very happy and smiling, perhaps after feeling worried about sth: *He was really depressed about the business last week, but he's all smiles now. A very big order has just come in.*

fortune smiles on sb ⇨ fortune; **raise a laugh/smile** ⇨ raise

smoke

go up in 'smoke (*informal*) **1** be destroyed by fire: *Their home went up in smoke before their eyes.* **2** (of plans, etc) be destroyed or ruined: *Her plans to become a member of parliament went up in smoke when the newspapers printed a story about her drinking problem.*

smoke like a chimney (*informal*) smoke a lot of cigarettes.

there is ,no ,smoke with,out 'fire (*saying*) if a lot of people are saying that sth bad is happening, it must be partly true.

put that in your pipe and smoke it ⇨ pipe

smokescreen

(put up) a 'smokescreen (do) sth that hides your real intentions, feelings, or activities: *She couldn't answer the question, so she tried to put up a smokescreen by talking angrily about the interviewer's rudeness.*

smooth

be (as) smooth as 'silk or (*informal, humorous*) **be (as) smooth as a baby's 'bottom** be very smooth: *He had just shaved. His chin was as smooth as a baby's bottom.*

smooth the path/way make it easier for sth to happen: *The President's speech smoothed the way for talks with the rebel leaders.*

a silver/smooth tongue ⇨ tongue; **take the rough with the smooth** ⇨ rough

snail

at a 'snail's pace (*informal*) very slowly: *My grandmother drove the car at a snail's pace.*

snake

a ,snake in the 'grass (*disapproving*) a person who appears friendly but is deceitful and dangerous.

snap

snap your fingers 1 attract sb's attention by making a sound with your thumb and middle finger: *Waiters don't like customers in restaurants who snap their fingers and shout 'waiter'!* **2** show you do not care about sb/sth: *He snapped his fingers at the committee and walked angrily out of the room.*

,snap 'out of it (*informal*) (sometimes used as a command) quickly stop being in a bad mood or depression: *For heaven's sake, Ann, snap out of it! Things aren't that bad!* ○ *She wouldn't talk to anyone for days, but her friends helped her to snap out of it.*

snappy

,make it 'snappy (*informal*) (often used as a command) hurry up: *If you don't make it snappy, we'll miss the train.* ○ *Come on, make it snappy! There's not much time left!*

sneak

a sneak preview an opportunity to look at or watch sth, for example a book or a film, before it is shown to the public: *She gave me a sneak preview of her latest book.*

sneezed

be not to be 'sneezed/'sniffed at (*informal*) be important or worth having: *If I were you, I'd take the job. A salary like that's not to be sneezed at.*

sniff(ed)

not get a sniff of sth (*informal*) not succeed in obtaining sth: *I worked in Hollywood for years, but I never got a sniff of the big money.*

be not to be sneezed/sniffed at ⇨ sneezed

snook cock a snook at sb/sth ⇨ cock

snuff

'snuff it (*informal*) die: *Old Jack was over 90 when he snuffed it.*

snug

be as snug as a bug in a rug (*informal, humorous*) be very comfortable and warm: *In his sleeping bag he'll be as snug as a bug in a rug.*

so

be not so much sth as sth be one thing but also something else which is more important: *He's not so much unintelligent as uninterested in school work.*

be ,so much/many 'sth be completely sth; be just or only sth: *All his fine speeches are so much rubbish if he doesn't keep his promises.* ○ *All these politicians are just so many names to me. I don't know any of them.*

or so (used for saying that an amount or period of time is approximate): *He stayed for a week or so.* ○ *Take a kilo or so of sugar....*

so 'be it (used to show that you accept a situation but do not like it): *He never wants to speak to me again? So be it.*

'so many/much (sth) a certain amount (of sth): *At the end of every working week I have to write in my notebook that I drove so many miles at so much per gallon.*

not so much as sth/doing sth *also* **without so much as sth/doing sth** (used for emphasizing that sb does not do sth) not even (do) sth: *He didn't so much as look at her when she came in.* ○ *She took the money without so much as a thank you.*

,so much for 'sb/'sth (used for showing the speaker's disappointment in sb/sth) I'm not going to think or talk about sb/sth any more: *She gave the job to the other manager. So much for all her promises to me.*

,so much 'so that to such an extent that: *His nose wouldn't stop bleeding – so much so that we had to take him to hospital.*

soaked

be/get ,soaked to the 'skin (of a person), be/get very wet: *Don't go out in this rain – you'll get soaked to the skin.*

sock(s)

put a 'sock in it (*British, very informal*) be quiet; stop talking or making a noise: *Put a sock in it, will you? I'm on the phone.*

pull your socks up ⇨ pull

sods   odds and sods ⇨ odds

soft

be soft in the head (*informal*) be stupid; be/become crazy or mad: *Sometimes I talk to myself in the street; people must think I'm soft in the head.*

have a soft 'spot for sb/sth (*informal*) particularly like sb/sth: *I've always had a soft spot for my little cousin Clare.*

a soft option an easier way of doing sth; an easier course of action: *If you want to go for the soft option, you can get the qualification in three years rather than two.*

an easy/soft touch ⇨ touch

softly

a/the softly-'softly approach a/the gentle, patient and careful way of doing sth, especially dealing with people: *The police are trying a more softly-softly approach with football hooligans.*

some

'some such (used to say that sth is similar to another thing or things): *I think this music's by Bartok or some such composer.*

something

or something (*informal*) or another similar thing: *Would you like some coffee or something?* ○ *Why won't you tell her? Are you frightened of her, or something?*

,something like 'sb/'sth similar or partly the same as/sth; approximately or about (a number): *'Is he a travel agent?' 'Yes, something like that.'* ○ *Something like twenty people came to the meeting.*

(be/have) something of a sth (be/have) quite or rather a sth; (be/have) sth to an extent: *He has something of a reputation as a sportsman.* ○ *Our walk home turned out to be something of an adventure.*

there is something about sb/sth sb/sth has a strange, attractive or unusual quality that influences you, but which is difficult to explain: *There's something about her I don't like, but I can't put it into words.*

son

a/the ,son of a 'bitch (*especially US, offensive*) a very unpleasant, offensive person; a person you feel very angry towards: *That's the son of a bitch who stole my* *car!*

like father/mother, like son/daughter
⇨ father; **the prodigal son** ⇨ prodigal

song

(go) for a 'song (*informal*) be sold for much less money than its real value: *also* **buy sth for a song** *I bought this car for a song.*

make a song and 'dance about sth (*disapproving*) worry or be excited about sth which is not very important: *My aunt makes a real song and dance about people arriving late, so hurry up.*

sing a different song/tune ⇨ sing

soon

none too soon **1** almost too late: *They were rescued none too soon; they'd already finished all the food and only had water for a couple more days.* **2** (used for saying that sb should have done sth a long time ago): *'I've mended the lamp in the children's room.' 'None too soon. It's been broken for weeks.'*

sb would (just) as soon do A (as B) sb wants to do one thing as much as another thing; it doesn't matter to sb what they do: *Susan can have my ticket for the show. I'd just as soon stay at home (as go out) anyway.* ○ *He'd just as soon have pizza as a hamburger.*

a fool and his money are soon parted ⇨ fool; **speak too soon** ⇨ speak

sooner

no ,sooner ,said than 'done (of a request) done immediately: *When he said he wanted to go to the zoo on his birthday it was no sooner said than done.*

no sooner...than (used to show that one thing, which is unexpected, happens immediately after another thing): *No sooner had she got in the bath than the front door bell rang.*

sooner or later (used when you want to say that sth will definitely happen) at some time, either now or later; eventually: *The police will find him sooner or later.*

sooner you, etc than me = rather you, etc than me ⇨ rather

sore

a ,sore 'point (with sb) a subject or matter that makes sb feel angry or hurt: *The tax increases are a sore point with Jake; he's*

going to lose a lot of money.

stand/stick out like a sore 'thumb (*informal*) be very obvious or easily noticed, possibly because sb/sth is unattractive or very different: *He's going to stick out like a sore thumb if he doesn't wear a suit to the wedding.*

be a sight for sore eyes ⇨ sight; **like a bear with a sore head** ⇨ bear

sorrow

do sth more in ,sorrow than in 'anger do sth with more regret or sorrow than anger: *One of the interrogators pretended to be acting more in sorrow than in anger.* (from Shakespeare's *Hamlet*)

drown your sorrows ⇨ drown

sorry

be/feel sorry for sb feel sympathy or pity for sb: *I feel sorry for all the people who are alone at Christmas.*

be/feel sorry for yourself (used for showing disapproval) be/feel unhappy because you think other people have treated you badly, etc: *You can't sit there feeling sorry for yourself all day.*

better safe than sorry ⇨ better

sort **kind/sort of** ⇨ kind; **nothing of the kind/sort** ⇨ nothing; **of a kind/sort** ⇨ kind

sorts

be out of 'sorts be feeling unwell or bad-tempered: *I was out of sorts for a couple of weeks after I came out of hospital.* ○ *What's the matter with Jane? She's rather out of sorts today.*

it takes all sorts (to make a world) (*saying*) different people like different things; different people have different characters and abilities: *'I don't understand Bill. He spends nearly all weekend cleaning and polishing his car.' 'Well, it takes all sorts.'*

soul

be the soul of sth a perfect example of a good quality or virtue: *She's the soul of discretion.*

bare your soul ⇨ bare; **bless your, etc heart/soul** ⇨ bless; **body and soul** ⇨ body; **heart and soul** ⇨ heart; **the life and soul of the party** ⇨ life; **search your**

heart/soul/conscience ⇨ search;　**sell your soul** ⇨ sell

sound

be/fall sound a'sleep be/become deeply and peacefully asleep: *He had fallen sound asleep in the chair by the fire.* ○ *The children are sound asleep upstairs.*

like, love, etc the ,sound of your own 'voice (*disapproving*) talk too much, usually without listening to others: *That man does like the sound of his own voice. We couldn't stop him talking.*

sound the 'death knell of sth be the reason why sth ends, goes out of fashion, or is replaced: *The arrival of large supermarkets sounded the death knell of many small local shops.*

safe and sound ⇨ safe; **strike/sound a false note** ⇨ false

soup

(be) in the 'soup (*informal*) (be) in trouble or difficulties: *If we don't get paid for the work soon, we'll be in the soup.* also **land yourself/sb in the soup** *I've really landed myself in the soup this time; I've crashed my father's car again.*

sour

go/turn 'sour become less enjoyable, pleasant or good: *Relations between China and Japan have recently gone sour.*

sour 'grapes (used to describe the behaviour of sb who pretends that sth they cannot have is of little value or interest): *She said she never wanted to go to university anyway, but I think that's just sour grapes.* (from one of Aesop's Fables. A fox cannot reach some grapes so he decides that they are not ready to eat.)

sow

sow your wild 'oats (*informal*) (usually used of young men) enjoy yourself before you get married and settle down: *The problem is that he never sowed his wild oats before he married, and he wants to sow them now.*

plant/sow the seeds of sth ⇨ seeds

space

in the space of a minute, hour, morning, etc during the period of a minute, etc: *I went from Glasgow to Edinburgh twelve times in the space of a few days.*

a breathing-space ⇨ breathing

spade **call a spade a spade** ⇨ call

span **spick and span** ⇨ spick

spanner

put/throw a 'spanner in the works (*informal*) spoil or prevent the success of sb's plan, idea, etc: *Let's get the job finished before the boss comes along and throws a spanner in the works.*

spare

go 'spare (*British, informal*) be very angry: *When she found the children painting the walls, she went spare.*

spare sb's 'blushes (*informal*) do not do sth which will embarrass sb: *Don't tell everybody about his excellent exam results. Spare his blushes.*

spare sb's 'feelings avoid hurting sb's feelings; avoid offending or upsetting sb: *Eric got no votes at all, but we didn't tell him because we wanted to spare his feelings.* ○ *She didn't spare my feelings at all; she told me exactly why she didn't like me.*

spare no expense/pains/trouble (to do sth/(in) doing sth) spend as much time, money or effort as is necessary: *His twenty-first birthday party was amazing; his parents had spared no expense.* ○ *The ship's crew will spare no pains to make your Mediterranean cruise unforgettable.* **no expense spared** *It will be a wonderful holiday, no expense spared.*

,spare the ,rod and ,spoil the 'child (*saying*) if you do not punish a child for behaving badly, she/he will behave badly in future.

a ,spare 'tyre (*humorous*) a roll of flesh around the waist: *He went on a diet to try and lose his spare tyre.*

spark(s) **bright spark** ⇨ bright; **the feathers/fur/sparks will fly** ⇨ fly

speak

nothing/not anything to speak of nothing very important or worth mentioning: *We looked through his private* *papers, but we didn't find anything to speak of.* ○ *He's got no money to speak of.*

speak for it'self/them'selves be so clear or obvious that no explanation or comment is needed: *The expressions on their faces spoke for themselves; they hated the film.*

speak for your'self (*humorous or offensive*) (said to sb who gives a personal opinion, but uses 'we' instead of 'I') that is your opinion, and I disagree with it: *'I think we've had enough cake, thank you.' 'Speak for yourself, Chris, I'm going to have some more!'*

speak highly of sb praise sb because you admire or respect their personal qualities or abilities: *His teacher speaks very highly of him.* ○ *Professor Heynman was very highly spoken of by his students.*

speak ill of sb speak unkindly about sb: *You shouldn't speak ill of the dead.*

speak your 'mind give your real opinion in an open, direct and fearless way: *I like a man who speaks his mind.*

speak too soon say sth, and find afterwards that what you said is not true: *'I'm glad Simon didn't come.' 'You spoke too soon. Here he comes now.'*

speak 'volumes (about/for sb/sth) show or express a lot about the nature or quality of sb/sth: *Her face spoke volumes. You could see how much she had suffered.* ○ *The progress he's made since the operation speaks volumes for his courage.*

so to speak = as it were ➪ **as; speak/ talk the same/a different language** ➪ language; **talk/speak of the devil** ➪ devil

speaking
be on 'speaking terms (with sb) 1 know sb well enough to speak to them, perhaps sb famous or important: *He's on speaking terms with a number of senior politicians.* **2** be talking to each other again after an argument: *Tony and Craig had a big row and are not on speaking terms.*

in a manner of speaking ➪ manner; **strictly speaking** ➪ strictly

spec
do sth on 'spec (*informal*) go somewhere without a ticket, reservation, appointment, etc in the hope that you will be able to get

sth you want: *'How did you get this job?' 'I just called into the office on spec one day and asked if they had any jobs.'*

spectacle
make a 'spectacle of yourself behave badly or oddly, or dress strangely in public, so that people look at you: *He made a spectacle of himself by shouting at the barman.*

speed at/with lightning speed ➪ lightning; **full steam/speed ahead** ➪ full; **full tilt/pelt/speed** ➪ full; **more haste, less speed** ➪ haste; **pick up speed** ➪ pick; **a turn of speed** ➪ turn

spell
(be) under sb's spell (*quite informal*) (be) so attracted to or fascinated by sb that you are in their power and will do what they say: *When he tells a story, the children are completely under his spell.*

spend
spend the 'night with sb/together (*quite informal*) have sex with sb: *James told me Kim and Robin spent the night together.*

spend a 'penny (*dated, informal*) go to the toilet; urinate.

spice variety is the spice of life ➪ variety

spick
,spick and 'span clean, tidy and fresh: *The boss likes everything spick and span in the office.*

spike
spike sb's 'drink add (more) alcohol or drugs to sb's drink, without their knowledge: *He spiked her drink because he wanted to get her drunk.*

spike sb's 'guns (*informal*) spoil sb's plans because you don't want them to succeed: *She was jealous of David's progress in the company, so she spiked his guns by telling the boss that David had a drinking problem.*

spill(s)
spill the 'beans (*informal*) tell a secret, news, or other information: *We were trying to keep it a secret from Pete, but Marcia spilled the beans.* ○ *Come on, spill the beans! What did your father say?*

thrills and spills ➪ thrills

spilt it's no good/use crying over spilt milk ⇨ crying

spin

spin (sb) a 'yarn tell (sb) a (usually long) story, often untrue: *She came an hour late and spun him a yarn about her car breaking down.*

spine

send a chill up/down sb's spine ⇨ send; **send a shiver up/down sb's spine** ⇨ send

spirit

(do sth) as/if/when the spirit 'moves you (do sth) when you want to, rather than when you have to or are forced to: *She works in the garden occasionally, when the spirit moves her.*

be with sb in spirit be thinking of sb who is in another place because you would like to be with them but cannot be: *I'm afraid I can't come to the wedding, but I'll be with you in spirit.*

the ˌspirit is ˌwilling but the ˌflesh (it) is 'weak (*saying*) a person's intentions and desires are good, but laziness, tiredness, love of pleasure, etc may stop them from acting in the right way. (from the Bible)

'that's the spirit! (used to encourage sb or to tell them that they are doing sth well): *'I'm rather tired, but I think I can run another mile.' 'That's the spirit!'*

the moving spirit ⇨ moving

spirits

be in high/low spirits *or* **in good/poor spirits** be happy and cheerful/sad and miserable: *John was in rather low spirits all evening.* **high-spirited, low-spirited** (*adjectives*)

raise sb's spirits ⇨ raise

spiritual

be sb's spiritual 'home be a place where sb could be happy, because they like the people, customs, culture, etc there: *I've always thought that Australia was his spiritual home.*

spit

spit and 'polish (*quite informal*) cleaning and polishing: *This table will look as good as new with a bit of spit and polish.*

spit it 'out! (*informal*) (a strong informal expression used when sb hesitates to tell you

sth important) tell me: *What did you tell her about me? Come on, spit it out!*

spite

(do sth) in spite of yourself (do sth) even though you do not want or expect to: *He was a bit depressed so I tried to cheer him up with a joke. He smiled in spite of himself.*

cut off your nose to spite your face ⇨ cut

spitting

within 'spitting distance (of sth) (*informal*) very near a place: *We live within spitting distance of the sea.*

splash

make, cause, etc a 'splash (*quite informal*) attract a lot of attention, for example in the newspapers, because you are famous: *Their wedding created quite a splash in the newspapers.*

spliced

get 'spliced (*informal*) get married.

split

split the 'difference agree on an amount (of money) which is halfway between two others: *John offered £60, but Peter wanted £100. Finally they split the difference and agreed on £80.*

split sth down the middle divide people into two groups, who disagree: *The local Conservative party is split down the middle on the matter of taxation.*

split 'hairs in a discussion or argument give too much importance to unimportant and small details or distractions; make unnecessary distinctions between one thing and another. **hair-splitting** (*adjective, noun*)

a ˌsplit 'second a very short time: *I heard a loud explosion and a split second later I was on the floor.* **split-second** (*adjective*) split-second timing/reactions

split your 'sides (laughing) *or* **split your sides (with laughter)** (*quite informal*) laugh a lot; laugh loudly: *When she started singing in that funny voice, we nearly split our sides.*

spoil

spoil the ship for a ha'porth/ha'penny-worth of tar (*saying*) spoil sth good because you didn't spend any or enough money on a small but essential part of it.

spare the rod and spoil the child ⇨ spare; **too many cooks spoil the broth** ⇨ cooks

spoiling
be spoiling for a fight, argument, etc want/be eager for a fight, etc: *Are you spoiling for a fight?* ○ *The teachers' union is spoiling for a fight with the Government.*

spoilt
be spoilt/spoiled for choice have so many opportunities or things to choose from that it is difficult to make a decision: *I've had so many job offers that I'm spoilt for choice.*

spoke
put a 'spoke in sb's wheel (*informal*) make it difficult for sb to do sth or to carry out their plans: *If the management try to cut our pay, we can put a spoke in their wheel by going on strike.*

sponge
throw in the sponge = **throw in the towel** ⇨ throw

spoon
born with a silver spoon in your mouth ⇨ born; **the wooden spoon** ⇨ wooden

spot
on the 'spot 1 at the place where sth is happening: *Our man on the spot is Geoff Davies. He's going to tell us exactly what's happening in Cairo.* 2 immediately; without any delay: *The policeman asked me for my driving licence and I gave it to him on the spot.*

put sb on the 'spot put sb in a difficult position, perhaps by asking them a difficult or embarrassing question: *Her question about my future plans really put me on the spot.*

bang/spot on ⇨ bang; **black spot** ⇨ black; **a/sb's blind spot** ⇨ blind; **have a soft spot for sb/sth** ⇨ soft; **the high spot of sth** ⇨ high; **a hot spot** ⇨ hot; **in a tight corner/spot** ⇨ tight; **rooted to the spot** ⇨ rooted

spots knock spots off sb/sth ⇨ knock; **a leopard cannot change its spots** ⇨ leopard

spout
(be) up the 'spout 1 (*informal*) (be) destroyed, ruined or wasted: *It looks like our holiday plans are up the spout.* 2 (*informal*) (be) wrong or mistaken: *This letter from the bank is totally up the spout.*

sprat
(be) a ˌsprat to catch a 'mackerel (*informal*) (be) a fairly small or unimportant thing which is offered or risked in the hope of getting sth bigger or better: *The competition and prize of a free car is a sprat to catch a mackerel. The publicity will mean good business for months to come.*

spread
spread like 'wildfire (especially of news or disease) travel or spread very quickly: *Rumours about a fall in the price of oil spread like wildfire in the city.* ○ *Cholera spread like wildfire through the camps.*

spread your 'net wide plan to attract or include as many people as possible with your business, with legislation, etc: *The Government has spread its net too wide with the tax relief – it should only be given to families who really need it.* ○ *Unless we spread our net a bit wider, this company will never get enough business.*

spread your 'wings try new activities and ways of living because you are now ready to: *Studying at university helps you to spread your wings and become independent.*

spring(s)
spring a 'leak (of a boat, roof, container, etc) start to let water in: *The boat sprang a leak halfway across the Atlantic.*

spring (in)to 'life/'action (of a person or thing) suddenly become active or start to work: *As soon as he heard the alarm bell, he sprang into action.* ○ *This machine will spring into life at the touch of a button.*

come/spring/leap to mind ⇨ mind; **full of the joys of spring** ⇨ full; **hope springs eternal** ⇨ hope

spur(s)
(do sth) on the ˌspur of the 'moment

(do sth) as soon as you think of it, without planning or preparation: *When they telephoned me with the offer of a job abroad, I decided on the spur of the moment to accept.* ○ *It was a spur-of-the-moment decision.*

win your spurs ⇨ win

spy

‚spy out the 'land find out about a situation, place, organization, etc before you make a decision: *The manager wants to send Mark to Iceland to spy out the land. He wants to know whether we can do business there.*

square

be/go back to square one or **start again from square one** (*informal*) start sth again from the beginning because your first idea, plan, action, etc has failed or has been stopped: *The experiment didn't work, so it's back to square one, I'm afraid.*

be (all) square (with sb) (*informal*) **1** have the same number of points or same score in a competition: *Liverpool were all square with Chelsea at half-time.* **2** (of two people) not owe money (or anything else) to each other: *Here's a pound; now we're square.*

be a square 'peg (in a round hole) (*informal*) not fit in well or easily into an organization, job, etc because you are different: *I don't have the right personality for the job. I feel like a square peg in a round hole.*

square your/an ac'count (with sb) or **square ac'counts (with sb)** **1** pay sb the money you owe them: *You can square your account at the end of the week.* **2** hurt sb or get revenge on sb because they have done sth bad to you: *I'm here to square accounts with Murphy for what he did to my sister.*

square the 'circle (try to) do sth that is or seems impossible: *The Government is trying to square the circle when it says it will spend more on the health service without raising taxes.*

a square 'meal a large and satisfying meal: *The children get three square meals a day.*

fair and square ⇨ fair

squeak a narrow escape/squeak ⇨ narrow

squeeze a tight squeeze ⇨ tight

squib a damp squib ⇨ damp

stab

have a stab at sth/doing sth (*informal*) try sth/doing sth especially if you have never done it before: *I had a stab at fishing once but I found it boring.*

stab sb in the back (*informal*) attack or harm sb who trusts you: *Jane promised to support me at the meeting, but then she stabbed me in the back by supporting David instead.* **a back-stabber, back-stabbing, a stab in the back** (*nouns*) *There is always a lot of back-stabbing in academic life.* ○ *This party is full of back-stabbers.*

stable

shut/lock/close the stable door after the horse has bolted take action to prevent sth bad from happening after it has already happened: *Last week all their silver was stolen; this week they're putting in a burglar alarm! That's really shutting the stable door after the horse has bolted.*

stacked

the cards/odds are stacked a'gainst sb/sth (*informal*) it is not likely that sb/sth will succeed, because she/he/it will have many problems or difficulties: *The cards are stacked against this plan. The public are against it.*

staff a skeleton crew/staff/service ⇨ skeleton

stage

be/go on the 'stage be/become an actor: *Maria has always wanted to go on the stage.*

set the scene/stage ⇨ set

stake

(be/have a lot, etc) at stake (of money, reputation, career, etc) at risk or in danger of being lost; depending upon the result of sth: *The team must win the game on Saturday to stay in the competition. With so much at stake, everyone's got to play their very best.* ○ *This decision has put our lives at stake.*

stake (out) a/your 'claim to sb/sth say that you have a special interest in sb/sth, or have a right to own sth, especially to warn other people not to take it: *Both countries have staked out a claim to the land.*

stand

sb can't 'stand (the sight/sound of) sb/sth (*informal*) sb dislikes or hates (seeing/hearing) sb/sth: *If you can't stand the sight of blood, you won't make a very good nurse! ○ I can't stand the sight of that woman.*

make a stand (against/for/over/ about/on sth) *or* **take a stand (on/ over sth)** argue, protest or fight because of sth you believe in: *This must never happen again; it's time to make a stand.*

not stand in sb's 'way not try to stop sb from doing sth: *If you want to become a singer, we won't stand in your way. In fact we'd encourage you.*

(not) stand a chance (of doing sth/ with sb) (not) have a chance (of doing, etc sth): *You stand a very good chance of winning the prize.*

stand 'firm not change your opinions or behaviour when other people want you to change them: *When he was arrested by the police, his friends stood firm in his support.*

stand sb in good 'stead be useful to sb: *Learning German at evening classes will stand her in good stead when she goes to work in the export department.*

stand on 'ceremony behave in a very formal way: *Come on – don't stand on ceremony! Start eating or the food will get cold!*

,stand on your 'dignity say firmly that you wish to be treated with the respect that you deserve: *The teacher stood on his dignity and insisted that the pupils be punished for being cheeky to him.*

stand on your own two feet not need the help of other people; be independent: *I left home to show my parents that I can stand on my own two feet. ○ Children have to learn to stand on their own two feet.*

stand or fall by sth succeed or fail, or be judged good or bad, because of one thing: *A salesman stands or falls by the number of sales he makes; if he doesn't make enough, he loses his job.*

(not) stand the pace not be able to work, live or compete under pressure: *You want to be a journalist? Are you sure you could stand the pace?*

stand a round (of drinks) buy a drink at the same time for each of your friends in a pub: *It's my turn to stand a round, so what are you all having?* (in Britain, if a group of friends go to a pub, each person stands a round in turn)

stand the test of 'time be considered valuable or useful by people for many years: *Dickens' books have stood the test of time – they are as popular now as they were a century ago.*

stand up and be counted make your opinion known to everyone, especially about an important or controversial subject: *I think that people who disagree with the government's education policy should stand up and be counted.*

as things stand ⇨ things; **hold/stand your ground** ⇨ ground; **know where you are/stand** ⇨ know; **last ditch stand/ attempt/effort** ⇨ last; **not have a leg to stand on** ⇨ leg; **a one-night stand** ⇨ one; **stand guard** ⇨ guard; **stand/ stick out like a sore thumb** ⇨ sore; **stand/stick out a mile** ⇨ mile; **stand/ turn sth on its head** ⇨ head

standing

do sth standing on your 'head (*informal*) do sth very easily, without any effort: *This exam's no problem. I could do it standing on my head.*

leave sb/sth standing ⇨ leave; **sure as I'm standing/sitting here = sure as eggs is eggs** ⇨ sure

stands

(know) how/where sb stands (know) what sb thinks about sth; know sb's opinion: *I don't know where she stands on nuclear weapons.*

it ,stands to 'reason (that...) it is quite clear, obvious or easy to understand: *It stands to reason that the less you eat, the thinner you get.*

sb's hair stands on end ⇨ hair

standstill grind to a halt/standstill ⇨ grind

stare stare/look you in the face ⇨ face

stark

be/go ,stark raving 'mad (*informal*) be/ become completely mad or crazy; become suddenly very angry with sb: *Are you stark raving mad, jumping off a moving train?* ○ *When I told her I'd crashed her car, she went stark raving mad.*

stars reach for the stars ⇨ reach; see stars ⇨ see; thank your lucky stars ⇨ thank

start

for a 'start *or* **to 'start with** *or* (*informal*) **for 'starters** (used for giving the first of several things, or reasons): *You're not going to marry him. For a start, you're much too young. For another thing, he hasn't got a job.*

'start something/anything (*informal*) begin a fight or argument: *Don't try to start anything with him, he carries a knife.* ○ *Are you trying to start something?*

a false start ⇨ false; **get off to a flying start** ⇨ flying; **set/start/keep the ball rolling** ⇨ ball; **start again from square one = be/go back to square one** ⇨ square; **start the wheels turning = put/set sth in motion** ⇨ motion

starters for starters = for a start ⇨ start

starts in fits and starts ⇨ fits

state

be in a 'state *or* **get into a 'state** (*informal*) **1** be/get worried, nervous or upset: *Her husband was killed in a car crash yesterday; she's in a terrible state.* ○ *He got into a state over his driving test.* **2** be/get dirty, untidy or messy: *What a state this house is in!*

a state of affairs circumstances or general situation: *We don't know very much about the present state of affairs in China.*

state of the art present stage of development of sth; the most recent or up-to-date model of sth: *This new computer uses state-of-the-art technology.*

the state of 'play what is happening now in a situation which is developing or changing: *We go to our Moscow correspondent for the latest state of play in the peace talks.*

in a good, bad state of repair = in good/ bad repair ⇨ repair; **lie in state** ⇨ lie

statesman an elder statesman ⇨ elder

stations action stations ⇨ action; panic stations ⇨ panic

status

a 'status symbol an expensive possession which shows people that you are rich: *These cars are status symbols in Britain.*

stay

stay 'put stay where you are; not travel, escape, look for another job, etc: *I'd like to move house, but my wife wants to stay put.*

be/keep/stay/remain in the swim ⇨ swim; **be/stay one jump ahead of sb/ sth** ⇨ jump; **steer/stay/keep clear** ⇨ clear

stead stand sb in good stead ⇨ stand

steady

go steady (with sb) (*becoming dated, informal*) have sb as a regular boyfriend or girlfriend: *Martin and Ingrid have been going steady for nearly a year.*

steady 'on! (*informal*) be more careful about what you do or say; slow down!: *Steady on, you two, don't get angry!* ○ *Steady on, you'll break it!*

steal

steal a 'glance at sb/sth look quickly at sb/sth, so that nobody notices you looking: *He stole a glance at her out of the corner of his eye.*

steal a 'march on sb do sth before sb else, and so gain an advantage: *The 'Daily News' stole a march on our paper by printing the story first.*

steal the 'show get more attention, praise or applause (especially unexpectedly) than other actors, performers, famous people, etc: *Actors don't like working with animals because they often steal the show.*

steal sb's 'thunder spoil sb's attempt to surprise or impress, by doing sth first: *He had planned to tell everyone about his discovery at the September meeting, but his assistant stole his thunder by talking about it before.*

beg, steal or borrow ⇨ beg

steam

get up/pick up steam **1** gradually

increase speed: *As the train came out of the tunnel, it picked up steam.* **2** gradually get bigger, more active or popular: *The election campaign is getting up steam now; it is only two weeks to election day.* ○ *I'm trying to get up enough steam to finish writing this book, but it's not easy.*

let off 'steam (*informal*) release energy, strong feelings, nervous tension, etc by intense physical activity or noisy behaviour: *He lets off steam by going to the gym after work.* ○ *All children need to let off steam from time to time.*

(do sth/go somewhere) ,under your own 'steam (do sth/go somewhere) without help from others: *Don't worry about arranging transport for us. We can get there under our own steam.*

full steam/speed ahead ⇨ **full**; **run out of steam** ⇨ **run**

steamed

be/get (all) steamed 'up (about/over sth) (*informal*) be/become very angry or excited (about sth): *There's no need to get so steamed up over such a small problem.*

steel **have nerves of steel** ⇨ **nerves**

steep

be a bit/rather steep (*informal*) (of a price or a request) be too much; be unreasonable: *£2.50? That seems a bit steep for a small piece of cheese.* ○ *It's a bit steep to expect us to work longer hours for no extra money.*

steer **steer/stay/keep   clear** ⇨ **clear**; **take/follow/steer a middle course** ⇨ **middle**

stem

stem the tide (of sth) stop the large increase of sth bad: *The government are unable to stem the rising tide of crime.*

step(s)

be in/out of step (with sth/sb) (not) think, act or behave like most other people; be compatible/incompatible (with sth): *He's completely out of step with other cancer specialists; his ideas about treatment are quite different.* ○ *The government no longer seems to be in step with the attitudes of the people.*

mind/watch   your   'step 1 walk carefully: *Mind your step, it's wet*

there.   **2** behave or act carefully: *You've got to watch your step with Simon. He gets angry very quickly.*

(do sth) ,step by 'step (do sth) slowly, one thing after another; (do sth) gradually: *If you take it step by step, learning a language is easy.* ○ *There are step-by-step instructions on how to build your bookcase.*

step into the 'breach take the place of sb who is not there: *The cook at the hotel fell ill, so the manager's wife stepped into the breach.*

step into sb's 'shoes take over a job from another person: *Mike stepped into his father's shoes when his father retired as director.*

'step on it or **step on the 'gas** (*informal*) drive a car faster; accelerate: *You'll be late if you don't step on it.*

step out of 'line behave in a way that annoys other people; break the rules: *The teacher warned them that she'd punish anyone who stepped out of line.*

take steps to do sth take the necessary action to achieve or get sth: *The government is taking steps to control the rising crime rate.*

tread/step on sb's toes ⇨ **toes**

sterner

be made of sterner stuff (of a person) have a strong character and be able to deal with difficulties and problems: *Did she cry? I thought she was made of sterner stuff.*

stew

be in a 'stew (about/over sth) or **get (yourself) into a 'stew (about/over sth)** (*informal*) be/become very worried or nervous (about sth): *She's in a stew over what she's going to wear at the party tonight.*

let sb stew in their own 'juice (*informal*) not help sb in a difficult situation, because you think it is their own fault and they do not deserve any help: *We told her not to trust him but she wouldn't listen – so let her stew in her own juice!*

stick

get/take 'stick from sb (*informal*) be angrily told you are wrong or at fault; be blamed or criticized: *The new centre forward took a lot of stick from the crowd. He played terribly.* ○ *The government has been getting a* *lot of stick from the press recently.*

give sb 'stick (*informal*) criticize sb: *The crowd gave the players a lot of stick for their terrible performance.*

,stick 'em 'up! (*informal*) (said for example by a robber with a gun) raise your hands above your head!

stick 'fast be firmly fixed in a place and unable to move or be moved: *The boat was stuck fast in the mud.*

stick in your 'mind (of a memory, idea, picture, etc) be remembered for a long time because it made a strong impression on you: *The image of the dead child's face stuck in my mind for ages.* ○ *That poem has always stuck in my mind.*

stick in your 'throat/'craw/'gullet (*informal*) sth is difficult or impossible to agree with or accept: *It really sticks in my throat that I get paid less than the others for doing the same job.*

stick your 'neck out (*informal*) do or say sth which other people are afraid to do, and as a result attract attention or trouble: *Joe stuck his neck out at the meeting this morning; he told the boss that the new sales policy wasn't working*

stick to your 'guns (*informal*) refuse to change your actions, opinions, etc despite criticism: *If the government sticks to its guns we'll get through this economic crisis.*

be in a cleft stick ⇨ cleft; **the carrot and/or stick** ⇨ carrot; **if you throw enough mud, some of it will stick = mud sticks** ⇨ mud; **poke/stick your nose in/into sth** ⇨ nose; **put/stick your oar in** ⇨ oar; **stand/stick out like a sore thumb** ⇨ sore; **stand/stick out a mile** ⇨ mile

sticks

(out) in the sticks (*informal, often humorous*) in the country, far from towns and cities: *I like living out in the sticks, but it can be a bit boring.*

up sticks (and go, etc) (*informal*) leave your home in order to move to another one: *So they upped sticks and went to Chicago.*

mud sticks ⇨ mud

sticky

(be on) a sticky 'wicket (*British,*

informal) (be in) a situation in which it is difficult to defend yourself against criticism or attack: *Don't be too confident about getting the contract. After our problems with the last contract we're on a sticky wicket there.* (from the game of cricket. A sticky wicket is difficult for the batsman to play on.)

come to a bad/sticky end ⇨ end; **go through, etc a bad/sticky patch** ⇨ patch

stiff

be (as) stiff as a 'board (of things) very stiff or rigid: *He left his gloves outside in the snow, and when he found them again they were as stiff as a board.*

be (as) stiff as a 'poker (*informal*) (usually of people) be very stiff or rigid (in the way you sit or stand): *The old lady was sitting upright in her chair, stiff as a poker.*

a stiff drink a strong alcoholic drink: *That was a shock – I need a stiff drink!*

(keep) a stiff upper lip appear very calm and self-controlled when in pain, trouble or danger: *The English gentleman is famous for his stiff upper lip.*

still

be still going 'strong (*quite informal*) **1** be still active, successful or working: *After nine hours of chess, both players are still going strong.* ○ *My car was made in the 'fifties, but it's still going strong.* **2** be still strong and healthy, despite being old: *She's 91 years old and still going strong.*

the still small voice the voice of your conscience, especially when you are thinking of doing sth wrong or bad.

still waters run 'deep (*saying*) a quiet person may have strong feelings or be very clever, etc; don't think that a quiet person has no emotions or nothing interesting to say.

be, etc stock still ⇨ stock; **even/much/still less** ⇨ less

sting

a ,sting in the 'tail (of sth written or spoken, for example a story) containing near or at the end sth very unpleasant or critical which is unexpected: *Roald Dahl's stories often have a sting in the tail; that's why I like them.*

take the sting out of sth (of a situation) take away the part that is unpleasant or dangerous: *We can pay the electricity bill in several stages if we want, which takes the sting out of it.*

stink
kick up/make/create/raise a 'stink (about sth) (*informal*) show that you are angry about a situation, often by protesting in public: *He kicked up a stink about the noise from the new nightclub, writing to all the papers and complaining to the council.*
smell/stink to high heaven ⇨ high

stinking
be 'stinking rich (*informal*) be extremely rich: *He doesn't need to work for a living – he's stinking rich.*

stint
do sth without 'stint (*quite formal*) do sth generously and in large amounts: *She praises her pupils without stint.*

stir
stir sb's/the blood make sb excited or enthusiastic: *His political speeches are designed to stir the blood.*

stitch
have not (got) a stitch 'on *or* **be without a stitch 'on** (*informal*) have no clothes on; be naked: *He was in the garden without a stitch on.*

a ,stitch in ,time saves 'nine (*saying*) if you act immediately when sth goes wrong, it will save you a lot more work later, because the problem will get worse if you leave it.

stitches
in 'stitches (*informal*) laughing a lot: *The film had the audience in stitches.*

stock
be, stay, stand, etc stock still be, etc very still or motionless: *When I heard footsteps on the stairs, I stood stock still and held my breath*

(be) in/out of stock (be) available/not available for sale in a shop: *Have you any mozzarella cheese in stock? ○ The book you want is out of stock at the moment.*

take stock (of sb/sth) think again

carefully (about sb/sth); think about what sth really means: *After a year in the job, she decided it was time to take stock* (think again whether it was the job she wanted). *○ He stopped to take stock of what he had read.*
lock, stock, and barrel ⇨ lock

stole
like the cat that got/ate/stole the cream ⇨ cat

stomach
have (got) no stomach for sth have no desire or appetite for sth because you find it unpleasant: *He has no stomach for this kind of job. He should never have become a salesman.*

sb's eyes are bigger than their stomach ⇨ eyes; **have a strong stomach** ⇨ strong; **on an empty stomach** ⇨ empty; **sick to your stomach** ⇨ sick; **turn sb's stomach** ⇨ turn

stone
a 'stone's throw a very short distance: *We're just a stone's throw from the shops.*

cast/throw the first stone ⇨ first; **have a heart of stone** ⇨ heart; **kill sth stone dead** ⇨ kill; **kill two birds with one stone** ⇨ kill; **leave no stone unturned** ⇨ leave; **like getting blood out of/from a stone** ⇨ blood; **a rolling stone** ⇨ rolling

stoned
be/get stoned out of your mind (*informal*) be under the influence of drugs, especially cannabis: *Last night I got stoned out of my mind.*

stones
people who live in glasshouses shouldn't throw stones ⇨ people

stools
fall between two stools ⇨ fall

stoop
stoop so low (as to do sth) lower your (moral) standards (and do sth bad, criminal or degrading): *I hope none of my friends would stoop so low as to steal. ○ She suggested advertising in a magazine for a boyfriend, but I'd never stoop so low.*

stop
stop at nothing do anything, even sth immoral or criminal in order to get sth: *He'd stop at nothing to make a success out of his business.*

stop (dead) in your 'tracks or **stop 'dead** stop suddenly because you are surprised or frightened. also **stop sb (dead in their tracks)** or **stop sb dead** *A sudden scream from the house opposite stopped him dead in his tracks.*

stop the rot stop sth getting worse, especially in politics or business: *Our company's profits were falling, so a new director was appointed to stop the rot.*

stop 'short **1** stop what you are doing because sth has surprised you or you have just thought of sth important: *When I read how many American soldiers had been killed, I stopped short and stared in disbelief at the newspaper.* **2** **stop short (of sth/of doing sth)** nearly but not actually do sth, for example because you are afraid or you think it is a bad idea: *The manager told her that he was unhappy with her work, but he stopped short of dismissing her from her job.*

come to a full stop ⇨ full; **full stop** ⇨ full

stops **the buck stops here** ⇨ buck; **pull out all the stops** ⇨ pull

store

be in store be coming in the future; be about to happen: *I can see trouble in store.* ○ *There's a surprise in store for you.*

store up trouble, etc for yourself have problems in the future because of things that you are doing or not doing now: *If you don't deal with the problem now, you'll be storing up trouble for yourself later.*

lie in store ⇨ lie; **set store by sth** ⇨ set

storm

the calm/lull before the storm a period of calm before sth terrible happens: *It was a strange war. For months nothing really happened and then suddenly there was bombing every night. It had been the lull before the storm.* (refers to the period just before a thunderstorm when the wind drops completely)

ride out/weather the 'storm (of sth) manage to survive a difficult period or situation, in which people are criticizing and attacking you: *The government has managed to ride out the recent storm.* ○ *Many companies are having difficulty weathering the present economic storms.*

(be) a storm in a 'teacup or (informal) **(be) a fuss about nothing** (be) a small or unimportant problem which is treated as much more serious than it really is: *Don't worry. It's a storm in a teacup. Everyone will have forgotten about it by tomorrow.*

take sb/sth by 'storm **1** take or seize a town, castle, building, etc with a sudden and fierce attack: *The police took the building by storm; two people were injured during the attack.* **2** make a great and favourable impression on the public; be very successful with the public: *ET took the whole world by storm; it was one of the most successful films ever made.*

any port in a storm ⇨ port

story

(quite) another 'story or **a (quite) different 'story** **1** very different from what has just been said: *Her English is excellent, but her French is another story.* **2** (used when you are talking about one thing and then mention another thing, which you are not going to talk about on that occasion): *I once met Marilyn Monroe, but that's another story. I'll tell you about that one day.*

it's the same old story also **it's the old, old story** something unpleasant or bad which happens again and again: *He says we haven't got enough money to go on holiday. It's the same old story every year.*

so the 'story goes (used when you are telling sb a rumour or story which you are not sure is true) people are saying (that...): *He used to be a doctor, or so the story goes.*

that's the ,story of my 'life (informal, humorous) (used for saying that sth that happens to you or to another person is typical of the bad luck you have always had): *'I meet somebody I really like and she tells me she's married. That's the story of my life!'*

a cock-and-bull story ⇨ cock; **a hard luck story** ⇨ hard; **a likely story** ⇨ likely; **a shaggy-dog story** ⇨ shaggy; **a side of the story/picture** ⇨ side; **a tall story/tale** ⇨ tall; **tell its own tale/story** ⇨ tell; **tell the same, a different, etc tale/story** ⇨ tell; **to cut a long story short** ⇨ cut

straight

be, etc (as) straight as an 'arrow be, etc in a straight line or direction: *You can't get lost if you follow this track. It runs as straight as an arrow through the middle of the wood.*

be, etc (as) straight as a 'die **1** be, etc in a straight line or direction: *The road runs northwards, as straight as a die.* **2** be honest: *Carol would never steal anything – she's as straight as a die.*

go straight (*informal*) (of a former criminal) live according to the law: *Many criminals find it very difficult to go straight.*

keep to, stay on, etc the ,straight and 'narrow live your life according to strict moral principles: *She's stopped drinking and now she's trying to stay on the straight and narrow.*

put sb straight (about sth) make sure that sb is not mistaken about the real facts in a situation: *He thought I was a doctor of medicine, so I put him straight and told him I was a doctor of philosophy.*

put sth straight make sth neat and tidy; organize or settle sth properly: *Please put all your papers straight before you leave the office.* ○ *When he discovered that he was dying, he started to put all his affairs straight.*

(keep) a straight 'face manage not to laugh: *When she told me about her accident with the pig, I couldn't keep a straight face.*

,straight 'up (*British, informal*) (used for telling sb that what you are saying is completely true): *'I got the best marks in the class.' 'Straight up?' 'Straight up.'*

tell, etc sb ,straight from the 'shoulder (that...) *or* **tell, etc sb straight 'out (that...)** tell, etc sb honestly and directly (that...): *He's an outspoken politician who speaks straight from the shoulder.* ○ *I told her straight out that she was wrong.*

get sth right/straight ⇨ right; **on the home straight/stretch** ⇨ home; **play it straight** ⇨ play; **right/straight away** ⇨ right; **think straight** ⇨ think

strain

strain at the 'leash (*informal*) want to be free from control; be eager to do sth: *Why don't you let her leave home? Can't you see she's straining at the leash?* ○ *He's straining at* the leash to leave Britain for somewhere sunnier.

strain every 'nerve/'sinew (to do sth) try as hard as you can (to do sth): *He strained every sinew to help us, but didn't succeed.*

strange

be/make strange bedfellows be two very different people or things that you would not expect to find together.

strapped

be ,strapped for 'cash (*informal*) have very little money: *I can't come to the cinema tonight. I'm a bit strapped for cash.*

straw

be the last/final straw *or* **be the straw that breaks the camel's back** be something bad or unwanted that happens to you after a series of other bad things, with the result that you cannot continue with sth or you break down: *I've had a terrible day, and this traffic is the last straw, I can't take any more.*

be a straw in the 'wind an unimportant incident or piece of information which shows you what might happen in the future: *Journalists are always looking for straws in the wind.*

clutch/grasp at a 'straw/'straws try to believe anything in a very difficult or desperate situation because you think it is your only hope: *The doctors have told him that he has only 6 months to live, but he won't accept it. He's going to a new clinic in Switzerland next week. He's just clutching at straws.*

draw the short straw ⇨ draw; **make bricks without straw** ⇨ bricks; **a man of straw** ⇨ man

strays **waifs and strays** ⇨ waifs

streak **a yellow streak** ⇨ yellow

stream

be/come on stream (of a factory, machine etc) be/start working or operating: *The new printing machines come on stream in March.* ○ *We're waiting for the new software to come on stream; it will make our jobs much easier.*

go, swim, etc with/against the stream/tide behave/not behave in the same way as most other people: *He's a fashion designer who's always swum against the stream; his work is very original.* ○ *Why do you always have to swim against the tide?*

street

be (right) up your street (*informal*) something which is suitable for you: *Why don't you apply for this job? It looks right up your street.*

be not in the same league/class/street ⇨ league; **the man in the street** ⇨ man

streets

be 'streets ahead (of sb/sth) (*quite informal*) be very much better (than sb/sth): *Japan is streets ahead of us in computer technology.*

on the streets (*informal*) **1** homeless: *He was weak and ill and he knew he wouldn't survive on the streets.* **2** be a prostitute: *She's been on the streets since she was fifteen.*

strength

be at full/be below full strength have/ not have the necessary number of people to do sth: *We're working below strength at the moment; it's not easy to deliver all the orders on time.* ○ *When we're working at full strength, we employ 1 300 people.*

go from strength to strength have more and more success: *Since she became the boss, the company's gone from strength to strength.*

on the strength of sth mainly because of sth: *I got the job on the strength of my experience in sales.* ○ *They were sent to prison on the strength of a tiny piece of evidence.*

a ,pillar/,tower of 'strength a person who gives you the courage and determination to continue when you are in a bad situation: *My wife has been a tower of strength during my illness.* ○ *During your five years in prison, Terry was a tower of strength.*

in force/strength ⇨ force

strengthen

strengthen your hand give you more power to do sth or act against sb/sth: *The new anti-drug laws will strengthen the hand of the police.*

stretch

at a stretch (of periods of time) without stopping; continuously: *She practises the piano for hours at a stretch.*

by 'no stretch of the imagination *or* **not by 'any stretch of the imagination** it is completely impossible to say; by no means: *By no stretch of the imagination could you call him clever.* ○ *You couldn't say that factory was beautiful, not by any stretch of the imagination!*

stretch your legs walk about after sitting or lying for a long time: *I'd been working at my desk all morning, so I went outside to stretch my legs for ten minutes.*

stretch a point allow sb to break the rules for a good reason: *You are usually only allowed one hour for lunch, but I'm prepared to stretch a point if there's an emergency.*

at full stretch ⇨ full; **bend/stretch the rules** ⇨ rules; **on the home straight/ stretch** ⇨ home

strictly

strictly speaking if we interpret these words or rules exactly or precisely, then sth is not really true or permitted: *Strictly speaking, nobody under 18 can join this club, but as you are nearly 18....* ○ *Strictly speaking, a tomato is a fruit, not a vegetable.*

stride(s)

get into your stride start to do sth well and confidently after a period of getting used to it: *She found the job difficult at first, but now she's got into her stride and she loves it.*

make great, rapid, etc strides (in sth/ doing sth) improve quickly or make fast progress (in sth/doing sth): *Tom has made enormous strides at school this year.* ○ *Ann's made huge strides in her piano-playing.*

put sb off their 'stride/'stroke disturb sb's concentration when they are doing sth: *All sorts of things can put a player off his stroke.*

take sth in your stride deal with a problem easily, without panicking or getting upset: *Joey was upset when we moved house, but Ben seems to have taken it all in his stride.*

strike(s)

strike a 'balance (between A and B) find a sensible middle point between two demands, extremes, course of action, etc: *We need to strike a balance between protecting him and letting him become more independent.* o *Children need to strike a balance between work and play at school.*

strike a 'bargain (with sb) come to an agreement (with sb), especially after a lot of discussion or argument: *They struck a bargain with the landlord to pay a lower rent in return for painting the house.*

strike a blow for/against sth act forcefully in support of/against sth (for example a belief, principle or group of people): *The workers saw the protest as a chance to strike a blow for freedom.* o *The new law would strike a blow against racism.*

strike a 'chord say or do sth which speaks directly to sb's emotions or memories: *His war poetry struck a chord with people who remembered that period.* o *The Queen's speech struck a chord with many people who were also worried about the problem.*

strike fear, terror, etc into sb/sb's heart make sb feel fear, etc: *His crimes struck horror into the nation's heart.*

strike 'gold (*informal*) find happiness, wealth, etc; find exactly what you need: *She hasn't always been lucky with her boyfriends, but I think she's struck gold this time.* o *We've struck gold here. This book has everything we need.*

,strike it 'rich (*informal*) become rich suddenly: *He struck it rich when a relative died and left him two million.*

strike (it) 'lucky (*informal*) have good luck: *We certainly struck it lucky with the weather – it's beautiful today.* o *He bets on the horses, and sometimes he strikes lucky.*

strike a pose sit, stand or lie in a position in order to attract attention: *He was striking a pose, leaning against the ship's rail.*

,strike while the ,iron is 'hot (*saying*) do sth immediately because now is a particularly good time to do sth: *He seems in a good mood. Why don't you strike while the iron is hot and ask him now?*

hit/strike home ⇨ home; **lightning never strikes twice** ⇨ lightning; **strike/ sound a false note** ⇨ false

striking
be within 'striking distance be near enough to be reached or attacked; near: *In one minute the aircraft can be within striking distance of the target.* o *There are lakes, mountains and forests all within striking distance.*

string(s)
another/a second/more than one 'string (to your bow) something else that you can use or do if the thing you are using or doing fails: *If I don't succeed as an actor, I've got another string to my bow because I'm a trained music teacher.*

(with) no 'strings attached *or* **without 'strings** with no special rules, conditions or limits: *A loan of £3000 with no strings attached.* o *It was a relationship without strings (without too much responsibility or commitment) which suited them both.*

pull strings ⇨ pull; **pull the strings** ⇨ pull

strip **tear a strip off sb** ⇨ tear

stroke
at a/one (single) 'stroke (something happens) as a result of one sudden action or event: *All my problems were solved at a stroke when an aunt left me some money.*

not do a stroke (of work) not do any work at all: *He's useless – he hasn't done a stroke of work today.* o *'Does your husband help in the house?' 'No, he doesn't do a stroke.'*

on/at the stroke of eight, midnight, etc at exactly eight o'clock, etc: *She gets to work at the stroke of nine every day.*

put sb off their stride/stroke ⇨ stride

strong
be your 'strong point/suit be a thing that you do well: *Writing letters has never been my strong point.* o *Logic is definitely not his strong suit.*

come on 'strong (with sb) (*quite informal*) speak forcefully or aggressively to sb: *Do you think I came on too strong at that meeting?*

have (got) a strong stomach not feel sick or upset when you see or experience things that are disgusting: *You've got to have a strong stomach to watch animals being killed.*

be still going strong ⇨ still

struck

be struck dumb (with sth) be suddenly unable to speak (because of shock, fear, etc): *We were struck dumb at the sight of three armed soldiers in the kitchen.* ○ *The witnesses were struck dumb with terror.* **be dumbstruck** (*adjective*) *When he told me I had won a million pounds, I was dumbstruck.*

stubborn **be stubborn as a mule** ⇨ mule

stuck

get stuck 'in(to sth) (*informal*) start doing sth eagerly or enthusiastically: *Here's your food. Now get stuck in (start eating).* ○ *We got stuck into the job immediately.*

stuff

do your 'stuff (*informal*) do sth you are good or skilled at (often while other people watch): *Joy got her guitar and went on stage to do her stuff.*

stuff him, that, etc! (*offensive*) (used to show strong dislike or rejection of sb): *'Switch that radio off, I'm trying to work!' 'Stuff you, I'll do what I like!'* ○ *He wants me to do extra work this week. Well, he can stuff it!*

'that's the stuff (*informal*) (used for telling sb that they are doing sth correctly or well, or doing sth good) that is good or what I needed: *'I'd like my hair cut shorter at the front.' 'Like this?' 'Yeah, that's the stuff.'*

be made of sterner stuff ⇨ sterner; **the hard stuff** ⇨ hard; **hot stuff** ⇨ hot; **kids' stuff** ⇨ kids; **know your stuff** ⇨ know

stuffed

a stuffed 'shirt (*informal*) a very formal and conventional person: *This office is full of stuffed shirts; there's no one friendly I can talk to.*

get knotted/stuffed ⇨ knotted

stuffing **knock the stuffing out of sb** ⇨ knock

style

be (not) sb's style be (not) the type of thing that sb enjoys; be (not) the way sb usually behaves: *Classical music's not my style; I prefer rock.* ○ *I don't like living in town much. The country is more my style.* ○ *I'm sure he didn't say that; it's not his style at all. He's* always so polite.

cramp sb's style ⇨ cramp

subject **change the subject** ⇨ change

substance

a woman, man, person, etc of substance a person who is important, powerful or rich: *In those days, a station master was a man of substance in the community.*

success **nothing succeeds like success** ⇨ nothing; **a roaring success** ⇨ roaring

such

as such **1** in the usual sense or meaning of the word: *There is no theatre as such in the town, but plays are sometimes performed in the town hall.* **2** considering sth only in theory, not in practice or in relation to a particular person or thing: *I am not interested in money as such, but I do like the freedom it can buy.* **3** because sb/sth is what it is: *The government is the main contributor and, as such, controls the project.*

such as (used for introducing examples) like: *Dairy products are things such as milk, butter, cheese or yoghurt.* ○ *'I met a lot of important people in England.' 'Such as?'*

,such as it 'is (used to say that sth is of poor quality, unsatisfactory or that there is not much of it): *You're welcome to join us for lunch, such as it is – we're only having soup and bread.* ○ *Later we went to the local nightclub, such as it was, but there was hardly anyone there.*

such is life (*informal*) (usually used for talking about sth unfortunate) that's what life is like: *He didn't get the prize he was hoping for. But such is life, I suppose.*

ever so/ever such ⇨ ever

suck **teach your grandmother to suck eggs** ⇨ teach

sudden

,all of a 'sudden (*informal*) suddenly and unexpectedly: *I was sitting reading my book when all of a sudden the lights went out.*

,sudden 'death a way of deciding who has won a game when both sides have equal points, by playing for one more point.

sudden-death (*adjective*) *They won the game after a sudden-death play-off.*

suffer

not suffer fools 'gladly not be patient or polite with people who are less intelligent than you: *He says what he thinks and doesn't suffer fools gladly. Some people consider him a bit arrogant.*

suffice

suffice it to say (that...) (used for saying that you could say much more about sb/sth but you do not want or need to): *I won't tell you all that was said at the meeting. Suffice it to say that they approved our plan.* ○ *Suffice it to say that the figures were not included in the official report.*

sugar

a 'sugar daddy (*informal*) an older man who has a much younger woman as a girlfriend and gives her presents, money, etc: *When you tell him that he's a sugar daddy, he gets very angry. He says she isn't interested in his money, only in him.*

sugar/sweeten the pill ⇨ pill

suit(s)

suit sb (right) ˌdown to the 'ground (*informal*) suit sb completely: *I've found a job that suits me down to the ground: the pay's great and I can work from home.* ○ *'We've only got beer, I'm afraid.' 'That suits me right down to the ground; that's just what I wanted.'*

be your strong point/suit ⇨ strong; **follow suit** ⇨ follow; **grey suits** ⇨ grey; **in/wearing your birthday suit** ⇨ birthday; **please/suit yourself** ⇨ yourself

summer

an Indian summer ⇨ Indian; **one swallow doesn't make a summer** ⇨ swallow

summon

pluck/summon up courage ⇨ courage

sun

under the 'sun of any kind; in the world: *He's tried every medicine under the sun, but nothing works.* ○ *I've got stamps from every country under the sun.*

catch the sun ⇨ catch; **make hay while**

the sun shines ⇨ hay; **a place in the sun** ⇨ place

Sunday(s)

your Sunday 'best (*informal*, *humorous*) your best clothes: *She got all dressed up in her Sunday best to meet her boyfriend's parents.*

a month of Sundays ⇨ month

sundry

ˌall and 'sundry (*informal*) everybody; people of all kinds: *I don't like you talking about my personal problems to all and sundry.*

sunshine

a ray of sunshine ⇨ ray

supply

be in short supply ⇨ short

support

moral support ⇨ moral

suppose

I don't suppose you could... (used as a very polite way of asking sb to help you) please...: *I don't suppose you could carry this bag for me, could you?* ○ *I don't suppose you could lend me £10, could you?*

I suppose so (used for showing that you agree but you are not happy about it): *'Can I borrow the car?' 'Yes, I suppose so, but be careful.'* ○ *'Can I invite him to the party?' 'I suppose so.'*

supposed

be (not) supposed to (do sth) **1** be (not) expected or required to do sth by rules, the law, an agreement, etc: *She's supposed to do an hour's homework every evening.* ○ *We're not supposed to be at the party for an hour yet.* **2** (used only in negative sentences) be not allowed to do sth: *You're not supposed to walk on the grass.*

what's 'that supposed to mean (*informal*) (used when you are angry about what sb has said, or do not fully understand it): *'You aren't the most popular person at school, you know.' 'What's that supposed to mean?'* ○ *'He says you're not suitable for the job.' 'What's that supposed to mean?'*

sure

for sure (*informal*) definitely: *'What time will you be here?' 'I don't know for sure yet.'* ○ *I'll be there for sure; don't worry.*

make sure **1** find out whether sth is as it should be or is true; check: *I think the door's locked, but I'd better go and make sure.* ○ *Have* *you made sure that we've got enough money?* ○ *I phoned to make sure the train had arrived.* **2** take action to check that sth is done or happens in the way you want: *I want to make sure that the party is a success.* ○ *Make sure there is enough to eat tonight.*

(as) sure as eggs is 'eggs *or* **(as) sure as I'm standing/sitting 'here** (*informal*) absolutely certain; without any doubt: *If he goes on driving at that speed, he'll end up in hospital, as sure as eggs is eggs.* ○ *That's exactly what she said, as sure as I'm standing here.*

(as) sure as hell (*US, informal*) certainly; without doubt: *Joe sure as hell won't want to dress up in a suit and tie.*

sure enough (*informal*) exactly as expected or as sb said: *She said she was going to give up her job and, sure enough, she did.* ○ *They said it would rain, and, sure enough, it did.*

,sure 'thing (*especially US, informal*) yes; of course: *'Will you come tonight?' 'Sure thing!'* ○ *'Can you help me with this table?' 'Sure thing.'*

surely slowly but surely ⇨ slowly

surface
below/beneath the surface what you cannot see but can only guess at or feel: *She seems very calm but beneath the surface I'm sure that she's very upset.* ○ *Beneath the surface of this beautiful city there is terrible poverty and suffering, that tourists never see.*

on the 'surface when you consider the obvious things, and not the deeper, hidden things: *On the surface she can be very pleasant and helpful, but underneath she's got problems.* ○ *The plan seems all right on the surface.*

scratch the surface ⇨ scratch

surprise
surprise, surprise (*informal, ironic*) (used when you are not surprised that sth has happened): *'There's nothing worth watching on TV tonight.' 'Surprise, surprise (there is usually nothing worth watching)!'*

take sb by sur'prise happen to sb unexpectedly; surprise sb: *The announcement of his death took us all by surprise.* ○ *They didn't know she was coming, so her arrival took them by surprise.*

suspicion
be a,bove/be,yond su'spicion be so good or honest that nobody thinks you would do sth bad: *He is absolutely beyond suspicion.*

be under su'spicion (of sth) be the person that the police think has committed a crime although they cannot prove it yet: *He was still under suspicion and he knew the police were watching him.*

swallow
one swallow doesn't make a summer (*saying*) you mustn't take too seriously a small sign that sth is happening or will happen in the future: *'We got a big order from Sweden this morning. Things are getting better.' 'One swallow doesn't make a summer, you know. Don't be too optimistic.'*

swallow the bait (*informal*) accept an offer, etc which has been made or prepared specially by sb in order to get you to do sth: *When people read the words 'Free Gift' on a magazine they usually swallow the bait and buy it.*

swallow your pride decide to act in a way you are ashamed of or embarrassed by because you want or need sth very much: *I didn't know what to do, so I swallowed my pride and asked my father for the money to pay the bill.* ○ *She is very independent and it was hard for her to swallow her pride and ask for help.*

swap
change/swap horses in midstream ⇨ horses

sway
hold sway ⇨ hold

swear
swear 'blind (that...) (*informal*) say emphatically that sth is true/not true: *She swore blind that she had not taken the money, and I believe her.* ○ *Peter swears blind he hasn't used the telephone, so it must be Janet who's been telephoning Australia.*

swear like a 'trooper use many swear words; use bad language: *She's only fourteen, but she swears like a trooper.* (a trooper is a soldier)

swear sb to 'secrecy make sb promise not to tell a secret: *Before telling her what happened, I had sworn her to secrecy.*

sweat
be in a sweat 1 *or* **be all of a 'sweat** (*informal*) be wet with sweat because it is hot or you have been running, etc: *I had to run to*

work this morning because I got up late. I was in a real sweat when I arrived. **2** or **be in a cold 'sweat** be very frightened or worried about sth: *I woke up during the night in a cold sweat worrying about the exam.*

no 'sweat (*very informal*) (used as a way of saying that sth is not difficult or any trouble): *'Thanks for driving me to the station.' 'No sweat (it is no trouble).'* ○ *'How was the exam?' 'I passed that one, no sweat.'*

sweat 'blood (*informal*) **1** work very hard; make a very great effort: *I sweated blood to get that essay finished on time.* **2** be very worried or afraid: *He sweats blood every time the telephone rings, in case it's the police.*

sweat it 'out (*informal*) suffer an unpleasant situation; wait for sth unpleasant to end: *I hate this job, but I'm going to sweat it out and hope something better comes along.* ○ *After the competition we just had to sit there and sweat it out until the result was announced.*

sweat like a pig (*very informal*) sweat very much: *It's 35 degrees inside the factory; the workers are sweating like pigs.*

sweep

sweep the 'board win all or most of the prizes, games, money, etc: *At the Oscar ceremony last night France swept the board, with six major prizes.*

sweep/brush sth under the 'carpet (*informal*) hide sth which might cause trouble, or which you do not want other people to know: *No matter how unwelcome the results of the enquiry may be, they must not be swept under the carpet.*

sweep sb off their feet (*informal*) attract sb very strongly because you are exciting, charming, etc: *She's waiting for a nice young man to come and sweep her off her feet.* ○ *I was swept off my feet by her wit and charm.*

make a clean sweep ⇨ clean

sweet

do sth in your ,own sweet 'time/'way (*informal*) do sth, taking as much time as you want or in the way that you want, usually despite the feelings or wishes of other people: *I tried to give her advice but she just went on in her own sweet way.* ○ *It's no use trying to hurry him. He'll do it in his own sweet time.*

have a sweet 'tooth like to eat sweet things: *I've got a sweet tooth, so I'd find it difficult to give up sugar in my tea.*

keep sb sweet (*informal*) be pleasant and nice to sb, so that they will treat you well: *I have to keep my mother sweet because I want to borrow the car.*

sweet F'A (*informal*) nothing; nothing important: *'What happened while I was away?' 'Sweet FA'* ('FA' stands for 'fuck all' (*offensive*) or the more polite 'Fanny Adams')

sweet 'nothings (*informal, usually humorous*) pleasant but unimportant words said by lovers: *He was whispering sweet nothings to somebody on the telephone.*

be short and sweet ⇨ short

sweeten sugar/sweeten the pill ⇨ pill

sweetness

be all ,sweetness and 'light (used to describe people or relationships) be (usually) friendly and reasonable: *She's all sweetness and light as long as you're doing what she wants.* ○ *Their quarrel seems to be over. Everything's all sweetness and light at the moment.*

swim

be/keep/stay/remain in the 'swim (*informal*) be, etc socially active, fashionable or aware of what is happening: *After being away for two years, it took a while before she was in the swim of things again.*

sink or swim ⇨ sink

swine cast pearls before swine ⇨ cast

swing(s)

get in/into the 'swing (of sth) (*informal*) become involved in sth and start to do it well and enjoy it: *I've only been at university a week, so I haven't got into the swing of things yet.* ○ *He was just getting in the swing of his performance when all the lights went out.*

go with a 'swing (*informal*) (of a party or entertainment) be lively, enjoyable and successful: *Their house-warming party really went with a swing.*

swing into 'action start to act efficiently and quickly: *When the police heard about the the bomb, they swung into action, searching the area with dogs and moving the public to safety.*

,swings and 'roundabouts (*especially*

British, informal) (used when you want to say that gaining one thing usually means losing another thing): *Higher earnings mean more tax, so it's swings and roundabouts.* ○ *What you gain on the swings you'll probably lose on the roundabouts.*

in full swing ➪ full; **no room to swing a cat** ➪ room

swoop at one fell swoop ➪ fell

sword(s) cross swords ➪ cross; **the pen is mightier than the sword** ➪ pen

syllable in words of one syllable ➪ words

symbol a status symbol ➪ status

system(s)
get sth out of your 'system (*informal*) **1** try to deal with and forget sth painful: *Tell him how angry you really feel. Get it out of your system.* **2** do sth that you have always wanted to do very much, and perhaps find that it is not right for you: *When I was a teenager I was obsessed with ballet, but by the time I left school I had got it out of my system.*

all systems 'go! (*informal, humorous*) let's go! let's begin!: *Have we got everything we need? Right, it's all systems go!*

T

T
to a 'T/'tee (*British, informal*) exactly; perfectly: *This new job suits me to a T (is exactly what I want).* ○ *This portrait is excellent; it's Rosemary to a T.*

tab pick up the tab ➪ pick

table(s)
on the 'table (*British*) (used in business, to talk about a suggestion, plan or amount of money which is being discussed or offered): *In today's meeting there were several new proposals on the table.* ○ *The company can put an extra one per cent on the table, in return for an agreement on overtime.*

drink sb under the table ➪ drink; **put/ lay your cards on the table** ➪ cards; **turn the tables** ➪ turn

tabs
keep tabs on sb/sth (*informal*) watch sb/ sth very carefully; keep informed about sb/ sth: *I'm not sure about Johnson – we'd better keep tabs on him until we know we can trust him.* ○ *I'm keeping tabs on the number of private phone calls David makes from the office.*

tacks get down to brass tacks ➪ brass

tail(s)
be, keep, etc on sb's 'tail (*informal*) (of

the police, a spy, etc) be, etc following sb closely (often in order to find out where they are going): *I had the feeling there was someone on my tail.*

have, etc your 'tail between your legs (*informal*) be weak, ashamed, humiliated or afraid, because you have been defeated or proved wrong: *They thought they would win easily, but they've gone home with their tails between their legs.*

(at) the tail end (of sth) (at) the final or last part (of sth): *I didn't hear most of the conversation – I only came in at the tail end.*

the tail is wagging the 'dog *or* **let the tail wag the 'dog** (*quite informal*) (used to describe a situation where a small, unimportant thing controls a larger, more important thing): *In this company the workers tell the manager what he can and cannot do. It's a real case of the tail wagging the dog.*

heads or tails ➪ heads; **(not) make head (n)or tail of sth** ➪ head; **a sting in the tail** ➪ sting; **turn tail** ➪ turn

take(s)
you can't take her, him, etc 'anywhere (*often humorous*) (used about a person who behaves badly in public and, as a result, embarrasses you): *You've got soup*

all over your shirt – I can't take you anywhere, can I?

take sth as it 'comes deal with difficulties as they happen, without worrying too much: *I don't plan for the future. I like to take life as it comes.*

take it (often used with can/could) (*informal*) be able to bear or tolerate sth difficult or unpleasant such as stress, criticism or pain: *They argued so much that finally he couldn't take it any more and he left her.* ○ *People are rude to her in her job, and she feels she's taken it for long enough.*

take it (that. . .) (used for checking with sb that sth is true) think or suppose (that sth is true, will happen, etc): *'I take it that you won't be back for lunch,' she said as they left.* ○ *You speak French, I take it?*

take it from here/there start doing sth on your own that another person has been doing before you, or has been explaining to you: *I explained how to start the machine, and let him take it from there.*

take it from 'me (that. . .) (*informal*) you should believe me, because I have personal experience of. . .: *Take it from me that it's not easy to become a professional writer.*

take it on/upon yourself to do sth decide to do sth without asking anybody for permission: *He took it upon himself to sack my secretary. He had no right to do that.*

take it 'out of sb *or* **take a lot 'out of sb** make sb very tired or weak: *Driving all day really takes it out of you.* ○ *Flu takes it out of you.*

take it out on 'sb/'sth (*informal*) behave towards sb/sth unpleasantly because you feel angry or upset about another person or thing: *I know you've had a bad day at work, but don't take it out on me.*

take sb 'out of herself/himself amuse or entertain sb and so make them feel less worried about their problems or less unhappy: *She was very depressed when her brother died. We took her on holiday to try to take her out of herself.*

it takes one to know one (*informal, saying*) (used for showing disapproval) you are the same kind of person as the person you are criticizing: *'Your brother is a real idiot.' 'Well, it takes one to know one.'*

tale **live to tell the tale** ⇨ live; **an old wives' tale** ⇨ old; **a tall story/tale** ⇨ tall; **tell its own tale/story** ⇨ tell; **tell the same, a different, etc tale/story** ⇨ tell

tales **tell tales** ⇨ tell; **tell tales out of school** ⇨ tell

talk

be all 'talk (and no action) (used for showing disapproval) be a person who talks a lot about what they are going to do or have done without doing much: *Don't listen to her promises – she's all talk and no action.*

be the talk of sth (*informal*) be sth that everybody is interested in and talking about: *His collection is the talk of the Milan fashion shows.*

'you can/can't talk (*informal*) you shouldn't criticize sb because you are also guilty of the same fault: *'He's always late for appointments.' 'You can talk! You're hardly ever on time yourself.'*

talk about. . . (*informal*) (used as an exclamation) very or extremely: *Did you watch the programme on the Labour Party last night. Talk about biased!*

talk 'big (used for showing disapproval) tell people how good you are or promise many things: *The President talks big but he doesn't do anything.*

talk dirty talk about sex: *I love it when you talk dirty.*

talk your 'head off (*informal*) talk a lot: *He talked his head off all evening.*

talk the hind legs off a donkey (*informal, humorous*) (mainly used with *can* or *could*) talk for a long time: *He would make a good politician – he could talk the hind legs off a donkey!*

talk 'shop talk about your work or business in a social situation with sb who works with you: *Are you two talking shop again? Why don't you forget business for a while and come and meet my friends?*

talk through the back of your head (*informal*) talk nonsense: *If he says that he's going to win the prize, he's talking through the back of his head.*

talk to a brick wall (*informal*) (used when sb refuses to listen to your advice, ideas, explanations, etc): *Talking to him is like* *talking to a brick wall. He just won't listen.*

talk 'turkey (*especially US, informal*) discuss the practical details of sth seriously and honestly: *Look, Mark, it's time we talked turkey. How much money can you invest in the company?*

talk your way out of sth/doing sth avoid trouble by talking or arguing cleverly: *He tried to talk his way out of it by saying someone else was responsible.* ○ *I'd like to see her talk her way out of this one (the present trouble).*

a pep talk ⇨ pep; **pillow talk** ⇨ pillow; **small talk** ⇨ small; **speak/talk of the devil** ⇨ devil; **speak/talk the same/a different language** ⇨ language

talking

now you're 'talking (*informal*) (used for showing interest and enthusiasm about sth just said, for example a good suggestion): *'Why don't we go to Paris for the weekend?' 'Now you're talking.'*

talking of sb/sth (used for saying that you intend to say more about sb/sth just mentioned): *'I was out last night with Dave, Mark and Angela...' 'Talking of Mark, did he tell you about his latest business idea?'*

know what you are talking about ⇨ know

talks **money talks** ⇨ money

tall

be a tall 'order be a very difficult task or request: *Finishing this work by the end of the week is a tall order, but I'll try.*

a tall 'story/'tale a story which is very difficult to believe: *What she says about her grandfather being a foreign prince sounds like a tall story to me.* ○ *There were many tall tales told later about the events of that day.*

great/tall oaks from little acorns grow ⇨ oaks; **walk tall** ⇨ walk

tandem

in tandem (with sb/sth) (*quite formal*) together (with sb/sth): *These two computers are designed to work in tandem.* ○ *She runs the business in tandem with her husband.*

tangent

go/fly off at a 'tangent change suddenly from talking or thinking about one thing to talking or thinking about another: *One moment the professor is working hard on a problem in physics, the next he's gone off at a tangent and he's talking about bees.*

tantrum

throw a tantrum/wobbly ⇨ throw

tap

(be) on tap (be) ready and available for immediate use: *I've got plenty of people on tap to help us if we need them.*

tape

red tape ⇨ red

tar

tar sb/sth with the same brush judge a whole group of people or things unfairly because of your bad experience with one or a few of them: *Because his older brother had been a troublemaker at the school, Paul was automatically tarred with the same brush. It wasn't fair!*

spoil the ship for a ha'porth/ha'penny worth of tar ⇨ spoil

target

a sitting duck/target ⇨ sitting

task

take sb to task (about/for/over sth) criticize sb forcefully (for doing sth wrong): *I was taken to task for arriving late.* ○ *She took the Government to task over its economic record.*

taste

an acquired taste ⇨ acquired; **be a taste of things to come = be the shape of things to come** ⇨ shape; **give sb a taste/dose of their own medicine** ⇨ medicine; **leave a bad/nasty taste in the/your mouth** ⇨ leave; **there's no accounting for taste(s)** ⇨ accounting

tat

tit for tat ⇨ tit

tatters

be in tatters **1** (of clothes) be ragged or torn: *He got into a fight and came home with his clothes in tatters.* **2** (*quite informal*) (used to describe a plan, idea, person's feelings, etc) be ruined or destroyed: *She's failed her exams, and now all her hopes of becoming a doctor are in tatters.* ○ *His career and his reputation are both in tatters after the scandal.*

tea

(would not do sth) for all the tea in 'China (*informal*) never; not for any reason at all: *'If you marry him you'll be a rich woman.' 'I wouldn't marry him for all the tea in China.'*

sb's cup of tea ⇨ **cup**

teach

teach your grandmother to suck 'eggs (*informal*) tell sb how to do sth or give advice to sb when they are more knowledgeable or more experienced than you.

teach sb a lesson *or* **teach sb (to do sth)** learn from a punishment or because of an unpleasant experience, that you have done sth wrong or made a mistake: *He needs to be taught a lesson* (he should be punished). ○ *Losing all his money in a card game taught him a lesson he's never forgotten.* ○ *That'll teach you! You'll be more careful with your money in future!*

(you can't) teach an old dog new 'tricks (*saying*) (you can't) make old people change their ideas or ways of working, etc: *My grandmother doesn't want a microwave. She says you can't teach an old dog new tricks.*

can/could teach/tell sb a thing or two = **know a thing or two** ⇨ **know**

teacup **a storm in a teacup** ⇨ **storm**

tear

tear your 'hair (out) (*informal*) be very worried or angry: *Why were you late home? Your mother and I were tearing our hair out wondering where you were!* ○ *The teacher nearly tore his hair out when he found the children had written in the register.*

tear sb 'limb from 'limb (*often humorous*) attack sb very violently: *Julian looked so angry that I thought he was going to tear his brother limb from limb.*

tear (yourself/sth) loose (from sb/sth) escape from sb/sth by using great force: *He put his arms round my neck but I tore myself loose and ran for help.*

tear a 'strip off sb (*becoming dated*) criticize sb because you are angry about sth they have said or done.

tear sb/sth to shreds/pieces criticize sb/sth; totally destroy sth: *The press tore the Government's economic plans to shreds.* ○ *The winger tore the Cardiff defence to pieces.* ○ *The Prime Minister tore his opponents' arguments to pieces.*

wear and tear ⇨ **wear**

tears

bore sb to death/to tears ⇨ **bore; crocodile tears** ⇨ **crocodile**

tee

to a T/tee ⇨ **T**

teeth

get your teeth into sth do sth with enthusiasm, for example a job which requires a great effort from you: *This job is too easy. Why can't they give me something I can really get my teeth into?*

(do sth) in the teeth of danger, opposition, etc (do sth) when or even though it is dangerous or people oppose it, etc: *The new law was passed in the teeth of strong opposition.* ○ *They crossed the Atlantic in the teeth of a force 10 wind.*

armed to the teeth ⇨ **armed; cut your teeth on sth** ⇨ **cut; do sth by the skin of your teeth** ⇨ **skin; fed up to the back teeth with sb/sth** ⇨ **fed; get/take the bit between your teeth** ⇨ **bit; grit your teeth** ⇨ **grit; kick sb in the teeth** ⇨ **kick; lie through your teeth** ⇨ **lie; set sb's teeth on edge** ⇨ **set; show your teeth** ⇨ **show**

teething

have, get, etc 'teething troubles (*quite informal*) experience small problems or difficulties in the development of a product, business, etc, or when sth new first becomes available to the public: *If your new car is having teething troubles, take it back to the garage where you bought it.* (refers to the problems babies have when their teeth first appear)

telegraph

bush telegraph ⇨ **bush**

telephone

be on the 'telephone/'phone **1** be speaking to sb by telephone: *Mr Perkins is on the telephone but he'll be with you in a moment.* **2** have a telephone at home: *They live on a small island and are not on the phone.*

tell

I/I'll tell you what or **I know 'what** (*informal*) (said before making a suggestion): *I tell you what – let's ask Fred to lend us his car.* ○ *I know what! Why don't you buy her a piano?*

I (can/can't) tell you (used for emphasis): *I tell you, we've got more unemployment in this country than ever before.* ○ *It's not as easy as it looks, I can tell you.* ○ *I can't tell you how happy I felt* (it is difficult to describe my happiness, because it was so great).

tell it how/like it is (*informal*) tell sth honestly and directly: *All right, I'll tell it like it is. I don't love you Rachel, and I never have.*

tell its own tale/story explain or show sth, without the need of any more explanations or comment: *The burned buildings and broken glass in the streets tell their own story.*

tell me another (*informal*) (used for saying that you don't believe sb because they are joking or exaggerating): *'I caught a fish that weighed 5 kilos on holiday.' 'Tell me another, will you. I bet it didn't even weigh a kilo.'*

tell the same, a different, another, etc tale/story (of sth) show the same, etc thing: *These two photographs of the city tell a very different story.* ○ *The faces of these children tell the same story of hunger and misery.*

tell 'tales (about sb) (*informal*) tell sb, especially sb in authority, that another person has done something wrong: *How did the boss know that I was late for work this morning? I think somebody's been telling tales about me.*

tell tales out of school talk about the private affairs of a group or organization, to people who do not belong to it: *I shouldn't tell tales out of school, but my company is in serious trouble.*

tell sb ,where to get 'off or **tell sb ,where they get 'off** (*very informal*) tell sb angrily that you do not like the way they are behaving and you no longer accept it: *He gets drunk every time we go to a party, so I've told him where to get off.*

tell the (whole) 'world tell sth to everyone; tell sth publicly: *Keep your voice down! We don't want to tell the whole world about it!*

you ,never ,can 'tell or **you can ,never 'tell** (*saying*) (often used to talk about people) you can never be sure; you can never know exactly what will happen: *'Is he happy?' 'I don't know. You can never tell with him.'* ○ *'Who's going to win?' 'In weather conditions like these you never can tell.'*

can/could teach/tell sb a thing or two = **know a thing or two** ⇨ know; **can/could tell/see a mile off** ⇨ mile; **live to tell the tale** ⇨ live; **not know/not be able to tell one end of sth from the other** ⇨ end; **time will tell** ⇨ time; **what did I tell you** ⇨ what

telling

you're telling 'me! (*informal*) (used for saying that you already know and completely agree with what sb has just said): *'Cooking for ten people is hard work.' 'You're telling me.'*

there is no knowing/saying/telling ⇨ knowing

temper

keep/lose your 'temper remain calm although you are annoyed/become very angry: *You must learn to keep your temper.* ○ *He loses his temper very quickly if you argue with him.*

temperature

get/have/run a 'temperature have a higher body temperature than normal: *She's got a headache and she's running a temperature.*

take sb's 'temperature measure the heat of sb's body, using a thermometer: *The nurse took my temperature; it was 38°.*

raise the temperature ⇨ raise

tempt

tempt 'fate/'providence take a risk or do something dangerous: *'I don't think I'll insure my boat.' 'Don't tempt fate. Insure it.'*

ten

ten to one (that...) (*quite informal*) it's very likely that...; very probably: *Ten to one they'll never find out who did it anyway.*

be two/ten a penny ⇨ penny; **nine times out of ten** ⇨ nine; **the top ten** ⇨ top

tender

(be) at a tender 'age or **(be) at the
tender ˌage of '8, '12, etc** (quite formal)
(be) young: *We were sent to boarding school at
a tender age.* ○ *At the tender age of seventeen I
left home.*

tenterhooks

be, etc on 'tenterhooks be, etc very
tense, excited or anxious about what might
happen: *We were kept on tenterhooks for hours
while the judges chose the winner.*

tenths
**possession is nine points/
tenths/parts of the law** ⇨ possession

term

**(do sth) in the 'long/'medium/'short
term** (do sth), looking or planning for a
long/medium/short time into the future: *In
the short term, we can send the refugees food
and clothing, but in the long term we must do
something about the basic problems.* **long-
term, short-term** (adjectives) *a long-term
approach* ○ *short-term problems*

terms

**be on good, bad, friendly, etc 'terms
(with sb)** have a good, etc relationship
(with sb): *He's not on very good terms with his
wife's family.*

come to terms with sth learn to accept
sth that is difficult or unpleasant: *He finally
came to terms with his father's death.*

do sth on sb's/your (own) terms do sth
in a way that sb chooses/you choose
because they/you are in a position of power:
*The Americans agreed to stop fighting, but on
their own terms: all prisoners to be released,
and talks to be held immediately.*

in terms of 'sth or **in 'sth terms** (used to
show how sth is explained, described or
judged): *In terms of money, it's a great job.* ○ *In
energy terms, this new power station can
produce ten times as much as the old type.*

on the same terms (as sb/sth) or **on
equal terms (with sb/sth)** with no
difference or advantage over another
person; as equals: *We're not competing on
equal terms; the other team has one more
player.* ○ *A good teacher should treat all her
pupils on the same terms.*

**on unfair/unequal terms (with sb/
sth)** with unfair/unequal conditions; not as

equals: *We are competing on unfair terms with
the steel industry in France.*

be on nodding terms with sb
⇨ nodding; **be on speaking terms**
⇨ speaking; **a contradiction in terms**
⇨ contradiction; **in glowing terms/
colours** ⇨ glowing; **say, tell sb, etc in no
uncertain terms** ⇨ uncertain

test

put sth to the 'test test sth; find out
whether sth is good, bad, true, real, etc: *The
second part of the contest will put your general
knowledge to the test.*

test the water/waters try to find out
whether sth is likely to succeed, by asking
people for their opinions before you do sth:
*Your idea might not be popular with people, so
before you start marketing it you should test the
waters.*

the acid test ⇨ acid; **stand the test of
time** ⇨ stand

tether **at the end of your tether** ⇨ end

Thames **not/never set the Thames/
world on fire** ⇨ set

thank

I'll thank you (not) to do sth or **I'll
thank you for sth/doing sth** (used
when you are angry or annoyed, to ask sb in
a formal way (not) to do sth): *I'll thank you
not to interfere in my personal affairs.*

thank 'God! or **thank 'goodness/
'Heaven(s)!** (used as an expression of
relief): *Thank God you've arrived. I was so
worried.*

thank your lucky stars (that...) be
very grateful (that...): *You should thank your
lucky stars that you're young and healthy.*

thankful
**be grateful/thankful for
small mercies** ⇨ small

thanks

(be) ˌno thanks to 'sb/'sth (informal) (be)
in spite of sb/sth: *It's no thanks to you that we
arrived on time – you kept wanting to stop!*

thanks to 'sb/'sth (informal) because of
sb/sth: *We won the game thanks to a lot of hard
work from everyone in the team.* ○ *We lost the
match, thanks to a few silly mistakes.*

a vote of thanks ⇨ vote

that

and (all) that (*informal*) and that sort of
thing; and all the other things: *My brother's
got a farm, with chickens, cows, pigs and all
that.* ○ *Her paintings are well done and all that,
but I find them rather boring.*

at that **1** when that happened: *He said
she was a fool. At that, she walked out of the
room.* **2** (*informal*) as well; either: *She
suggested that we should write to our Member
of Parliament, and it's not such a bad idea at
that.*

is that so? (*informal*) **1** (used for telling
sb that you are not frightened by their
actions or threats): *'If you don't shut your
mouth I'll kick you out of the house.' 'Is that so?
You just try it!'* **2** (used to express surprise
or interest at what sb has said): *'He owns
twenty cats.' 'Is that so?'*

(just) like that without hesitating: *I asked
him for £100 and he gave it to me just like that.*

that is (to say) **1** in other words: *I'm
between jobs at the moment; that's to say
unemployed.* ○ *It cost him a week's wages, that
is, £300.* **2** (used to give more
information or to correct what has already
been said): *She's a housewife – when she's not
teaching English, that is.* ○ *Let him explain it –
if he can, that is.* ○ *Nobody wants to do it.
Nobody except me, that is.*

that's a good one (*informal*) **1** (said in
reply to a joke or clever remark). **2**
(*ironic*) (said in reply to a stupid remark or
action): *'Can you make dinner? I'm tired.'
'Tired? That's a good one. I've been working all
day and you've done nothing.'*

that's (about) 'it (*informal*) **1** (used for
saying that an activity, job, etc is finished):
That's it for today. We can go home now. ○
*That's about it. I've said all I wanted to
say.* **2** (used to agree with or confirm
what sb has just said): *'You mean you won't
get more than £5 000.' 'That's about it.'*

that's just 'it or **that's just the
'trouble** (*informal*) that is exactly the
problem: *'You only need to spend £5 more and
you can get a really good dictionary.' 'That's
just it, I'm afraid – I haven't got another £5.'*

that's more 'like it (*informal*) that is
better: *Turn the music up louder! That's more
like it!*

(and/so) ,that's 'that (used to show that

sth is finished or decided, and there should
be no more discussion or argument): *So
that's that. At last we're all agreed.* ○ *You're
going to bed now, and that's that! I don't want
any argument!*

them

,them and 'us (used to describe a situation
in which two groups are opposed to each
other, often with one group more powerful
than the other): *We should try to get away
from a 'them and us' attitude between
employers and workers.*

theme **variations on the theme of sth**
⇨ variations

then **now and again/then** ⇨ now; **then
again = there again** ⇨ there; **then and
there = there and then** ⇨ there; **there
and then** ⇨ there

there

be not all there *or* **be not quite there**
(*informal*) think slowly because of low
intelligence, illness, drugs, etc: *Are you sure
he's all there?*

so there! (*informal*) (used for emphasizing
your satisfaction with sth or for
emphasizing a refusal, etc): *I got a better
mark than you. So there!* (usually used by
children and considered unpleasant)

there again *or* **then again** (*informal*)
(used for introducing an extra piece of
information which explains sth or gives
another explanation): *I thought you loved me,
but then again I was never really sure.*

(do sth) ,there and 'then *or* **(do sth)
,then and 'there** (do sth) at that time and
place: *I took one look at the car and offered to
buy it then and there.*

there ,is 'that (said when agreeing with
sth): *'Flying is quick, but it's very expensive.'
'Yes, there is that.'*

(and/but/so) there it 'is *or* **(and/but/
so) there you 'go** *or* **(and/but/so) there
we/you 'are** (said to show acceptance of a
situation that you do not like and that you
would change if you could) that is the
situation; those are the facts: *I don't like my
job, but I need the money, so there it is.* ○ *Soup
and bread isn't the best of meals, but there you
go.*

'there's a good boy, girl, dog, etc

(*informal*) (used to praise or encourage small children or animals): *Finish your dinner, there's a good lad.* ○ *Sit! There's a good dog.*

,**there, 'there!** (*informal*) (used to comfort a small child): *There, there! Never mind, you'll soon feel better.*

,**there you 'are** **1** (used when you give sth to sb): *I've got your newspaper. There you are.* **2** (used when you are explaining how to do sth) it is done or ready: *You cook it on both sides for three minutes and there you are. The perfect steak.* **3** (used when sth happens which shows that you were right): *There you are. I told you we'd miss the train.*

there you 'go (*informal*) (used when you give sb sth): *There you go. That's £5.29 change.*

there you 'go (a'gain) *or* **there sb 'goes (a'gain)** (used to criticize sb because they are behaving badly again or saying the same things again and again): *There you go again – as soon as we disagree you start shouting at me!* ○ *There he goes again – always complaining about something.*

here and there ⇨ here; **here, there, and everywhere** ⇨ here

thick

be (as) thick as 'thieves (with sb) (*informal*) (of two or more people) be very friendly with each other.

be (as) thick as two short 'planks be very stupid.

give sb/get a thick 'ear (*very informal*) hit sb/be hit on the side of the head, as a punishment: *If you don't behave yourself you'll get a thick ear.*

(be) in the thick of sth/doing sth (be) in the busiest or most active part of sth/ doing sth; (be) in the most crowded part of sth: *He was in the thick of preparing the food for the party, so I didn't interrupt.* ○ *If there's trouble, you usually find him in the thick of it.*

,**thick and 'fast** quickly and in great numbers or quantities: *Replies to our advertisement are coming in thick and fast.* ○ *By midnight, the snow was falling thick and fast.*

(be) thick with sth/sb (be) full of sth/sb: *The air was thick with the scent of roses.* ○ *The street was thick with reporters and photographers.*

through ,thick and 'thin despite all the difficulties and problems; in good and bad times: *He's been a good friend to her through thick and thin.*

a bit thick/strong ⇨ bit; **get sth into your/sb's thick head** ⇨ head; **a thin/ thick skin** ⇨ skin

thickens the plot thickens ⇨ plot

thicker blood is thicker than water ⇨ blood

thief

like a thief in the night secretly or unexpectedly. (from the Bible)

thieves be thick as thieves ⇨ thick

thin

appear, etc out of thin air appear, etc suddenly from nowhere or nothing: *The car seemed to appear out of thin air. I didn't have time to brake.* ○ *She seems to conjure wonderful costumes out of thin air.*

as thin as a 'rake too thin: *You're as thin as a rake. You certainly don't need to diet.*

be/get thin on top (*informal*) be/go bald: *Max is only 30 but he's already getting a bit thin on top.*

disappear, etc into thin air disappear suddenly and mysteriously: *The money vanished into thin air. Nobody knows what happened to it.*

have a thin 'time (of it) be in an unsuccessful period in your business: *Small businesses are having a thin time of it at the moment; a lot are closing down.*

the thin end of the 'wedge (used for saying that you fear that one small request, order or act, etc is only the beginning of sth larger and more serious or harmful): *The government says it only wants to privatize one or two railway lines, but I think it's the thin end of the wedge. They'll all be privatized soon.*

thin on the ground not easy to find because they are scarce: *Good science teachers are thin on the ground.*

be skating on thin ice ⇨ skating; **a thin/ thick skin** ⇨ skin; **through thick and thin** ⇨ thick; **wear thin** ⇨ wear

thing

be just the thing *or* **be the very thing**

be exactly what you need or want: *Hot lemon juice and honey is just the thing for a cold.* ○ *A holiday by the sea, with plenty of swimming and walking, would be the very thing.*

be a near/close thing *or* **be a close-run thing** (*informal*) **1** a competition, election, race, etc which you only just succeed in winning: *I know we won, but believe me, it was a near thing. They could easily have beaten us.* **2** a punishment, accident, etc which you only just avoided: *The police searched the house but they didn't find him. It was a close thing.*

be on to a good 'thing (*quite informal*) be in a position or situation which brings you a lot of benefits: *They've offered her a company car, a month's holiday and a huge salary. She's on to a good thing there.*

do your own 'thing (*informal*) live, act or behave as you want, not as others tell you to do; be independent: *Mark's father wanted him to be a doctor, but Mark wanted to do his own thing and run an art gallery.*

the done 'thing the socially correct way to behave: *Smoking while somebody else is eating is not the done thing.* ○ *It's the done thing to dress for dinner in this hotel.*

have (got) a thing about sb/sth (*informal*) have very strong feelings, either positive or negative, about sb/sth: *I think she's got a thing about David. She keeps looking at him.* ○ *I've got a thing about smoking, and I don't allow anybody to smoke in my house.*

it's ,one thing to do ,X, it's (quite) a,nother (thing) to do 'Y (used for saying that you find the first thing acceptable or possible but the second thing definitely unacceptable or impossible): *It's one thing to write a short article; it's quite another to write a whole book on the subject.*

make a (big) 'thing (out) of sth (*informal*) make sth seem much more serious or important than it really is: *It was only a small mistake, but he made a really big thing out of it.*

the thing 'is (used before an explanation, objection or further information about sth already said) the problem, the question, the fact, etc is: *You want to expand the business. The thing is, we haven't got the money to do that.*

amount/come to the same thing ⇨ same; **can/could teach/tell sb a thing or two = know a thing or two** ⇨ know; **chance would be a fine thing** ⇨ chance; **first thing** ⇨ first; **for one thing…** ⇨ one; **a good job/thing** ⇨ job; **a good job/thing too** ⇨ job; **know a thing or two** ⇨ know; **last thing** ⇨ last; **the next best thing** ⇨ next; **the next thing** ⇨ next; **not know the first thing about sb/sth** ⇨ know; **one thing and another** ⇨ one; **the real thing/McCoy** ⇨ real; **sure thing** ⇨ sure

things

all things con'sidered considering all the facts, especially the problems or difficulties, of a situation: *She's had a lot of financial problems since her husband died but she seems very cheerful, all things considered.*

as things 'stand the present situation is that: *As things stand, we won't finish the job on time; but if we get some extra help, we might.*

be all things to all men (*saying*) change the way you behave or what you say to try to please the people you are with: *The President's attempts to be all things to all men had disastrous consequences.*

in all things (*formal*) in every situation; always: *I believe in honesty in all things.* ○ *Moderation in all things is my motto.*

(just) one of those things (used when sth unfortunate has happened) unfortunate things do happen sometimes and we must accept this fact: *He doesn't love me any more and there's absolutely nothing I can do about it. It's just one of those things.*

other/all things being 'equal if nothing else changes; if other conditions remain the same: *Other things being equal, prices will rise if people's incomes rise.*

these ,things are sent to 'try us (*saying*) (said to sb sympathetically when sth bad has happened) problems like this are sent (by God) to test our patience, courage, etc: *'My car broke down again.' 'Oh well, these things are sent to try us.'*

,things that go ,bump in the 'night (*humorous*) strange or frightening noises, or things that cannot be explained by science: *I don't believe in ghosts or spirits, or things that go bump in the night.*

as it/things turned out ⇨ turned; be/
feel out of it/things ⇨ out; be the shape
of things to come ⇨ shape; be a taste
of things to come = be the shape of things
to come ⇨ shape; by/from the look of it/
things ⇨ look; first things first ⇨ first;
have your mind on other things
⇨ mind; in the nature of things
⇨ nature; one of those things ⇨ one;
overdo it/things ⇨ overdo; put things
right ⇨ right; the scheme of things
⇨ scheme; see things ⇨ see

think

anyone would think (that...) *or* **you
would have thought (that...)** (used to
talk about sb's unreasonable or surprising
behaviour) if you did not know the truth, it
would seem that...: *Don't be so nervous!
Anyone would think you'd never been to a party
before!*

come to think of it *or* **thinking about
it** (*informal*) (said when you suddenly
remember or realize sth): *I first met her in
1987. No, come to think of it, it was 1986.*

give sb sth to think about (*informal*) do
or say sth to sb which shows how angry or
determined you are: *This letter will give him
something to think about.*

have (got) another think 'coming
(used for saying that sb's opinion about a
future event is wrong because sth quite
different will happen): *If she thinks that
married life is going to be easy, she's got
another think coming.*

I should think 'so/not *or* **I should
think she, etc 'is/'does/'did, etc** (used
for emphasis when agreeing that sth is right
or correct): *'He didn't give the waiter a tip.' 'I
should think not, after such bad service.' ○ 'He
finally apologized for what he said.' 'I should
think so.' ○ 'I'm very angry with my son.' 'I
should think you are. He's behaved very badly
indeed.'*

just think (used when you feel interest,
shock or excitement at sth): *Just think of the
money we spend renting this place. ○ I'll be on
television in front of millions of viewers! Just
think!*

not think of sth/doing sth (used with
wouldn't, couldn't, won't or *can't*) not do sth
(in any circumstances); never do sth: *I
wouldn't think of buying one of those ugly*
*modern houses. ○ A famous man like him can't
think of answering all his letters personally.*

that's what 'sb thinks (*informal*) what sb
thinks will happen will not happen,
especially because the speaker is going to do
sth to prevent it: *'Your team doesn't have a
chance of winning.' 'That's what you think.'*

,think a'gain consider a decision again
very carefully and perhaps change your
opinion; reconsider sth: *I'd advise you to think
again before leaving your wife.*

,think a'loud *or* **,think out 'loud** speak
your thoughts about sth, for example a
problem, to yourself or to others, probably
without organizing them as in normal
speech.

think 'better of sth/doing sth decide
not to do sth that you were going to do: *He
was about to say something, but then he
thought better of it and kept quiet.*

think big (*quite informal*) have big plans for
the future; be ambitious: *If you want to be
successful in life, you've got to think big.*

think highly of sb/sth have a very high
opinion of sb/sth: *His paintings are highly
thought of by the critics. ○ Her teachers think
highly of her.*

think nothing of sth/doing sth *or* **not
think anything of sth/doing
sth** **1** consider (doing) sth as normal or
easy, when other people consider it as
difficult, dangerous, etc: *He thinks nothing of
working 14 hours a day.* **2** think that sth is
not important or significant: *I saw a man
outside the door, but I didn't think anything of it
at the time. I realized later that he must have
been the thief.*

think nothing 'of it (said as a polite reply
to apologies or thanks): *'I'm terribly sorry for
all the trouble I've caused you.' 'Think nothing
of it.'*

think on your feet think very quickly:
*When he asked me why I wasn't at work, I had
to think on my feet and I invented an excuse
about going to see the doctor. ○ Lawyers in
court need to be able to think on their feet.*

think positive think in a confident way
about what you can do: *If you don't think
positive, you won't win.*

think straight think clearly and
reasonably: *You're not thinking straight. If*

you leave your job, how will you support your family?

(not) think twice about sth/doing sth
(not) think carefully about sth/doing sth; (not) hesitate: *You should think twice about employing someone you've never met.* ○ *If they offered me a job abroad, I wouldn't think twice about taking it!*

think the world of sb/sth like, admire or respect sb/sth very much: *The children think the world of their new teacher.*

to think that. . . how surprising, exciting, sad, etc it is to think that. . .: *I can still hardly believe it! To think that the President stayed at my hotel!* ○ *To think that he was killed on the last day of the war.*

who does sb think they are? (*informal*) (said when you are angry about sb's behaviour) sb has no right to behave in a certain way: *Who do you think you are, taking my books without asking?* ○ *She just walked into my office without knocking! Who does she think she is?*

can't hear yourself think ⇨ hear; **I shudder to think** ⇨ shudder; **see/think fit** ⇨ fit

thinking
put your 'thinking cap on (*informal*) try to solve a problem by thinking hard about it: *Now, how are we going to find this money? Let's put our thinking caps on.*

wishful thinking ⇨ wishful

third
(give sb) the ,third de'gree question sb intensively for a long time, perhaps also using physical methods of torture, in order to make them confess to a crime or give secret information: *The soldiers were given the third degree in order to make them reveal the information.*

this
,this and 'that *or* **,this, ,that and the 'other** (*informal*) a number of different things: *We talked about this and that for a while and then had dinner.*

this is it (*informal*) **1** (said when you are agreeing that a point made by sb is important): *'People prefer their cars to public transport, you see.' 'Well, this is it.'* **2** (said when you have come to an important

moment): *Well this is it, Mike. Good luck in Australia. Don't forget to write. . . .*

thither **hither and thither** ⇨ hither

Thomas **a** **doubting** **Thomas** ⇨ doubting

thorn
be a thorn in your flesh/side be a person or thing that continually annoys you or stops you doing sth: *This patient is a real thorn in my side. He is always complaining of feeling ill and I can never find anything wrong with him.*

thought
I 'thought as ,much that is what I thought or expected: *'She's been lying to you; she hasn't really got any money at all.' 'I thought as much.'*

it's the thought that counts (*saying*) the fact that sb remembered about sth is more important than the size or value of a present: *She didn't send him a present for his birthday, only a card, but it's the thought that counts.*

food for thought ⇨ food; **perish the thought** ⇨ perish; **a school of thought** ⇨ school; **the wish is father to the thought** ⇨ wish

thoughts **have** **second** **thoughts** ⇨ second; **on** **second** **thoughts** ⇨ second; **a penny for your thoughts** ⇨ penny; **read sb's mind/thoughts** ⇨ read

thousand **a** **hundred/thousand/ million and one** ⇨ hundred; **not a hundred, etc miles away from here** ⇨ mile; **the sixty-four thousand dollar question** ⇨ sixty

thread
thread your way through (sth) move through a place by moving round and between people or things: *I threaded my way through the busy streets.*

hang by a thread ⇨ hang; **lose the drift/ thread of sth** ⇨ lose

threads **the** **loose** **ends/threads** ⇨ loose; **pick up the threads** ⇨ pick

three

three bags 'full (*becoming dated, humorous*) (said when you agree to do sth that sb asks you but think that they are rather rude or unreasonable): *Our new manager doesn't want to hear our opinions, all he wants is, 'Yes sir, no sir, three bags full sir.'* (from the nursery rhyme, 'Baa, baa, black sheep')

(give) three cheers (for sb/sth) shout 'hurray' three times to show admiration or support for sb/sth: *You all deserve three cheers for working so hard.* ○ *'Three cheers for the winner – hip, hip, hurray!'*

the three 'Rs reading, (w)riting and (a)rithmetic as the basic school subjects.

threshold

be on the threshold of sth be at an important moment when sth begins, changes or develops: *The country seemed to be on the threshold of war.* ○ *Now, on the threshold of a new career in industry, he seems confident and happy.*

thrilled

thrilled to 'bits (*informal*) be very pleased; be very excited: *We're thrilled to bits that you two are getting married!* ○ *The children were thrilled to bits with their presents.*

thrills

(the) thrills and spills (of sth) the exciting mixture of sudden successes and difficulties: *He loves the thrills and spills of Grand Prix motor racing.*

throat(s)

(be) at each other's throats *or* **(be) at one another's throats** (be) angrily fighting or arguing with each other: *Within six months of their marriage, Sue and Rodney were at each other's throats.*

ram, force, thrust, etc sth down sb's 'throat (*informal*) try to make sb accept or believe an idea or belief by talking about it all the time: *I'm tired of having religion rammed down my throat all the time!* ○ *He was always forcing Marxist theories down our throats.*

clear your throat ⇨ clear; **cut your own throat** ⇨ cut; **have a frog in your throat** ⇨ frog; **jump down sb's throat** ⇨ jump;

a lump in your throat ⇨ lump; **stick in your throat/craw/gullet** ⇨ stick

throes

(be) in the throes of sth/doing sth (be) doing a difficult task; (be) experiencing a difficult period or event: *The film's about a country in the throes of change.* ○ *He's in the throes of divorce at the moment.*

throne

be the power behind the throne ⇨ power

through

,through and 'through completely (typical of sb/sth): *He's a gentleman through and through.* ○ *This letter is my bank manager through and through.*

throw

throw the baby out with the bathwater (*informal*) mistakenly or stupidly throw away the good or best of sth together with the bad part: *It's stupid to say that the communist system was all bad; there were some good things about it. The baby was thrown out with the bathwater.*

throw the book at sb (*informal*) punish or criticize sb for as many things as possible: *The police stopped me for speeding and threw the book at me for everything – faulty lights, dangerous tyres, no insurance....*

throw caution to the wind(s) (*often humorous*) stop being careful or sensible and do sth risky or rash: *I decided to throw caution to the winds and buy myself a really smart pair of shoes.*

throw down the 'gauntlet invite sb to compete with you; challenge sb: *They have thrown down the gauntlet to the Prime Minister by demanding a referendum.* (A gauntlet is a kind of glove. In medieval times a knight threw his gauntlet at the feet of another knight as a challenge. In order to show that he accepted the challenge to fight, the other knight would pick up the glove.)

throw good money after bad spend more money in an attempt to get back the money which has been lost, although this is unlikely to be successful: *The Government was investing money in industries that would never make a profit; it was throwing good money after bad.*

throw your 'hand in (*informal*) stop trying to do sth; resign or give up: *If I fail again this time, I shall throw my hand in.* (when you have no chance of winning in a game of cards, you throw your hand (cards) into the middle of the table)

throw in your lot with sb decide to join a person or organization, so that you share their luck, both good and bad: *He left his job in the National Theatre to throw in his lot with a small travelling theatre company.*

throw in the 'towel *or* **throw in the 'sponge** (*informal*) stop doing sth because you know that you cannot succeed; admit defeat: *It's a bit early to throw in the towel – you've only just started the job.* (from boxing: throwing in the towel or sponge is a sign that a fighter accepts defeat)

throw your money about/around (*informal*) spend money freely, usually on extravagant or unnecessary things: *He's always throwing his money around to try to impress people.*

throw money at sth spend a lot of money trying to do sth which will probably not succeed: *They threw money at the business, but it failed in its first year.* ○ *The government throws money at social problems but it doesn't do much good.*

throw sth overboard reject or get rid of sth: *All ideas of reform were thrown overboard when the new government came to power.*

throw yourself at sb's feet ask humbly for sb's help, protection or forgiveness: *He threw himself at her feet and asked her forgiveness.*

throw yourself on sb's mercy ask sb to treat you kindly, especially when you have done sth wrong: *Throw yourself on the mercy of the court, and they might not send you to prison.*

throw a tantrum/wobbly (*informal*) suddenly become very or uncontrollably angry: *Your mother would throw a wobbly if she knew what we'd been doing.* ○ *When you were a child, you were always throwing tantrums.*

throw sb to the 'wolves/'lions allow sb to be attacked or remain in a difficult situation, perhaps because they are no longer useful or important to you: *When he became politically unpopular the rest of his party just threw him to the wolves.*

throw up your hands/arms in horror, despair, etc (*often humorous*) show that you disagree strongly with sth, or are very worried about sth: *When she said she wanted to get a motor bike, her parents threw up their hands in horror.*

throw your weight about/around (*informal*) use your authority over other people aggressively and insensitively: *He started throwing his weight around, shouting at everyone and telling them what to do.*

cast/shed/throw light on sth ⇨ light; **draw/throw/cast a veil/a curtain over sth** ⇨ veil; **fling/sling/throw mud** ⇨ mud; **have/throw a fit** ⇨ fit; **if you throw enough mud, some of it will stick = mud sticks** ⇨ mud; **people who live in glasshouses shouldn't throw stones** ⇨ people; **pour/throw cold water on sth** ⇨ cold; **put/throw sb off the scent** ⇨ scent; **put/throw a spanner in the works** ⇨ spanner; **a stone's throw** ⇨ stone

thrown **jump in/be thrown in at the deep end** ⇨ deep

thrust **cut and thrust** ⇨ cut

thumb

thumb your nose at sb/sth show that you have no respect for sb/sth, sometimes by making a gesture with your thumb against the end of your nose: *A photograph shows one of the crowd thumbing his nose at the speaker.* ○ *This new rule says there is strictly no smoking in here but people are just thumbing their noses at it.*

(be) under sb's 'thumb (*informal*) (be) completely controlled or influenced by another person: *Now that they're married, she's completely under his thumb and never sees her old friends.*

a green thumb = green fingers ⇨ green; **a rule of thumb** ⇨ rule; **stand/stick out like a sore thumb** ⇨ sore; **thumb/hitch a lift** ⇨ lift

thumbs

be all (fingers and) 'thumbs be unable to hold sth without dropping or damaging it; be clumsy: *He's all thumbs when it comes to fixing machines.*

(give sb/sth) the thumbs 'up/'down
(show your approval/disapproval of sth/sb):
*I asked him whether I could borrow the car, and
he gave me the thumbs up* (said yes). ○ *I'm
afraid it's thumbs down for your new proposal;
the boss doesn't like it.* also **get the thumbs
up/down** *We've got the thumbs up for the
new swimming pool.* (in contests in ancient
Rome the public put their thumbs up if they
wanted a gladiator to live, and down if they
wanted him to be killed)

twiddle your thumbs ⇨ twiddle

thunder blood and thunder ⇨ blood;
steal sb's thunder ⇨ steal

tick

get, buy, etc sth on tick (*especially
British, informal*) get food or other goods and
pay for them later: *You can only buy things on
tick in small shops where they know you well.*

tick sth off on your fingers check a list
of things by saying them aloud, and
touching your fingers one after another at
the same time.

what makes sb 'tick (*informal*) what
makes sb behave or think in the way they
do: *I've never really understood what makes her
tick.* ○ *Money is what makes him tick.* (tick is
the sound a watch or clock makes every
second)

ticket just the job/ticket ⇨ job

tickle catch/take/tickle sb's fancy
⇨ fancy; **slap and tickle** ⇨ slap

tickled

be tickled 'pink *or* **be tickled to
'death** (*informal, becoming dated*) be very
pleased or amused: *My grandmother will be
tickled pink to get an invitation to the wedding.*

tide

the tide turns things change, especially
for the better: *For a long time there has been
little political freedom, but slowly the tide is
turning.*

go, etc with/against the stream/tide
⇨ stream; **stem the tide** ⇨ stem

tie

tie sb's hands stop sb doing sth, by taking
away their power or freedom: *Employers
now have the right to sack workers who go on*
*strike and this has tied the unions' hands
considerably.* **sb's hands are tied** a person
cannot do sth because he/she does not have
the permission or authority: *Unless I get
permission from the manager, I can't help you;
my hands are tied.*

tie the knot (*informal*) get married: *When
did you decide to tie the knot?*

tie yourself (up) in 'knots *or* **get tied
(up) in 'knots** (*quite informal*) become
confused when trying to say or explain sth:
*He tied himself up in knots when he tried to
explain why he had lipstick on his face.*

tie sb up in knots (*informal*) confuse sb
and make them uncertain by using clever
arguments against them: *The interviewer tied
the Prime Minister up in knots. He looked a
complete fool.*

bind/tie sb hand and foot ⇨ hand; **the
old school tie** ⇨ old; **with one hand tied
behind your back** ⇨ hand

tiger a paper tiger ⇨ paper

tight

in a tight corner/spot (*informal*) in a
very difficult situation: *He's in a bit of a tight
spot at the moment. The bank has given him one
week to find £20 000.*

keep a tight 'rein on sb/sth control sb/
sth very carefully; give sb/sth very little
freedom: *The company must keep a tight rein
on spending.* ○ *She kept a tight rein on all her
children to make sure they didn't get into
trouble.*

a ˌtight 'squeeze a situation where you do
not have much space to put things in: *We
managed to get all the luggage in the car but it
was a tight squeeze.*

run a tight ship ⇨ run; **sit tight** ⇨ sit;
sleep tight ⇨ sleep

tighten

tighten your 'belt spend less money, eat
less food, etc because there is little available:
In wartime everyone has to tighten their belts. ○
*We'll have to tighten our belts if we want to
save any money for our holidays this year.*

tightrope walk a tightrope ⇨ walk

tiles a night on the town/on the tiles =
go, etc (out) on the town ⇨ town

till

have your fingers/hand in the till
(*informal*) steal, especially small amounts of
money from a shop, business, etc where you
work: *He was sacked after they found he'd had
his hand in the till.*

till/until kingdom come ⇨ kingdom

tiller **at the helm/tiller** ⇨ helm

tilt **full tilt/pelt/speed** ⇨ full

time

(and) about 'time ('too) *or* **(and) not
before 'time** (*informal*) (said when the
speaker is pleased that sth has happened but
thinks that it should have happened
sooner): *Here comes the bus – and about time
too.* ○ *'She finally repaired the window.' 'Not
before time.'*

'any time (used after sb has thanked you
for helping them, etc): *'Thanks for the lift.'*
'Any time.'

at the 'time at a certain moment in the
past; then: *I remember watching the first men
on the moon on television; I was only six at the
time.*

at my, your, etc time of life at my, your,
etc age (usually used about older people):
'Learn to drive at my time of life? Don't be silly!'

**be ahead of/before/in advance of
your 'time** have ideas or invent things a
long time before people are ready to accept
them: *He was sure that it was possible to fly to
the moon, but he was ahead of his time and
people laughed at him.* ○ *She was a feminist
before her time.* ○ *Her ideas on women's
education were very much in advance of her
time.*

be, etc ahead of/behind 'time be, etc
early/late: *He arrived ahead of time, and had to
wait.* ○ *The trains are running behind time
again today.*

be before sb's 'time be before the period
that a person can remember or was involved
in: *The Beatles were a bit before my time.* ○
*There used to be fields behind this house, but
that was before your time* (before you started
living here).

be, etc (right) on 'time *or* (*informal*) **be,
etc bang on 'time** at the correct time,
neither early nor late; be, etc punctual: *I
always have to wait for you – you're never on*
time. ○ *The train came in bang on time.*

do/serve 'time (*informal*) be in prison: *He
had done time for robbing a bank.* ○ *Two of the
gang are serving time for murder.*

for the nth time (*informal*) (used for
expressing annoyance, impatience, etc at
the number of times sth happens or is
necessary): *I told him, for the nth time, to tidy
his room but he's done nothing to it at all.*

for the time 'being *or* **for the
'moment/'present** now, and for a short
time in the future: *He can stay with us for the
time being until he finds a place of his own.* ○
*We're happy living in a flat for the moment, but
we might want to move into a house quite soon.*

from/since ˌtime imme'morial from
ancient times; from a very long time ago:
*The Barton family have lived in this village
since time immemorial.*

from ˌtime to 'time occasionally;
sometimes: *We go to the cinema from time to
time.*

**give sb a rough, hard, bad, etc 'time
(of it)** (*informal*) make sb's life very difficult
because you don't like them, etc: *Ever since I
started work here, she's been shouting at me
and giving me a hard time.*

have an easy 'time of it (*informal*) be in a
very favourable situation: *She has a very easy
time of it in her job – she only works about 20
hours a week.*

have (got) a lot of time for sb/sth
(*informal*) like, admire or respect sb/sth very
much: *I've got a lot of time for the police. I think
they've got a very difficult job.* also **have (got)
no time for sb/sth** dislike and have no
respect for sb/sth: *I've got no time for people
who tell lies.*

**have a (hard, rough, bad, etc) time of
it** (*informal*) experience difficulties,
problems, etc: *We're having a time of it at the
moment with the builders in the house.* ○
*Businesses are having a hard time of it at the
moment.*

have the ˌtime of your 'life (*informal*)
enjoy yourself; be very happy or excited: *The
children had the time of their lives at the circus.*

have (got) time on your hands
(*informal*) have more free time than you
want or need: *Now the children have left
home, she's got a lot of time on her hands.*

in good time well before the time sth starts or happens: *Make sure you get there in good time to buy your ticket.*

(do sth) in your own good 'time (do sth) when you want to, and not when other people tell you to: *There's no point in getting impatient. She'll finish the job in her own good time.*

(do sth) in your own time (do sth) in your free time, and not at work: *Please make private phone calls in your own time, Mr Davies, not when you are at work.*

in 'time 1 not late: *Make sure that you get here in time for the concert.* **2** after quite a long time; eventually: *You will feel better in time.* **3** (play, sing, or dance to music) at the right speed: *The violins didn't seem to be in time with the rest of the orchestra. also out of time The violins were out of time.*

it is high/about 'time (that...) (used for saying that sth should be done or happen immediately or very soon): *It's high time that this room was properly cleaned!* ○ *So you've started work! It's about time* (you should have started a long time ago)!

it is only, just, etc a matter/a question of 'time (before...) (used to say that a thing will definitely happen in the future, although it may not happen immediately): *Don't worry, you'll get a job if you keep looking. It's just a matter of time.* ○ *It's only a question of time before the fighting spreads to the city.*

keep 'time 1 (of a clock or watch) always show the correct time: *It's an old watch, but it keeps very good time.* **2** sing, play, or dance to music at the right speed: *Keep time with the music, Fiona. You're singing too fast.*

lose/waste no time (in doing sth) do sth quickly and without delay: *As soon as she arrived back home, she lost no time in visiting all her old friends.*

make good, etc 'time go as fast as, or faster than you expected or hoped: *On the first part of the trip we made good time.*

make time (to do sth) make sure you have enough time to do sth: *I'm very busy, but I'll try to make time to do it.*

make up the time do sth at a different time, because you cannot do it at the usual or correct time: *He had a long lunch break on Tuesday and so he made up the time by working late on Wednesday.*

(there is) no time like the present (*saying*) the best time to do sth is now.

of all time that has ever been made, lived, etc: *Which do you think is the best film of all time?* **all-time** (*adjective*) *My all-time favourite film is 'Gone with the Wind'.*

one, two, etc at a 'time singly, or in groups of two, etc at the same time or together: *I want to see you one at a time.*

take your 'time (over sth/to do sth/ doing sth) 1 do sth as slowly as you like; do not hurry: *There's no rush – take your time.* **2** be late; do sth too slowly: *You certainly took your time to get here. I've been waiting an hour!* ○ *The shop assistant took her time serving me.*

there's no time to lose *or* **there's no time to be lost** (*saying*) you must act quickly: *Come on, there's no time to lose! The plane leaves in half an hour!*

time after 'time *or* **time and a'gain** very often; many times, repeatedly: *He makes the same mistake time after time.* ○ *Time and again she's tried to give up smoking, but she never succeeds.*

time 'flies (*saying*) time seems to pass very quickly: *How time flies! I've got to go now.* ○ *Time has flown since the holiday began.* (translation of the Latin 'tempus fugit')

time hangs/lies heavy (on your 'hands) time seems to pass very slowly because you are bored or have nothing to do: *In prison, time hangs heavy.*

time is getting on it is getting late; there is not much time left: *We'd better hurry up and finish; time's getting on.*

time is money (*saying*) time is valuable, and should not be wasted.

time is on sb's 'side sb has enough time to do sth; the more that time passes, the more sb will be helped: *Although she failed the exam, time is on her side; she is young enough to take it again next year.* ○ *The longer we wait to sell the house, the more it will be worth, so we've got time on our side.*

the time is ripe (for sb) (to do sth) *or* **the time is ripe for sth/doing sth** it is the right time to do sth: *I think the* *time's ripe for him to leave home if he wants to.* ○ *The time is ripe for a change in this country.*

time (alone) will 'tell (*saying*) (used when you are wondering what the future results of an action or decision will be) we cannot know what will happen before it happens.

work, etc against 'time work, etc under pressure and very quickly, because you must finish sth by a certain time: *We've only got two days to find a replacement, so we're racing against time.*

beat time ⇨ beat; **bide your time** ⇨ bide; **buy time** ⇨ buy; **do sth in your own sweet time** ⇨ sweet; **half the time** ⇨ half; **have a thin time** ⇨ thin; **in the fullness of time** ⇨ fullness; **in half the time** ⇨ half; **in less than no time** ⇨ less; **in the nick of time** ⇨ nick; **in no time at all = (in) next to no time** ⇨ next; **live on borrowed time** ⇨ live; **long time no see** ⇨ long; **mark time** ⇨ mark; **(in) next to no time** ⇨ next; **once upon a time** ⇨ once; **pass the/your time** ⇨ pass; **pass the time of day** ⇨ pass; **play for time** ⇨ play; **quite some time** ⇨ quite; **stand the test of time** ⇨ stand; **a stitch in time saves nine** ⇨ stitch; **there's a first time for everything** ⇨ first; **a whale of a time** ⇨ whale

times

at 'times sometimes: *At times I wonder whether he'll ever get a job.*

be behind the 'times be old-fashioned in the way you live, work, think, etc: *You're behind the times if you think a visit to the dentist has to be painful.*

keep up, move, etc with the 'times change in the same way as the rest of society changes: *In business it's important to go with the times.* ○ *People's tastes change with the times.*

at the best of times ⇨ best; **fall on hard times** ⇨ fall; **for old times' sake** ⇨ old; **nine times out of ten** ⇨ nine; **ninety-nine times out of a hundred = nine times out of ten** ⇨ nine; **a sign of the times** ⇨ sign

tip

be on the tip of your 'tongue (used when you are speaking and cannot remember a word, name, etc but feel that you will remember it very soon): *What's her name? You know, that tall Italian girl...it's on the tip of my tongue...Claudia, that's it!*

be the tip of the 'iceberg what you can see of a problem or difficult situation is only one small part of a much larger (hidden) problem: *The 1 000 homeless people in London sleeping in night shelters are only the tip of the iceberg. There are many thousands of homeless people in the capital.*

tip the 'balance/'scales be the reason that finally causes sb to do sth or sth to happen in one way rather than another: *They were both very good candidates for the job but she had more experience and that tipped the balance.*

tip sb the 'wink (*informal*) give sb a helpful piece of (confidential) advice which puts them in an advantageous position to do sth, perhaps before other people: *'How did you know that this job was available?' 'A friend tipped me the wink and so I telephoned you immediately.'*

tired

be/get tired of sth/doing sth be bored or annoyed with sth/doing sth: *We got tired of the country and we moved into town.* ○ *I'm tired of listening to his complaints.*

tissue

a tissue of lies a false story; untrue statements: *Don't believe her – the whole thing is a complete tissue of lies.* ○ *This official report on the nuclear energy industry is a tissue of lies.*

tit

tit for 'tat (do) sth unpleasant to sb because they have done sth unpleasant to you: *He hit me, so I hit him back – it was tit for tat.*

tizzy

be/get in/into a tizzy/tizz (about sth) (*informal*) become excited, nervous or confused, especially about sth unimportant: *He was in such a tizz about his homework.*

to

to and 'fro from one place to another and back, repeatedly; from side to side repeatedly: *travel to and fro between London and Paris* ○ *She held the baby in her arms and rocked her to and fro.*

toast

toast **be warm as toast** ⇨ warm

toe

toe the 'line or (US) **toe the 'mark** obey the orders and accept the ideas, aims and principles of a particular group or person: *The Prime Minister is angry because some members of the government are not toeing the line.*

from head to foot/toe ⇨ head; **from top to toe** ⇨ top

toes

be, etc on your 'toes be, etc alert and ready for action: *We were all on our toes, waiting for the game to begin.*

keep sb on their toes (*informal*) make sure that sb is active and alert; be the reason for sb being active, etc: *A good boss keeps his workers on their toes.* ○ *This job really keeps me on my toes.*

tread/step on sb's 'toes (*informal*) offend or upset sb by criticizing them or by interfering in things that they are responsible for: *It's difficult to criticize the plan without treading on somebody's toes.*

together

get sth/it/your act to'gether (*informal*) manage to organize or control sth (better than you have done previously): *He's been trying to get his life together.* ○ *If Sally got her act together she'd be a great musician.* ○ *He seems to be getting it together at last.*

pull yourself together ⇨ pull

toing

toing and 'froing movement from one place to another and back, repeatedly: *There's been a lot of toing and froing next door today. I wonder what's happening.*

token **by the same token** ⇨ same

told

all 'told (used with numbers) with everything/everyone included: *So far there have been fourteen arrests all told.*

I told you so = what did I tell you? ⇨ what

toll

take a (heavy) toll (of sth) or **take its toll (on sb/sth)** cause a high number of unfortunate things, for example deaths,

injuries, accidents, bankruptcies; cause a lot of harm or damage: *Smoking continues to take its toll; it is killing more and more people each year.* ○ *The present economic crisis is taking a heavy toll. Thousands of firms have gone bankrupt.* ○ *His job is taking its toll on him. He needs a holiday.*

Tom

every/any Tom, Dick and/or 'Harry any ordinary person; people of no special value to you: *We don't want any Tom, Dick or Harry marrying our daughter.*

a peeping Tom ⇨ peeping

tomorrow

do sth like there's no tomorrow or **do sth as if there's no tomorrow** (*informal*) do sth with a lot of energy, as if this is the last time you will be able to do it: *She's spending money like there's no tomorrow.*

ton

come/be down on sb like a ton of 'bricks (*informal*) tell sb off angrily because they have done sth wrong: *The first time I made a mistake, he came down on me like a ton of bricks.* ○ *If I find anyone drunk in this factory I'll be down on them like a ton of bricks.*

weigh a ton ⇨ weigh

tone **set the tone** ⇨ set

tongs **go/be at sb/sth hammer and tongs** ⇨ hammer

tongue

get your 'tongue round/around sth manage to say a difficult word correctly: *I sometimes find it difficult to get my tongue around the word 'sixth'.*

a silver/smooth tongue the ability to talk in a very pleasing and polite way, to make people do what you want: *It was his silver tongue that got him the job.* **silver-tongued, smooth-tongued** (*adjectives*) *smooth-tongued salesmen*

(with) tongue in 'cheek or **with your tongue in your 'cheek** not meant seriously; jokingly or ironically: *I never know if Charlie's serious or if he is speaking tongue in cheek.* **tongue-in-cheek** (*adjective*) *a tongue-in-cheek remark*

be on the tip of your tongue ⇨ tip; **cat**

got your, etc tongue? ⇨ cat; **find your tongue** ⇨ find; **have a sharp tongue** ⇨ sharp; **hold your tongue** ⇨ hold; **your mother tongue** ⇨ mother; **a slip of the tongue/pen** ⇨ slip

tongues

tongues wag (*informal*) there is a lot of talk or gossip about sb's private life, etc: *Don't tell anyone your secret – you know how tongues wag around here.* also **set tongues wagging** *That remark really set tongues wagging.*

too

be too much (for sb) **1** be stronger or better than sb; beat sb: *Oxford were too much for Cambridge in the boat race.* **2** be more than sb is able to do: *A cycling holiday would be too much for an unfit person like me.* **3** (used for expressing annoyance): *His rudeness towards her is just too much.*

tools **down tools** ⇨ down

tooth **fight tooth and nail** ⇨ fight; **go over/through sth with a fine-tooth comb** ⇨ fine; **have a sweet tooth** ⇨ sweet; **long in the tooth** ⇨ long

top

at the top of your 'voice very loudly: *We shouted at the top of our voices.*

be/go ,over the 'top (*especially British, informal*) behave in a wild, excited or extreme way; (of sth) be unnecessarily extreme: *She drank a bottle of champagne, danced on the table and took all her clothes off. She went completely over the top.* ○ *His remarks were a bit over the top.*

come out on 'top (of sth) (*informal*) become, etc more successful than others: *It was a hard match but Sampras came out on top in the end.* ○ *The firm's new model has come out on top in export markets this year.*

from ,top to 'bottom completely and thoroughly: *We searched the house from top to bottom.*

from ,top to 'toe from the head to the feet; completely: *He was all in green from top to toe.* ○ *We were covered in mud from top to toe.*

get/be on top of sth (*informal*) be able to manage and control problems and difficulties successfully: *I've finally got on top*

of my new job but it took a long time.

get on top of sb (*informal*) (of a problem, too much work, etc) make sb feel very worried or depressed: *She's letting things get on top of her at work.*

off the ,top of your 'head (*informal*) as a guess; without having time to think carefully: *Off the top of my head I'd say it would cost £1 000 to do the repairs.* ○ *'What's the population of Liverpool?' 'I'm afraid I couldn't tell you off the top of my head.'*

on top of sb/sth **1** in addition to sth; also: *On top of his salary, he gets about £100 in commission every week.* **2** too close to sth/sb: *These houses are all built on top of one another.* ○ *He was right on top of* (driving very close behind) *the car in front.*

on top of the world (*informal*) very happy; in very good form: *I'm on top of the world; I've just had a baby son.* ○ *You'll feel on top of the world after a good holiday.*

take it from the top start again from the beginning (especially used about playing music, acting or performing): *OK, take it from the top, and no mistakes this time!*

to top/cap/crown it all (*informal*) (used for introducing the last undesirable thing in a list) in addition to (all the things already mentioned): *We went to a horrible restaurant. The food was awful, the music was far too loud, and to top it all, the waiter was rude to us.*

(the) ,top 'brass (*informal*) people with power and authority: *The top brass got a huge pay rise.*

,top 'dog (*informal*) a person, group or country that is better or more powerful than all the others: *He's top dog in BBC drama now.*

(be) ,top 'secret (used to describe very secret government information): *These defence plans are top secret, known only to a very few people.* ○ *The file was marked TOP SECRET.*

the ,top 'ten, 'twenty, etc the ten, twenty, etc best-selling pop records each week: *The song didn't make* (get into) *the top twenty.*

(at) the top of the 'tree/'ladder (at) the highest position in a career: *Anyone can get to the top of the ladder if they try hard enough.*

up top (*informal*) (used to talk about sb's intelligence): *He doesn't have much up top, I'm* *afraid.*

at the bottom/top of the pile ⇨ pile; **be/ get thin on top** ⇨ thin; **blow your top** ⇨ blow; **head/top the bill** ⇨ bill; **sleep like a log/top** ⇨ sleep

toss

toss a coin throw a coin in the air to decide sth, for example who begins a game. Before the coin is thrown, one person chooses either 'heads' (the side of the coin marked with a head) or 'tails' (the other side). If the side chosen lands upwards this person 'wins the toss' and the other person 'loses the toss'.

touch

be, etc in/out of 'touch (with sth) have/not have recent knowledge or news of sth, and so fully/not fully understand it: *I try to keep in touch with what's happening by reading the newspapers.* ○ *Our politicians are old and out of touch* (unaware of people's real feelings).

be/keep in touch (with sb) communicate with sb regularly: *We are in touch with our central office every day.* ○ *I still keep in touch with some of my university friends.*

be touch and go (whether. . .) be very uncertain or risky (whether sth will happen or not): *It was a very dangerous operation. It was touch and go several times.* ○ *It was touch and go whether the building would be finished in time.*

an easy/a soft 'touch (*informal*) a kind and perhaps easily deceived person whom people ask for money, help, etc: *Ask Tony to lend you some money. He's a soft touch.*

get in touch with sb/sth make contact with sb/sth (by phone, letter, visit, etc): *Here's my phone number in case you need to get in touch with me.*

have, etc a touch of class have, etc quality, in design, character, etc: *His clothes are old and unfashionable, but nevertheless he has a real touch of class.*

not touch sb/sth with a 'bargepole (*British, informal*) strongly dislike or distrust sb/sth; not want to be involved or associated with sb/sth: *I don't know why she's marrying that man. I wouldn't touch him with a bargepole.* ○ *I wouldn't touch the job with a*

bargepole.

put sb in touch with sb/sth arrange for sb to contact, meet, etc a person you already know: *He put me in touch with the British Council in Paris.*

touch 'wood *or* (*US*) **knock on 'wood** (*often humorous*) (used for expressing the hope that your good luck will continue): *We haven't had a serious accident yet, touch wood.* (many people touch a piece of wood when they say this)

the finishing touch(es) ⇨ finishing; **hit/ touch a (raw) nerve** ⇨ nerve; **lose your touch** ⇨ lose; **lose touch/contact** ⇨ lose; **the Midas touch** ⇨ Midas; **touch/tug your forelock** ⇨ forelock

tough

be/get 'tough (with sb) be strict with sb whose behaviour you do not like; be ready to punish sb: *It's time to get tough with football hooligans.* ○ *be tough on lawbreakers*

be (as) tough as old 'boots (*informal*) **1** (of food) be very tough and difficult to chew: *This steak's as tough as old boots.* **2** very strong and able to bear pain, criticism, etc without complaining or giving up: *Don't worry, she'll soon recover. She's tough as old boots.*

a tough customer (*informal*) a very difficult person to deal with.

a 'tough guy (*informal*) a strong, independent-minded person who seems to be afraid of nothing: *The most famous 'tough guy' in American films was John Wayne.*

bad/hard/tough luck! ⇨ luck; **a hard/ tough nut** ⇨ nut

tour **a whistle-stop tour** ⇨ whistle

tow

in tow (*informal*) following closely behind; with you: *Mrs Bridge arrived at the playgroup with her four children in tow.*

towel **throw in the towel** ⇨ throw

tower **an ivory tower** ⇨ ivory; **a pillar/ tower of strength** ⇨ strength

town

go, etc (out) on the 'town *or* (**go for, have, etc) a night (out) on the 'town/on the 'tiles** go, etc out to enjoy yourself at night, for example to the theatre, pub, nightclub, etc: *For a birthday treat they took him out on the town.* ○ *The students went for a night on the tiles after the last exam.*

go to 'town (on/over sth) (*informal*) put a lot of money, energy, etc into sth: *When they give parties they really go to town* (spend a lot of money, invite a lot of people, etc). ○ *She decided to go to town and redecorate all the rooms in the house.*

a one-horse town ⇨ one; **paint the town red** ⇨ paint

trace(s)

sink, vanish, etc without trace disappear completely: *The boat sank without trace.* ○ *Many pop stars sink without trace. After five years no one can even remember their names.*

kick over the traces ⇨ kick

track

be on the right/wrong 'track be thinking or acting in the right/wrong way to find the answer to a problem: *We haven't found a solution to the problem yet, but I think we're on the right track.* ○ *You're on the wrong track, I'm afraid. The information you want isn't here.*

keep/lose track (of sb/sth) keep/not keep informed about sb/sth; remember/ forget about the number of sth, the time, etc: *It's hard to keep track of what's happening in Russian politics.* ○ *I've lost track of the number of times I've been to Paris.*

a 'track record all a person's or an organization's successes or failures in the past: *In business your track record is more important than your qualifications.*

have a one-track mind ⇨ one; **off the beaten track** ⇨ beaten

tracks

make 'tracks (for sth) (*informal*) leave one place to go to another: *It's getting late; I think we'd better make tracks.*

cover your tracks ⇨ cover; **stop in your tracks** ⇨ stop; **the wrong side of the tracks** ⇨ wrong

trade(s)

a trade secret 1 a secret about a particular company's method of production:

The ingredients of Coca-Cola are a trade secret. **2** (*humorous*) a secret about how you make or do sth: *'Can I have a recipe for this cake?' 'No, you can't. It's a trade secret.'*

do a roaring trade ⇨ roaring; **a jack of all trades** ⇨ jack; **the rag trade** ⇨ rag; **the tricks of the trade** ⇨ tricks

trail   **blaze a/the trail** ⇨ blaze

train

in train (*quite formal*) being prepared; happening: *The plans for the Queen's birthday celebrations are all in train.* ○ *Changes to the law have been set in train.*

the gravy train ⇨ gravy

transports

(be) in transports of joy, delight, etc (be) feeling very great joy, etc: *They were in transports of delight at the news.*

trap   shut your mouth/trap/face/gob! ⇨ shut

travel

travel 'light travel with very little luggage: *We're travelling light with one small bag each.*

tread

,tread the 'boards (*humorous*) be an actor: *He has recently been treading the boards in a new play at the National.*

,tread 'water 1 stay upright in the same place in water by making treading movements with your legs. **2** stay in a situation without making progress: *For the past year I've been treading water, in a boring job with no hope of promotion.*

tread/step on sb's toes ⇨ toes

treat

go down a treat (*informal*) be very successful or enjoyable: *'Did the children like the story?' 'Yes, it went down a treat.'* ○ *Mm! Strawberries and cream. That'll go down a treat.*

treat sb like 'dirt (*informal*) treat sb very badly and without respect: *He treated his wife like dirt. She finally left him after ten terrible years.*

tree(s) **bark up the wrong tree** ⇨ bark; **the top of the tree/ladder** ⇨ top; **money doesn't grow on trees** ⇨ money; **not see the wood for the trees** ⇨ see; **up a gum tree** ⇨ gum

trembling in fear and trembling ⇨ fear

trial(s)
by ˌtrial and ˈerror trying different ways of doing sth until you find the right one: *I didn't know how to use the camera at first, so I had to learn by trial and error.*

a ˌtrial ˈrun a first try at doing sth, to test it or for practice: *Take the car for a trial run before you buy it.*

ˌtrials and tribuˈlations difficulties and troubles: *The film is about the trials and tribulations of adolescence.*

tribute pay tribute to sb/sth ⇨ pay

trick
use, try, etc every trick in the ˈbook try any method you know to get sth or get sb to do sth you want: *He'll use every trick in the book to try and stop you.*

do the job/trick ⇨ job; **have an ace/trick up your sleeve = have sth up your sleeve** ⇨ sleeve; **not miss a trick** ⇨ miss

tricks
be up to your (old) ˈtricks (*informal*) be acting in your usual way, which the speaker does not like: *Tom's up to his old tricks again. He's having an affair with his secretary.*

how's ˈtricks? (*informal, becoming dated*) (used when you meet a friend you haven't see recently) how are you? how are things going?

the ˌtricks of the ˈtrade clever or expert ways of doing things, especially used by people in their jobs: *She's only been here a couple of months, so she's still learning the tricks of the trade.*

teach an old dog new tricks ⇨ teach

trim
be/keep in ˈtrim be/remain fit and healthy: *For a man of his age he keeps in good trim.*

Trojan work like a dog/slave/Trojan ⇨ work

trooper swear like a trooper ⇨ swear

trot
on the ˈtrot (*informal*) one after the other: *The bus has been late for five days on the trot.*

trouble
take trouble over sth/with sth/to do sth/doing sth *or* **go to the trouble/a lot of trouble to do sth** use a lot of time, care and effort in doing sth: *She takes a lot of trouble with her writing, which is why it's so good.* ○ *I went to a lot of trouble to find a nice birthday present, but he doesn't like it.* ○ *I don't want you to go to too much trouble.*

there's trouble brewing (*informal*) a difficult situation is starting to develop: *There's trouble brewing in the car industry.*

a trouble shared is a trouble halved (*saying*) if you talk to sb about your problems and worries, instead of keeping them to yourself, they seem less serious.

ask for trouble/it ⇨ ask; **spare no expense/pains/trouble** ⇨ spare

troubled pour oil on troubled waters ⇨ pour

troubles have, etc teething troubles ⇨ teething

trousers catch sb with his pants/trousers down ⇨ catch; **wear the trousers** ⇨ wear

truant play truant ⇨ play

truck
have no truck with sb/sth not want to deal with or be involved with sb/sth: *He'll have no truck with anyone on the political left.*

true
come ˈtrue (of a hope, wish, etc) really happen: *What the fortune-teller said about your future really came true.* ○ *Her dreams came true when she won the gold medal at the Olympics.*

so bad, stupid, etc it isn't true (*informal*) (used for emphasis) very bad, etc: *His brother is so lazy it isn't true!*

sb's true ˈcolours (often used for showing disapproval) what a person is really like: *Once he got into power he showed his true colours.*

(happen, go, etc) true to form (happen, etc) in the usual or typical way or as you expect: *True to form, he arrived early.* o *The meeting went true to form, with a lot of boring speeches.*

hold good/true ⇨ hold; **ring true/false/hollow** ⇨ ring; **too right/true** ⇨ right

truly **well and truly** ⇨ well; **yours truly** ⇨ yours

trumpet **blow your own trumpet** ⇨ blow

trumps

come/turn up 'trumps (*informal*) **1** be very helpful or generous to sb who has a problem: *I asked a lot of people if they could lend me the money, but finally it was my sister who came up trumps.* **2** do better than expected: *On the day of the match the team turned up trumps (won the match).*

trust

trust sb/sth to do sth (*informal*) (used to express annoyance or disappointment when sb does sth typically silly or bad, or when sth happens as usual): *Trust you to forget my birthday!* o *Trust it to rain at the weekend!*

truth

truth will out (*saying*) the truth about sth cannot be hidden for ever.

a home truth ⇨ home; **the moment of truth** ⇨ moment; **the naked truth** ⇨ naked; **the truth/fact of the matter** ⇨ matter

try

try your hand (at sth/doing sth) try sth for the first time, for example a skill or a sport: *I've always wanted to try my hand at painting.*

try it on (with sb) (*informal*) do sth that you know is wrong, in order to see if sb will accept this behaviour or not: *The price he asked was far too much. I think he was just trying it on.* o *Don't try it on with me, pal, or you'll be sorry.*

try your luck try to do or get sth, hoping you will succeed: *A friend told me the job was available, so I thought I'd try my luck.*

do/try your damnedest ⇨ damnedest; **do/try your level best** ⇨ level; **these things are sent to try us** ⇨ things

trying **like looking for/trying to find a needle in a haystack** ⇨ needle

tug

tug at sb's heartstrings (*informal*) (often used for showing disapproval) make sb feel very strong emotions like sadness and pity: *These photographs of starving puppies are designed to tug at your heartstrings.*

touch/tug your forelock ⇨ forelock

tune

be ,in/,out of 'tune (with sb/sth) 1 be on/not on the right musical note: *singing out of tune* **2** be in/not in agreement with sb/sth; be/not be happy or comfortable with sb/sth: o *He's out of tune with modern ideas about education.* o *I don't like London – I just don't feel in tune with city life.*

to the tune of £500, etc (*informal*) (used for saying that an amount of money is larger than expected or more than is right) at the cost of £500, etc: *We're paying rent to the tune of £200 a week.*

call the shots/the tune ⇨ call; **change your tune** ⇨ change; **he who pays the piper calls the tune** ⇨ pays; **sing a different song/tune** ⇨ sing

tunnel

(have) tunnel vision (used to show disapproval) (have) an interest in only one small part of sth instead of the whole of it: *He's got tunnel vision about music. He thinks only the classics are worth listening to.*

light at the end of the tunnel ⇨ light

tuppence

not care/give 'tuppence for/about sb/sth (*informal*) think sb/sth is not important; not care about sb/sth: *She loves him, but he doesn't care tuppence for her.* o *The police don't give tuppence for our rights.*

turkey **talk turkey** ⇨ talk

turn

at every 'turn everywhere; all the time: *I keep meeting her at every turn.* o *My plans go wrong at every turn.*

be on the 'turn be about to change, often for the better: *That's the third time they've won this week. I think their luck is on the turn.*

by turn(s) (used when talking of contrasting feelings or actions which follow each other): *He looked surprised, worried and angry by turn.* ○ *When they told me I had got the job in New York, I felt by turns excited and anxious.*

do sth ,out of 'turn 1 do sth when you have no right to do it because another person should have done it before you; not in the correct order: *There was an argument in the doctor's waiting room because somebody had gone in to see him out of turn.* 2 say or do sth that you should not say because you have no right to or because it's not the right time or place to say it: *It is not the first time that Julia has said something out of turn.*

do sb a (good) 'turn be helpful or unhelpful to sb; do sb a favour: *She's done the family a lot of good turns in the past.* ○ *I did you a good turn, now you do me one.*

in turn 1 one after another: *The Queen spoke to all of us in turn.* 2 (used for introducing the result of sth just mentioned): *She was very angry with me and I in turn was very upset.*

not turn a 'hair not show strong emotion like fear, surprise or excitement, when others expect you to: *He didn't turn a hair when the judge gave him 20 years in prison.*

one good turn deserves another (*saying*) if sb helps you with sth, you should help them in return.

a practical, scientific, etc turn of 'mind a practical, scientific, etc kind of mind: *He's got a very practical turn of mind. He can mend anything.*

take a turn for the better/worse become better/worse: *The weather is taking a turn for the worse, I'm afraid.*

turn and turn about (of two people) (do sth) one after the other repeatedly: *'Who drove to Germany?' 'We did the driving turn and turn about.'*

turn your back on sb/sth refuse to help or support sb who needs it: *She turned her back on her family when she became famous.*

turn a blind 'eye (to sth) pretend not to see sth or know about sth: *There's so much suffering in the world, you can't just turn a blind eye to it.* ○ *The police here turn a blind eye to a lot of drug taking; they're really only interested in the big drug dealers.*

turn the 'corner pass the most dangerous point of an illness or the most difficult part of sth, and begin to improve: *Now that the company is beginning to pay back the money it owes, I feel we've turned the corner.* ○ *The doctors say she's turned the corner now. She should be out of hospital soon.*

turn a deaf 'ear (to sth) refuse to listen (to sth); ignore sth: *She turned a deaf ear to her husband's advice and ordered another large whisky.*

turn in her/his 'grave (used for expressing disapproval of sth) a person who is dead would be shocked by or angry about sth if she/he were still alive: *Beethoven would turn in his grave if he could hear the way they're playing his music.*

turn sth inside 'out/upside 'down search for sth by looking everywhere, and probably make a mess at the same time: *The thieves turned the office upside down but they didn't find anything valuable.* ○ *I've turned this drawer inside out but I can't find my passport.*

turn it in! (*very informal*) stop making a noise! Stop doing that!: *Hey, you! Turn it in, I'm trying to get some sleep!*

turn your 'nose up at sth (*informal*) refuse or reject sth because you don't think it is good enough for you: *The cat turned up his nose at the food.*

a/the ,turn of e'vents the way things happen, especially when this is not expected: *Because of a strange turn of events at work, she has unexpectedly been offered a very good job in the sales department.*

a ,turn of 'phrase a particular way of saying sth or describing sth: *She has a very amusing turn of phrase.*

a ,turn of the 'screw another problem or difficulty added to a situation which is already very bad: *In this recession a rise in interest rates is just another turn of the screw for businesses.*

a ,turn of 'speed a sudden increase in speed: *She put on a turn of speed at the end of the race and won easily.*

the ,turn of the 'year/'century the time when a new year/century starts: *He was born around the turn of the century.*

,turn ,on the 'heat (*informal*) put

increased pressure on sb in order to make them do sth: *If he doesn't pay us we'll have to turn on the heat.*

turn on your 'heel suddenly turn around and leave, often because you are angry or annoyed: *Quite unexpectedly he turned on his heel and walked out of the door.*

turn the other 'cheek refuse to react violently or critically to sb who has been violent or critical to you: *It's hard to just turn the other cheek when people are criticizing you unfairly.* (from the Bible)

turn over a new 'leaf change your way of behaving and start a better life: *This is a new project to help ex-prisoners turn over a new leaf.*

turn round and do sth (*informal*) say or do sth unexpected and unfair: *He just turned round and told her that he was leaving. She couldn't believe it.*

turn sb's 'stomach or **make sb's 'stomach turn** make sb feel sick or disgusted: *The thought of eating a raw egg turns my stomach.*

turn the 'tables (on sb) do sth which means that you now have an advantage over sb who previously had an advantage over you: *Oxford beat us 3-0 last year, but we turned the tables on them this year – we won 5-0.*

turn 'tail (and run, flee, etc) quickly go back in the direction you have just come from because you are frightened: *As soon as he saw the police he turned tail and fled.*

turn sth to your (own) ad'vantage or **turn sth to great ad'vantage** do sth which helps you benefit from an unfavourable or difficult situation: *She had three empty rooms in the house after her children left home, so she decided to turn this to her advantage and rent them out to students.* ○ *I once knew a blind teacher who turned his blindness to great advantage in the classroom.*

turn 'turtle (*informal*) (of a boat) turn upside down: *We turned turtle right in front of the yacht club. It was so embarrassing.*

a 'turn-up for the book(s) (*informal*) an unusual or unexpected event: *Everyone thought John would win, so when Richard won it was a real turn-up for the books.*

turn up like a bad 'penny appear at a meeting, party, etc when you are not wanted or made welcome by the people there: *He turns up like a bad penny every time there's a chance of a free meal or a drink.*

go/turn sour ➪ sour; **not know which way to turn** ➪ know; **put/set/turn your mind to sth** ➪ mind; **put/turn the clock back** ➪ clock; **put/turn/send sb out to grass** ➪ grass; **serve his, etc turn = serve the purpose** ➪ serve; **stand/turn sth on its head** ➪ head; **turn/put sth to good account** ➪ account

turned

as it/things turned 'out as later events showed: *I didn't need my umbrella as it turned out* (because it didn't rain later).

be well, badly, etc turned 'out be well, etc dressed: *Her children are always smartly turned out.*

the wheel has come/turned full circle ➪ wheel

turns

take turns doing sth or **take it in turns to do sth** do sth one person after another: *My wife and I take it in turns to write to our daughter in Canada.* ○ *There weren't enough computers for everybody, so we had to take turns using them.*

the tide turns ➪ tide; **the worm turns** ➪ worm

turtle **turn turtle** ➪ turn

twice

be 'twice the man/woman (that sb is) be much better, stronger, healthier, etc than sb or than before: *How dare you criticize him? He's twice the man that you are!* ○ *I saw him today for the first time since his heart operation. He's twice the man he was.*

lightning never strikes twice ➪ lightning; **once bitten, twice shy** ➪ once; **(not) think twice about sth/doing sth** ➪ think

twiddle

twiddle your thumbs (*informal*) do nothing (while you wait for sth): *I had to sit at home twiddling my thumbs, waiting for the phone to ring.*

twinkling

(do sth) in the ,twinkling of an 'eye

twist

(do sth) very quickly: *Her mood can change in the twinkling of an eye.*

twist

,twist sb's 'arm (*quite informal, often humorous*) force or persuade sb to do sth, but not by using physical force: *'Do you think Jane will lend us her car?' 'I think we could probably twist her arm.'* ○ *'Have another whisky, Mike.' 'OK, if you twist my arm.'*

twist sb (a)round your little 'finger (*informal*) be able to persuade or influence sb very easily usually because they like you: *I can twist my parents round my little finger.*

get/have your knickers in a twist ⇨ knickers; round the bend/twist ⇨ round

'twixt there's many a slip 'twixt cup and lip ⇨ slip

two

be in two 'minds about sth/doing sth be unable to decide about sth: *I was in two minds about leaving London; my friends were there, but at the same time I really wanted to work abroad.*

for two pins (*informal*) (used for saying that it would not take very much to persuade you to do sth but you cannot because it would cause problems for you or for other people) for any small reason or excuse; willingly: *I spend so much money on this car. For two pins I'd sell it.*

it takes two (to do sth) *or* it takes two to tango some things cannot be the fault or responsibility of one person alone: *You have only heard his side of the story. It takes two to quarrel, you know.* ○ *The company is ready to sign the agreement now, but it takes two to tango and the negotiations may continue for several days yet.*

(there are) no two ways a'bout it (*informal*) (used for saying that you are giving the only possible correct interpretation or opinion about sth): *There are no two ways about it – these sales figures are terrible!*

not have (got) two pennies to rub together (*British, informal*) have very little

money: *How can they afford a holiday? They haven't got two pennies to rub together.*

put ,two and ,two to'gether from what you know, have seen or heard about sb/sth, make a guess which is probably correct: *Sue's car is often outside his house, but only when his wife is at work; so it's not difficult to put two and two together.*

that makes 'two of us (*saying*) I agree with your opinion; I am in the same situation: *'I think he's behaving very badly.' 'That makes two of us.'* ○ *'I'm bored with this job.' 'That makes two of us.'*

two can play at 'that game *or* a game that 'two can play (*saying*) (used when you threaten to behave as unpleasantly, badly, etc as sb has just behaved towards you): *'He told the boss that you were going home early every day.' 'Oh did he? Well, two can play at that game. I think I'll tell the boss about him getting to work late every morning.'* ○ *Pointing out other people's mistakes in public is a game that two can play, so you'd better stop.*

two heads are better than 'one (*saying*) two people who are trying to solve a problem together achieve more than one person who works alone.

two wrongs don't make a right (*saying*) (used for saying that it is wrong or useless to harm sb because they have harmed you): *Don't be stupid! You want to crash his motorbike just because he crashed yours! Two wrongs don't make a right, you know.*

two's 'company (three's a crowd) (*saying*) two people, especially two lovers, are happier alone than within a group of three.

be two/ten a penny ⇨ penny

type

be (not) sb's type (*informal*) be (not) the kind of person that sb likes: *Mark isn't really her type – she prefers quiet, sensitive men.* ○ *Gerry is more her type.*

revert to type ⇨ revert

tyre a spare tyre ⇨ spare

U

ugly

an ˌugly ˈduckling (*informal*) an unattractive or uninteresting child who develops into a very attractive or interesting adult: *He's got the looks of a film star now, but he was a real ugly duckling as a child.* (from a story by Hans Christian Andersen in which a young swan is raised with ducklings. They have to stop teasing him about his ugliness when he becomes a beautiful swan)

be miserable/ugly as sin ⇨ **sin**

um

um and aah (about sth) *or* **hum/hem and haw** (*informal*) speak but say nothing important because you need more time to think about a problem, matter, etc: *He ummed and aahed for about half an hour and then finally said he would lend me the money.*
umming and aahing (*noun*) *After a lot of umming and aahing, he finally said yes to the plan.*

umbrage

take ˈumbrage (at sth) (*formal*) be offended or angry because of sth: *She took umbrage at my remarks about her hair.*

unawares

catch/take sb unaˈwares surprise sb; do sth when sb does not expect it: *Her sudden refusal took me unawares.* ○ *You caught us unawares by coming so early.*

uncertain

say, tell sb, etc (sth) in ˌno unˌcertain ˈterms say, etc (sth) clearly and forcefully: *I told him in no uncertain terms what I thought of his behaviour.*

uncle   Bob's your uncle ⇨ Bob

uncrowned

(be) the ˌuncrowned ˈking/ˈqueen (of sth) (*informal*) a person who is recognized unofficially as being a leader or the best at an activity.

undivided

get/have sb's undivided attention receive sb's full attention: *I'll just finish writing this sentence, and then you'll have my undivided attention.* also **give sb your undivided attention**

unequal   on   unfair/unequal   terms
⇨ terms

unknown

(be) an ˌunknown ˈquantity (be) a person or thing that you do not know anything or enough about: *His ability to make decisions in a crisis is an unknown quantity.* ○ *Our new director is still an unknown quantity.*

unstuck

ˌcome unˈstuck (*informal*) be unsuccessful; fail: *His plan to escape came badly unstuck.* ○ *She came unstuck in the last part of the exam.*

unturned   leave no stone unturned
⇨ leave

up

be/get up to sth (*informal*) be doing sth, possibly sth that you should not be doing: *What are those children up to?* ○ *We used to get up to all sorts of things when we were that age.*

be on the ˌup and ˈup (*informal*)   **1** (*British*) be getting better, becoming more successful, etc: *Her health is on the up and up. Soon she'll be out of hospital.* ○ *Business is on the up and up.*   **2** (*US*) be honest: *Before we give him the job, are you sure he's on the up and up?*

be up against it (*informal*) be in a difficult situation: *Two of the staff are ill and the order has to be ready for delivery by this evening, so we're really up against it.*

be ˌup and aˈbout/aˈround be out of bed after being ill or sleeping: *She was off work for a week, but she's up and about again now.* ○ *On a Saturday he's not up and around till about eleven o'clock.*

be ˌup and ˈdown (*informal*) (of the way a person feels) change often, for example from happy to sad, healthy to unhealthy, etc: *One moment he seems well, the next he's ill again –*

he's up and down all the time.

be up for grabs (*very informal*) be available to anybody who is interested in getting, buying, etc it: *The contract for repairing the damaged buildings will soon be up for grabs.*

be up to sb **1** be sb's right to decide: *Shall we have an Indian or a Chinese meal? It's up to you.* ○ *The decision's not up to me.* **2** be sb's responsibility or duty: *It's up to us to help people in need.* ○ *Repairs to the house are up to the owner, aren't they?*

(not) be 'up to sth/doing sth *or* **(not) feel 'up to sth/doing sth** **1** (not) be well enough or not too tired to do sth: *I had a terrible cold and didn't feel up to going to work.* ○ *At my age, I just don't think I'm up to climbing 200 steps.* **2** not be of a high enough quality or standard; not be good enough: *He's just not up to the job, I'm afraid.*

be up with sb/sth be wrong with sb/sth: *'What's up? You look really worried.' 'I've just had a very unpleasant letter from my bank manager.'* ○ *Something's up with the car. It won't start.*

be well up on sth know a lot about sth: *Are you well up on the latest developments?* ○ *She's very well up on modern Chinese literature.*

have had it up to here (with sth/sb) (*very informal*) not be able to bear a problem, situation, etc any longer: *I've had it up to here with tax demands.* ○ *I've had it up to here. I'm going!* (when using this idiom, you often raise your open hand to the side of the top of your head)

up and down sth all over sth; everywhere in a place: *People up and down the country are giving money to the earthquake appeal.*

up and leave, go, etc (*informal*) leave, etc quickly and unexpectedly: *Without saying anything, she just upped and went.*

(be) up to your ears/eyes/eyeballs/ neck in sth (*informal*) have too much of sth, for example work, problems, etc; be deeply involved in sth: *He was up to his eyes in debt.* ○ *She was up to her eyeballs in washing-up so I offered to help.*

look sb up and down ⇨ **look**

upon once upon a time ⇨ **once**; **take it on/upon yourself to do sth** ⇨ **take**

upper

get, have, gain, etc the upper 'hand (over sb) get, etc power or control over sb, especially in a fight, competition, etc: *Our team gained the upper hand in the second half of the match.* ○ *The police now have the upper hand in their fight against the drug dealers.*

the upper crust (*informal*) people who are in the highest social class.

a stiff upper lip ⇨ **stiff**

ups

ups and 'downs times of success, happiness, etc and times of failure, unhappiness, etc: *I suppose every marriage has its ups and downs.* ○ *I've watched the ups and downs of his business with great interest.*

upset

upset the/sb's 'apple-cart (*informal*) do sth that spoils a plan or stops the progress of sth: *Another, much cheaper hairdresser has opened next door, which has upset the apple-cart.*

upstairs kick sb upstairs ⇨ **kick**

uptake

be ,quick/,slow on the 'uptake (*informal*) understand things quickly/ understand even simple things with difficulty: *He's a very good worker but he's a bit slow on the uptake sometimes. You have to explain everything at least twice.*

use

be in/out of 'use be (not) being used: *We'll have to find a classroom that's not in use.* ○ *The road's out of use while it's being repaired.*

be of use (to sb) be useful (to sb): *These maps might be of use to you on your holiday.* ○ *Was the book of any use?*

,come into/,go out of 'use start/stop being used: *When did this word come into common use?* ○ *The present phone boxes will go out of use next year.*

have no use for sb/sth strongly dislike sb/sth: *I have no use for people like John. You can never trust them.*

I, etc could use a 'drink, etc (*informal*) I, etc need a drink, etc: *We could use some extra help just at the moment.*

it's no use (doing, etc sth) it will not achieve anything; it is pointless: *'It's no use* running. The bus has already gone.' ○ It's no use. I just can't remember the word.

make use of sth use sth for your own advantage: *Make full use of every chance you get to speak English.*

put sth to good 'use benefit from using sth: *She'll be able to put her experience to good use in the new job.*

use your loaf (*informal*) think carefully; use your intelligence: *Use your loaf! Meena can't read English, so there's no point in writing her a letter!* (*a loaf of bread* is Cockney rhyming slang for 'head')

what's the use (of doing, etc sth)? *or* **what use is there (in doing, etc sth)?** (used for emphasizing that you think an action, etc will not achieve anything): *What's the use of worrying about the weather on your wedding day? You can't do anything*

about it.

a fat lot of use/help ⇨ fat; **be no good/ use to man or beast** ⇨ man; **no earthly use** ⇨ earthly

useful
make yourself useful help other people: *Come on, Hannah. Make yourself useful and peel those potatoes for me.*

come in handy/useful ⇨ handy

usual as per usual/normal ⇨ per; **it's business as usual** ⇨ business

utmost
do/try your 'utmost (to do sth) try as hard as you can (to do sth): *I tried my utmost to stop them.* ○ *Don't blame her – she did her utmost to finish it on time.*

V

vacant situations vacant ⇨ situations

vacuum
do sth in a 'vacuum do sth alone, without contact with other people, things, events, etc: *No novel is written in a vacuum. There are always influences from past writers.* ○ *These decisions are not made in a vacuum.*

vain take sb's name in vain ⇨ name

value
a 'value judgement (*disapproving*) a judgement about sth that is based on sb's personal opinion and not on facts: *'She's quite a good driver for a woman.' 'That's a real value judgement, Simon. Women drive just as well as men.'* ○ *make value judgements*

take sb/sth at face value ⇨ face

variations
variations on the theme of sth different ways of doing or saying the same thing: *Her new book of short stories offers variations on the the theme of man's cruelty to woman.*

variety
variety is the spice of life (*saying*) a variety of different activities, interests,

places or people in your life makes it more enjoyable.

veil
draw/throw/cast a veil over sth say nothing or no more about something unpleasant: *Most of us prefer to cast a veil over subjects like illness and death.* ○ *It is kinder to draw a veil over some of his later films.*

velvet an iron fist/hand in a velvet glove ⇨ iron

vengeance
do sth with a 'vengeance (*informal*) to do sth with great energy or force: *After the holiday I need to start working with a vengeance.* ○ *The rain came down with a vengeance.*

ventured nothing ventured, nothing gained ⇨ nothing

vent
give (full) vent to something express a strong (negative) feeling freely and forcefully: *I tried to stop myself giving full vent to my anger.*

verge

on/to the verge of sth at or close to the point or time when sth begins: *We're on the verge of war and nobody seems really worried.* ○ *Her unhappiness brought her to the verge of a mental breakdown.*

verse chapter and verse ⇨ chapter

very

can/could not very well do sth (*informal*) (used to say that sth is not the right thing to do): *You can't very well change the arrangements now. It's too late to inform people.*

very good (*rather formal*) (used for saying 'yes' when a person in authority gives you an order): *'Brown, bring me a bottle of champagne and two glasses, please.' 'Very good, Sir.'*

very much so (*rather formal*) (used for emphasizing 'yes'): *'I understand you are interested in German politics.' 'Yes, very much so.'*

very well (*quite formal*) (used to accept sth or agree to sth, especially when you do not really want to): *'Please could I go home an hour early today, Mrs Smith?' 'Very well Emma, if you really must.'*

vessel burst a blood vessel ⇨ burst

vested

have (got) a vested interest (in sth) have a special interest in sth, because you may benefit from it: *He has a vested interest in Mona leaving the firm* (because he may get her job).

vexed

a vexed ʹquestion a difficult problem that people often talk and argue about: *They're discussing the vexed question of private health insurance.*

vice a den of iniquity/vice ⇨ den

vicious

a vicious ʹcircle a difficult situation or problem where one thing makes another thing happen, which then makes the first thing happen again: *He spends too much on drink because he's worried about his financial problems, and so the situation gets worse and worse. It's a vicious circle.*

victory a Pyrrhic victory ⇨ Pyrrhic

view

(have, etc sth) in ʹview (*quite forma*) (have, etc sth) as an idea, plan, etc in you mind: *What the President has in view is world without nuclear weapons.*

in view of sth because of sth; considerin sth: *In view of all this rain, I suppose we better stay at home today.*

(be) on ʹview being shown or displayed t the public: *A lot of exciting new designs are o view at the Boat Show this year.*

take a dim/poor ʹview oʹf sb/sth (*qui informal*) disagree with or dislike sb/st} *Farmers tend to take a dim view of the publ walking over their land.* ○ *The judge said he too a very poor view of their behaviour.*

take the view (that) (*quite formal*) it i my, etc opinion that...: *I take the view tha medical care should be provided by the State.*

(do sth) with a view to sth/doing st} (do sth) with the plan or hope of sth/doin sth: *He is painting and decorating the hous with a view to selling it for a good price.*

a bird's eye view ⇨ bird; **have a ringsid seat/view** ⇨ ringside; **in full view** ⇨ fu| **a point of view** ⇨ point; **take the lon view** ⇨ long; **a worm's eye view** ⇨ worm

villain

the ʹvillain of the piece (*often humorous* a person or thing that is responsible for certain problem, difficulty, etc: *Nicolette's th villain of the piece; she's the person who starte this trouble.* (refers to the principal ev character in a book, play, etc)

vine wither on the vine ⇨ wither

violet a shrinking violet ⇨ shrinking

virtue

by virtue of sth (*formal*) because of sth: *was invited to a party at the embassy simply b virtue of being British.*

make a virtue of necessity act in a goo or moral way, and perhaps expect praise fo this, not because you chose to but becaus in that particular situation you had n choice.

virtue is its own reward (*saying*) th reward for acting in a moral or correct wa is the knowledge that you have done so, and you should not expect more than this, for example praise from other people or payment.

a paragon of virtue ⇨ paragon

vision tunnel vision ⇨ tunnel

visit a flying visit ⇨ flying; **pay sb/sth a visit** ⇨ pay

voice
be in good, poor, etc 'voice be singing well, badly, etc: *The soprano was in excellent voice.*

keep your voice down (used to tell sb to speak more quietly): *Keep your voice down, will you? There are people trying to sleep!*

make your voice 'heard express your opinions, feelings, etc so that other people hear or notice: *This programme gives ordinary people a chance to make their voices heard.*

a voice (crying) in the wilderness a warning of a danger given by a person or small group which most people do not pay any attention to: *A few scientists in the early 1980s were warning of the dangers of AIDS but nobody took them seriously. They were just a voice in the wilderness.* (from the Bible)

at the top of your voice ⇨ top; **like, love, etc the sound of your own voice** ⇨ sound; **raise your voice** ⇨ raise; **raise a voice against sb/sth** ⇨ raise; **the still small voice** ⇨ still; **with one voice** ⇨ one

void null and void ⇨ null

volume speak volumes ⇨ speak

vote
put sth to the 'vote decide sth by asking people for their votes: *OK, I'll put it to the vote. Put up your hands if you think religion should be taught in schools.* ○ *The issue was put to the vote.*

a ,vote of 'thanks (*quite formal*) a short speech, usually at a meeting or social occasion, to thank sb, or to ask people to clap to show that they enjoyed sth: *I'd like to propose a vote of thanks to Mrs Warren for her interesting talk.*

vote with your feet show that you dislike or disagree with sth by leaving a place or organization: *If shoppers don't like the new market, they'll vote with their feet and go elsewhere.*

W

wag let the tail wag the dog = the tail is wagging the dog ⇨ tail; **tongues wag** ⇨ tongues

wagging set tongues wagging = tongues wag ⇨ tongues; **the tail is wagging the dog** ⇨ tail

wagon
be/go on the 'wagon (*informal*) no longer drink/decide to stop drinking alcohol usually for a short period of time: *My brother-in-law goes on the wagon for a month after Christmas every year.* ○ *'Would you like a gin and tonic?' 'No thanks. I'm on the wagon.'*

waifs
waifs and strays homeless people, especially children in a big city; (*humorous*) lonely people with nowhere else to go: *There are lots of waifs and strays living on the streets here.* ○ *My wife is always inviting various waifs and strays from work to our house. She seems to attract them.*

wait(ing)
,wait and 'see wait patiently to find out what will happen (before doing sth): *'Where are you taking me?' 'Wait and see.'* ○ *There's nothing we can do at the moment. We'll just have to wait and see.*

wait for it (*formal*) **1** wait until you receive the order or signal to do sth: *Are you all ready? Wait for it! Now!* **2** (used for telling sb that you are about to say sth amusing or surprising): *'What did you have?' 'We had roast duck and wait for it – caviar!'*

(play) a 'waiting game delay making a decision or doing sth because this puts you in a stronger position: *They're playing a waiting game, delaying their own offer until they know what the others are offering.*

wait on sb hand and 'foot do almost everything for sb, for example cook meals, bring everything they ask for, etc: *My father expects my mother to wait on him hand and foot.*

(just) you 'wait (*informal*) (said to warn sb that you will punish them or get your revenge on them later): *All right, so you won – just you wait till next time! ○ Just you wait till your father gets home!*

lie in wait ⇨ lie; **time and tide wait for no man** ⇨ time

wake

in the wake of sth coming after and resulting from sth; behind sth: *Disease began spreading in the wake of the disaster. ○ The tourists left all sorts of rubbish in their wake.* (as a ship moves through the water, it leaves a wake (disturbed water) behind it)

wake the 'dead (of a noise) be very loud: *He must have heard it – that doorbell's loud enough to wake the dead.*

walk

from every walk/all walks of 'life from all parts of society: *The people at the meeting came from all walks of life – students, writers, business people, and so on. ○ Gardening appeals to people from every walk of life, from bus drivers to company directors.*

take a walk (*especially US, offensive*) (said when you are angry with sb) go away: *She told him to take a walk.*

walk all over sb (*informal*) **1** treat sb very badly or unkindly: *Tell him what you think of him – don't let him walk all over you like that.* **2** completely defeat sb in a competition: *The only time I played chess with my wife, she walked all over me.* **'walkover** (*noun*) an easy victory: *We beat them 12-0: it was a walkover.*

walk it (*informal*) win easily in a competition: *If you play like that on the day of the match, you'll walk it.*

walk sb off their 'feet (*informal*) make sb walk so far or so fast that they are exhausted: *She may be over seventy, but I'm sure she could walk some of you younger ones off your feet.*

walk on air (*informal*) be very happy about sth: *When I passed my driving test, I was walking on air for days.*

walk 'tall feel proud and confident: *When I finally got a job after years of unemployment, I felt I could walk tall again.*

walk a tightrope *or* **be on a tightrope** be in a situation where you must act very carefully: *I'm walking a tightrope at the moment; one more mistake and I might lose my job.* (a tightrope is a rope high up in the air that an acrobat walks along at a circus)

run before you can walk ⇨ run

walking

be a walking 'dictionary, encyclo'pedia, etc (*informal*) be an expert on sth whom other people can consult for advice: *Geoff is a walking encyclopedia. He knows about everything.*

wall(s)

drive/send sb up the 'wall (*informal*) make sb very annoyed; drive sb crazy: *That noise is driving me up the wall.* also **go up the 'wall** (*informal*) become very annoyed.

go to the wall be defeated or ruined: *Smaller companies are always the first to go to the wall in an economic recession.*

,walls have 'ears (*saying*) somebody may be listening, so be careful what you say.

bang, etc your head against a brick wall ⇨ head; **a fly on the wall** ⇨ fly; **have your back to the wall** ⇨ back; **talk to a brick wall** ⇨ talk; **the writing on the wall** ⇨ writing

wand wave a wand ⇨ wave

wane

be on the 'wane be becoming smaller or less strong: *Her interest in the project is on the wane. ○ Their political power is on the wane.* (when the moon is on the wane it appears smaller in the sky)

wax and wane ⇨ wax

want

for want of sth because sth needed is either absent or impossible: *For want of a better name, I'm calling this book 'My Early Years'. ○ We went to the cinema for want of* *anything better to do.*

not want to 'know (about sth) (*quite informal*) not care (about sth); not want to become involved (with sth): *She was in desperate need of help but nobody seemed to want to know.* ○ *If she wants money, I don't want to know about it*

want for nothing have everything you need or want: *They both earn good salaries; their children want for nothing.*

have/want none of it/that ⇨ none; **not for lack/want of trying, being told, etc** ⇨ lack; **want the moon = cry/ask for the moon** ⇨ moon

war

a war of 'nerves a situation where two people, groups, or countries try to defeat one another by using threats, warnings, and other psychological pressure (but not violence or war): *ICI is trying to take over our company; it's a real war of nerves.*

all's fair in love and war ⇨ fair

warm(ed)

be (as) warm as 'toast (*informal*) be pleasantly warm compared to the cold air outside etc: *I'll light the fire and we'll soon be as warm as toast in here.*

keep sb's 'seat, etc warm (for them) (*informal*) remain in a job, official position, etc until sb is ready to take it so that a third person cannot do so: *She's not the regular gardener – she's just keeping his place warm for him until he gets back.*

like death warmed up ⇨ death

warpath

be/go on the 'warpath (*informal*) be angry and ready for an argument or a fight about sth: *Look out – the boss is on the warpath again!*

warrant sign your own death warrant ⇨ sign

wars

in the 'wars (*informal or humorous*) (especially of children) slightly injured because you have been in a fight or have hurt yourself in an accident: *My nephew Ben is always in the wars. Whenever I see him, he's covered in plasters.*

warts

warts and all (*often humorous*) including all the faults as well as the good points: *This new book on Churchill describes him warts and all. It gives a very complete picture.* (Oliver Cromwell asked the painter Sir Peter Lely to portray him 'warts and all')

wash

(all) come out in the 'wash (*informal*) **1** (of mistakes, problems, difficulties, etc) be corrected after a while, without any great harm being done: *'Some of the documents still haven't arrived!' 'Don't worry, there's probably been a slight mix-up – it'll all come out in the wash.'* **2** (of a secret) be revealed: *You can't hide what you've done for ever. It'll come out in the wash, you know.*

wash your dirty linen in 'public (*quite informal*) talk or write about unpleasant or embarrassing private difficulties in public: *Nobody must mention these problems at the meeting. I don't want our dirty linen washed in public.*

wash your hands of sb/sth refuse to deal with or be responsible for sb/sth any longer: *After the way she's behaved, I'm never going to help her again! I wash my hands of her!* ○ *I can't just wash my hands of the whole business. I've got responsibilities.* (refers to Pontius Pilate in the Bible who refused to take a decision about what should happen to Jesus)

waste

go/run to 'waste be unused and therefore wasted: *What a pity to see all that food go to waste!*

waste your 'breath (on sb/sth) speak (to sb or about sb/sth) but not have any effect: *Don't waste your breath on her. She doesn't take advice from anybody.*

,waste not, 'want not (*saying*) if you never waste anything, for example food or money, you will have it when you need it.

don't waste your breath = save your breath ⇨ save; **lay sth waste** ⇨ lay; **lose/waste no time** ⇨ time

watch

be on the 'watch (for sth) be carefully watching (so you are ready when a thing happens): *The police warned people to be on the watch for car thieves.*

keep 'watch (for sb/sth) stay awake or alert (to be ready for danger, etc): *I'll keep watch while you sleep.* ○ *The doctors are keeping watch for any change in her condition.*

watch the 'clock (*informal*) often check what time it is, because you are impatient for sth to finish or to happen: *She sits at home each evening watching the clock until her husband comes in.* ○ *Someone who spends all his time watching the clock is usually not a good worker.* **clock-watching** (*noun*) *Don't spend the afternoon clock-watching.*

'watch it (*informal*) **1** (used to warn sb to be careful): *Watch it! There's a car coming.* **2** *or* **watch your step** (used to tell sb that they are behaving badly and will be punished if they continue): *I'm in control now, so watch it!* ○ *If you do that again, there'll be trouble, so watch your step.*

watch sb/sth like a hawk (*quite informal*) watch sb/sth very carefully: *Unless you watch him like a hawk, he'll go off without finishing the work.*

watch the 'world go by watch what is happening around you, but do little yourself: *The old people sit at their windows and watch the world go by.* ○ *It was one of those cafés with a terrace where you can sit and watch the world go by.*

mind/watch your step ➪ step

watched

a watched pot never boils (*saying*) when you wait impatiently or anxiously for a thing to happen, it seems to take longer: *Looking out of the window won't make him arrive any quicker! Don't you know that a watched pot never boils?*

water

be (like) water off a ,duck's 'back (*quite informal*) (of criticism) have no effect on sb: *His book got bad reviews, but it was all water off a duck's back – he doesn't care what they say.*

be (all) water under the 'bridge be an event, mistake, etc that has already happened and cannot be changed (so you should not worry about it): *We had a terrible quarrel five years ago but that's all water under the bridge.*

like 'water (*informal*) in large amounts; in great quantity: *They're spending money like*

water. ○ *Champagne was flowing like water at the party.*

a lot of water has passed, etc under the 'bridge (since then) it's a long time ago; a lot of things have happened (since then) and the situation is different now: *You keep talking about our problems ten years ago. A lot of water has flowed under the bridge since then.*

blood is thicker than water ➪ blood; **come hell or high water** ➪ hell; **deep water** ➪ deep; **a fish out of water** ➪ fish; **high water mark** ➪ high; **hold water** ➪ hold; **in hot water** ➪ hot; **keep your head above water** ➪ head; **like a duck to water** ➪ duck; **make sb's mouth water** ➪ mouth; **pass water** ➪ pass; **pour/throw cold water on sth** ➪ cold; **test the water/waters** ➪ test; **tread water** ➪ tread; **you can take/lead a horse to water, but you can't make it drink** ➪ horse

Waterloo **meet your Waterloo** ➪ meet

waters **muddy the waters** ➪ muddy; **pour oil on troubled waters** ➪ pour; **still waters run deep** ➪ still

wave(s)

make waves (*informal*) cause trouble or a change in a situation which most people want to keep stable or calm: *It's taken us a long time to find an answer to this problem, so please don't make waves now.*

wave a (magic) wand (and do sth) find a quick and easy way of doing sth that is very difficult or impossible; do sth as if by magic: *I'm sorry, but I can't just wave a magic wand and solve your problems.* ○ *If you could wave a wand, what sort of house would you like?*

the crest of a wave ➪ crest

wavelength

be on the same wavelength/on different wavelengths (*informal*) have the same/different, etc opinion(s) or feelings about sth: *I find him difficult to talk to – we're on completely different wavelengths.* ○ *On the subject of marriage, Judith and I are on the same wavelength.*

wax

,wax and 'wane become continually

stronger and then weaker, or more important and then less important: *The government's popularity has waxed and waned over the past year.* (refers to the changing shape of the moon in the sky)

way

be in a bad 'way be very ill or in serious trouble: *He was attacked in the street last night and he's in quite a bad way, I understand.* ○ '*I hear the company's in a bad way.' 'Yes, it's lost a lot of money.'*

be, etc in/out of the 'way (of sb/sth) be, etc (not) stopping sb/sth moving freely; be, etc (not) stopping sb doing sth: *I'm afraid your car's in the way – I can't get out.* ○ '*Why did you leave?' 'Well, she had a lot of work to do, and I felt I was in the way.'* ○ *He was busy cooking, so I got out of the way.*

be on the way 'out/'in be becoming unfashionable/fashionable: *Short skirts are on the way out.* ○ *Long hair is on the way back in.*

be on the/your way to/towards sth be about to achieve sth in the near future (usually sth good): *We're on the way towards an election victory.*

be under 'way have started and be now progressing or taking place: *A major search is under way to find the escaped prisoners.* ○ *Negotiations are under way to resolve the dispute.*

be with sb all the way support sb completely: *You can count on my support, Steve. I'm with you all the way.*

by the way 1 (used for introducing sth you have just thought of, which may or may not be connected to what has just been said): *I had lunch with Graham at work today... by the way, I've invited him and his wife to lunch on Sunday.* **2** (used for saying that sth is not important or relevant to the present situation or discussion): *Her academic qualifications are by the way. What we need is someone dynamic and creative.*

by way of sth 1 (of a journey) passing through a place: *They're going to Poland by way of France and Germany.* **2** as a kind of sth; as sth: *What are you thinking of doing by way of a holiday this year?* ○ *The flowers are by way of a 'thank-you' for all her help.*

come your 'way happen to you or come

into your possession, temporarily or permanently: *Some good luck came his way.* ○ *When my grandmother dies, quite a lot of money will be coming my way.*

do sth in a big/small 'way do sth to a great/small extent; do sth on a large/small scale: *He's got himself into debt in a big way.* ○ *She collects antiques in a small way.*

do sth on/along the 'way 1 do sth as you go somewhere: *Buy a hamburger and eat it on the way.* **2** do sth while you do sth else; do sth during the process of doing sth else: *I've succeeded in this business, and met a lot of nice people along the way.*

get sth out of the way deal with a task or difficultly so that it is no longer a problem or worry: *I'm glad I've got that visit to the dentist out of the way.*

give 'way break or collapse: *The bridge gave way under the weight of the lorry.* ○ *Her legs suddenly gave way and she fell to the floor.*

give 'way (to sb/sth) 1 allow sb/sth to go first: *Give way to traffic coming from the right.* **2** feel and express a strong emotion, without trying to hide it or stop it: *She refused to give way to despair.* ○ *As soon as she was alone, she gave way to tears.* **3** allow sb to have what they want: *In arguments, I'm always the first to give way.* ○ *We must not give way to their demands.* **4** be replaced by sth: *The storm gave way to bright sunshine.*

go out of your way to do sth make a special effort to do sth, usually to help or please sb: *She went out of her way to cook a really nice meal.* ○ *I went out of my way to be nice to her.*

go your own 'way do what you want, especially against the advice of others: *Teenagers always go their own way, and it's no use trying to stop them.*

go sb's way 1 travel in the same direction as sb: *I'm going your way. Do you want a lift?* **2** (of events) be favourable to sb: *Did you hear Alan got the job? It seems that things are going his way at last.*

go the way of all 'flesh (*often humorous*) die.

have/get your (own) 'way *or* **have it/ things/everything (all) your (own) 'way** get, believe or do what you want, usually despite the wishes or feelings of others: *She always gets her own way in the end.* ○ *All right, have it your own way – I'm tired of arguing.*

have a way of doing sth often do sth, usually sth you do not like: *He has a way of arriving when you're not expecting him.*

have a way with sb/sth have a special ability to deal with sb/sth: *She's a very good teacher. She has a way with children.* ○ *He's always had a way with horses.* ○ *She has a way with words* (she speaks or writes well).

in a 'way *or* **in 'one way** *or* **in 'some ways** to a certain extent (but not completely): *In a way, living in the town is better than the country, because there's much more to do.* ○ *In one way, I'm sorry we didn't stay longer.* ○ *In some ways I agree with you.*

a lot, not much, etc in the way of sth a lot, etc of sth: *We don't do a lot in the way of exercise.* ○ *She doesn't have much in the way of clothes.*

make 'way (for sb/sth) make enough space for sb/sth; allow sb/sth to pass: *Could you move your books to make way for the food?* ○ *People made way for my wheelchair.*

make your way (to/towards sth) go (to/towards sth): *Would passengers please make their way to gate 15 for the flight to Paris.*

make your way in sth succeed in sth, especially a job: *She's trying to make her way in the fashion business.* ○ *The time had come to leave home and make his way in the world.*

‚no 'way (*informal*) definitely not; never: *'Are you going to stay at school after you're 16?' 'No way. I want to get a job.'* ○ *No way am I going to speak to him again.*

(be) on the 'way (*informal*) (of a baby) not yet born: *She's got two children and another one on the way.*

(be) on your/the 'way (be) coming; (be) going: *If she phones again, tell her I'm on my way* (coming to see her). ○ *I'd better be on my way soon* (leave soon). ○ *I bought some bread on the way home.*

that's the way (*informal*) (used for showing pleasure or approval of what sb is doing or has done): *That's the way. Just keep playing like that and you'll win.*

that's the way the cookie crumbles *or* **that's the way it goes** (*informal*) (used when sth unpleasant or

unfortunate has just happened) that is what can happen in a situation like this and you must accept it because you can't change it: *She met somebody else and left me. That's the way the cookie crumbles, I suppose.*

'way back (*informal*) a long time ago: *We've known each other since way back.* ○ *I first met her way back in the fifties.*

the ‚way of the 'world what often happens; what is common: *Marriages don't always last for ever. That's the way of the world, I'm afraid.*

'work, etc your way through sth read or do sth from beginning to end: *He worked his way through the dictionary learning ten new words every day.* ○ *He's eating his way through all the restaurants that are recommended in the Good Food Guide.*

she/he couldn't punch her/his way out of a paper bag ⇨ punch; **do/learn sth the hard way** ⇨ hard; **do sth in your own sweet time/way** ⇨ sweet; **downhill all the way** ⇨ downhill; **feel your way** ⇨ feel; **go a long way = go far** ⇨ far; **have come a long way** ⇨ long; **in the family way** ⇨ family; **know your way about/around** ⇨ know; **lead the way** ⇨ lead; **lie your way into/out of sth** ⇨ lie; **look the other way** ⇨ look; **not know which way to look** ⇨ know; **not know which way to turn** ⇨ know; **not stand in sb's way** ⇨ stand; **one way and another/the other** ⇨ one; **out of harm's way** ⇨ harm; **pave the way** ⇨ pave; **point the way** ⇨ point; **rub sb up the wrong way** ⇨ rub; **see your way to doing sth** ⇨ see; **see which way the wind blows/is blowing** ⇨ see; **smooth the path/way** ⇨ smooth; **talk your way out of sth/doing sth** ⇨ talk; **thread your way through** ⇨ thread; **where there's a will there's a way** ⇨ will; **work your way up** ⇨ work

ways

in more ways than one (used to show that sth that has been said has more than one meaning): *She's a big woman, in more ways than one* (she is big in size, and also important or powerful).

‚ways and 'means methods or ways, especially unofficial or illegal ones: *'How will you get the money?' 'Don't worry, there are* *ways and means.'*

be set in your ways ⇨ set; **you, etc can't have it both ways** ⇨ both; **cut both/two ways** ⇨ cut; **the error of your ways** ⇨ error; **go your separate ways** ⇨ separate; **mend your ways** ⇨ mend; **no two ways about it** ⇨ two; **the parting of the ways** ⇨ parting

wayside **fall by the wayside** ⇨ fall

weak

be/go ,weak at the 'knees (*informal*) be/become weak because of illness, strong emotion, etc: *He felt dizzy and a bit weak at the knees.* ○ *Her smile made me go weak at the knees* (with nervousness, love, etc). **weak-kneed** (*adjective*) not brave or determined.

a weak 'moment *or* **a moment of 'weakness** a time when you do or agree to sth you would not normally do: *In a weak moment I agreed to let them stay at our house, but later I wished I hadn't.* ○ *I was on a very strict diet but in a moment of weakness I ate a cream cake.*

the spirit is willing but the flesh is weak ⇨ spirit

wear

,wear and 'tear damage or loss of quality because of normal use: *After having the car for five years you expect some wear and tear.* ○ *The guarantee does not cover normal wear and tear.*

wear your ,heart on your 'sleeve show other people your emotions, especially love: *He wears his heart on his sleeve and often gets hurt.* (from Shakespeare's *Othello*)

wear 'thin begin to become less; become less interesting or amusing: *My patience is beginning to wear very thin.* ○ *Don't you think that joke's wearing a bit thin? (because we have heard it many times before).*

wear the 'trousers *or* (*US*) **wear the 'pants** (*informal*) be the partner in a marriage who makes the decisions and tells the other what to do: *It's not difficult to see who wears the trousers in their house!*

the worse for wear ⇨ worse

wearing **in/wearing your birthday suit** ⇨ birthday

weather

be, etc under the 'weather (*informal*) feel, look, etc a bit ill or depressed: *She was off work for two weeks and she still seems a bit under the weather.*

keep a weather eye on sth/open for sth watch sth very carefully for signs of change so that you will be prepared for a problem, difficulty, etc: *It's an ambassador's job to keep a weather eye open for any important political changes.*

make heavy weather of sth ⇨ heavy; **ride out/weather the storm** ⇨ storm

wedding **a shotgun wedding** ⇨ shotgun

wedge **drive a wedge between A and B** ⇨ drive; **the thin end of the wedge** ⇨ thin

week

today, tomorrow, Monday, etc 'week seven days after today, tomorrow, etc: *I'm leaving on Tuesday week.*

week ,in, week 'out (used for emphasis) every week: *I'm tired of the same old routine week in, week out.* (*day*, *month*, and *year* can be used in a similar way to *week* in this expression)

a week last 'Monday, 'Tuesday, etc *or* **a week 'yesterday, to'morrow, etc** seven days before last Monday, etc: *It was a week yesterday that we heard the news.*

weekend **a dirty weekend** ⇨ dirty

weigh

weigh 'anchor (of a ship and its passengers) leave a place: *We weighed anchor in the afternoon and started for the Phillipines.*

weigh on your mind (of a problem or difficulty) make you feel continually worried and anxious: *The safety of the missing children was weighing on their minds.*

weigh (half) a 'ton (*informal*) be very heavy: *These suitcases weigh a ton! What have you got in them?*

weigh your 'words carefully choose the words you use when you speak or write: *He spoke slowly, weighing his words.*

weight

take the 'weight off your feet (*informal*)

(used to tell sb who is tired to sit down): *Here, take the weight off your feet and I'll bring you a cup of tea.*

(do sth by) weight of 'numbers (do sth by) having more people in one group than in another; (do sth by) the strength of many people: *They got what they wanted by sheer weight of numbers.*

be worth your/its weight in gold ⇨ worth; **carry weight** ⇨ carry; **a load/ weight off sb's mind** ⇨ mind; **pull your weight** ⇨ pull; **throw your weight about/around** ⇨ throw

weird

weird and wonderful clever (and attractive) but unusual or strange: *People were wearing all sorts of weird and wonderful clothes.*

welcome

outstay/overstay your 'welcome (of a guest) stay too long so that you are no longer welcome: *We visited some friends in France, but we didn't want to overstay our welcome and left after a couple of days.*

you're welcome (used as a polite reply when a person thanks you): *'Thanks for your help.' 'You're welcome.'*

well

all being well if everything happens as you expect and hope: *We'll see you at Christmas then, all being well.*

all's well that 'ends well (*saying*) if the final result is good, earlier difficulties and problems are not important. (the title of a play by Shakespeare)

be ,all very 'well (for sb to do sth) but. . . *or* **be all well and good (for sb to do sth) but. . .** *or* **be all very fine (for sb to do sth) but. . .** (used for saying that sth, for example a suggestion, opinion or piece of advice, that appears to be reasonable or acceptable to other people is not to you): *'Why don't you try to relax more?' 'Look, it is all very well to say that, but how can I possibly relax with four small children in the house?'* ○ *It's all very well for you to suggest a skiing holiday but where are we going to find the money?*

be (just) as 'well (to do sth) be a good, sensible or advisable thing (to do sth): *It's just as well to lock the door even if you only go out of the house for a few minutes.*

be well aware of sth *or* **be well aware that. . .** know very well about sth: *I'm well aware of the dangers involved.* ○ *She's well aware that not everyone agrees.*

be 'well away (*informal*) **1** be making good progress; be succeeding: *If I had another £10000 to invest in this business, I'd be well away.* **2** be drunk: *He's well away; he's been drinking all evening.*

be well 'off 1 be wealthy enough to have a high standard of living: *Her parents are both doctors so they're quite well off really.* **2** be in a fortunate situation: *Some people don't know when they're well off. If they realized how millions of people in this world live, they wouldn't complain all the time.*

be well ,off for 'sth have as much of sth as you need or want: *We're very well off for computers in this school.*

be ,well 'out of sth (*informal*) be lucky that you are not/no longer doing sth or involved in sth: *'I've left my job in advertising.' 'You're well out of it, John. The firm is in terrible financial trouble.'*

do well by sb treat sb kindly or generously: *He did well by me when I needed money, and I shall always be grateful to him.*

do well to do sth (often used when giving advice or a warning) act wisely or sensibly: *You'd do well to remember that I'm paying the bill.* ○ *They did well to sell when the price was high.*

it's (just) as 'well (that . . .) it's a good thing (that . . .); it's lucky (that . . .): *It's as well that we brought an umbrella.* ○ *'She was wearing a crash helmet, fortunately.' 'Just as well.'*

leave/let well alone not try to change sth or get involved in sth: *Arguments between other couples should be let well alone.*

may/might (just) as well (do sth) (used for saying that you will do sth although you do not feel happy or enthusiastic about it): *Since nobody else wants the job, I might as well give it to him.* ○ *'Are you coming to the pub?' 'Might as well.'*

,well and 'truly (used for emphasis) completely: *We were in the middle of the forest, and well and truly lost.*

,well I 'never! (*informal*) (used to express surprise): *Well I never! Fancy meeting you here!*

be well up on sth ⇨ up; know sth very/ perfectly well ⇨ know; sb may/might as well be hanged/hung for a sheep as a lamb ⇨ hanged; mean well ⇨ mean; only too well ⇨ only; pretty well/much/ nearly ⇨ pretty; sb/sth promises well ⇨ promises; very well ⇨ very; wish sb/ sth well/ill ⇨ wish; you know as well as I do ⇨ know

wet

be ,wet behind the 'ears (*informal, disapproving*) be young and with very little experience: *He's a young teacher, still wet behind the ears.*

wet the baby's head (*informal*) have a drink to celebrate the birth of a baby: *Jack phoned me from the hospital and then we met in the pub to wet the baby's head.*

a ,wet 'blanket (*informal*) sb who spoils other people's enjoyment of sth by refusing to join in an activity; sb who is miserable and negative: *She was such a wet blanket at the party that they never invited her again.*

wet your 'whistle (*dated, informal*) have an alcoholic drink.

whale

(have) a 'whale of a time (*informal*) (have) a very enjoyable time: *The children had a whale of a time at the beach and didn't want to go home.*

what

and 'what not *also* (and) what 'have you (*informal*) and other (similar) things: *The shop sells nails, screws, hammers and what not.* ○ *He does all sorts of things – building, gardening, fencing and what have you.*

give sb/get what 'for (*informal*) punish sb/be punished, usually severely: *I'll give her what for if she does that again.* ○ *If you steal any more of my apples, you'll get what for.*

or what? 1 (used after a number of different choices to indicate that there are more): *Do you want blue shoes, black shoes, brown shoes, or what?* 2 (*informal*) used, slightly aggressively, at the end of a question to suggest that the speaker thinks that the answer is clear or obvious: *Are you stupid or*

what? ○ *Come on! Are we going or what?*

so 'what? *or* what 'of it? (*informal*) (used for showing that you don't care about what sb has just told you and that you think it is unimportant) what difference does it make?; what does it matter?: *'Your sister did much better than you in the exam.' 'So what?'* ○ *'We're going to be late for the party.' 'So what, who cares?'*

what did I 'tell you? *also* I 'told you so (used for telling sb who did not listen to your warnings or take your advice that they were wrong and you were right): *'I've got terrible stomach ache.' 'What did I tell you? You should never have drunk the tap water.'* ○ *'She didn't like the present.' 'I told you so. I knew she didn't like perfume.'*

what if...? 1 what would happen if ...?: *What if the car breaks down?* 2 why should I care if ...? what does it matter if ...?: *'You'll fail the exam if you don't work harder, Carol.' 'What if I do? It's not the end of the world.'* ○ *What if people are starving? It doesn't affect me.*

what with sth (*informal*) because of sth or a series of things: *What with the weather and my bad leg, I haven't been out for weeks.* ○ *I've not had time to sit down, what with one thing and another.*

what's all this/that (...)? (said when you are annoyed) why is this/that happening?: *What's all this I hear about you wanting to leave?*

what's it to you, him, her, etc? (*informal*) 1 (said when you are annoyed) you, etc have no right to know sth; what does it matter to you, etc: *What's it to her how I spend my money?* ○ *What's it to them if public transport is getting worse? They never have to use it.*

(and) what's more *or* what is more (and) more importantly; (and) in addition: *I don't like pubs. They're noisy, smelly, and what's more, expensive.*

what's yours? (*informal*) (said in a pub or bar) what would you like to drink?

what's this, etc in aid of? ⇨ aid

wheat separate the wheat from the chaff ⇨ separate

wheel(s)

(be) at/behind the 'wheel (of sth)

driving a car: *Who was at the wheel when the car crashed?*

take the wheel start to drive a car, replacing sb else: *When we got halfway, Sarah took the wheel and I had a rest.*

,**wheel and 'deal** (*disapproving*) (especially in business and politics) act in a clever but often dishonest or unfair way to get sth you want: **wheeling and dealing** (*noun*) *I don't want to go into politics; there's too much wheeling and dealing.* **wheeler-dealer** (*noun*)

the wheel has come/turned full circle (*saying*) sth that changed greatly has now returned to its original state or position: *How long does it take for the wheel of fashion to come full circle?*

(there are) ,wheels within 'wheels (used to explain that you don't understand a situation because it is very complicated and difficult to understand, as there are many people taking part in it, all with different motives and acting under different influences): *In making political agreements there are always wheels within wheels.* (from the Bible)

a big cheese/wheel ⇨ big; **oil the wheels** ⇨ oil; **put a spoke in sb's wheel** ⇨ spoke; **set the wheels in motion = put/set sth in motion** ⇨ motion

where
be where it's 'at (*informal*) be where the most exciting things are happening (in music, art, etc): *For dance music, New York's where it's at right now.*

wherefores the whys and wherefores ⇨ whys

whet
whet sb's appetite make sb feel hungry; make sb interested in sth: *Don't eat too much of this dish. It's only to whet your appetite for the main course.* ○ *One of my teachers lent me a book about fishing, and it really whetted my appetite.*

while
while away the time, etc (doing sth) pass the time (doing sth), usually because you are waiting for sth or have nothing better to do: *I had ten hours to wait in Rome, so I whiled away the time wandering around the*

museums.

be, etc worth sb's while ⇨ worth; **make sth worth sb's while** ⇨ worth; **once in a while** ⇨ once

whip
get, have, hold, etc the whip hand (over sb) have power or control (over sb): *The government knows that the army have the whip hand.* ○ *Our opponents had the whip hand over us from the beginning.*

a fair crack of the whip ⇨ fair

whipping
a whipping boy sb who is punished for the mistakes of another person: *The directors are clearly responsible for what happened, but no doubt they will find a whipping boy lower down the company.* ○ *'It was your fault, and I am not going to be your whipping boy.'*(in the past when a royal prince made a mistake in his lessons, another boy was whipped (punished) for his mistakes)

whirl
give sth a 'whirl (*informal*) try sth, to see if it is enjoyable, interesting, etc: *I've never had Indonesian food but I'll give it a whirl.*

(be) in a whirl (feel) confused and excited: *My mind was in a whirl as I realized that this decision would change our lives.*

whisker(s)
do sth by a 'whisker (*informal*) do sth, but nearly fail; do sth, but only just: *He missed the first prize by a whisker.* ○ *You escaped serious injury by a whisker, so consider yourselves lucky.*

whiskers the cat's whiskers/pyjamas ⇨ cat

whistle
you, etc can whistle for it (*informal*) I'm not going to give you, etc what you, etc want: *'The boss wants that sales report this afternoon.' 'Well, he can whistle for it.'*

whistle in the 'dark try not to show that you are afraid, are in danger, etc: *He seems confident, but he's whistling in the dark. He knows he's going to lose the election.*

a whistle-stop tour short visits to different places made by a politician, etc during an election campaign, etc: *The Prime Minister is on a whistle-stop tour of the north of*

England today. ○ *The new manager's gone on a whistle-stop tour of all the offices today.*

blow the whistle ⇨ blow; **wet your whistle** ⇨ wet

white

(be/go) (as) ˌwhite as a ˈsheet/ˈghost (*informal*) (be/become) very pale in the face, because of illness, fear or shock: *She went as white as a sheet when she heard the news.*

a white Christmas a Christmas when it snows.

a white elephant something expensive but useless and unwanted: *That theatre is a real white elephant. It cost a lot to build and nobody goes there.*

a white ˈlie a small or harmless lie that you tell to avoid hurting sb.

black and white ⇨ black; **bleed sb dry/white** ⇨ bleed; **in black and white** ⇨ black

whizz

a ˈwhizz kid (*informal*) a highly intelligent and dynamic young man or woman who has already risen high in his/her profession, etc: *'Who's the new manager?' 'A whizz kid from the Harvard Business School.'*

who

know, learn, etc who's ˈwho know, etc people's names, jobs, positions, etc: *You'll soon find out who's who at the office.*

who am ˈI, are ˈyou, is ˈshe, etc to do sth? (used when you think a person has/you have no right or authority to do sth): *Who are you to tell me I can't leave my bicycle here? It's not your house.* ○ *I don't agree, but then who am I to say what she should do?*

whole

as a ˈwhole considered as one general group: *The population as a whole were not very interested in the issue.*

go the ˌwhole ˈhog (*informal*) do sth completely or thoroughly, and perhaps excessively: *They painted the kitchen and then decided to go the whole hog and do the other rooms as well.*

on the whole considering everything; in general: *On the whole her work is improving, though her spelling is still poor.*

why(s)

why ˈever (used to express surprise or annoyance) why: *Why ever didn't you tell us?*

why ˈnot? (*informal*) (used to make a suggestion, or agree to a suggestion): *'Why not go and see a film?' 'OK.'* ○ *'Let's go and see a film.' 'OK, why not?'*

the whys and (the) wherefores (of sth) the reasons (for sth): *I don't want to know all the whys and the wherefores. Just tell me what happened.*

wick

get on sb's ˈwick (*British, informal*) annoy or bother sb: *She's always talking – she gets on my wick.*

wicket a sticky wicket ⇨ sticky

wide

be/fall wide of the ˈmark *or* **be (a long) way off the ˈmark** be not at all correct or accurate: *No one knew where Bangalore was, and their guesses were all wide of the mark.*

be wide ˈopen (of a competition, election, etc) with no predictable or obvious winner: *The presidential election is wide open.*

give sb/sth a wide ˈberth avoid meeting sb; avoid going near or using sth: *He's so boring I always try to give him a wide berth at parties.* ○ *The roads are very dangerous there – I'd give them a wide berth and go by train.*

a ˈwide boy (*disapproving, informal, dated*) sb who is dishonest in business: *If he offers you a business deal, say no. He's a bit of a wide boy.*

(lay/leave yourself) wide open (to sth) (put yourself) in a situation where you can easily be criticized, blamed, attacked, etc: *By not saying anything in your defence, you're leaving yourself wide open to their accusations.* ○ *The soldiers were wide open to attack.*

far and wide ⇨ far

wife the world and his wife ⇨ world

wild

a ˌwild-ˈgoose chase (*quite informal*) a (long) search for sth that you cannot find because you have been given the wrong information: *He gave us the wrong directions to the station and that led us off on a wild-goose* *chase.* ○ *Peter's story sent the police on a wild-goose chase. They soon realized he had been lying.*

wild horses couldn't/wouldn't drag sb there, prevent sb doing sth, etc (*informal, humorous*) nothing would make or persuade sb to go somewhere, do sth, etc: *Wild horses wouldn't keep me at home on a Saturday night.*

run wild ⇨ run; **sow your wild oats** ⇨ sow

wilderness

(be) in the 'wilderness (of politicians) no longer having power, influence or importance because they no longer hold high office: *After a few years in the wilderness she was allowed to return to a job in the government.*

a voice in the wilderness ⇨ voice

wildest

be, etc beyond your wildest 'dreams (*quite informal*) be, etc, much greater or better than you ever expected: *It succeeded beyond our wildest dreams.*

wildfire **spread like wildfire** ⇨ spread

will

(do sth) against your 'will (do sth) without wanting to: *I was forced to sign the agreement against my will.*

do sth at 'will do sth when, where, how, etc you want to: *The animals are allowed to wander at will in the park.* ○ *The younger soldiers started shooting at will* (they fired their guns without waiting for the order).

where there's a ‚will there's a 'way (*saying*) a person who really wants something very much and is determined to get it will find a way of getting it or doing it.

(do sth) with a 'will (do sth) with energy and enthusiasm: *She started digging the garden with a will.* ○ *With a will they set to work.*

with the best will in the world ⇨ best

willing **God willing** ⇨ God; **the spirit is willing but the flesh is weak** ⇨ spirit

win

I, you, etc ‚can't 'win (*informal, saying*) whatever you do, you can't succeed

completely or please everybody: *If I spend time with Phil, she's unhappy. If I spend time with her, he's jealous. I just can't win.* ○ *We try to eat a healthy diet, but there are so many chemicals in food nowadays that you just can't win.* **no-win situation** (*noun*) a situation where you cannot succeed: *They are in a no-win situation at the moment. Whatever they do, someone criticizes them.*

you can't win them 'all (*informal*) (used after sb has been involved in a failure or loss) sometimes you succeed; sometimes you fail: *'I made a terrible speech this evening.' 'Well, you can't win them all. Don't worry about it.'*

win sb's heart (*quite formal*) gain the love or admiration of sb: *The children have won the old man's heart.* ○ *The actress who played 'Natasha' won the hearts of the audience.*

win your 'spurs (*dated or humorous*) become successful or famous: *You'll win your spurs as a teacher if you can control class 5.*

ask for/win sb's hand ⇨ hand; **carry/win the day** ⇨ day; **win/beat sb hands down** ⇨ hands

wind

get wind of sth hear indirectly about sth secret; hear a rumour about sth: *I got wind that there might be a job, so I went to see the manager.* ○ *A journalist got wind of a story of the nuclear research centre.*

go, run, etc like the 'wind go, etc very fast: *We had to drive like the wind to get there in time.* ○ *She ran like the wind.*

(be) in the 'wind (especially of sth which is being planned or prepared) (be) going to happen: *I can see some changes in the wind.* ○ *The soldiers sensed that something was in the wind.*

put the 'wind up sb make sb frightened about sth: *He really put the wind up her with his descriptions of the rats in the kitchen.*

take the 'wind out of sb's sails (*informal*) make sb feel much less confident, proud or self-satisfied: *Getting beaten in the first race took the wind out of her sails.*

a wind of 'change a change: *There is a wind of change in the attitude of voters.* ○ *Winds of change were sweeping over Eastern Europe.*

a straw in the wind ⇨ straw; **break wind** ⇨ break; **get your second wind**

⇨ second; **it's an ill wind** ⇨ ill; **sail close to the wind** ⇨ sail; **see which way the wind blows/is blowing** ⇨ see; **throw caution to the wind(s)** ⇨ throw

window

be, go, etc out (of) the window (*informal*) (of a chance, an opportunity, a job, etc) disappear; be lost: *All my hopes of finding a good job in television have gone out of the window.* ○ *Don't throw this opportunity to work in the USA out of the window.*

a window of opportunity a limited period of time when you can do something that you want to do or need to do: *The government's difficulties provided the left with a window of opportunity to present an alternative policy to the voters.*

a window on the 'world a way of learning about other people and other countries: *News programmes try to provide a window on the world.*

wine

,wine and 'dine (sb) entertain sb at a good restaurant: *Our hosts wined and dined us very well.* ○ *Too much wining and dining is making him fat.*

wing

on the 'wing (of a bird) flying: *photograph a bird on the wing*

take/have sb under your 'wing give sb help and protection: *When new children arrive at the school, she takes them under her wing.*

take 'wing (of a bird or aircraft) start flying away: *With a roar of engines, the plane took wing.*

wings

(wait, stand, etc) in the 'wings (wait, etc), ready to do sth, especially to take the place of another person: *If the party leader should resign, there are plenty of other politicians waiting in the wings.* ○ *There are many younger tennis players in the wings, waiting for the chance to show their abilities.*

clip sb's wings ⇨ clip; **spread your wings** ⇨ spread

wink(s) forty winks ⇨ forty; **a nod is as good as a wink** ⇨ nod; **not sleep a wink** ⇨ sleep; **tip sb the wink** ⇨ tip

wipe

wipe the 'floor with sb (*informal*) defeat sb completely and easily in an argument, competition, etc: *They started arguing about the education reforms, and she wiped the floor with him.* ○ *Italy wiped the floor with Austria, beating them 5-0.*

wipe sth off the ,face of the 'earth *or* **wipe sth off the 'map** completely destroy sth: *In the event of nuclear war, whole cities would be wiped off the face of the earth.* ○ *The fall in prices wiped a lot of businesses off the map.*

wipe the 'slate clean forget the bad things a person has done in the past; forgive sb: *We're both to blame. Let's wipe the slate clean and start again.*

wipe the/that 'smile, 'grin, etc off your/sb's face (*informal*) **1** (often used as an order) stop smiling, etc: *Wipe that smile off your face or I'll send you out of the classroom.* **2** make sb feel less happy or satisfied with sth: *The news from the stock market soon wiped the smile off his face.* ○ *I'm going to wipe that smile off his face one day.*

wire(s) get your lines/wires crossed ⇨ crossed; **a live wire** ⇨ live

wisdom pearls of wisdom ⇨ pearls

wise

be ,wise after the e'vent know what should have been done in a particular situation, but only after it has happened: *'If we'd been more careful, the fire would never have happened.' 'It's no good being wise after the event – we can't do anything now.'*

be/get wise to sth/sb (*informal*) be/become aware of sth or aware of sb's (usually bad) behaviour: *When did you first get wise to what was happening?* ○ *He thought he could fool me but I'm wise to him.* also **put sb 'wise (to sb/sth)** make sb aware of sb/sth

a 'wise guy (used for showing disapproval) a man who speaks or behaves as if he knows much more than other people.

wiser

be none the 'wiser/no 'wiser *or* **not be any the 'wiser** still not know or understand sth: *The meeting lasted three hours but I was none the wiser at the end of it.*

wish(es)

(just) as you 'wish I will do what you want; I will agree with your decision: *We can meet at my house or yours, as you wish.*

if wishes were horses, beggars would/might ride (*saying*) wishing for sth doesn't make it happen.

the wish is father to the thought (*saying*) we believe a thing because we want it to be true. (from Shakespeare's *Henry IV*: 'Thy wish was father, Harry, to that thought.')

wish sb/sth 'well/'ill hope that sb/sth succeeds or has good luck/hope that sb fails or has bad luck: *I wish you well in your new job.* ○ *She said she wished nobody ill.*

would not wish sth on my, etc worst enemy (*informal*) (used for saying that sth is so unpleasant, painful, etc that you would not like anybody to experience it): *It's a terrible job; it's dirty, it's noisy, it's boring, the people are awful. I wouldn't wish a job like that on my worst enemy.*

your wish is my com'mand (*humorous*) I am ready to do anything you ask: *'Put the kettle on, will you?' 'Your wish is my command.'*(the words of the genie in the story about Aladdin in *The Thousand and One Nights*)

wishful

,wishful 'thinking believing or hoping that sth unlikely is true, because it is what you want: *Prices seem to have stopped rising in the shops, or is that just wishful thinking on my part?*

wit

to 'wit (*rather formal, sometimes humorous*) (used for introducing further, more precise information about sth just mentioned) that is to say: *I told him I only spoke one foreign language – to wit, French.*

with

be with sb **1** understand what sb is saying or explaining: *I'm sorry, but I'm not with you. What exactly did you mean by 'cut and paste'?* ○ *'Are you with me?' 'No, you've lost me. Can you explain it again?'* **2** be in support of or agreement with sb: *'What do you think, Jonathan?' 'I'm with Sarah on this.'* **3** (used especially by a waiter, shop assistant, etc when a customer is waiting to be served) please wait a moment until I serve you: *'I'm just serving this lady. I'll be with you in a minute.'*

be, etc 'with it (*informal*) **1** (*becoming dated*) (of sb/sth) fashionable and up to date: *Her clothes are very with it, aren't they?* **with-it** (*adjective*) *He was wearing very with-it sunglasses.* **2** be thinking quickly and clearly: *I'm a bit tired this morning. I'm not really with it.*

get 'with it (*informal*) become aware of the most recent ideas, developments, events, etc: *You never seem to know what's happening around you. Get with it, Paul. Start reading, start talking to people.*

wither

wither on the vine gradually come to an end or stop being effective: *He used to be so ambitious, but his ambition seems to have withered on the vine.*

without

without without so much as sth/ doing sth = not so much as sth/doing sth ⇨ so

wits

be at your wits' 'end be so confused or worried that you don't know what you should do: *I can't pay the bills, the bank won't lend me any money, and I don't know what to do – I'm at my wits' end.*

collect/gather your 'wits try to become calm and think clearly: *After such a shock I found it difficult to gather my wits.*

have/keep your 'wits about you be/ remain quick to think and act in a demanding, difficult or dangerous situation: *Mountaineering is dangerous, so you need to keep your wits about you.*

drive sb out of their mind/wits ⇨ drive; **frighten/scare sb to death/out of their wits** ⇨ frighten; **live by/on your wits** ⇨ live; **pit your wits** ⇨ pit

wives an old wives' tale ⇨ old

wobbly throw a tantrum/wobbly ⇨ throw

woe

woe be'tide sb (*dated, often humorous*) there will be trouble for sb: *Woe betide anyone who arrives late!*

wolf

keep the 'wolf from the door make sure that you have enough money to pay for the basic things like food, rent, heating, etc: *Their wages are hardly enough to keep the wolf from the door.*

a wolf in sheep's 'clothing (*quite informal*) a person who appears friendly and nice but is really dangerous.

cry wolf ⇨ cry; **a lone wolf** ⇨ lone

wolves throw sb to the wolves/lions
⇨ throw

woman

(speak, talk, etc) woman to woman *or* **(speak, talk, etc) man to man** speak, etc honestly and clearly: *Let's talk woman to woman about this problem.* ○ *We had a chat, man to man, about what to do.*
woman-to-woman *or* **man-to-man** (*adjective*) *a man-to-man talk*

the inner man/woman ⇨ inner; **a man/ woman of few words** ⇨ few; **old woman** ⇨ old

wonder(s)

I ,shouldn't 'wonder (if . . .) (*informal*) I should not be surprised to find out (that . . .): *It's paid for with stolen money, I shouldn't wonder.*

it's a wonder (that). . . it is surprising or puzzling (that). . .: *Did you see the car after the crash? It's a wonder that they survived!*

(it's) no/small/little 'wonder (that . . .) it's not surprising: *If you walked all the way, it's little wonder you're late.* ○ *'The heating's gone off.' 'I thought it was cold. No wonder!'*

,wonders will ,never 'cease (used to express surprise and pleasure at sth): *'The train was on time today.' 'Wonders will never cease (I am surprised, because usually it is late).'*

a nine days' wonder ⇨ nine; **work/do wonders/miracles** ⇨ work

wonderful weird and wonderful
⇨ weird

wood

not be out of the wood(s) 'yet (*quite informal*) not be free from dangers or difficulties yet: *Our sales figures look much better this month, but we're not out of the woods yet.*

dead wood ⇨ dead; **knock on wood** = **touch wood** ⇨ touch; **not see the wood for the trees** ⇨ see; **touch wood** ⇨ touch

wooden

the ,wooden 'spoon the prize for being last in a race or competition. (usually said as a joke, and not actually given)

woods in your, etc/this neck of the woods ⇨ neck

wool pull the wool over sb's eyes
⇨ pull; **wrap sb up in cotton wool**
⇨ wrap

word

be as ,good as your 'word do what you have promised to do: *You'll find that she's as good as her word – she always comes if she says she will.*

be a woman/man of her/his 'word be a person who always does what she/he has promised to do: *If he said he'd help you, he will – he's a man of his word.*

by word of 'mouth in spoken, not written, words: *The news spread by word of mouth.*

(do sth) from the word 'go (*informal*) (do sth) from the very beginning: *I knew from the word go it would be difficult.*

(not) get a word in 'edgeways (*informal*) (usually used with *can* or *could*) (not) be able to say sth, because other people are talking too much: *I tried to tell him what I thought, but I couldn't get a word in edgeways.*

give sb your 'word (that. . .) *or* **have sb's 'word for it (that. . .)** promise sb/be promised (that. . .): *I give you my word that I'll pay you tomorrow.* ○ *I've got his word for it that he'll fix the car by the weekend.*

go ,back on your 'word not do what you have promised; break a promise: *He said he wouldn't charge more than £100, but he went back on his word and gave me a bill for £120.*

have, etc a (short) 'word (with sb) (about sth) *or* **have, etc, a few (short) words (with sb) (about sth)** speak to sb briefly about sth, especially in private: *Can I have a word, Marie? It's about Jane.* ○ *We've* *had a few short words about the matter.*

have a word in sb's 'ear speak to sb in private: *Can I have a word in your ear, John?* ○ *I must have a word in her ear before the others arrive.*

in a 'word (used for introducing the main point or conclusion of what you have just said) in short: *In a word, 'stupid' is how I'd describe him.*

keep/break your 'word do/fail to do what you have promised: *Do you think she'll break her word and tell everyone?*

(upon) my 'word! (*dated*) (used to express surprise): *My word! That was quick!*

not be the word for it (used to say that a word or expression does not describe sth fully or strongly enough): *Unkind isn't the word for it! I've never seen anyone treat an animal so cruelly!*

not/never have a good word to 'say for/about sb/sth (*quite informal*) not/ never have anything positive to say about sb/sth: *She rarely has a good word to say about her neighbours.* ○ *Nobody has a good word to say for the new computer system.*

not a 'word (to sb) (about sth) do not say anything (to sb) (about sth): *Not a word to Jean about the party – it's a surprise!* ○ *Remember, not a word about how much it cost.*

put in a (good) 'word (for sb) say sth good about sb to sb else in order to help them: *If you put in a good word for me, I might get the job.*

the spoken/written 'word the language, in speaking/writing: *The spoken word is often very different from the written word.*

take sb at their'word act according to the exact or literal meaning of what sb said although this may not really have been what they intended or meant: *She said I could go and stay in her flat in Paris whenever I wanted, so I took her at her word.*

take sb's 'word for it (that...) believe sth that sb has said, (which is that...): *You know more about cars than I do, so if you think it needs a new gearbox, I'll take your word for it.* ○ *Can I take your word for it that the text has all been checked?*

word for 'word in exactly the same words; in an exact translation from another

language: *I repeated what you said, word for word.* ○ *It probably won't sound very natural if you translate it word for word.* **word-for-word** (*adjective*) *a word-for-word account, translation, etc*

sb's ,word is (as ,good as) their 'bond (*quite formal*) sb always does what they promise: *Don't worry, you can trust my brother. His word's as good as his bond.*

sb's word is law sb has complete power and control: *Their father is very old-fashioned. His word is law in their house.*

sb's ,word of 'honour (often used when making promises) sb's promise: *He gave me his word of honour that he'd never drink again.*

(not) breathe a word ⇨ breathe; **a dirty word** ⇨ dirty; **a four-letter word** ⇨ four; **have, etc the last word** ⇨ last; **a household word/name** ⇨ household; **the last word** ⇨ last; **your last word** ⇨ last; **leave word** ⇨ leave; **mum's the word** ⇨ mum; **not know the meaning of the word** ⇨ know; **pledge your word** ⇨ pledge; **the printed word** ⇨ printed; **say the word** ⇨ say

words

have 'words (with sb) (about sth) (*informal*) argue or quarrel with sb because you don't like the way they have behaved: *I had to have words with him about his behaviour.* ○ *They both got angry and had words.*

in 'other words expressed in a different way; that is to say: *'I don't think this is the right job for you, Pete.' 'In other words, you want me to leave. Is that it?'*

(not) in so many 'words (not) clearly and explicitly: *'Have you told John that you are leaving him?' 'Not in so many words, no. I just said I thought it might be better if we lived apart.'* ○ *Did you actually tell her in so many words that there was no hope of a cure?*

in words of one 'syllable using very simple language so that sb will understand: *They didn't seem to understand my explanation, so I explained it all again in words of one syllable.*

a man/woman of few words a person who does not talk much: *Mr Robins was a man of few words, but his opinions were always respected.*

put 'words in(to) sb's mouth say or suggest that sb has said sth, when they have not: *You're putting words in my mouth. I didn't say the whole house was dirty, I said the front room needed a clean.*

take the words out of sb's 'mouth *or* **take the words right out of sb's 'mouth** say exactly what another person was going to say: *'The speed limit on motorways should be raised.' 'I agree completely! You've taken the words right out of my mouth!'*

too funny, sad, etc for 'words extremely funny, etc: *The man in the post office was too stupid for words.*

words 'fail me (often said because the speaker is too embarrassed, surprised, angry, etc) I cannot express or describe sth: *Words fail me! How could you have been so stupid?*

actions speak louder than words ⇨ actions; **at a loss for words** ⇨ loss; **eat your words** ⇨ eat; **famous last words** ⇨ famous; **hang on sb's words/ every word** ⇨ hang; **mark my words** ⇨ mark; **not mince your words = not mince matters** ⇨ mince; **a play on words** ⇨ play; **weigh your words** ⇨ weigh

work

all work and no 'play (makes Jack a dull boy) (*saying*) it is not healthy to spend all your time working, you need to relax too.

be at 'work be having an influence or effect: *Why did they lose the election? Several factors were at work. . . .* ○ *Evil forces are at work in this country.*

go/set about your 'work start to do your work: *She went cheerfully about her work.*

go/set to 'work (on sth) *also* **get (down) to 'work (on sth)** start working on a particular task: *I set to work on the car, giving it a good clean.* ○ *I ought to get to work on that essay.*

have your 'work cut out (to do sth/ doing sth) (*informal*) **1** find it very difficult to do sth: *You'll have your work cut out to get there before nine. It's 8.30 already.* **2** be very busy: *I won't be able to come with you today. I've got my work cut out at the moment.*

in/out of 'work having/not having a paid job: *I've been out of work for a year.* ○ *Is your husband in work at the moment?* **out-of-work** (*adjective*) *an out-of-work actor*

put/set sb to 'work (on sth) make sb start work (doing sth): *On his first day in the office they put him to work on some typing.*

work all the hours God sends (*informal*) work all the time: *'You look tired, Jane.' 'I'm working all the hours God sends at the moment trying to finish my thesis.'*

work your fingers to the bone (*informal*) work very hard: *It's not fair – I work my fingers to the bone all day and then I have to cook and clean in the evenings.*

work like a 'charm (*informal*) quickly have the effect you want; work like magic: *I don't know what she said to him, but it worked like a charm – he's much more cooperative now.*

work like a dog/slave/Trojan (*informal*) work very hard: *She worked like a slave to pass her exams.*

'work things, it, etc (so that) plan sth carefully to get the result you want; organize or arrange sth: *Can you work it so that we get free tickets?* ○ *I worked things so that I could take all my holidays in July and August.*

work your way through 'college, etc have a paid job while you are a student: *She had to work her way through law school.*

work your way 'up start with a badly-paid, unimportant job and work hard until you get a well-paid, important job: *He's worked his way up from an office junior to managing director.*

work/do 'wonders/'miracles (for/on/ with sb/sth) (*informal*) have a very good effect (on sb/sth); quickly succeed: *Getting the job did wonders for her self-confidence.* ○ *This is a washing powder that works miracles on difficult stains.* **miracle-worker** (*noun*) *I just don't have enough time to finish it. I'm sorry, but I'm not a miracle-worker.*

work yourself/sb to death (*informal*) (make sb) work very hard: *That company is working him to death.* ○ *She works herself to death and nobody ever thanks her for anything.*

all in a day's work ⇨ day; **the devil makes work for idle hands** ⇨ devil; **the donkey work** ⇨ donkey; **make hard**

work of sth ⇨ hard; **make light work of sth** ⇨ short; **make short work of sth/sb** ⇨ short; **many hands make light work** ⇨ hands; **a nasty piece of work** ⇨ nasty; **nice work** ⇨ nice; **too much like hard work** ⇨ hard; **work/go like a dream** ⇨ dream

worker a fast worker ⇨ fast

working

have a working knowledge of sth know sth well enough to be able to use it: *I speak good French and I have a working knowledge of Italian and Spanish.* ○ *I've worked with this software a bit so I do have a working knowledge of it.*

in (full/good) working order *or* **in running order** (of a machine) in good condition; working well: *For Sale. Sewing machine in good working order. £50.*

works gum up the works ⇨ gum; **put/throw a spanner in the works** ⇨ spanner

world

be, live, etc in a world of your own (*informal*) seem not to be aware of things happening around you; be a person who has ideas that other people think are strange.

be/mean (,all) the 'world to sb be very important to sb; be loved very much by sb: *Her job means the world to her.* ○ *They've only got one child and he's all the world to them.* also **think the world of sb** *My daughter thinks the world of her drama teacher.*

come/go 'down/'up in the world become less/more successful; become poorer/richer: *He's come up in the world since I last saw him. That was a Mercedes he was driving, wasn't it?* ○ *Since she left Cambridge she's gone down in the world.*

for all the 'world as if/though... *or* **for all the 'world like...** (used to express surprise or wonder) very much or exactly as if, like...: *She stood up and screamed at him, then sat down and continued her work for all the world as if nothing had happened.*

have (got) the world at your feet have many advantages, and so opportunities to choose from: *If you're young and you've got a good education you've got the world at your*
feet. ○ *She's got money; she's well-educated; the world is at her feet.*

not (do sth) for (all) the 'world not for anything; never: *I wouldn't sell that picture for all the world.*

out of this 'world (*informal*) unusually good: *She cooked a meal which was out of this world.*

there's a 'world of difference (between A and B) there's a lot of difference (between A and B): *There's a world of difference between records and CDs.*

what is the world 'coming to? *or* **I don't know what the world's 'coming to** (*saying*) (used as an expression of anger, shock, complaint, etc, at changes in people's behaviour, the political situation, etc): *When I read the news these days I sometimes wonder what the world's coming to.* ○ *Instant tea? What is the world coming to?*

a woman/man of the 'world a person with a lot of experience of life, business, etc, especially someone who is not easily surprised or shocked: *She's a woman of the world. She won't mind if you talk frankly about sex.*

(all) the ,world and his 'wife (*informal*) everybody; crowds of people: *Don't put our address in the newspaper. I don't want all the world and his wife knocking on the door.* ○ *The world and his wife were in Brighton that day.*

the ,world is your 'oyster you have the freedom to do what you want, go where you want, etc in the future because you are young, successful, rich, talented, etc

the (whole) world 'over everywhere in the world: *People are the same the whole world over.* ○ *Writers the world over joined in protest against her imprisonment.*

(think) the world owes you a 'living (*disapproving*) (think that) society is responsible for doing everything for you and that you shouldn't have to make any effort yourself: *Why don't you go out and get a job? The world doesn't owe you a living, you know.* ○ *Young people today seem to think the world owes them a living.*

the bottom drops/falls out of sb's world ⇨ bottom; **brave new world** ⇨ brave; **dead to the world** ⇨ dead; **do sb/sth a power/world of good** ⇨ power; **how, etc**

on earth/in the world... ⇨ earth; **it's a
small world** ⇨ small; **the next world**
⇨ next; **not be the end of the world**
⇨ end; **not long for this world** ⇨ long;
not/never set the Thames/world on fire
⇨ set; **the outside world** ⇨ outside; **see
the world** ⇨ see; **tell the world** ⇨ tell;
think the world of sb/sth ⇨ think; **on
top of the world** ⇨ top; **watch the world
go by** ⇨ watch; **the way of the world**
⇨ way; **a window on the world**
⇨ window; **with the best will in the
world** ⇨ best

worlds

be 'worlds away (from sth) *or* **be a
'world away (from sth)** be very different
(from sth): *Life in the country today is worlds
away from how it was a hundred years ago.*

be poles/worlds apart ⇨ poles; **the best
of both worlds** ⇨ best

worm

a worm's eye view the opinion of sb who
is closely involved in sth.

the ,worm 'turns (*informal*) even a
patient, calm person will get angry if they
are continually badly treated: *He's often rude
to his secretary and she doesn't say anything
&m; but one day the worm will turn.*

the early bird catches the worm ⇨ early

worry

,not to 'worry (*informal*) don't worry; it
doesn't matter: *'Oh, damn! We've missed the
train!' 'Not to worry. There'll be another one in
five minutes.'*

worry sb to death (*informal*) worry sb
very much: *It worries me to death when he
goes climbing.* ○ *Where have you been? I've
been worried to death.*

'you should worry! (*informal*) (used for
telling sb that they are worrying completely
unnecessarily): *You think you're going to fail
the exam! You should worry! You're the best in
the class.*

worse

**we, you, he, etc can/could/might do
'worse (than do sth)** it is a good idea to do
sth; sth is a good decision: *If you're looking for
a good career, you could do worse than a job in
banking.*

go from ,bad to 'worse (of an already bad

situation) become even worse: *Under the
new management things have gone from bad to
worse.*

none the 'worse for sth **1** not less
valuable, attractive, enjoyable, useful, etc
because of sth: *It's rather old-fashioned but
none the worse for that.* ○ *She's a very strict
teacher, but none the worse for that.* **2** not
injured or damaged by sth: *One of the drivers
had been in a crash but, luckily, was none the
worse for the experience.*

(be) the ,worse for 'drink (*quite formal*)
(be) drunk: *He was the worse for drink when
the time came for his speech.*

(be) the ,worse for 'wear (*informal*) (be)
damaged; (be) tired or drunk: *Your
dictionary is looking a bit the worse for wear.* ○
*Ellen came back from the pub rather the worse
for wear.*

'worse ,luck (*informal*) (used to express
disappointment) unfortunately: *I'm working
tonight, so I can't come to the party, worse luck.*

for better or worse ⇨ better; **so much
the better/worse** ⇨ better

worst

be your ,own worst 'enemy be a person
who often creates problems or difficulties for
herself/himself: *He spends all his money on
drink, and then finds that he's got nothing left to
live on – if you ask me, he's his own worst
enemy.*

do your 'worst be as harmful, unpleasant,
violent, etc as you can: *I refuse to pay this bill.
Let them do their worst.* ○ *They did their worst
and cut off the electricity supply.*

get the 'worst of it *or* **come off worst**
be defeated in a fight, etc; be affected more
seriously than other people, etc: *The dog had
been fighting and had obviously got the worst of
it.* ○ *Small businesses have come off worst in the
present economic crisis.*

if the ,worst comes to the 'worst if the
most unpleasant or unfortunate thing
happens: *If the worst comes to the worst and
all the hotels are full, you could come and stay
with us.*

at best/worst ⇨ best

worth

be 'worth it be worth the time, money
effort, risk, etc you have spent/taken doing

sth: *A dishwasher costs a lot of money, but it's worth it.* ○ *Don't drink and drive. It's not worth it.*

be ,worth your/its ,weight in 'gold be very useful or valuable: *A good manager is worth his weight in gold.* ○ *A reliable car is worth its weight in gold.*

be, etc (well) worth sb's 'while (to do sth) be, etc a good idea for sb to do sth, because they will find it interesting, useful, profitable, etc: *It would be well worth your while to come to the meeting.*

do sth for ,all you are 'worth (*informal*) do sth with as much energy and effort as possible: *I shouted for all I was worth but no one heard me.*

for ,what it's 'worth (*quite informal*) (used when you're not sure about the value or importance of what you are about to say, etc): *That's my opinion, for what it's worth.* ○ *This is the first drawing I made, for what it's worth.*

make sth worth sb's 'while (*informal*) pay sb well for doing sth for you: *If you can work on Saturdays and Sundays, we'll make it worth your while.*

not be worth the paper it's 'written on (of a written agreement, document, report, etc) be worthless: *The promises in this letter aren't worth the paper they're written on.*

(be) ,worth your 'salt (be) a person who does their job well and deserves the money they get for doing it: *Any teacher worth his salt knows that students who enjoy a lesson learn the most.*

a bird in the hand is worth two in the bush ➪ bird; **the game is not worth the candle** ➪ game; **get/give/have your money's-worth** ➪ money

worthy

worthy of the 'name *or* **worth the 'name** deserving to be called good: *Any doctor worthy of the name would help an injured man in the street.*

wound(s)

cut/wound sb to the quick ➪ quick; **rub salt into the wound/into sb's wounds** ➪ rub; **lick your wounds** ➪ lick

wrap(s)

keep sth, stay, etc under 'wraps

(*informal*) keep sth, stay, etc secret or hidden: *These letters of Winston Churchill's have lain under wraps since the 1940s.*

wrap sb up in cotton 'wool (*informal*) protect sb too much from dangers or risks: *If you keep your children wrapped up in cotton wool, they'll never learn to be independent.*

wreak play/wreak havoc with sth
➪ havoc

wring

,wring your 'hands twist and rub your hands together because you are very worried, upset or anxious: *It's no use just wringing our hands – we must do something.* ○ *He stood there, wringing his hands in despair.*

,wring sb's 'neck (*informal*) (used as an expression of anger or as a threat): *If I find the person who did this, I'll wring his neck!* (to 'wring the neck' of a chicken, turkey, etc is to kill it by strangling it)

wrist a slap on the wrist ➪ slap

write

be nothing, not much, etc to write 'home about *also* **be nothing, not much, etc to shout about** (*informal*) not be very good or special; be ordinary: *The play was OK, but it wasn't anything to write home about.* ○ *The food was nothing much to shout about.*

writing

the ,writing (is) on the 'wall a sign that sth terrible is going to happen soon: *The writing is on the wall for the club unless they can find £20 000.* ○ *The President refuses to see the writing on the wall* (that he will soon be defeated). (from the Bible)

written

be written all over sb's 'face (*informal*) (of an emotion) be clearly seen on sb's face: *You could see he was guilty; it was written all over his face.*

have (got) sb/sth written all 'over it (*informal*) show the influence or characteristics of sb/sth: *It's been badly organized, as usual – it's got the council written all over it.*

not be worth the paper it's written on ➪ worth

wrong(s)

get sb 'wrong (*informal*) think that a person means sth else; misunderstand sb: *Please don't get me wrong, I'm not criticizing you.*

get (hold of) the ,wrong end of the 'stick (*informal*) completely misunderstand sb/sth: *You've got the wrong end of the stick. He doesn't owe me money, I owe him!*

go 'wrong **1** make a mistake: *It doesn't work. We must have gone wrong somewhere. Pass me the instructions book.* **2** (of a machine) stop working correctly: *This television is always going wrong. I'm fed up with it.* **3** not progress or develop as well as you expected or intended: *Their marriage started to go wrong when he lost his job.*

(be) in the wrong be the person who is responsible for a mistake, an accident a quarrel, etc: *She is clearly in the wrong. She had no right to take the book.* ○ *The accident wasn't my fault. The other driver was totally in the wrong.*

the wrong side of the 'tracks (*informal*) be from or living in the part of a town which is considered socially inferior: *I was born on the wrong side of the tracks.*

bark up the wrong tree ⇨ bark; **be on the right/wrong side of 40, 50, etc** ⇨ side; **be on the right/wrong track** ⇨ track; **get/keep on the right/wrong side of sb** ⇨ side; **get out of bed on the wrong side** ⇨ bed; **get your priorities right/wrong** ⇨ priorities; **not far off/out/wrong** ⇨ far; **not/never put/set a foot wrong** ⇨ foot; **rub sb up the wrong way** ⇨ rub; **two wrongs don't make a right** ⇨ two

Y

year(s)

,all (the) year 'round all year; all the time: *It's open to visitors all the year round.*

from, since, etc the year 'dot (*informal*) from, etc a very long time ago: *The case contained old papers going back to the year dot.*

put 'years on sb make sb feel or look much older: *The shock of losing his job put years on him.*

take 'years off sb make sb feel or look much younger: *The new hairstyle takes years off her.*

year ,in, year 'out (used for emphasis) (all year and) every year: *He had travelled on the 7.40 train to London year in, year out for thirty years.*

yellow

a 'yellow streak (*disapproving*) cowardice; being afraid: *He won't fight? I always thought he had a yellow streak.*

yes

yes and no (said when you cannot answer either 'yes' or 'no' because the situation is not simple): *'Have you got a car?' 'Well, yes*

and no. We have, but it's not working at the moment.'

yet

as 'yet (used with negative words) until now/then: *As yet little is known about the disease.*

you

,you and 'yours (*informal*) you and your family: *You must provide a safe future for you and yours.*

you 'what? (*informal*) (said when you have not heard sth properly or do not understand sth, to ask sb to repeat or explain it).

young

be, stay, etc, young at 'heart (of an old person) still feel and behave like a young person: *He said that the secret of living to 100 was to remain young at heart.*

(be) with 'young (*formal*) (of an animal) (be) pregnant: *The lioness was with young.*

younger

not be getting any 'younger (*informal*) be getting older: *I can't possibly walk all the* *way to the beach; I'm not getting any younger, you know.*

yours

up 'yours! (*very informal, offensive*) (used for showing that you do not accept sb's criticism or for expressing strong disagreement with sb/sth): '*Your work just isn't good enough for this company.*' '*Oh, up yours! I'll find another job then.*'

yours 'truly (*informal, often humorous*) I/me: *Steve came first, Robin second, and yours truly came last.* ○ *And of course, all the sandwiches will be made by yours truly.*

you and yours ➪ you

yourself

please/suit yourself (*informal*) (used for expressing annoyance at sb's decision): '*I don't want anything to eat, I'm on a diet.*' '*All right, please yourself!*' ○ '*I don't want to see that film.*' '*Oh, suit yourself then.*'